Crew Resource M

Crew Resource Management

Third Edition

Edited by

Barbara G. Kanki
Retired, NASA, Ames Research Center, Moffett Field, CA, United States

José Anca
Faculty of Science, Engineering and Technology, Swinburne University of Technology, Hawthorn, VIC, Australia

Thomas R. Chidester
Federal Aviation Administration, Civil Aerospace Medical Institute, Oklahoma City, OK, United States

ACADEMIC PRESS

An imprint of Elsevier

Academic Press is an imprint of Elsevier
125 London Wall, London EC2Y 5AS, United Kingdom
525 B Street, Suite 1650, San Diego, CA 92101, United States
50 Hampshire Street, 5th Floor, Cambridge, MA 02139, United States
The Boulevard, Langford Lane, Kidlington, Oxford OX5 1GB, United Kingdom

Notices
Knowledge and best practice in this field are constantly changing. As new research and experience broaden
our understanding, changes in research methods, professional practices, or medical treatment may become
necessary.

Practitioners and researchers must always rely on their own experience and knowledge in evaluating and
using any information, methods, compounds, or experiments described herein. In using such information or
methods they should be mindful of their own safety and the safety of others, including parties for whom
they have a professional responsibility.

To the fullest extent of the law, neither the Publisher nor the authors, contributors, or editors, assume any
liability for any injury and/or damage to persons or property as a matter of products liability, negligence or
otherwise, or from any use or operation of any methods, products, instructions, or ideas contained in the
material herein.

British Library Cataloguing-in-Publication Data
A catalogue record for this book is available from the British Library

Library of Congress Cataloging-in-Publication Data
A catalog record for this book is available from the Library of Congress

ISBN: 978-0-12-812995-1

For Information on all Academic Press publications
visit our website at https://www.elsevier.com/books-and-journals

Working together
to grow libraries in
developing countries

www.elsevier.com • www.bookaid.org

Publisher: Nikki Levy
Acquisition Editor: Emily Ekle
Editorial Project Manager: Barbara Makinster
Production Project Manager: Vijayaraj Purushothaman
Cover Designer: Mark Rogers

Typeset by MPS Limited, Chennai, India

Contents

12. Crew Resource Management and Line Operations Safety Audit 343

Bruce A. Tesmer

13. Maintenance Resource Management for Technical Operations 357

Manoj S. Patankar

Part III
CRM Perspectives

16. A Regulatory Perspective

Kathy H. Abbott

22. The Future of CRM 581

Thomas R. Chidester, Barbara G. Kanki and José Anca

A Story of Robert L. Helmreich: A Convergence of Friends and Colleagues

Thomas R. Chidester

Federal Aviation Administration, Civil Aerospace Medical Institute, Oklahoma City, OK, United States

Dr. Robert L. Helmreich pioneered research in aviation, medicine, and space operations. With Janet Spence, he wrote definitive conceptualizations of masculinity, femininity, and their psychological correlates. Along the way, he trained and inspired a generation of researchers and changed how the known universe thinks about safety in a variety of environments. I was among many students for whom he served as a mentor and dissertation supervisor, and then became a lifelong colleague. In this tribute, I review a number of those key contributions, but wherever possible, those who collaborated with him at the time have offered their insight into the person and his accomplishments. Here is Bob:

1 LIFE HISTORY

Bob was born in Kansas City, Missouri on April 29, 1937. His father, Ralph, became an Assistant Vice President at Bell Laboratories and moved the family to New Jersey. On February 6, 1958, his hometown newspaper reported, "Cited for academic honors at Yale University are two Summit Area students. They are Robert L. Helmreich, son of Mr. and Mrs. Ralph L. Helmreich of 105 New England Avenue ..." (Summit Herald & Record, 1958). Bob received his Bachelor's degree from Yale in 1959 and was commissioned into the US Navy. His undergraduate thesis was published in *Science* (Helmreich, 1960). After serving as the Executive Officer on the *USS Decatur*, Bob received his discharge and returned to Yale, entering the doctoral program in Social Psychology. While there, he began research in isolated and confined environments on Project Sealab, work that would lead to both advising NASA on space flight issues and form the intellectual and methodological bases for many of his later accomplishments in aviation and medicine. Completing his PhD in 1966, Bob was hired as an assistant professor at The University of Texas at Austin, where he gained tenure and was promoted to associate professor in 1969 and professor in 1973. He retired in 2007, and passed away on July 7, 2012 (Wilhelm & Domjan, 2013).

2 UNDERSEA HABITATS—SEALAB II AND TEKTITE

For his dissertation project at Yale, Bob had the opportunity to support the Sealab II project under an Office of Naval Research grant (Radloff & Helmreich, 1968). The experience would influence much of his career. Sealab I and II were designed to enable the opening of the ocean floor to human work by showing that divers could live and perform effectively in saturation conditions.

Sealab I had been in clear, warm Atlantic waters near Bermuda. Sealab II was designed to be more challenging and representative of work that habitat diving might support in the future. Deployed offshore of La Jolla, California, Sealab II sat in cold water with poor visibility, and the ocean floor and habitat were not level. For the aquanauts, it was dangerous. They could not ascend to the surface immediately in an emergency. "To do so would mean certain, rapid, and painful death from an explosive embolism" (p. 8). They were 35 hours of decompression time away from the normal world. Should a porthole break, the habitat would immediately flood; escape was not certain. During work dives, SCUBA equipment could malfunction and alternative breathing umbilicals could tangle, leading to drowning. One could get lost in low visibility and be unable to reach the habitat before exhausting life support. Scorpion fish inhabited the ocean floor surrounding the habitat; stings were typically painful, but capable of causing seizures. Adding discomfort to danger, a helium-oxygen atmosphere was required because nitrogen becomes a narcotic and oxygen causes anemia and edema at high pressures. This results in constriction of the vocal chords (and a high-pitched helium voice) and difficulties in body temperature control (when sleeping, one could feel freezing on one side while sweating on the other). Mercury astronaut Scott Carpenter, who set records for time at depth in Sealab II, described saturation diving and living in the habitat as more challenging than his experiences in space flight (p. 1).

Roland Radloff and Bob saw Sealab II as an ideal laboratory for understanding the impact of prolonged stress on individual and group performance and well-being. Both saw the habitat as an analog to extended space flight—humans would be isolated to a workplace from which physical return to the normal world is possible only through exceptional circumstances outside the individual's control. They collected a variety of self-report and observational measures among 28 aquanauts divided among three 14-day missions. They found that the teams recognized the stress, adapted, and maintained group cohesiveness well for the most part, and performed effectively. All of the aquanauts found their participation highly rewarding, and some saw it as something of a peak experience. However, some described maintaining group relations as effortful and reported feelings of isolation and overt hostility towards remote operational personnel. "In the final analysis, the characteristics which the aquanauts had in common may have become more important than any differences" (p. 108). This was somewhat different from what had been observed in contemporary laboratory studies of isolation and confinement, which could fairly be described as leading to individual alienation and group disintegration. Bob and Roland proposed a framework conceptualizing Sealab as a high cost, high reward environment, suggested its potential motivation for crew success, and argued that laboratory studies had subtracted from both the cost and reward components of the equation. From a biographical perspective, one should make note of the approach—Bob immersed himself in the operating theater, he sought ecologically valid measures of participant thought and behavior, he compared results with similar laboratory experimentation, and he leveraged those comparisons towards theory. This would recur throughout his career.

I first met Bob when he was a graduate student at Yale in the 1960s and I worked at the Yale Computer Center as a systems programmer. In those early days of computers, the psychologists were delighted to find an easier and less error-prone way to compute their statistics and part of my job was to help them. I even wrote some custom programs for Bob and his advisor and I shared the occasional evening beer at our favorite watering hole with him, which made me familiar with his dissertation work on Sealab II. Bob's delight in fast cars was already well developed in those days, and one evening he asked me to go with him to the local car dealership to look at a Chevy Corvette. The salesman exuded 1960s-style sleaze. At one point, he looked Bob earnestly in the eye and asked, "Do you think you're man enough for this car?" With monumental effort we managed not to break down laughing—does this guy know he's talking to a psychologist?—but Bob walked out with a shiny blue Corvette, a picture of which his friends will remember hanging on the wall at the lake house. I think I was Bob's second PhD, which means I remember well the green Jaguar that followed the blue Corvette, and remember with affection the man who set me on a satisfying life course. (Roger Bakeman).

Bob would continue undersea research with Project Tektite at the Brookings Institution in Washington. There, he observed and identified predictors of substantial between-crew variability in performance, observed systematic variation in performance within crews over time, and reported that two-way closed-circuit video between the habitat and surface control room appeared to reduce reports of isolation and hostility towards surface personnel (Helmreich, 1971). Today saturation diving habitats are typically housed aboard ship, with divers transitioning in pressure vessels to and from the worksite, greatly increasing their safety.

Dr. Bob, as he was affectionately called, first influenced my life when I was an undergraduate with no declared major at The University of Texas at Austin in 1968. Bob was a new professor who was a mesmerizing lecturer in the "Introduction to Psychology" class I took. I did well in his class and attended some great parties at his house where I met other undergraduate and graduate students. Out of the sky came an invitation to work as a College Work Study student for him, quarter time. Yee, haw! I couldn't believe it! He quickly became a mentor and steered me into Social Psychology. I got my Master's degree under his tutorship and worked on research projects as his project manager until my retirement from UT in 2003. In my senior year, Bob called me into his office, where he was puffing away on cigarettes and literally bouncing up and down with excitement. He had just received word that he was going to be funded for an underwater project where we were to observe scientist and engineer men and (gasp) women 24 hours a day working in a confined, hostile environment as an analog for humans in space. Bob quickly put together an enthusiastic team of undergraduate and graduate students who had to work in—poor us—the US Virgin Islands. On this project I learned some lessons in bureaucracy. We were expected to serve as support for the dive project and to provide our own equipment. You can imagine the grilling that the UT procurement office gave us when a Psych professor wanted to buy a Zodiak rubber boat to use on a research grant in the Caribbean! After daily use by us rowdy folks and many patches from holes punched by anchors, etc., we had to retire the poor old thing. Then we started to get letters from the inventory people demanding to know where the boat was! They expected it to be returned as excess inventory. A trip to the Dean's office was in order. (John Wilhelm)

3   RECONCEPTUALIZING PSYCHOLOGICAL MASCULINITY AND FEMININITY

A decade after Sealab, Janet Spence and Bob published their seminal monograph on psychological dimensions associated with gender (Spence & Helmreich, 1978). Their work was supported by grants from the National Institute of Mental Health. In biographies of Janet Spence, initiation of this work is described as a reaction to Helmreich, Aronson, and LeFan (1970). They had focused on the likeability of men who were seen as competent, finding that men liked competent men. Noticing the gender bias, Janet recruited Bob to study reactions to competent women (Spence, 1988).

Bob Helmreich was my teacher and mentor. Dr. Helmreich and I both arrived at the University of Texas at Austin in the fall of 1966—he, as an assistant professor in the psychology department, and I, as a freshman. The first psychology course I took was in the fall of 1967. The young Dr. Helmreich taught "Introduction to Psychology" to several hundred students in Batts (yes, Batts) auditorium. It was the usual survey course, but Dr. Helmreich gave wonderful lectures, making the material come alive. I decided to major in psychology as well as math. The following year, I took Dr. Helmreich's "Introduction to Social Psychology" course, and I loved it. His enthusiasm was infectious. As an undergraduate, I did a little work in Bob's (no longer "Dr. Helmreich") lab on projects he was doing with Elliot Aronson, and I decided I wanted to go to graduate school in social psych. Bob was a wonderful teacher, and he was recognized by the Cactus yearbook in 1970 with the Cactus Teaching Excellence Award. I went off to graduate school in California in 1970, but returned to UT after a year to work with Bob, who was now assistant chair of the psychology department. On the other side of the department office was the department chair, Janet Taylor Spence. Propinquity makes things happen, and in this case, it led to one of the great research collaborations in psychology. Janet was intrigued by a study Bob had done with Elliot Aronson that, among other things, looked at the effects of perceived competence on interpersonal attraction. Because the participants were male and the stimulus person was male, Bob and Janet set out to answer the question, "Who likes competent women?" In the early 1970s, the study of gender roles and other gender-related phenomena was ground-breaking. At that time, Sandra Bem was developing a competing conceptualization of the issues. Her measurement instrument (Bem Sex Role Inventory; Bem, 1974) hit the streets shortly before the Personal Attributes Questionnaire. In 1978, Janet and Bob's book Masculinity and Femininity: Their Psychological Dimensions, Correlates and Antecedents, was a landmark in psychological research and the study of gender. I was privileged to be part of this collaboration. It seemed like almost every day we went to lunch, and after we reviewed the latest revelation in the Watergate scandal, we would talk about the research. It was exciting to participate in the exchange of ideas. In those years, I spent a lot of time at Bob's wonderful house in West Lake Hills where he was always a gracious host. He had a computer terminal at home that hooked up with the mainframe on campus—this was long before Apple II and PCs. This was old-time batch processing. One night when I arrived for dinner, Janet grabbed me by the ear and pointed out that I had mistakenly given her a 3 x 2 ANOVA instead of a 2 x 3. I was promptly escorted (by the ear) to Bob's home office where I sat down at his terminal and submitted another job with the correct parameters. Only then was I given a drink and invited to the table. And sure enough the revised analysis made a lot more sense. (Joy Stapp).

The answer to "Who likes competent women?" was complex. Spence and Helmreich (1972a) found that female subjects preferred competent women whether they were performing traditionally masculine or feminine tasks, but male subjects most preferred a competent woman performing a masculine task and least preferred a less competent woman performing a traditionally masculine task. Women performing traditionally feminine tasks received intermediate ratings from male subjects, regardless of competence. This study was followed by a series of psychometric instruments that disentangled psychological "masculinity" and "femininity" (and achievement motivation) from gender:

- Attitudes Toward Women Scale (AWS; Spence & Helmreich, 1972b);
- Personal Attributes Questionnaire (PAQ; Spence, Helmreich, & Stapp, 1974);
- Work and Family Orientation Questionnaire (WOFO; Helmreich & Spence, 1978); and
- Male-Female Relations Questionnaire (MFRQ; Spence, Helmreich, & Sawin, 1980).

Similar to Bakan's (1966) competing concepts of agency and communion, Spence and Helmreich described traits of *Instrumentality* and *Expressiveness*. But, they found the psychological traits to be nearly orthogonal and only moderately correlated with—not definitional of—gender. The means of the dimensions differed by gender, but their multivariate distributions overlapped tremendously, leaving the sexes with perhaps as much in common as in difference. There are both highly expressive men and highly instrumental women, and any given individual may be high or low on either or both dimensions. But perhaps the most successful people have elevated levels of both—they seek to influence their environment to achieve and accomplish *and* they care about people, emotions, and community. Many found this concept both intellectually compelling and personally liberating. Men could seek emotional intimacy in their relationships without being any less masculine. Women could be highly motivated to achieve and be competent in a field of their choosing without sacrificing their femininity. These insights would lead to theories of attainment that applied equally well to both genders (Helmreich, Beane, Lucker, & Spence, 1978).

In August of 1977, I applied for the Graduate Social Psychology administrative assistant position at UT Austin. While interviewing with Dr. Helmreich, I mentioned that my cousin Joe Burleson was a psychology graduate student but I didn't know in which department. Bob was thrilled, as Joe was in his program and was highly admired, which provided me with an unexpectedly successful reference. When the school year started, Bob told Joe that he really needed to meet the new admin assistant and brought Joe into my office. Joe was happily surprised to see me and Bob got a real kick out of his joke! As a newly out lesbian, I could not have asked for a more supportive, positive atmosphere in which to nurture my growing self-awareness. Reading and assisting with publication tasks for Masculinity & Femininity: Their Psychological Dimensions, Correlates, & Antecedents supported my personal insights and gave me the courage to truly be myself for the first time in my 27-year-old life. I owe Bob, and also Dr. Janet Spence and John Wilhelm, a huge debt of gratitude as excellent role models. (Pamela Cobb)

Bob would later apply these concepts to the selection of airline and space crewmembers—seeking to select those with the "right stuff," for leadership positions in small groups performing challenging tasks. Of course, this right stuff was not traditional stereotypically masculine characteristics, but rather both highly achievement oriented and highly interpersonally skilled. In the late 1980s he argued that core dimensions of the PAQ and WOFO could be used to predict performance of groups conducting challenging tasks. Instrumentality, Expressiveness, Work Motivation, and Mastery Motivation could be used as positive predictors, while Negative Instrumentality, Negative Communion, Verbal Aggressiveness, and Interpersonal Competitiveness could serve as negative predictors. A series of validation studies by Bob, colleagues, and students yielded promising results, culminating in training assessment and simulation studies that found leaders (airline Captains) with a cluster of these positive traits fostered crews that worked together and were more likely to perform well during a crisis. They could be contrasted by performance of leaders with the "wrong stuff"—mostly high Positive and Negative Instrumentality combined with interpersonal competitiveness—whose crews seemed to perform poorly initially but adapt over time, and those with generally low motivation—what Bob affectionately called "no stuff"—whose crews did not perform well and did not adapt over time (Chidester, Helmreich, Gregorich, & Geis, 1991; Chidester, Kanki, Foushee, Dickinson, & Bowles, 1990). Musson (2003) would later establish the correlation of these personality dimensions to measures of the "Big Five" conceptualization of personality (McCrae & Costa, 1990). Spence and Helmreich's scales could be construed as more specific subcomponents of four of the five dimensions (Conscientiousness, Agreeableness, Extraversion, and Neuroticism), including both positive and negative correlates. Only the dimension of Openness was not well-represented in their instruments. Musson, Sandal, and Helmreich (2004) found, disappointingly, that neither the Spence/Helmreich measures nor the Neuroticism-Extraversion-Openness Five Factors Inventory (NEO-FFI) (McCrae & Costa, 2010) dimensions reliably predicted which applicants would be selected into the astronaut corps. Their impact upon astronaut *performance* remains to be determined.

I had the honor of being a post-doctoral student of Bob's during the late 1970s at the height of airline deregulation. Bob asked me to be involved in studying crew coordination at a start-up airline "People Express" more specifically in picking crews for the airline. Because of this opportunity I learned that flight decks were in many ways similar to small businesses. I learned that what motivated a good pilot also motivated a successful entrepreneur. Because of Bob I became one of the first entrepreneurship professors in the United States. Clearly he motivated me to explore topics many applied psychologists only later discovered as important. (Alan Carsrud)

4   DEVELOPING COCKPIT RESOURCE MANAGEMENT

In the early 1980s Bob turned his full attention to performance of crews in the cockpit. Bob's former student, Clay Foushee (1984) described how aviation accidents had become increasingly attributed to human error, and that this description was not a satisfactory explanation. Human error is a *result* of contextual, individual, and process factors present in a situation, not a sufficient *explanation* for accident causation. Foushee further argued that many concepts of small group research could be applied to the task of operating modern aircraft.

> *Bob Helmreich influenced my life and career more than any other mentor. I've been gifted with several, but he was the "uber-mentor." However, my affiliation with him was accidental, unplanned, but ultimately quite profound. As a Duke undergraduate, I worked with two luminaries of academic, social psychology, Jack Brehm and Edward E. Jones. I applied to the PhD programs of several highly-ranked departments, all of which were classic, experimental social psychology programs. I was fortunate to have my choice of several, and I chose Texas, in part, because it had a great reputation, and in larger part, because they offered me a "full-ride" research fellowship. I had every intention of following in the laboratory tradition of Elliott Aronson, David Glass, E. E. Jones, and Jack Brehm. Bob Helmreich wasn't even on my radar screen. At Texas, I started down that very path, but I found myself intrigued by the energy and brilliance of the research team led by the legendary Janet T. Spence and Robert L. Helmreich. I was honored to be invited into the team doing pioneering research on masculinity, femininity, and achievement motivation. I spent my entire graduate career doing classic, experimental social psychology research. As I was writing my doctoral dissertation on achievement motivation, I was immersed in a similar existential crisis to the one Bob had experienced years before. I wanted be involved in helping to solve "real-world" problems, as opposed to documenting the behavior of college sophomores in groups, when they are required to participate in psychology experiments. That was 1978, and Bob mentioned to me that John Lauber, and his colleagues at the NASA-Ames Research Center, had invited him to speak at a workshop on "Cockpit Resource Management." He invited me to go with him. That meeting of airline training managers and NASA human factors researchers was my professional "epiphany," and shortly thereafter, I was offered a position at NASA-Ames, where I reported for duty in 1979. It was also the beginning of our 14-year research partnership in aviation human factors research, which charted me on a professional course that I could never have imagined. I left the research world in 1992 to accept an offer as the VP of Flight Operations at Northwest Airlines, but my mentor was always with me. In 2004, Bob called to let me know that I would be receiving the University of Texas, Department of Psychology, Distinguished Alumnus Award, and asked me to deliver a*

commencement address to the graduating class of psychology majors. Throughout that incredible weekend in Austin, I was rather dumbfounded that this legendary man had arranged this honor for me, and thinking he was the one who should have been on that stage delivering my message: "Just exactly what does one do with a degree in psychology?" Bob's students were his children, and he was my daughter's godfather. I was privileged to have been taken under his wings at the onset of this important era in aviation safety, which brought about a wholesale cultural change in the way crews are selected, trained, and operating procedures are designed, among other things. I think about him often and miss him greatly. (Clay Foushee)

Bob would offer and validate definitions of and behavioral markers evidencing effective Cockpit (and later, Crew) Resource Management (CRM), advocate full-mission in addition to part-task simulator training, develop and validate measures of attitudes associated with those behaviors, chronicle and advance the evolution of training, and articulate concepts that dominate modern flight training curricula. His work was supported by grants from the Federal Aviation Administration (FAA) and National Aeronautics and Space Administration (NASA).

In the early 70s, I had the good fortune to work with the likes of Charlie Billings, H. P. Ruffell Smith, George Cooper and others at NASA Ames. In these early days of the HF program there, we had done several analyses of aircraft accident data, and a limited amount of incident data, and were in the process of analyzing the rich data coming from the Ruffell Smith full-mission simulation study. We gradually formed the idea that human error was a critical issue in aviation, and that specifically, it seemed that such error wasn't coming from a lack of technical knowledge or skill, but more from an inability to effectively utilize the vast array of resources available to flight crews—other crew members, equipment in the aircraft, ATC, support from airline maintenance and operations centers, and even cabin crew. It seemed to be the kind of issue that was being addressed in business management training programs, and from this nascent idea came the term "cockpit resource management." In about 1974 or so, I was discussing this work and these ideas with another colleague from the now politically-incorrectly named Man-Machine Integration Branch at NASA Ames, Trieve Tanner. Trieve was the NASA project leader for a study of social-psychological issues involved in long-term manned space flight, and was the contract monitor for a study that used extended underwater habitats as an analog for long-duration space missions. During my discussion with Trieve, he suggested that I might find it worthwhile to have this same discussion with the Principal Investigator for that study, a guy named Helmreich. We did, and it became immediately clear that Bob was closely tuned to wavelengths similar to those we were exploring; only he was focused on human performance in space, via the depths of the ocean, and we were focused on human performance in airplanes. In the end, it was clear that these were largely overlapping issues, and to my knowledge, it was Bob's first look at aviation human factors. Bob took a concept and ran with it and is directly responsible for the central place "CRM" now occupies in the art and science of human factors, not just in aviation, but in a broad array of systems that depend upon the exquisite and unique capability of humans to work effectively as teams to achieve some desired outcome—safe flight, safe navigation of ships, safe surgery, fire-fighting, and on and on. I continue to be amazed at how many explicit and implicit references to "CRM" in its many variations can be found in a very diverse set of human activities. It was largely Bob who made this possible in several ways. First as a scholar and scientist, he was a rich source of endless new ideas, new ways of looking at the problem, new solutions. Second, and equally importantly, as a teacher and mentor, reflected in the manifold contributions of his students, research assistants, associates and colleagues. His infectious enthusiasm for concepts and ideas, his competence as a researcher and practitioner, and his great ability to form effective teams from disparate groups of people, from pilots to physicians, mechanics to firemen, across all cultures national and corporate, and his genuinely warm personality allowed him to occupy a unique place in the history of "human factors." Our world is a better one because of him. (John Lauber)

From this initial work would come the Cockpit Management Attitudes Questionnaire (CMAQ; Helmreich, 1984), a measure to allow airlines to assess how well their training programs were meeting their knowledge and attitudinal objectives. It included scales focusing on communication and coordination, command responsibility, and recognition of stressor effects (Gregorich, Helmreich, & Wilhelm, 1990). Later versions would incorporate use of cockpit automation and characteristics of national culture (Helmreich & Merritt, 2001). Helmreich and Foushee (1993) concluded that measureable positive changes in these attitudes followed classroom and simulator training in CRM. Not satisfied with attitude change, Bob and the airlines he worked with developed a checklist of behavioral markers of effective CRM, assessed during simulator training by supervisory pilots given specialized training in observational methodology. Similar positive changes in behavior following training were observable in the simulator.

I was the manager of the budding CRM program at Continental Airlines when I first met Bob in 1983. That started a collaboration, which continued until I retired in 1999. He along with John Lauber (NTSB), Clay Foushee (NASA) and Earl Wiener (University of Miami) were extremely helpful in starting what was originally called CRM but morphed into Human Factors, Error Management, and finally Threat and Error Management. The programs were not initially met with enthusiasm (that's an understatement) and we struggled with making the workshops as meaningful as possible from the pilots' view-point. We had to stay away from what crews called "touchy feely stuff." One of the continuing problems was the material; although applicable, it got stale

*quickly, which required the CRM team to continually reinvent the curriculum.
That's where Bob was most helpful; he continued to assist us in creating a targeted lesson plan that was palatable to the crews. We used mainly accident
case studies with the appropriate lesson objective highlighted within the tragic
event. We at Continental along with most of the other major airlines consistently drew from Bob his expertise in making the workshops fresh and as
appealing as could be. He worked tirelessly for us whenever we asked for his
assistance. (Frank Tullo)*

5 DEVELOPING LINE OPERATIONS SAFETY AUDITS

The drive to understand whether and how CRM training affected performance carried over from how pilots performed in the "laboratory" of simulation to how they performed in daily flight operations. While most of us now
would accept as given the value of what Antonsen (2009) described as the
second historical phase of accident investigation and corrective action
response, this was far from certain in the early 1990s. Unlike the prior phase,
focused upon technical failures of equipment, ground structures, and systems,
resulting in a clear downward trend in the fatal accident rate in aviation,
CRM focused on operator behavior. Its impact upon accident rates was
unknowable for many years, leading the airlines to seek the most valid process measures they could create. Working primarily with James Klinect,
Ashleigh Merritt, and John Wilhelm, Bob developed Line Operations Safety
Audits (Helmreich, 2001). This technique trained cadres of supervisory
pilots, and often line pilots, to standards of evaluation using a library of
video scenarios, then deployed them to large numbers of representative
flights to collect standardized observational data from the cockpit jumpseat.
When accomplished multiple times within an airline, or compared to a body
of data collected at other airlines, this method provided a benchmark allowing participants to assess how well their behavioral goals were being met
and identify areas for potential improvement. By the close of the 20th century, almost every major US airline had participated and in 2001, the
International Civil Aviation Organization (ICAO) endorsed LOSA as a program to provide safety data comprised of normal operations in technical and
human performance areas. Bob and Bruce Tesmer (Continental Airlines
Captain and Safety Department program developer) were corecipients of the
2001 Aviation Week and Space Technology Laurel Award for Commercial
Aviation. They were recognized for bringing LOSA from a research concept
to a mature flight safety data collection program in just 5 years.
Continental's willingness to participate and fund LOSA development, their
proximity to Austin, and active management collaboration (Captains Frank
Tullo and Deb McCoy) enabled five consecutive LOSA development audits

to be performed through the UT Human Factors Research Project between 1996 and 2001.

In the mid 90s, the Philippines was going through significant political tur-moil—we were having coup d'états every six months. Bob and I had completed our final analytics of the airline's CMAQ. I sent him first class tickets to come over to Manila to deliver the final report. Unfortunately, his profound amaze-ment with the airline's upper-deck first class B747-400 beds (which predated A380 first class by 20 years, outshining it by far) was ended when the flight was diverted to Cebu, yes, because of a coup. I rang him through the airline's station agents (no cell phones then yet) and said a million apologies and asked him how he was. His response was that all was okay. He said, the CMAQ report was very encouraging and he did not expect a huge turnout of data (which made NASA and the FAA happy). He said to me that he was hoping to fly to Manila (coup or no coup) on the same first class B747 bed because he was running out of floor tiles to count whilst stranded at Cebu Airport! We sent a Beech King Air to fetch him from Cebu. Bob was the only passenger. We put him up at the Manila Hotel but could not billet him at the Douglas MacArthur Suite—it was occupied. I suppose this is a lesson for young researchers, where Bob exemplified humility (yes, and patience). Bob was cul-turally adept and accommodating of the shortfalls of airlines that he worked with. Humility and empathy strikes a vibrant chord in Bob's life. (Joey Anca)

Working in "real-world" settings continued to push the administrative enve-lope at UT. We had finally received funding for a project observing airline pilots at work in the cockpits of regularly-scheduled aircraft with passengers in the back. Our travel department insisted on three-month prior authorization for travel payments to international destinations and one-month prior authori-zation for domestic travel. When we proposed sending trained observers on the UT payroll out to "ride the flight lines" to both domestic and international destinations on an impromptu basis with the expectation of having hotels and per-diem paid, UT responded, "Absolutely no way." So...another trip to the Dean's office, then to the President of the University, resulted in a special "blanket" travel authorization for our observers. (John Wilhelm)

Though John describes what was required to accomplish LOSA develop-ment, conflicts over applied research logistics and their prioritization relative to other department, school, and University objectives strained Bob's rela-tionships with University faculty.

6 CONCEPTUALIZING FLIGHT AS THREAT AND ERROR MANAGEMENT

Through the 1980s, most university researchers avoided developing CRM curricula and it became a market captured by management development training professionals, with mixed acceptance and impact. This was suboptimal for training managers, the airlines, and the traveling public (Chidester, 1993). By 1995, CRM would probably have been described in terms of the attitudes measured in the CMAQ and behaviors conceptualized in Bob's behavioral marker work. That was certainly true of curricula for the program I managed at American Airlines, which used accident and incident data and scenarios to enable classroom instruction of concepts relating to situation awareness, automation management, communication, and team coordination. In the simulator, training scenarios challenged the same constructs and were debriefed by supervisory pilots who had received the same conceptual curricula. That it was consistent, but not sufficient was revealed by the accidents of the 1990s and a series of changes in the process data available to the industry.

The FAA introduced its Advanced Qualification Program (AQP; FAA, 2015) allowing airlines to customize their training content and footprint to their unique requirements. Prior to that, training content and performance standards were driven by appendices to Part 121 of the Federal Aviation Regulations, with innovation allowed only through petition for exemption (Northwest Orient Airlines developed Line-Oriented Flight Training through such an exemption, which led to an Advisory Circular authorizing LOFT in any Part 121 recurrent training program). AQP allowed an airline to conduct task analyses of flight operations for each aircraft type and design a training footprint and qualification standards to those analyses. But the FAA also insisted that training innovation be evaluable through data, yielding many observations of training and line performance. At the same time, Bob's team was accumulating a body of LOSA data enabling a degree of benchmarking, and at least two airlines were actively engaged with that team as they developed their AQP. Concurrently, Captain Scott Griffith at American Airlines proposed, and its management, the Allied Pilots Association, and the FAA agreed, to experimental development of Aviation Safety Action Partnerships (ASAP; FAA, 2013a), which allowed pilots (and subsequently all certificated airmen) to report without penalty any safety concern they observed, even if their actions caused or contributed to the problem. In parallel, United Airlines brought the European concept of Flight Operations Quality Assurance (FOQA; FAA, 2013b) to the United States. FOQA programs download from onboard recorders many parameters recorded on each flight, allowing at a minimum, identification of the frequency, location, and context of exceedances of desired aircraft states, such as unstable approaches. The nature of process information available to the airlines fundamentally changed and expanded exponentially. While most operations were safe, deviations from what airline safety professionals would desire were more frequent and geographically widespread than we imagined. Bob organized colleagues within academia and the airlines to respond.

In the late 1990s, I was working at American Airlines as manager of their human factors training program and also serving as the primary analyst, publication, and outreach liaison for the review team of its ASAP program. Bob was consulting with both Continental and Delta Air Lines to help them develop their next generation of classroom CRM and line-oriented simulator training. He called me at some point and explained what they were developing, which focused on errors that occur in the cockpit and strategies to ensure they were caught and corrected, rather than allowed to escalate to incident or accident. He was thinking of calling the approach, "Error Management." Bob asked what I thought, and I told him I found it pretty compelling. Having just come through the investigation of the Flight 965 accident in Cali, Columbia, I would have wished to have designed training that wasn't only situationally preventive in nature (don't be confused by automation modes or inputs; practice operating in all levels of available automation, and choose the level most appropriate to the situation), but offered resiliency (position yourself to catch and correct deviations from your intended flight path). One thing bothered me though, and I said to Bob that my impression from reviewing, by then, hundreds of ASAP reports was that most errors were provoked. Something occurred in the operating environment that caused a response that was either facilitative or dysfunctional. What we saw in ASAP reports tended to be things corrected somewhere along the line; some quickly, some much later, and some serious enough that had the correction not happened, the aircraft could have been lost. About a week later, Bob called me and asked what I would think about an approach called "Threat and Error Management." He then spelled out for me most of what would appear in the first publication of the concept and would form the core of airline human factors training for years to come—including at American. For me, that was the type of person Bob was. He would reach out to colleagues to seek input on concepts. He would listen and adapt. And then he would bring back something that was far more than one imagined from the conversation. (Tom Chidester)

I too, was around when Bob needed to move forward from just having human error as the bad guy of flight crew performance, with CRM as the solution. The reality is that there is no such thing as a "normal" flight! Each is unique. The difference between the pristine and the flight from hell is the difference in the numbers of encountered threats and errors. Consider two flights from Houston Intercontinental to Newark, NJ that are two hours apart. The first flight is all in clear weather, on time, with no ATC delays, with an aircraft with no inoperative components and having no malfunctions, and no passenger or cabin issues. The second flight has thunder showers in the area and along the flight planned route, multiple ATC required altitude and course corrections, heavy arrival traffic with holding required, a difficult instrument approach required to a landing near the maximum crosswind limit. The questions we ask about each flight are how tough was it and how did the crew handle it? The airline knows only whether or not the aircraft made it and whether or not it was on time. From the start of the first Line Operations Safety Audit, at Continental Airlines, Bob wanted to understand the thought process of the pilots when they encountered things in flight that required time and attention of the crew (hazards that were realized). As the data started to come in, we all could see that crew errors (slips, lapses or mistakes) were mostly made in completion of required normal procedures and were routinely trapped with crew run checklists, call-outs or monitoring by the other pilot. What was unclear was the relationship of system and environmental threats and the action/reaction of the crews to those threats. Bob always included all the individual perspectives of the project team when deriving a hypothesis on what was actually happening to the crews when threats were encountered. That discussion was spirited and from all the input Bob developed the Threat and Error Management Model. That model has withstood the questions from all users and critics as to its reality and usefulness. One thing I always appreciated about working with Bob was that he included all input from the team and when he was convinced that the data showed the truth of the path he did not shy away from taking a stand on what the data meant. I also appreciate the fact that Bob saw merit in my belief that valid data could be obtained from flight crew performance monitoring of "normal" flight operations. On the lighter side, when we were looking at the data for unstable approaches and landings, James Klinect developed the concept of the "blue box." This was a time along the flight path that allowed the flight crew the opportunity to slow from cruise speed and altitude to achieve a descent path enabling the aircraft to maintain a stable final approach and landing. When a flight did not start down from within the blue box, the crew would be unable to maintain a stable approach, resulting in a fly through, a go-around or long landing out of the touchdown zone. When Bob was pressed for a warning to give the flight crews about this effect, Bob just told us all to promote the wisdom of the Klinect prospective: "tell them to get their s... together, before it hits the fan." Everyone seemed to agree that for solutions to common sense predicaments you needed a common sense solution. Tell it like it is. (Bruce Tesmer)

As an aside, that "blue box" concept would subsequently emerge empirically from analyses of FOQA data that searched for flights that were multivariate-statistically extreme during the descent phase of flight, compared to masses of similarly-situated flights. A high energy state (being too high and too fast, resulting in high potential and kinetic energy) that develops while maneuvering from cruise altitude to the approach frequently results in go-arounds and unstable approaches, with only some of the latter corrected before touchdown (Chidester, 2007). Uncorrected unstable approaches are at greater risk of accident. Here, multiple sources of data on crew performance converged on an issue requiring industry and government intervention.

Helmreich, Klinect, and Wilhelm (1999) articulated the Threat and Error Management Model (TEM) for flight operations. TEM suggests that most adverse events can be described in terms of risks or challenges present in an operational environment (threats) and the actions of specific personnel that potentiate or exacerbate those threats (errors). The goal of safe operations, then, is to identify likely threats in the operating environment or the current unique sequence of actions, mitigate those threats, and trap and correct any erroneous actions by team members. TEM has been widely applied in the aviation industry and suggests that some risks are constant, but many are contingent by situation and vary by phases of activity. This regularity may be used to predict and prevent error. The utility of TEM has been demonstrated for analyzing accidents, incidents, and safety reports. It has been adapted for developing training programs that teach pilots, dispatchers, and mechanics to identify and mitigate threats before a hazardous situation can occur. This approach now guides much airline training development and the capture of feedback from training, ASAP reports, and FOQA.

My first meeting with Bob was in late 1992 or early 1993. I had been reading an aviation magazine in the months prior and learned that some top researchers in Cockpit (now Crew) Resource Management (CRM) were in Austin, the city where I lived. At that time, I was looking for an internship project to complete my undergraduate degree from Southwest Texas State University (now Texas State) in San Marcos. One of my reasons for attaining the Bachelor's degree was to get into the airline industry as a pilot. Here I saw an opportunity to learn about the new hot topic, CRM, from the very people that were making the difference in the airline industry, and complete my university degree. I had no idea that when I walked in the door to meet Bob Helmreich that my life would be forever changed. The NASA/UT/FAA Aerospace Crew Research Project (NASA/UT) was a collection of offices and desks with mostly PhD candidates working toward their degrees as well as some professional researchers and data crunchers. All these people were working under the guidance of Bob Helmreich. Lou Montgomery headed up the front office and did a thousand tasks including grammatical reviews of papers and life counseling. I came through the NASA/UT door a few minutes early and met Lou. She asked me to have a seat and she then advised Dr. Helmreich that I was there for our meeting. Bob was soon off the phone and invited me into his office. We had a chat about who I was and what I hoped to achieve in a one semester internship. I clearly remember that Bob said "That is quite an ambitious project for one semester." Bob made it clear to me that the best we could achieve in one semester was to make a good start since the nature of scientific research is to continually gather empirical evidence and make revisions as necessary to improve the precision and validity of research methods. Bob asked me how I would deal with the possibility of an uncertain outcome. I told him that I was sure that we could come up with at least one "thing" and my documentation of

*the process would achieve the purpose of my occupational education intern-
ship. Bob looked pensive. He had his hands together in front of him with just
the finger tips touching. "If we come up with something solid would you be
willing to continue the work beyond the semester?" he asked me. Not entirely
sure where that might lead, but I do love an adventure and a project, I said
"yes." Bob asked if I drank coffee. "Love it" I replied. We had a spontaneous
laugh, got up, and together made a pot of coffee. Over that cup Bob told me
that he had an area of crew interaction that was not well studied and that he
had just been talking to a friend about it. (I shared my results with and later
met Dr. Earl Wiener of the University of Miami.) The area of interest was the
"shift change" in what he called "ultra long haul" flights. Being a Flight
Engineer on the C5 Galaxy for the USAF Reserve I had some experience in
those long duty days and the sometimes "here, you've got it" handover briefings. I was now quite interested in that topic. The one "thing" that my internship developed was a focus on the flight crew shift change in the form of one
question that went into the Flight Management Attitudes Questionnaire
(FMAQ). To me that was quite a good result. Many years later in April 2005 I
joined British Airways (BA) and on Day One of training I found the European
evolution of Bob Helmreich's behavioral markers on the wall in the CRM
class. I asked the trainers if they knew of Bob and the UT research group.
They not only knew of Bob but acknowledged that he was very influential in
making CRM what it is today. Things tend to happen slowly at most airlines
and it was only a few years ago that BA put out a detailed Crew Handover
Briefing as a section of our hand held checklist. That made me very happy.
The work that we started in Austin looking into industrial shift change procedures and asking questions of major players in the aviation arena furthered the
discussion of how to handle the crew shift change in order to "keep it safe."
Today at work I use a checklist that the research group and I, with Bob
Helmreich's guidance, began in 1993. CRM has been a while developing but
we are all safer for it. I've told many people at work of my internship with the
"NASA/UT" research group and how "we" planted a seed. In my view that
seed has grown and evolved to become the way business is done. I am pleased
to say that Bob flies with me. (Leslie Partridge)*

7 CARRYING GROUP PERFORMANCE CONCEPTS AND METHODS INTO MEDICINE AND BEYOND

Bob argued that physicians and care teams working in the operating room
experience safety challenges similar to pilots flying aircraft, that they must
quickly resolve the ensuing crises to prevent loss of patient life, and that
negative outcomes are probably comparable to flight, but less observable
(Helmreich, 2000; Sexton, Thomas, & Helmreich, 2000). His work was supported by grants from the Agency for Healthcare Research and Quality and

the US Public Health Service. A number of medical researchers moved this idea forward. Rall and Gaba (2005) redefined CRM as Crisis Resource Management, developed core concepts, and advocated training using patient simulation. Sexton et al. (2006) published a Safety Attitudes Questionnaire (SAQ), adapted from the CMAQ, to measure a snapshot of safety culture through surveys of front-line worker perceptions. It has been completed by over 10,000 healthcare professionals in over 200 settings in three countries, and its psychometric properties are well documented with benchmarks available. Ruskin et al. (2013) proposed a threat taxonomy for anesthesia as part of adapting the TEM approach to the operating room.

I first met Bob in 1992 at the Second Australian Aviation Psychology Association Symposium in Manly, Australia, where he gave the keynote address, "Fifteen years of the CRM Wars: Report from the Trenches." Bob described seeing the history and evolution of CRM as a series of battles, for example, a "battle to convince skeptical management of the value of CRM" and a "battle to develop ways to deal with CRM 'failures.'" Bob then took the audience through the history and evolution of CRM, which he was careful to say was colored by his perspective which was largely that of experiences in the United States. Bob was not only a good scientist; he was a kind and tactful man. He described three generations of CRM:

- *The "Stone Age — Clubs and Rocks", focusing on fixing the "wrong stuff;"*
- *The "Bronze Age — Lances and Spears," focusing on concepts and models;*
- *The "Iron Age — Muskets and Sabres," focusing on a systems approach.*

He cited the research supporting CRM, including work from Clay Foushee, John Lauber, Michael Baetge, Dorothea Atcomb, Tom Chidester, Court Dickinson, Stephen Bowles, Earl Wiener, Barbara Kanki, Judith Orasanu and Stephen Predmore. Bob was very good at both encouraging and crediting others. He then concluded his presentation with an "agenda for the renaissance," which included "CRM with an electronic crew member" and the "need to consider specific operations with respect to glass cockpit operations". Bob came up and introduced himself after my presentation on analogous safety concepts between aviation and anesthesiology. "Splendid!" he said. He then asked if I knew of a European anesthesiologist by the name of Hans-Gerhard Schaefer. Bob and Hans were working together on a new survey, the Operating Room Management Attitudes Questionnaire (ORMAQ), derived in part from the CMAQ. The end result of that conversation was that in 1994 I joined Bob and Hans to work on the Team Oriented Medical Simulation (TOMS) project at the University Hospital (Kantonsspitals Basel), University of Basel. This project was a collaboration between the University of Texas at Austin, NASA and the Kantonsspitals Basel. The team included Dr. Thomas Kocher, the simulator's surgeon, whose ingenuity and surgical skills meant that the patient, Wilhelm Tell, actually bled realistically when blood vessels were cut. The other team member was Dr. Dieter ('Betsi') Betzendoerfer, an anesthesiologist and vitally important computer expert. One of Bob's students from Austin, Bryan Sexton, also became involved in the project, as did Dr. Ron Westrum, Professor of Sociology and Interdisciplinary Technology at Eastern Michigan University. The TOMS project was the first time that a complete (and real) Operating Room (OR) team had participated in simulation. Up till then, most OR simulation had focused on testing a staff anesthesiologist staff or resident, who was put in the hot seat to work out the 'problem of the day'. The rest of the OR team was composed of volunteers, sometimes acting in roles such as the surgeon. But in Basel, the team that was booked in a certain room on the real OR slate actually went to work in the simulator, instead of in the OR. And preliminary results showed the utility of the model, as long-standing hierarchies were broken down and team functioning improved. I spent just over a week with the team in Basel. The days were filled with working on the simulation scenarios and debriefing, and giving lectures to the operating room staff. The evenings were spent exploring Basel, window shopping and choosing different restaurants to try. On the weekend Bob and I wandered further from the town center until pulled back by the lure of an organ recital in the cathedral. Our discussions were similarly diverse, encompassing aviation, health care and culture. Bob threw himself into this work. He was fascinated by healthcare, with its superficial similarities to aviation and its deeper differences, which he was careful to note and respect. And although the simulator project was halted by Dr. Schaefer's tragic death in 1995, Bob's interest in healthcare did not stop. We continued to collaborate on projects and to publish together, and Bob was a frequent, enthusiastic and highly acclaimed speaker at many healthcare conferences, including the Halifax Series: The Canadian Healthcare Safety Symposia. But like all great men, Bob had a weakness that I only discovered when he came to Calgary in 1996 to present at Combined Anesthesia and Surgery Grand Rounds and to the Calgary Medical-Legal Society. All went well until the last day when we had planned an excursion to Lake Louise. Not unusually for Calgary in May, there was fresh snow. On seeing this, Bob declared that the warm winds of Texas were preferable and he left early! (Jan Davies)

8 RETIREMENT TO GRANITE SHOALS, TEXAS

Bob retired in 2007 and spent his remaining years traveling, boating, collecting cars, relaxing in his lakefront home, and enjoying University of Texas football. He was a student of the game and could analyze strengths and weaknesses of the offense or defense as if he were an experienced coach. (He also introduced me to Heisman Trophy-winning former Texas Longhorn and Houston Oilers running back, Earl Campbell, at a University function during one of my poststudent visits!)

In the spring of 2000, while leading Delta's new captain's course,("In Command") I conceived of a lifetime achievement award to be given very selectively—to those persons who had, through their continuing work, contributed most significantly to aviation safety through the power of their ideas, their efforts, and their character. Following intense discussion, we chose to call this award the "Dr. Earl Wiener Lifetime Achievement Award." Logically, Dr. Earl was chosen to be the first recipient at that year's "Captain's Leadership Symposium" (CLS) conceived of and hosted by my staff at Delta. Many of the great luminaries of our profession were in attendance at the CLS. Academics, government officials, and many pilots and human factor specialists were present along with all the major US carriers and many of the regional airlines. The first evening of our event, we convened to the 1848 House restaurant in Marietta, Ga. for an evening of Southern hospitality and conversation with Earl Wiener as our featured speaker. As Earl was introduced, we brought his award forward and made the presentation to his astonishment—a Don Lilly hand blown glass sculpture of aircraft in flight complete with contrails. In early 2001, we made the 2nd presentation of the Dr. Earl Wiener award to Captain Al Haynes of United 232 fame while he was speaking before Delta's Flight Operations department. Which brings us to the 3rd and final presentation of the Dr. Earl Wiener award—to Bob Helmreich upon his retirement celebration on the 9th of June, 2007. No one was more deserving; no one was more surprised. Bob's friends, colleagues, staff and others had gathered in the Longhorn Room at University of Texas stadium for an evening to remember and reflect upon Bob's career and accomplishments. At a predetermined point in the program, I was called forward for a special presentation. Delta Captains Ray Justinic, Kurt Shular, Lloyd Sauls, and Steve Paul joined me as we called Bob to the dais and showered him with love, affection, and genuine praise for all the had accomplished, and for all his life had meant to our industry. Truly, he has been a lifesaver for thousands of passengers who will never know that their benefactor was a humble man named Bob Helmreich. During our remarks, Dr. Earl Wiener phoned in to congratulate Bob on receiving this most distinguished of awards. As both he and Earl have flown west, it is appropriate to remember him with the words inscribed on the sculpture:

The Dr. Earl Wiener Lifetime Achievement Award — Presented to Dr. Bob Helmreich June 9, 2007

"Teacher — Leader — Mentor — Friend: He conceived the future and made it reality. With great affection and humble gratitude for your exceptional contributions to flight safety."

Bob was humbled and appreciative, reflective and humorous as he received this recognition before his peers. (Alan Price)

9   IMPACT

In an introduction to a one of the core texts in Aviation Human Factors, Bob said of his own career, that he had not originally even been aware of the field while in graduate school.

My doctoral training at Yale University was in social psychology. Yale had no courses or program in human factors. Indeed, the zeitgeist there and in much of academic psychology was that the only valid approach to research was through carefully controlled laboratory experiments using as data sources two- (or four-) legged subjects—usually bored undergraduates fulfilling a course requirement. Before entering graduate school, I spent four years as a destroyer officer in the U.S. Navy. My naval experience included searching for Russian submarines off Cuba during the missile crisis. When I arrived at graduate school fresh from sea I was directed toward laboratory studies, trying to change student attitudes about mundane issues. As a president was assassinated, riots broke out in American cities, and the country continued in a frenzied race to land humans on the moon, I became less and less enamored with my research path. Because of my military background, I was given the opportunity for my doctoral dissertation to study the behavior of aquanauts living on the ocean floor during Project Sealab. Using in-habitat video cameras and open microphones, the crew's behavior in an extremely dangerous and stressful environment could be captured and analyzed—a precursor of today's confidential observations of flightdeck behavior. I certainly did not realize that my study could best be classified as research into the human factors of an extreme environment.

Salas, Jentsch, & Maurino, 2010, p. xi.

His career would define many curriculum elements for the Human Factors science that grew around him and other leaders of his time. Bob's life and work put things and people into action, and they mattered, particularly to the safety of those who travel by air or receive critical medical care.

In the mid-1980s I started working with Bob as a graduate student research assistant. Originally, and incorrectly, I considered Bob's work to be the stuff of traditional organizational research. Around the same time, I was taking a course offered by another professor on research designed to inform policy decisions. In that course, I was taught that policy decisions optimally are informed by input from several sources, including individuals who serve the role of 'advocate' as well as others who serve the role of 'expert.' In that world-view, advocates are knowledgeable members of the policy-related community, or stakeholders; experts are knowledgeable individuals who are external to the community and are objective and dispassionate about the decisions at hand, e.g., scientists. At the time, a strict separation of the advocate and expert roles was intuitively appealing to me. Scientists must maintain their objectivity, after all. I told Bob about that perspective; mostly, I expected that he would agree with it. I am eternally grateful that he immediately and passionately disagreed. He explained that there is no inherent conflict with an individual acting as both advocate and scientific expert. More to the point, he felt strongly that separating the two roles would diminish the policy-related impact that any one person could have. My lesson was solidified over the years as I watched him work. Bob was the exemplar of how simultaneously to serve the roles of advocate and expert without letting one role contaminate or diminish the other. (Steven Gregorich)

I could write many anecdotes about Robert Helmreich and the many lovely, sometimes humorous, events we shared over our long relationship. I choose to write about my first encounter with him because it illustrates the true nature of Bob. He was driven by passion for improving transportation safety and driven by compassion for sharing his time, knowledge and expertise with those individuals working in the field. I have experienced both, first, as a graduate student then for many years as manager of Bob's FAA research grants. During 1989–1990 I was doing my doctoral research with Army pilots at Fort Rucker. I was a grad student at George Mason University and an intern with The Army Research Institute. The army was interested in determining if personality played a role in pilot error. In my study, I administered several personality, attitude, and performance measures. One was The University of Texas CMAQ. During data analysis, results from the CMAQ were not consistent with other measures. I needed to solve that part of the puzzle. I had never had any contact with UT or Bob's group but I decided to call Austin for information on the CMAQ. Fully expecting to get a brief brush off and maybe a reference to an article, I was totally surprised that Bob took my call. After our discussion he invited me to come to Austin, bring my data, and offered that he and staff would help me sort out the problem. WOW! A lowly grad student from another University getting this attention from this revered group at UT!! I took him up on the offer and went to Austin many times. I worked with Bob, John Wilhelm, Steve Predmore, Steve Gregorich and others in that office. They spared no time or expense to help me with this project. (A problem in CMAQ data collected, analyzed, and forwarded to me by Army personnel turned out to be the root cause.) We became friends over those many trips and many months. They included a little fun, wine and dining during my visits. I was so fortunate to have this introduction to the broad world of the NASA/UT crew project. In doing this Bob had no idea where I would end up professionally; neither did I. Bob's commitment and unselfish motive in helping me was to further research in aviation safety. After my dissertation was complete and I was working for the FAA, I was assigned our first research program in CRM. And so began my professional association with Bob. I was assigned his FAA research grant. What a coincidence! Now I was managing Bob, and did so for 23 memorable and way too short years. I might add, I never really managed Bob! It was a

delight working with him and the UT group, they are the ultimate profes-
sionals. When Bob retired and closed the UT lab it was a huge loss for FAA
research and aviation safety. When Bob passed away I lost a friend and col-
league. Without Bob's help so many years before my path might have been dif-
ferent. He is missed. (Eleana Edens)

Bob was a frequent contributor to Division 21 activities within the American Psychological Association. His first invited address was in 1966 and discussed Sealab II research; the last occurred in 2008, and was titled, From *Charm School to Threat and Error Management: The Evolution of Human Factors Training in Aviation and Medicine.* In between, he would present research findings on theory and perspectives on social interaction, behavioral manifestations of negative components of masculinity and femininity, achievement motivation and scientific attainment, and social-psychological research in space flight. He served as editor of the Group Processes and Individual Differences section of the *Journal of Personality and Social Psychology* from 1983 to 1985. He was a Fellow of the American Psychological Association and the American Psychological Society. In 2007, he received the Franklin V. Taylor Award for Outstanding Contributions in the Field of Applied Experimental/Engineering Psychology. He also received formal recognition from the Flight Safety Foundation, *Aviation Week and Space Technology*, and the Royal Aeronautical Society, among others (Wilhelm & Domjan, 2013).

Bob enabled his students to create productive careers that improved human performance.

Through the years, there was a steady, slow assembly line of brilliant graduate
students working on their PhDs. They learned quickly that Bob wasn't going to
guide them closely. What we did for most was to "dress them up" and get them
out into real-world corporate, aviation and medical situations where they could
use their psychology "tool bag" to provide useful information to the organiza-
tions while collecting data to feed their dissertations. And each year there
were those bright undergraduates who would show up at my office, much to
my surprise, saying, "Dr. Bob told me to show up today for work." After warm
welcome, we would go off to our departmental procurement office to try to
work a payroll miracle for these surprise employees. I never forgot that I was
once one of these youngsters trying to find a place to hang my hat at the big
University and a direction for my life. (John Wilhelm)

Bob was many things to his graduate students—teacher, mentor, father-figure,
and friend. My anecdote highlights the care and concern he felt for us. It was
January 1991 and I was starting my last semester with Bob. I was an Air
Force pilot with a B.S. in engineering. The Air Force had selected me for a 2-
year master's degree in social psychology, focusing on Crew Resource
Management (CRM). The plan was to have me teach at the Air Force Academy

and enhance Air Force CRM. Bob graciously took me on as one of his students. As I was in the final stretch of drafting my thesis, Operation DESERT STORM broke out in Iraq. My friends and those I had trained to fly the KC-135 Stratotanker were deployed, flying in a hostile environment. I was so very frustrated. I had been trained for just such an event. Our Nation called upon her military and I was sitting safe and sound in Austin, TX. Bob noticed that I had become withdrawn and not as focused on my research. One afternoon, he casually caught me in the hallway and asked how I was doing. (Personally, I believe he was watching for me.) I explained how frustrated I was at not being at the controls of my aircraft when air refueling assets were needed in the fight. The naval officer in Bob shown through and he told me he understood exactly how I felt. And, then he looked me in the eyes and with a gentle smile said, "I need you here, too. You are doing great things here." I took a deep breath, smiled back at him, and attacked my thesis with great enthusiasm. That was Bob—watching over us, understanding how we felt, and letting us know how much he valued us being on his team. It was an honor to know him. (Cathy McClain)

Bob was well known for championing those others would have given only second, third or even fourth thought. After wandering leisurely though my undergraduate education over 11 years, I decided I wanted to settle on a career in psychology and get involved in the space program. I was delighted to discover the perfect mentor already busily contributing to aviation and space at UT Austin. I was confident that graduating from one of the UT daughter schools in San Antonio, my native Texan status, and my decision to pursue a doctorate would certainly be sufficient to achieve admittance to the psychology program at Austin. I was not discouraged when I failed to be selected in the first round of applications. Although I lived an hour and a half away outside of San Antonio, I drove to UT and introduced myself to everyone in the department indicating my intention to achieve admittance to graduate school and registered as a special student in one of Bob's summer seminar classes. Bob remarked later that my efforts were largely viewed with benign bemusement by the faculty, including himself. That attitude was very likely strengthened when the fall semester rolled around and I showed up in class seven months pregnant with my second child. I continued to commute the three hour round trip twice a week, growing noticeably more 'prego' by the day. As the baby begin doing the typical in- utero calisthenics common in the ninth month, my small exclamations during class apparently became most unnerving. I arrived at class one day to be met by Dr. Bob grinning from ear to ear. "Go home!" he ordered. "Do you realize you are an hour and half minimum from your doctor?" "Yes….so?" I replied cautiously. "I am NOT going to deliver your baby! Go home. We'll let you into the program next fall. I'll send you the letter next week. Just go home and have that kid," he insisted emphatically. "Ok! See you then!" And off I went. Over the next five years, I'm sure there were times, especially in the first two years, when he wondered if he had made a good bargain. Maybe delivering my son during class would have been the easier route. There were also times when I wondered if that wouldn't have been the better outcome. There was the time I scheduled an appointment with Bob to discuss my dissertation idea and he showed up an hour late, completely forgetting we were supposed to meet. And he did the same thing again the next four mornings in a row. Some would have questioned whether such absent-mindedness was genuine or not. However, Tom Chidester squatted down beside me in the hallway where I sat glumly waiting on the third no-show morning and told me not to take it personally...he was actively working on his own dissertation and it had taken him two weeks to finally pin the good Doctor down for a face-to-face. Tom may never know what a lifeline that kindness represented. In the end, Bob stood as my champion on a dissertation that others thought couldn't be pulled off. And while he confessed he had had his own doubts, he never did more than mildly 'suggest' a reemphasis here or a more narrow focus there. I was proud to be one of Helmreich's 'empirical/applied' gang, whether we were bleary-eyed from hours of VHS tape transcriptions of simulator flight data, chasing down dinner-platter sized 'floppy' discs, experimenting with the early internet systems to talk to NASA Ames or listening to horrifying recordings of airline crashes. We were part of legacy that started with Bob's graduate work on the Sealab II, and continued to his passing. He vastly changed the field of aviation and space for the better. And the same could be said of those of us passing through his care as mentees. Ad Astra, Bob. (Sheryl Bishop)

Around 1993 or so, I was a Ph.D. student from the Management department in the business school at the University of Texas at Austin, looking around for a psychology elective to take. I happened to come across the description for a group dynamics course that sounded interesting, including the fact that it met off campus. What was that about? The time to meet was also listed as TBD. So I called the professor to inquire. Bob answered the phone. "Well, when would you like the class to meet?" he asked. What kind of prof was this? "Um... Wednesdays at 10:00 would work for me," I stammered. "Ok then, that's when it will meet. And we're on Shoal Creek Drive—much more fun than campus." This was very convenient to my apartment, and I signed up for the course—my very first in psychology. And what a course it was. My classmates were wonderful psychology students working with Bob, and we discussed, argued (mostly nicely), probed, and laughed our way through a collection of classics and not-yet-published work on group dynamics in a way that certainly changed the course of my academic life. Gosh, you could actually publish research with fascinating teams like flight crews? By the end of the semester, I wanted to be a group and team dynamics researcher. Twenty-three years later, after studies of flight crews, nuclear power plant crews, seaport teams, mine rescue teams... I've never looked back. But Bob was more than a mere instigator for me. The way he invited me into the fold, the way his students and staff accepted me as one of the crew, and the way he provided opportunities for us to combine the academic with the practical all served to set the tone for me for what a program of consequential research could look like. Bob became my dissertation committee co-chair along the way, and was a wonderful coach and mentor for academics and beyond. I was so nervous to defend my dissertation—a study of flight crews, air traffic control dyads, and airport ground operations crews—in the business school; I think Bob was concerned I might simply implode. So he told me he would pick me up at my apartment and drive me to the defense. That morning, I put on my one good suit and probably spent an hour on my hair. And then Bob drove up all right—in his huge lumbering Cadillac with the top down. By the time we got to school, my hair was a mop, but he had me laughing so hard, I didn't care at all. The defense went well, although some business professors were still dubious about my career prospects given this aviation bent, and I went on to an academic career that has given me the opportunity to train my own Ph.D. students. I have failed to deliver any of them to their dissertation defenses in a convertible; however, all of them have produced research in group dynamics, and many of them are now training their own Ph.D. students. And truly, it is all due to Bob's ability to recognize and fan a student's ember of tentative interest and possibility, and to do so with humor, kindness, understanding, occasional ire, and a continuous enveloping acceptance. Thank you, Bob. (Mary Waller)

I first stumbled across Bob Helmreich and his colleagues' work in 1990 while earning a Master's in Counseling Psychology at Rutgers University. Something in one of my class assignments led me to become interested in how people worked together under conditions of stress, time pressure, and risk. The paper I had found was about the effects of stress and isolation on overwinter crews at Antarctic research stations. Intrigued, I wrote to Bob (on paper, using a pen, sent in a stamped envelope) telling him I enjoyed the research write-up and I was interested in doing work in this area. I never received a response to that letter, but I applied to the University of Texas at Austin's Psychology program anyway. To my surprise and delight, I was accepted to the program and received a personal note from Bob mentioning that he was happy to have me join the research collective. Fast forward a few years. I've survived my comprehensive exams, just started observing flight crews from the jumpseat, and I'm feeling the stress of figuring out what my dissertation topic should be. After about a dozen jumpseat rides, it started to sink in that there was something ... different ... about how pilots worked together on the new "glass cockpit" transports such as the A320, 757/767, and newer 737's. I mentioned my observations to Bob. He told me that the effect of automation on crew communication and coordination was turning into an important area of inquiry. He encouraged me to read "Normal Accidents" by James Perrow, as well as to reach out to his co-author Earl Weiner. It's fair to say that his advice put me on the path I've been on ever since that day somewhere in 1993 or '94. I don't work in aviation directly anymore, but the knowledge I gained studying automation in aviation always informs my approach to the enterprise software systems design and testing that I perform. (Paul Sherman)

I first met Bob in the spring of 1989. I had done a bit of research and a lot of consulting in the area of team-skills training in the nuclear industry, and I was intrigued by the close parallels between that setting and the airline cockpit. I wanted to broaden my understanding of team development by devoting my sabbatical year 1989—90 to studying with the best. I had read some of Bob's work, and so he was on my initial hit list, but the thing that attracted me most was that whomever I talked with about my sabbatical interest, invariably they mentioned Bob as someone I "must talk to." I talked to a lot of people, and it was always the same. So I contacted Bob, and set up a visit to Austin to see the place, talk about how the sabbatical-in-residence might work, meet the other folks in his research group, and see if it all fit. My first hint that there might be just a touch of eccentricity there came when I was arranging for Bob to meet me at the airport. I asked him what I should look for and he said "I'll be driving the 1972 avocado green Cadillac convertible." And indeed he was. I quickly fell in with the most amazing and talented bunch of colleagues that I could have ever imagined. They included, among many others, Steve Gregorich, Cathy Clothier [McClain], Steve Predmore, John Wilhelm, and Lou Montgomery. Wrapped in the warm, playful, loving, frenetic chaos of that place and time, we all were happy and productive, and while I have been blessed to do some pretty cool things in my life, only a few compare to that incredible year in Austin. Bob made a tremendous difference in how modern aviation works, and in how we understand teams and teamwork. I greatly admired his scholarship, his unparalleled ability to collect amazing colleagues and students, and his extraordinary personal and professional generosity to so many, including me. I am so glad that the luminaries I spoke with so many years ago all said with complete unanimity that this was the guy I must talk to. (John Kello)

Bob was on my dissertation committee. After the committee met to decide my fate I came back into the room noting the congratulations for meeting the requirements for the Ph.D., Bob was the one who said, "If no one else will say it, I'll be pretentious and tell you, 'Welcome to the community of scholars.'" It was a nice moment and another warm memory of Bob's kindness. (Torsten Neilands)

Bob would often be consulted by media. For example:

Even the experts agree: cabin fever is rampant. "I believe in cabin fever, the sense of being trapped in a situation you can't leave," said Robert L. Helmreich, a professor of psychology at the University of Texas, who studies how astronauts and undersea explorers cope with confinement. When small *groups of people have to function in "extreme environments," as in submarines or space shuttles, "they tend to get irritable, and there's depression," Dr. Helmreich said. He added, "I consider being snowed in with kids an extreme environment." Aside from turning to arts and crafts, here are some experts' tips for dealing with cabin fever:*

- *Don't compete. "The Russians discovered that one of the worst things people can do is play competitive games" when they are confined together, said Dr. Helmreich of Texas, referring to research on long space flights. "They found chess games could lead to violence. It was, 'You won; I'll kill you.'"*
- *Clean the closets. "We learned that if people work on cooperative projects, it makes for very positive feelings and increases the harmony of the group," Dr. Helmreich said (Rubenstein, 1994).*

And his work sometimes intersected with popular culture. Mirabile (2015) cited Chidester et al. (1991) in discussing how leader characteristics and behavior might influence survival during a zombie apocalypse.

10   THE PRIVATE MAN

Bob was a proud gay man, out to most faculty and students at the University of Texas. And yet, I suspect many of his airline and medical acquaintances first learned this in his obituary, acknowledging his lifetime partner, Carlos Canales. This reflects the times in which Bob lived; the private was separate from the public. Activists might challenge this, because knowing the private man could have been a strong and positive influence for social change. For example, "Americans who have a close friend or family member who is gay or lesbian are 27 points more likely than those who do not to favor allowing gay and lesbian couples to legally marry (63% vs. 36%)" (Jones, Cox, & Navarro-Rivera, 2014, p. 2). As a 21-year old graduate student in 1980s America, knowing my mentor was gay influenced my beliefs, attitudes, and choices for the better. But we must also acknowledge that some in academia, government, and industry would have dismissed Bob's ideas and contributions, solely on the basis of his sexuality. This conflict is a tragic legacy of our shared history. Less than a decade has passed since he retired and only 6 years since he passed way. But much has happened since. Bob did not live to see *Obergefell v. Hodges* (2015). Supreme Court Justice Kennedy wrote in the majority opinion, "[the plaintiffs'] hope is not to be condemned to live in loneliness, excluded from one of civilization's oldest institutions. They ask for equal dignity in the eyes of the law. The Constitution grants them that right." When the decision was announced, I first thought of my friends who would soon marry and gain full governmental acknowledgment of their relationships. And then I thought of Bob and Carlos, and wished they had

had that opportunity. No couple I knew lived with more dignity or was more deserving of that validation.

I think I first met Bob at John Wilhelm's house in Manchaca, Texas about 25 years ago ... those were the days. Then the fun times moved to Bob's house on Lake Austin, where we always celebrated every ones' birthdays. Soon Bob, Carlos Canales and I were on the road to adventure. First to the steamy jungle of Puerto Vallarta, Mexico—what fun we all had. Next off to Costa Rica and Bob's zip line jungle ride—he was a trooper and we could not hold him back as he flew through the tops of trees 100 feet off the ground. At least he was not reading a book when he did this. We cooked up a trip to Turkey with Carlos, John and me in tow. I'm still sore from the hours of our bus ride. Did Bob ride the camel? I can't remember. How did I talk them into a trip to Bali? Just a little Merlot will do the trick—a magical journey into the mystical Hindu culture. Great memories of Bob in his sarong we had to wear into the temple grounds and of the big pink hat Bob had to wear to keep the sun from his head on the beach. Throw in many good times fishing and football games and several bottles of wine at their home at Lake LBJ. Love you Bob and will miss you so ... it will be hard to not have you there when the Longhorns kick off this year. (Joe McAlister).

So Long, Bob. We know it's not tootlepip, Helmreich. There's another Lab you are working on in some other space.

REFERENCES

Antonsen, S. (2009). *Safety culture: Theory, measurement, and improvement.*. Burlington, VT: Ashgate.

Bakan, D. (1966). *The duality of human existence.*. Reading, PA: Addison-Wesley.

Bem, S. L. (1974). The measurement of psychological androgyny. *Journal of Consulting and Clinical Psychology, 42*, 155–162.

Chidester, T. R. (2007). Intramural monitoring. In I. C. Statler (Ed.), The aviation system monitoring and modeling project: A documentation of its history and accomplishments: 1999–2005. *NASA Technical Publication, TP-2007-214556*. Washington, DC: National Aeronautics and Space Administration.

Chidester, T. R. (1993). Critical issues for CRM training and research. In E. L. Wiener, B. G. Kanki, & R. L. Helmreich (Eds.), *Cockpit resource management.*. San Diego, CA: Academic Press, Inc.

Chidester, T. R., Helmreich, R. L., Gregorich, S. E., & Geis, C. (1991). Pilot personality and crew coordination: Implications for training and selection. *International Journal of Aviation Psychology, 1*, 23–42.

Chidester, T. R., Kanki, B. G., Foushee, H. C., Dickinson, C. L., & Bowles, S. V. (1990). Personality factors in flight operations: I. Leader characteristics and crew performance in full-mission air transport simulation. *NASA Technical Memorandum 102259*. Moffett Field, CA: NASA-Ames Research Center.

Federal Aviation Administration. (2013a, April 11). *Aviation Safety Action Program*. Retrieved from FAA.GOV: http://www.faa.gov/about/initiatives/asap/.

Federal Aviation Administration. (2013b, March 19). *Flight Operational Quality Assurance (FOQA)*. Retrieved from FAA.GOV: http://www.faa.gov/about/initiatives/atos/air_carrier/foqa/.

Federal Aviation Administration. (2015). *Advanced Qualification Program (AQP)*. Retrieved from FAA.GOV: http://www.faa.gov/training_testing/training/aqp/.

Foushee, H. C. (1984). Dyads and triads at 35,000 feet—Factors affecting group process and aircrew performance. *American Psychologist, 39*(8), 886–893.

Gregorich, S. E., Helmreich, R. L., & Wilhelm, J. A. (1990). The structure of cockpit management attitudes. *Journal of Applied Psychology, 75*(6), 682–690.

Helmreich, R. L. (1960). Regulation of reproductive rate by intra-uterine mortality in the deer mouse. *Science, 13,* 417–418.

Helmreich, R. L. (1984). Cockpit management attitudes. *Human Factors, 26*(5), 583–589.

Helmreich, R. L. (2000). On error management: Lessons from aviation. *British Medical Journal, 320,* 781–785.

Helmreich, R.L. (2001). The Line Operations Safety Audit (LOSA) and safety culture. In *Proceedings of the first LOSA week*. Cathay City, Hong Kong.

Helmreich, R. L., Aronson, E., & LeFan, J. (1970). October). To err is humanizing—Sometimes: Effects of self-esteem, competence, and a pratfall on interpersonal attraction. *Journal of Personality and Social Psychology, 16*(2), 259–264.

Helmreich, R. L., Beane, W. E., Lucker, G. W., & Spence, J. T. (1978). Achievement motivation and scientific attainment. *Personality and Social Psychology Bulletin, 4,* 222–226.

Helmreich, R. L., & Foushee, H. C. (1993). Why Crew Resource Management? Empirical and theoretical bases of human factors training in aviation. In E. Wiener, B. Kanki, & R. Helmreich (Eds.), *Cockpit resource management*. San Diego, CA: Academic Press.

Helmreich, R. L. (1971). Behavioral program conclusions and recommendations. In J. Miller, J. VanDerwalker, & R. Waller (Eds.), *Scientists in the Sea: Tektite 2.*. Washington: Department of the Interior. Downloaded from: https://archive.org/stream/tektitescientis00-mill/tektitescientis00mill_djvu.txt.

Helmreich, R. L., Klinect, J. R., & Wilhelm, J. A. (1999). *Models of threat, error, and CRM in flight operations. Proceedings of the tenth international symposium on aviation psychology*. Columbus, OH: The Ohio State University.

Helmreich, R. L., & Merritt, A. C. (2001). *Culture at work in aviation and medicine: National, organizational, and professional influences*. Farnham: Ashgate.

Helmreich, R. L., & Spence, J. T. (1978). The Work and Family Orientation Questionnaire: An objective instrument to assess components of achievement motivation and attitudes toward family and career. *JSAS Catalog of Selected Documents in Psychology, 8,* 35.

Jones, R. P., Cox, D., & Navarro-Rivera, J. (2014). *A shifting landscape: A decade of change in american attitudes about same-sex marriage and LGBT issues*. Washington, DC: Public Religion Research Institute.

McCrae, R. R., & Costa, P. T. (1990). *Personality in adulthood.*. New York: The Guildford Press.

McCrae, R. R., & Costa, P. T., Jr. (2010). *NEO inventories: Professional manual.*. Lutz, FL: Psychological Assessment Resources, Inc.

Mirabile, S. (2015). The psychology of surviving the zombie apocalypse. In A. L. Thompson, & A. S. Thompson (Eds.), *But If a Zombie Apocalypse Did Occur: Essays on Medical, Military, Governmental, Ethical, Economic, and Other Implications.*. Jefferson, NC: McFarland & Company.

Musson, D.M. (2003). Personality determinants of professional culture: Evidence from astronauts, pilots, and physicians (Unpublished doctoral dissertation). The University of Texas at Austin.

Musson, D. M., Sandal, G. M., & Helmreich, R. L. (2004). Personality characteristics and trait clusters in final stage astronaut selection. *Aviation, Space, and Environmental Medicine, 75*, 342–349.

Obergefell v. Hodges, 576 U.S. (United States Supreme Court, June 26, 2015).

Radloff, R., & Helmreich, R. L. (1968). *Groups under stress: Psychological research in SEALAB II.*. New York: Appleton-Century-Crofts.

Rall, M., & Gaba, D. (2005). Human performance and patient safety. In R. Miller (Ed.), *Miller's anesthesia*. London: Elsevier.

Rubenstein, C. (1994). It may be cold outside, but inside, it's crazy. *The New York Times*. Retrieved from http://www.nytimes.com/1994/02/03/garden/it-may-be-cold-outside-but-inside-it-s-crazy.html?pagewanted = all.

Ruskin, K. J., Stiegler, M. P., Park, K., Guffey, P., Kurup, V., & Chidester, T. (2013). Threat and error management for anesthesiologists: A predictive risk taxonomy. *Current Opinion in Anesthesiology, 6*, 707–713.

Salas, E., Jentsch, F., & Maurino, D. (2010). *Human factors in aviation.*. Cambridge, MA: Academic Press.

Sexton, J., Helmreich, R., Neilands, T., Rowan, K., Vella, K., Boyden, J., ... Thomas, E. (2006). The Safety Attitudes Questionnaire: Psychometric properties, benchmarking data, and emerging research. *BMC Health Services Research, 6*(44), 1–10.

Sexton, J. B., Thomas, E. J., & Helmreich, R. L. (2000). Error, stress, and teamwork in medicine and aviation: Cross sectional surveys. *British Medical Journal, 320*, 745–749.

Spence, J. T. (1988). Janet Taylor Spence. In A. N. O'Connel, & N. F. Russo (Eds.), *Models of achievement: Reflections of eminent women in psychology* (Vol. 2). Hillsdale, NJ: Lawrence Erlbaum Associates.

Spence, J. T., & Helmreich, R. (1972a). The Attitudes toward Women Scale: An objective instrument to measure attitudes toward the rights and roles of women in contemporary society. *JSAS Catalog of Selected Documents in Psychology, 2*, 66–67.

Spence, J. T., Helmreich, R., & Stapp, J. (1974). The personal attributes questionnaire: A measure of sex-role stereotypes and masculinity-femininity. *JSAS Catalog of Selected Documents in Psychology, 4*, 43–44.

Spence, J. T., & Helmreich, R. L. (1972b). Who likes competent women? *Journal of Applied Social Psychology, 2*, 197–213.

Spence, J. T., & Helmreich, R. L. (1978). *Masculinity and femininity: Their psychological dimensions, correlates, and antecedents.*. Austin: University of Texas Press.

Spence, J. T., Helmreich, R. L., & Sawin, L. L. (1980). The Male-Female Relations Questionnaire: A self-report inventory of sex role behaviors and preferences and their relationships to masculine and feminine personality traits, sex role attitudes, and other measures. *JSAS Catalog of Selected Documents in Psychology, 10*, 87.

Summit Herald and Record (1958, February 6). *Digifind-it. com*. RetrievedAugust 22, 2016, from Innovative Document Imaging: www.digifind-it.com/summit/DATA/newspapers/herald/1958/1958-02-06.pdf.

Wilhelm, J., & Domjan, M. (2013). Robert (Bob) L. Helmreich (1937-2012). *American Psychologist, 68*(6), 470.

FURTHER READING

Wiener, E., Kanki, B., & Helmreich, R. (Eds.), (1993). *Cockpit resource management.*. San Diego, CA: Academic Press.

List of Contributors

Kathy H. Abbott United States Federal Aviation Administration, Washington, DC, United States

José Anca Faculty of Science, Engineering and Technology, Swinburne University of Technology, Hawthorn, VIC, Australia

Thomas R. Chidester Civil Aerospace Medical Institute, Federal Aviation Administration, Oklahoma City, OK, United States

Michael Curtis University of Central Florida, Orlando, FL, United States

Pamela Farago Psychology Department, College of Behavioral, Social, & Health Sciences, Clemson University, Clemson, SC, United States

Douglas R. Farrow Federal Aviation Administration (retired), Washington, DC, United States

Rhona Flin Aberdeen Business School, Robert Gordon University, Aberdeen, Scotland

H. Clayton Foushee Office of Audit and Evaluation, Federal Aviation Administration, Washington, DC, United States

Robert C. Ginnett Retired, United States Air Force Academy, Colorado Springs, CO, United States

Charles Hagan Flight Training International, Denver, CO, United States

Robert G. Hahn US Navy School of Aviation Safety, Pensacola, FL, United States

Brenton J.H. Hayward Dédale Asia Pacific, Albert Park, VIC, Australia

Robert L. Helmreich[†]

Florian Jentsch University of Central Florida, Orlando, FL, United States

Barbara G. Kanki Retired, NASA Ames Research Center, Moffett Field, CA, United States

Candace K. Kolander Formerly with the Association of Flight Attendants-CWA, Washington, DC, United States

Robert W. Koteskey San Jose State University Research Foundation, NASA Ames Research Center, Mountain View, CA, United States

Katherine A. Lemos, Ph.D

Eric T. Lish Private Consultant, Denver, CO, United States

[†]Deceased

Andrew R. Lowe Dédale Asia Pacific, Albert Park, VIC, Australia

Wayne L. Martin University of Southern Queensland, Cairns, QLD, Australia

Ryan McKendrick, Ph.D

Gregg Montijo Crew Training International, Inc., Memphis, TN, United States

Kathleen L. Mosier San Francisco State University, San Francisco, CA, United States

Robert Nullmeyer Aviation Programs, Arizona State University, Mesa, AZ, United States

Judith Orasanu-Engel NASA-Ames Research Center, Moffett Field, CA, United States

Linda M. Orlady Orlady Associates, Maple Valley, WA, United States

Paul O'Connor National University of Ireland, Galway, Ireland

Manoj S. Patankar School of Aviation and Transportation Technology, Purdue University, West Lafayette, IN, United States

Eduardo Salas Department of Psychological Sciences, Rice University, Houston, TX, United States

Marissa L. Shuffler Psychology Department, College of Behavioral, Social, & Health Sciences, Clemson University, Clemson, SC, United States

Robert L. Sumwalt

Bruce A. Tesmer[†]

Matthew J.W. Thomas Westwood-Thomas Associates, Adelaide, SA, Australia

Frank J. Tullo Embry-Riddle Aeronautical University, Daytona Beach, FL, United States

---

[†]Deceased

Foreword

I was privileged to write the Foreword for the 1993 first edition of *Cockpit Resource Management* and for the second, retitled 2010 edition of this book. Now I'm honored to write the Foreword for the third edition of *Crew Resource Management*. I am pleased to set the stage for the remainder of this volume which describes the latest research and the most recent developments and applications of the basic principles of crew resource management. More significantly, it lays out a map for future researchers, developers, and practitioners of this fundamentally important set of methods and processes for studying and shaping complex human behavior in organizational and team settings.

Although by some accounts we are on the threshold of revolutionary developments in artificial intelligence that will fundamentally alter the roles of humans and machines, I am fully confident that the material presented here will remain highly relevant, probably even beyond *The Singularity* that some foresee as marking an end to human development as we know it. These prognosticators may be right, but meanwhile we have airplanes to fly, ships to sail, trains to roll, nuclear power plants to operate, fires to fight, and surgical procedures to perform. Clearly, it is to the ultimate benefit of all that we undertake these endeavors using the best available methods for achieving maximal performance of pilots, ship's officers, locomotive engineers, control room operators, firefighters, and surgeons and nurses (and many others) both as skilled individuals and as members of their respective teams. That's fundamentally what this book is all about.

In the two previous editions of this book, I cited several examples of major airline crashes, both to illustrate what can happen when highly-trained, highly-skilled *individuals* fail to operate effectively as an integrated *team* (the 1972 crash of Eastern Flight 401 in the Everglades), and what can happen when they do (United Flight 232 at Sioux City, IA in 1989). I also cited some relevant statistical data—the hull-loss accident rate for global scheduled air transport operations fell from 1.9 per million flights in 1993 to just under 1.0 per million flights in 2010, a factor of two. That rate has halved again in the intervening years, and we have reached a point where some of us refer, albeit with some hesitation, to a "near-zero" accident rate for such operations. There are many changes that have helped drive those rates ever-downward, but certainly one of those has been the universal adoption and application of CRM principles in airline operations worldwide. I have also had the opportunity to observe how the maritime community, both civil and military, have integrated CRM principles in training members of deck and engine room crews, and I've personally seen similar developments in training for surgical teams. Examples in other domains can easily be found through searches on the internet.

In 1993 I said, "Like most good concepts, CRM is not new," and discussed the origin of the term as it emerged from the collective work of many airlines along with findings from ongoing research conducted at NASA-Ames Research Center and elsewhere. These organizations recognized the importance of addressing such concepts as leadership, followership, decision-making, monitoring, distraction management, communication skills, and other elements of team performance. As an aside, since my retirement nearly 10 years ago I've had opportunity to revisit some of the literary classics and was surprised and pleased to see that the importance of CRM was recognized 2700 years ago, as described by Homer in *The Iliad*. In a 1974 translation by Robert Fitzgerald[1] we find in Book 10 the following: the Greeks are in camp the night before a bloody battle with the Trojans. Lord Agamemnon is consulting with his officers regarding strategy and tactics for the day to come. Nestor suggests great acclaim will come for the one among them who could successfully scout the enemy encampment and return with useful intelligence. Diomedes volunteers, "Nestor, pride and excitement urge me on to make a foray into the enemy camp so close at hand here. If some other soldier goes along, it will be better, though—more warmth to it. *Two men can make a team: one will catch on quicker than the other when there's a chance of bringing something off, while one man's eyes and wit may move more slowly*" (emphasis added. Fitzgerald, p. 230). Something tells me that Bob Helmreich would have loved this passage.

In 1993, I concluded "(CRM) is an exciting story, and one which offers great personal gratification. There are few more rewarding efforts than those which result in the saving of lives." In the intervening years, the exciting story and the demonstrated benefits have generated nearly universal application of CRM principles in virtually thousands of settings. This is a direct result of evolutionary developments in concept and practice honed by a multitude of dedicated researchers and practitioners. These data and others show convincingly that countless lives have been saved by the collective efforts of those whose works are chronicled here. I'm proud to have been one of the players in this remarkable story.

John K. Lauber
Vaughn, WA

---

1. *Homer—The Iliad*, translated by Robert Fitzgerald. Farrar, Straus and Giroux, 2004 ISBN-13:978-0-374-52905-5.

Preface

In 1993, Cockpit Resource Management (CRM) was celebrated as the convergence of a concept, attitude, and practical approach to pilot training. Equally important was the convergence and enthusiastic support of the research community, aviation regulators, transport operators, and pilot organizations. CRM training was being implemented and continuing to develop at the same time.

It was always said that if CRM succeeded, it would disappear as standalone training as it became fully integrated into an airline's training program. As early as 1990 the Federal Aviation Administration (FAA) provided a mechanism for achieving just that, in the form of the Advanced Qualification Program (AQP). But CRM grew in many other directions as well. Many years later, CRM concepts have endured not only by disappearing into the fabric of training, but by expanding the team concept, integrating into a higher level of safety and risk management goals, and inspiring training innovations.

Even in 1993, it was evident that CRM was being applied beyond the cockpit and we acknowledged that "CRM" more appropriately stood for Crew Resource Management. While we continued to focus on CRM in the cockpit, we also emphasized that the concepts and applications provided generic guidance for a wide variety of "crews" in the broader aviation system and in complex, high-risk nonaviation settings as well.

In the late 1970s, when our late colleague H. Patrick Ruffell Smith launched his classic study of flight crew performance in a Boeing 747 simulator, he could not have foreseen what would be inspired by that project. The experiment originally investigated pilot vigilance, workload, and response to stress. A testament to that early research, we continue to make effective use of the simulator to investigate vigilance (situational awareness), workload management, and response to stress—as well as a host of other human factors affected by the continually evolving aircraft and airspace system. Ruffell Smith's use of simulation opened the door to researching human factors and to a useful methodology for observing crew performance and the reliability of instructor and evaluator assessments.

CRM training, like any new approach to a well-established, tradition-bound enterprise, was not universally acclaimed in its early years. Many airline managers dragged their feet; they claimed that they were doing it anyway, just not under the name of CRM. And, who had any proof that the new training was effective? The FAA initially viewed the approach with a degree of skepticism as well, in spite of a string of recommendations from the National Transportation Safety Board (NTSB) that CRM training be required of the nation's airlines.

In the original 1993 edition of *Cockpit Resource Management*, it was clear that momentum was taking hold, not only in US commercial aviation, but in the military and abroad. While Advanced Qualification Program (AQP) was still under development, US and international operators, pilot organizations, investigators, regulators, researchers, and others in the industry grew to be an active CRM community that experimented with training concepts and shared its results. Continuing in the spirit of successful collaboration, the 2010, 2nd Edition, *Crew Resource Management*, incorporated a mix of US and non-US, commercial and military, researchers, training organizations, and regulators. Our authors personally remembered the beginnings of CRM and helped to support and develop enhancements and new directions for CRM training. The development continued to flourish, and we have tried to capture this progress in the chapters to follow.

As in previous editions, *Crew Resource Management*, 3rd Edition, consists of three main sections: (1) Nature of CRM; (2) CRM Training Applications; and (3) CRM Perspectives. In addition to the Preface and Foreword preceding Part 1, Edition 3 includes a dedication to Dr. Robert L Helmreich, one of our original editors. His contribution to this field as a researcher and supporter of the concept development as well as the implementation of effective training programs, was unmatched. When Prof. Helmreich passed away in 2012, we were initially reluctant to start working on a new edition of this book. But at the suggestion of Elsevier, we realized that a new edition would give us the opportunity to pay tribute to our friend, mentor, and colleague.

In Edition 2 we had noted exciting, new CRM applications outside aviation; some of these new domains, most notably, medical, have already established their own communities of practice through research, conferences, and domain-specific publications. We therefore reduced our focus outside aviation in order to focus on the growth of CRM within aviation. Aside from this small shift in focus, Edition 3 is largely comprised of updates from most of our Edition 2 authors, but we are pleased to introduce a number of new authors and new topics. We have tried to maintain a balance between US and non-US applications and to preserve the perspectives unique to military operations, regulators, and accident investigators. Following are brief descriptions of each section of this 2018 edition.

PART 1: NATURE OF CRM

Part 1 begins with the historical account from the 1993 and 2010 editions in which the empirical and theoretical bases of Human Factors Training were described. Chapters 2 through 4 are updates to the familiar CRM concepts and skills: teamwork, leadership, communication, and decision-making. Much of the original research and early initiatives are preserved in these pages and it is gratifying to see how far the concepts have grown, not only from a theory perspective, but how they have matured into useful skills that are being trained and utilized in operations. Chapter 5, Flight Crew Decision-Making, recasts CRM (Nontechnical) skills from the European point of view and includes associated guidance updates. Part 1 concludes with two new chapters. First, while CRM skills are based on the team concept, there is a crucial relationship to individual resilience that is discussed in Chapter 7, Crew Resource Management and Individual Resilience. Second, connections between resource management and risk management are discussed in Chapter 8, Crew Resource Management, Risk, and Safety Management Systems, both conceptually and in the context of safety management systems.

PART 2: CRM TRAINING APPLICATIONS

Part 2 contains chapters that describe some of the many innovations that have developed while transforming CRM concepts to practice. Over the years, the implementation of CRM training has generated major enhancements and lessons learned. Chapter 9, The Design, Delivery, and Evaluation of Crew Resource Management Training, gives a broad discussion of the design, delivery, and evaluation of CRM training with practical guidelines for ensuring training effectiveness. Chapter 10, Line Oriented Flight Training: A Practical Guide for Developers, and Chapter 11, Line Operations Simulation Development Tools, focus on CRM training in the simulator, providing guidance and tools for CRM developers of scenarios and assessment strategies. Audit tools that are used in line operations are addressed in Chapter 12, Crew Resource Management and Line Operations Safety Audit. Chapter 13, Maintenance Resource Management for Technical Operations, Chapter 14, Flight and Cabin Crew Teamwork: Improving Safety in Aviation, and Chapter 15, The Migration of Crew Resource Management Training, discuss CRM applications beyond the cockpit. Chapter 13, Maintenance Resource Management for Technical Operations, and Chapter 14, Flight and Cabin Crew Teamwork: Improving Safety in Aviation, describe training application within aviation organizations, namely, Maintenance Resource Management in technical operations, and joint CRM training for flight and cabin crews. Chapter 15, The Migration of Crew Resource Management Training, closes Part 2 with a discussion of CRM migration to teams outside aviation (e.g., maritime operations, health care, rail).

PART 3: CRM PERSPECTIVES

While flight department trainers in both commercial and military transport operations were the original practitioners of CRM training, CRM also influenced organizations outside the actual "crews" practicing CRM. For example, CRM affected the way regulators and investigators understood, assessed, and analyzed human performance. This is described in Chapter 16, A Regulatory Perspective, Chapter 17, A Regulatory Perspective II, and Chapter 18, The Accident Investigator's Perspective. Part 3 also includes chapters that address the way organizational and national culture affects CRM implementation. Chapter 19, The Military Perspective, describes CRM training in military operations (e.g., US Navy, Air Force, Army, Coast Guard). In addition to traditional piloted flights, this chapter considers CRM in unmanned aircraft systems (UAS). Chapter 20, Cultural Issues and Crew Resource Management Training, provides a discussion of the variety of ways CRM may be affected by national culture. In spite of widespread migration of CRM concepts and training approaches outside the United States, many key areas of CRM training design and implementation have required cultural adaptation. The final two chapters of Part 3 are commentaries on the state of CRM training today with a perspective that looks forward to challenges ahead. Chapter 21, Airline Pilots, Training, and CRM in Today's Environment, presents a pilot's point of view describing the operational environment in which CRM is now practiced. Because many of the training challenges involve increasingly automated aircraft, the manufacturer's role is discussed. Finally, Chapter 22, The Future of CRM, points to three key areas that affect CRM training effectiveness: (1) sound guidance materials that are consistent with research and operations; (2) CRM training that is integrated and informed by safety management systems; and (3) CRM training that evolves to keep up with technological advances in aircraft and airspace systems.

In sum, we have tried to capture the breadth and depth of CRM topics, applications, and perspectives for a global audience including training practitioners, managers, corporate decision-makers, regulators, investigators, and researchers. In addition, we hope that all aviation work groups, as well as nonaviation teams, will find topics that are useful in developing CRM programs for their own work settings. We believe CRM presents a success story as it has transcended its own training roots and followed a path of adaptation and expansion that addresses larger, safety management objectives. It is a model which—in spite of cultural barriers, economic setbacks, and bureaucratic complexities—has become a household word in aviation.

We thank our authors for a job well done and for helping to preserve this documentation of CRM history, knowledge, and practical advice. We are also grateful to the staff at Elsevier for their very professional help and encouragement. Finally, we respect and honor the aviation crews throughout the world whose participation and experiences continue to perpetuate CRM success.

Barbara G. Kanki, José Anca and Thomas R. Chidester

Part I

The Nature of CRM

Chapter 1

Why CRM? Empirical and Theoretical Bases of Human Factors Training*

Robert L. Helmreich[†] and H. Clayton Foushee
Office of Audit and Evaluation, Federal Aviation Administration, Washington, DC, United States

1.1 THE EVOLUTION AND GROWTH OF CRM

1.1.1 Introduction

One of the most striking developments in aviation safety during the past decade has been the overwhelming endorsement and widespread implementation of training programs aimed at increasing the effectiveness of crew coordination and flightdeck management. Civilian and military organizations have developed programs that address team and managerial aspects of flight operations as complements to traditional training that stresses the technical, "stick-and-rudder" aspects of flight. The original, generic label for such training was *cockpit resource management*, but with recognition of the applicability of the approach to other members of the aviation community including cabin crews, flight dispatchers, and maintenance personnel, the term *crew resource management* (CRM) is coming into general use.

Just as CRM has evolved from "cockpit" to "crew" over its short history, the field of human factors has similarly changed in its scope. From an initial marriage of engineering and psychology with a focus on "knobs and dials," contemporary human factors has become a multidisciplinary field that draws on the methods and principles of the behavioral and social sciences, engineering, and physiology to optimize human performance and reduce human

---

* Author's note: This chapter has been preserved intact from the previous edition of this book as a tribute to the incredible legacy created during the distinguished career of Dr. Robert L. Helmreich, who passed away in 2012. In reviewing the previous edition of this chapter for updates, the second author concluded that the content is as relevant today as it was when written, and it remains an important historical piece.

[†] Deceased 7 July 2012.

Crew Resource Management. DOI: https://doi.org/10.1016/B978-0-12-812995-1.00001-4

error (National Research Council, 1989). From this broader perspective, human factors can be viewed as the applied science of people working together with devices. Just as the performance and safety of a system can be degraded because of poor hardware or software design and/or inadequate operator training, so too can system effectiveness be reduced by errors in the design and management of crew-level tasks and of organizations. CRM is thus the application of human factors in the aviation system. John K. Lauber (1984), a psychologist member of the National Transportation Safety Board (NTSB), has defined CRM as "using all available resources—information, equipment, and people—to achieve safe and efficient flight operations" (p. 20). CRM includes optimizing not only the person—machine interface and the acquisition of timely, appropriate information, but also interpersonal activities including leadership, effective team formation and maintenance, problem-solving, decision-making, and maintaining situation awareness. Thus training in CRM involves communicating basic knowledge of human factors concepts that relate to aviation and providing the tools necessary to apply these concepts operationally. It represents a new focus on crew-level (as opposed to individual-level) aspects of training and operations.

This chapter's title inquires why an industry would embrace change to an approach that has resulted in the safest means of transportation available and has produced generations of highly competent, well-qualified pilots. In seeking the answer, we examine both the historic, single-pilot tradition in aviation and what we know about the causes of error and accidents in the system. These considerations lead us to the conceptual framework, rooted in social psychology, that encompasses group behavior and team performance. In this context we can look at efforts to improve crew coordination and performance through training. Finally, we discuss what research has told us about the effectiveness of these efforts and what questions remain unanswered.

1.2 THE SINGLE-PILOT TRADITION IN AVIATION

The evolution of concern with crew factors must be considered in the historical context of flight. In the early years, the image of a pilot was of a single, stalwart individual, white scarf trailing, braving the elements in an open cockpit. This stereotype embraces a number of personality traits such as independence, machismo, bravery, and calmness under stress that are more associated with individual activity than with team effort. It is likely that, as with many stereotypes, this one may have a factual basis, as individuals with these attributes may have been disproportionately attracted to careers in aviation, and organizations may have been predisposed to select candidates reflecting this prototype.

As aircraft grew more complex and the limitations and fallibility of pilots more evident, provision was made for a copilot to provide support for the pilot, to reduce individual workload and decrease the probability of human error. However, these additional crewmembers were initially perceived more as redundant systems to be used as backups than as participants in a team endeavor. Ernest K. Gann (1961) and other pioneers of air transport have documented the distinctly secondary role played by the copilot in early airline operations.

The tradition in training and evaluation has similarly focused on the individual pilot and his or her technical proficiency (Hackman & Helmreich, 1987). This begins with initial selection and training, which have historically used aptitude and performance standards developed for single-pilot operations. Indeed, the first critical event in a pilot's career is the solo flight. Even in multipilot operations, the major emphasis continues to be on evaluating the individual proficiency of crewmembers. Regulations surrounding the qualification and certification of pilots reinforce these practices and can even result in negative training. For example, in crewmembers are cautioned not to provide assistance to pilots whose proficiency is being evaluated, a model of individual instead of team action is being reinforced. Indeed, in 1952 the guidelines for proficiency checks at one major airline categorically stated that the first officer should not correct errors made by the captain (H. Orlady, personal communication cited in Foushee & Helmreich, 1988). The critical point is that the aviation community has operated on the assumption that crews composed of able and well-trained individuals can and will operate complicated aircraft in a complex environment both safely and efficiently.

1.3   HUMAN ERROR IN FLIGHT OPERATIONS

The introduction of reliable turbojet transports in the 1950s was associated with a dramatic reduction in air transport accidents. As problems with airframes and engines diminished, attention turned to identifying and eliminating other sources of failure in flight safety. Fig. 1.1 gives statistics on the causes of accidents from 1959 through 1989, indicating that flightcrew actions were casual in more than 70% of worldwide accidents involving aircraft damage beyond economical repair. Recognition of this human performance problem stimulated a number of independent efforts to understand what the term "pilot error" encompassed and what could be done to reduce it.

The formal record of investigations into aircraft accidents, such as those conducted by the NTSB, provides chilling documentation of instances where crew coordination has failed at critical moments.

- A crew, distracted by the failure of a landing gear indicator light, failing to notice that the automatic pilot was disengaged and allowing the aircraft to descent into a swamp.

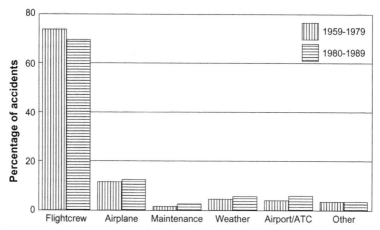

FIGURE 1.1 Primary causes of hull loss accidents (excluding military and sabotage): worldwide commercial jet fleet, 1959–89. Data from Boeing Aircraft Company.

- A copilot, concerned that take-off thrust was not properly set during a departure in a snowstorm, failing to get the attention of the captain with the aircraft stalling and crashing into the Potomac River.
- A crew failing to review instrument landing charts and their navigational position with respect to the airport and further disregarding repeated Ground Proximity Warning System alerts before crashing into a mountain below the minimum descent altitude.
- A crew distracted by nonoperational communication failing to complete checklists and crashing on take-off because the flaps were not extended.
- A breakdown in communication between a captain, copilot, and Air Traffic Control regarding fuel state and a crash following complete fuel exhaustion.
- A crew crashing on take-off because of icing on the wings after having inquired about deicing facilities. In the same accident the failure of a flight attendant to communicate credible concerns about the need for deicing expressed by pilot passengers.

The theme in each of these cases is human error resulting from failures in interpersonal communications. By the time these accidents occurred, the formal study of human error in aviation had a long tradition (e.g., Davis, 1948; Fitts & Jones, 1947). However, research efforts tended to focus on traditional human factors issues surrounding the interface of the individual operator with equipment. This type of investigation did not seem to address many of the factors identified as causal in jet transport accidents, and researchers began to broaden the scope of their inquiry.

In the United States, a team of investigators at NASA–Ames Research Center began to explore broader human factors issues in flight operations.

Charles Billings, John Lauber, and George Cooper developed a structured interview protocol and used it to gather firsthand information from airline pilots regarding human factors in crew operations and "pilot error" accidents. At the same time, George Cooper and Maurice White analyzed the causes of jet transport accidents occurring between 1968 and 1976 (Cooper, White, & Lauber, 1980), while Miles Murphy performed a similar analysis of incidents reported to NASA's confidential Aviation Safety Reporting System (Murphy, 1980). The conclusion drawn from these investigations was that "pilot error" in documented accidents and incidents was more likely to reflect failures in team communication and coordination than deficiencies in "stick-and-rudder" proficiency. A number of specific problem areas were identified, including workload management and task delegation, situation awareness, leadership, use of available resources including other crewmembers, manuals, air traffic control, interpersonal communications (including unwillingness of junior crewmembers to speak up in critical situations), and the process of building and maintaining an effective team relationship on the flightdeck.

In Europe, Elwyn Edwards (1972) drew on the record of accident investigation and developed his SHEL model of human factors in system design and operations. The acronym represents *software*, usually documents governing operations; *hardware*, the physical resources available; *liveware*, consisting of the human operators composing the crew; and *environment*, the external context in which the system operates. Elaborating his model to examine the functioning of the liveware, Edwards (1975) defined a new concept, the transcockpit authority gradient (TAG). The TAG refers to the fact that captains must establish an optimal working relationship with other crewmembers, with the captain's role and authority neither over- nor underemphasized.

In the operational community in the early 1970s, Pan American World Airways management became concerned about crew training issues following several "pilot error" accidents in the Pacific. In 1974, a flight operations review team headed by David D. Thomas, retired Deputy Administrator of the Federal Aviation Administration (FAA), examined all aspects of flightcrew training and made a number of significant recommendations. The foremost of these was to utilize "crew concept training." Under this approach, both simulator training and checking were to be conducted not as single-pilot evolutions but in the context of a full crew conducting coordinated activities. At the same time, Pan Am manuals were revised to incorporate crew concepts and to explain more completely responsibilities for team activities and communications. These actions represented a fundamental change in the operating environment and provided an organizational framework for more effective crew coordination. Although the focus in training was now on crew activities, the shift was not accompanied by a program of formal instruction in communications and coordination. Crewmembers were mandated to operate as effective teams but were left to develop means of achieving this goal without formal guidance and instruction.

Identifying crew-level issues as central to a high proportion of accidents and incidents was a significant achievement in the process of understanding the determinants of safety in flight operations. However, development of successful strategies to improve crew performance requires an understanding of the determinants of group behavior and how they can be influenced. In the following section we describe a model of group processes and performance and its implications for training and organizational actions.

1.4   GROUP PROCESSES AND PERFORMANCE IN THE AVIATION ENVIRONMENT

The study of group behavior has historically been the province of social psychology and provides the conceptual basis for the three-factor model of the determinants of group performance we presented in an earlier discussion of flightcrew interaction and performance (Foushee & Helmreich, 1988; McGrath, 1964). Subsequent research has enabled us to expand and refine the model, and we present it as a framework for discussing issues surrounding CRM training. The model defines three major components of group behavior: *input factors*, which include characteristics of individuals, groups, organizations, and the operational environment; *group process factors*, which include the nature and quality of interactions among group members; and *outcome factors*, which include primary outcomes such as safety and efficiency of operations and secondary outcomes such as member satisfaction, motivation, attitudes, and so on. The underlying assumption of the model is that input factors both provide the framework and determine the nature of group processes that lead, in turn, to the various outcomes. Fig. 1.2 shows the three factors and their interrelationships. A central feature of the model

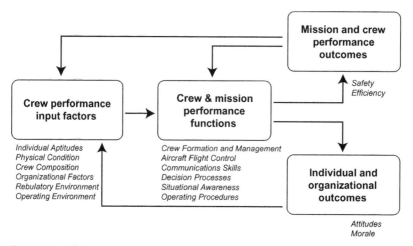

FIGURE 1.2   Flightcrew performance model.

is feedback loops among the factors. Outcomes (right side of figure; either positive or negative) may change components of input factors (left side; e.g., attitudes and norms), and these changes may alter subsequent group processes (middle) and outcomes. Outcomes may theoretically also influence group processes without being directly mediated by input factors. It is the iterative nature of the factors determining group performance that makes its study both complex and challenging.

1.4.1   Outcome Factors

Primary outcome factors are readily recognizable and relatively easily quantifiable. In flight operations safety is paramount, but the efficient completion of missions and compliance with organizational and regulatory requirements are also important. Both experience and training can create changes in crew attitudes and norms regarding appropriate flightdeck management. The quality of group processes, influenced by organizational, group, regulatory, and environmental factors, determines the satisfaction crews experience with operations and their motivation for future operations.

Outcome factors form the criteria against which the impact of interventions such as training or organizational policy changes are measured. While the most compelling measure of effectiveness in aviation would be a decrease in the frequency of accidents, such events are (happily) already so infrequent that reliable statistical evidence can only be found by aggregating data over extremely long periods of time. Accordingly, criteria of group performance need to be drawn from surrogate measures such as records of operational errors, expert ratings of crew effectiveness, and measures of attitude and job satisfaction.

1.4.2   Input Factors

A number of qualitatively different variables form the inputs to group processes. These have multiple components that, singly and in combination, influence the way teams interact. Fig. 1.3 expands the input factors portion of the model to include lower-order variables that have a demonstrated influence on group processes and outcomes.

Individual Factors

Consideration of a flightcrew's job in today's airspace brings to mind a number of background or input factors that can influence the effectiveness of crew activities even before an engine is started. Teams are composed of individuals who bring to the flightdeck their knowledge, skills, personalities, motivation, and physical and emotional states. Each of these characteristics has been identified as causal in one or more aircraft accidents.

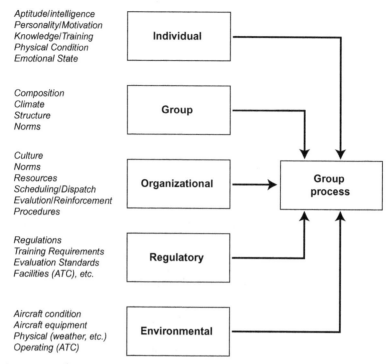

Aptitude/intelligence
Personality/Motivation
Knowledge/Training
Physical Condition
Emotional State

Individual

Composition
Climate
Structure
Norms

Group

Culture
Norms
Resources
Scheduling/Dispatch
Evalution/Reinforcement
Procedures

Organizational

Group process

Regulations
Training Requirements
Evaluation Standards
Facilities (ATC), etc.

Regulatory

Aircraft condition
Aircraft equipment
Physical (weather, etc.)
Operating (ATC)

Environmental

FIGURE 1.3   Flightcrew performance model: expanded input factors.

Physical condition includes fatigue, which can undermine vigilance in a knowledgeable and motivated pilot. Emotional state is determined by a variety of life stresses (e.g., marital discord or worries about the financial condition and viability of an airline) that cannot be left at the gate and can subtly undermine effectiveness. Aptitude (including intelligence and psychomotor skills) has long been recognized as critical to success as a pilot, and selection has emphasized these attributes. Recent research has also confirmed that personality factors are significant determinants of individual and team performance. A full-mission simulation study was run with volunteer, three-person crews in the NASA—Ames Boeing 727 simulator. The study explored the impact of leader personality factors on crew performance (Chidester, Kanki, Foushee, Dickinson, & Bowles, 1990). Crewmembers participating in the study were pretested on a personality battery that had been validated as predictive of flightcrew behavior (Chidester, Helmreich, Gregorich, & Geis, 1991). Three experimental groups were composed on the basis of the captain's personality constellation. One group was led by captains high on both goal orientation and interpersonal skills. A second group had captains who were high on goal orientation but relatively low on the interpersonal dimension. The third group was led by captains who were quite low on both goal orientation and positive interpersonal dimensions.

Each crew flew five complete flight segments spread across 2 days. On two of the legs, mechanical malfunctions occurred which were compounded by poor weather conditions at the destination airport. Crew performance was rated by expert observers, and technical errors were coded from computer records and videotapes of the flights. The data showed significant differences in performance between groups that could be attributed to the leader's personality. Crews led by captains high in both achievement needs and interpersonal skills performed uniformly well across all segments. In contrast, crews led by captains low on both of these dimensions were significantly less effective across all flights. Those in the third group, with captains high in achievement needs but low in interpersonal traits, were given poorer performance ratings initially but improved substantially by the fifth leg. One interpretation of this finding is that crews in this condition learned over time how to adapt to this difficult but motivated type of leader. The point relevant to this discussion is that a single input factor (personality) can be isolated as an influence on the performance of a well-trained and qualified crew in a controlled research setting.

Attitudes serve as guides for behavior and are another of the input factors that crews bring to the flightdeck. The *Cockpit management attitudes questionnaire (CMAQ*, Helmreich, 1984; Helmreich, Wilhelm, & Gregorich, 1988) is a 25-item, Likert-scaled battery that allows quantification of attitudes regarding crew coordination, flightdeck management, and personal capabilities under conditions of fatigue and stress. Attitudes measured by the *CMAQ* have been validated as predictors of outcome factors in the form of expert ratings of performance in line operations (Helmreich, Foushee, Benson, & Russini, 1986), thus demonstrating the linkage between input and outcome factors. Measures such as the *CMAQ* can be used both to assess input factors in organizations and as measures of outcomes to determine whether programs such as CRM can change attitudes.

Group Factors

Crews are composed of individuals who bring with them all the attributes noted above. They may be cohesive and effective or divisive, rancorous, and ineffectual depending on the mix of individuals and their states that comes together at any given time. The climate that develops in a group is multiply determined by the characteristics of individual members, by the structure imposed by the formal and informal norms of the organization, and by the quality and style of leadership present. Because of the many individual and group factors identified, research into these issues and their effects is difficult and time-consuming. As a result there is not an extensive literature on the outcome effects of systematically varying multiple individual- and group-level variables, especially in the aviation environment.

Organizational Factors

The culture of an organization is a critical input factor. If an organization sanctions individual actions rather than team coordination, both processes and outcomes are likely to have a very different flavor from those in organizations that stress crew actions and responsibility. The level of training and type of formal evaluation given to crews are also influential. Manuals and formal procedures also form part of the operational setting, as do the resources that the organization has and makes available for crews (including crew scheduling practices, maintenance support, flight planning, dispatching, etc.).

Another NASA simulation study examined the performance implications of several individual- and group-level factors. Foushee, Lauber, Baetge, and Acomb (1986) examined the interactions and performance of experienced two-person jet transport crews flying a realistic scenario in a Boeing 737 simulator. NASA was directed by the US Congress to investigate the operational significance of pilot fatigue—an individual factor driven by organizational and regulatory practices. The experimental design reflected this concern and divided crews into two groups, preduty (defined as flying the scenario after a minimum of 2 days off as if it were the first leg of a 3-day trip) and postduty (flying the scenario as the last segment of a 3-day trip). The scenario was characterized by poor weather conditions that necessitated an unexpected missed approach that was complicated by a hydraulic system failure. Following the hydraulic failure, crews were faced with a high-workload situation involving the selection of an alternate destination while coping with problems such as the requirement to extend gear and flaps manually and fly an approach at higher than normal speed.

Crews in the postduty condition had less presimulation sleep and reported significantly more fatigue, as expected from the research design. The surprising finding, however, was that fatigued crews were rated as performing significantly better and made fewer serious operational errors than the rested, preduty crews. This finding was counterintuitive but had major implications relevant to the importance of team formation and experience. By the nature of the scheduling of flight operations, most crews in the postduty condition had just completed 3 days of operations as a team, while those in the preduty condition normally did not have the benefit of recent experience with the other crewmember. When the data were reanalyzed on the basis of whether or not crews had flown together recently, the performance differences became even stronger. The findings suggest that crew scheduling practices that result in continuing recomposition of groups and a need for frequent formation of new teams can have significant operational implications. For example, three recent takeoff accidents in the United States (one involving a stall under icing conditions, one an aborted takeoff with an over-run into water, and one a runway collision after the crew became lost in dense fog) involved crews paired together for the first time.[1] The implications of crew pairings are discussed further in the chapter by Hackman.

Environmental Factors

Weather conditions constitute an environmental input factor outside the control of flightcrews. The ability of organizations and the government to provide accurate, timely information on weather constitutes one of the factors governing both group processes and outcomes. The physical condition of the aircraft (including inoperative equipment, etc.) also determines part of the field in which the crew must operate as does the availability and quality of navigational aids.

Regulatory Factors

Regulatory practices also influence the nature of crew interaction and performance. For example, the "sterile cockpit" rule in the US proscribes nonoperational communications below 10,000 ft. As described above, the focus of regulation has been on individual training and evaluation, and this has been echoed in organizational policies (recall the prohibition on first officers correcting captain's mistakes during proficiency checks). Ambiguity in regulations can also impact crews' decisions and actions. If the regulations governing an operation are unclear, responsibility shifts to the organization that can direct operations to meet operational goals and to the captain who must take ultimate responsibility for decisions regarding the safety of flight.

1.4.3 A Case Study: The Interplay of Multiple Input Factors in a Crash

Investigation of the human factors surrounding the crash of a Fokker F-28 on takeoff in Canada demonstrates the interplay of input factors at the regulatory, organizational, environmental, and individual levels. In this accident it can be seen how all of these can intersect to create an operational environment that fails to provide needed safeguards against pilot error (Helmreich, 1992; Moshansky, 1992). On a snowy winter afternoon the crew of Air Ontario Flight 1363 attempted a takeoff from Dryden, Ontario, with an accumulation of snow and ice on the wings and crashed because the aircraft could not gain enough lift to clear trees beyond the end of the runway. In the crash and resulting fire, 29 passengers and crewmembers, including both pilots, were killed. In attempting to understand how a crew with many years

---

1. One involved a DC-9 taking off in a snowstorm at Denver, the second a rejected take off by a B-737 at New York-LaGuardia, and the third a DC-9 that erroneously taxied onto the active runway and collided with a B-727 taking off.

of experience operating in the severe winter, weather of northern Ontario could make such a serious operational error, a number of input factors were uncovered which, operating in concert, set the stage for a tragically wrong decision.

At the *environmental* level, the weather was poor and deteriorating, forcing the crew to select distant alternate landing sites and to carry extra fuel. Because of the poor weather, the flight was operating more than an hour late and was full, operating at maximum gross weight. The aircraft itself had a number of mechanical problems, the most serious of which was an inoperative auxiliary power unit (APU). With an inoperative APU, it was necessary to keep an engine running during stops at airports without ground start capabilities. Dryden had no such facilities.

At the *regulatory* level, the Canadian regulations regarding deicing prohibited an aircraft from commencing a flight "when the amount of frost, snow, or ice adhering to the wings, control surfaces, or propeller of the aeroplane may adversely affect the safety of flight" (Moshansky, 1989).[2] The problem facing the crew under existing regulations was how, under time and operational pressures, to determine what constituted enough contamination to "adversely affect" safety of flight. The regulation as written made the takeoff decision at the captain's discretion and, at the same time, failed to provide safeguards against personal and organizational pressures to complete the mission at all costs.

The regulatory agency's surveillance of the airline had not focused on the newly initiated jet operation. While an audit of the airline's operations had been completed during the preceding year, the audit did not include the F-28 operation. A more complete examination might have revealed procedural and organizational discrepancies in the F-28 operation, as noted below.

A number of *organizational* factors served to increase the stress level of the crew. The airline had just begun operating jet transports and had little operational experience with this type of equipment. Initial crews for the Fokker had been trained at two different US airlines before the operation was initiated. The airline had not developed its own operating manuals, and some crewmembers were carrying manuals from one airline and others from another. The organization had not developed an approved minimum equipment list (MEL) specifying what equipment could be inoperative in normal passenger operations. Dispatchers had received only minimal training for this type of aircraft and were experienced only with small propeller-driven equipment. The flight release for the day of the accident contained a number of errors. In sum, the crew was operating without a high level of organizational support and resources.

---

2. In response to a recommendation by the Commission of Inquiry into the crash, the regulation was changed to prohibit operation with any contamination of lifting surfaces.

The airline itself was the product of the merger of two regional airlines with very different operational cultures. One had operated in the north of Canada as what was often called a "bush" operation. The other had operated in southern Ontario in a more traditional airline environment. The chief pilot of the Fokker fleet had come from the northern operation and had himself had two serious incidents involving take-offs with ice on the wings—experiences that had earned him the nickname of "Iceman." These practices suggest the possibility that norms and pressures existed to operate with wing contamination. The ambiguous regulation (see p. 13) provided no safeguard against such norms and pressures.

As *individuals*, both crewmembers had extensive experience in Canadian operations. The captain had more than 24,000 flight hours and the copilot more than 10,000. However, neither had much experience in jet transport operations, the captain having accumulated 81 hours in the F-28 and the first officer 65. The captain had been a chief pilot and instructor and was known for adherence to procedures. The first officer was a former captain described as having a somewhat abrasive personality. He also had a history of difficulties in completing some stick-and-rudder maneuvers and had required additional supervision and training before qualifying in new aircraft.

As a *group*, the crew had only flown together for 2 days. The fact that the crew lacked operational familiarity with each other and with the aircraft, along with the fact that both were accustomed to flying as captains, may have influenced the processes surrounding their conduct of the flight. In addition, the captain came from the more structured southern airline, while the first officer's experience was in the less formal northern operation.

When the aircraft landed to pick up passengers at Dryden, the crew faced a complex and stressful situation. Weather was deteriorating further, with heavy snow falling. Refueling was needed before departure, but this would necessitate keeping an engine running because of the inoperative APU. The cabin manual prohibited refueling with passengers aboard and an engine running, but the cockpit manuals were silent on this issue. The flight attendants were not alerted to the need to refuel with an engine running. The manufacturer's manual further prohibited deicing with an engine running because of possible ingestion of fluid into the powerplant. The flight was falling further behind its schedule, and many passengers were facing the prospect of missing connecting flights if there was an additional delay for deicing.

Faced with these contingencies, the crew chose to refuel with passengers aboard and an engine running. It is known that the captain considered deicing, because he inquired about the availability of equipment and was told that it could be provided. Ultimately, however, the crew chose to take off without deicing. Having reached this decision, a further environmental factor intervened in the form of a small plane, flying under visual flight rule (VFR) conditions, which made an emergency landing, causing additional delay until the runway was cleared.

There were also several experienced pilots, including two airline captains, seated as passengers in the main cabin. They survived and testified to being aware of the need for deicing and the associated threat to safety. One of them expressed his concerns about icing to the lead flight attendant but was told (falsely) that the aircraft had automatic deicing equipment. These credible concerns were never communicated to the flightdeck by the flight attendants. This failure in communication is understandable in light of organizational norms regarding cabin—cockpit communication on safety issues. One of the managers of flight attendant training testified that flight attendants were trained not to question flightcrews' judgment regarding safety issues.

Because the cockpit voice recorder was destroyed in the fire following the crash, it is impossible to reconstruct the interaction processes that led to the decision to depart Dryden without deicing. While there was unquestionably human error in that decision, to stop at this conclusion would be to ignore the extent to which the input factors set the stage for the outcome.

1.4.4   Group Process Factors

Group process factors have historically been the least studied and least understood aspects of team performance. Much of the research that has been done, especially in operational settings, has looked at input and outcome factors, leaving the intervening process as a block box (e.g., Foushee & Helmreich, 1988; Foushee, 1984; Hackman & Morris, 1975). Input factors are manifested in the types of interactions that occur when individuals and machines come together to execute complex tasks in a complex environment. The fact that process variables have been largely ignored in research does not indicate a lack of awareness of their importance; rather, it reflects the difficulty of conceptualizing and measuring them. There are a number of important and theoretically interesting questions regarding flightcrew group processes: (1) How do individuals come together as strangers and forge a cohesive team that can operate effectively after only a brief acquaintance? (2) How is team workload managed and delegated? (3) What means are used to integrate ambiguous and incomplete data to reach optimum decisions? (4) How does stress induced by fatigue, emergencies, and personal experiences influence the way teams communicate and operate? (5) What is the nature of effective and ineffective leadership among flightcrews?

Group processes are manifested primarily through verbal communications, and these provide the record that we can use to understand how teams function in flight operations. Fortunately, there is a growing base of empirical research on group processes among flightcrews, much of it from experimental flight simulations. As Foushee (1984) has pointed out, modern flight simulators provide investigators with an extraordinarily useful research setting. Simulation provides high experimental realism including visual, motion, and auditory cues. Major aspects of flight operations can be reproduced, including mechanical problems, weather, air-to-ground communications, and cabin—cockpit interactions. Flight-plans can be generated and normal and abnormal operations between real airports simulated. Having experienced crews "fly" familiar equipment using normal procedures and manuals further enhances the external validity and generality of findings from simulations. Participants in experimental simulations report that realism is high and that motivation is comparable to that in regular line operations. Because simulators can be programmed to provide an identical operating environment for each crew, it is possible to gain statistical power by exposing many crews to the same conditions. To isolate causal factors, operational factors can be experimentally varied for different subgroups of participants: for example, the manipulation of recent experience in the simulation addressing fatigue. The simulator computer provides a record of the crew's physical actions controlling the aircraft, while video and audio recordings capture the interpersonal aspect of flight. The simulations described earlier have yielded important data on the impact of input factors such as operational experience and personality and have also allowed quantification of the processes involved.

Although not designed as a study of group processes, an experimental simulation sponsored by NASA and conducted by the late H. Patrick Ruffell Smith (1979) is a powerful demonstration of the operational significance of crew interactions. Eighteen airline crews flew a two-segment flight in a Boeing 747 simulator. The scenario consisted of a short flight from Washington, DC, to John F. Kennedy Airport in New York and a subsequent leg from New York to London. After departing from New York, the crew experienced an oil pressure problem that forced them to shut down an engine. Because the flight could not be completed with a failed engine, the crew had to decide where to land. This decision was complicated by the further failure of a hydraulic system, deteriorating weather at possible landing sites, complex instructions from air traffic control, and a cabin crewmember who repeatedly requested information and assistance from the flightdeck at times of high workload. The study showed a remarkable amount of variability in the effectiveness with which crews handled the situation. Some crews managed the problems very well, while others committed a large number of operationally serious errors, including one miscalculation of more than 100,000 pounds in dumping fuel. The primary conclusion drawn from the study was that most problems and errors were induced by breakdowns in crew coordination rather than by deficits in technical knowledge and skills. For example, many errors occurred when individuals performing a task were interrupted by demands from other crewmembers or were overloaded with a variety of tasks requiring immediate action. In other cases, poor leadership was evident and resulted in a failure to exchange critical information in a timely manner.

The cockpit voice data from the study were subsequently analyzed by Foushee and Manos (1981) to quantify the processes related to variability in group performance. Their approach grew out of social psychological research into information flow within groups (e.g., Bales, 1950) and involved classifying each speech act as to type (i.e., observations regarding flight status, inquiries seeking information, etc.). The findings were clear: crews who communicated more overall tended to perform better and, in particular, those who exchanged more information about flight status committed fewer errors in the handling of engines and hydraulic and fuel systems and the reading and setting of instruments.

This methodology has been subsequently refined by Barbara Kanki and her colleagues at NASA—Ames Research Center and applied to communications records from additional experimental simulations. Kanki, Lozito, and Foushee (1989) and Kanki and Foushee (1989) examined communications patterns among crews in the previously described fatigue simulation (Foushee et al., 1986). For example, in the Kanki et al. study, sequences of communications were classified in terms of initiator and target as well as content. Initiating communications were classified as *commands, questions, observations*, and *dysfluencies* (e.g., ungram-matical or incomplete statements), while responses were classified as *replies* (responses greater than simple acknowledgments), *acknowledgments*, or *zero response*. Over and above the typical (and prescribed) occurrences of command–acknowledgment sequences, this study found that greater information transfer in the form of "commands" structuring activities and acknowledgments validating actions was associated with more effective crew performance.

Communications sequences were contrasted between crews committing a large number of operational errors and those making few. Although some specific patterns (such as that noted above) are worth special note, the primary finding of the study was the homogeneity of patterns characterizing the low-error crews. This was interpreted as the adoption of a more standard, hence more predictable form of communication. High-error crews, in contrast, showed a great diversity of speech patterns. Kanki further discusses the status of communications research as it relates to flightcrews in Chapter 4.

Orasanu (1991) has conducted additional analyses of decision-making by crews in this simulation and has identified four components that support the decision process and differentiate effective from ineffective crews. This decision strategy includes *situation assessment, metacognitive processes* in forming action plans, *shared mental models* based on intracrew communication of both situation assessment and plans, and *resource management* that encompasses task prioritization and delegation of specific responsibilities. Orasanu's formulation is congruent with basic principles of CRM and can be translated into prescriptive training. Several airlines have incorporated these findings and concepts into their CRM training. This research and a growing empirical and theoretical literature question traditional theories of decision-making that are based on the assumption of a "rational," but biased, Bayesian decision maker (e.g., Klein, Orasanu, Calderwood, & Zsambok, in press). In particular, this approach emphasizes differences between decision-making by experts in natural settings with high stakes and time pressure, and the processes employed by naive subjects in the constrained, laboratory environments frequently employed in decision research. Orasanu summarizes the state of knowledge in this area in her chapter.

Data from the Chidester et al. (1990) simulation involving personality factors were coded and analyzed to isolate decision-making processes while crews dealt with multiple inflight abnormalities—a jammed stabilizer and low oil pressure on one engine (Mosier, 1991). It was found that the majority of crews utilized a strategy consistent with Thordsen and Klein's (1989) team decision model. Sampling of information and repeated verification of the accuracy of situation assessment continued throughout the decision process. Many crews made preliminary, revocable decisions as soon as they felt they had enough critical data about the problem. The implication of this finding is that, while thorough assessment of the situation is critical, crews make decisions without having all relevant information. Indeed, the best-performing crews collected information pertinent to situation evaluation *after* making a final decision as a means of confirming the decision. In contrast, high-error crews showed a diverse pattern of interactions.

In a field investigation of group formation and interaction processes among three-person airline crews, Ginnett (1987) observed crews from their formation on the ground prior to the first flight of a multiday trip, and in the cockpit on each flight segment. He found that the quality of the initial briefing was associated with better crew performance throughout the trip. Captains of effective crews communicated the team concept and elaborated or affirmed the rules, norms, and task boundaries that constitute the organizational structure (what Hackman, 1987; has called the "organizational shell") in this first encounter. Leaders of less effective crews showed a variety of interaction patterns. Thus in both studies there was consistency among crews rated as performing well and diversity among the less effective teams. These team issues are discussed in the chapter by Ginnett.

1.4.5   Elaborating Group Process Factors

Building on research with flightcrews and theoretical conceptions of group process mediators of aircrew performance, we should be able to fill in the black box with a more complete description of the processes that influence outcomes. Helmreich, Wilhelm, Kello, Taggart, and Butler (1991) have developed an evaluation system for systematic observation of flightcrews in line operations and simulations. The methodology grew out of findings from small group research and investigations of accidents and incidents. Group processes identified during flight operations fall into two broad categories.

One consists of the *interpersonal and cognitive functions*. The second includes *machine interface tasks*. The latter category reflects the technical proficiency of the crew. It is a given that optimal team interactions and decision-making will be of little value if the crew cannot also integrate them with technical execution of maneuvers and procedures needed for safe flight. There is also ample evidence from review of the accidents cited earlier that competence in machine interface tasks alone does not guarantee operational safety.

Fig. 1.4 shows the expanded group process model as it flows into outcome factors. In theory, the two categories of group processes containing human factors and technical components must be integrated operationally to produce effective overall performance. Note that the final box in Fig. 1.4 is labeled "Integrated CRM and Technical Functions" to emphasize the fact that the two components need to come together in the group process phase, which then flows into desired outcomes of safe and efficient mission completion.

Breaking the subordinate categories down further, die interpersonal and cognitive functions can be classified into three broad clusters of observable behaviors: team formation and management tasks, communications processes and decision tasks, and workload management and situation awareness tasks. The machine interface tasks fall into two clusters, the actual control of the aircraft (either manually or through computer-based flight management systems) and adherence to established procedures for the conduct of flight.

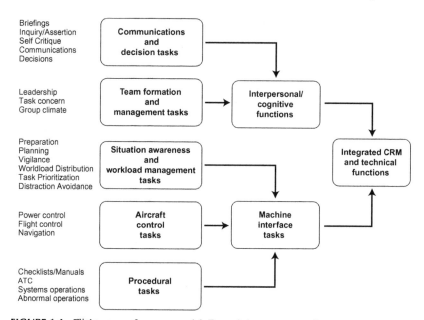

FIGURE 1.4 Flightcrew performance model: Expanded group process factors.

Team Formation and Management Tasks

The first cluster deals with the formation of the crew as an operating team, including cabin as well as flightdeck personnel. As Ginnett's (1987) research has demonstrated, there is a formation process for teams during which patterns of communication and interaction are established. Once established, the process continues and leads to activities that can maintain patterns of effective (or ineffective) group interaction. The process of formation and maintenance can be categorized into two broad areas, *leadership, followership, and task concern;* and *interpersonal relationships and group climate.*

Flightcrews are teams with a designated leader and clear lines of authority and responsibility. Not surprisingly, the captain, as leader, can and should set the tone of the group. Effective leaders use their authority but do not operate without the participation of other team members. As demonstrated in the Chidester et al. (1990) simulation study, captains' attributes such as personality play a role in determining group processes and outcomes. Two negative patterns of leadership have been isolated in the investigation of accidents. One consists of a strong, autocratic leader who chills input from subordinates and conducts operations as if the flightdeck were a single-seat fighter. The "macho pilot" tradition discussed by Foushee and Helmreich (1988) represents the prototype of such a leadership style and is typified by an incident reported by Foushee (1982) in which a copilot's attempts to communicate an air traffic control speed restriction were met with an order to "just look out the damn window." Equally destructive are leaders who abdicate responsibility and fail to control activities on the flightdeck. An example of this type of leadership is seen in the crash of a B-727 at Dallas—Fort Worth because the crew was distracted and failed to confirm that flaps were set prior to take-off (NTSB, 1989). In this case, the first officer became involved in a lengthy social conversation with a flight attendant during taxi. Although not participating extensively in the conversation, the captain failed to control the group processes and did not establish work priorities or demonstrate a concern for operational duties.

One of the observable components of group processes is the quality of interpersonal relationships and the resulting group climate. Effective crews maintain a group climate that encourages participation and exchange of information. The group climate does not reflect the crew's concern with effective accomplishment of required tasks, but it is axiomatic that, other things being equal, crews functioning in a positive environment will be more motivated and will participate more fully in team activities.

Communications Processes and Decision Tasks

As data from experimental simulations have shown, the processes of information transfer and decision-making are prime determinants of crew performance, and higher levels of communication are associated with fewer operational errors. Critical elements in this process include *briefings* and the extent to which free and open communications are established and practiced. Briefings need to address team formation issues as well as technical issues anticipated during operations. Although categorized as part of the communications cluster, briefings are one of the demonstrated means of forming effective teams and establishing a positive group climate.

Inquiry, advocacy, and *assertion* define behaviors meant to ensure that necessary information is available and that required communications are completed at appropriate times (e.g., initiating and completing checklists, alerting others to developing problems). The accident literature is replete with examples of crewmembers failing to inquire about actions being taken by others. It is critical to safety and team action that crewmembers request clarification when they are unclear about the current operational situation or planned actions. Paralleling the need to gain operational data is the willingness of crewmembers to advocate effectively courses of action that they feel essential to safe and efficient operations. In cases such as the Air Florida crash in Washington, DC (NTSB, 1982). The voice recorder shows that one crewmember is uneasy about the takeoff but fails to express his concern strongly and to advocate an alternative action strategy. Concerns and suggestions for needed actions must be communicated with sufficient assertiveness to ensure that others are aware of their importance. It is noteworthy that the NTSB's first call for something like CRM was in the form of a recommendation for "assertiveness training" for junior crewmembers after investigation of a crash that was caused by fuel exhaustion during a hold to investigate a warning light (NTSB, 1979). In this accident, the second officer repeatedly reported that the fuel state was critical, but without sufficient assertiveness to elicit action on the part of the captain. The willingness of crewmembers to advocate the course of action they feel best, even when it involves disagreements with others, is an essential attribute of an effective team. When crewmembers have differing views of proper courses of action and advocate their preferred course of action, interpersonal conflict may result. The observable behaviors resulting from disagreement are the means used for conflict resolution. Conflict may result in either careful consideration of alternatives, or a polarization of positions and a negative group atmosphere. Effective conflict resolution is focused on *what* is right rather than *who* is right.

Active participation in decision-making processes should be encouraged and practiced, including questioning actions and decisions. When decisions are made, they need to be clearly communicated and acknowledged. *Crew self-critique* is another essential component of effective group processes. Teams need to review their decisions and actions with the goal of optimizing future team activities. Effective critique includes the *product or outcome*, the *process*, and the *people involved*. Critique can and should occur both during and after completion of activities. Critique is not the same as criticism. Indeed, review of effective team performance is a powerful reinforcer.

Situation Awareness, Workload Management Tasks

The third grouping of crew effectiveness markers is labeled Workload Management and Situation Awareness. The crew's awareness of operational conditions and contingencies, usually defined as situation awareness, has been implicated as causal in a number of incidents and accidents. However, situation awareness is an outcome rather than a specific set of mission management behaviors. The specific factors that are defined for this cluster are *preparation/planning/vigilance, workload distribution,* and *distraction avoidance.*

Preparation, planning, and vigilance behaviors reflect the extent to which crews anticipate contingencies and actions that may be required. Excellent crews are always ahead of the curve while poor crews continually play catch-up. Vigilant crews devote appropriate attention to required tasks and respond immediately to new information. However, a crew indulging in casual social conversation during periods of low workload is not lacking in vigilance if flight duties are being discharged properly and the operational environment is being monitored; the crew may be using this time for team formation and maintenance.

As the Ruffell Smith (1979) study demonstrated clearly, when abnormal situations arise during a flight, particular crewmembers may become overloaded with multiple tasks and/or become distracted from primary responsibilities. One of the observables of group process is how well crews manage to distribute tasks and avoid overloading individuals. By prioritizing activities, teams can avoid becoming distracted from essential activities, as was the crew whose concentration on a burned-out light bulb kept them from noticing that the autopilot had become disengaged and that the aircraft was descending below the proper flight path (NTSB, 1972).

Machine Interface Tasks

The flight control and procedural tasks that constitute the machine interface portion of group processes represent the traditional model of flight training and evaluation. The model proposed here, with its inclusion of interpersonal and cognitive processes, in no way downplays the continuing importance of these activities. Rather it reflects the fact that both are essential to safe and efficient operations.

If the proposed model does indeed reflect the major input and process determinants of flightcrew performance, it should provide insights into how training programs can best address the group processes of flight. In the following section we discuss theoretical approaches to maximizing the impact of CRM.

1.5   THEORETICAL LEVERAGING OF CRM TRAINING

The model indicates that there are multiple determinants of crew effectiveness among both input and process factors. In theory, organizations should achieve the greatest impact on crew performance when they address and optimize as many input and group process factors as possible. In this section we consider how programs can be designed to accomplish this. This discussion is cast in terms of an integrated approach to technical and human factors training.

1.5.1   Optimizing Input Factors

Individual Factors

We suggested in an earlier article on crew interaction and performance that the selection of individuals more predisposed toward team activity and crew coordination concepts could provide one means of achieving more effective crew Performance (Foushee & Helmreich, 1988). Subsequent research has supported this contention as personality factors have been linked to crew performance in experimental simulations (Chidester et al., 1990), to acceptance of CRM training and changes in attitudes regarding flightdeck management (Chidester et al., 1991; Helmreich & Wilhelm, 1989, 1991; Helmreich, Wilhelm, & Jones, 1991), and to fatigue and health complaints in short- and long-haul operations (Chidester, 1990). The chapters by both Hackman and Chidester discuss the need for innovations in this area. Selection represents a long-term strategy, but one that should be entertained. In the short term, however, efforts should concentrate on enhancing training for the existing workforce.

All effective training programs have an information base. In the case of CRM, the goal is to communicate new knowledge about effective team performance and, concurrently, to change or reinforce attitudes regarding appropriate flightdeck management. Changed attitudes, in turn, should be reflected in improvements in group process and ultimately in better crew performance.

Organizational Factors

There are a number of issues that organizations can address that should, in theory, increase crew effectiveness. Foremost, of course, is to demonstrate a commitment to developing and implementing training of the highest quality. However, unless the concepts presented in training are consistent with the organization's culture and practices, they are not likely to have a major impact. Several steps are necessary to ensure that the culture and norms are congruent with CRM. One is to stress training using a crew rather than an individualistic model. Another is to make checklists and other cockpit documents consistent with crew concepts (Pan American Airways took this step in the early 1970s in response to a number of crew-induced accidents). An additional step is to address communications issues between flightcrews and other operational units including dispatchers, cabin crews, and the maintenance force. The interface between the cockpit and these elements forms a significant component of group processes and can either support or hinder effective team performance.

An essential means of making organizational culture and norms congruent with CRM concepts is by providing role models who practice and reinforce them. In most organizations, check airmen, instructors, and chief pilots are highly respected and experienced pilots who are looked to as exemplars of the organization's norms and requirements (Helmreich, 1991a, 1991b; Helmreich et al., 1991). Selection of individuals for these positions should include assessment of interpersonal as well as technical expertise. Special training in evaluating and debriefing group processes can help them establish and maintain norms supportive of good CRM practices.

Regulatory Factors

In 1986, following a crash caused by a crew's failure to complete pretake-off checklists and to extend flaps, then FAA Administrator T. Allen McArtor called a meeting of airline managers to discuss the implementation of human factors training. This resulted in the formation of a government—industry working group that drafted an Advisory Circular (AC) on cockpit resource management (FAA, 1989, 1993). The AC defines the concept, suggests curriculum topics, and recognizes that initial CRM training provides only basic awareness of CRM issues. It further points out that awareness must be followed by a practice and feedback phase and a continual reinforcement phase. Full mission simulation training (line-oriented flight training, LOFT) is highly recommended as the most effective means of continual reinforcement. The content of the AC is consistent with generally accepted principles of learning and reinforcement and with the theoretical model of flightcrew performance being discussed here. Although CRM has not been mandated as a requirement for air carriers, the AC clearly encourages US carriers to develop such programs. Efforts are further under way to mandate CRM training for all air transport.

Also growing out of this government—industry collaboration has been a Special Federal Aviation Regulation—Advanced Qualification Program (FAA SFAR 58, AQP) issued in 1990. AQP is described in detail in the chapter by Birnbach & Longridge. It is a voluntary regulation for airlines that allows much more flexibility and innovation in training. In exchange for this flexibility in conducting training, participating airlines are required to provide CRM training, LOFT, and to initiate formal evaluation of crew as well as individual proficiency. Organizations that operate under AQP should find the regulatory environment supportive of CRM training efforts.

1.5.2   Enhancing Group Process Factors

In theory, the point of greatest impact on flightcrew behavior should be the group process itself. This should be accomplished effectively by full mission simulation training (LOFT), where crews have an opportunity to experiment with new interaction strategies and to receive feedback and reinforcement. The FAA supported this approach and issued an Advisory Circular (FAA, 1978) establishing guidelines for the conduct of LOFT. NASA hosted an industry conference on LOFT in 1981 that resulted in two volumes providing a review of techniques and formal guidelines for its conduct (Lauber & Foushee, 1981). The principles espoused include establishing high levels of realism, conducting normal flight operations as well as creating emergency and abnormal situations, and nonintervention by instructors into group processes, decisions, and actions. CRM LOFT is defined as training rather than formal evaluation, with the goal of allowing crews to explore the impact of new behaviors without jeopardizing their certification as crewmembers.

LOFT should influence subsequent behavior most strongly when scenarios are crafted to require team decision-making and coordinated actions to resolve in-flight situations. The debriefing of LOFT is also a critical element in achieving impact. Skilled instructors should guide crews to self-realization rather than lecture them on observed deficiencies. Instances of effective team behavior should be strongly reinforced. The use of videotapes of the simulation can provide crews with the opportunity to examine their own behavior with the detachment of observers (Helmreich, 1987).

In addition to the practice and reinforcement provided later by LOFT, initial CRM training, usually conducted in a seminar setting, should allow participants to observe and experiment with behavioral strategies and to receive individual and group feedback. Instruction that allows participants to experience processes is more meaningful than lectures where ideas are presented to a passive audience. Introductory training in CRM provides the conceptual framework needed to understand the processes that will later be encountered in LOFT.

It is also necessary to identify and reinforce effective group processes in normal line operations as well as in the training environment. We earlier identified check airmen as key agents and role models. To help transfer concepts from training to the line, check airmen should address not only technical performance but also interpersonal and cognitive issues in their conduct of periodic evaluations of crew performance line operations (line checks).

As we pointed out in describing Fig. 1.4, process factors from both the interpersonal and machine interface components need to be integrated as the team performs its duties. The corollary of this is that the most effective training should bring together technical and human factors aspects of each maneuver taught, so crewmembers can recognize that every technical activity has team-level components essential to its successful completion. For example, the V_1 cut[3] is a maneuver in which crews are required to demonstrate proficiency. It involves the loss of power at a point when it is too late to abort the take-off. Crews are required to climb out, reconfigure the aircraft, communicate with the tower, and return for landing. While this is often seen as primarily a technical exercise, in fact it requires concerted activity by the full crew along with rapid, accurate information transfer within the cockpit and between cockpit and cabin and cockpit and ground. If training in basic flight maneuvers stresses the human factors as well as technical components, the likelihood that crews will demonstrate effective, integrated group processes should be increased.

In a similar vein, the specificity of concepts communicated and reinforced should determine their acceptance and adoption. Individuals may accept, in principle, abstract ideas of open and complete communication, team formation, situation awareness, and workload management, but may find it difficult to translate them into concrete behaviors on the flightdeck. In theory, individuals who understand both the conceptual bases of effective crew coordination and their specific behavioral manifestations should be able to put them into practice readily and should be able to evaluate their success in accomplishing them.

As part of a research effort to evaluate the impact of CRM training and to train observers to judge crew effectiveness, Helmreich et al. (1991) have attempted to define behavioral markers of the three clusters of interpersonal and cognitive tasks. These are observable behaviors that reflect the concepts central to CRM training. Forty discrete markers have been isolated and utilized in observations of line operations and LOFT (Clothier, 1991a). The data suggest that these behaviors can be reliably measured. Fig. 1.5 shows the ten markers associated with the Situation Awareness/Workload Management cluster. It can be argued that programs that employ concrete, behavioral examples should have a greater impact on crew processes and outcomes than those that deal with abstract concepts.

In this section we have tried to derive approaches to CRM training that should theoretically have the greatest leverage on crew performance. This analysis suggests that programs need to attack a number of areas in concert if they are to achieve maximum influence on behaviors and attitudes. In the following section we discuss efforts to achieve these goals and describe some of the major developments in CRM training over the last decade.

---

3. V_1 is the decision speed for take-off. When an aircraft reaches V_1 the crew is committed to take-off. It is a function of runway length and condition, aircraft weight, temperature, etc. We are indebted to Captain Kevin Smith for his analysis of actions required during the maneuver.

- Avoids "tunnel vision", being aware of factors such as stress that can reduce vigilance
- Actively monitors weather, aircraft systems, instruments, and ATC, sharing relevant information
- Stays "ahead of curve" in preparing for expected or contingency situations
- Verbally insures that cockpit and cabin crew are aware of plans
- Workload distribution is clearly communicated and acknowledged
- Ensures that secondary operational tasks are prioritized
- Recognizes and reports work overloads in self and others
- Plans for sufficient time prior ro maneuvers for programming of automation
- Ensures that all crewmembers are aware of status and changes in automation
- Recognizes potential distractions caused by automation and takes appropriate preventive action

FIGURE 1.5   Behavioral markers for workload distribution/situational awareness.

1.6   THE EVOLUTION OF CRM TRAINING

Formal training in human factors aspects of crew operations was beginning to take root by the 1970s. For example, the late Frank Hawkins (1984) had initiated a human factors training program at KLM, Royal Dutch Airlines, based on Edwards' (1972, 1975) SHEL model and TAG. Operational and theoretical concerns with human factors aspects of flight came together in a NASA/Industry workshop held in 1979. At this gathering, managers from worldwide aviation met with the members of the academic and government research community concerned with human performance. Research into the human factors aspects of accidents was reviewed (e.g., Cooper et al., 1980) along with the seminal findings from the Ruffell Smith (1979) study. Many of the participants left the meeting committed to developing formal training in crew coordination.

A number of different CRM courses began to emerge in the early 1980s. The focus of most early training was on input factors, especially in the areas of knowledge and attitudes. Much of the emphasis was on the review of human factors aspects of accidents, with the goal of changing attitudes regarding appropriate flightdeck management. Many of these courses were presented in a lecture format, and some consisted only of videotaped presentations. Other training, growing out of management development programs, included tests and exercises designed to provide self-awareness and to demonstrate general concepts of group processes. What was not present in early efforts was a focus on organizational issues and flightcrew group processes, including reinforcement of effective process behavior. Many early CRM courses faced considerable resistance from crewmembers who expressed concerns about both the motivation for and possible outcomes of the training. Some saw it as unwarranted psychological meddling, equating the training with clinical psychology or psychotherapy. Others feared that captains' authority would be eroded by a kind of Dale Carnegie charm school approach to developing harmonious interpersonal relations, without regard for operational effectiveness.

The first CRM course integrated with LOFT was developed by United Airlines following the NASA workshop. The course, called Command, Leadership, and Resource Management, was the result of a collaboration among United flight training personnel, members of the Air Line Pilots' Association, and Drs. Robert Blake and Jane Mouton. Blake and Mouton were social psychologists who had developed training programs aimed at improving managerial effectiveness for a number of major corporations. The centerpiece of their training approach is providing participants with insights into their personal managerial styles (an individual input factor) using the managerial grid (Blake & Mouton, 1964) as a means of classifying managers along independent dimensions of task and interpersonal orientations. The multiday training program that emerged is intensive and interactive, requiring participants to assess their own behaviors and those of peers. Operational concepts stressed in the training include process factors such as inquiry, seeking of relevant operational information; advocacy, communicating proposed actions; and conflict resolution, decision-making, and critique, reviewing actions taken and decisions reached. The unique aspect of the United approach was that the initial training was followed by recurrent review of CRM concepts. The program also demonstrated a major commitment to group process factors by providing annual CRM LOFT sessions. These allow crews to practice the human factors concepts covered in the seminar and recurrent training. One of the major innovations in United's LOFT was the use of a video camera in the simulator to record crew interactions. By replaying the tape of their LOFT, crews gain the ability to review their actions and decisions and to obtain insights into their behavior, guided by the LOFT instructor.[4] This program represents the first integration of multiple input and group process factors that also recognized the need for continuing practice and reinforcement.

NASA and the Military Airlift Command of the US Air Force jointly sponsored a workshop on developments in CRM training in May, 1986 (Orlady & Foushee, 1987). This conference demonstrated the striking spread of CRM training throughout the world since the first workshop in 1979. Reports were presented on the implementation of CRM courses at United Airlines (Carroll & Taggart, 1987), Pan American World Airways (Butler, 1987), People Express Airlines (Bruce & Jensen, 1987), Continental Airlines (Christian & Morgan, 1987), Japan Air Lines (Yamamori, Orlady, & Foushee, 1987), Trans Australia Airlines (Davidson, 1987), in units of the

---

4. The videotape is always erased following the LOFT debriefing to preserve the confidentiality of the training and behaviors observed.

Military Airlift Command (Cavanagh & Williams, 1987; Halliday, Biegelski, & Inzana, 1987), and in corporate and regional operations (Mudge, 1987; Schwartz, 1987; Yocum & Monan, 1987).

In the late 1980s a second generation of CRM training began to emerge in the United States. Pan American World Airways and Delta Airlines both initiated CRM courses that included recurrent classroom training and LOFT. In addition, these programs addressed organizational input factors by providing additional training for check airmen and instructors with the goal of increasing impact on group process factors through reinforcement of effective behaviors both in LOFT and in line operations.

Although there has been a great proliferation of CRM courses, there has not been a parallel growth in the use of CRM/LOFT to provide practice and reinforcement. At the time this is written, in the United States only United, Horizon Airlines, Delta, Continental, and units of military aviation have integrated CRM/LOFT programs, although a number of other organizations including Northwest Airlines, US Air, and Comair are in the process of implementing them. There are a number of reasons why more comprehensive programs have been slow in emerging. One is certainly economic. As Chidester points out in his chapter, at a time of great financial distress in the industry, innovative and relatively expensive programs that are not formally mandated by regulations must compete with other operational needs for scarce resources. Indeed, regulations in the United States have tended to operate against the adoption of LOFT because it is necessary to meet many formal, technical requirements each year and because requirements for recurrent training for captains are semi-annual but annual for first officers and flight engineers, making it difficult to schedule complete crews for LOFT.[5] The previously mentioned Advanced Qualification Program both removes some of the regulatory barriers to comprehensive CRM/LOFT and provides incentives for their adoption. Additional resistance to changes in training may also come from awareness that the aviation system has an excellent safety record when compared with all other forms of transportation and from the fact that empirical evidence for increased safety of flight as a result of CRM training has been lacking until very recently.

At the present time a third generation of CRM training is emerging. This approach continues the practices of integrating CRM with LOFT but also takes a systems approach to multiple input factors including organizational cultures and group and individual factors. Evaluation and reinforcement in line operations are also cornerstones of this approach. In addition, new programs are becoming more specific in focus and are defining and directly addressing optimal behaviors (e.g., behavioral markers). Efforts are

---

5. United Airlines, Pan American Airlines, and Delta Airlines have received exemptions from some training requirements to facilitate training complete crews on an annual basis in exchange for implementation of integrated CRM/LOFT programs.

underway in several organizations (stimulated in part by requirements of AQP) to remove the distinction between technical training and evaluation and CRM, with the goal of implementing a training philosophy where both components are addressed in every aspect of pilot qualification.

An additional characteristic of evolving programs is the extension of CRM training beyond the cockpit to other operational areas. Joint training for cabin and cockpit crews has been initiated at America West Airlines, and programs are being developed at a number of other carriers. American Airlines is including dispatchers in CRM training in recognition of common concerns and responsibilities and the need for effective, open communication. Pan American and later Continental Airlines developed CRM programs for maintenance personnel. Efforts are also underway to implement similar training within the FAA for Air Traffic Control personnel who also operate in a team environment but have historically received little or no formal instruction in human factors issues relating to their jobs.

Looking at the growth and evolution of CRM training, one is struck by the willingness of very disparate organizations to embrace a training concept that counters many of the traditions of an industry. In the following section we consider factors that may have facilitated this acceptance.

1.7   CRM AND TRADITIONAL MANAGEMENT DEVELOPMENT TRAINING

From an observer's perspective, the philosophical and pragmatic bases of CRM are consistent with programs that have been used in management development training for several decades. Concerns with self-assessment, managerial styles, interpersonal communications, and organizational influences on behavior have academic roots in social, industrial, and clinical psychology, sociology, and schools of business. Programs to translate empirical and theoretical knowledge about groups into practical training have been employed with differential acceptance in many segments of industry and government. Indeed, many of the initial CRM programs, such as that at United Airlines, were adaptations of existing management training courses. What is striking about CRM is the rapidity of its spread and the enthusiasm with which it has been accepted. What is unique about its implementation in this setting? What can convince fiscally conservative managers to commit scarce resources and highly experienced crewmembers to reevaluate their approach to a highly structured task?

Part of the answer rests in the nature of the flight environment. Operating an aircraft with a multiperson crew is a structured and bounded endeavor with clear lines of authority and responsibility. The inherent activities involved in taking an aircraft from one point to another are similar in organizations throughout the world. Although aircraft differ in design and sophistication and in number of crewmembers required for operation, the basic tasks are generic. One implication of this is that the types of problems in flight-deck management found in one organization or flightcrew have a high probability of occurring in others. Findings regarding crew contributions to accidents can be easily recognized as generic rather than as unique occurrences in unique organizational cultures and operating environments. It can be inferred that similar approaches to improving crew effectiveness should work throughout the industry despite differences in the culture, history and health of organizations.

In aviation the results of breakdowns in flightcrew group processes are dramatic and highly visible and provide an unequivocal outcome criterion. In contrast, outcome criteria in industry such as profits or productivity are relatively diffuse and subject to qualification by industry-specific and organization-specific factors. Given an overall performance criterion that represents a common, desired outcome, it is understandable that a similar approach would be recognized and embraced.

Again, in contrast to the diversity found outside aviation, the range of decisions and behaviors that faces flightcrews is constrained and can be incorporated in a fairly simple model. Because of this behavioral specificity, training can be more sharply focused than it normally is in courses developed for generic managers. This clearer definition of issues and processes should lead both to greater acceptance by participants and to more tangible, positive outcomes.

Another distinctive feature of the aviation environment is the ability to use highly realistic simulation to practice behaviors and receive feedback and reinforcement. Unlike many of the exercises that are used in general management training, LOFT provides a valid representation of the actual task setting with measurable outcomes. This allows crews to observe the discrete components of group processes as they flow into outcomes. LOFT provides compelling evidence of the validity of the concepts being trained.

The ultimate question, of course, is how well the training achieves its stated goals. In the following section we review preliminary results from evaluation of CRM courses in a number of organizations.

1.8 RESEARCH FINDINGS

Although the process of research is necessarily slow and incremental, a number of consistent findings have emerged regarding the effects of CRM programs. Our goal is to provide a brief overview of what research has told us about the impact of CRM and to point out some of the gaps in current knowledge. It should be noted that the research to be discussed regarding the effectiveness of CRM training comes from evaluation of intensive programs integrated with LOFT and not from brief lecture or discussion sessions called

CRM that may be included in crew training. Strategies for the investigation of CRM-related behaviors and concepts are discussed further in Helmreich (1991b).

1. *Crewmembers find CRM and LOFT* to *be highly effective training.* Survey data from more than 20,000 flight crewmembers in civilian and military organizations in the United States and abroad show overwhelming acceptance of the training. The vast majority of crewmembers find the training both relevant and useful (Helmreich & Wilhelm, 1991). Fig. 1.6 shows the distribution of responses in five airlines to a posttraining survey question regarding the utility of the training. A similar pattern of endorsement is found in evaluations of the value of LOFT. Wilhelm (1991) has analyzed reactions to LOFT from more than 8,000 participants in the training at four organizations. Crewmembers overwhelmingly feel that it is important and useful training and that it has value on the technical as well as the human factors dimensions. Fig. 1.7 shows the distribution of mean ratings of the usefulness of LOFT in four airlines, broken down by crew position. Clearly, acceptance of training is a necessary but not sufficient indicator of its effectiveness. If crews do not perceive training as useful, it is unlikely that it will induce behavioral change. On the other hand, the training may be perceived as useful, but because behavioral tools are not provided to help participants apply the concepts, the result may be increased awareness of CRM concepts but little change in observable behavior.

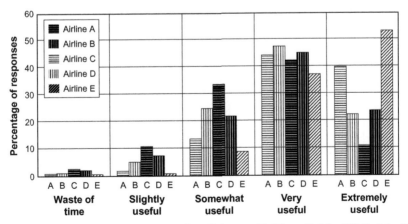

FIGURE 1.6 Responses to the question, "Overall, how useful did you find the CRM training?" in five organizations (A, B, C, D, E).

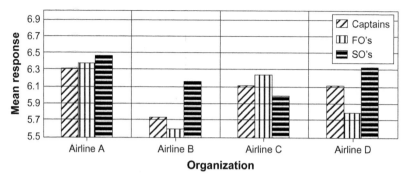

FIGURE 1.7 Average ratings for the item, "Overall, LOFT is an extremely useful training technique," in four organizations (A, B, C, D). Scale: 1, strongly disagree: 4, neutral: 7, strongly agree.

2. *There are measurable, positive changes in attitudes and behavior follow-ing the introduction of CRM and LOFT,* Changes in attitudes regarding flightdeck management measured by the *CMAQ* (Helmreich, 1984) can be used as a measure of training impact. Typically, attitudes show signifi-cant positive shifts on the three scales of the *CMAQ*, Communications and Coordination, Command Responsibility, and Recognition of Stressor Effects (Helmreich & Wilhelm, 1991). As Fig. 1.8 illustrates for the Communications and Coordination scale in six organizations, there is a consistent increase in the positivity of reactions, although the magnitude of change (along with the baseline attitudes) varies between organiza-tions. The *CMAQ* findings suggest that participants do relate the concepts being taught to specific attitudes regarding the conduct of flight operations.

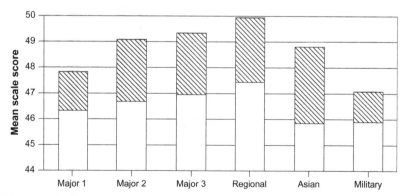

FIGURE 1.8 Pretest (unshaded) and posttraining (shaded) attitudes on the CMAQ Communications and Coordination scale. All differences significant ($P < .01$): scale range, 11−55.

Because the linkage between attitudes and behavior is less than perfect (e.g., Abelson, 1972), it is critical to the validation of CRM training effectiveness that there be observable changes in crewmembers' behaviors on the flightdeck. Data have been gathered both by independent observers and by check airmen and instructors given special training in observational methodology (e.g., Clothier, 1991b). Data collected across time show changes in behavior in the desired direction. Fig. 1.9, for example, shows shifts in observed behavior during line operations over a 3-year period on 14 observed categories of process behavior following the introduction of CRM and LOFT in one major airline. All mean differences are statistically significant. It can be noted that the behavioral effects continue to grow across time. A reasonable interpretation of this trend is that, as concepts become more widely accepted, organizational norms shift and exert pressure on crewmembers to conform to the new standards of behavior.

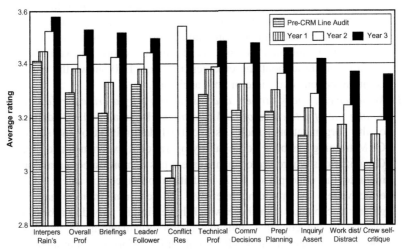

FIGURE 1.9 Average crew performance ratings in one organization across time. Scale: 1, poor; 5, excellent.

Significant differences have also been found when crew behavior is aggregated and contrasted in terms of the level of flightdeck automation (Butler, 1991; Clothier, 1991a). Crews observed in advanced technology aircraft are rated as more effective in LOFT than those flying conventional aircraft on a number of human factors dimensions. The causes and extent of these differences remain for further research to clarify. Issues surrounding cockpit automation, crew coordination, and LOFT are discussed in the chapter by Wiener.

As we have noted, the number of accidents involving crews with formal training in CRM and LOFT is too small to draw any statistical inferences regarding the role of these experiences in helping crews cope with serious emergency situations. There are, however, a growing number of anecdotal reports that the training does provide valuable resources for crews faced with major inflight emergencies. Two recent accidents have involved United Airlines crews with both CRM and LOFT experience. In one, a cargo door blew off in flight on Flight 811, a Boeing 747, causing considerable structural damage and the loss of two engines. In the other, the catastrophic failure of the center engine on a McDonnell Douglas DC-10, Flight 232, resulted in the loss of all hydraulic systems and flight controls. Both crews were able to minimize loss of life by coping effectively with the problems, and both acknowledged the role of CRM in enabling them to cope with their novel emergencies. Crew communications taken from the cockpit voice recorder transcripts have been coded in terms of content and frequency and analyzed by Steven Predmore (1991). The coding system classifies communications in terms of CRM concepts including inquiry, command and advocacy, reply and acknowledgment, and observation (communication of operational information). Both crews maintained a high level of communication and verification of information throughout the emergencies. Fig. 1.10 shows the pattern of communications over time in both accidents.

3. *Management, check airmen, and instructors play a critical role in determining the effectiveness of CRM training.* Hackman's (1987) delineation of the "organizational shell" as a critical determinant of the success of CRM training has been borne out by operational experience and research. Organizations where senior management has demonstrated a real commitment to the concepts of CRM and its importance for safety and crew effectiveness by providing intensive and recurrent training have found greater acceptance than those which have simply provided a brief introduction to the concepts. Indeed, several organizations in which flight operations management made a concerted effort to communicate the nature of CRM training and the organization's dedication have noted significant improvement in cockpit management attitudes even before formal training was instituted. The pivotal position of check airmen and instructors as primary role models and agents of reinforcement has also become increasingly recognized (Helmreich, 1987; Helmreich et al., 1991). Consistent with the theoretical model, the extent to which these key individuals endorse, practice, and emphasize CRM concepts both in the training and checking environment seems largely to determine program acceptance.

4. *Without reinforcement, the impact of CRM training decays.* Data indicate that even intensive, initial CRM training constitutes only an awareness phase and introduction to the concepts, and that continuing reinforcement

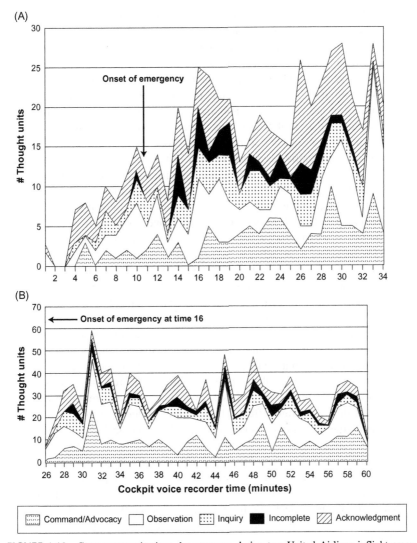

FIGURE 1.10 Crew communications, by category, during two United Airlines inflight emergencies: (A) Flight 811; (B) Flight 232.

is essential to produce long-term change in human factors practices. Some of the most compelling evidence of the need for ongoing emphasis on CRM comes from revisiting organizations where well-received initial CRM training has not been accompanied by an organizational commitment to continuing the effort (Helmreich, 1991a). In one organization, when the *CMAQ* was readministered more than a year after the completion of initial training, attitudes had reverted to near their baseline, pre-CRM levels. In this organization many open-ended comments written by respondents expressed concern over the fact that some outspoken opponents of CRM concepts continued management styles antithetical to good human factors practice. In another organization, recurrent CRM and LOFT were provided, but management support was weak, there was high turnover in training and checking personnel, no formal human factors training for new check airmen and instructors, and limited efforts to revise and update LOFT scenarios. When attitudes regarding the value of CRM training and LOFT were assessed more than 2 years later, they had become significantly less positive than in the first year. These longitudinal findings have major operational significance as they reinforce the notion that organizations desiring to maintain the momentum provided by initial CRM training must make a formal commitment to provide the resources necessary for continuing training and reinforcement.

5. *A small but significant percentage of participants "boomerang" or reject CRM training.* Although the self-report reactions and attitude change findings discussed above show the overall positive impact of initial CRM training, some participants fail to see its value and some even show attitude change in a direction opposite to that intended. These individuals have been described as showing a "boomerang effect" (Helmreich & Wilhelm, 1989). Similarly, some crews observed in line operations following initial CRM seminars do not practice the concepts espoused in training. The fact that reactions to CRM are not uniformly positive does not negate the value of the training, but this undesired outcome is reason for some concern. Research has shown that there are multiple determinants of the boomerang effect (Helmreich & Wilhelm, 1989). Some resistance to the training is rooted in individual personality characteristics. Crewmembers who are lacking in traits associated with both achievement motivation and interpersonal skills are initially more prone to reject CRM concepts. In addition, the group dynamics of particular seminars also appear to influence reactions. The presence of a charismatic participant who openly rejects the training can influence the level of acceptance by other crewmembers and poses a major challenge to those conducting the training.

1.9 OPEN ISSUES FOR RESEARCH

There are a number of open questions that require sustained research efforts to assist CRM training in reaching its full potential. One is to determine the long-term impact of the training on crew behavior and system safety. Many of the measures employed to evaluate crew performance and attitudes are still under development and require refinement through research. Part of the measurement effort has been directed toward the development of consistent classification strategies for human factors aspects of aviation incidents and accidents. These can generate extremely important research databases, and investigations supporting this effort are much needed. Such data should facilitate continual refinement of programs and will take into account changes in the aviation system itself (e.g., the development of more digital data links between aircraft and Air Traffic Control).

Another urgent need is to learn how to maximize the role of LOFT in reinforcing and extending human factors training. Recent data suggest that there are great differences in the perceived value of different scenarios and in the quality of their implementation (Wilhelm, 1991).

Several critical topics need much additional research before they can be translated into basic CRM training. Research into fundamental aspects of interpersonal communications, such as that described in the chapter by Kanki, has much to offer those developing CRM programs, but the knowledge base remains relatively undeveloped. Another critical area is decision-making. As Orasanu points out in her chapter, substantial progress has been made toward understanding decision-making in natural situations, but much remains to be done before full operational benefits can be gained. In particular, additional research into individual and group decision-making under highly stressful conditions (such as high time pressure, fatigue, life stresses, and life-threatening emergencies) should have high priority. Indeed, the whole topic of psychological stress and its behavioral impact has languished in the research community and needs renewed attention. Not until the research base is extended will we be able to mount effective programs of stress management and evaluate their operational impact.[6]

Given the lack of empirical data on the impact of system automation on crew coordination, it is also difficult to specify how best to train crewmembers to interact most effectively with "electronic crewmembers." Clearly this effort will be enhanced by further research.

We also need to know whether the boomerang reaction to CRM training is transitory or enduring. It is characteristic of human nature to question new and alien concepts on first encounter. Some exposed to CRM for the first time may show initial hostility to the concepts but may, after time and with peer pressure, later become enthusiastic advocates of CRM concepts. Only longitudinal research strategies that revisit and reassess individual reactions across time can determine the long-term reactions of the "boomerang" group. An associated question is whether different training strategies or interventions may be needed to gain acceptance from this subset of individuals.

Human factors concepts and training need to be further integrated with traditional technical training. To a considerable extent, CRM has developed outside the boundaries of the traditional training and evaluation of technical proficiency. As CRM has matured and become a part of organizational

---

6. A related question is what level of stress needs to be imposed on training to maximize the probability that human factors concepts will generalize to operational emergencies.

cultures, awareness of the fact that there are vital human factors components of all aspects of flight training has grown. As the theoretical model suggests, the effectiveness of both CRM and technical training should be enhanced when trainers stress the human factors components of every aspect of flight. Only basic research and operational evaluation can optimize these efforts. In the same vein, such research should provide guidance for incorporating human factors training into initial pilot training as well as training for experienced crewmembers.

1.10   CONCLUSIONS

Recognizing the critical role of human factors in determining the effectiveness of technically proficient flightcrews in both normal and emergency situations, the aviation community has embraced the concept of CRM training. The spread of CRM programs has proceeded faster than the accumulation of knowledge regarding their operational impact, reflecting the perceived importance of the issues. However, research findings to date suggest that this faith has not been misplaced. Crewmembers value the training, and available data suggest that it does have a positive impact on crew behavior and, by inference, on the safety of the aviation system.

The theoretical model of flightcrew group processes suggests that the most effective CRM courses will simultaneously address multiple input and group process factors and will be developed with awareness of the particular cultures in which they are embedded. Impact should also be enhanced when participants are not forced to make large generalizations from abstract concepts to their normal work setting, but rather receive training that communicates psychological concepts in terms of shared everyday experiences and clearly defined behaviors. Successful programs appear to provide not only basic psychological concepts, but their translation into operational terms.

It seems likely that if research and evaluation proceed in tandem with the implementation of continuing human factors training, courses of the future will evolve continually and make today's efforts look as antiquated as the Link Trainers of World War II. The open exchange of information that has developed surrounding CRM training has provided an environment conducive to rapid evolution.

1.11   CRM REDUX (2010)

Revisiting words written 15 years ago was a chastening experience for me. While the superordinate goals of CRM training—safe and efficient flight—are the same, its scope and practice have changed dramatically. Developments in CRM training and guidance for its delivery are provided in an updated Advisory Circular (120.51) of the US Federal Aviation Administration (Federal Aviation Administration, 2004). The aviation system has also undergone massive upheaval: a faltering economy has resulted in bankruptcies and mergers, airline fleets have been reduced in size, and operations have been shifted to more efficient, highly automated aircraft flown by two-person crews. Extremely long-haul flights, for example, Houston to Tokyo, have also been established. On very long flights a full relief flight crew (captain and first officer) is required, raising issues of command and leadership in the event of an in-flight emergency.

One of the factors we did not recognize in 1993 was the powerful influence of national culture on flight crew behaviors and the diverse approaches needed for delivery and acceptance of CRM programs in different cultures (Helmreich & Merritt, 1998; Merritt & Helmreich, 1996c). Another growing realization has been that CRM is not for the cockpit alone. (I must confess that as the first edition was going to press there was heated debate among the editors about whether the title of the volume should be Crew or Cockpit Resource Management. The three of us, Earl Wiener, Barb Kanki, and myself, ultimately agreed that it should have been Crew Resource Management.

1.11.1   Culture

I observed a wide range of cockpit behaviors from the jumpseat (despite assurances from managers and check airmen that pilot behavior was highly standardized in their airline). To explore this rather startling finding, I designed and administered a survey of pilot attitudes, the *Cockpit Management Attitudes Questionnaire* (CMAQ: Helmreich, 1984). The CMAQ was completed by pilots from a number of countries. It queried them about their beliefs regarding appropriate cockpit leadership and management of the flight deck. Analyzing the data, I was struck by highly significant differences in response as a function of aircraft fleet, pilot background, and, especially, national culture. It remained for my former student and colleague Ashleigh Merritt to develop a new survey, the Flight Management Attitudes Questionnaire based on the CMAQ (FMAQ: Helmreich & Merritt, 1998). The FMAQ draws on the multidimensional conceptualization of culture developed by the Dutch psychologist Geert Hofstede (Hofstede, 2001). The FMAQ has been administered to flight crews in more than 30 countries. Examining the cross-national data, the most diagnostic of Hofstede's dimensions has proved to be power distance (PD). In high PD cultures it is accepted and expected that leaders behave in an autocratic manner and it is unacceptable for copilots and other junior crew to question the captain's decisions and acts (Helmreich, Wilhelm, Klinect, & Merritt, 2001). Asian and Latin American cultures tend to be high in PD with Australia anchoring the egalitarian pole and the US falling in an intermediate position. One first officer from a high PD culture said to me, "I would rather die than challenge the captain's actions." Sadly, this statement has been borne out in more than one accident (Helmreich, 1994).

After administering the FMAQ to pilots from an airline in an extremely high PD culture, I presented the survey results through a translator to a meeting of senior managers and chief pilots. As always I stressed the importance of the first officer speaking up when the situation is deteriorating and the aircraft is standing into danger. I was informed later by a bilingual, expatriate pilot at the meeting that while I was talking a senior manager announced to all present that they should disregard everything I said.

In the most egalitarian cultures, however, status inequalities are prevalent. In one airline from a very low PD culture, organizational rules require that on overnight stops the captain must always have a room on a higher floor than the rest of the crew.

Even without managerial sabotage, gaining acceptance of CRM concepts that run counter to culture is a daunting enterprise—especially in cultures where juniors should not question or contradict their seniors. I was astonished and delighted to hear how a senior captain, head of the CRM program in one Asian carrier, got the CRM message across. His admonition to junior pilots was "Think of yourself as the eldest son in a traditional family. Your task is to protect your father from harm. Thus it is essential that you speak up and warn him if his actions are leading the flight into danger."

Clay Foushee and I described CRM as being in its third generation in our chapter in the first edition. In the following 15 years another three generations can be identified (Helmreich, Merritt, & Wilhelm, 1999). The fourth generation stressed the definition of procedures that include the behaviors exemplifying effective cockpit resource management. The fifth generation, known as error management, was short-lived and unpopular. As one captain remarked to me, "I feel insulted being labeled as an 'error manager'—it implies that my job is to screw up and then correct my mistakes."

Under the leadership of Captains Bruce Tesmer and Don Gunther of Continental Airlines, a sixth generation of CRM emerged, known as *threat and error management* or TEM. TEM is defined and described in the Line Operations Safety Audit (LOSA) Advisory Circular 120.70 of the US Federal Aviation Administration (Federal Aviation Administration, 2006). TEM gained immediate acceptance from pilots, managers and regulators (Helmreich, 1997). TEM accurately depicts the role of flight crews—piloting and navigating the aircraft from point A to point B while coping with threats to safety in the system and managing errors originating in the cockpit. External threats include air traffic controller errors, severe weather, terrain, and a host of others. The TEM concept can be applied in all components of an organization—maintenance, dispatch, ramp operations, etc. Threat and error management has also proved to be a valuable framework for the analysis of CRM-related behaviors in the investigation of air crashes (Helmreich, 1994).

One of the critical issues facing airlines, given the cost of developing and delivering training to highly paid staff who expect to be paid for their participation, was whether CRM programs change pilot behavior and increase system safety. After experiencing a series of embarrassing incidents (including landing at the wrong airport and shutting down the good engine after failure of the other), Delta Airlines developed and conducted an intensive 3-day CRM course for all its pilots. The course led to significant, positive changes in attitudes about CRM but Delta management wanted to know if the training also led pilots to change their behavior in normal operations. The University of Texas Human Factors Research Project was asked to determine how well crews practiced CRM during normal line flights. With my colleague John Wilhelm, retired Pan American World Airways captain Roy Butler, and a team of trained observers, we collected data on crew behavior during regularly scheduled flights. To code observations we adapted the systematic observational methodology that I had employed studying the behavior and performance of aquanauts living in a habitat on the ocean floor in Project Sealab (Radloff & Helmreich, 1968) and that John Wilhelm and I had used in observing the behavior of aquanauts living on the bottom of the Caribbean in Project Tektite (Helmreich, 1972, 1973). We observed 291 Delta domestic and international flights. The results were most reassuring: Delta crews were practicing CRM on normal flights as evidenced by their effective use of the behavioral indicators of good CRM.

The observational methodology we employed evolved into the *Line Operations Safety Audit* (LOSA) under the guidance of James Klinect, PhD, a graduate of our program and principal of the LOSA Collaborative. CRM is an essential component of LOSA. LOSA's strength is in the use of expert observers riding the cockpit jumpseat with total assurance of confidentiality to capture not only real-time behaviors including task performance and CRM practices of crews but also the context of behavior and the outcomes—errors committed or managed and threats managed or mismanaged. LOSA and CRM have been mandated by the International Civil Aviation Organization for all the world's airlines (ICAO, 1998, 2002).

LOSA in the United States was nearly sabotaged by the terrorist attacks on the World Trade Center in 2001 following which an FAA edict specified that only crewmembers could have access to the cockpit during flight. Continental Airlines responded to this situation by giving me an ID showing me in full captain's uniform, although they were wise enough not to let me fly one of their aircraft.

CRM rapidly infiltrated other components of the aviation system—soon we had Dispatch Resource Management and Maintenance Resource Management addressing team and intergroup issues. CRM training for air traffic controllers also emerged.

After Southwest Airlines had completed initial CRM training for its pilots, I presented the results (observations and attitude change) to management. Southwest CEO Herb Kelleher attended and rose to speak after presentations by me and the managers and instructors of the CRM program. Herb said that it was not fair for pilots to be the only beneficiaries of such training—thus was born Management Resource Management at Southwest Airlines.

1.11.2 Acquiring and Using Safety Data

Any successful program designed to improve CRM attitudes and behaviors needs to be based on valid data. As we have noted, the CMAQ and later the FMAQ provide reliable baseline information on the cognitive acceptance of CRM. LOSA, with guarantees of anonymity for those observed, provides a real-time snapshot of actual behavior. Another source of data also yields unique insights into organizational practices and CRM—confidential incident reporting systems. The Aviation Safety Reporting System (ASRS) managed by NASA has been in existence for more than 30 years and has amassed an enormous national database of events, but ASRS reports lack organizational specificity and don't give airlines useful information on conditions in their own organization. American Airlines, under the leadership of Dr. Thomas Chidester, then at American and now at the FAA, helped institute a local reporting system, the Aviation Safety Action Program (ASAP: AC 120-66, Federal Aviation Administration, 2002), which provides protection from disciplinary action for those reporting threats to safety and errors to their own organization. These reports are processed at the organizational level and provide useful insights into local issues. An ASAP committee including management and pilots' association members reviews each report and develops a strategy to deal with the issues raised. A high percentage of ASAP narratives deals with CRM issues. Data from these sources combined with data-driven CRM training contribute to the development of an organization's safety management system and safety culture (Helmreich & Merritt, 2000).

1.11.3 Expansion of CRM Into New Domains

Medicine

In 1994 I met an anesthesiologist, Hans-Gerhard Schaefer, from the University of Basel/Kantonsspital in Switzerland. Hans had heard of CRM and decided that it might be just the thing to improve teamwork in the operating theaters of Basel. Hans traveled to Austin and spent a year in our lab at the University of Texas. During his stay in Texas he observed all aspects of teamwork and team training in aviation. Following his return to Switzerland, I was invited to spend a year as a visiting professor in Basel where, assisted by Bryan Sexton, a student of mine from the University of Texas, we observed physician and staff behavior in operating theaters during surgeries. We also participated in development of a Critical Incident Reporting System

(CIRS) to allow professionals to share information on safety-related issues—especially CRM issues surrounding the interfaces between surgeons, anesthesiologists and nurses.

A few years later the United States Institute of Medicine (IOM) issued a highly influential report documenting the scope of preventable medical error. The IOM report concluded that more than 90,000 people a year may die needlessly in the United States from preventable medical error (Institute of Medicine, 1999). Comparing medicine and aviation, I discovered many similarities between the two professions. Stunned by the implications of the data, a number of medical organizations began to realize that they might benefit from adopting aviation's approaches to safety (Helmreich, 1997). The *British Medical Journal*, one of the most prestigious medical publications, placed a crashed aircraft on the cover of its issue containing articles by me and others about adapting aviation safety approaches to healthcare (Helmreich, 2000). Contrasting death rates from errors in the two professions, it is apparent that your doctor is more likely to kill you than your pilot. The data also suggest that significant improvement may come from embracing aviation's safety strategies including CRM (Helmreich & Sexton, 2004a, 2004b; Thomas & Helmreich, 2002).

Facing the reality of becoming an increasing consumer (and potential victim) of the healthcare system as I age, I became more involved in patient safety issues and in designing appropriate CRM training for healthcare professionals. In the United States, one of the barriers to the effective information exchange needed to optimize CRM in medicine is that, unlike aviation, there is no immunity from punishment or malpractice lawsuits for those who report and acknowledge their errors. Indeed, in Texas until recently a nurse who committed an error, even the administration of the wrong medication because of an error in the pharmacy, faced potential loss of license. The workaround for lack of protection for those who disclose errors has been to limit reports submitted to threat and error databases to near misses with no adverse impact on patients. I do not see this as a critical problem because near miss data usually have as much diagnostic value as information from events with less happy outcomes. In the absence of a more coherent healthcare system, it remains to be seen how useful these data will prove to be and if medical CRM training enhances safety significantly.

Firefighting

Of all the professions in the United States firefighting has the second highest incidence of line of duty death (behind mining) with 114 fatalities in 2008. CRM training has been provided for firefighters to help them cope as individuals and teams with complex, dangerous, and frequently changing situations where information is often incomplete. I had the privilege of working with the International Association of Fire Chiefs as they developed and implemented a national, internet-based close-call reporting system (www.firefighternearmiss.com). Their firefighter reporting system asks respondents to identify multiple causal and contributing factors and to provide a narrative describing the event. Contributing and causal factors in the reports provide insights into team coordination issues and decision-making. In larger fires there are frequently multiple units from different stations on the scene. This type of situation requires effective leadership as well as inter- and intrateam coordination.

1.11.4 The Future

I have been amazed and delighted at the proliferation of CRM in extremely diverse professions. The basic concepts of CRM clearly address critical safety issues. Cooke and Durso (2007), in their assessment of failures and successes, apply psychology to settings as different as minefields, the operating room, and the performance of elderly drivers. I feel confident that, in its threat and error management identity, CRM will continue to play a significant role in the training of professionals who work in areas where teams must interact successfully for safe and efficient task performance.

ACKNOWLEDGMENTS (1993)

Research by the first author has been supported by a Cooperative Agreement with NASA—Ames Research Center, NCC2-286, Robert L. Helmreich, Principal Investigator, and by a contract with the FAA, DTFA-90-C-00054. The cooperation of many airlines and flightcrews in the United States and around the world allowed the research for this chapter to take place. Special thanks are due John K. Lauber, who motivated us both to enter this research area and who has served as mentor for many years. Don Burr, former CEO of People Express Airlines, provided great assistance by opening the organization for research into determinants of crew performance. Captain Roy E. Butler, formerly of Pan American World Airways, assisted in the design and execution of research into the impact of CRM and LOFT and has subsequently become a colleague. Captain Reuben Black of Delta Airlines has also been instrumental in the implementation of integrated CRM/LOFT and the collection of data to assess the process. Captain Milt Painter and the CRM team at Southwest Airlines contributed their time and talent to the development of LOFT videos for calibrating evaluators. John A. Wilhelm has been a close collaborator for many years and remains master of the data, while William R. Taggart has provided invaluable counsel and assistance in the design and delivery of training for evaluation of crew performance. Finally, current and former graduate students at the University of Texas have been instrumental in all stages of the project. This group includes Cathy Clothier, Thomas R. Chidester, Steven E. Gregorich, Cheryl Irwin, Sharon Jones, Randolph Law, Terry McFadden, Ashleigh Merritt, Steven Predmore, and Paul Sherman.

REFERENCES

Abelson, R. (1972). Are attitudes necessary? In B. T. King, & E. McGinnies (Eds.), *Attitudes, conflict, and social change*. New York: Academic Press.

Bales, R. F. (1950). *Interaction process analysis: Theory, research, and application*. Reading, MA: Addison-Wesley.

Blake, R. R., & Mouton, J. S. (1964). *The managerial grid*. Houston: Gulf Press.

Bruce, K. D., & Jensen, D. (1987). Cockpit resource management training at people express: An overview and summary. In H. W. Orlady, & H. C. Foushee (Eds.), *Cockpit resource management training: Proceedings of the NASA/MAC workshop (NASA CP-2455)* (pp. 50−55). Moffett Field, CA: NASA-Ames Research Center.

Butler, R. E. (1991). *Lessons from cross-fleet/cross airline observations: Evaluating the impact of CRM/LOS training*. Proceedings of the Sixth International Symposium on Aviation Psychology (pp. 326−331). Columbus: Ohio State University.

Butler, R. E. (1987). Pan Am flight training—A new direction: Flight operations resource management. In H. W. Orlady, & H. C. Foushee (Eds.), *Cockpit resource management training: Proceedings of the NASA/MAC workshop (NASA CP-2455)* (pp. 61−67). Moffett Field, CA: NASA-Ames Research Center.

Carroll, J. E., & Taggart, W. R. (1987). Cockpit resource management: A tool for improved flight safety (United Airlines CRM training). In H. W. Orlady, & H. C. Foushee (Eds.), *Cockpit resource management training: Proceedings of the NASA/MAC workshop (NASA CP-2455)* (pp. 40−46). Moffett Field, CA: NASA-Ames Research Center.

Cavanagh, D. E., & Williams, K. R. (1987). The application of CRM to military operations. In H. W. Orlady, & H. C. Foushee (Eds.), *Cockpit resource management training: Proceedings of the NASA/MAC workshop (NASA. CP-2455)* (pp. 135−144). Moffett Field, CA: NASA-Ames Research Center.

Chidester, T. R. (1990). Trends and individual differences in response to short-haul flight operations. *Aviation, Space, and Environmental Medicine, 61*, 132−138.

Chidester, T. R., Helmreich, R. L., Gregorich, S., & Geis, C. (1991). Pilot personality and crew coordination: Implications for training and selection. *International Journal of Aviation Psychology, 1*, 23−42.

Chidester, T. R., Kanki, B. G., Foushee, H. C., Dickinson, C. L., & Bowles, S. V. (1990). *Personality factors inflight operations: Vol. 1. Leader characteristics and crew performance in full-mission air transport simulation (NASA Technical Memorandum 102259)*. Moffett Field, CA: NASA-Ames Research Center.

Christian, D., & Morgan, A. (1987). Crew coordination concepts: Continental Airlines CRM training. In H. W. Orlady, & H. C. Foushee (Eds.), *Cockpit resource management training: Proceedings of the NASA/MAC workshop (NASA CP-2455)* (pp. 68−74). Moffett Field, CA: NASA-Ames Research Center.

Clothier, C. (1991a). Behavioral interactions in various aircraft types: Results of systematic observation of line operations and simulations. Unpublished Master's thesis, The University of Texas at Austin.

Clothier, C. (1991b). *Behavioral interactions across various aircraft types: Results of systematic observations of line operations and simulations*. Proceedings of the Sixth International Symposium on Aviation Psychology (pp. 332−337). Columbus: Ohio State University.

Cooke, N. J., & Durso, F. (2007). *Stories of modern technology failures and cognitive engineering successes*. New York: CRC Press.

Cooper, G. E., White, M. D., & Lauber, J. K. (Eds.), (1980). *Resource management on the flight-deck: Proceedings of a NASA/Industry workshop (NASA CP-2120)*. Moffett Field, CA: NASA-Ames Research Center.

Davidson, J. (1987). Introduction to Trans Australia Airlines CRM training. In H. W. Orlady, & H. C. Foushee (Eds.), *Cockpit resource management training: Proceedings of the NASA/ MAC workshop (NASA CP-2455)* (pp. 88–89). Moffett Field, CA: NASA-Ames Research Center.

Davis, D. R. (1948). *Pilot error: Some laboratory experiments*. London: His Majesty's Stationery Office.

Edwards, E. (1972). *Man and machine: Systems for safety. Proceedings of British Airline Pilots Association Technical Symposium* (pp. 21–36). London: British Airline Pilots Association.

Edwards, E. (1975). Stress and the airline pilot. Paper presented at British Airline Pilots Association Medical Symposium: London.

Federal Aviation Administration. (1978). *Federal Aviation Administration. Line Oriented Flight Training (Advisory Circular AC-120-35A)*. Washington, DC: Author.

Federal Aviation Administration. (1989). *Federal Aviation Administration. Cockpit Resource Management (Advisory Circular120-51)*. Washington, DC: Author.

Federal Aviation Administration. (1993). Crew Resource Management (Advisory Circular 120-51A). Author, Washington, DC.

Federal Aviation Administration. (2002). Aviation Safety Action Program (Advisory Circular 120-66). Author: Washington, DC.

Federal Aviation Administration. (2004). Cockpit Resource Management (Advisory Circular 120-51E). Author: Washington, DC.

Federal Aviation Administration. (2006). Line Operations Safety Audits (Advisory Circular 120-70). Author: Washington, DC.

Fitts, P. M., & Jones, R. E. (1947). *Analysis of 270 "pilot error" experiences in reading and interpreting aircraft instruments (Report TSEAA-694–12A)*. Wright-Patterson Air Force Base, OH: Aeromedical Laboratory.

Foushee, H., & Manos, K. L. (1981). Information transfer within die cockpit: Problems in intracockpit communications. In C. E. Billings, & E. S. Cheaney (Eds.), *Information transfer problems in the aviation system (NASA TP-1875)*. Moffett Field, CA: NASA-Ames Research Center.

Foushee, H. C. (1982). The role of communications, socio-psychological, and personality factors in the maintenance of crew coordination. *Aviation, Space, and Environmental Medicine, 53*, 1062–1066.

Foushee, H. C. (1984). Dyads and triads at 35,000 feet: Factors affecting group process and aircrew performance. *American Psychologist, 39*, 886–893.

Foushee, H. C., & Helmreich, R. L. (1988). Group interaction and flight crew performance. In E. L. Wiener, & D. C. Nagel (Eds.), *Human factors in aviation* (pp. 189–227). San Diego, CA: Academic Press.

Foushee, H. C., Lauber, J. K., Baetge, M. M., & Acomb, D. B. (1986). *Crew performance as a function of exposure to high density, short-haul duty cycles (NASA Technical Memorandum 88322)*. Moffett Field, CA: NASA-Ames Research Center.

Gann, E. K. (1961). *Fate is the hunter*. New York: Simon and Shuster.

Ginnett, R. G. (1987). *First encounters of the close kind: The first meetings of airline flight crews. Unpublished doctoral dissertation*. New Haven, CT: Yale University.

Hackman, J. R., & Helmreich, R. L. (1987). Assessing the behavior and performance of teams in organizations: The case of air transport crews. In D. R. Peterson, & D. B. Fishman (Eds.), *Assessment for Decision* (pp. 283–316). New Brunswick, N.J: Rutgers University Press.

Hackman, J. R., & Morris, G. (1975). Group tasks, group interaction process, and group performance effectiveness: A review and proposed integration. In I. Berkowitz (Ed.), *Advances in Experimental Social Psychology* (Vol., 8, pp. 45−99). New York: Academic Press.

Hackman, J. R. (1987). Organizational influences. In H. W. Orlady, & H. C. Foushee (Eds.), *Cockpit resource management training: Proceedings of the NASA/MAC workshop (NASA CP-2455)* (pp. 23−39). Moffett Field, CA: NASA-Ames Research Center.

Halliday, J. T., Biegelski, C. S., & Inzana, A. (1987). CRM training in the 249th military airlift wing. In H. W. InOrlady, & H. C. Foushee (Eds.), *Cockpit resource management training: Proceedings of the NASA/MAC workshop (NASA CP-2455)* (pp. 148−157). Moffett Field, CA: NASA-Ames Research Center.

Hawkins, F. H. (1984). *Human factors of flight. Aldershot*. England: Gower Publishing Co.

Helmreich, R. L. (1973). Psychological research in TEKTITE 2. *Man Environment Systems, 3*, 125−127.

Helmreich, R. L. (1984). Cockpit management attitudes. *Human Factors, 26*, 583−589.

Helmreich, R. L. (1987). Exploring flight crew behaviour. *Social Behaviour, 21*, 63−72.

Helmreich, R. L. (1991a). *Strategies for the study of flightcrew behavior. Proceedings of the Sixth International Symposium on Aviation Psychology* (pp. 338−343). Columbus: Ohio State University.

Helmreich, R.L. (1991b). The long and short term impact of crew resource management training. In: Proceedings of the AIAA/NASA/FAA /HFS conference, Challenges in aviation human factors. The national plan: Vienna, VA. January 1991.

Helmreich, R. L. (1994). Anatomy of a system accident: The crash of Avianca Flight 052. *International Journal of Aviation Psychology, 4*(3), 265−284.

Helmreich, R. L. (1997). Managing human error in aviation. *Scientific American*, 62−67, May.

Helmreich, R. L. (2000). On error management: Lessons from aviation. *British Medical Journal, 320*, 781−785.

Helmreich, R. L., Foushee, H. C., Benson, R., & Russini, W. (1986). Cockpit management attitudes: Exploring the attitude-performance linkage. *Aviation, Space, and Environmental Medicine, 57*, 1198−1200.

Helmreich, R. L., & Merritt, A. C. (1998). *Culture at work in aviation and medicine: National, organizational, and professional influences*. Aldershot, UK: Ashgate.

Helmreich, R. L., & Merritt, A. C. (2000). Safety and error management: The role of Crew Resource Management. In B. J. Hayward, & A. R. Lowe (Eds.), *Aviation Human Factors* (pp. 107−119). Aldershot, UK: Ashgate.

Helmreich, R. L., Merritt, A. C., & Wilhelm, J. A. (1999). The evolution of Crew Resource Management in commercial aviation. *International Journal of Aviation Psychology, 9*(1), 19−32.

Helmreich, R. L. (1972). The TEKTITE 2 human behavior program. In J. W. Miller, J. Vanderwalker, & R. Waller (Eds.), *The TEKTITE 2 Project*. Washington: Government Printing Office.

Helmreich, R. L. (1992). Human factors aspects of the Air Ontario crash at Dryden, Ontario: Analysis and recommendations. (Commissioner) In V. P. Moshansky (Ed.), *Commission of Inquiry into the Air Ontario Accident at Dryden, Ontario: Final report. Technical appendices*. Ottawa, ON: Minister of Supply and Services, Canada.

Helmreich, R. L., & Sexton, J. B. (2004a). Group interaction under threat and high work load. In R. Dietrich, & T. M. Childress (Eds.), *Group interaction in high risk environments* (pp. 9−23). Aldershot, UK: Ashgate.

Helmreich, R. L., & Sexton, J. B. (2004b). Managing threat and error to increase safety in medicine. In R. Dietrich, & K. Jochum (Eds.), *Teaming up: Components of safety under high risk* (pp. 117–132). Aldershot, UK: Ashgate.

Helmreich, R. L., & Wilhelm, J. A. (1989). *When training boomerangs: Negative outcomes associated with cockpit resource management programs. Proceedings of the Sixth International Symposium on Aviation Psychology* (pp. 92–97). Columbus: Ohio State University.

Helmreich, R. L., & Wilhelm, J. A. (1991). Outcomes of crew resource management training. *International Journal of Aviation Psychology, 1*, 287–300.

Helmreich, R.L., Wilhelm, J.A., Gregorich, S.E. (1988). Revised versions of the cockpit management attitudes questionnaire (CMAQ) and CRM seminar evaluation form. NASA/The University of Texas Technical Report 88-3-revised 1991. Austin.

Helmreich, R. L., Wilhelm, J. A., & Jones, S. G. (1991). *An evaluation of determinants of CRM outcomes in Europe*. Austin: NASA/University of Texas Technical Report, 91–91.

Helmreich, R. L., Wilhelm, J. A., Kello, J. E., Taggart, W. R., & Butler, R. E. (1991). *Reinforcing and evaluating crew resource management: Evaluator/LOS instructor reference manual* (pp. 90–92). Austin: NASA/University of Texas Technical Manual.

Helmreich, R. L., Wilhelm, J. A., Klinect, J. R., & Merritt, A. C. (2001). Culture, error and Crew Resource Management. In E. Salas, C. A. Bowers, & E. Edens (Eds.), *Improving teamwork in organizations: Applications of resource management training* (pp. 305–331). Hillsdale, NJ: Erlbaum.

Hofstede, G. (2001). *Culture's consequences, comparing values, behaviors, institutions, and organizations across nations*. Thousand Oaks, CA: Sage Publications.

International Civil Aviation Organization (ICAO).(1998). Human Factors Training Manual. Canada: Montreal.

International Civil Aviation Organization (ICAO). (2002). Line Operations Safety Audit (LOSA). ICAO Document 9803. Canada: Montreal.

Institute of Medicine. (1999). To Err is Human: Building a Safer Healthcare System. Canada: Washington, DC. Montreal.

Kanki, B. G., & Foushee, H. C. (1989). Communication as group process mediator of aircrew performance. *Aviation, Space, and Environmental Medicine, 60*, 402–410.

Kanki, B. G., Lozito, S., & Foushee, H. C. (1989). Communication indices of crew coordination. *Aviation, Space, and Environmental Medicine, 60*, 56–60.

Klein, G., Orasanu, J., Calderwood, R., & Zsambok, C. (Eds.). (in press). Decision making action: Models and methods. Norwood, NJ: Ablex.

Lauber, J. K. (1984). Resource management in the cockpit. *Air Line Pilot, 53*, 20–23.

Lauber, J. K., & Foushee, H. C. (1981). *Guidelines for line-oriented flight training (Volume 1, NASA CP-2184)*. Moffett Field, CA: NASA-Ames Research Center.

McGrath, J. E. (1964). *Social psychology: A brief introduction*. New York: Holt, Rinehart, and Winston.

Merritt, A. C., & Helmreich, R. L. (1996c). Human factors on the flightdeck: The influences of national culture. *Journal of Cross-Cultural Psychology, 27*(1), 5–24.

Moshansky, V. P. (1989). *Commission ofInquiry into the Air Ontario Accident at Dryden, Ontario: Interim report*. Ottawa, ON: Minister of Supply and Services, Canada.

Moshansky, V. P. (1992). *Commission of Inquiry into the Air Ontario Accident at Dryden, Ontario: Final report (Volumes1–4)*. Ottawa, ON: Minister of Supply and Services, Canada.

Mosier, K. (1991). *Expert decision making strategies. Proceedings of the Sixth International Symposium on Aviation Psychology* (pp. 266–271). Columbus: Ohio State University.

Mudge, R. W. (1987). Cockpit management and SBO's. In H. W. Orlady, & H. C. Foushee (Eds.), *Cockpit resource management training: Proceedings of the NASA/MAC workshop (NASA CP-2455)*. Moffett Field, CA: NASA-Ames Research Center.

Murphy, M. (1980). Review of aircraft incidents. Cited in Cooper et al.

National Research Council. (1989). *Human factors research and nuclear safety*. Washington, DC: National Academy Press.

National Transportation Safety Board. (1972). Aircraft Accident Report: Eastern Airlines, Inc., Lockheed L-1011, N310EA, Miami, Florida, December 29, 1972. Author: Washington, DC. (Report No. NTSB-AAR-73-14).

National Transportation Safety Board. (1979). Aircraft Accident Report: United Airlines, Inc., McDonnell Douglas DC-8-61, N8082U, Portland, Oregon, December 28, 1978 (Report No. NTSB-AAR-79-2). Author: Washington, DC.

National Transportation Safety Board. (1982). Aircraft Accident Report: Air Florida, Inc., Boeing B-737-222, N62AF, Collision with 14th Street Bridge, Near Washington National Airport, Washington, D.C., January 13, 1982 (Report No. NTSB-AAR-82-8). Author: Washington, DC.

National Transportation Safety Board. (1989). Aircraft Accident Report: Delta Air Lines, Inc., Boeing 727-232, N473DA, Dallas-Fort Worth International Airport, Texas, August 31, 1988 (Report No. NTSB-AAR-89-04). Author: Washington, DC.

Orasanu, J. (1991). *Information transfer and shared mental models of decision making. Proceedings of the Sixth International Symposium on Aviation Psychology* (pp. 272–277). Columbus: Ohio State University.

Orlady, H. W., & Foushee, H. C. (1987). *Cockpit Resource Management training (NASA CP 2455)*. Moffett Field, CA: NASA-Ames Research Center.

Predmore, S. C. (1991). *Microcoding of communications in accident analyses: Crew coordination in United 811 and United 232. Proceedings of the Sixth International Symposium on Aviation Psychology* (pp. 350–355). Columbus: Ohio State University.

Radloff, R., & Helmreich, R. L. (1968). *Groups under stress: Psychological research in SEALAB II*. New York: Appleton-Century Crofts.

Ruffell Smith, H. P. (1979). *A simulator study of the interaction of pilot workload with errors, vigilance, and decisions (NASA Technical Memorandum 78482)*. Moffett Field, CA: NASA-Ames Research Center.

Schwartz, D. (1987). CRM training for FAR Parts 91 and 135 operators. In H. W. Orlady, & H. C. Foushee (Eds.), *Cockpit resource management training: Proceedings of the NASA/MAC work-shop (NASA CP-2455)*. Moffett Field, CA: NASA-Ames Research Center.

Thomas, E. J., & Helmreich, R. L. (2002). Will airline safety models work in medicine? In M. M. Rosenthal, & K. M. Sutcliffe (Eds.), *Medical error: What do we know? what do we do?* (pp. 217–234). San Francisco: Jossey-Bass.

Thordsen, M.L. & Klein, G.A. (1989). Cognitive processes of the team mind. 1989 IEEE International Conference on Systems, Man, and Cybernetics Proceedings 1, 46–49.

Wilhelm, J. A. (1991). *Crewmember and instructor evaluations of Line Oriented Flight Training. Proceedings of the Sixth International Symposium on Aviation Psychology* (pp. 362–367). Columbus: Ohio State University.

Yamamori. (1987). Optimum culture in the cockpit. In H. W. Orlady, & H. C. Foushee (Eds.), *Cockpit resource management training: Proceedings of the NASA/MAC workshop (NASA CP-2455)* (pp. 75–87). Moffett Field, CA: NASA-Ames Research Center.

Yocum, M., & Monan, W. (1987). CRM training in corporate/regional airline operations: Working group V Report. In H. W. Orlady, & H. C. Foushee (Eds.), *Cockpit resource management training: Proceedings of the NASA/MAC workshop (NASA CP-2455)* (pp. 238−240). Moffett Field, CA: NASA-Ames Research Center.

FURTHER READING

Merritt, A. C., & Helmreich, R. L. (1996a). Creating and sustaining a safety culture: Some practical strategies. In B. Hayward, & A. Lowe (Eds.), *Applied aviation psychology: Achievement, change and challenge* (pp. 20−26). Sydney: Avebury Aviation.

Merritt, A. C., & Helmreich, R. L. (1996b). CRM in 1995: Where to from here? In B. Hayward, & A. Lowe (Eds.), *Applied aviation psychology: Achievement, change and challenge* (pp. 111−126). Sydney: Avebury Aviation, where to from here.

Sexton, J. B., Grommes, P., Zala-Mezo, E., Grote, G., Helmreich, R. L., & Hausler, R. (2004). Leadership co-ordination. In R. Dietrich, & T. M. Childress (Eds.), *Group interaction in high risk environments* (pp. 166−184). Aldershot, UK: Ashgate.

Chapter 2

Teamwork and Organizational Factors

Frank J. Tullo

Embry-Riddle Aeronautical University, Daytona Beach, FL, United States

INTRODUCTION

No single word describes what we now call "Crew Resource Management (CRM)" better than the first word in the title of this chapter: TEAMWORK. This hybrid word (TEAM + WORK) conveys a simple concept, but as you will see it carries. The observations in this chapter are clinical, the result of long experience in the aviation industry, both as a pilot and as a flight operations manager. My opinions have been formed through involvement in numerous industry councils, committees, and task forces. They are the product of the many opportunities for teamwork I have enjoyed over the last half century in our industry.

The last five decades has seen an enormous change in the commercial airline business—especially within the cockpit of our aircraft. Changes in the systems that individuals utilize have revolutionized the industry, while an equal change has occurred in the knowledge of the human factors that affect those involved in operating in this environment. Over this period, the concept of teamwork has spiraled outward from the cockpit. While our industry initially focused on ensuring the cockpit crew organized itself by critical actions of the Captain, First Officer, and (then) Flight Engineer (and now International Officers, where required for long-duration flights), we quickly realized the importance of and connections with other frontline employee workgroups. Flight attendants have access to information unavailable in the cockpit. Mechanics, dispatchers, fuelers, loaders, gate agents, and ground crew must work effectively with the cockpit during critical phases of flight. And many of the precursors of error and potential for corrective action reside in those groups and in our interfacing procedures. This outwardly spiraling conception of teamwork is reflected in the organization of the chapter.

I begin by discussing the evolution of teamwork on the flight deck, as exemplified by the advent of CRM, spelling out several meanings the term

Crew Resource Management. DOI: https://doi.org/10.1016/B978-0-12-812995-1.00002-6

has acquired during the past decades. I offer a new definition of CRM to remove ambiguities and clearly identify its meaning and focus. This discussion leads to recognition of a good leader's attributes and to the realization and acceptance of the ubiquity of errors in the aviation industry. There will also be a discussion of the importance of standard operating procedures (SOPs) and the role they play in the safety culture of organizations.

These five decades have seen a notable improvement in the safety record of the world aviation industry, most notable in the United States. This record is often attributed to improvements in the "safety culture" of our industry. But these changes came through organizational learning and cumulative experience of different subcultures at the corporate and administrative level in our industry. I conclude by addressing leadership issues, since a true safety culture can only be achieved if it starts at the top and it will not permeate the entire organization unless it has the support and backing, in writing, of the organization's leaders.

2.1 UPDATING THE DEFINITION OF CRM

Prior to the embrace of CRM by most major United States airlines, pilot training and evaluation emphasized the skill level of the individual pilot, and the notion that pilots could be trained to operate in an error-free manner. This zero-defects approach was inherited from the military model that was in use during the 1960s. As recently as the 1980s commercial pilots were rated almost solely on their ability to handle the aircraft, know the rules and performance data, and deal with contingencies. The primary objective of training and evaluation was to produce a pilot who would—at least during a check ride—turn in an error-free performance. Little emphasis was placed on working as a team to anticipate and avoid errors. Crewmembers passed or failed based on his or her individual performance. Strikingly, individual performance was emphasized to the extent that the nonflying crewmembers were often told *not* to help the flying pilot during his portion of the evaluation. The check pilot's (and his flight operations superiors') main task was to "wash out" those individuals who did not have the "right stuff" (to use the term made famous by author Tom Wolfe, 1979). The bottom line of training was to eliminate, as much as possible, all human error from the cockpit.

Now, over 40 years later, the industry evaluates a cockpit team's performance or teamwork using "CRM." Summed up, this new standard can best be explained in a statement made by former FAA administrator Donald Engen who said, "pilots do not cause accidents—*crews* do." The unspoken concept behind his statement is that line managers need to look beyond an individual's performance and judge that person's skills as a team member.

Granted, we cannot completely disregard individual performance. However, this matter is best addressed when an individual is first hired and/or during training for a new position or new equipment. Too much emphasis is still placed on this aspect of aviation training. In the new CRM model, individual performance should not be the focus during the plethora of training/checking events a pilot must endure: line checks, proficiency check/recurrent training, line operational evaluation (LOE), or line oriented flight training (LOFT), etc. Rather the focus should be on how well the individual works in a team. Once an individual has been successfully qualified in a crew position the emphasis should then become how well he or she can predict or prevent errors through threat analysis, detect the inevitable errors made by the crew, and correct those errors before negative consequences occur. *The true definition of "teamwork" or CRM is its focus on the proper response to threats to safety and the proper management of crew error.*

The focus on "threat and error management" (TEM) does not mean a lowering of performance standards. While we accept the inevitability of errors we must nevertheless maintain performance standards. Error management demands that we distinguish between an individual's recklessness or disregard for SOPs and mistakes that are simply the product of human limitations. CRM requires that we reach beyond evaluation of individuals to that of the entire team responsible for safety in flight.

2.2 THE TEAM AT THE SHARP END

For our present purposes, we need to make clear what constitutes a "team" in CRM. Broadly speaking, everyone who participates in moving a flight from A to B is a member of the team—including management, ground services, and even Air Traffic Control (ATC). But for this discussion, the key members of a team are on board the aircraft, those who manipulate the controls and manage the aircraft systems, and handle the human and other cargo from gate to gate. In other words, the team consists of the cockpit crew and flight attendants.

There is in addition another member of the team onboard the flight: the fitted equipment designed to reduce workload and increase safety in coordination with the flight crew. This "member," usually described using the simplistic and misleading term "automation," and thought of as "dutiful and dumb," has become increasingly important in CRM due to the reduction in crew size and the increasing complexity of automated systems onboard. In present day aircraft, this silent member of the team that accomplishes so much of the work in the cockpit will dutifully do any task it has been asked to do, whether it makes sense or not (it can also simply disconnect and hand the problem to you with an array of failure messages, if it has insufficient system input to perform its functions, as in Air France 447). Failure to understand and integrate this member into the flight team has, since the introduction of automation, provided many painful lessons of the need to include this cockpit resource into flight management.

From the beginning, the focus of CRM has been the attitude, behavior, and performance of individual pilots. The objective was to eliminate the "wrong stuff" from pilots and replace it with skills that ensured good team performance. Good CRM was defined as a captain that creates an atmosphere where crewmembers feel comfortable to speak up and state opinions, ask questions, and challenge if necessary. Indeed, the captain should insist on this behavior and praise it when it is present—not only to talk the talk but also to walk the walk. As early in the flight as possible, the captain should look for a situation in which the other crewmember(s) input information, and use that instance to praise the crewmember, thanking him or her for the teamwork. This has a positive teambuilding effect and is most important in a crew that has never flown with each other before; and it is necessary even with a familiar crew. In this model, the captain is charged with reinforcing good performance and helping other crewmembers improve their responses to threats and their recognition of errors.

The other crewmembers are charged with speaking up regardless of the atmosphere created by the captain. This may, at times, require an aggressive posture by the crewmembers, which flies in the face of the common misconception that good CRM is "getting along in the cockpit." Good CRM is recognizing and identifying threats, preventing errors if possible, catching those that will inevitably take place, and to the extent possible, through resistance and resolution, mitigating the consequences of those that have occurred.

The threat and error model shown in Fig. 2.1 illustrates the flow of this process. The only terms that require some explanation are "RESIST," and "RESOLVE." The term RESIST represents those aviation safety systems in the cockpit, in the ATC controller's suite and on the ground, which create resistance to errors. RESIST includes systems such as Enhanced Ground Proximity Warning Systems (EGWPSs), wind shear warning systems on the aircraft and the ground, and a Traffic Collision Avoidance System (TCAS).

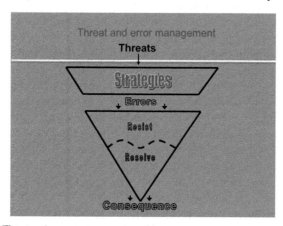

FIGURE 2.1   Threat and error management model.

There is also a Minimum Safe Altitude Warning System (MSAWS) in the control towers warning of dangerously low altitudes, just to mention a few. As a result of the success of these systems Controlled Flight into Terrain (CFIT) is no longer the number one cause of fatalities in our industry. Increasingly important in modern flight management are the automated systems designed to "resist" threats (altitude deviation, conflicting traffic, menacing weather) before they become unmanageable.

"RESOLVE" on the other hand is what the human brings to aviation safety—proficiency, experience, effective monitoring, and communicating, etc. Together resistance and resolution filter out errors that may inevitably occur and prevent negative consequences.

While CFIT is no longer the major threat (because advanced Terrain Awareness and Warning Systems incorporated in the late 1990s comparison of present position to terrain databases, generating alerts or displaying threatening terrain long before potential conflict), "Loss of Control" is now the leading cause of accidents in our industry. This points to the inability of the crewmember to successfully recognize and recover (RESOLVE) from a situation into which automation or human mismanagement has placed the aircraft. The questions must be asked: has the use of automation played a role in the degradation of basic flying skills? Has the reliance on automation eroded the proficiency required to take over when automation fails? Are the regulatory agencies and the training facilities of the industry recognizing the need for pilots to demonstrate adequate manual flying proficiency in addition to the proper use of automation?

In the model illustrated in the figure, the top level "STRATEGY" may be thought of as "managing our future" by recognizing threats and creating error-blocking strategies in advance. If, STRATEGY notwithstanding, a threat goes unrecognized or an error occurs, the subsequent levels (RESIST and RESOLVE) may be thought of as "managing our past," whether by catching errors or by mitigating negative consequences. These levels of error management may appear inferior, but in fact are at least as effective in generating good outcomes as the STRATEGY level.

The industry has come to understand and accept the ubiquity of error in our complex and dynamic aviation system. Hopefully, the industry is now moving toward a robust error management system in which a well-trained and focused crew can be very effective in accomplishing safe, economical, and efficient flight.

In the early decades of aviation, the model of cockpit "pecking order" had it that the captain, like the 19th century ship captain, acted like a monarch in charge of his small kingdom. The copilot was the pilot not flying (PNF), sometimes given smaller tasks when the captain doled them out—handling the landing gear, flaps, and communication, etc. In the 21st century the industry, for the most part, has now come to prefer the term "pilot monitoring" (PM) in place of PNF to indicate the crewmember not primarily manipulating the controls. The implication of this change in terminology is that the PM is, in fact, an active participant in crew operations and is eminently as responsible for the safe conduct of the flight as is the "pilot flying" (PF).

It is time to change the emphasis of the team and refocus on their resistance to error. Moving away from the individual accomplishment culture toward a true team accomplishment culture is indeed a very hard task, for it is truly not only embedded in our national, industry, and organizational culture but is also part of our basic human makeup. This individualistic orientation begins at the very onset of a pilot's career and is constantly reinforced in proficiency checks, during advancements to new positions in the currently flown aircraft, or in moving into new aircraft. A pilot would much prefer to be known as a "good stick" rather than a good team member. This makes the formation of a good error detecting team all the more difficult to create.

2.3   TRAITS OF A GOOD COCKPIT TEAM

Is there is a difference in the attributes or traits of a good leader or a good follower? Experience has taught us that they are almost always the same. There are no absolutes in this world, but history has strongly indicated that a good follower will make a good leader and vice versa. There are many instances in our industry where the role of leader and follower flowed back and forth between crewmembers as the flight progressed. There is no argument that the captain is the team leader and will make the final decision, but there will be times when he or she will be, and should be, in the role of a follower. That being said, let's examine some of the traits of good team members, leaders, and followers.

There can be little argument that the hallmark of an effective team is *proficiency*. The forgone conclusion is that each member of the team will be proficient at the task they are assigned to perform. This is the responsibility of the director of flight operations: the person responsible for ascertaining the ongoing proficiency and competency of the individual assigned a position in the team. This is something that airlines do very well. The training departments of the large airlines are extremely effective in turning out exquisitely prepared crewmembers and the certified training organizations, which do so much of the training for smaller outfits, do just as well. This is further assured by the Federal Aviation Administration (FAA) which sets the minimum standards required for positions within the cockpit.

Proficiency must include the commitment to comply with SOPs. This may not seem a serious problem, but Boeing statistics kept since 1959 have shown that deviation from SOPs is a contributing cause in over one-third of all hull loss and fatality accidents worldwide. This deviation may take the form of omission, such as failing to do something that should have been done (perform a checklist), or commission, such as accomplishing an action incorrectly or doing something that should not be done (e.g., checklist from memory, descent below minimums). The slippery slope here is that every time a deviation from SOPs is successful, it reinforces the act of getting away with it. This can lead to the "normalization of deviance" (Vaughn, 1997) where the crewmember doesn't even recognize it as a deviation because it has been done so often and sometimes by so many. Deviation from SOPs is an ever-present problem in our industry and must not be tolerated by aviation organizations and agencies.

Just as important as proficiency is effective *communications*. This of course includes the ability to communicate between team members and between the team and others outside their environment. Automation in our industry has increased the need for effective communication between members of a team. As we will discuss later, automation does so much of the handling of the aircraft that it becomes extremely important that the crewmembers *verbalize, verify*, and *monitor* any instructions or changes to instructions given to automation.

Miscommunication between the pilot and the controller is the leading item cited in the NASA-managed Aviation Safety Reporting System (ASRS). Failure to communicate clearly can be especially dangerous and has been cited as a causal factor in a number of major accidents. Some of the worst examples of teamwork have been characterized by poor communications between the team members and also between the crew and those outside the cockpit. Conversely, one of the best examples of superior communication was the United DC-10 accident at Sioux City, Iowa. The crew, including a company pilot who was riding in the back, did a remarkable job of communicating within and outside the cockpit and was able to bring the flight to the best possible outcome considering the horrible situation. Robert Helmreich of the University of Texas studied the cockpit voice recorder and judged that at some points in the emergency the crewmembers were processing as much as one item of information per second, a remarkable accomplishment considering the amount of stress under which the crewmembers were working.

Effective communication can take many forms, both verbal and nonverbal. One of the most effective verbal communications takes the shape of briefings and debriefings of the entire crew. As the complexity of the industry has grown, preflight briefings have become increasingly more important, both between the company (dispatcher) and the crewmembers and also within the team itself in the form of a preflight briefing when the entire team comes together prior to the flight. Given the increasing size of some of the crews in modern aircraft this can be a daunting task—but is all the more important. These briefings are necessary to clarify the task responsibilities of the crew and the environment in which the flight will be conducted. This will assure the entire crew is of the same mindset. Debriefings are also a very important part of communications. It is the best opportunity to highlight and praise good teamwork and also point out areas needing improvement. The most important thing when debriefing a negative event is to emphasize "what went wrong," not "who was wrong"—and how to prevent it from happening again.

Effective *monitoring* is also one of the more desirable traits of an effective team. As mentioned earlier, the industry has embraced the concept of the PM versus the PNF. This is a subtle change, but the implications are large. The PM has many tasks to accomplish in support of the PF but the primary job of the PM is to observe the progress of the flight and the PF's performance in order to detect any threat or error that can lead to negative consequences. If a threat or an error is detected, that crewmember's job then becomes making an assertive challenge to identify the threat so the error does not occur, or identify the error so there are no negative consequences.

A study identified the failure to monitor and challenge by low-time-in-type copilots as being especially prevalent (Flight Safety Foundation, 1994). Whether this was the result of an inexperienced pilot who didn't monitor the error, or the insecure pilot who saw the error but failed to challenge, will never be known. The study was backed up recently with similar results (Dismukes, Berman, & Loukopoulos, 2007). Both of these studies highlight the need for training and evaluating monitoring skills.

Effective monitoring is a skill that has to be trained, practiced, and evaluated. This is something that has not been emphasized in training programs to date, yet is so important to the successful accomplishment of TEM. One of the most effective ways of providing pilots with the motivation to be good monitors is to always evaluate them as a crew and hold them responsible for that skill in a training setting. LOFT and LOE sessions are the ideal vehicles for accomplishing this. However, monitoring should be evaluated anytime a crew is being observed. The need for good monitoring skills can easily be emphasized during any training session. When an error is made by the PF, the instructor should ask the PM why he or she allowed the error to occur. While this is a major shift in the way crewmembers are trained, it accomplishes two things. It identifies the primary role of the PM, while de-emphasizing the focus on the individual performance and refocusing it on the team and the role of each team member.

Included in the skill of monitoring is vigilance and, more important, knowing when to be vigilant. A crew cannot and need not be vigilant all of the time. Knowing when to be vigilant and when to relax a little is important especially in today's environment with aircraft having such long flight endurance including ultralong flights.

Another important trait of a good team is *modeling*. It is an excellent way for a leader or follower to demonstrate a personal example of compliance with all SOPs. Modeling is a method of giving positive feedback or sharing knowledge without appearing to critique or give a "flying lesson." It was Albert Einstein who said "Setting an example is not the main means of influencing others; it is the only means." Conversely, there are few things worse in this industry than presenting a bad example. A role model or leader does immeasurable damage when he or she does not adhere to SOPs. The "do as I say not as I do" performance by a person in a position of power can have a negative effect far in excess of the one incident that is observed. It can also add to the previously mentioned dangerous problem in air transportation, the "normalization of deviance" (Vaughn, 1997). The damage that can be done by even one individual with this attitude is considerable. The modeling of dignity and the respect of conduct consistent with standards is a very powerful tool that can and should be used by a leader and a follower.

Envisioning is just another way of saying what pilots have heard from their first flight: "stay ahead of the aircraft." This skill creates and shares a plan for the entire crew and is an absolute necessity for good situation awareness (SA). It provides meaning and direction for the task at hand, and along with a good briefing creates operational clarity and sets workload management parameters. One of the more meaningful sayings heard in aviation circles is "never take your aircraft any place your mind hasn't been 5 minutes earlier." This is the essence of envisioning.

Leaders and followers must also be *adaptable*. The ability to adjust to changes is an absolute necessity in air transport operations. "Decision bias and plan continuation" has been cited as causal factors in many aircraft accidents over the years. The resistance to change is something inherent in all humans. The adjustment to changes that occur in flight and the willingness to build and share a new plan are hallmarks of good airmanship. Flying is so dynamic that what is an issue requiring attention at the present time can easily change very quickly. Teamwork requires a balance between structure, which all humans require, and the ability to recognize a changing environment requiring the flexibility to adjust as necessary.

When a crewmember pays attention to another's ideas, concerns, or questions, that person is demonstrating *receptiveness*. This skill, along with adaptability and the willingness to change are key elements of a safe cockpit. Listening to suggestions and adopting the suggestion when appropriate are very powerful teambuilding tools. Even when one disagrees with the idea it is an important part of crewmember teambuilding. The recognition of the input and the appreciation that should be voiced by the receiver of the input will strengthen the cohesiveness of the crew. There will be times when a suggestion or concern is not adapted during flight but it is important that it be acknowledged even if the end result is the "agreement is to disagree." The cockpit is not a democracy. The captain is the final authority and will make the final decision.

Using logic and tact, a leader/follower can *influence* others and obtain a commitment to ideas or actions. This is an especially important attribute when faced with incomplete or conflicting information from varied sources or when there is a need to assess novel situations and devise appropriate solutions. Situations like this require the use of all available resources and may include a junior crewmember being assertive enough to convince a senior crewmember to take a desired action.

And finally, when a crewmember begins an appropriate action, within bounds and without direction, that person is exhibiting *initiative*. This leader/ follower attribute is especially important when an action is begun to correct an operational deficiency. This may take the form of a pilot tactfully correcting another pilot when that person is doing something nonstandard, or it may be an action taken to find a more effective way to accomplish something— again, within bounds.

2.4   ERRORS AND THE SUPPORT TEAMS AND PROCESSES THAT RESOLVE THEM

Errors are an inevitable part of flying. The aviation industry has been laboring long and hard to eliminate as many errors as possible and have done a reasonably good job. Truth is, however, that error is ubiquitous and probabilistic and can never be eliminated completely. New systems (resistance in the TEM model) installed in our aircraft and in ATC suites have gone a long way toward protecting the pilots and controllers from error-producing situations. This is borne out by the remarkable safety record that our industry has been enjoyed over the past decades. However, the fact remains that the elimination of all errors will never be achievable in an industry as dynamic as air transportation.

This industry operates within a society or culture of blame. This is most evident when a negative event occurs. The hunt for the individual villain begins immediately. Conversely, the positive event results in a similar hunt for the hero. Too often the attitude has been that the crew caused the accident because they made errors central to the events leading up to the accident. It appears that we are convinced that human error is a cause of trouble in an otherwise safe system, when in fact the conventional theory is that human error is not a cause but a symptom. It is a by-product of hard working crewmembers trying to pursue success in a resource-constrained, uncertain, imperfect system. That is the underlying assumption in error management. Anytime a human is used to operate equipment, no matter how well selected, how well trained, or how optimally used, the human is subject to limitations. The flip side of human performance is human error.

Jerome Lederer, a leading pioneer in aviation safety, said the following in a lecture given to the Royal Aeronautical Society in 1952:

> ...*The average man has only one head, two eyes, two hands, two feet, his response to demands cannot be guaranteed within plus or minus five per cent; his temperature cannot be allowed to vary more than a few degrees; his pump must operate at constant speed and pressure; his pressure containers, both*

hydraulic and pneumatic, have limited capacity; his controls are subject to fatigue, illness, carelessness, anger, inattention, glee, complacency and impatience. This mechanism was originally designed to operate in the Stone Age; it has not since been improved. The problem consists of permitting this ancient mechanism designed to function within narrow tolerances to control its destiny in a strange environment of very wide ranges in operating conditions.

Recognizing these limitations, a change has to occur in the training and evaluation of our crewmembers. The performance of a team should not be based on error-free operation but instead the emphasis should be on threat recognition, detecting errors, and managing, to the extent possible, the consequences of errors. Traditionally, flight instructors have trained by rewarding error-free performance. Errors have always counted against a pilot. The consequences are usually lower grades, further training, debriefing, etc. This is often true even if an error is caught before it becomes a serious problem. In the conventional approach to training and evaluation the fact that an error was committed becomes the center of attention. If error is inevitable because of the threats present in all work environments, and its correction is essential to survival, where should an instructor devote his attention? I would suggest to the threats, their mitigation, and correction of any resulting errors.

More is known about a crew that makes an error and manages it than is known about the crew that doesn't make the error.

At the heart of this is a desire to eliminate, as much as possible, errors during instruction and evaluation. If there were a finite number of errors that could occur in aviation it might be possible to train crewmembers to eliminate them. However, history has shown us that the number is infinite. Murphy's Law is alive and well in our industry and if something can possibly happen, it will happen. The challenge is to create an error management system in which the crewmembers recognize threats that can cause errors, guard against the errors that will inevitably occur, and correct errors before there are any negative consequences. More is known about a crew that makes an error and manages it than is known about the crew that doesn't make the error.

The way that instructors conduct training and evaluating is extremely important. Instructors have to move away from the "blame and train" method of training and concentrate on the crew's ability to work together recognizing threats, detecting and managing errors. The instructor still must detect errors made by the crew, and eventually point them out. However, when crewmembers detect and resolve an error quickly, for all practical purposes, *the error did not occur.* This is exactly the behavior we desire in our industry and it must be recognized and rewarded. In good error management training, it is possible for a crew to make an error, detect and resolve it and actually be graded higher on that particular event or the entire training period.

As stated earlier, effective monitoring by the crewmembers is an all-important element of error management. In training, the PM should be held responsible for monitoring the performance of the PF and maintaining SA of the progress of the flight. This implies that there will be a grading system established whereby monitoring can be graded.

2.5 STRUCTURING TEAMWORK THROUGH STANDARD OPERATING PROCEDURES

Airline management must provide great clarity about the day-to-day task responsibilities of crewmembers; these tasks and how they are to be performed must be spelled out explicitly in great detail in flight operations policy manuals. The importance of good, well-thought-out SOPs cannot be overemphasized. Experience has shown that the degree to which these procedures are adhered to is usually a good measure of the quality of the airline and a very good measure of the quality of the airline's instructors, check airmen, and management pilots. It is also an indication of the quality of the captains of the airline. If junior officers are found to be deviating from SOPs it is a strong indication that the captains with whom they have been flying have allowed these deviations and not taken action to stop this type of behavior—or worse, they are deviating themselves. An essential axiom of error management is that a *behavior uncorrected is a behavior condoned*.

If crewmembers are not given clear direction on how tasks are to be performed they tend to "do their own thing," and this can have dire consequences. Even when the task is clearly defined there are crewmembers that will deviate from normal procedures. Psychologists learned long ago that the more ambiguity there is in a situation, the more personality differences show themselves (Dismukes et al., 2007).

SOPs ensure that crewmembers that have never flown with each other before will come together with the knowledge that the flight will be flown by the book, and know exactly what to expect from each other. The procedures set forth in flight operations should be time-tested methods of assuring the flight will be safely and efficiently flown. This can only be accomplished if the procedures make sense to the pilots and they feel they have a stake in the formation of the procedures. To get buy-in from the crews, it is extremely important that these procedures be reviewed on a regular basis and that there is line pilot input. The feedback stream should be from the line pilot upward through management and every recommendation should be considered carefully. At the same time, it is incumbent on the management of the organization to check and evaluate all crewmembers on their adherence to SOPs. Deviation from SOPs cannot be tolerated and should be dealt with on the spot. In some cases, disciplinary steps may be necessary.

Of course, there will be times when the crew has to use whatever means they deem necessary to accomplish the flight safely. This is addressed in the

Emergency Powers of the Captain granted by the FAA in federal regulations. There will also be times when the crew has to use their leadership skills to deal with an ambiguous or unique situation. Management can assist the crewmembers by providing clear and challenging direction about the desired end-states that ensure efficient, on-time performance and customer satisfaction. This is when the ability of the human far surpasses that of a computer. The creative and innovative abilities of the human to deal with this type of dilemma and make split second decisions in situations never faced before is when a crew "earns its pay." One of the most remarkable examples of this is the "miracle on the Hudson" when the crew of a US Airways Airbus 320 made a successful, rarely ever before accomplished, water ditching of a modern jet aircraft. The successful accomplishment of this extremely unusual emergency water landing with no loss of life is an astonishing feat and speaks to the professionalism of our pilots and flight attendants.

2.6   THE AIRLINE AND ITS CULTURES

There is a strong belief that each organization has its own individual culture; however, experience has shown that there can be many subcultures within an organization. It is expected that an organization would take on the personality of its leader, good or bad. In general, the industry has found this to be true but there are many mid-level managers that can create subcultures within the major organization, again good or bad. How well an organization recognizes and deals with these subcultures is a measure of the health of the organization and its safety culture. An extensive dialog will clearly define a safety culture later in this chapter. But first it is important to discuss the development and refinement of SOPs, which is the first step in creating a safety culture.

2.7   DEVELOPING SOPS

The flight management department of any aviation organization has the responsibility to create a crystal-clear set of guidelines governing flight operations. This is separate from the organization's "vision" and "mission" statements, although these documents will still play a role in the operation of the flight department. This can be accomplished in four steps as shown in Fig. 2.2, which follows a well-developed human factors paradigm known as the "Four Ps" (Degani & Wiener, 1994).

The first step is for the most senior management person in the flight operations department to create a *philosophy*; this is usually the vice president of flight operations in a major airline. This should be a broad statement outlining, in general terms, how the department should go about conducting safe, efficient operations which ensure regulatory compliance and customer satisfaction. This can also include wide-ranging guidance on the use of

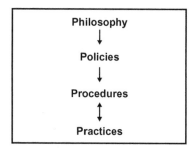

FIGURE 2.2 Four Ps model.

automation. In fact, it was the introduction of highly automated aircraft that created the need for a philosophy of automation, which defined the different levels of automation available and their use under varying circumstances. This is certainly a necessary piece of the overall philosophy.

The second step is for the next level of management, usually directors, to draw upon the broad philosophical statement to create *policies* that further define the desired goal and focus on the methods used to accomplish the desired outcome. This level of management is closer to the everyday operation of the organization and is therefore the appropriate level to create policy. Upper management should delegate this task to the directors and not micromanage the accomplishment of the policies. Micromanagement is the quickest and surest way to create problems in a flight department.

The third step is for the managers, supervisors, and flight instructors to create *procedures* that complement the policies set forth by the directors. It is of utmost importance that the crewmembers on the line play a role in creating these procedures. In addition, the procedures must be constantly reviewed and revised if necessary. The model should end at this point, but real-world experience shows there is often a disconnect between procedures and the next and fourth step—*practices*. This disconnect is also known as procedural noncompliance and can be prevalent in any organization that doesn't work hard to minimize it. Practices are the measure to which the procedures have been accepted and are followed by the average crewmember. Another definition of practices is "how it's really done around here" or "norms." Norms are described as "a practice bought into or tolerated by the majority" and are very hard to reverse. They may be so prevalent that crewmembers are unaware that they are deviating, and they may be around for years, undetected, until something happens that highlights their existence. James Reason labels this a "latent failure" or hazard (Reason, 1993). Once a norm exists it is very hard to rid the organization of it.

An important feature in Fig. 2.2 is that the arrow between procedures and practices goes both ways. This is an important flow of information that serves to minimize procedural deviations. Managers and supervisors should constantly watch for procedures that are not being followed and look for the reasons. It may be that crewmembers have devised a better way to accomplish the task and it should be adapted as a procedure; this is a win−win situation. Of course, it may also be that crewmembers have found an easier or quicker, but not necessarily a safer, way to get the task done. Procedural deviation is hard to detect and rarely surfaces during normal checks such as proficiency checks or yearly line checks because crewmembers are at their best behavior during these occasions. One of the most effective ways of detecting them is during audits such as line operations safety audits (LOSAs), a nonjeopardy audit that many airlines around the world have adopted for just this reason. A description of LOSAs will be addressed in the next section on safety cultures.

2.8   THE ORGANIZATIONAL CULTURE LINK TO SAFETY

There is one extremely important rule about an organization's culture—it is created at the top and permeates the entire organization. However, it is always measured at the bottom where the work is being done. This fact points out a critical aspect of safety cultures—the highest level of management must be fully committed, lead the way, and be the loudest and strongest proponents of the safety culture and all its ingredients. A recent article in *Aviation Week and Space Technology* stated the following:

> *Investing the time and money needed to get at the root cause of a problem takes total commitment at the most senior levels of a company or organization. In most organizational settings, communicators learn early in life how bad news can impact their leaders. If the news is valued and the communicator is protected, there is a real chance information can and will routinely flow upward in time for proper action to be taken.*

The unspoken word here is *trust*! Company personnel must feel protected and this protection should come, in writing, from the highest levels of the organization. Nonjeopardy programs are the finest examples of this type of protection. This does not mean that willful violations or dangerous and reckless behavior will be tolerated; this type of behavior should be acted upon harshly and swiftly. These programs do recognize, however, that learning how, where, and when a human error has occurred is much more important than placing blame, and can be useful in preventing a reoccurrence.

As previously stated, we live in a blame society. This means that whenever there is a negative event there is always a rush to find the villain or villains. This need to place blame gets in the way of the ultimate objective of preventing the event from happening again. Corporate leadership and middle managers must recognize that the value of this information far outweighs the small satisfaction gotten from placing blame and punishing.

One of the most effective programs of this type in current use at many major air carriers is the Aviation Safety Action Program (ASAP; FAA, 2002), a nonjeopardy partnership that encourages corporate-specific voluntary safety reporting. Management and unions play a vital role in these programs and their support cannot be overemphasized. A strong union is an asset for an organization with the skill to use this vital resource and the wisdom to capitalize on their talent. There is no stronger program in an organization than one that has the combined backing of management and union officials. Unions usually have committees that deal with safety, training, and professional standards. These groups can play a crucial role in the effectiveness of the operation; management should make the most of this source of manpower and intelligence.

Another excellent source of support is the Airlines for America (A4A) and for international carriers, the International Air Transport Association (IATA). These organizations and their councils, committees, and task forces are invaluable resources available to an air carrier. They have led the way in many of the safety initiatives of the past few decades, such as wind shear, traffic collision avoidance, and terrain avoidance systems, and have been successful in lobbying in favor of beneficial programs for our industry at the government level.

The subject of corporate culture has been a much-discussed item for many years and our industry has seen startling examples of both good and bad. At a Symposium on Corporate Culture and Transportation Safety in 1997 the honorable Jim Hall, a former chairperson of the NTSB, had these comments on the subject:

> We have found through 30 years of accident investigation that sometimes the most common link is the attitude of corporate leadership toward safety. The safest carriers have more effectively committed themselves to controlling the risks that may arise from mechanical or organizational failures, environmental conditions and human error.

2.9 SAFETY CULTURE

A safety culture has been described as the product of the individual and group values, attitudes, competencies, and patterns of behavior that determine the commitment to, and the style and proficiency of an organization's health and safety programs. James Reason has taken this description one step further by breaking down the individual parts necessary to create a safety culture. Dr. Reason says there are four parts to an effective safety culture, an informed culture, a reporting culture, a just culture, and finally a learning culture (Reason, 1993). Let's discuss each one of these individually.

An *informed culture* is one in which an organization collects and analyzes the right kind of data to keep it informed of the safety health of the organization. This collection can be done in a number of ways. One of the easiest ways is to analyze data from the training department in the form of satisfactory and unsatisfactory performance during check rides. Depending on an organization's grading system, there may be invaluable data from proficiency checks, recurrent training, and LOFT performances that identify the need to develop focused training. For instance, items that are graded poor or unsatisfactory more often than other items in the check rides may indicate the need for emphasis on those particular items.

Another excellent source of data for an organization is the FAA Flight Operations Quality Assurance (FOQA) program, which flags data from the digital flight recorder in flight that exceed certain parameters. If collected and analyzed correctly, the data will show trends such as flap speed exceedances, excessive speed below 10,000 feet, unstabilized approaches, etc. If a trend is detected, the organization now has options on how to reverse the trend. This may not always be a flight crew problem, which can be addressed with bulletins and training. Experience has shown us that at times, a particular destination with a rash of flap speed exceedances may indicate a poor arrival profile. This is where union committees and A4A committees can be of great value. Sharing the data and working with other organizations experiencing the same problem in the industry have been very successful in resolving such problems.

An organization with a robust informed culture can create a safety information system that collects, analyzes, and disseminates information on incidents and near misses, as well as proactive safety checks. The key word here is disseminating. Information of this type is of no value unless it is sent through the proper channels and to the right people so that action is assured.

A *reporting culture* is one in which employees are encouraged to report safety problems. The most important ingredient of this culture is *trust*. They must feel confident they will not be punished or ridiculed for reporting (shoot the messenger). This trust can best be achieved if a written nonreprisal policy exists, signed by the most senior management as mentioned earlier in this discussion. This assumes confidentiality will be maintained or the data are de-identified. Lastly, they must have confidence the information will be acted upon if found to be meaningful.

A *just culture* exists if the employees realize they will be treated fairly. Recognizing the ubiquity of error, organizations will not punish those who error or commit unsafe acts so long as the error was unintentional. However, it must be perfectly clear that those who act recklessly or take deliberate and unjustifiable risks will be punished. Willful violations and reckless operation will not be tolerated and will be acted upon swiftly and painfully if necessary.

The final part of an effective safety culture is a *learning culture*. In short, the organization is able to learn and change from its prior misdirection or mistakes. This may seem an oversimplification but those who study management know how difficult change can be. Human beings are inherently resistant to change. The enemy of any organization is "business as usual." Even after a problem has been identified and corrective action initiated, it is not unusual for the day-to-day operation to slip slowly back to the old routine. One of the definitions of insanity is doing the same thing over and over again and expecting a different outcome. Yet this is something we see organizations doing constantly. The ability to correct operations that are going wrong is truly a skill fraught with apprehension and angst. It takes a strong leader with a clear vision of what he or she wants and, even better, an understanding of how to get there and what it looks like to achieve true and lasting change.

Experience has shown that although an organization can have an overall healthy safety culture it is possible for departments within the company to differ greatly. For instance, when a new aircraft type is introduced into an organization, the new fleet manager(s) usually incorporate the latest concepts in training for technical proficiency and human factors skills. This is a positive step forward because all aspects of the training and operation tend to be scrutinized and optimized. Using lessons learned by others already flying the aircraft type may also benefit the new fleet in creating the best possible procedures.

However, the older fleet types don't necessarily benefit from this optimization or may resist changing from the way they have historically done things. This is one of the easiest ways for cultures within an organization to drift apart. As more modern aircraft are brought into the fleet, the older aircraft fall further and further behind in the way they operate. This change is so slow and insidious that it is hard to detect. Sometimes this problem does not come to light until an incident or accident highlights the problem and the fix is a reactive one.

One of the most successful ways of overcoming this problem is through a robust trend analysis and auditing system. LOSA is undoubtedly one of the most effective ways to accomplish this task proactively, and provides a unique and insightful view of an operation. LOSA will be covered in depth in Chapter 12, Crew Resource Management (CRM) and Line Operations Safety Audit (LOSA).

2.10 SUMMARY

I conclude that crewmembers and organizations can capably manage their errors and that this is the key function of teamwork. Error management is not a new concept; it has been around since the earliest days of CRM. In the early 1980s, at one of the first CRM meetings, Clay Foushee (then of NASA Ames) used the term when talking about LOFT. Unfortunately, at the time, we in the industry were so focused on the "wrong stuff" pilot we didn't appreciate the relevance of his statement.

Hopefully, this chapter will play a role in the way we look at errors. We need to convince those in our industry who regulate, manage, train, and evaluate crewmembers that accident and incident-causing errors are actually symptoms of an imperfect system in which imperfect humans operate. If that can be established, we can maximize the effects of the newest version of CRM—TEM. This includes the concept that even the finest of crews can make errors, and when they occur they are able to trap and correct those errors, and should be subsequently rewarded for their actions.

This chapter has highlighted, if not exhaustively discussed, the optimum traits and attributes of crewmembers, the need for organizations to continually audit and evaluate their performance, and the many methods that now can be used to analyze trends in the industry and make systemic corrections. Perhaps this chapter will provoke thought and action on how crewmembers are motivated, trained, and evaluated. The myriad of brilliant members in our industry will create and implement the next generation of human factors training and many excellent ideas and concepts that are sure to come.

REFERENCES

Degani, A., & Wiener, E. L. (1994). Philosophy, policies, procedures, and practices: The Four "P"s of flight deck operations. In N. Johnston, N. McDonald, & R. Fuller (Eds.), *Aviation psychology in practice* (pp. 44−67). Hants, UK: Avebury Technical.

Dismukes, R. K., Berman, B. A., & Loukopoulos, L. D. (2007). *The limits of expertise*. Burlington, VT: Ashgate Publishing.

Federal Aviation Administration. (2002). Aviation Safety Action Program (ASAP). Advisory Circular 120-66B. Washington, DC. Retrieved from: https://www.faa.gov/regulations_policies/advisory_circulars/index.cfm/go/document.information/documentID/23207.

Flight Safety Foundation. (1994). Flight Safety Foundation. A review of flightcrew-involved major accidents of U.S. air carriers 1978 through 1990. (1994) Flight Safety Digest: Alexandria, VA, 12(4).

Reason, J. (1993). *Review. Vol. I management overview*. London: British Railways Board.

Vaughn, D. (1997). *The challenger launch decision: Risky technology, culture, and deviance at NASA*. Chicago: University of Chicago Press.

Wolfe, T. (1979). *The right stuff*. New York: Farrar, Straus, and Giroux.

FURTHER READING

Billings, C. E. (1997). *The search for a human-centered approach*. Mahwah, NJ: Lawrence Erlbaum Associates.

Dekker, S. (2006). *The field guide to understanding human error*. Burlington, VT: Ashgate Publishing.

Dyer, W. G. (1977). *Team building issues and alternatives*. Reading, MA: Addison-Wesley Publishing Co.

Foushee, H. C. (1984). Dyads and triads at 35,000 feet: Factors affecting group process and aircrew performance. *American Psychologist, 39*, 885−893.

Maurino, D. E., Reason, J., Johnston, N., & Lee, R. B. (1995). *Beyond aviation. Human factors*. Burlington, VT: Ashgate Publishing.

Orlady, H. W., & Orlady, L. M. (1999). *Human factors in multi-crew flight operations.* Brookfield, VT: Ashgate Publishing.

Tullo, F. J. (2001). Viewpoint: Responses to mistakes reveal more than perfect rides. *Aviation Week and Space Technology, 21,* 106, May.

Tullo, F. J., & Dismukes, K. (2000). Aerospace forum: Rethinking crew error. *Aviation Week and Space Technology, 17,* 63, July.

Wiener, E. L., & Nagel, D. C. (1988). *Human factors in aviation.* San Diego, CA: Academic Press.

Chapter 3

Crews as Groups: Their Formation and Their Leadership

Robert C. Ginnett

Retired, United States Air Force Academy, Colorado Springs, CO, United States

3.1 INDIVIDUAL VERSUS CREW ORIENTATION

On January 15, 2009, the "miracle on the Hudson" occurred. Shortly after takeoff from New York's LaGuardia Airport, US Airways Flight 1549 struck a flock of birds and the unthinkable occurred—both Airbus A320 engines lost power. In command, Captain Chesley "Sully" Sullenberger soon determined he would not be able to make Teterboro's Runway 1 as assigned by New York's TRACON and the best alternative would be to ditch in the Hudson River. The individual airmanship displayed by Captain Sullenberger in guiding what had become a commercial glider safely down to a water landing is unquestioned and truly remarkable. Individual airmanship will always be essential, especially in emergency situations. But even Captain Sullenberger has noted that the safety and survival of all 155 aboard was a crew accomplishment, and that notion is the essence of this chapter.

The objective of this chapter is to change the focus of crewmembers from solely a perspective of competent individuals coming together to do work to a perspective that acknowledges that a crew, group, or team has certain unique characteristics that cannot be explained at the individual level. Further, these group concepts are critical for performance and should be understood and leveraged by anyone who considers leading a team.

At this point, it is prudent to clarify what we mean by crews, groups, and teams. I assume that crew is self-explanatory to anyone who has decided to read a book entitled *Crew Resource Management*. Groups and teams might not be so self-evident, as we shall see later. The most generic of these terms is group. For purposes of this chapter, a group is defined as two or more people coming together with a common task or objective, with differentiated roles, and interdependence. First, we are only talking about task groups. This does not mean that the factors discussed here don't apply to social groups or identity groups; they may, but those groups have not been studied by this

Crew Resource Management. DOI: https://doi.org/10.1016/B978-0-12-812995-1.00003-8

author. Secondly, the members of the group must have different roles. So a whole room full of accountants all working as equal contributors would not qualify as a group. A high school football team with linemen, receivers, punters, and quarterbacks would qualify as a group. And lastly, the members of the group must be mutually interdependent upon each other to complete the task. So a number of people waiting at the bus stop for the next bus would not constitute a group because they don't have differentiated roles and they are not in the least interdependent. An airline crew composed of a captain, a first officer, and a number of flight attendants qualifies.

What about teams? Again, for our purposes here, a team is a group with the same characteristics listed above but more highly specialized. There is no clear-cut difference between a task group and a team. Rather, it is matter of degree. In this chapter, the terms crew, group, and team may be used interchangeably even though many of the examples will be from aircraft crews. But what is important here is to make clear to the reader the vast and distinct difference between "individual work" and "crew, group, or team work."

To accomplish this objective, we will first look at some examples of crew failure and then introduce a few critical group-based concepts. Paramount among these will be group dynamics and leadership (yes—leadership is a group concept, not an individual concept). Then I will briefly review a NASA-funded research project I conducted examining the importance of leadership during the formation process of crews and discuss some of the unexpected results of that study. The concept of organizational shells will be introduced to help explain the surprising findings. Lastly, the implications for effective crew leadership will be discussed.

A crew is a group and possibly the most critical resource in Crew Resource Management. It is also the primary and fundamental issue if we are to improve the work outcome for those who fly airplanes in the crew environment. But it goes far deeper than just the work in crew-served aircraft. Across the United States, we are discovering the difficulty of making the transition from individual work to group work in many of our industrial settings. And on that note, this chapter certainly applies to crews—but arguably more than any other chapter in this book, the concepts here apply to any task group. Airline crew or surgical team, Navy SEAL team or high school basketball team; it makes no difference from a group perspective because it is not about the task—it is about the team.

Our tendency not to think in group concepts is itself a group issue. We are an individualistic culture (Triandis, 1995). From birth through college, we nurture and praise the individual accomplishments of our offspring. Whether in academics or athletics, in myth or in history, we focus on, and reinforce, individual accomplishments. This is not to say that group-oriented activity is ignored, but rather to say that we do not focus as much attention on the accomplishments of groups as we do on the accomplishments of individuals. Being a member of the NCAA championship football team is obviously cause for celebration. But are we more inclined to remember the team that won the national championship 5 years ago or the winner of the Heisman trophy from 5 years ago? Being a member of the national collegiate debate team is something to be proud of—but in our culture being a Rhodes Scholar carries more prestige.

Even our educational systems are based upon individual competition rather than group collaboration. At the US Air Force Academy a group of fellow faculty members and I came to believe that the entire system—from elementary school through undergraduate pilot training—evaluated and rewarded individual performance. At the same time, we began to recognize and acknowledge that once finished with the formal "training" portion of the lives of our pilots, the subsequent "work" which was to be done depended largely on the ability to work in a group. This notion was reinforced in the extreme when F-16 pilots from Nellis Air Force Base requested our research results on crew performance. As they noted, F-16 pilots work in "two-ships" or "four-ships," and even though they were in separate cockpits, they needed to work as a group or team to be effective.

We have imported and strengthened this individualistic orientation in the aviation community. From the early days of flight training, the goal is to "solo." I am hard pressed to come up with a more individualistic term than "solo." Historically, the airline industry and those responsible for its oversight have been primarily interested in the qualifications and performance of the individual even though the individual was to be inserted into a crew-served cockpit. Airline companies have traditionally hired many of their pilots from the military, which assured them some reasonable minimum standard of training and experience in flying modern aircraft. Other pilots hired by the major companies have had to demonstrate comparable levels of qualifications. Likewise, the Federal Aviation Administration (FAA) certifies individual pilots on their technical skills at flying the airplane (for the captain and the first officer) or at managing the aircraft systems (for the flight engineer). For example, pilots are asked to demonstrate in recurrent simulator training procedures for difficult and infrequently encountered conditions, such as steep turns, multiengine failures, recovery from wind shear stalls on takeoff, and go-arounds in weather conditions with less than minimum visibility. Scheduling in most major airlines is driven by individual considerations, with seniority of the individuals in each of the positions being the principal factor. Only within the last few decades have we begun to consider this issue of crews and groups (which is quite foreign to our culture) in the training of teams that fly commercial aircraft.

Before one gets the idea that this chapter is "anti-individual," let me lay those fears to rest. As noted in the opening paragraph briefly describing Captain Sullenberger's remarkable water landing skills in a circumstantial glider, nothing in this chapter suggests we need any less individual competence if we are to enhance crew performance. As we shall see later, individual skills are critical in aviation performance and should continue to be developed and rewarded. However, we have reached a point in aviation history (and in American business as well, I might argue) where we need to take the next step and go beyond the individualistic focus. That next step requires that we learn about groups.

Sometimes we hear the argument that "groups are nothing more than the collection of individuals making up the groups." Such statements ignore a growing body of evidence in both the research literature and in the annals of aviation mishaps. Rather than citing evidence from both of these sources, let me provide a very simple example to show how group work can be quite different, and to someone with little group experience, even counterintuitive, from individual work (Langfred, 2000). Again this example comes from athletics.

As a culture built on valuing individual performance, we are sometimes given individual advice which will not necessarily result in quality team outcomes. For example, often team members are told by their coach that they all need to do their absolute best if the team is going to do well (at least, that is what my coaches told me on more than one occasion). But from systems theory we know that for a team to do well, sometimes the individuals comprising the team must not maximize their individual effort. Referred to as subsystem nonoptimization, this concept is not intuitively obvious to either many team members or their coaches. But consider a high school football team which has an extremely fast running back and some very competent, but measurably slower, blocking linemen. If our running back does his absolute best on a sweep around the end, he will run as fast as he can. By doing so, he will leave his blocking linemen behind. The team is not likely to gain much yardage on such a play, and the back, who has done his individual best, is apt to learn an important experiential lesson about teamwork. The coach would get better results if he or she worked out an integrated coordination plan between the back and the linemen. In this case, the fast running back needs to slow down (i.e., not perform maximally) to give the slower but excellent blockers a chance to do their work. After they have been given a chance to contribute to the play, the back will then have a much better chance to excel individually, and so will the team as a whole. Good teamwork is sometimes on a different plane (no pun intended) from good individual work.

Unfortunately, we find repeated evidence of poor crew work resulting in errors, accidents, and incidents in the aviation community. Three of the more publicized examples should be sufficient to illustrate this problem. The first example is taken from a National Transportation Safety Board investigation (NTSB, 1979, pp. 23–29). It illustrates both the pervasiveness of the captain's authority and the group's failure to demand that attention be focused on a critical aspect of the flight:

The crew of Flight 173 had experienced only routine conditions as they brought the four-engine DC-8 into the Portland, Oregon traffic pattern. However, on final approach as they lowered their gear for landing, they heard a dull thump from what seemed to be the main gear area. The captain elected to abort the landing and was put into a holding pattern until they could determine if there was a problem and whether or not it warranted further emergency precautions.

The aircraft proceeded in a large holding pattern while the captain directed the crew in attempting to determine the possible cause of the noise. This pattern was maintained for approximately one hour at the captain's insistence. During this time, both the first officer and the flight engineer warned the captain on four separate occasions that they were running out of fuel and needed to make a decision about landing. In spite of these repeated cautions, the captain insisted that they continue to circle. Finally, as the first of the four engines flamed out, the captain ordered the plane toward the field while demanding that the flight engineer explain the cause of the engine failure. With all fuel tanks now dry, the other engines began to fail in sequence and the DC-8 nosed downward.

About 1815 PST, Flight 173 crashed into a wooded, populated area, killing 8 passengers and 2 crew members, and seriously injuring 21 passengers and 2 other crew members. The National Transportation Board determined that the probable cause of the accident was the failure of the captain to monitor properly the aircraft's fuel state and to properly respond to the low fuel state and the crew members' advisories regarding fuel state. This resulted in fuel exhaustion to all engines. Contributing to the accident was the failure of the other two flight crew members to fully comprehend the criticality of the fuel state or to successfully communicate their concern to the captain.

The Safety Board believes that this accident exemplifies a recurring problem—a breakdown in cockpit management and teamwork during a situation involving malfunctions of aircraft systems in flight. To combat this problem, responsibilities must be divided among members of the flight crew while a malfunction is being resolved. . .

Admittedly, the stature of a captain and his management style may exert subtle pressure on his crew to conform to his way of thinking. It may hinder interaction and adequate monitoring and force another crew member to yield his right to express an opinion.

The second example, taken from a confidential report submitted to the NASA/FAA Aviation Safety Reporting System (ASRS) (Foushee, 1984, p. 888), describes a more blatant example of an overbearing and intimidating captain. Here is the first officer's report:

I was the first officer on an airline flight into Chicago O'Hare. The captain was flying, we were on approach to 4 R getting radar vectors and moving along at 250 knots. On our approach, Approach Control told us to slow to 180 knots. I acknowledged and waited for the captain to slow down. He did nothing, so I figured he didn't hear the clearance. So I repeated, "Approach said slow to 180," and his reply was something to the effect of, "I'll do what I want." I told him at least twice more and received the same kind of answer. Approach Control asked us why we had not slowed yet. I told them we were doing the best job we could and their reply was, "You almost hit another aircraft." They then asked us to turn east. I told them we would rather not because of the weather and we were given present heading and to maintain 3000 ft. The captain descended to 3000 ft. and kept going to 2500 ft. even though I told him our altitude was 3000 ft. His comment was, "You just look out the damn window."

This last example illustrates the tragic consequences of a captain from the other extreme—one who would not make a decision when one was required (Burrows, 1982; Foushee, 1984; NTSB, 1982):

"Slushy runway. Do you want me to do anything special for it or just go for it?" asked the First Officer of Air Florida's Flight 90, as he peered into a snowstorm at Washington National Airport....

"Unless you got anything special you'd like to do," quipped the plane's 34-year-old captain. Shortly after brake release, the first officer expressed concern with engine instrument readings or throttle setting. Four times during takeoff roll he remarked that something was "not right," but the captain took no action to reject the takeoff. (Air Florida operating procedures state that the captain alone makes the decision to reject.)

Seconds later, Flight 90 came back down, hitting the 14th Street Bridge before it crashed into the ice covered Potomac River, killing 74 persons on the aircraft and four motorists on the bridge.

The NTSB ruled that the captain of the aircraft did not react to the copilot's repeated, subtle advisories that all was not normal during the takeoff. Moreover, in recommending that pilot training include "considerations for command decision, resource management, role performance, and assertiveness," the Board implied that the copilot's lack of assertiveness (possibly induced by the inherent role structure of the cockpit) may have been a causal factor. (NTSB, 1982, pp. 67–68)

It is obvious that some crews do not work as well as they should. Yet in the course of our research on crews we have seen evidence of crews that go well beyond the call of duty—crews that do better than the collection of individual skills available to them. For a truly remarkable account of a leader and crew "flying an unflyable aircraft," readers should review the NTSB account of United Flight 232 captained by Al Haynes, which will be briefly described later in this chapter. If we are to understand effective crew performance, it is essential that we move beyond our focus on the individual to a broader level. We must begin to pay serious attention to the crew as a group if we are to optimize cockpit resources.

3.2   CREWS, GROUPS, AND TEAMS

Groups fly crew-served airplanes, for a number of reasons. "As a direct result of the limitations and imperfections of individual humans, multipiloted aircraft cockpits were designed to ensure needed redundancy" (Foushee, 1984). Furthermore, the Federal Aviation Regulations require at least a second-in-command if the aircraft is designed to carry more than 10 passengers (FAR 135.99). At a minimum then, commercial flights will have a dyad (the smallest group) in the cockpit. The other extreme observed in our research was a crew of 25 aboard a military C-5 Galaxy. Whether a dyad, a triad, or a crew of 25, these are all groups and as such share the potential strengths and weaknesses that are inherent in groups.

As illustrated earlier, groups are something more than merely a collection of the individuals comprising them. Some groups do remarkably well with no particularly outstanding individuals. Other groups, made up almost exclusively of high-performing individuals, do not do at all well as a team. A review of the performance of some of the US Olympic teams illustrates this phenomenon quite well. The 1988 US Olympic basketball team is remembered, if at all, for not winning the gold medal. Yet the team had high-performing individuals, many of whom went on to play in the National Basketball Association, and the coach was highly respected. How could this happen, many asked? In the view of color commentator and former coach Al McGuire, the problem was that they did not have a "team," but merely a collection of high-performance individuals. As McGuire recalls, the United States had a history of putting together basketball teams by selecting the best individuals available but doing little to foster or coordinate teamwork. In previous Olympics, when our individuals were much superior to the rest of the world's individual players, we could win in spite of our lack of true teamwork. But as the rest of the world improved, particularly in the work of their teams as a whole, individual ability could no longer do the job. In what may be McGuire's most remembered quote, he said "You have to remember, there's no 'I' in team." He also noted that if we want to win, we have to quit building "all-star teams" and instead build a team. "Team" is precisely what coach Mike Krzyzewski focused on with his US basketball team in the 2008 Olympic Games in China.

Perhaps an even more extreme example was the famous 1980 US Olympic hockey team, which is remembered for "the impossible dream come true" as it beat the Soviet team. Here was a team of no overwhelmingly great individuals—but a great team. They practiced over 100 games together as a team. Rather than being rewarded solely as individuals for goals, assists, saves, and the like, they were rewarded for the play of their lines (the five-man subgroups that take the ice together) and for the performance of the team as a whole. They learned to work as a team and found that a team can overcome individual inadequacies, deficiencies, and errors.

Although these are excellent examples of team performance (or lack thereof), one does not have to go to the intense level of Olympic competition to demonstrate the same phenomenon. A technique used widely in helping groups to understand the value-added from team performance is a classroom exercise designed to demonstrate *synergy*. In this exercise, individuals are presented with a hypothetical scenario which places them in an uncommon setting and asks them to rank order a limited number of items critical to their ultimate survival. While the specific task can vary widely (from "Lost on the Moon" to "Desert Survival"), the procedures remain common. After the individuals have completed their own rank orderings, they are placed in a group which represents the other survivors in this unique setting. The group's task is to arrive at a consensus rank ordering of the same set of critical items. Upon completion of the rankings, both the individual and group rankings are compared to an ordering by experts in the particular setting (e.g., desert survival experts). Regardless of the specific nature of the setting, the results are virtually always the same (Kerr & Tindale, 2004). The most common result is that all of the groups' performances will exceed the performance of any individual in any group.

The parallel between lessons learned from this exercise and those learned in many aircraft accidents is more than casual. The characteristic of the classroom task that results in such predictable outcomes is its high degree of ambiguity to the participants. None of us has been lost on the moon, and it is such a unique environment that our experiences as individuals here on Earth are not particularly useful. Only when we integrate a number of varied experiences are we likely to arrive at a high-quality solution. Similarly, we seldom crash airplanes when we know exactly what the problem is and how to handle it. Even with major problems in critical periods of flight (such as loss of one engine at Vr), we are trained to handle them. In many accidents in today's complex systems and environment, it is common to find that some aspect of the environment or situation created ambiguity which, by definition, eliminated a structured solution. After all, if you do not know what the problem is, it is unlikely that you know what the solution is! But if you can get two or three independent critical thinkers involved, you will have a better chance of ruling out individual biases and will be on the road to a more effective solution. It is important to acknowledge, even in these hypothetical examples, that there must be time available to have effective group work. As I note in a later section, time-critical emergencies drive different strategies.

In order to better understand group behavior and the impact of the group on the individual, it is necessary to become familiar with conditions that are uniquely associated with groups themselves. These are characteristics that can either only be defined relative to the group or, if associated with individuals, only make sense in a group setting.

3.2.1   Boundaries

Boundaries for a group are like the fence around a piece of property. A group boundary allows us to know who is in the group and who is not, whether or not we are a member of the group. It defines both physically and psychologically who the members of the group might rely on within their own group's boundaries and thus indicates when it may be necessary to go beyond their own group for assistance or resources. A cockpit crew has a number of members defined by the design of the aircraft. A Boeing 757 has seats for two cockpit members, and hence there is an expected boundary of two for the crew of that airplane.[1] A psychosocial boundary might also define the limits of tolerable deviance for group members. For example, all the types of socially acceptable and unacceptable behaviors are never made absolutely clear and are seldom written down. Thus, if a group can identify a boundary maintainer (usually someone close to the edge of acceptable behavior), they will have some means of gauging their own behavior as to its acceptability.

3.2.2   Roles

A role is a set of expected behaviors associated with a particular position (not person) in a group or team. In any group setting over time, various roles will emerge. Some people will assume roles that are focused on accomplishing the task while others will take on behaviors associated with maintaining relationships within the group. Still others may take on roles that are counterproductive or even destructive to the group. Examples of some of the group roles which have been identified are listed in Table 3.1.

Airline crews have clearly defined roles for the most part. The captain is the leader of the crew, followed by the first officer and second officer in turn. The lead flight attendant occupies a similar leadership position for the flight attendants. Some aspects of these roles are defined by law. Federal Aviation Regulation 91.3 states, "The pilot in command (i.e., the captain of

---

1. Sometimes technology overtakes original design. For example, on a C-141 aircraft there is a seat and workstation for a navigator. But the incorporation of inertial navigation systems and GPS has eliminated the requirement for the navigator position. Interestingly, this crew restructuring has also changed the social dynamics of the crew as predicted by sociotechnical systems theory, but that is another story for another chapter.

TABLE 3.1 Commonly Identified Group Roles

Task Roles	Maintenance Roles	Blocking Roles
Initiator contributor	Harmonizer	Dominator
Information seeker	Encourager	Blocker
Information giver	Gatekeeper	Aggressor
Evaluator	Compromiser	Disruptor
Summarizer		

a commercial aircraft requiring more than one pilot) of an aircraft is directly responsible for, and is the final authority as to, the operation of that aircraft." Other role expectations are defined by the organization, or even by the crew itself.

To the extent roles are clear and independent, the group will tend to function well, at least from a role standpoint. However, there can be role problems which will cause stress for the individuals involved and typically decreased performance from the group. Two kinds of role problems are most common.

Role Conflict

When the individual is getting contradictory messages or expectations about his or her behavior, he or she is experiencing role conflict. These conflicts can come from several different sources. Perhaps most common is where the person is receiving two different signals about the expectations for a particular role. We can attach a label to this kind of role conflict depending upon from whom the signals are emanating. If the same person is giving you conflicting signals, we call that intrasender role conflict. ("I want you to do a high-quality, detailed job and I need it in two minutes.") If two different people are providing differing expectations about your role, that is labeled intersender role conflict. Sometimes the conflict can be between two different roles held by the same person. For example, a newly upgraded first officer may have conflicts between his role as father and Little League baseball coach and his flying schedule, which is now based on low seniority. This is referred to as interrole conflict. Last is the situation where the expectations of a role violate the role occupant's personal expectations or values. This is known as person/role conflict. Person/role conflict can also develop as the expected role migrates from initial expectations. An extreme example might be a person who was recruited by an intelligence agency to conduct analysis and, through a series of unexpected changes, is asked to engage in covert operations.

Role Ambiguity

In role conflict, one receives clear messages about expectations but the messages are not all congruent. In situations of role ambiguity, the problem is that one cannot be sure what the expectations are at all. The information about the role is either lacking or not clearly communicated. Role ambiguity is more apt to occur in management positions than in traditional cockpit crew roles.

3.2.3   Norms

Norms are the informal rules that groups adopt to regulate group members' behaviors. Although these norms are infrequently written down or openly discussed, they often have a powerful, and consistent, influence on group members' behavior (Hackman, 1976). One might reasonably ask, "if norms are powerful (so they are something I need to know about) but they aren't written down and aren't discussed, how am I supposed to figure them out?" Fortunately, most of us are rather good at reading the social cues that inform us of existing norms. When we first enter a work situation, even though there may not be a dress code, we are fairly astute at determining that "everybody around here wears a suit." We also are apt to notice a norm if it is violated, even though we may have been unable to articulate the norm before its violation was apparent (e.g., the guy wearing jeans when everybody else is wearing a suit).

Another fortunate aspect of norms is that they do not govern all behaviors, just those behaviors that the group feels are important. Feldman (1984) has outlined four reasons why norms are likely to be enforced. He suggests norms are more apt to be enforced if they (1) facilitate group survival; (2) simplify, or make more predictable, what behavior is expected of group members; (3) help the group avoid embarrassing interpersonal problems; or (4) express the central values of the group and clarify what is distinctive about the group's identity.

An outsider is often able to learn more about norms than an insider for several reasons. First, the outsider (not necessarily being subject to the norms herself) is more apt to notice them. In fact, the more "foreign" the observer is, the more likely the norms are to be perceived. If one is accustomed to wearing a tie to work, one is less likely to notice that another organization also wears ties to work, but more likely to note that a third organization typically wears sweaters and sweatshirts around the office. Another lesson the outsider can learn by observing other groups' norms is something about his or her own group's norms. In a recent consulting project, our research team was struck by the failure of the client organization to share information with us—not proprietary information, but information that impacted our own ability to work with them. In a moment of reflection on this situation, we realized that our work group norm was very different from theirs. Our team had a norm that encouraged open sharing of information with each other—but prior to seeing a very different norm in a different group, none of us could have articulated our own norm of openly sharing information.

3.2.4 Status

Status is the relative ranking of individuals within a group setting. In an airline cockpit crew, status is typically associated with the roles of captain, first officer, and, if appropriate, second officer. In these cases, status comes with the position. Status, like roles, determines appropriate behaviors for all group members. Usually a high-status person has more power and influence, and thus the lower-status members of a group tend to defer to the higher-status members. Again, crossing cultures gives us interesting insights into status impact. In Eastern cultures, age is given status and younger people will bow to older people. Since Western culture lacks castes or clear-cut status lines, it is sometimes difficult to figure out who has the most status. Status incongruence can result in stress for the individuals and less than satisfactory work outcomes. Tom Wolfe in *The Right Stuff* (1979) describes the status incongruence that occurred between the flight surgeons (who believed they were the most important people in the manned space flight program—after all, they could reject an unfit "subject" with the stroke of a pen), and the test pilots who were to become the astronauts (who believed they were the very reason there was a manned space flight program).

3.2.5 Authority

Technically, authority is the right to use power and influence. People derive authority in the group setting from the legitimate power given them by the organization. The captain has the authority to order a drunken or abusive passenger off the airplane or to not accept a flight that he or she believes is unsafe. Authority can also be granted on the basis of recognized expertise or expert power. Again, the group can get into trouble when differing sources of authority clash. There have been numerous reports of accidents caused by confused authority dynamics in the cockpit. For example, several accidents have occurred in military cockpits when a higher ranking (status) officer was assigned as a check pilot for a junior ranking crew and then became involved in giving directions during an actual emergency. The confused authority dynamics were directly responsible for accidents of this nature.

Authority dynamics have their roots in the dependency relationships we have developed from birth. As children, we were dependent on our parents and accepted their authority. As we grew and became more independent, we had to work through the evolving authority relationships. Even today, we are all dependent at certain times. Passengers in commercial aircraft are dependent on the crew. A "dead-heading" first officer with 10,000 hours of flying

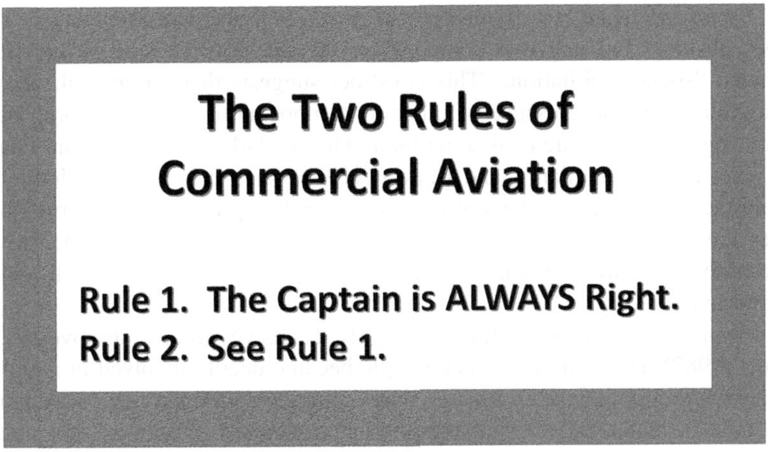

The Two Rules of Commercial Aviation

Rule 1. The Captain is ALWAYS Right.
Rule 2. See Rule 1.

FIGURE 3.1   Sign posted on an airline crew bulletin board.

time is still dependent on the crew flying in the cockpit. There is nothing good or bad about being dependent unless we mismatch the degree of dependency and the situation. A passenger who decides to take over the airplane has inappropriately usurped authority. At the other extreme, a first officer who becomes overly dependent on the captain for decision-making is not likely to help the crew either. Yet authority dynamics can result in just such occurrences. In an investigation conducted by Harper, Kidera, and Cullen (1971) at a major air carrier, captains feigned incapacitation at a predetermined point during final approach in simulator trials characterized by poor weather and visibility. In that study, approximately 25% of these simulated flights "hit the ground" because, for some reason, the first officers did not take control even when they knew the plane was well below glide slope. We can assume from this research and from other artifacts (see below) that the authority dynamic surrounding the role of the captain must be extremely powerful. Fig. 3.1, which depicts a sign found on a bulletin board in a commercial carrier's operations room, is only partly facetious.

3.2.6   Group Dynamics

Clearly, all the topics in this section on groups could fall under the general heading of group dynamics, since they are all dynamic characteristics that only occur in a group setting. Recognizing the confusing nature of groups themselves, especially in our culture, it seems best to discuss a few group dynamics topics separately. There are, of course, many more group topics than I have space to discuss here. However, in closing we should note two remaining dynamics of groups.

Social influence is a by-product of group activity. Unfortunately, it has both positive and negative components. On the positive side is an effect labeled "social facilitation." This construct suggests that, in general, people are aroused by the presence of others and more motivated to perform well, knowing that others are evaluating them. On the dark side of social influence is what Latane, Williams, and Harkins (1979) have called "social loafing." Here the individual members of the group feel less pressure to perform when they are working with others. The researchers believe this may happen when the individuals are only carrying part of the load and no one can tell which member is loafing.

Groupthink is another flaw of highly cohesive groups, discovered by Janis (1982). He found that when people became deeply involved in a highly cohesive group, they often became more concerned with striving for unanimity than in realistically appraising alternative courses of action. This condition can be exacerbated when the leader promotes his or her preferred solution and when the group is insulated from expert opinions outside the group. Janis believed that groupthink accounted for a number of historic fiascos, including the United States' failure to heed warnings of the impending attack on Pearl Harbor, the decision processes leading up to the failed Bay of Pigs invasion, and the Watergate cover-up.

3.3 GROUP PROCESS AND LEVERAGE

Having briefly discussed some of the characteristics associated with groups, teams, and crews, we may now begin to consider a model for improving their output. Merely, the mention of the word "output" leads us to begin thinking in the language and models of systems theory with its familiar terminology of "input-process-output." While that concept may be useful for considering group work, interventions or corrections based on systems theory have not been too successful. In systems theory, inputs are generally "givens" and outputs are "desired." If the outputs are not meeting expectations, then the corrective intervention most typically occurs somewhere in the "process" stage of the system. Since the 1970s, much of our group-oriented corrective interventions have pursued this course of action by attempting to intervene in the process stage of the group's work (see Schein, 1969, for a discussion of process interventions). After all, that is where the problems were most obvious—why not fix them where you see them? Unfortunately, years of evidence did not support that concept (Kaplan, 1979). That does not mean that process interventions cannot be helpful, but they should not be expected to fix all the problems encountered by groups either. If one buys an extremely cheap automobile, no amount of work by a mechanic will make it perform and ride like a Mercedes-Benz. Some things are far better incorporated in the design (input) phase than in the maintenance (process) phase.

Hackman (1987) and Ginnett (Hughes, Ginnett, & Curphy, 2015) have proposed models to design groups for output effectiveness. Their models suggest that the organization should be set up to support group work and also that the group should be designed to accomplish output objectives. Two important points should be noted in these models. First, the output is not unidimensional—it is not exclusively focused on satisfying the organizational or client needs. Certainly, that is an important consideration, but both Hackman and Ginnett also note that the group must be able to continue to perform in the future, and the individuals making up the group should obtain at least as much satisfaction as dissatisfaction from working in the group. For example, if a cockpit crew flies a "safe and efficient" leg in a trip, that would meet the first criterion. But if, in the process of the trip, there was so much interpersonal tension that the crew felt they could no longer work together on subsequent legs, the output of the group would not be labeled as effective.

Most organizations (airlines included) cannot afford to wait until their teams disintegrate or fail to perform their required tasks successfully before taking corrective action. This is where process criteria can be helpful, not as points for intervention but as points for diagnosis. By paying attention to how the group is going about its work, we may infer that their ultimate performance may have problems as well. But rather than intervening first at the process level, it makes more sense to use leverage at the input level. Ginnett's model discusses factors at the organizational, team, or group level and at the individual level which can support group-level work. It is at the team or group level of leverage that we will focus our attention.

3.4 LEADERSHIP

Having just stated the focus to be group design and then labeling this section "leadership" might trigger a few questions if not alarms. Two such questions might be: (1) How can we do anything about group design—aren't cockpit crews based on the design of the cockpit? and (2) What does leadership have to do with groups—I thought leadership was about leaders?

Let me address the second question first. Leadership is about leaders. But it is not about leaders in a vacuum—it is about leaders in relation to followers in a particular setting. Is there such a thing as leadership without followers? And since we have already agreed that any two people comprise a group, if there is a leader and at least one follower, we are in the group realm. The fact is leadership is a group phenomenon.

This contributes directly to our answer to the first question. Anyone who has spent much time watching groups operate in organizational environments will tell you that they do not all work equally well. Some cockpit crews cause accidents (as we have already noted), yet other cockpit crews exceed our greatest expectations. As one example, Captain Al Haynes and the crew of United 232 en route from Denver to Chicago suddenly found themselves in a situation that was never supposed to happen. After a catastrophic failure of the DC-10's number 2 engine fan disabled all three hydraulic systems, this crew was left with little or no flight controls. Captain Haynes enlisted the assistance of another captain traveling in the passenger cabin and, with his newly expanded crew, literally developed their own emergency procedures on line. In the midst of crisis the crew of United 232 managed to get the crippled airliner within a few feet of the Sioux City airport before impact. Remarkably, this crew performed even better than subsequent crews in simulator reenactments—even when those crews were comprised of test pilots. If some crews work better than others in the same organizational setting, then something about those crews must be different, and it must have something to do with the design of the groups. For airline crews, this "crew design" begins to occur when the crew first forms. But what is responsible for the difference?

In numerous interviews with crewmembers about this variation among crews, the same consistent answer emerged. Whether a crew works well or not is a function of the captain. One typical example of interviews of subordinate air crewmembers conducted by this author (Ginnett, 1987) illustrates this point:

> *RCG: Are all the [captains] you fly with pretty much the same?*

> *PILOT: Oh no. Some guys are just the greatest in the world to fly with. I mean they may not have the greatest hands in the world but that doesn't matter. When you fly with them, you feel like you want to do everything you can to work together to get the job done. You really want to do a good job for them. Some other guys are just the opposite... you just can't stand to work with them. That doesn't mean you'll do anything that's unsafe or dangerous but you won't go out of your way to keep him out of trouble either. So you'll just sit back and do what you have to and just hope that he screws up.*

> *RCG: How can you tell which kind of guy you're working with?*

> *PILOT: Oh, you can tell.*

> *RCG: How?*

> *PILOT: I don't know how you tell but it doesn't take long. Just a couple of minutes and you'll know.*

Not only does this illustrate the perception of the impact of the leader (the captain), but it also points to the critical nature of the crew formation (i.e., "Just a couple of minutes and you'll know").

The pervasive impact of the leader has been demonstrated in controlled research settings as well. I have already cited the feigned incapacitation study by Harper et al. (1971), in which the authority dynamics associated with the captain's role impacted the performance of the first officers. In another simulator study, Ruffell Smith (1979) designed an experiment where crews were given an interactive problem soon after departing on an intercontinental flight. The problem required a return to a short, wet runway with a number of interrelated mechanical problems and a critical fuel dump. The workload burden fell on the engineer, so the most obvious predictions about which crews would be able to safely return centered around the engineer's performance. A very detailed analysis of the number and type of errors showed great variations among the crews. As it turned out, the variable of most significance was not the flight engineer's behavior but the behavior of the captain. If the captain recognized the problem as a crew problem and managed the problem accordingly, the crew did well. However, if the captain handled the problem as "a piloting problem," the crew did not fare as well. Apparently, the captain's behavior carries considerable weight in the way the crew works. And if the interview data are valid, the leadership impact begins early in the crew's life.

3.5 LEADERSHIP AT FORMATION: A CRITICAL LEVERAGE POINT

The first phase of our NASA research set out to address the question of what actually goes on in the formation process of cockpit crews (Ginnett, 1987). Of particular interest was the behavior of captains who, prior to observation, were assessed by check airmen as being exceedingly good at creating highly effective teams (the HI-E captains) versus their counterparts who received low ratings on this same ability (LO-E captains). In accordance with accepted research procedures, the category of the captain to be observed was not revealed until after all data collection and content analyses were completed.

It may be helpful to briefly explain the context within which the first phase of the research occurred. Phase One was conducted entirely with crews assigned to 727-200 aircraft so the technology, crew size, and training were standardized. The particular airline company in which these first data were collected used a fairly typical bid system for crew scheduling. As a result, the crews were quite likely never to have worked together prior to coming together for an assigned trip. Of the 20 different three-person crews observed in the first phase of the research, none had ever worked together prior to the observation period. In fact, of the 60 dyads within the 20 crews, only eight had ever flown together before, and seven of those eight had done so only once. Their operations manual required a formal crew briefing before the first leg of each new crew complement. This briefing, conducted 1 hour before scheduled departure, was held in a designated room in the terminal unless there were late arrivals, in which case the briefing would occur on the aircraft. It is important to note that whether an organization requires a formal briefing or not (as was the case in subsequent organizations researched), there will be a crew formation process. If the organization does not legitimize this process with a required briefing, then whether the formation process occurs by design or by chance is very much up to the captain.

Based on extensions of the normative model by Hackman and Walton (1986) and observations of team formations in organizations other than airlines, I had certain expectations of what effective leaders would do when forming a team that had never worked together before. It seemed reasonable to expect a team leader to:

1. Discuss the task to be accomplished by the group.
2. Discuss the relevant team boundaries. Since this was a team that had never worked together before, I expected the leader to build a tight-knit working group.
3. Discuss relevant norms for the group's effective performance.

There were some surprises in what I found.

3.5.1 Task Findings

Contrary to expectations, the HI-E captains hardly discussed tasks at all.

Even when tasks were mentioned (e.g., closing the cabin door, retracting the aft air stairs, or keeping the cockpit door open prior to pushback), they were more about boundary issues (to be discussed in the next section) than about the tasks themselves. The only other exceptions which generated some task discussion occurred when there were unusual conditions such as weather or performance limitations due to deferred maintenance items on the aircraft. In contrast, some of the LO-E captains spent inordinate amounts of time discussing minute task requirements for the flight attendants which had little to do with boundary requirements or any other critical aspect of team performance. One LO-E captain went into great detail about procedures for bagging the cabin garbage!

But the general absence of task discussion was far from the predicted behavior—or from behavior exhibited by leaders in other task groups. For example, in problem-solving groups (often assembled in organizational settings as ad hoc committees), the bulk of the first meeting is spent defining and clarifying the task at hand. How can we explain the lack of task discussion by HI-E captains, and in sharp contrast, the focus on even trivial tasks by LO-E captains?

3.5.2 Boundary Findings

As noted earlier, it might appear that an airline cockpit crew, or even the total crew including the attendants, is a fairly well-defined and bounded group. After all, when you seal a work team in a pressurized aluminum cabin at 35,000 feet, there is little chance of someone leaving the group. In fact, based on the behaviors of the HI-E captains, they felt the groups were potentially overbounded. The HI-E captains worked both in the briefing and at other opportunistic times to expand the relevant team boundary and to make the boundary more permeable. They always talked about "we" in terms of the total flight crew, as opposed to some of the LO-E captains who referred to the cockpit crew as "we" and the flight attendants as "you." The HI-E captains also worked to create a larger vision of the relevant work group— one that exceeded the bounds of the aircraft. They took pains to include (at least psychologically) gate personnel, maintenance, and air traffic controllers as part of the group trying to help them, not as an outside hostile group trying to thwart their objectives. One HI-E captain routinely reminded the crew that the passengers could be a relevant part of their team if the crew made the effort to listen to passengers, particularly if they were expressing some concern about the aircraft.

3.5.3   Norms Findings

Norms can be communicated in a variety of ways. Certainly, the captain can make explicit the standards and expected behaviors of the crew. She can communicate the importance of a subject merely by including it in the briefing, or he can talk explicitly about its importance. The captain can also communicate normative information through a modeling process. This may include specific descriptions of intended behaviors or, more subtly, be expressed through actual behavior in the briefing and at other times in the presence of the crew. For example, a captain may quite subtly transmit the importance of exchanging information as the group goes about its work by merely taking time to exchange information (two-way communication) in the time allotted for the crew briefing. The norm that "communication is important" is expressed in the series of exchanges including: (1) I need to talk to you; (2) I listen to you; (3) I need you to talk to me; or even (4) I expect you to talk to me.

There was no single norm that was explicitly communicated by all of the highly effective captains. However, there were three norms most frequently communicated as important to the effective work of the group. These were the importance of safety, effective communication, and cooperation between crewmembers. Perhaps most surprising is that "safety" should need to be mentioned at all! Is that not the most important consideration anyway? That safety should be emphasized also seems to be contrary to the finding regarding tasks which were not mentioned much at all by the HI-E captains. These apparently conflicting and confounding findings are explained later in the section on "organizational shells."

3.5.4   Authority Dynamics Findings

While not a factor outlined in Hackman and Walton (1986) as something to which the leader should attend in group formation, the authority dynamic was such a powerful finding that it could not be overlooked. In fact, interpersonal relationships, authority dynamics, and control systems (basically, authority systems built into the organization's structure) were recognized as such critical factors, they received a prominent place in Ginnett's Team Leadership Model[©] (Hughes et al., 2015). Certainly, the use of influence and authority are common issues in leadership writings as far back as Lewin, Lippitt, and White (1939) and often are an integral part of leadership definitions. To understand the authority dynamics for airline cockpit crews it will first be necessary to provide a small amount of background information. The authority relationship between the captain and the rest of the crew is inexorably bound to aviation history, regulations, and often to the characteristics of the crewmembers themselves. This combination of history, regulation, and crewmember characteristics has established an authority dynamic that has undoubtedly positively impacted the aviation safety record. In those situations requiring immediate response to a single authoritative command, airline crews work particularly well. However, this tendency toward the high-authority end of the continuum has resulted in crewmembers not speaking up when necessary, as in the previously cited study and accident investigation. This inclination may also result in excessive psychological dependence on the captain as leader to the extent that individual contributions to problem-solving are neither voiced nor attempted. For example, one captain with whom I flew made a particularly poor approach which resulted in an excessive dive on short final, thus setting off numerous alarms. In reviewing the crewmembers' inactions afterward, the young second officer (who literally said nothing during the final approach) admitted that he had never seen an approach quite like that, but figured "the captain must know what he's doing."

If we plot authority dynamics along a continuum (as opposed to Lewin et al., 1939, who used nominal categories), the history, regulations, and individual characteristics of crewmembers all tend to be forces pushing toward the high end of authority use and response (Fig. 3.2).

As noted above, there are occasions in aviation where the extreme high end is appropriate, and most of us would agree that we cannot afford (nor do we personally want) the low end to occur. Given the existing history, regulations, and backgrounds, the latter condition is unlikely to occur. In fact, if we exclude hijackings and suicides, a review of the records of aviation accidents cannot produce a single incidence of "accident due to mutiny."

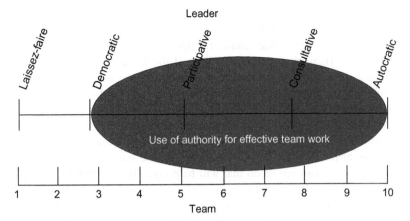

FIGURE 3.2   Range of authority dynamics in crew work.

Establishing Appropriate Authority

One might expect HI-E captains to deliberately move the authority dynamic back down from its preexisting extreme point to a level more appropriate for group-level work (i.e., somewhere in the middle of the continuum). Under such a hypothesis, the leader might operate solely in a more democratic or participative fashion. Such a finding would be simple and prescriptive. Unfortunately, that simplistic approach is not what happens.

Rather than operating at some specific point between complete democracy and complete autocratic behavior, the highly effective captains shifted their behavior during the formation process all along the continuum between the extremes of the effective range. Again, note that the highly effective captains never exhibited laissez-faire behaviors. Three methods were used to build an effective leader/team authority relationship: (1) establish competence; (2) disavow perfection; and (3) engage the crew.

1. *Establish competence.* In addition to the other statements made by the HI-E captains during their briefings (like establishing norms for crew behavior), they demonstrated their capability to assume the legitimate authority given them in three ways. First, the briefing was organized along some logical parameter (e.g., temporal, criticality, etc.). This helped to establish competence by demonstrating the captain had given some thought to the work they were about to engage in and he or she was able to present this in an organized manner, thus indicating rationality. Second, the briefing always contained elements of technical language specific to the vocation of flying. And finally, they were comfortable in a group setting—the environment of leadership. Like norms, this fact escaped recognition until its absence was observed among some of the LO-E captains.

2. *Disavow perfection.* All the HI-E captains established competence by exhibiting the above behaviors, but that only provided their crews with evidence that there was cause for the captain to exercise legitimate authority. Then, these captains balanced the leader/crew relationship by having the crewmembers take responsibility for the work of the group as well. This is important if the crew is not to completely rely on the captain, especially when he or she is in error. This was first noted in a captain's statement prior to an extremely effective crew performance in a simulator: "I just want you guys to understand that they assign the seats in this airplane based on seniority, not on the basis of competence. So anything you can see or do that will help out, I'd sure appreciate hearing about it." As simple as that sounds, it seems to underlie the basic behavior that HI-E captains use in disavowing perfection. They make a statement suggesting they don't know something about a particular issue even though the information is often quite readily available. This is a delicate balance: they do not contradict the competence they have established regarding their ability as a captain. Rather, they typically make some comment about their lack of knowledge (although not on a critical task) or about some personal shortcoming. They are open about dealing with their own vulnerabilities.

3. *Engaging the crew.* The HI-E captains became involved with and included the crews in the process of the briefing and in the social process of group formation. Content analysis of the briefing process showed specific instances where the HI-E captains were engaging the crew through real-time interactions. They dealt with the situations that could potentially impact the particular crew they were briefing as they learned about them in the course of their interactions. They interacted on a personal level with the other people who were filling the crew roles. (For literature supporting the importance of leader/team interaction, see Kozlowski & Bell, 2003.) They did not present a "canned briefing," nor did they provide a briefing that could just as well have been given to a group of mannequins. They interacted in the here-and-now with the other people with whom they would work. By dealing in real time with the people who were filling the roles, they conveyed important normative information about themselves and the value of the individuals who made up this particular group. They often did this with humor but it was not humor to isolate (canned jokes) but rather humorous responses to real-time interactions. The HI-E captains also spent more "nondirective" time with the group. It is not the case that these captains spent significantly more total time in the briefing with the crew than did the LO-E captains. Nor is it the case that they spent more time than the LO-E captains actually talking to the crew. There was, however, a significant difference between the HI-E captains and the LO-E captains in the amount of time that other members of the crew talked while the captain was present. The highly

effective captains allowed and encouraged conversation by the other crewmembers, particularly if it was related to the task. They always asked if there were any questions, and several of them solicited comments about any behaviors on other crews or with other captains that might be troublesome. By establishing their competence, disavowing perfection, and engaging the crew in the course of the briefing, the HI-E captains actually covered the range on the continuum of authority in which groups most effectively operate. Rather than demonstrate only one type of leadership authority which would be inappropriate across the range of requirements in a typical line operation (see Ginnett, 1990), these captains established, early on, an authority basis that would change according to the situation. This contingent authority pattern ranged from direct statements by a competent, legitimate authority figure to a human who recognized and was comfortable with his own imperfections. They further provided a mechanism for correcting these errors by ensuring that the crew was engaged and active in the task work already begun in the briefing.

In summary, the HI-E captains did not dwell on the task, expanded the boundaries to include others who could help the group in its work, made explicit certain important performance norms, and created an expectation of flexible authority contingent upon the situation.

What remains unresolved are (1) explanations of the unexpected or surprising findings concerning the absence of task discussion in contrast to the explicit discussion around norms associated with safety; (2) some understanding of how the leaders of these groups were able to accomplish the formation process so quickly; and (3) what the differing leadership behaviors had to do with subsequent performance. Fortunately, the concept of organizational shells[2] can help answer these questions.

3.6   ORGANIZATIONAL SHELLS

The origin of organizational shells is similar in concept to shells in chemistry or shells in computer science. In chemistry, a shell is a space occupied by the electrons or protons and neutrons in an atomic structure. The shell can be qualitatively pictured as the region of space where there is a high probability of finding the particle of interest. Similarly, the organizational shell for a group will not guarantee that every component for its formation will be established. It merely suggests that somewhere within the bounds of the

---

2. The concept of organizational shells emerged in a working session between this author and Richard Hackman. Although we both remember that the concept first appeared "on the flip-chart on the back of the door," neither of us recalls who used the term first. Hence, we agreed to jointly assume responsibility for the concept.

shell, one might expect to find certain behaviors, roles, norms, or dynamics occurring.

In computer science, a shell provides a predefined set of interactions between various aspects of the system. Typically, these predefined sets of interactions occur between the computer and the operator. Analogously in organizational settings, a shell serves the same function—it provides a predefined or expected set of interactions between various elements of the system which permits simpler and more efficient interactions. With these two concepts as background, it is now possible to examine the data in light of the concept of the shell.

The research described in part here was designed to examine the captain's behavior during the formation process of crews in their organizational setting with all the relevant contextual information in place. This preexisting context provides critical information for the forming group. Just as it was important for the reader to have some understanding of the relevant background of aviation-related authority dynamics to make sense of the findings in that area, so too is it important to recognize that all the task work described here occurs in an ongoing organizational and environmental context. The crews do not form in isolation but rather in an embedded system of intraorganizational, industry, and environmental conditions (see Fig. 3.3).

One can see from this diagram that information critical to group work can come from a variety of sources and in varying amounts. For example, the environment and industry may provide a sufficient guarantee of capability such that the organization (or lower levels) need not expand upon these. In the case of the airlines, industry-level agencies such as the FAA and the Air Line Pilots Association provide minimum certification requirements for commercial pilots. Other requirements for effective group work may be left solely to the crew, and these elements may be added at the formation or other opportunistic moments later in the crew's life. In light of this understanding of the concept of the shells, let us examine a few of the apparent anomalies in the data.

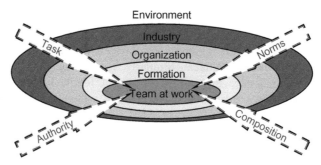

FIGURE 3.3 Organizational shells.

How is it that HI-E captains forming their crews for the first time do not spend much time at all discussing the task? In contrast, since safety would seem to be the most important factor for commercial air travel (at least from the perspective of passengers), why is it that the HI-E captains do take time to discuss safety? And how is it that even the LO-E captains produce teams that, under normal conditions, perform satisfactorily?

The answer to the first question lies in the nearly total fulfillment of task information from the shells outside of crew formation. All the individuals coming together to form the crew bring with them the knowledge, skill, and training necessary to perform the group's work. At increasingly redundant levels, the environment, the industry, and the organization test and certify these abilities. Unlike a randomly selected group of college sophomores forming to complete a novel task in a social science laboratory, all these crewmembers were highly qualified in the task requirements of a role that was designed to enable the group to work. Knowing that the outer shells have satisfied these task requirements, it would be extremely redundant for the leader to further discuss them. This is also consistent with the predictions of leader effectiveness according to path/goal theory as described by House and Mitchell (1974). In fact, when a LO-E captain spends time discussing obvious tasks, the crew begins to develop a very different picture of how life will be with him or her as their leader.

But this explanation might seem to confound expectations regarding the time spent by the leaders in explicitly discussing safety. Certainly, the outer shells contain some normative expectations concerning safe operations. And if one were to ask any individual crewmember whether safety was important, it is reasonable to assume they would answer affirmatively. Then why spend time talking about a norm everyone accepts? The answer again is found in the shells, but in a more complex and ambiguous manner. Within the various shells there are numerous normative expectations for performance, among them safety. Unfortunately, not all the norms are congruent. A specific example will help to clarify this.

Beyond the norm of safety which exists in all the shells, a highly supported norm from airline management (within the organizational shell) is fuel conservation. For a commercial carrier, fuel is typically the second highest expense, so anything that can be done to save fuel is reinforced. Thus, when takeoff delays are anticipated, captains will instruct their crews to delay starting all engines as a fuel conservation measure. This tactic has virtually no confounds with safety. But another fuel conservation technique might be to keep the airplane "as clean as possible for as long as possible." Pushing this technique to the extreme, a crew may delay extension of flaps and gear until late in the approach. The problem is that this practice might be in conflict with safety, which might prescribe an earlier and more gradual configuration for landing. By prioritizing potentially conflicting norms, the HI-E captains have clarified in advance their expectations, thus reducing ambiguity and potentially enhancing performance on the line. This will help the crew in routine operations and will be critical to effective performance in demanding or emergency situations.

Lastly, the shells for airline crews provide sufficient structure to allow them to perform at some minimal level in spite of ineffective leader behavior. It is important to note in this context that we are not considering "optimal" group performance across normal line operations, but rather "satisficing" group performance (cf. Chapter 5: Flight Crew Decision-Making). This type of minimally acceptable behavior may well be less than necessary in demanding situations where crew resource management is essential. For a more in-depth discussion of the leader's transformational behavior enhancing the safety behaviors in followers, see Barling, Loughlin, and Kelloway (2002).

It is critical to stress the importance of understanding the contribution made by the shells for the particular group under examination. This means that the particular findings from these groups should not be extrapolated directly to other groups unless their shells are similar. In these airline crews, the HI-E captains did not spend much time in the formation process dealing with the task because the task information was imported from the shells. However, in the first meetings of other groups (e.g., B-1 bomber crews on a new low-level night mission, or ad hoc task groups) it may be most appropriate for the leader to spend considerable time discussing the task to be performed, since the shells offer insufficient information about the group's impending assignment.

If we return to Hackman and Walton's (1986) normative model, which suggests that the leader can make a contribution to the group at the critical formation period by discussing the task, the boundaries, and the norms of the group, we may now be able to improve those prescriptions. First, authority dynamics must be added to the list (as noted before in Ginnett's Team Leadership Model© (Hughes et al., 2015). The leader needs to consider the preexisting (shell-provided) authority issues and modify them in the direction of group effectiveness. For airline captains, the shell structure for authority was almost exclusively in the direction of the autocratic power of the leader. While that is sometimes appropriate, it may not be the best for effective group work, and so the leader should attempt to shift authority down the continuum while maintaining a contingency approach. Second, rather than suggesting the leader spend time discussing tasks, boundaries, norms, and authority issues, it is more appropriate to say the leader should consider these issues and ensure information about them is provided in sufficient quantities for the group to get started and work effectively. The shells may provide all the necessary information for some groups and virtually none for others. In the former groups, discussion might be redundant, while in the latter case, discussion (in the absence of information) or clarification (in the event of conflicting information) may be the most important function the leader can perform at the group's formation. Which behavior is most important can only be determined by understanding the data inherent in higher levels of the shells.

3.7   IMPLICATIONS FOR EFFECTIVE CREW LEADERSHIP

From the research described here, it should be fairly obvious that the captain can make a difference. Assuming we have an organizational context that supports and sustains crew and team effectiveness, the captain has available to him or her the critical period of crew formation. This is where the captain breathes life into the shell which is filling with others who will play predefined roles. How well or how poorly the crew performs is, in large part, established in the course of the first meeting (Ginnett, 1987; Weick, 1985).

I have already detailed four specific areas in which the captain can create effective conditions for crew work. Beyond this are four more general categories which describe the captain's overall response to the shells at the group level.

3.7.1   Undermining

A captain who "undermines" actively countermands the conditions inherent in the shell that each member imports to the crew situation. These are the captains who, through their behaviors (including explicit statements), redefine in a more restrictive and unconstructive manner the tasks, boundaries, norms, and authority dynamics which will guide the crew's operations. These captains create conditions that undermine crew effectiveness. In an organization with established shells that foster effective crew work, undermining captains negate the preexisting and positive shells. Not only can they reduce and restrict positive aspects of the shell by explicitly undermining them, but their general tendency to undermine is extrapolated to other areas of the shell they do not mention. If a captain says he does not want flight attendants to get off the aircraft to talk to gate personnel without his permission, the flight engineer who overhears this may well wonder whether he or she needs the captain's specific approval to conduct a walk-around inspection of the aircraft. Worse yet, should he or she take the initiative to plan ahead for the crew's benefit or wait to see if it is "what the captain wants?" If captains go against procedures on one aspect of performance, what can they be expected to do on others? The most widespread negative effect of undermining behavior is that, like a cancer, it metastasizes throughout the organization. Unfortunately, the reduced shells that result from interaction with an undermining captain may be subsequently imported to other crews with the same potentially negative impact. If a captain can behave inappropriately (as defined by existing organizational shells) and the organization fails to correct that inappropriate behavior, the other members of the crew will doubt the validity of the shells and hence expect less of subsequent captains and crews.

3.7.2 Abdicating

Captains who "abdicate" neither confirm the preexisting shell nor deny it.

They add nothing to the shell, nor do they confirm what the environment and organization have put in place. Crews under these kinds of captains are "not sure"—they are left with whatever shell they arrived with, minus any confirmation of its current utility or appropriateness. Not only is the shell for this particular crew left unverified, but each crewmember's shell used for defining the role of "captain" is reduced because of this particular captain's performance. They leave with a "less clearly defined and potentially poorer" shell of what the organization expects of its captains. This is because it is very likely that the organization, if not the environment, has authorized the captain to clarify and even modify the shell, and this captain has failed to do that. Therefore, extrapolations regarding his or her self-imposed diminished authority in a more general sense are apt to be the result. By *abdicating*, the captain has unwittingly exhibited some of the behaviors inherent in the previous category.

3.7.3 Affirming

At a minimum for crew effectiveness, the captain should affirm the constructive task definitions, boundary conditions, norms, and authority dynamics that the environment and the organization have structured into the shell. These behaviors would not expand the shell but would help solidify the crew's understanding and acceptance of it. In effect, each crewmember arrives with a shell that has generally defined appropriate crew behaviors in the past. The "affirming" captain "fills in the existing dotted lines" so the crew can proceed with behaviors based on their imported expectations. To the extent the organization and the environment have provided a shell appropriate for crew effectiveness, the crew under an affirming captain can be expected to perform well.

3.7.4 Elaborating and Expanding

These are the behaviors of the best leaders. They appreciate and exploit the opportunity for crew effectiveness provided them at the time of crew formation. They expand the existing shell and create new ways to operate within and outside of its boundaries. These are the leaders who expand and create new opportunities for constructive interactions among crewmembers. They tend to elaborate and enlarge the boundaries of the individual roles and of the crew as a whole. They also create semipermeable boundaries for the crew (not so underbounded that the crew operates only as individuals, but not so overbounded that they exclude information or assistance available outside their group per se) which can be useful later in the conduct of work on the line. They elaborate and expand the norms regarding safety, cooperation, and communication. Under their leadership, new ways to share their authority emerge, and hence the total authority of the cockpit and cabin crews expands and becomes more effective. They create conditions which can lead to better crew performance by expanding previously defined shell structures. These behaviors also tend to enlarge each crewmember's concept of what the shell can be for an effective crew, and this improved image can be imported into the shells of subsequent crews of which they will be a member.

3.8 CONCLUSION

Prior to the first meeting of the crew, we find a collection of individuals, each with his or her own perception of the shells for crew behavior. That imported shell is only that—a shell which the captain can enhance or diminish. Captains can expand it or undermine it; they can affirm it or abdicate. But when the first meeting is over and the crew goes to work, they are some sort of a team. They may start work envisioning new and creative ways to improve team effectiveness, or they may be wondering what this crew is really going to be like. In one form or another, this new team now has its own shell, one shaped by the captain's behavior regarding the tasks, by the boundary definitions the captain described, by the transmission of implicit and explicit norms, and by the authority dynamics demonstrated by the captain. If we assume that the company believes in CRM and provides sufficient shell support for crew work, then whether the captain enhances or impedes a crew's ability to perform well is really up to him or her.

ACKNOWLEDGMENTS

The research reported here was supported by Cooperative Agreement NCC 2-324 between NASA-Ames Research Center, Yale University, and the United States Air Force Academy.

REFERENCES

Barling, J., Loughlin, C., & Kelloway, E. (2002). Development and test of a model linking safety-specific transformational leadership and occupational safety. *Journal of Applied Psychology, 87*, 488–496.

Burrows, W. E. (1982). Cockpit encounters. *Psychology Today December, 16*(11), 42–47.

Feldman, D. C. (1984). The development and enforcement of group norms. *Academy of Management Review, 9*(1), 47–53, January.

Foushee, H. C. (1984). Dyads and triads at 35,000 feet: Factors affecting group process and aircrew performance. *American Psychologist, 39*, 885–893.

Ginnett, R. C. (1987). *First encounters of the close kind: The formation process of airline flight crews. Unpublished doctoral dissertation.* New Haven, CT: Yale University.

Ginnett, R. C. (1990). Airline cockpit crews. In J. Richard Hackman (Ed.), *Groups that work.* San Francisco, CA: Jossey-Bass.

Hackman, J. R. (1976). Group influences on individuals. In M. Dunnette (Ed.), *Handbook of industrial and organizational psychology* (pp. 1455–1525). Chicago, IL: Rand McNally.

Hackman, J. R. (1987). The design of work teams. In W. Lorsch Jay (Ed.), *Handbook of organizational behavior.* Englewood Cliffs, NJ: Prentice-Hall.

Hackman, T. R., & Walton, R. E. (1986). Leading groups in organizations, Associates In P. S. Goodman (Ed.), *Designing effective work groups* (pp. 72–119). San Francisco, CA: Jossey-Bass.

Harper, C. R., Kidera, G. L., & Cullen, L. F. (1971). Study of simulated airline pilot incapacitation: Phase II, subtle or partial loss of function. *Aerospace Medicine, 42,* 946–948.

House, R. L., & Mitchell, T. R. (1974). Path-goal theory of leadership. *Contemporary Business, 3,* 81–98.

Hughes, R. L., Ginnett, R. C., & Curphy, G. J. (2015). *Leadership: Enhancing the lessons of experience* (8th ed., pp. 415–429). Boston, MA: McGraw-Hill Irwin.

Janis, I. L. (1982). *Groupthink* (2nd ed.). Boston, MA: Houghton Mifflin.

Kaplan, R. (1979). The conspicuous absence of evidence that process consultation enhances task performance. *Journal of Applied Behavioral Science, 15,* 346–360.

Kerr, N. L., & Tindale, R. S. (2004). Group performance and decision making. *Annual Review of Psychology, 55,* 623–655.

Kozlowski, S. W. J., & Bell, B. S. (2003). Work groups and teams in organizations. In W. C. Borman, & D. R. Ilgen (Eds.), *Handbook of Psychology: Industrial and Organizational Psychology.* (Vol. 12, pp. 333–375). New York: Wiley & Sons.

Langfred, C. W. (2000). The paradox of self-management: Individual and group autonomy in work groups. *Journal of Organizational Behavior, 21,* 563–585.

Latane, B., Williams, K., & Harkins, S. (1979). Social loafing. *Psychology Today, 13,* 104.

Lewin, K., Lippitt, R., & White, R. K. (1939). Patterns of aggressive behavior in experimentally created social climates. *Journal of Social Psychology, 10,* 271–301.

National Transportation Safety Board. (1979). *Aircraft Accident Report: United Airlines, Inc., McDonnell-Douglas DC-8-61, N8082U, Portland, Oregon, December 28, 1978 (NTSB-AAR-79-7).* Washington, DC: Author.

National Transportation Safety Board. (1982). *Aircraft Accident Report: Air Florida, Inc., Boeing 737-222, N62AF, Collision with 14th Street Bridge, Near Washington National Airport, Washington D.C., January 13, 1982 (NTSB-AAR-82-8).* Washington, DC: Author.

Ruffell Smith, H.P. (1979). *A simulator study of the interaction of pilot workload with errors, vigilance, and decisions (Report No. TM-78482).* NASA-Ames Research Center: Moffett Field, CA.

Schein, E. H. (1969). *Process consultation: Its role in organization development.* Reading, MA: Addison-Wesley.

Triandis, H. C. (1995). *Individualism and collectivism.* Boulder, CP: Westview Press.

Weick, K. E. (1985). Systematic observational methods. In (3rd ed.) G. Lindzev, & E. Aronson (Eds.), *Handbook of Social Psychology.* (Vol. 2). New York: Random House.

Wolfe, T. (1979). *The right stuff.* New York: Farrar, Straus, and Giroux.

Chapter 4

Communication and Crew Resource Management

Barbara G. Kanki

Retired, NASA Ames Research Center, Moffett Field, CA, United States

INTRODUCTION

Communication is a topic with many meanings and many uses because it is so fundamental to human endeavor. Whether written, verbal or nonverbal, face-to-face or remote, communication is an essential part of human behavior in the social sciences: psychology, sociology, political science, sociolinguistics, etc. In addition to traditional academics, communication is pragmatic; that is, we communicate in order to acquire what we need and to accomplish goals. Thus, we are likely to think of communication in terms of effectiveness; you are understood or misunderstood; information is transmitted or it is not; you are persuaded or unmoved. Communication skills help to determine the success or failure in attaining goals; when one's goals are linked to high stakes, communication effectiveness is essential.

There is no doubt that operating in today's airspace is a high-stakes profession since lives and costly assets are invested in every flight. As in other complex, socio-technical systems, communication plays an important role in accomplishing goals, and coordinating individuals and tasks. In this chapter, the importance of effective communication for safe and efficient flight operations supported by crew resource management (CRM) is addressed.

This chapter retains much of the structure from the 1993 and 2010 chapters as the basic concepts and history retain relevance today. However, the contents have been updated to reflect how communication as a CRM skill has evolved and how it relates to changes in the operational environment, enhanced technology aircraft and airspace systems. In addition, the communication concept is considered beyond the flight deck including cross-functional teams and the organization as a whole. Training and evaluation—particularly in the simulator—has evolved, and communication indicators are tied to specific performance objectives within flight phases and under particular

Crew Resource Management. DOI: https://doi.org/10.1016/B978-0-12-812995-1.00004-X

operational conditions. While optimized for assessing within-cockpit communication, training and evaluation for the larger "team" will require further innovations, research, and development for optimal implementation.

4.1 HISTORICAL VIEW OF COMMUNICATION AND FLIGHT SAFETY

4.1.1 NTSB Accident Reports

Many of the most dramatic and compelling demonstrations of the link between communication and flight safety come from accident investigations. Consider the example of Avianca Flight 052, a Boeing 707B from Medellin, Columbia, to John F. Kennedy International Airport (JFK), New York, which ran out of fuel over Long Island on January 25, 1990 (NTSB, 1991). Several critical failures in communication were evident; specifically, the crew failed to communicate to air traffic control (ATC) the information that they were desperately low on fuel and needed immediate clearance to land. Poor weather conditions led to the flight being held three times by ATC for a total of 1 hour and 17 minutes. Not until the third period of holding did the flight crew report that:

1. The airplane could not hold longer than 5 minutes.
2. It was running out of fuel.
3. It could not reach its alternate airport, Boston-Logan International.

Following the execution of a missed approach to JFK, the crew experienced a loss of power to all four engines and crashed approximately 16 miles from the airport.

The NTSB attributed probable cause of the accident to the failure of the flight crew to manage the airplane's fuel load adequately and their failure to communicate an emergency fuel situation to ATC before fuel had been exhausted. Additional problematic communication links included the following:

1. Pilot responsibilities and dispatch responsibilities regarding planning, fuel requirements, and flight following during international flights.
2. Pilot to controller communications regarding the terminology to be used to convey fuel status and the need for special handling.
3. ATC flow control procedures and responsibilities to accommodate aircraft with low fuel state.
4. Flight crew coordination and English language proficiency of foreign crews (NTSB, 1991, p. v).

In Fig. 4.1 critical communication links are depicted by bidirectional arrows. Although the probable cause of the accident is attributed to Link #2, at least four sets of communication/information links were called into question.

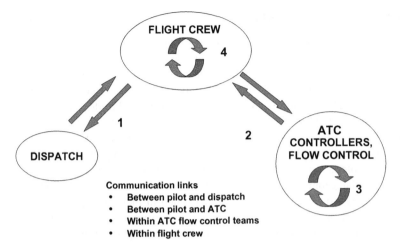

FIGURE 4.1 Critical information links in the Avianca Flight 052 accident (NTSB, 1991).

Effective communication among crewmembers has always been an essential component of the concept of crew coordination. The first NTSB mention of "flight deck resource management" was made in the report filed on the crash in 1978 in Portland, Oregon, of United Airlines Flight 173 (NTSB, 1979). The probable cause was determined to be failure of the captain to monitor aircraft fuel state, which resulted in total fuel exhaustion. Contributing causes included "the failure of the other two flight crewmembers either to fully comprehend the criticality of the fuel state or to successfully communicate their concern to the captain" (NTSB, 1979, p. 29).

Resulting from that investigation was the FAA Air Carrier Operations Bulletin Number 8430.17 (Change 11), which included instructions regarding resource management and interpersonal communications training for air carrier flight crews. This action was taken in response to one of the four recommendations made by the NTSB that focused on both participative management for captains and assertiveness training for other cockpit crewmembers. Since 1979, the NTSB has continued to consider the possible impact of CRM and crew communication in accident sequences.

NTSB investigations also acknowledge instances of exemplary CRM in their findings on the basis of communication data provided by the cockpit voice recorder (CVR). Two dramatic cases are United 811 (NTSB, 1990a) and United 232 (NTSB, 1990b), in which flight crew interactions were "indicative of the value of cockpit resource management training which has been in existence at UAL for a decade" (NTSB, 1990b, p. 76). An analysis of the CVR communications (Predmore, 1991) has identified specific communication patterns that may have contributed to the exemplary CRM (described in Section 4.2.4).

4.1.2   Incident Reports

In contrast to accident reports, incidents reports are generated and collected in far greater numbers by a variety of organizations (e.g., airlines, unions, and nationwide databases such as the NASA Aviation Safety Reporting System (ASRS), and FAA Aviation Safety Information Analysis and Sharing (ASIAS)). These reports are usually voluntarily submitted and cannot be assumed to represent an unbiased perspective on all parts of the aviation system. Nevertheless, greater frequency of particular classes of events can indicate recurrent trouble spots. The US-wide sample of reports tells us whether these problems occur across the aviation system or whether they are specific to particular geographic regions, weather conditions, airports, airspace, etc.

Because voice recordings are not included in incident reports, the role of communication is not directly observed. For example, an incident classified as a "workload management" problem may be, in part, brought about by an ineffective communication style but not recognized as such by the individual reporter. However, incident data, due to a large database, can accommodate more generalizable analyses. For instance, Billings and Cheaney (1981) analyzed transfer of information problems in the aviation system and found that over 70% of 28,000 reports submitted by pilots and air traffic controllers (during 1976–81) fell in this category. Reports focused on pilot/controller interactions and controller to controller communications more often than within-cockpit communications.

> Close examination of ASRS reports led to the finding that information transfer problems…did not ordinarily result from an unavailability of information nor because the information was incorrect at its source…Instead, the most common findings showed that information was not transferred because (1) the person who had the information did not think it necessary to transfer it or (2) that the information was transferred, but inaccurately.
>
> Billings and Cheaney (1981, p. 2).

Thus, incident reports can be extremely useful for identifying more widespread problem areas in the aviation system. Communication problems involve a variety of individual failures (e.g., distraction, failure to monitor, complacency) as well as system factors (e.g., radio frequency saturation, high workload) that interfere with successful information transfer (see Billings & Cheaney, 1981, p. 86). The identification of such behaviors and system factors not only informs the operational community but assists system designers and researchers by pointing out areas of risk. For instance, how are communications affected in an automated environment or in conjunction with visual displays with aural alerts? How do information transfer problems surface under conditions of work overload, ambiguous data, or failing equipment?

Based on reports to ASRS, it is concluded that information transfer problems are responsible for many potentially serious human errors in aviation operations. Voice communications, in particular, are a pervasive problem. Technological solutions exist for many problems related to information transfer. These solutions, however, may give rise to serious new problems unless they are implemented with an understanding of the capabilities and limitations of the humans who operate the aviation system.

Billings and Reynard (1981, p. 13).

4.1.3 Early Communication Research

Early analyses of aircrew communication used three different data sources:

1. accident transcripts from the CVR;
2. real-time field observations; and
3. full-mission simulations.

Each of these sources provided different types of data; therefore they required different analysis methods.

Accident Cockpit Voice Recorder Transcripts

Outside the realm of official investigations, one of the first systematic analyses of communications from CVR data was performed by Goguen, Linde, and Murphy (1986). Hypotheses grew out of the recognition that assertiveness training may be needed for junior crewmembers, as recommended by the NTSB (NTSB, 1979). In order to study crewmember assertiveness, a classification scheme was devised to distinguish levels of mitigation (i.e., direct communication vs softened communication), and included speech types such as planning, explanation, and command and control. For example, a command stated in the imperative form is less mitigated than a suggestion which is often spoken as a question. In order to consider whether captains were engaging crewmember participation, levels of mitigation were compared across positions, captain versus first officer (FO), or second officer. Results, based on eight transcripts and 1725 speech acts, included the following:

1. Subordinate crewmembers were characterized by a more mitigated (softened) style of making requests.
2. Mitigated speech was associated with subsequent changes of topic and ungratified commands, indicating that mitigated communications were less successful.
3. Requests were less mitigated during conditions of recognized emergencies or problems.

While mitigated requests appeared to be less effective at eliciting a response in general, this speech pattern usually occurred during less critical phases of flight. In contrast, requests were less mitigated (hence more effective) during times when there were recognized problems. In short, the use of mitigated speech did not seem to be a simple or general practice. Rather, mitigated communications seemed to be serving different purposes during different flight conditions. For example, the use of suggestions rather than commands during a predeparture briefing may be a means of encouraging crewmember participation even though it may be an ineffective strategy during a critical phase.

Field Studies

Field studies have the advantage of having uncompromised face validity; that is, there is no question that the behaviors observed are relevant to operations. While observations may be limited to what can be documented in real time and may represent mostly routine conditions, observations during actual operations can be an effective way to identify problem areas, generate hypotheses, and understand the operational context in which the actions of interest take place.

Field studies can go beyond mere observations. Costley, Johnson, and Lawson (1989) were among the first to develop a real-time communication coding system for making systematic observations during flight. They investigated communication differences across aircraft types—B737-200, B737-300, and B757—which represented three levels of aircraft automation. The coding system included speech categories such as commanding, reacting, information processing, giving explanation, checking, summarizing, asides (jokes, quips), and questioning. From ten observation flights, two main communication differences were included:

1. Lower communication rates in more automated aircraft (B737-200 vs B757) with no accompanying decrease in operational actions.
2. Of the categories of speech affected, less questioning in more automated aircraft was the primary difference.

While these data are suggestive of potential problem areas, the differences in communication were not linked to observed differences in performance.

In general, if performance differences are not found to be linked to differences in communication patterns, we can assume they may be differences of lesser consequence. However, if (as discussed by Costley et al.) communication differences are linked to performance decrements under specified operational conditions, there could be serious implications for communication training and interventions. For instance, the results of this field work could be further tested by additional field work or in a flight simulator where some of the uncontrolled variables could be systematically manipulated or held constant.

Simulation Studies

Analyses of accident transcripts and field research began to shed light on the role of communication in crew performance and flight safety. But high-fidelity full-mission simulation research introduced a compelling dimension to assessing crew performance. Because flight scenarios and conditions could be controlled and variables manipulated, flight crew performance could be measured with more statistical rigor. Unlike any previous source of communication data, the entire flight performance (including prepushback and post-touchdown) could be videotaped. With this new opportunity to investigate the relationship of communications to performance differences, full-mission simulation became a unique and powerful tool for communication researchers.

The Ruffell Smith (1979) simulation at NASA Ames Research Center was a landmark study. In addition to demonstrating the yet untapped potential of high-fidelity, full-mission simulators for research and training purposes, it confirmed what instructors, practitioners, and accident investigators already knew. Technical skills alone were not enough to guarantee effective crew performance. More important, it proved that specific CRM behaviors, such as crew communication, and timely coordination could be clearly identified and characterized.

Foushee and Manos (1981) expanded the Ruffell Smith study by analyzing the communication behaviors. The methodology included:

1. a systematic "speech act" coding of verbatim transcribed speech;
2. an exploration of communication patterns that reliably related to differences in crew performance;
3. a test of specific effects of crew factors; and
4. control for operational conditions (e.g., normal vs abnormal operations) that could influence the use of particular speech patterns.

The overall objective was to identify specific communication patterns associated with effective CRM outcomes so that training of best practices could be developed.

While simulation methodology clearly offered the most research control and ability to investigate specific hypotheses, field studies and analyses from CVR data continued to contribute to identifying issues and specific research questions. Regardless of the research method, it was useful to fit these research questions into a conceptual framework that described the relationships among the variables and outcomes of interest.

4.1.4 The Communication Concept

The relationship between communication patterns and practices with crew performance constitutes two parts of a three-part conceptual model of factors affecting group performance. This model, derived from McGrath's (1984) theoretical framework of input, process, and output variables, was altered to fit the aircrew work environment. See Chapter 1, Why CRM? Empirical and Theoretical Bases of Human Factors Training, for a discussion of the models depicted in Figs. 1.2 and 1.3.

To briefly review the model, input variables refer to a wide range of factors: attributes of individuals, characteristics of the group itself, and factors related to the physical environment including specific task elements that define the workplace. *Individual-level input factors* include any aspect of a group member that could conceivably affect that person's ability to be an effective crewmember, such as flying skills, personality, motivation, physiological state, and interpersonal skills. *Group-level factors* are aspects of the group as a whole: structure, size, collection of skills, etc. Clearly, flight crews are relatively standardized since there are many individual requirements (pilot certification standards) as well as requirements demanded by the aircraft type and task that should ensure a common level of competency. *Environmental input factors* are focused on characteristics of the operating work environment; aspects of the task, level of difficulty and stress involved, design factors such as flight deck configuration including displays and specialized equipment. External environmental factors such as weather and aircraft conditions also fall in this category. It is in this area that we find research examining the effects of automation on performance and crew communication (Wiener et al., 1991; Wiener, 1989). The importance of this area since 1993 has grown exponentially and will continue to do so in the future. In the current era of next generation initiatives, new technologies (data communications, electronic flight bag, advanced navigation aids) as well as procedural changes to match new ATC technologies and procedures make this "input" area very relevant and dynamic.

Outcome variables shown in Fig. 1.2 refer to the individual, organizational, mission, and crew performance outcomes such as safety and efficiency, but the most salient output concern is the relative success or failure of a group to achieve the mission and crew performance objectives. Performance errors and crew ratings have typically been the chief outcome measures in communication research.

Group process variables represent mediators between inputs and outcomes; they refer to the means by which crews achieve specific performance outcomes. As shown in Fig. 1.3, these processes are affected by the various inputs that feed into it. Communication processes are of central importance to the group activities that rely on verbal exchanges and information transfer. In addition, communication is often the behavioral indicator of other CRM functions such as decision-making, problem-solving, resource and workload management. While a more traditional research paradigm focuses on the relationship between input and output (performance variables), there is growing recognition of the importance of group processes as intermediate predictors of group success (Foushee & Manos, 1981; Foushee, Lauber, Baetge, & Acomb, 1986; Kanki, Lozito, & Foushee, 1989). Group process variables are behavioral sequences that describe the interactions of group members. They include communication patterns as well as other resource management strategies.

This level of specificity is important for training because it demonstrates what constitutes effective communication practices and allows specific communication sequences to be identified and evaluated.

Process variables have also been directly associated with performance as predictors of outcomes, independent of input variables. For example, Foushee et al. (1986) demonstrated that patterns of communication among air transport crews who had recently flown together were more clearly associated with higher levels of performance than the patterns of crews who were flying together for the first time. These have been further investigated and described in research by Kanki and Foushee (1989) and Kanki et al. (1989; Kanki, Greaud, & Irwin, 1991a) which indicates that crews that share similar communication patterns appear to perform better as a team. Thus, group process analyses have shown that communication patterns can be associated with performance differences.

Communication analyses involve exploring relationships between group processes and both input and output variables. Although the overall direction of influence in the model (Fig. 1.2) flows from left to right (i.e., culminating in outcome), it must be noted that group processes are dynamic and change over time. The model also contains continual feedback loops because performance outcomes can and do reflect back onto ongoing group processes. How a crew prepares and communicates during preflight affects takeoff and departure phases just as planning and preparing during cruise can greatly affect the arrival and landing phases. Consequently, crews that plan ahead may never experience high workload, therefore they may never need to invoke workload management strategies. In contrast, crews that "get behind the aircraft" may have to redouble their efforts in order to "get everyone back in the loop." An early outcome of a well-organized contingency plan may lead to a relatively "quiet" cockpit with respect to communication, while an early outcome of ill-timed preparation may lead to a flurry of communications needed to reprioritize tasks, solve problems, and manage workload in a compressed time period. The final performance outcome, however, may be similar for both crews if the latter crew is able to catch up.

In addition to the normal interdependence of actions that flow from one flight phase to the next, the dynamic nature of group process and communication arises from the changing state of the aircraft and conditions affecting flight. Even with highly routine forms of communication such as checklists and briefings, other aspects of the operational environment (aircraft malfunction, weather, traffic) may create the need for immediate changes in communication content and form. When it does not, there can be a marked lack of leadership or information exchange. Kanki and Smith (2001) describe the nearly complete lack of communications from the Air Florida Flight 90 accident:

> When Air Florida Flight 90 (NTSB, 1982) crashed into Washington DC's Fourteenth Street Bridge, it was in a full stall, yet both pilots, qualified in stall recovery procedures since primary flight training, failed to verbalize any-thing...that would have triggered an automatic stall recovery response, that is, applying full power. Instead, the inadequate communication that did occur...was more an acceptance of fate than a last-ditch effort to correct the problem. (p. 114)

In contrast to the Air Florida crew, who either did not recognize a problem or who did not communicate an emergency response, is the case where a crewmember actively shuts down the communication. From an ASRS report, a FO attempted to assist an extremely "negative" captain by reminding him of the correct speed, heading, and altitude during an approach into Chicago O'Hare. The captain's response, "You just look out the damn window," is a good example of a situation in which authoritarian control was excessive, inappropriate, and unsafe (Foushee & Manos, 1981, p. 70).

In summary, the communication concept is one that describes a dynamic process in which communication is a primary means by which individuals develop and coordinate activities in order to achieve goals. Variations in communication patterns are useful indicators of effective crew solutions as well as crew problems. In any case, communications must be interpreted within a task, operational environment, and interpersonal context which change dramatically over time, sometimes in expected, routine ways and occasionally, in unexpected and startling ways.

As both a skill and a tool for achieving objectives, communication patterns and practices can be linked to crew performance outcomes and CRM. However, some differences can be considered simple individual styles or even cultural differences that do not affect crew performance at all. How do we decide what communication patterns are important to crew performance and which are not? The answer can be found in the key functions that communication serves.

4.2 FUNCTIONS OF COMMUNICATION

The philosopher John L. Austin in an entertaining book called *How to Do Things with Words* (1962) described how words can be "used" in much the same way bricks and boards are used to build things. Austin discussed the ability of language not only to "say" things but to "do" things as well. For instance, saying "I promise to do X" means you have actually "made a promise" (as long as you were sincere and understood what you were saying). Speech not only accompanies actions but is action itself.

Because communication serves so many functions, it provides an effective index of crew performance. By listening to the communications during a flight, we get many indicators of whether tasks are being performed according to normal procedures or whether problems are occurring. When problems do occur, we can tell if they are handled in a timely way or if the crew is falling behind the curve. With respect to CRM, we outlined five functions in the 1993 chapter which are only slightly paraphrased below. Although these might have been categorized a little differently, these five are still among the most significant ways that communication affects crew performance. In some cases, it is the actual communication content that is most important; in other cases, communication is a tool for achieving CRM objectives:

1. Communication conveys information.
2. Communication establishes interpersonal/team relationships.
3. Communication establishes predictable behavior and expectations.
4. Communication maintains attention to task and situational awareness.
5. Communication is a management tool.

Although each of these communication functions can be studied as a topic in its own right, in reality, most communications fulfill several functions at the same time. For example, if the captain makes it a point to bring flight and cabin crews together for a predeparture briefing, his or her communications serve several functions simultaneously. They provide operational information relevant to the flight; they allow the captain to establish a leadership relationship with the rest of the crew, and, finally, they help to establish predictability, because the crewmembers now know something about the captain's management style and expectations. Even if the captain said something as simple as "we'll follow standard operating procedures (SOP)," this assures crewmembers that company protocol will be expected and should be followed.

In communication research, any one of these functions may be investigated directly, or, as in most accident investigations, all functions may be considered in one analysis. To return to the Avianca Flight 052 example, four of the five functions are illustrated in the safety issues raised:

1. The communications between pilots and dispatch point to a failure on the part of the pilots to manage or effectively utilize their resources from dispatch.
2. The communications between pilots failed in terms of situation awareness and monitoring.
3. The communications between pilots and ATC illustrate the failure to transfer information, namely, their "emergency" status.
4. The communication exchanges exemplify a lack of predictable behavior patterns, since the language difference between pilots and controllers failed to provide the usual redundancy of information (via intonation and other paralinguistic cues) pertaining to emergency states.

TABLE 4.1 Communication Functions and Some of Their Associated Problems

Communication Functions	Related Problems
Communication provides information	Lack of information, incomplete or inaccurate information
Communication establishes team relationships	Interpersonal strain, ambiguity, lack of leadership or role clarity
Communication establishes predictable behaviors (SOPs and best practices)	Nonstandard, unpredictable behavior
Communication maintains attention to task and monitoring (situational awareness)	Lose of vigilance, monitoring, situational awareness
Communication is a management tool: resources, time, workload	Lack of or misdirected management of task, time, resources, workload

Since communications are typically multifunctional, any given flight may be analyzed on any or all of these dimensions. However, each of the five communication functions above is typically associated with a subset of potential problems that can result in crew performance decrement (see Table 4.1). The next five sections discuss each of the communication functions and their associated problems. There will be overlap across topics, but each function is critical to key CRM elements.

4.2.1 Information Transfer

The traditional view of communication highlights the information transfer function of language. In the cockpit, there are numerous information sources used in flight including: crewmembers, ATC, company, manuals, maintenance log, checklists, etc. In addition, information is obtained from aircraft instruments, light indicators, aural alerts, and from the outside world (e.g., weather, other aircraft and airport conditions). Information (often communicated in numerical form) is often safety critical and therefore required to be discussed and implemented in a predefined standardized manner (e.g., briefings and checklists). SOPs not only specify when information must be obtained and acted upon, but often include a verification component as well (e.g., cross-check, or readback).

However, when operations are normal and repetitive, the information exchange can easily slip into rote recitation. Even when the actual words are "correct," the timing, intonation, and attention may influence whether the communication is actually successful. There are critical differences between simply repeating a statement versus verifying the statement versus questioning the statement. Take the following statement as an example: "This reads in the normal range." If the statement was repeated by FO with a questioning intonation, it may be that FO did not hear the captain. If it was said with the same rising intonation by the FO but it was not a simple repetition, it may have been the case that the FO was questioning whether the reading was "normal." If the FO made the statement after the captain read an instrument, it may have been a verification of the captain's reading. In short, intonation and other contextual features contribute to the intention and interpretation of a statement.

Information transfer is crucial in problem-solving situations because the resolution of the problem relies on gathering and communicating pertinent information. The types of speech acts that become salient in problem-solving include statements that: (1) recognize problems; (2) state goals and subgoals; (3) plan and strategize; (4) gather information; (5) alert and predict; and (6) explain (see Orasanu, 1990). Based on the communications from previous simulation studies (Chidester, Kanki, Foushee, Dickinson, & Bowles, 1990; Foushee et al., 1986), these categories of problem-solving talk were compared across normal and abnormal phases of flight for high-performing crews versus low-performing crews.

Highlighting the information function of communication, it is not simply gathering task-relevant information that ensures good performance, but also the patterning of these communications that is critical. In Orasanu's (1990) study, better performing teams generated communication patterns showing problem-solving talk during low-workload phases and increased interchanges of planning and strategy formation. Poorer teams failed to engage in planning communication during low-workload periods. Thus, when workload became high, the information gathering increased but was not as effective.

Each scenario and specific problem generates its own list of pertinent information and speech categories that are tied directly to these points. For example, in the analysis of expert decision-making strategies, Mosier (1991) developed an information transfer matrix containing "items evaluated as important to making the critical decisions of each flight segment, as well as the checklists and procedures associated with the abnormalities of that scenario...Information solicitation and transfer were coded on the matrices beginning with the onset of the abnormal situation" (p. 268). The general strategy was (1) to consider how correctly and completely the communication data from each flight crew filled out the matrix and (2) to assess whether performance and correctness of decision outcomes were related to this measure of situation assessment.

Both studies are good examples of how communications serve an informational function to problem-solving and decision-making. Communication analyses help to delineate what information is critical, when it should be solicited, the best way in which it should be integrated, who the possessors of information are, and whether specific patterns can be linked to more or less effective performance outcomes.

Moving beyond the cockpit, every flight has numerous information transfer events between pilots and ATC that are still conducted voice-to-voice on specified radio frequencies. While most of these communications are routine, errors are made both in speaking and hearing, which requires the process to be augmented by a verification step (readback or hearback). As mentioned in the ASRS incident research, information transfer has been a problem area for many years. A 2009 Safety Publication focuses on continuing pilot/ATC communication problems involving (1) false anticipation of ATC calls based on expectations, (2) language problems, and (3) call sign confusion (NASA, 2009).

4.2.2 Interpersonal/Team Relationships

Communication serves a social function when it helps to form team relationships and creates a work atmosphere that affects how crews perform their duties. This is one reason why the prebriefing of the captain to crew is so important. As discussed in Chapter 3, Crews as Groups: Their Formation and Their Leadership, part of the leadership role is to establish the social climate in which crewmembers are encouraged and expected to provide and receive information. In Ginnett's field study of team building (1987) many of the leadership attributes suggested the types of speech acts that would distinguish effective leaders. For example, effective leaders:

- Explicitly affirm or elaborate on the rules, norms, task boundaries that constitute the normative model of the organizational task environment.
- Establish clear authority dynamics, as well as their own technical, social, and managerial competence during team creation prior to flight.

These findings help to clarify the types of communications that enable effective leadership as well as when these communications are likely to occur.

Personality of crewmembers also seems like an obvious determinant of interpersonal relationships. For example, several lines of research investigated the links between personality and performance (Chidester et al., 1990; Chidester, 1990; Helmreich & Wilhelm, 1989), and between personality and communication (Kanki, Palmer, & Veinott, 1991b). Summarizing some of the findings from the Chidester et al. (1990) simulation study of "leader personality" there were found to be three personality groups of captains.[1] The first group consisted of *positive, instrumental skill/expressive* (IE +) captains who were highly motivated, goal-oriented achievers and who were also

---

1. Personality type was determined by a battery of instruments including the Expanded Personal Attributes Questionnaire (Spence, Helmreich, & Holahan, 1979), the Work and Family Orientation Questionnaire (Spence & Helmreich, 1978), and the Revised Jenkins Activity Survey C.

concerned with the interpersonal aspects of crew performance. The second group of *negative instrumental* (I-) captains were also high on goal achievement, but had little regard for interpersonal issues. The third group consisted of *negative expressive* (Ec-) captains who had lower motivation for achieving goals and toward enhancing interpersonal relationships with other crewmembers. Results showed that the lower-performing crews were led by the Ec- captains whereas the higher performing crews were led by the IE + and I- captains. It was somewhat surprising that I- captains (the "authoritarian" captain) would show no decrement in crew performance since they had the potential to shut down communication. On the other hand, these captains were probably quite clear about their role, unlike the Ec- captains who, in essence, abdicated their leadership role.

Kanki et al. (1991b) investigated the links between the three captain personality types and communication patterns. This analysis involved 12 three-person crews grouped by captain personality type. In spite of a small number of crews, the findings suggested that the negative expressive (Ec −) captains initiated communication proportionately less than the other captains. Specifically, they provided fewer observations and questions while their FOs asked more questions possibly compensating for an information deficit. Positive instrumental (IE +) captains initiated speech marginally more than their crews but did not dominate in terms of overall speech ratios.

The research on communication and personality was interesting with respect to leadership, or lack of it. But of most importance was the ability to characterize poorer performance or lack of leadership in terms of communication patterns since changing one's personality or affecting airline hiring practices was rarely feasible. However, one could develop good policies, procedures or practices involving requesting and providing information.

4.2.3   Predictable Behavior

Effective team performance in complex task environments requires team members to integrate their activities in an organized, timely fashion and to make their actions and intentions known to others. Some tasks are completed simultaneously (CA and FO predeparture flows), some tasks in sequence (performing the steps in emergency procedures), but all need to be completed at the appropriate times. For example, entering descent phase requires a sequence of tasks performed by pilot flying and pilot monitoring that allows changes to aircraft configuration, altitude, speed, and course to be accomplished in a timely but controlled manner.

Coordination of tasks among crewmembers is facilitated by the fact that pilots share knowledge and skills to a great extent. SOPs extend the shared knowledge base by setting up expectations about who is doing what and when. To the extent that both pilots have the same cognitive or mental representation regarding the general state of the aircraft (i.e., location, course, altitude, flaps configuration, etc.), the simultaneous or sequential coordination of tasks can be smooth and predictable. Using SOPs frees busy crewmembers from having to spend valuable time searching for and validating routine information and is designed to allocate workload in an effective way.

Communication is an important way to accomplish SOPs. In checklists, for example, communication specifies what tasks need to be done, who should do them, in what order, and when they should be completed (see Degani & Wiener, 1990). SOPs may also arise out of company policies that become conventionalized ways of performing tasks and/or communicating. For example, the task of operating radios during flight typically falls to the pilot monitoring. The pilot flying can then assume that all incoming and outgoing communications are being dealt with and that the pilot monitoring can relay the relevant information upon request.

From a communication perspective, conventionalized patterns of information exchange serve a similar purpose, that is, to create expectations about how and when information is available. When information is made available in a predictable way, more efficient understanding and utilization of that information is possible. For example, the use of standard statements like "positive rate, gear up" makes accurate information transfer easier. Even if only part of the phrase is heard in a noisy cockpit, pilots will know what is being communicated and can act accordingly. The notion of conventionalized communication patterns also refers to the standardized exchanges between pilot roles. For example, captains may be expected to issue more commands than FOs, and FOs may be expected to use more acknowledgments of communications (e.g., commands) than do captains. Other less obvious patterns (best practices) may distinguish high-performance crews from less effective crews.

In a study of communication processes and crew familiarity, Foushee et al. (1986) conducted a full-mission simulation study and found that crews that flew the simulator immediately after completing a trip together (postduty condition) performed better than crews that had the benefit of rest before the simulation but had not flown together (preduty condition).[2] Expanding on these findings, postduty crews, in general, used more statements of intent to perform actions, more acknowledgments of others' communications and a greater amount of communications overall. Interestingly, FOs in postduty crews expressed more disagreements with captains than FOs in preduty crews.

It has been suggested (Foushee et al., 1986; Kanki & Foushee, 1989) that the time spent flying together before the simulation increased the ability of crewmembers to anticipate each others' actions and understand the style and

---

2. The study was originally investigating the effect of fatigue on aircrew performance. But when the "rested" crews (preduty condition) performed less well compared to the "fatigued" crews (postduty), the results of which were counterintuitive (fatigued crews flew better than rested crews), the data were reanalyzed focusing on the preduty vs. postduty factor.

content of their communication. Postduty crews therefore could adopt a more informed or "familiar" style in which FOs might be more willing to initiate directives or question captains' decisions. Furthermore, while there may have been stronger flow of "bottom-up" communication (i.e., from FO to captain), the authority structure was not impaired (captains still issued more commands than FOs).

Taking a different approach with these data, Kanki et al. (1989, 1991a) have shown that similarity of communication patterns may be a distinguishing feature of high-performance crews. This research has attempted to demonstrate that high-performance crews (regardless of whether or not they had flown together) share similar communication patterns, while lower-performing crews show dissimilar patterns. For example, consistent with the earlier findings (Foushee et al., 1986) in four of five best-performing crews, captains and FOs generated essentially the same proportions of speech types (commands, questions, acknowledgments, etc.). The five lower-performing crews used in these analyses showed no consistent pattern of speech types. These analyses suggest that high-performance crews share similar patterns of communication. Thus, regardless of amount of time spent flying together, high-performance crews appear to have very quickly reached levels of efficient information transfer and crew coordination, perhaps because their communications followed a more predictable form.

4.2.4 Task Monitoring and Situation Awareness

It should be obvious by now that many of the communication functions overlap. For instance, problem-solving and decision-making require situation assessment and the planned sequential acquisition of pertinent information. Furthermore, CRM principles that underlie good management and leadership skills are linked to achieving team situational awareness and effective distribution of workload across crewmembers. However, safe operations depend on maintaining vigilance during normal and nonnormal operations alike; from extremely low workload to extremely high workload. From a communication standpoint, we are interested in what kinds of communication patterns contribute to maintaining attention to tasks, effective monitoring and situation awareness under any of these various conditions.

NTSB investigations have singled out several instances of exemplary CRM behaviors in the face of extreme emergency. United Flight 811 (NTSB, 1990a) and United Flight 232 (NTSB, 1990b) were two such flights. In both cases the captain cited training in CRM as contributing significantly to the overall effectiveness of the crews. With these characterizations in hand, an analysis of the verbal behavior of each crew was undertaken to explore how catastrophic events impacted the dynamics of crew interaction, and how CRM principles contributed to successful crew performance under stressful, emergency conditions (Predmore, 1991).

Similar to other studies, the verbatim transcripts from the CVR were broken into units of analysis classified by speaker, target (of the communication), time of onset and speech type. Categories of speech acts included:

1. command-advocacy;
2. incomplete-interrupted;
3. reply-acknowledgment;
4. observation; and
5. inquiry.

Larger units of speech called action decision sequences (ADSs, roughly representing topics or types of operational subtasks) were then delineated. These included: (1) flight control; (2) damage assessment; (3) problem solution; (4) landing; (5) emergency preparations; and (6) social.

Once all speech was categorized, the distribution of communication units was graphically presented on timelines. For example, a graph depicting speech act categories is shown in Fig. 1.10. Timelines were constructed that depicted ADS units broken down by crewmembers (captain, FO, flight engineer, check airman). These graphs show that the distribution of topics or attention shifts drastically over time. As one would expect, some topics (such as social) completely drop out because other ADSs, such as flight control and landing, are now assigned high priority. This form of analysis allows us to see where problem solution and damage assessment fall in the timeline and how they gained attention without loss of attention to other ADSs. While we already know something about effective communication patterns related to problem-solving (see prior discussion on information transfer), these patterns show how multiple tasks are distributed and monitored over time. As stated by Predmore (1991), "The interactions of the crew of United Flight 232 were marked by an efficient distribution of communications across multiple tasks and crewmembers, the maximum utilization of a fourth crewmember, the explicit prioritizing of task focus, and the active involvement of the Captain in all tasks throughout the scenario" (p. 355). In addition to pointing to the information transfer, team relationships, and crew and workload management functions of the communications, these analyses provide graphical descriptions of how and when effective task monitoring is achieved under the most demanding emergency conditions.

4.2.5 Crew and Workload Management

To many, the management function of communication is at the heart of CRM (e.g., management of resources, time, crew, and workload). Consider the following characteristics of a hypothetical crew:

1. The interpersonal atmosphere of the cockpit is conducive to a good working relationship among crewmembers.

2. Standard procedures and crewmember expectations are known and reliable.
3. Information is available and accessible.
4. Crewmembers are in the loop and ahead of the airplane (i.e., situationally aware).

In short, we have a "CRM-ready" crew. All that is lacking is the actual implementation of the plans, problem solutions, decisions, etc. that constitutes "CRM in action." To state it sequentially, crews "form, storm, and norm" and are now ready to "perform" (see Ginnett, 1987; Tuckman, 1965). To enable performance a manager must lead, distribute tasks, oversee and monitor the whole process. Enter the captain who holds command authority and ultimate responsibility.

But captain leadership is only half of the equation. The other side of leadership is followership. There is a strong implication that all crewmembers participate to some extent in the management function, since each is a player who contributes to the coordination of the crew as a team. Consider a multiple team environment such as the C-5 military transport (pre C-5A/B/C/M), in which there are several levels of "teams." The entire flight crew, led by the aircraft commander (AC), consists of pilots, at least two flight engineers, and as many loadmasters as are needed to carry out the mission. The crew is also composed of three operational subteams, each of which has its own leader, namely the AC, the primary engineer and the primary loadmaster who oversee each work group. There are many periods when these subteams work autonomously, while at other times the team is called together into a single unit led by the AC. For instance, before takeoff and on approach, the AC makes a "crew report call to stations," which assemble the team as one.

Even within a two-person cockpit, there are continual shifts between times when both pilots are working together and when each is working alone (e.g., one is flying the airplane and the other is communicating with ATC). Each of these team combinations consists of some predetermination of roles and tasks. One can even characterize the pilot/ATC relationship as a "team" and discuss the predetermined roles and tasks implicit in the meaning and significance of their communications.

Whether the actions taking place are produced by a single team unit or by subteams working in parallel, they must fit into a single flow. It is to this end that communication takes a management function, coordinating the crew's actions. We typically think of directive speech acts as commands and suggestions, but this does not imply that managers/leaders necessarily accomplish their tasks by dictating crew actions in an authoritarian way. In fact, recalling the results of Orasanu's (1990) work, directive speech during abnormal operations will not promote smooth crew coordination if the proper groundwork (e.g., planning and sharing of information) has not already been

TABLE 4.2 Typology of Management Strategies

	Aircraft	Environment	People[a]
Planning	Studying approach procedures	Planning routes	Prioritizing tasks
Acting	Following glideslope	Implementing routes	Assigning tasks
Evaluating/ monitoring	Assessing pitch of aircraft	Reporting a navigational fix reached	Evaluating crew experience with task

[a]*Cells in the People column represent the management of crew resources, task management, and workload distribution.*

accomplished. The good manager knows when to take the control and when to let the crew do their jobs; when to direct and when to monitor.

Other studies have looked directly at management functions. For example, Conley, Cano, and Bryant (1991) analysis of communication takes a task management perspective and all communications were coded into a 3×3 matrix that differentiated aspects of crew coordination during flight (i.e., planning, acting, and evaluating/monitoring) by content domain (i.e., aircraft, environment, and people). In the Conley, Cano, Bryant, Kanki, and Chidester (1990) study, this matrix was used to classify the management strategies shown in Table 4.2. Task management from the CRM perspective is best represented by the three coordination techniques under the "people" content domain. Note that commands probably fall most often in the "action" cell of the matrix, while planning and evaluating cells may contain any variety of speech acts.

Managing crew resources in the modern airspace system is a complex task which may involve coordinating teams within teams and tasks within tasks, both within the aircraft and with others in the system. The ability to manage communication must be cultivated, for it is through good communication skills that effective crews invite the participation and contributions of a diverse group of team members, direct and integrate a complex flow of tasks, and monitor a dynamic operation that may require changes at any moment.

4.3   ISSUES AND ADVANCES IN COMMUNICATION

4.3.1   Communication Research

A primary issue in the discussion of CRM research is the degree to which results generalize to the "real world." A first limitation is imposed by *research approach.* For example, field research in which a study is conducted during operations has face validity that is hard to match by other methods. However, field studies often require spending many hours traveling with flight crews and this may limit the number of crews that can be reasonably sampled. In addition, a researcher has limited control over the environmental or operational conditions and therefore cannot easily control factors of interest. On the other hand, laboratory studies often lack the operational realism to confidently generalize findings to the real world, even if the conditions are carefully controlled and the data are reliable. Full-mission simulation offers an excellent compromise, providing enough control to develop operationally realistic scenarios with experimental conditions. The benefits of full-mission simulation for research are even greater in the realm of training and evaluation.

The high-fidelity full-mission simulation paradigm introduced by Ruffell Smith (1979) not only represented a methodological breakthrough for CRM researchers but was a useful vehicle for conducting CRM research that would advance the training potential. However, it is important to keep in mind that even in the best full-mission simulation, choices have been made by researchers based on *research focus.* These choices result in the selection of particular conditions and scenario manipulations that best fit the research question. At the same time these choices limit the findings to a reduced set of real-world operations. For example, specific kinds of problems are built into scenarios to create opportunities to observe pilots' decision-making and crew coordination skills. But every scenario is necessarily bound to the particular conditions and problems incorporated, thus excluding many other variations. Care must be taken to qualify the conclusions made on the basis of a single full-mission study, or a single scenario.

Finally, *problem focus* is constrained by simulation limitations. For example, from a CRM perspective, we often concentrate on communications within the flight deck and do not look deeply at the pilot/ATC linkages even though they have been shown to be crucial in accident and incident reports. A study of pilot/controller collaboration (Morrow, Lee, & Rodvold, 1991) found that procedural deviations were more likely to have been made by pilots when ATC economized their workload by composing longer messages. In addition, procedural deviations were also associated with nonroutine transactions (e.g., clarifications, interruptions/repeats, corrections, etc.). The results pointing to these potential pilot/ATC tradeoffs suggest that (1) studies of pilot communication and workload may be defining the problem space too narrowly and should consider that both pilot and controller performances are affected by their negotiations, and (2) there may be important training implications for both pilots and controllers when their communications are directly assessed. This is not to imply that all studies must incorporate pilot/ATC processes, but care must be taken to qualify conclusions made on the basis of studies that omit certain aspects of flight operations.

For example, while there is mention of ATC and company, these functions are not usually incorporated into line operational simulation (LOS) in a realistic way (Burki-Cohen, Kendra, Kanki, & Lee, 2000). When Lee (2001) conducted a simulator study in which crews given realistic radio communications (RRC) (including simulated ATC, dispatch, and frequency chatter) were compared to nonrealistic radio communication crews, the average time to execute a go-around more than doubled for the RRC crews. In short, RRCs actually require much more time due to increased captain coordination with FO and FO with ATC.

4.3.2 Communication and Investigation

Widespread use of communication analysis in both aviation and space event investigation makes use of verbal recordings and transcripts. Investigators have always used the CVR data to help understand the events and circumstances surrounding an accident, but with the awareness and acceptance of CRM concepts, investigators began to adopt systematic methods of analyzing CVR transcripts and focus on CRM behaviors as a part of the more general consideration of human performance. It is now common in many countries to see a systematic analysis of communication from the CVR and a consideration of CRM behaviors (see Chapter 18). Such analyses have also been applied to space operations (Kanki, 1995; NTSB, 1993).

Communication analysis methodologies have incorporated some of the communication principles mentioned earlier in this chapter; for example, critical functions that communication serves. An obvious example is the use of communication protocols especially in radio communications and the use of verbal SOPs such as checklists and briefings. Another common example is the use of communication data to support the presence or absence of team relationships. In some cases, communications may indicate confusion about leadership or tension that shuts communications down. Similarly, communications are examined for their role in maintaining vigilance and situation awareness or for managing task priorities and workload.

Pegasus Launch Procedures Anomaly

On February 9, 1993, in the final few minutes of countdown for the commercial launch of two satellites, confusion in the control room resulted in the continuation of the launch in spite of range safety's call for abort. The communication timeline starting at 59 seconds before launch is shown in Table 4.3. The timeline is simplified since the personnel locations and team roles are not indicated, but the communications show how the incident unfolded.

Underlying the basic miscommunication were a number of contributing factors, many of which reflected CRM inadequacies such as: misuse of

TABLE 4.3 Simplified Timeline of Communications for Pegasus Launch Procedure Anomaly (NTSB, 1993)

Time	Communication
T −3.28	Discussion of an altitude deviation found in the data
T −.59	RSO calls for mandatory Abort; stops countdown clock
T −.44	TC tells NASA-1 of Abort, but recycle possible
T −.34	NASA-1 tells B52 "Abort"
T −.29	Abort discussion between TC, RCO and RS3: TC misinterprets nonverbal wave from RS3 to mean Negative on Abort
T −.23	Negative on Abort? discussion TC, NASA-1 and B52 pilot
T −.18	NASA-1 to B52 "Keep going"
T −.08	TC "Go for launch"
T −.06	NASA-1 to B52 "Go for launch"
T −.04	B52 "Go for launch"
T −.02	RCO "Are you saying Abort"
T .00	RCO "Abort Abort"
T .00	B52 "Pegasus Away"

TC is the test conductor; RSO is range safety; NASA-1 is the communicator to B52 launch pilot; RCO is range control; RS3 is on range safety support staff.

communication channel assignments resulting in lack of cross-team access to information; confusion about leadership authority; inconsistent use of communication protocols; lack of situation awareness; and ineffective problem-solving, decision-making, and time management.

Communication Context

In addition to serving many functions, communication occurs in a context. Information from these contexts contributes to how communication is conducted, what is communicated and how effectively communication is received. At least four contexts are relevant when considering communication events: (1) the physical context; (2) the social and organizational context; (3) the task and operational context; and (4) the speech and linguistic context. When interpreting what is communicated, these four contexts typically come into play; thus, they must also be considered when interpreting or evaluating crew communication.

The physical context includes aspects of the work environment such as a noisy or quiet cockpit. It also includes whether communication takes place face-to-face or remotely. Face-to-face speech is often abbreviated because the communicators share the same situation and may be looking at the same thing. Speech may also be accompanied by pointing (to an indicator or display), gaze direction, etc. In an analysis of a transcript there may be no hope of understanding a statement like "It doesn't look right" if you have no visual reference to what "it" is.

The social and organizational context pertains to work role differences such as pilot-to-pilot speech compared to pilot-to-ATC communication. In each case, there are roles and responsibilities that greatly narrow the meaning of the communication. A role difference within the cockpit is captain versus FO where the authority difference changes the meaning of statements that might otherwise seem identical. When the captain says "Would you like to pull out the checklist," it is probably a command; when the FO says the same words, it is probably a question. In the analysis of an accident transcript, these roles and organizational contexts are often preestablished by regulations and company policies and need to be understood by the analyst.

The task and operational context is generically described by the phases of flight and routine versus nonroutine operations. Recalling the results of the early communication by Goguen et al. (1986), mitigated speech (which was found to be a less effective form of making requests) was not as frequently used during conditions of recognized emergencies or problems. In short, speech patterns were used differently during critical flight phases and may have served different functions for captains versus subordinate crewmembers. In accident transcripts there is not always an opportunity to compare normal phases of flight compared to nonnormal phases, but what is critical is whether the crew recognizes their operational state.

The speech and linguistic context consists of the grammatical and discourse rules of the language that would specify such patterns as "answers follow questions," or the difference between completed speech versus speech fragments. It may also reflect language or cultural differences that could lead to misunderstandings of particular terms or phrases as in the Avianca accident. Aviation is considerably more standardized in its use of procedural speech than many other professions, but these regularities may fall short under unusual or emergency conditions.

4.3.3 Communication and CRM Training

In the early days of CRM, communication was considered one of a number of CRM skills. In the curriculum suggested in the NASA/MAC CRM Workshop (Orlady & Foushee, 1987), communication was listed as one of seven major topic areas:

1. communication;
2. situation awareness;

3. problem-solving/decision-making/judgment;
4. leadership/followership;
5. stress management;
6. critique; and
7. interpersonal skills.

As a stand-alone skill, communication skills were described in a laundry list of examples such as "polite assertiveness and participation," "active listening and feedback," "legitimate avenue of dissent," etc. (Orlady & Foushee, 1987, p. 199). Such examples were right on point, but training communication as a stand-alone skill was hard to pin down. As Kanki and Smith (2001):

> ... *communication often is relegated to a module in the Human Factors or CRM syllabus...When trainers isolate communications as a stand-alone "soft" CRM skill, they overlook the limitless potential of communication—the mechanism for achieving proficiency in technical, procedural and CRM skills. The implications of communication as a tool for achieving objectives permeates all aspects of instruction and evaluation, just as it does in actual flight operations. (pp. 110–111)*

Once communication was also considered as an enabling skill for technical, procedural, and CRM objectives, it became much easier to specify communication indicators. In the FAA Advanced Qualification Program (AQP) the distinction between performance objectives and enabling objectives provided an appropriate and systematic way to link communication to the wide variety of objectives it can support.

When communication is also considered in its operational context, the finer details of communicator roles (CA vs FO, pilot flying vs pilot monitoring), flight phases, and routine versus nonroutine are incorporated. At times communication behaviors are proceduralized (ATC communications, checklists, briefings), but often they are simply the tools for accomplishing a performance objective. Adapted from Kanki and Smith (2001), Table 4.4 provides examples of the main communication enabling skills used by pilots in routine operations and the functions that are added in nonroutine operations.

4.3.4   Communication and CRM Evaluation

As an enabler for technical, procedural, and CRM objectives, communications are often the prime indicator for an evaluator to assess whether specific objectives were achieved. In the LOS environment, major advances in event set methodology have improved the evaluation process. At the same time, it has allowed evaluators to use communications as indicators of technical, procedural, and CRM objectives in a fairly straightforward way. Other chapters

TABLE 4.4 Communication Enabling Skills for Achieving Objectives During Routine Versus Nonroutine Operations

	Routine Functions	Additional Nonroutine Functions
Technical Objectives		
	Flight Control: standard commands, minor workload redistribution	*Flight Control:* time critical diagnosis, crew coordination
	Navigation: clarify and execute flight plan, contingency plans, programming FMS	*Navigation:* complex planning with ATC and company
	Systems Management: adjustments, monitoring	*Response to Hazard:* enhanced, verbalized situation awareness
		Systems Management: responding to uncertain requirements and changes
Procedural Objectives		
	Checklists: normal	*Checklists:* nonnormal/ emergency
	Briefings: standard	*Briefings:* standard and contingency
	ATC: standard	*Procedures:* identification and performance of nonnormal procedures
		ATC: problem resolution
CRM Objectives		
	Leadership: set the tone, vigilance, team building	*Leadership:* set the tone, utilizing resources, setting priorities
	Monitoring: normal systems, route, traffic, flight efficiency, weather	*Monitoring:* normal and nonnormal, continual; dynamic event consequences, time management
	Task/Workload Management: minor adjustments, adherence to established routines and procedures	*Task/Workload Management:* major adjustments, crew coordination
		Problem-Solving: time limited inquiry, assertiveness, advocacy of changes
		Decision-Making: time critical, risk sensitive, explicit online planning and executing

discuss LOS scenario development and instructor/evaluator tasks in detail, but it is because LOS has incorporated a systematic method for designing a system of triggers and behavioral indicators that evaluations can be more easily and reliably performed. As long as we can clearly identify the proficiency objectives and their enablers, we can know what to look and listen for. In many cases they will be communications.

Event sets within flight phases provide specific operational contexts within which certain crew behaviors are expected to occur. Behaviors are even more finely distinguished by role (CA vs FO) or (pilot flying vs pilot monitoring). While many technical objectives and procedural objectives are required in every scenario because they are a part of normal operations, key behaviors can be evaluated by designing-in operational factors that require the target behaviors. Since the scenario is controlled, pilot options can be relatively well controlled and certain target behaviors should occur within a particular window of time.

Because of the ability to design-in specific challenges, it is an excellent opportunity to test, train, and evaluate new procedures and technologies. With the appropriate changes in policies, procedures, and possible new best practices, observing crew performance in the simulator can be an effective way to judge the adequacy of the new procedures and technologies as well as a way to determine what training will be needed.

4.3.5   Cross-Functional Communication

In recent years, cross-functional CRM training (primarily across pilot, flight attendant, and dispatch work groups) has been rediscovered. Other groups within the company also deserve attention (e.g., maintenance, ramp crews), but pilots, flight attendants, and dispatch interface on every flight and have roles and responsibilities that are operationally and procedurally coordinated during emergencies as well as normal operations. As described by Farrow (in Chapter 17: A Regulatory Perspective II), cross-functional CRM training originally took the form of a "simple combination of multiple work groups attending the same classes in the same room." In the face of economic and logistical challenges of convening groups face-to-face, a wide range of media options have been explored that vary the level of participant interaction, and whether or not it is facilitated. An example of the lowest level of interaction might be the use of videotapes that describe to individual pilots at their computer, the work of flight attendants. While informative, no direct interaction is experienced by the participants. The level of interaction may be increased by the use of real-time video conferencing that allows participants from different groups to interact with one another in a discussion led by an online facilitator. While less overall content may be covered, the pilot/flight attendant interface may be covered in more depth and problem areas may be identified. In future technologies, interaction may be enhanced through the use of sophisticated scenario interaction by an online avatar without other group participants or facilitator physically present. However, the incorporation of interactive qualities (e.g., participant real-time decision-making, procedural responses) requires a greater depth of knowledge by the training developer to make it a realistic training experience for all work groups.

When different work groups interact, the most obvious interface may be procedural communications which are fairly standardized, but circumstances (particularly abnormal situations) may call for more creative information transfer. Each group must know more than their own role and responsibility in order to transfer and receive information appropriately. For instance, pilots must know the boundaries of the flight attendant's roles and the basic requirements for managing passengers. Similarly, the flight attendant must know the pilots' responsibilities and understand their task priorities. Group interactions are also facilitated by some knowledge of the timing of tasks, for instance, when workload is likely to be high. Not every aspect of coordination can be covered by known rules and procedures, but a general appreciation of each work group's general timeframe of duties can facilitate smooth coordination.

In addition to procedural communications and simple information transfer, communication serves as an indicator of other CRM behaviors, such as leadership, situation awareness, and decision-making. In order to judge CRM effectiveness, the cross-functional CRM instructor/evaluator must have an understanding of what counts as behavioral indicators for within-group CRM as well as across-group CRM. For this reason, cross-functional CRM training is often developed through a collaboration between different work group instructors. Once the expanded knowledge base is available, development of scenarios and targeting the cross-functional elements for training and evaluation, the general guidelines of LOS development can be applied.

4.3.6 Effect of Digital Technologies on Communication

The most obvious technology affecting communication in the cockpit is data communications (Data Comm or datalink) which enables controllers and pilots to communicate with digitally delivered messages, rather than radio voice communications alone. Flight deck communication and Data Comm have been extensively researched, with many of the studies published prior to 2000. For example, controller pilot voice communication issues prior to 2000 is summarized by Prinzo and Britton (1993) as well as Cardosi, Falzarano, and Han (1999). Earlier Data Link research is summarized through the reviews of Navarro and Sikorski (1999) and Rehmann (1997) who presented the human factors issues as well as general benefits and risks of Data Link. Cardosi et al. (1999) summarize earlier ASRS research on controller pilot communications focusing on three types of communication errors pertaining to readback/hearback.

Data Comm technology has been discussed for decades but slow to be implemented. Progress is finally being seen in the United States under the FAA NextGen program that is developing a system of new technologies in a coordinated way. Even so, implementation of Data Comm is piecemeal beginning with the delivery of digital tower departure clearance services, including route revisions (FAA, 2016). According to NextGen Update 2017, Data Comm tower services are operating at 56 airports. In the timeframe of 2019−21, Data Comm services will be implemented in en route airspace, enabling controllers to provide frequency handoffs, altitude changes, and inflight reroutes, and enabling pilots to send digital messages to controllers (FAA, 2017). Intended benefits include increased controller and pilot productivity, the potential reduction of miscommunications, improved routing around weather and congestion, and increased accommodation of user requests. However, as new technologies are implemented there are always "bugs" to work out as discussed in NASA's ASRS Callback Issue 443 (NASA, 2016) on Controller Pilot Data Link Communications Departure Clearance Services (CPDLC-DCL). In short, reports received describe a variety of problems crews are having using CPDLC-DCL (e.g., ambiguous syntax, display architecture that inhibits "search," clearance procedures that differ from airport to airport and in different aircraft).

In addition, there are risks related to the change of communication modality that must be appreciated and mitigated. For example, the readback/callback practice in voice communication has been a useful way to target potential barriers to communication. The readback of clearances or instructions (including flight call sign) by the pilot to the controller helps to ensure to the controller that the information was received correctly and completely. On the basis of hearback, the controller has the opportunity to correct errors or omissions. Certainly the acknowledgment function can be reinvented digitally or, in some cases, require hybrid systems (including voice). The point to be made is that functions that enhance safety and effective information transfer are recognized and retained in an appropriate form. This may require some research and testing.

As discussed in earlier sections, communication accomplishes more than information transfer. Digital transmissions may fulfill this basic function but we must consider whether voice communications provide other CRM benefits. When voice communications are on radio heard by both pilots, the shared situational awareness may not transfer one-to-one to digital communications. Again, an appropriate digital solution may require further research and testing.

4.3.7   Organizational Communication Concepts

Over the years of CRM implementation, the importance of organizational buy-in and support has become better understood. Economic downturn and airline mergers have put significant strain on organizations who are simply trying to survive. But to borrow Degani and Wiener (1994), CRM must be evident in the organization's philosophy, policies, procedures, as well as practices. CRM behaviors are trained and evaluated at the procedures and practices level but must be consistent with the company's policies and philosophy of training, SOPs, automation, etc. If we consider that CRM is the effective utilization of all resources and we apply this concept at the organizational or corporate level, effective communication implies that communication is open and multidirectional. Just as we want all flight crewmembers to feel free to speak up when necessary, senior management, in accordance with organizational policy, should support communication and participation at all levels of the company.

For example, in response to the 2001 Space Shuttle Columbia disaster and in addition to the investigation of technical causes reported by the Columbia Accident Investigation Board (NASA, 2003), a team was appointed to investigate failings of NASA's safety culture. The Diaz Report (NASA, 2004) made a total of 85 recommendations, observations and findings which fell into seven categories: (1) Leadership; (2) Learning; (3) Communication; (4) Processes and Rules; (5) Technical Capabilities; (6) Organizational Structure; and (7) Risk Management. In the Communication category, it was recommended that a communication philosophy be adopted that promotes a diversity of viewpoints, eliminates fear of retribution, and provides a process for the workforce to allow for dissenting opinions and intervenes when retribution is suspected. While an organizational philosophy may stand some distance from practical real-time communication, it sets the appropriate tone for CRM and other human factors programs such as Aviation Safety Action Programs (event reporting) and Line Operational Safety Audits.

Generalizing from the original communication concept between captains and FOs, a company-wide communication concept would facilitate effective information flow and other CRM functions horizontally (within and across work groups) as well as vertically, upward from the workforce and downward from senior management.

4.4 SUMMARY

Communication has always been a part of CRM but it was originally considered a stand-alone skill. Accidents and incidents pointed to numerous examples of communication failures but the examples covered a wide range of communicators and situations. As result of a growing understanding of how CRM could affect crew performance, accident investigators and researchers began to systematically analyze communication that came from CVR transcripts, field studies, and simulation studies. Several fundamental concepts became evident.

1. *Communication is a tool for achieving technical, procedural, and CRM objectives.* It may be proceduralized speech following explicit policies or it may be shaped by training as best practices. In LOS scenarios, it may be considered a behavioral indicator for specified performance objectives.
2. *Communications serve many functions.* As a vehicle for: (1) information transfer; (2) establishing interpersonal or team relationships; (3) predictable behavior; (4) maintaining task monitoring and situation awareness; and (5) ensuring effective crew and workload management, communication is both an enabler and indicator of these and other aspects of CRM. Any of these CRM objectives can be targeted with an appropriately designed LOS scenario.
3. *Communication occurs in a context and is interpreted in a context.* These include: (1) the physical context; (2) the social and organizational context; (3) the task and operational context; and (4) the speech and linguistic context. A part of training and assessing communication skills is knowing when communication is "appropriate" and "effective," and much of this is determined by who the communicators are (social/organizational context), where the communication takes place (physical context), during what flight phase and under what operational conditions (task/operational context), and whether the communication is grammatically and culturally understood (speech/linguistic context). Using LOS event set methodology and invoking a well-designed scenario, all of these contexts are easily incorporated and serve as an information backdrop for evaluating communication effectiveness.

As a skill, communication serves CRM training and evaluation well. Within the CRM and AQP framework, and utilizing LOS event sets, observed communications are the behavioral indicators for many procedural and CRM objectives. Thus, communication as a practical skill has found a useful place in simulator training that can be scarcely matched.

It is natural to also consider communication in the context of the larger system of teams (e.g., cross-functional teams). While this requires a foundation of knowledge of each work group as well as the interfaces between groups, this knowledge plus the safety data that points to current weaknesses can lead to the development of robust and targeted training scenarios. An enhanced knowledge base and the promise of new technologies that solve logistical issues and make cross-functional team interaction possible are exciting challenges for the future.

In the meantime, there is ongoing work to be done in the areas of Data Comm and the pilot/ATC interface. Because we are observing a shift in communication modality from voice to digital display, new procedures related to data communications and navigation need to be smoothly incorporated into the controller's and pilot's tasks. Communication can take any number of forms but as always, we need to consider the context in which they occur. If digital forms interfere with situational awareness because pilots are "heads down" when they could be "heads up" and communicating by voice, the benefits may not be a net gain. Ideally, some form of operational simulation or testing with pilots and controllers can serve to evaluate and improve the processes and procedures as they are being developed rather than after they are implemented.

Finally, as we acknowledge communication across multiple groups within and outside the cockpit, the Degani and Wiener 4 P's (1994) are again relevant. Not only should communication practices and procedures support good CRM but company policies and philosophy should ensure overall consistency and guard against communication barriers across departments and work groups.

ACKNOWLEDGMENTS

In 1993, we acknowledged support from NASA (the Office of Space Science and Applications) and the Federal Aviation Administration (FAA). In 2010, the FAA continued to support this work under the AFS-230, Voluntary Programs Office. We acknowledge their support over many years and their active role in enhancing its CRM knowledge base through industry collaboration and improvement of guidance materials. As in 1993 and 2010, we above all, acknowledge the generous and active participation of the transport operators who have turned concept to practice with their dedicated hard work.

REFERENCES

Austin, J. L. (1962). *How to do things with words*. London: Oxford University Press.
Billings, C. E., & Cheaney, E. S. (1981). *Information transfer problems in the aviation system (NASA Technical Paper 1875)*. Moffett Field, CA: NASA Ames Research Center.
Billings, C. E., & Reynard, W. D. (1981). Dimensions of the information transfer problem. In C. E. Billings, & E. S. Cheaney (Eds.), *Information transfer problems in the aviation system (NASA Technical Paper 1875)*. Moffett Field, CA: NASA Ames Research Center.
Burki-Cohen, J., Kendra, A., Kanki, B.G., & Lee A.T. (2000). *Realistic radio communications in pilot simulator training. Final Report No (2000)*. DOT-VNTSC-FAA-00-13.
Cardosi, K., Falzarano, P., & Han, S. (1999). *Pilot-controller communication errors: An Analysis of Aviation Safety Reporting System (ASRS) Reports*. DOT/FAA/AR-98/17). Federal Aviation Administration.
Chidester, T. R. (1990). Trends and individual differences in response to short-haul flight operations. *Aviation, Space, and Environmental Medicine, 61*, 132−138.
Chidester, T. R., Kanki, B. G., Foushee, H. C., Dickinson, C. L., & Bowles, S. V. (1990). *Personality factors in flight operations I: Leader characteristics and crew performance in full-mission air transport simulation (NASA Technical Memorandum 102259)*. Moffett Field, CA: NASA Ames Research Center.
Conley, S., Cano, Y., & Bryant, D. (1991). *Coordination strategies of crew management. Proceedings of the Sixth International Symposium on Aviation Psychology* (pp. 260−265). Columbus, OH: Ohio State University.

Conley, S., Cano, Y., Bryant, D., Kanki, B., & Chidester, T. (1990). *Beyond standard operating procedures: Crew dynamics in the B-727. Unpublished Technical Report.* Moffett Field, CA: NASA Ames Research Center.

Costley, J., Johnson, D., & Lawson, D. A. (1989). *Comparison of cockpit communication B737–B757. Proceedings of the Fifth International Symposium on Aviation Psychology* (pp. 413–418). Columbus, OH: Ohio State University.

Degani, A. S., & Wiener, E. L. (1990). *Human factors of flight-deck checklist: The normal checklist (NASACR 17549).* Moffett Field, CA: NASA Ames Research Center.

Degani, A. S., & Wiener, E. L. (1994). Philosophies, policies, procedures, and practices: The four 'P's of flight deck operations. In N. Johnston, N. McDonald, & R. Fuller (Eds.), *Aviation psychology in practice* (pp. 44–67). Routledge.

Federal Aviation Administration. (2016). *FAA's NextGen Implementation Plan 2016* (p. 11) Washington, DC: FAA Office of NextGen.

Federal Aviation Administration. (2017). *NextGen update 2017, progress and plans: Data communications.* Available from www.faa.gov/nextgen/where_are_we_now/nextgen_update/progress_and_plans/data_comm/.

Foushee, H. C., Lauber, J. K., Baetge, M. M., & Acomb, D. B. (1986). *Crew factors in flight operations III: The operational significance of exposure in short-haul air transport operations (NASA Technical Memorandum 88322).* Moffett Field, CA: NASA Ames Research Center.

Foushee, H. C., & Manos, K. (1981). Information transfer within the cockpit: Problems in intra-cockpit communications. In C. E. Billings, & E. S. Cheaney (Eds.), *Information transfer problems in the aviation system (NASA Technical Paper 1875).* Moffett Field, CA: NASA Ames Research Center.

Ginnett, R. G. (1987). *The formation of airline flight crews. Proceedings of the fourth international symposium on aviation psychology* (pp. 399–405). Columbus, OH: Ohio State University.

Goguen, J., Linde, C., & Murphy, M. (1986). *Crew communication as a factor in aviation accidents (NASA Technical Report 88254).* Moffett Field, CA: NASA Ames Research Center.

Helmreich, R. L., & Wilhelm, J. (1989). *Validating personality constructs for flightcrew selection: Status report on the NASA/UT Project, NASA/UT Technical Memorandum.* (pp. 89–93). Austin: University of Texas.

Kanki, B.G. (1995). Communication research in aviation and space operations: Symptoms and strategies of crew coordination. In *Proceedings of the International Aerospace Congress, IAC'94, Moscow, Russia* (pp. 160–165).

Kanki, B. G., & Foushee, H. C. (1989). Communication as group process mediator of aircrew performance. *Aviation, Space, and Environmental Medicine, 60*(5), 402–410.

Kanki, B. G., Greaud, V. A., & Irwin, C. M. (1991a). Communication variations and aircrew performance. *International Journal of Aviation Psychology, 1*(2), 149–162.

Kanki, B. G., Lozito, S. C., & Foushee, H. C. (1989). Communication indices of crew coordination. *Aviation, Space, and Environmental Medicine, 60*(1), 56–60.

Kanki, B. G., & Smith, G. M. (2001). Training aviation communication skills. In E. Salas, C. Bowers, & E. Edens (Eds.), *Applying resource management in organizations: A guide for training professionals* (pp. 95–127). Mahwah, NJ: L. Erlbaum Associates, Inc.

Kanki, B. G., Palmer, M. T., & Veinott, E. (1991b). *Communication variations related to leader personality. Proceedings of the sixth international symposium on aviation psychology* (pp. 253–259). Columbus, OH: Ohio State University.

Lee, A. T. (2001). *Radio communication simulation and aircrew training (BRI Tech. Report BRI-TR-130901)*. Los Gatos, CA: Beta Research, Inc.

McGrath, J. E. (1984). *Groups: Interaction and performance*. Englewood Cliffs, NJ: Prentice-Hall.

Morrow, D. G., Lee, A. T., & Rodvold, M. (1991). *Collaboration in pilot-controller communication. Proceedings of the sixth international symposium on aviation psychology* (pp. 278—283). Columbus, OH: Ohio State University.

Mosier, K. (1991). *Expert decision making strategies. Proceedings of the sixth international symposium on aviation psychology* (pp. 266—271). Columbus, OH: Ohio State University.

National Aeronautics and Space Administration. (2003). *Columbia Accident Investigation Board Report Volume 1*. National Aeronautics and Space Administration and the Government Printing Office.

National Aeronautics and Space Administration. (2004). *A renewed commitment to excellence. An assessment of the NASA agency-wide applicability of the Columbia Accident Investigation Board report*. Washington, DC: National Aeronautics and Space Administration.

National Aeronautics and Space Administration. (2016). *Aviation safety reporting system callback: Controller pilot data link communications*. Issue Number 443, December 2016. Available from https://asrs.arc.nasa.gov/publications/callback/cb_443.html.

National Aerounautics and Space Administration. (2009). Aviation safety reporting system, callback: Communication factors in ASRS reporting. Issue Number 354, June, 2009. Available from http://asrs.arc.nasa.gov/publications/callback/cb_354.html.

National Transportation Safety Board. (1979). *Aircraft accident report: United Airlines, Inc., McDonnell-Douglas DC-8-61, N8082U, Portland, Oregon, December 28, 1978 (NTSB-AAR-79-7)*. Washington, DC: Author.

National Transportation Safety Board. (1982). *Aircraft accident report: Air Florida, Inc., Boeing 737-222, N62AF, Collision with 14th Street Bridge, Near Washington National Airport, Washington DC, January 13, 1982 (NTSB-AAR-82-8)*. Washington, DC: Author.

National Transportation Safety Board. (1990a). *Aircraft accident report: United Airlines, Flight 811, Boeing 747-122, N4713U, Honolulu, Hawaii, February 24, 1989 (NTSB/AAR/90/),01)*. Washington, DC: Author.

National Transportation Safety Board. (1990b). *Aircraft accident report: United Airlines, 232, McDonnell Douglas DC-10-10, Sioux Gateway Airport, Sioux City, Iowa, July 19, 1989 (NTSB-AAR-90-06)*. Washington, DC: Author.

National Transportation Safety Board. (1991). *Aircraft accident report: Avianca, The Airline of Columbia, Boeing 707-321B. HK2016, Fuel exhaustion, Cove Neck, New York, January 25, 1990 (NTSB-AAR-91-04)*. Washington, DC: Author.

National Transportation Safety Board. (1993). *Special investigation report: Commercial space launch incident, launch procedure anomaly, Orbital Sciences Corporation, Pegasus/SCD-1, 80 Nautical Miles east of Cape Canaveral, Florida, February 9, 1993 (NTSB/SIR-93/02)*. Washington, DC: Author.

Navarro, C., & Sikorski, S. (1999). Data link communication in flight deck operations: A synthesis of recent studies. *International Journal of Aviation Psychology*, 9(4), 361—376.

Orasanu, J. M. (1990). *Shared mental models and crew decision making (Cognitive Science Laboratory Report #46)*. Princeton, NJ: Princeton University.

Orlady, H. W., & Foushee, H. C. (1987). *Proceedings of the NASA/MAC Workshop on Cockpit Resource Management (NASA Conference Publication 2455)*. Moffett Field, CA: NASA Ames Research Center.

Predmore, S. C. (1991). *Microcoding of communication in accident investigation: Crew coordination in United 811 and United 232. Proceedings of the sixth international symposium on aviation psychology* (pp. 350–355). Columbus, OH: Ohio State University.

Prinzo, O. V., & Britton, T. W. (1993). *ATC/Pilot voice communications − a survey of the literature*. Washington, DC: Office of Aviation Medicine.

Rehmann, A.J. (1997). *Human factors recommendations for Airborne Controller-Pilot Data Link Communications (CPDLC) Systems: A synthesis of research results and literature (FAA/CT-TN97/6)*. Washington, DC: U.S. Department of Transportation, Federal Aviation Administration.

Ruffell Smith, H. P. (1979). *A simulator of the interaction of pilot workload with errors, vigilance, and decision (NASA Technical Memorandum 78482)*. Moffett Field, CA: NASA Ames Research Center.

Spence, J. T., & Helmreich, R. L. (1978). *Masculinity and femininity: Their psychological dimensions, coordination and antecedents*. Austin: University of Texas Press.

Spence, J. T., Helmreich, R. L., & Holahan, C. K. (1979). Negative and positive components of psychological masculinity and femininity and their relationships to self-reports of neurotic and acting out behaviors. *Journal of Personality and Social Psychology, 37,* 1573–1682.

Tuckman, B. W. (1965). Developmental sequence in small groups. *Psychological Bulletin, 63,* 384–399.

Wiener, E. L. (1989). *Human factors of advanced technological ("glass cockpit") transport aircraft (NASA Contractor Report No. 177528)*. Moffett Field, CA: NASA Ames Research Center.

Wiener, E. L., Chidester, T. R., Kanki, B. G., Palmer, E. A., Curry, R. E., & Gregorich, S. E. (1991). *The impact of cockpit automation on crew coordination and communication: I. Overview: LOFT evaluations, error severity, and questionnaire data (NASA Contractor Report No. 177587)*. Moffett Field, CA: NASA Ames Research Center.

Chapter 5

Flight Crew Decision-Making

Judith Orasanu-Engel[1] and Kathleen L. Mosier[2]

[1]*NASA-Ames Research Center, Moffett Field, CA, United States,* [2]*San Francisco State University, San Francisco, CA, United States*

INTRODUCTION

Flight crews make decisions throughout their flights, from the captain's acceptance of the aircraft and flight plan prior to departure to blocking in at the gate after landing. Unfortunately, the decisions that get the most attention are those that result in disasters, for example, the decision to take off with snow and ice on the aircraft after the de-ice time had expired at Washington National Airport (NTSB, 1982), or the decision to take off without being sure the runway was clear of traffic in heavy fog at Tenerife, the Canary Islands (Comision de Accidentes, 1978). However, commercial aviation remains an incredibly safe mode of transportation, in good part due to the skills and judgment of its flight crews, both in the air and on the ground.

Despite high overall safety, an analysis by the National Transportation Safety Board (NTSB, 1994) of 37 commercial aircraft accidents between 1978 and 1990 in which flight crew behavior contributed to the accident revealed that 25 (or 68%) involved what the Board considered "tactical decision errors." This finding has been replicated in both military (Shappell & Wiegmann, 2004) and international flights (e.g., Li & Harris, 2008).

Given the infrequency of air accidents, line operations safety audits (LOSAs) provide observations of crew behaviors during a wide range of normal flights and provide insight into decision errors, potential negative consequences, and how they are handled (Helmreich, Klinect, & Wilhelm, 1999). Observations from hundreds of flights conducted by both domestic and foreign airlines found that decision errors were among the least likely type of error to occur ($\sim 6\%$), but they were more likely (57%) to become consequential (e.g., result in a hazardous aircraft state) than other types of errors (Klinect, Wilhelm, & Helmreich, 1999; also see Thomas, 2004). These live flight observations show that safe flight operations depend on effective crew decision-making to avoid significant negative consequences, especially under high-threat conditions (Helmreich, Klinect, & Wilhelm, 2001).

Crew Resource Management. DOI: https://doi.org/10.1016/B978-0-12-812995-1.00005-1

Equally important, observations carried out during normal flights (LOSAs) describe how crews successfully manage threats and errors, including error trapping and threat mitigation, behaviors that are typically invisible because they are part of everyday safe operations. These safety behaviors illustrate the positive side of crew coordination, situation awareness, problem-solving, decision-making and resource management, crew resource management (CRM) skills that are a source of crew resilience, often in the face of seemingly insurmountable conditions. An example of outstanding crew coordination and threat management is seen in response to loss of both engines of an Airbus A-320 aircraft due to a bird strike during takeoff from LaGuardia Airport in New York (NTSB, 2010). The crew had several options: return to their departure airport, divert to a nearby airport (Teterboro, NJ, 6 miles away), or ditch in the Hudson River. The Captain rapidly assessed their situation: engine conditions, altitude, airspeed and location. He determined that they had insufficient altitude and airspeed to divert to Teterboro, and that returning to LaGuardia would entail flying over heavily populated Manhattan. He decided the only workable solution was to ditch in the Hudson River, a feat the crew accomplished, miraculously, it seemed, with no loss of life (NTSB, 2010).

This case illustrates unexpected and potentially catastrophic conditions that required consequential decisions to be made, the stresses and threats under which the crew was operating, and the complexity of the decision: sizing up the situation, assessing the level of risk and time available to make a decision, examining the constraints on their options, and evaluating potential outcomes. The crew needed to develop a shared model of the emerging situation (shared also with air traffic control (ATC) and other ground support personnel), plan how to carry out their decision, assign tasks, monitor the unfolding situation, and keep everyone in the loop as they executed their plans (Orasanu, 1994).

Because of the difficulty of making effective decisions under challenging conditions, aircraft designers, carriers, and the Federal Aviation Administration (FAA) aim to simplify and support crew decision-making by establishing standard procedures and checklists to cover anticipated failures or emergencies (Burian, Barshi, & Dismukes, 2005), and by designing automated decision support systems (Billings, 1991; Wiener, 1998). Given the impossibility of designing procedures and error-proof or fully automated systems that cover all contingencies, the last line of defense is the flight crew. Thus, the bottom line is: How can flight crews be trained and supported to make the best possible decisions, and to demonstrate resilience and adaptability under challenging high-risk conditions? To address these issues, answers to the following questions are needed:

1. What TYPES OF DECISIONS do flight crews actually make?
2. HOW do effective crews make decisions? What behaviors are targets or leverage points for training and design of procedures?

3. What factors contribute to ERRORS or decisions that increase risk and likelihood of undesired outcomes?
4. How can crews be TRAINED to make effective decisions, essentially boosting novice or intermediate decision-making to an expert level?

These questions and the theoretical and behavioral frameworks used to address them serve as the broad organizing structure of this chapter.

5.1 NATURALISTIC DECISION-MAKING—A THEORETICAL FRAMEWORK FOR AERONAUTICAL DECISION-MAKING

Naturalistic decision-making (NDM) is the theoretical framework for flight crew decision-making described in this chapter (Klein, 2008; Klein, Orasanu, Calderwood, & Zsambok, 1993). NDM describes how people with domain expertise use their knowledge to make decisions, typically in dynamic and safety-critical environments (Cannon-Bowers, Salas, & Pruitt, 1996; Zsambok et al., 1997). The research approach originated from studies of fire ground commanders (both wildfire and urban) as they faced fires and developed plans for extinguishing them (Klein, Calderwood, & Clinton-Cirocco, 1986). This original work addressed the question of how fire commanders could develop an effective plan quickly in the face of high-risk, dynamically changing conditions, working with uncertain or incomplete knowledge. Through on-site observations and follow-up interviews, Klein and his team discovered that the commanders used a process that bore little resemblance to classical decision-making (CDM) models (Klein, 1989, 1993a; Lipshitz, Klein, Orasanu, & Salas, 2001).

CDM emphasizes a thorough evaluation of all the options, taking into consideration all available information. Multiple options are assessed in parallel to choose the optimal solution. In classical decision paradigms, options are typically available to the decision-maker; domain knowledge is not needed to assess the situation and generate candidate options. The emphasis in CDM is on the *choice* process. Some aviation decision training models reflect a CDM framework, as defining and selecting among options are primary components (see Section 5.5). But the CDM approach gives little consideration to the process of applying expert knowledge to shape the problem space, what has been called the "front-end" process (Kahneman, 2011; Mosier & Fischer, 2010).

In contrast to what CDM models advocate, Klein's research team found that the commanders surveyed a fire situation and quickly sized it up, classifying the problem space based on their prior experience with similar types of fires. Their recognition of the problem facing them called to mind a solution that had worked in the past with similar fires. They then evaluated that candidate response by mentally simulating how it was likely to play out. If it appeared the response would satisfy their goals and the constraints of the present situation, they adopted it. If not, they generated a second response option and similarly evaluated it. If they still could not achieve a satisfactory response, they reassessed their understanding of the problem and sought to clarify and revise it based on plausible "stories" for how the current fire situation came about. Klein and colleagues called this process "Recognition-Primed Decision-making" or RPD (Klein, 1989, 1993a). Klein's team conducted similar studies in other high-risk domains, including aviation and medicine. Based on these studies, the researchers concluded that the RPD model accounted for approximately 80% of the decisions they observed (Klein, 1998). Thus, a new approach to studying decision-making "in the wild," as Hutchins (1995) put it, was born.

NDM is characterized by several features that distinguish it from CDM (Dawes, 1988; Hogarth, 1987). First, as evident from the firefighter example, NDM decisions are *integral to accomplishing a meaningful task* in the real world, and are made in order to achieve operational goals, such as putting out the fire or transporting air passengers to their destinations while managing threats to safety. This contextualized decision process contrasts with the context-free stand-alone decision problems used in CDM research.

Second, decision-makers' *knowledge*, acquired through many years of training and experience, is central to the decision process. Unlike in classical decision research, where knowledge is seen as a variable to control, in NDM knowledge is the basis for recognizing situations that require a decision to be made and appropriate responses to them (Klein, 2008; Lipshitz et al., 2001).

Third, as evident in the firefighter example, decisions in familiar situations typically are made by retrieving and evaluating a *single option* at a time rather than by engaging in a deliberate analytic process involving thorough information search and concurrent evaluation of all options to choose the best, as in CDM. A corollary to this NDM strategy for choosing an option is the *criterion* for selection: an option is selected if it is workable and meets the decision-maker's goals, a process Simon (1991) called "satisficing." In CDM the criterion is to optimize based on a comprehensive review of all available information and options. However, human information processing limitations[1] preclude the exhaustive information search and simultaneous comparison of multiple options in real-world, dynamic decision situations required by CDM.

Fourth, in CDM the focus is exclusively on the *choice* process. NDM focuses on a new component that may broadly be called *situation assessment* (SA). It includes noticing that a problem exists that requires a decision to be made and determining what the problem's essential features are. This has led to a distinction between two types of processes: "front-end" (SA) and "back-end" (choice of a course of action (CoA)) (Mosier & Fischer, 2010). NDM

---

1. Simon (1991) has termed this characteristic of the human cognitive system "bounded rationality."

research focuses largely on the front-end processes because they constrain the choice of action.

Finally, a process orientation (*how* experts make decisions) replaces the input−output orientation that emphasizes prediction of outcomes from knowing a person's values and goals. Context-sensitive informal models replace CDM formalism. NDM decision models are descriptive rather than prescriptive (Lipshitz et al., 2001).

5.1.1 The Role of Expertise

Expertise contributes to NDM in three ways. First, expert knowledge is the foundation for rapid and accurate perception of information that signals a problem (Cannon-Bowers et al., 1996). This knowledge supports recognition of cues and stored condition−action patterns, the basis for recognition-primed decisions (Klein, 1989, 1993a). Second, expert knowledge provides a basis for risk assessment and for estimating the likelihood of various outcomes (Fischer, Orasanu, & Wich, 1995). Third, expert knowledge includes mental models (Chi, Glaser, & Farr, 1988; Larkin, McDermott, Simon, & Simon, 1980) that are the basis for mental simulation and evaluation of candidate options (Klein, 1993a, 2008).

Expert knowledge confers an advantage for problems that are meaningful within the expert's domain (Klein, 1998). For example, chess masters show remarkable memory for the location of chess pieces that represent positions during legitimate play, a basis for strategic moves (Chase & Simon, 1973). But if those same pieces are placed randomly on the chessboard, the masters' recall is no better than that of novices'. This set of findings reflects organized patterns of knowledge in memory (mental models; Chi et al., 1988; Larkin et al., 1980) that support both rapid perceptual recognition of meaningful cue patterns and retrieval of associated actions, a foundation of expert decision-making.

Knowledge is not a shield against errors. Expertise is the foundation for heuristics, or rules of thumb, which may result in poor judgments if inappropriately applied. Deep knowledge is responsible for efficient functioning most of the time, but occasionally leads one astray. Heuristics such as *availability* and *representativeness* (Kahneman, 2011; Tversky & Kahneman, 1974) may lead the decision-maker to choose a typical and highly used response, even in situations when it is not appropriate, otherwise known as "habit capture" (Nowinski, Holbrook, & Dismukes, 2003).

5.1.2 Domain-Specific Models

Given that NDM decision models are *descriptive* of what people actually do rather than *prescriptive* of what they should do (Lipshitz et al., 2001), it follows that models for different operational domains will have somewhat different features. A major factor that distinguishes domains is the source of information available to decision-makers. In aviation, information sources vary in the extent to which they are digital and technology-based, which induces analytic processing for SA; on the other hand, "analog" data such as visible weather features, distinctive sounds, vibrations, or smells permit rapid intuitive perception and recognition of the situation. This distinction between analytic and intuitive processes is the basis for Hammond's "cognitive continuum" theory (Hammond, Hamm, Grassia, & Pearson, 1987), which posits that decision-makers shift between the two types of decision processes depending on the type of data that signal a decision problem. Similarly, Kahneman (2011) distinguishes between System 1 and System 2 thinking: System 1 thinking is fast and intuitive, whereas System 2 thinking is slow and analytic.

Back-end processes for choosing a CoA also differ across domains. Aviation is highly proceduralized. Decisions benefit from extensive operating procedures, checklists, and aids that specify what should be done when certain threats or problems occur. They provide diagnostic guidance to verify the nature of the threats stemming from system failures, weather, and traffic. Emergency checklists support decision-making when the pilots are under stress and little time is available (Burian et al., 2005). These resources provide flight crews with a rich level of decision support that is not available in many domains, where decision-makers must rely on their own accumulated experience.

5.1.3 Methods for Conducting Naturalistic Decision-Making Research

The features that distinguish NDM reflect not only a distinct theoretical framework, but also imply major differences in the methods used to conduct research compared to traditional CDM decision-making research. Three major factors set the NDM approach apart: the participants of interest, the research setting, and the methods used. First, NDM focuses on experts (rather than college students or other nonselected group), because of their demonstrated ability to make effective knowledge-based decisions under challenging conditions.

Second, NDM research typically is conducted not in a laboratory, but in the field where experts engage their decision-making processes in response to emergent problems under typical conditions. These conditions often include time pressure, ambiguous or conflicting problem information, dynamically changing situations, uncertain decision outcomes, high workload, high risk, shifting goals and significant consequences for poor decisions (Orasanu & Connolly, 1993).

Third, the methods used by NDM researchers are borrowed from ethnography, cognitive anthropology, sociolinguistics, and other disciplines engaged primarily in descriptive field research (Hoffman, Crandall, & Shadbolt, 1998), rather than hypothetico-deductive laboratory approaches. Typically, the methods involve a bottom-up approach: investigators describe what expert decision-makers know and do when making meaningful decisions in their fields of expertise. Developing this knowledge typically involves critical task analysis methods such as think-aloud procedures (Ericsson & Smith, 1991) and concurrent or retrospective structured interviews, including the Critical Decision Incident technique (Flanagan, 1954; Hoffman et al., 1998; Militello, Wong, Kirschenbaum, & Patterson, 2011). Investigators then may test hypotheses about these processes in the laboratory or other realistic simulations.

5.2 A NATURALISTIC AERONAUTICAL DECISION-MAKING MODEL (NADM)

5.2.1 NDM Methodology and Data Sources for NADM

Working within the NDM framework, several methods were used by the Team Performance research group at NASA Ames Research Center over the past 20 + years to understand how fight crews make effective decisions under routine and off-nominal conditions. Orasanu and Fischer (1997) analyzed ASRS incident reports, National Transportation Safety Board (NTSB) accident reports, including cockpit voice recorder data (Orasanu, Martin, & Davison, 2002), observations of flight crews in complex flight simulations (Orasanu, 1994), and laboratory research (Fischer & Orasanu, 2001).

Archival Data. Archival data from accident (NTSB) and incident (ASRS) reports provided diverse examples of the kinds of decisions pilots make, externalized or self-reported processes used to make those decisions, and factors that contributed to poor or effective decisions. Accident reports with CVR data provided insights into what the crew was thinking and doing in response to threats that prompted decisions.

Interviews. Critical incident interviews (Militello et al., 2011) were used to elicit information from pilots flying in Alaska concerning decisions they made under threats from weather, terrain, fatigue, lack of ATC support, passengers or organizational pressures.

High-Fidelity Flight Simulations. High-fidelity simulators enabled observations of certified air transport pilots as they responded to normal and emergency flight scenarios that required decisions in response to threats encountered during full-mission "flights." One study examined spontaneous monitoring and challenging strategies in response to scripted errors, either originating outside the cockpit or introduced by one of the crewmembers (a research team member) (Orasanu et al., 1998). Other high-fidelity simulation studies examined crew responses to system failures and weather issues (Orasanu, 1994).

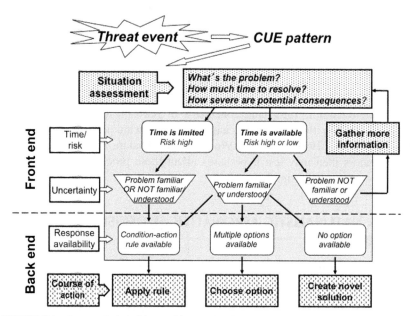

FIGURE 5.1   Aeronautical decision-making model. The inner shaded area describes the types of decisions flight crews may encounter. The outer area represents the decision processes involved in situation assessment (front-end process) and choosing a course of action (back-end process).

Laboratory studies. Hypotheses generated from the above three data sources were put to the test in laboratory studies that focused on specific aspects of the decision process. For example, to address possible differences between captains and first officers in how they perceived risks in various decision situations, the research team used a sorting task followed by multi-dimensional scaling and hierarchical clustering analysis (Fischer et al., 1995). Another study addressed the effectiveness of various error correction strategies (Fischer & Orasanu, 2000). Using multiple methods allowed us to validate findings across studies.

The resultant aeronautical decision-making model described in Orasanu (2010) still holds, with some minor adjustments as shown in Fig. 5.1. The model involves the two major components common to all NDM models: SA, the front-end or recognitional component, and choosing a CoA, the back-end component (Mosier & Fischer, 2010).

5.2.2   An Updated Aeronautical Decision-Making Model

This model captures information about both (1) the kinds of decisions flight crews are called upon to make in response to different situational demands, and (2) the processes by which flight crews make those decisions under different contextual conditions. In Fig. 5.1 the features that define decision types are located within the central shaded rectangle. Three dimensions comprise the front-end component: available time, risk level, and familiarity or clarity of the problem. One feature characterizes the back-end component: how defined or prescribed the CoA is. These range from procedural condition—action decisions to ill-structured decisions in which neither the problem situation nor the response is clear-cut.

How these situational features influence the decision-making process is described in the next section. In Fig. 5.1, the front-end and back-end processes are illustrated in the activities outside the central rectangle.

Front-End Processing: Situation Assessment

Aviation decisions typically are prompted by off-nominal or unanticipated events that require adjustment of the planned CoA. SA involves interpreting the pattern of cues that define the nature of the problem, assessing the level of risk associated with the situation, and determining the amount of time available to reach a solution.

Time available. Available time appears to be a major determinant of decision strategies. The time dimension is relative and depends on how quickly a negative consequence may evolve in a specific situation if nothing is done. Threatening events may either be fast evolving, as when traffic is rapidly approaching an aircraft and an evasive maneuver is needed, or may evolve slowly, allowing time for the crew to gather sufficient information to understand the problem and come to a reasoned decision. For example, failure of a landing gear component while a flight is still far from its destination would not pose an imminent threat, though the crew would certainly want to deal with the problem expeditiously in order to be prepared when they must later execute the resulting plan.

If a threat situation is not understood, diagnostic actions are needed, but sufficient time may not be available. External time pressures may be mitigated by crews to support information search and problem solution (Orasanu & Strauch, 1994), for example, crews may buy time through holding, or reprioritize tasks to reduce workload and assure that critical tasks are addressed (cf. Wickens & Raby, 1991). If risk is high and time is limited, mitigating action may be taken without thorough understanding of the problem.

Risk Assessment. Risk typically is defined as the likelihood of a negative consequence and its severity (Slovic, 1987; Yates & Stone, 1992). Events that score high on both dimensions pose severe consequences and demand immediate attention, for example, fire, rapid decompression, engine failures, or loss of control of the aircraft. In aviation, events with the most severe consequences occur quite infrequently (Klinect et al., 1999; Thomas, 2004). Other threats are more common, stemming from, for example, traffic, weather, or runway changes, which vary in their potential for severe consequences (Martin, Davison, & Orasanu, 1999; Thomas, 2004). Low-probability serious problems may trigger development of a contingency plan, just in case. Likely problems that have no serious consequences may not be seen as threats, and therefore not require any immediate action.

Risk typically is considered to be a subjective judgment that varies with the decision-maker's domain knowledge and prior experience with the threat (Slovic, 1987; Yates & Stone, 1992). A highly experienced crew with a well-developed mental model for the situation is likely to have a more realistic understanding of the risk, as well as ability to cope with it. They also are likely to have a more realistic judgment about the time course of the event. A study comparing captains' and first officers' perceptions of a variety of flight scenarios using a sorting task analyzed through multidimensional scaling found that the primary dimension captains used to classify the decision situations was potential risk, followed by time pressure. Potential risk actually included a time component: it ranged from no risk to present risk to risk in the future. In contrast, first officers, who had less experience, were concerned with how much time was available and how well defined the CoA was (Fischer et al., 1995). These differences in perceptions appear to reflect differing crew roles, rather than simply years of experience.

While relatively little research has been conducted on risk perception in aviation (but see O'Hare & Smitheram, 1995), Fischer, Davison, and Orasanu (2003) conducted a study that clearly demonstrated the role of risk perception in decision-making. Using a think-aloud protocol with dynamically evolving ambiguous flight situations, the investigators analyzed the information pilots requested in terms of risk, awareness of ambiguity, time available, and goal conflicts, as well as their ultimate decisions and risk management strategies. Findings from this low-fidelity study show that decisions—either accepting or avoiding risks—depended on how the pilots perceived the ambiguous conditions. If they felt conditions were not too severe, they were willing to take a risk while seeking to mitigate its possible negative consequences, but if the risk level passed a subjective threshold, they avoided the risk by deciding, for example, to delay their takeoff or diverting to an alternate.

Problem familiarity or clarity. Problems vary in the degree to which their nature is clearly evident to the crew and whether the crew recognizes the problem as familiar. Less mental effort is required when the problem is clear and/or familiar than when it is neither. If the problem is clear but not familiar, the crew may not have an appropriate response associated with it, and hence must search for one. If the problem is unclear, the crew must do additional work to assess the nature of the problem, a process that may require considerable time. Lack of clarity can arise from several conditions: inherently ambiguous cues (especially external perceptual ones), or partial, conflicting, or misleading cues. In these cases, the crew may engage in the macrocognitive process of sensemaking (Klein et al., 2003; Mosier, Fischer, Hoffman, & Klein, in press) in order to determine the nature of the problem.

Back-End Processing: Choosing a Course of Action

After the problem is recognized or defined and the conditions are assessed, a CoA is chosen based on the structure of the options present in the situation. Building on Rasmussen (1985), Orasanu and Fischer (1997) specified three types of response structures: rule-based, choice and creative. All involve application of knowledge but differ in the degree to which the response is determined by the situation. The appropriateness of a CoA depends on the affordances of the situation: Sometimes a single response is prescribed in company manuals or procedures. At other times, multiple options exist from which one must be selected. On some rare occasions, no option is readily available and the crew must invent a CoA. In order to deal appropriately with the situation, the decision-maker must be aware of what constitutes a situationally appropriate process.

Rule-based or RPD Decisions

Single-response situations correspond to Klein's (1989, 1993a) recognition-primed decisions and Rasmussen's (1985, 1993) rule-based actions. Single option cases are the most straightforward because they require the least cognitive work.

In many high-risk and time-pressured situations, such as smoke in the cockpit, an engine stall, or rapid decompression, an action is prescribed in response to those specific situation cues. These and other abnormal situations are deemed to be sufficiently consequential that procedures are specified to reduce the crew's need to invent solutions for the problem while they may be experiencing considerable stress and workload (Orasanu, 1997). The primary process is recognizing the pattern of situational cues, and the primary decision is whether any circumstances suggest that the predefined response should not be implemented.

A "go/no go" decision is a form of rule-based decision: an action may be planned or in process and a stimulus triggers a question—whether to continue or to terminate the action. Stimulus conditions that elicit this response may be quite diverse. For example, a rejected takeoff may be triggered by an explosive engine failure, cargo door light, runway traffic, compressor stall, or engine overheat lights (also see Chamberlin, 1991). Likewise, a missed approach—a decision to terminate a landing—may be triggered by inability to see the runway at decision height, by air or ground traffic, autopilot disengagement, or an unstable approach.

Rule-based decisions involve risk assessment, particularly when ground speed or altitude is near a decision threshold. Environmental conditions, like a wet runway or system malfunction that result in poor braking, may complicate the otherwise correct decision to terminate the plan. Even though the basic condition—action pairing is quite straightforward, the issue is: can I make this response under the present circumstances?

Decision-making in aviation differs from many other high-consequence domains in that many rule-based decisions are codified in FAA regulations or company operations manuals. Klein (1989, 1998) observed that recognition-based decision-making in diverse fields, such as firefighting, medicine, and the military, was based on previous experience with similar problems. But whether the response to a defined problem situation is grounded in formal protocol, as in aviation, or the decision-maker's own experience, the retrieved response option is evaluated by mentally simulating its consequences to determine whether the response will satisfy the decision-maker's goals and the constraints in the situation. If so, the action is accepted. If not, another option is generated and evaluated, or the situation is reassessed. Klein (2008) has noted that his RPD model applies primarily to time-limited decision-making for problems that are typical in the decision-maker's domain of expertise. When the decision is complex, with greater ambiguity and uncertainty, and when more time is available for situation analysis, expert decision-makers will take that time to explore the problem more thoroughly.

Multiple-Option Decisions

Some flight decisions involve choice from among alternatives present in the situation. These cases may map most closely onto our everyday notion of decision-making and to CDM models. For example, a crew may need to select an alternate landing site in response to an onboard medical emergency in bad weather. Landing alternates are prescribed in the flight plan in case weather conditions at the destination fall below minimums, and procedure manuals provide guidance on how to deal with medical emergencies. However, weather conditions may be deteriorating at the nearest airport that offers appropriate medical facilities, and precious time may be required to reach a different airport. In this case, the crew needs to weigh the risks of trying to land in borderline weather conditions versus the possible danger to the passenger of flying to a more distant airport.

Strategies used by crews to select from among alternatives vary, but observations to date (Klein, 1993a; Orasanu, 2010) suggest that they do not correspond to the full concurrent analysis of options recommended by CDM models but rather reflect NDM processes. A full analysis would involve evaluation of each possible option in terms of all variables relevant to the decision (e.g., weather, fuel consumption, runway length, airport facilities), and a mathematical formula would be used to combine all the information to yield the optimal choice. In fact, crews appear to make decisions in the most economical way, taking shortcuts in this process. They work toward a suitable—but not necessarily the best—decision, investing the least possible cognitive work. Several authors have pointed out that thorough analysis of multiple options in terms of the decision-maker's goals and values as specified by the CDM models exceeds human information processing capacity. This is especially true when time is limited, potential consequences are severe, and relevant information is not readily available.

In some cases options are eliminated from consideration because they fail to meet a criterion on a critical feature and are out of the running thereafter, unless no suitable option can be found and the SA process must be reopened. This is essentially an elimination-by-aspects strategy (Tversky, 1972). Usually, the most safety-critical constraint prevails, such as weather or fuel available. In fact, the decision to ditch US Airways 1549 in the Hudson River described earlier was reached following sequential evaluation of two other options, both of which were eliminated based on failure on critical criteria. The first option was returning to the departure airport (LGA), but this choice would have been irrevocable and would have entailed zero room for error, a risky proposition. It also would have meant flying over highly populated Manhattan, with the possibility of catastrophic injuries on the ground. The second option was diverting to Teterboro, NJ. This option was rejected because of the aircraft's current airspeed, altitude, and location. The remaining option was landing on the Hudson River. This was accepted based on favorable conditions: relatively calm winds and water surface, good visibility, little river traffic, and the captain's experience flying gliders.

Ill-Defined Problems

Two other types of decisions hardly look like decisions at all. They consist of ill-defined problems that may or may not be clarified in the process of SA. Ambiguous cues may make it challenging to define the problem that needs fixing. Two strategies may be used to cope with this type of situation: manage the situation as though it is an emergency without clearly defining the problem (*procedural management*), or diagnose and define the problem, and then generate a novel solution (*creative problem-solving*) because no prescribed procedures exist for dealing with it.

Procedural management: Certain cues are ominous but leave the crew without a clear idea of the underlying problem. Various noises, thumps, vibrations, rumblings, pressure changes, or control problems indicate that something has happened, but not necessarily what. The cues signal potentially dangerous conditions that trigger emergency responses, regardless of the source of the problem. Smoke, loss of pressure, an acrid smell, an explosion, or loss of control all signal "Land now." Little time is available to determine the source of the cues. All energies are devoted to finding an appropriate airport, running necessary checklists, getting landing clearance, declaring an emergency, dumping fuel, and landing. These problems are essentially treated as RPD situations, with the condition broadly labeled as "emergency landing."

The cognitive work done for this class of decision is primarily risk assessment. Responses are clearly prescribed and highly procedural—once the situation is defined as an emergency. If the risk is judged to be high, then emergency procedures are undertaken to manage the situation. If the risk is not defined as an immediate emergency, then additional energy may be devoted to situation diagnosis after actions have been taken to "safe" the situation. When workload is relatively low, as in cruise, and time is available, the crew may try to diagnose and fix the problem. But even if diagnostic efforts do not lead to repair of the malfunction, the information acquired can turn the problem into one with a better-defined response (e.g., essentially a recognition-primed decision). Defining the problem clearly may lead to a more specific response than simply treating it as an emergency.

Creative problem-solving. Perhaps the most difficult type of decisions are those requiring creative problem-solving. This approach to decision-making is required when the problem is unique: the nature of the problem is unclear and no procedures are available for dealing with it. Diagnosis is needed to understand what the problem is; then a solution must be invented that will satisfy the crew's goals and the situational constraints. These cases tend to be low-frequency events; neither aircraft designers nor operations personnel imagined such situations would arise, so no checklists or procedures were designed to cope with them.[2]

Accurate diagnosis in these situations is critical and typically involves causal reasoning, which is reasoning backward from effects to cause (Patel & Groen, 1991), as well as hypothesis generation and testing. Recognitional processes may not be applicable because the situation is unfamiliar; few crews are likely to have experienced similar situations.

Even if the nature of the problem has been determined, no ready solutions are prescribed for some problems. Perhaps the most celebrated case of creative problem-solving was United Airlines Flight 232 (NTSB, 1990) in which the DC10 lost all hydraulic systems due to an explosion in the number two engine. The captain invested considerable energy on SA, determining what capability remained after the hydraulic failure (Predmore, 1991). The two outboard engines were still running, but no flight controls were operative. Knowing that the only control they had was engine thrust, the crew determined that they could use asymmetrical thrust to turn the aircraft and could use power levels to (somewhat) control the altitude.

---

2. Following the bird strike and subsequent loss of both engines, the crew of US Airways Flight 1549 had to make do with a checklist designed for loss of both engines at high altitude. No checklist or procedures had been developed for low altitude birdstrikes and loss of two engines because aircraft designers and engineers thought that condition was highly unlikely. The NTSB (2010) recommended that such procedures be developed and implemented based on its analysis of the US Airways event.

While the case of UAL 232 is extreme, ASRS reports indicate that crews do, in fact, encounter novel situations that are not included in operations manuals, minimum equipment lists, or checklists. For example, the captain of a large transport on a cross-country flight reported a low level of oxygen in the crew emergency tanks while at FL310. No guidance concerning how to proceed was available in company manuals. The cause of oxygen depletion could not be determined in flight, nor could the problem be fixed. Regulations require emergency oxygen in the flight deck in case of rapid decompression. Descending to 10,000 feet would have eliminated the need for the O_2—but would have meant the flight would not have had sufficient fuel to reach its destination in case of rerouting around bad weather. Rather than landing immediately or diverting to a closer airport and disrupting the passengers' travel plans, the crew came up with a creative solution. They descended to FL250 and borrowed the flight attendants' walk-around oxygen bottles. (Different O_2 requirements are specified for flight attendants above and below FL250.) This solution allowed them to continue to their destination.

This example is interesting because it illustrates consideration of multiple options, creation of a novel solution, sensitivity to constraints, and explicit risk assessment. In creating this solution, the captain was aware that he would not be able to communicate with ATC in an emergency if he were using the walk-around O_2 bottle, as it had no microphone. But he judged the likelihood of a rapid decompression to be sufficiently low that he chose this option. Another constraint was fuel; the captain wanted to conserve fuel because of the possibility of a missed approach or diversion due to poor destination weather. An early decision to divert would have been the most conservative decision, but it would not have met the goal of getting the passengers to their destination in a timely manner.

The above-described effort to classify decisions in terms of situational demands and affordances is a first step toward understanding what makes certain kinds of decisions difficult, the cognitive effort they require, possible weak links, and leverage points for supporting the crew. The various types of decisions fall on a continuum ranging from simple to complex, requiring little cognitive work to considerable effort. One reason for laying out these differences is to create an appreciation for the fact that no single decision method will work for all types of situations.

5.3 WHAT FACTORS MAKE DECISIONS DIFFICULT?

Before examining factors that make decisions difficult and contribute to errors, the concept of "decision error" within an NDM framework must be considered.

5.3.1 Decision Errors: Outcome Versus Process

Defining decision errors in naturalistic contexts is fraught with difficulties. First, errors typically are defined as *deviations from a criterion of accuracy* (Reason, 1990). However, defining "accuracy" in a natural work environment is problematic given that there is no mathematically optimal decision. Second, a *loose coupling* of decision processes and event outcomes works against using outcome as a reliable indicator of decision quality. Redundancies in the system can "save" a poor decision from serious consequences. Conversely, even the best decision may be overwhelmed by events over which the decision-maker has no control, resulting in an undesirable outcome. A third problem is *hindsight bias*. Fischhoff (1975), Hawkins and Hastie (1990), and others point out a tendency to define errors after the fact by their consequences: that is, a decision must have been faulty because the situation turned out badly (or *good* if it turned out well). But in natural contexts the analyst does not know how often exactly the same decision process was used or the same decision was made in the face of similar situations with no negative consequences. Were those prior decisions also "errors"?

Consistent with our aeronautical decision model, the following definition is adopted: decision errors are "deviations from some standard decision process that increase the likelihood of bad outcomes" (Lipshitz, 1997, p. 152). Within NDM, the decision process that serves as the "standard" is the collective judgment of experts in a particular domain, rather than a formal analytic process that exhaustively takes all information into consideration to yield an optimal solution. Although outcome alone may not be a reliable indicator of decision quality, the decision-maker's goal or *intended* outcome remains important. In natural work contexts, decisions contribute to performance goals. Decisions do not stand alone as events to be judged independent of the broader task.

5.3.2 How Can Decision Processes Go Wrong?

Decision errors may arise within the two major components of the aviation decision model: (1) pilots may develop an incorrect interpretation of the situation, which leads to an inappropriate decision; or (2) they may establish an accurate picture of the situation, but choose an inappropriate CoA. In both cases, they may not appropriately assess the risks inherent in the situation.

Faulty Situation Assessment

SA errors can be of several types: cues may be misinterpreted, misdiagnosed, or ignored, resulting in an incorrect picture of the problem (Endsley, 1995); risk levels may be misassessed (Johnston, 1996; Orasanu, Fischer, & Davison, 2004); or the amount of available time may be misjudged (Keinan, 1988; Maule, 1997; Orasanu & Strauch, 1994). Problems may arise when conditions change and pilots do not update their situation models (Woods & Sarter, 1998).

For example, one accident that can be traced to an incorrect assessment of the situation was the decision by the crew of a B-737 to shut down an engine; unfortunately, the wrong one:

> *The crew sensed a strong vibration while in cruise flight at 28,000 ft. A burning smell and fumes were present in the passenger cabin, which led the crew to think there was a problem in the right engine (because of the connection between the cabin air conditioning and the right engine). The captain throttled back the right engine and the vibration stopped. However, this was coincidental. In fact, the left engine had thrown a turbine blade and gone into a compressor stall. The captain ordered the right engine shut down and began to return to the airport. He again questioned which engine had the problem, but communication with air traffic control and the need to reprogram the flight management computer took precedence, and they never did verify the location of the problem. The faulty engine failed completely as they neared the airport, and they crashed with neither engine running.*

> AAIB (1990).

The problem was incorrectly defined because the cues (vibration and burning smell) supported the interpretation of a right engine problem. The crew did not verify this interpretation using other engine indicators before taking an action that was irrevocable at that point in the flight.

Susceptibility to Automation Bias

Automation and automated decision aids for the most part facilitate accurate decision-making, but may sometimes lead to faulty SA and automation bias, that is, errors resulting from the use of automation as a heuristic replacement for vigilant information search. Reliance on automation may lead to *omission* errors—failure to take appropriate action when not informed of a situation by the automation, or *commission* errors—erroneous actions resulting from inappropriately following automated information or directives (Mosier & Skitka, 1996; see Mosier & Fischer, 2010; for a review). Early research found that experts and novices alike were susceptible to automation bias (Mosier, Skitka, Heers, & Burdick, 1998; Skitka, Mosier, & Burdick, 1999), especially under time pressure (Mosier, Sethi, McCauley, Khoo, & Orasanu, 2007); however, recent work found differences in sensitivity to automation bias between new and experienced pilots (de Boer, Heems, & Hurts, 2014). De Boer and colleagues measured the time to detection of a system failure that occurred at the top of descent and was not alerted by automation (no warning message on the ECAM), but was signaled by other cockpit indicators. Only four out of 35 participants detected the failure within the norm time of 45 seconds, and 12 did not detect the failure before the bottom of descent. More experienced pilots as a whole were less susceptible to automation bias (lower cumulative stimulus probability) and novice pilots exhibited a greater variation in performance.

Experts must also take care not to "pattern recognize" a situation that is not within their scope of experience. The Air Florida Flight 90 pilots who crashed during takeoff in January, 1982, Washington, DC, thought they recognized the cockpit readings; tragically, they did not:

> *Their cockpit voice recording suggests that the crew did notice that the engine power instrument readings were well in excess of normal takeoff thrust, even though the throttle settings corresponded to normal takeoff power. Rather than imagining the readings to be faulty, the pilot's comments indicate clearly his judgment that the apparent increase in power must be due to what were for him unusually cold conditions. In other words, he apparently thought that the engines were more efficient in the cold!*
>
> paraphrased from Maher (1989), and Nagel (1989, pp. 289–290)

Faulty Selection of Course of Action

Errors in choosing a CoA may also be of several types. In rule-based decisions, the appropriate response may not be retrieved from memory, either because it was not known or because some contextual factor such as stress mitigated against it. Conversely, an inappropriate rule may be applied, especially a frequently used one, essentially habit capture. In choice decisions, some workable options may not be considered. Constraints that determine the adequacy of various options may not be used in evaluating them.

An accident in which an inappropriate CoA was chosen with fairly complete information about the nature of the problem involved loss of both generators about 2 minutes into a night flight in a commuter aircraft. Despite the fact that the crew knew that backup battery power would only last for about 30 minutes, they opted to continue to their destination airport 45 minutes away. A complete electrical failure and subsequent loss of flight instruments critical for IFR flight led the plane to crash (NTSB, 1985).

Years later, even with sophisticated equipment and displays, a similar decision situation resulted in an emergency landing and runway overrun. An American Airlines B-757 aircraft en route from Seattle to New York and equipped with modern electronic displays experienced electrical problems preflight and then approximately 30 minutes after takeoff:

> *... Several cockpit lights flickered; multiple EICAS messages appeared, including the AIR/GRD SYS caution message; the Standby Power OFF light illuminated; the autopilot disconnect warning sounded; and the autothrottles disconnected. The first officer turned the Standby Power selector to the BAT position based on the checklist.... Although the QRH did not instruct the crew to divert to the nearest suitable airport, it indicated that the battery would supply bus power for approximately 30 minutes; the captain reported to*

maintenance that the battery would be depleted. After consulting with company maintenance specialists, the crew elected to continue the flight. Battery power was depleted and numerous essential aircraft systems began to fail about 2 hours and 24 minutes after the flight crew switched the Standby Power selector to the BAT position. . . .. The flight diverted to the closest airport (ORD), an emergency was declared, and the airplane was cleared to land on the 7,500-foot-long runway . . . To avoid over-running the end of the runway, the captain veered off the runway into the grass, where the airplane came to rest with seven of the eight main gear tires either blown out or deflated. There were no injuries to passengers or crew.

NTSB (2008).

The central question is why did the crew decide to continue the cross-country flight with the electrical failures, knowing that the battery would only supply power to flight instruments and some controls for a short time? They had the information they needed based on the checklists, but they did not consider the loss of standby power to constitute an emergency and a basis for immediate diversion. As in the earlier commuter case, the crew made a decision based on a flawed SA—they did not understand the ramifications of the electrical failure, despite sophisticated support and discussions with two technical specialists on the ground. This decision suggests a tolerance for risk or "best case reasoning," even when essential information was displayed and sufficient time was available to engage in the metacognitive processes of questioning their interpretation of the situation and simulating the consequences of their decision to continue to their destination.

Inappropriate CoAs also may occur when operational goals conflict or when no good choice is available. These types of decision dilemmas were reported by airline captains in a survey concerning factors that made decisions difficult (Orasanu et al., 2004). For example, weather at the destination airport might be satisfactory when the plane takes off, but may deteriorate and be below minimums by the time the flight arrives. The alternate airport may have clear weather, but it may be more distant, straining fuel resources. Risk assessment may result in no low-risk option being found. Then risks must be considered in terms of what will be gained in each case, factoring in the crew's level of confidence that they can follow through with their choice. The crew needs to think about what *might* happen down the line. They are in a dynamic state; their equipment, the weather, and their location all will be changing over time. Under these circumstances the cognitive load on the crew may increase substantially, thereby increasing the probability of an error due to insufficient updating of situation awareness over time.

Inadequate Risk Assessment

Poor decisions may arise when a flight crew is aware of a threat that requires a response, but underestimates the likelihood or severity of possible consequences, especially when conditions are changing dynamically. For example, when approaching Dallas for landing, the first officer of an L-1011 commented on lightning in the storm lying on their flight path (NTSB, 1986a). Yet, the crew flew into it and encountered windshear, subsequently crashed, suggesting an underestimate of the risk. We know that pilots are concerned with managing risks during flight based on several sources of evidence: Potential risk was the dominant dimension considered by captains from several airlines when making judgments about flight-related decision situations (Fischer et al., 1995). Decisions that involved safety conflicts, especially those conflicting with organizational goals, and situations in which no good options are available were listed by captains as the most difficult decisions they encountered (Orasanu et al., 2004).

Actual data on flight penetration of thunderstorms (NWS level 3 +) over a destination airport illustrates the conflicts that can arise. Facing poor weather at the destination, pilots tended to divert (74% of flights) when they were more than 25 km from the airport. However, when a flight was more than 15 minutes behind schedule, the likelihood of penetrating the thunderstorms rather than diverting increased to 51% versus 15% of on-time flights (Rhoda & Pawlak, 1999). The question is why crews appear to tolerate risk in potentially dangerous situations.

One possible explanation is that crews lack the relevant experience or fail to retrieve the knowledge needed to assess risk appropriately in those specific circumstances (cf. Klein, 1993b). Another arises from pilots' routine experience. If similar risky situations have been encountered in the past and a particular CoA has succeeded, the crew may expect to succeed the next time with the same response, a phenomenon Reason (1990) called "frequency gambling." Given the uncertainty of outcomes, in many cases they will be correct, but not always. Hollenbeck, Ilgen, Phillips, and Hedlund (1994) found that past success influences risk-taking behavior. Baselines become misrepresented over time as a situation becomes familiar and the individual becomes more comfortable with it. Likewise, Sitkin (1992) argued that uniformly positive experiences provide no baseline by which to determine when the situation is becoming more dangerous. In a variety of experiments, Tversky and Kahneman (1974) identified an "optimism bias" and a "planning bias" that could also be driving what appears to be inappropriate evaluation of risk, or overconfidence in the decision-maker's ability to cope with the situation.

Plan Continuation Errors

Examination of decision errors in the NTSB's (1994) analysis of 37 crew-involved accidents revealed an emergent theme: about 75% of the decision errors ($n = 51$) involved continuation of the original flight plan in the face of cues that suggested changing the CoA (Berman, 1995). These included taking off in snowy conditions, landing during an unstable approach, or continuing a VFR flight in instrument conditions (cf. O'Hare & Smitheram, 1995). More recent analyses confirm this pattern, called "plan continuation errors" (or PCEs) (Berman, 1995; Orasanu et al., 2002) or "plan continuation biases" (Dismukes, Berman, & Loukopoulos, 2007).

Although it is not possible to determine the cause of these choices from post hoc analyses, our efforts were drawn to examining factors that might lead crews to demonstrate plan continuation. Both contextual and cognitive factors were hypothesized as potential contributors to these types of decision errors. In many cases it appeared that the crew failed to appreciate the risks inherent in the evolving conditions or those associated with pressing on with their original CoA, perhaps because they did not consider the relevant information. Consistent with this explanation, crews who decided to reroute during a risky situation shared more information about the nature of the problem than those who focused on past actions and procedures—and stuck with the original flight plan (Bourgeon & Navarro, 2013).

5.3.3   Error Inducing Contexts

Three types of contextual factors extracted from accident analyses were associated with poor aviation decisions including PCEs: (1) poor quality information, including ambiguous dynamic conditions or poorly displayed information; (2) organizational pressures; and (3) environmental threats and stressors.

Information Quality

Cues that signal a problem are not always clear-cut. Poor interface design that does not provide adequate diagnostic information or action feedback can lead a crew astray (Woods & Sarter, 1998). For example, in the crash in Kegworth, UK, information about which engine had a problem was poorly displayed, contributing to the flight crew shutting down the wrong engine (AAIB, 1990). Conditions can deteriorate gradually, and the decision-maker's situation awareness may not keep pace (Sarter & Woods, 1995), especially if automation that is not sensitive to changes in context displays outdated or irrelevant information (Mosier, Fischer, Burian, & Kochan, 2017), or when design choices about what to display do not include essential diagnostic data (Degani, Barshi, & Shafto, 2013). Ambiguous cues permit multiple interpretations. If ambiguity is not recognized, a crew may be confident in its understanding of a situation, when in fact they are wrong.

In addition to making it difficult to assess the situation, ambiguity can influence the decision indirectly. A crewmember may recognize that something "doesn't seem right" (as stated by the first officer in the Air Florida takeoff crash in Washington, DC, during heavy snow with a frozen pitot tube, NTSB, 1982), but may find it difficult to justify a change in plan when cues are ambiguous. For decisions that have expensive consequences, such as rejecting a takeoff or diverting, the decision-maker may need to feel very confident that the change is warranted. Ambiguity thus may contribute to PCEs.

Organizational Pressures

An organization's emphasis on productivity may inadvertently set up goal conflicts with safety. As Reason (1997) has documented, organizational decisions about levels of training, maintenance, fuel usage, keeping schedules, and so on, may set up latent pathogens that undermine safety. For example, on-time arrival rates are reported to the public. Companies also emphasize to their pilots the importance of fuel economy and getting passengers to their destinations rather than diverting, inadvertently sending mixed messages concerning safety versus productivity. Mixed messages, whether explicit or implicit in the norms and organizational culture, create conflicting motives, which can affect pilots' risk assessment and the CoA they choose.

Environmental Threats and Stressors

Operational factors that may affect pilots' ability to make effective decisions include stressors such as high workload, limited time, heavy traffic, poor weather, last minute runway changes, and schedule delays, among others. An extensive literature documents the deleterious effects of stress on cognitive functioning (Hancock & Desmond, 2001; Hockey, 1979), especially on attentional focus, working memory capacity, and risk taking. These influence decisions through their effects on information scanning, cue detection, hypothesis generation, and option evaluation. Stress and fatigue also may affect crew communication, which can interfere with building shared situation models, updating information, contingency planning, and error trapping (Harville, Lopez, Elliott, & Barnes, 2005).

One of the few studies to examine stress and pilot decision-making found that stress had little effect on decisions that drew on domain expertise and relied on perceptual knowledge, that is, recognition-primed decisions (Stokes, Kemper, & Kite, 1997). This is consistent with the notion that the most difficult decisions are associated with ill-defined problem situations that require integration of data from diverse sources to analyze the problem plus creation of a unique response.

Certain phases of flight typically induce higher levels of stress due to heavy workload, traffic, and little room for error recovery (Strauch, 1997), such as during takeoff and from top of descent to landing (Flight Safety Foundation, 1998). Under stress, decision-makers often fall back on familiar responses (Hockey, 1979), but these responses may not be appropriate to the current situation. For example, about 1 minute after takeoff the captain of a four-engine aircraft retarded power on all four engines in response to a vibration throughout the aircraft, an action that resulted in a crash (NTSB, 1986b). Reducing power so close to the ground was not appropriate because insufficient time was available for recovery, though this action may have been appropriate at a higher altitude.

Other potentially dangerous conditions may permit more time to diagnose the problem and consider what to do (e.g., fuel leaks, or hydraulic, electrical, or communication failures). However, under stress, people often behave *as though* they are under time pressure, when in fact they are not (Keinan, 1988), and truncate their SA prematurely.

5.3.4   Cognitive Factors in Decision Errors

Ambiguous cues, dynamically changing risks, organizational pressures, and environmental stressors may not in themselves be sufficient to cause poor decisions. However, when the decision-maker's cognitive capacities are stressed, these factors may combine to induce errors.

Lack of Knowledge

Consider that almost half of the decision errors (22 out of 51) in the NTSB (1994) database of crew-involved accidents were considered errors of *commission* (NTSB, 1994). These are cases in which crews took actions that were not prescribed or were out of the ordinary, for example, attempting to blow snow off their aircraft using the engine exhaust from the aircraft ahead of them (NTSB, 1982). These cases may reflect "buggy" mental models or gaps in knowledge (Van Lehn, 1990). Buggy models may lead to success in some cases, so decision-makers may have confidence in them.

Novices are at a disadvantage in making decisions because they lack the deep and well-integrated knowledge of experts (Chi et al., 1988; Klein, 1998). This may be manifest in what appears to be inadequate SA or choice of risky options. For example, Driskill, Weissmuller, Quebe, Hand, and Hunter (1998) found that general aviation (GA) pilots only matched experts' choices of options under a variety of flight conditions in terms of their "riskiness" 50% of the time, presumably due to their less-informed risk models. When Fischer et al. (2003) asked GA and commercial pilots to categorize flight scenarios on the basis of risk, novices focused only on the severity of the consequences, whereas experts included both the timeline (How long do I have to make a decision?) and controllability (What can I do about the situation?).

Expert–novice differences were manifest in behaviors of more and less experienced pilots in several low-fidelity simulations involving deteriorating weather conditions. More experienced pilots made decisions earlier and traveled less far into bad weather prior to diverting than did less experienced pilots (Wiegmann, Goh, & O'Hare, 2002), suggesting the junior pilots had less adequate situation awareness stemming either from lack of knowledge or different risk standards. Expert–novice differences also have been found in the ability to recall weather information; more experienced pilots were able to remember more from traditional destination weather reports (METARs) than less experienced pilots (O'Hare & Waite, 2012), likely reflecting their deeper and more integrated knowledge structures.

Schema-Based Decisions or Habit Capture

Having sufficient knowledge does not in itself prevent errors. Over half of the decision errors (29 out of 51) in the NTSB (1994) database involved *omissions*, or failures to do something that should have been done. Crews may have been captured by a familiar schema in these cases, leading them to do what they normally do, that is, to carry on with the usual plan, even though another action was called for and intended by the crew. When a habit prevails over a conscious goal, it results in "habit capture," a "strong but wrong" response (Reason, 1990). Some of these errors may result from a lack of attention or failure of conscious monitoring. Nowinski and colleagues noted that instances of habit capture occurred when the crew was busy, fatigued, or interrupted (Nowinski et al., 2003). More experienced pilots are more likely to be victims of habit capture due to their strong overlearned habits (Dismukes et al., 2007).

Navigating the Hybrid Ecology

Even when knowledge and information are present, pilots may not synthesize it appropriately. Automated cockpits contain a complex array of instruments and displays in which information and data are layered and vary according to display mode and flight configuration. Most of the advances in automation are geared toward decision-making—assuring that information is available, analyzing data, providing alerts, or improving or integrating system and navigation displays. These systems reduce the ambiguity inherent in naturalistic cues, as they process probabilistic cues from the outside environment and display them as highly reliable and accurate information.

The availability and capability of electronic systems has transformed flight decks into complex *hybrid* ecologies. They are *deterministic* in that much of the uncertainty has been engineered out through technical reliability, but they are also *probabilistic* in that conditions of the physical and social world (including ill-structured problems, ambiguous cues, time pressure, and rapid changes) interact with and complement conditions in the electronic world (Mosier, 2002, 2008). In a hybrid ecology, ambiguous probabilistic cues originating in the physical environment, such as noise or smoke, must be integrated with information from onboard electronic deterministic systems. Moreover, SA processes must be tailored to the information source. Naturalistic cues may be quickly perceived as patterns, which can be matched to experts' experiential stores. In the electronic world however, expertise affords only limited shortcuts, as characteristics inherent in automated systems such as layered data, multiple modes, and opaque functioning demand analytical processing even from experts. For example, in the Strasbourg A-320 accident in which pilots flew a −3300 ft/min descent into a mountain, the cockpit setup for a flight path angle of −3.3 degrees in the desired flight mode looked almost the same as the setup for a −3300 ft/min approach in a different, incorrect flight mode (Ministre de l'Equipement, des Transports et du Tourisme, 1993).

When crews make decisions and take actions based on faulty mental models of system state, the results can be disastrous. For example, the divergence between the flight crew's mental model of system functioning and the actual system state was a factor in the 2013 Asiana 214 accident at San Francisco. The crew thought that their auto-throttle was active and would capture approach speed; however, the system was actually in dormant mode and was set in idle position (NTSB, 2013). Silva and Hansman (2015) developed and tested a framework to understand the mechanisms underlying divergence of flight crew mental model and actual system state for the case of auto-throttle mode confusion. They found that a successful recovery was dependent on the time to reconvergence of mental models: crews needed to quickly recognize divergence and update their SA to avoid accidents.

5.3.5 Personal and Social Factors

Personal stressors include concern with family matters, job security, or health issues. While some pilots may be able to put these matters out of mind on the flight deck, others may be distracted by them, resulting in loss of attentional focus, working memory capacity, or mental simulation ability. These personal factors may affect decision-making also by interfering with sleep, which can have negative effects on alertness, attention, mood, and crew communication (Harville et al., 2005; Hockey, 1979). Ill-structured problems and organization-related goal conflicts require high levels of cognitive effort, which may be compromised in conjunction with other stress factors such as high workload and threats (Cannon-Bowers & Salas, 1998). Limitations on working memory capacity (Hockey, 1979) can limit a decision-maker's ability to entertain multiple hypotheses or to mentally simulate the consequences of options, essential aspects of NDM (Wickens, Stokes, Barnett, & Hyman, 1993).

Social factors may create goal conflicts that increase decision difficulty. Perceived expectations among pilots may encourage risky behavior or may induce one to behave as if one were knowledgeable, even when ignorant. For example, a runway collision in near zero visibility due to fog resulted when one aircraft stopped on an active runway because the crew did not realize where they were (NTSB, 1991). The captain was unfamiliar with the airport and was making his first unsupervised flight after a long period of inactivity. The first officer boasted of his knowledge of the airport but, in fact, gave the captain incorrect information about taxiways. Rather than questioning where they were, the captain went along.

Based on critical incident interviews with pilots flying in the extreme conditions of Alaska, Paletz and colleagues characterized several social phenomena that may lead crews into taking risks and perhaps into PCEs (Paletz, Bearman, Orasanu, & Holbrook, 2009). These include:

- *Informational social influence*: accepting information obtained from another as *evidence* about reality, as in follow-the-leader behavior.
- *Foot-in-the-door persuasion technique*: agreement to a small request increasing likelihood of agreement to a large one later.
- *Normalization of deviance*: an incremental acceptance of a progressively lower level of safety by a group of people.
- *Impression management*: wanting not to look bad to themselves or to others.
- *Self-consistency motives:* acting in ways consistent with one's beliefs.

5.4 BEHAVIORS THAT CHARACTERIZE EFFECTIVE CREW DECISION-MAKING

Behaviors associated with effective crew decision-making have been identified from research in both high- and low-fidelity flight simulations (Orasanu, 1994), and validated in actual line operations, primarily through LOSA that target nontechnical skills (Flin, O'Connor, & Crichton, 2008; Klinect et al., 1999; Thomas, 2004). Both sources provide evidence of how crews manage threats, trap errors, and maintain positive and coordinated crew interactions essential to making good decisions.

These behaviors can be broken down into taskwork skills and teamwork skills (Cannon-Bowers, Salas, & Converse, 1990). The taskwork skills that have been identified correspond to many of the "macrocognitive" functions identified by the NDM research community such as problem detection, sensemaking, planning, adaptation, and coordination (Klein et al., 2003; Schraagen, Klein, & Hoffman, 2008). These functions are supported by a number of team processes: managing attention; maintaining common ground and developing mental models for the situation; mental simulation by running the models; managing uncertainty and risk; and identifying leverage points. While one may quibble with the distinction between functions and general processes, all of these elements have been observed in flight crews as they coped with threats embedded in flight scenarios in high-fidelity simulators (Fischer, Orasanu, & Montalvo, 1993; Orasanu & Fischer, 1992, 1997; Orasanu et al., 2002; Orasanu, 1994).

5.4.1 Taskwork Skills

Situation Awareness. Effective crews are vigilant. They monitor the environment for threats that may require a response, as well as monitoring progress of the flight according to the operative plan. They gather additional information to clarify threats.

Shared Situation Models. Effective crews build shared situation models when threats arise. They assess and communicate the nature of the threat, the degree of risk, and time available. By sharing information, crewmembers co-construct a working model of the emerging situation as well as plans for dealing with it (Orasanu & Fischer, 1992; Resnick, Salmon, Zeith, Wathen, & Holowchak, 1993; Van den Bossche, Gijselaers, Segers, Woltjer, & Kirschner, 2011). These shared situation models are grounded in the crewmembers' individual mental models for the task, the equipment, and the crew. Maintaining "common ground" is essential in dynamically changing situations (Klein, Feltovich, Bradshaw, & Woods, 2005).

Plan Updates. Effective crews are adaptive. They adjust to dynamically evolving conditions and update plans as needed (in part to avoid PCEs). This includes building contingency plans to cope with uncertain situations. Threats may require that goals be updated to support threat management while maintaining the overall plan.

Task and Workload Management. Effective crews revise task priorities and reassign tasks to manage workload. Revising task priorities or plans may allow them to "buy time" to assure thorough SA and consideration of options.

Option Evaluation. Effective crews project the consequences of various options to decide what to do. They are sensitive to competing goals and risks, such as safety, productivity, economic, and professional consequences.

Metacognitive Strategies. Effective crews are reflective. They check their assumptions, question missing information, consider what might go wrong with their plans, how likely negative consequences are, and how serious they would be (Cohen, Freeman, & Wolf, 1996). These skills may be among the most trainable (Means, Salas, Crandall, & Jacobs, 1993), given that they have been taught to a diverse set of participants for self-regulation, including children (Brown, Armbruster, & Baker, 1986; Moritz, Kerstan, Veckenstedt, Randjbar, Vitzthum, Schmidt et al., 2010).

5.4.2 Teamwork Skills

Effective taskwork depends on effective teamwork. One of the earliest observed causes of crew-involved aviation accidents was poor teamwork (Helmreich & Foushee, 2010). This observation led to establishment of the initial CRM training programs and to their evolution as threat and error management (TEM) programs (Helmreich, 2002). Maintaining a positive crew climate and trust in each other is essential for assuring that all crew-members, especially junior ones, contribute to problem assessment and decision-making (Helmreich & Foushee, 2010; Salas, Sims, & Burke, 2005). Trust and openness are the basis for error trapping.

Crew Climate. Positive crew climate begins with the captain's preflight briefing (Ginnett, 1993), which establishes a climate of openness and partici-pation. Low-fidelity studies show that effective crews are characterized by active participation of all crewmembers (Fischer, McDonnell, & Orasanu, 2007; Parke, Kanki, Nord, & Bianchi, 2000) in updating situation awareness and developing plans and strategies for coping with a problem.

Error Trapping. When errors occur, members of effective crews are able to disrupt the error chain by calling out the error and correcting it (or even preventing it from occurring by being pro-active). Accident investigations repeatedly point out the role of "monitoring-challenging" failures as links in the accident chain (NTSB, 1994). These failures are more frequent when the captain is the one making the error than when both crewmembers are respon-sible or when the error arises outside of the flight deck (Orasanu et al., 1998; Thomas, 2004).

While junior crewmembers may be reluctant to challenge an error commit-ted by the captain, they are more likely to be effective in preventing or trap-ping errors by using certain communication strategies: clearly describing the nature of the problem, offering a suggestion for solving it while leaving the decision up to the captain, and providing justification for the suggestion (*why* it's a good idea) (Fischer & Orasanu, 2000). Challenges that are too direct or too mitigated (weak) are not likely to be effective, the former because they may disrupt crew climate, the latter because they don't convey the seriousness of the problem. Effective challenges invoke a crew orientation reflected by use of "we" rather than "you" or "I" in the suggestions, for example, "*We* need to turn 15 degrees north about now" (Fischer & Orasanu, 2000).

Back-up Strategies. Finally, members of effective crews monitor each other for stress, fatigue, or workload and back up each other or reassign tasks as needed. More effective crews use compensatory strategies to manage fatigue or stress, such as double-checking information, status, or plans (Petrilli, Roach, Dawson, & Lamond, 2006).

5.5 TRAINING CREWS TO MAKE BETTER DECISIONS

Team training approaches that focus on team process skills appear to be most effective in developing resilient teamwork essential to effective crew decision-making (Klein, Salas, DiazGranados, Burke, Stagl, Goodwin et al., 2008; Salas, Nichols, & Driskell, 2007). Cannon-Bowers and Bell (1997) recommend validated team process skills as training targets, including SA and risk assessment, domain-specific reasoning, problem-solving, and mental simulation, with specific attention focused on difficult-to-perceive cue patterns. Decision strategies are learned most effectively in conjunction with domain-specific content (Glaser & Bassok, 1989), a principle guiding the integration of CRM skills with technical training for pilots under the FAA's Advanced Qualification Program (AQP) (FAA Advisory Circular #120-54 A, 6/23/06).

A recent meta-analysis of 51 controlled studies that aimed to improve teamwork and team performance in several domains verified previous findings of positive effects for team training interventions on both teamwork and team performance (McEwan, Ruissen, Eys, Zumbo, & Beauchamp, 2017; Salas et al., 2008). Active learning practices such as workshops in which team members, for example, played roles or analyzed positive and negative cases of team behaviors, simulations (low- or high-fidelity), guided practice, and team behavior reviews were found to be significantly more effective than passive lecture methods. While most studies focused on performance-related teamwork skills, others targeted interpersonal team dynamics, such as managing interpersonal conflict or providing social support. The analysis found that team performance in fact benefitted from interpersonal dynamics training. Marks, Zaccaro, and Mathieu (2000) commented that interpersonal processes lay the foundation for the effectiveness of other processes, a factor recognized in CRM training (Helmreich & Foushee, 2010).

5.5.1 Aeronautical Decision-Making Training

Several decision training models have been developed in the aviation industry, some of which are used by major international carriers. For example, DODAR stands for Diagnosis, Options, Decide, Assign tasks, Review (Walters, 2002). FOR-DEC stands for Facts, Options, Risks and Benefits— Decide, Execute, Check (Hoermann, 1995). While both include steps of gathering information, deciding on actions based on anticipated consequences, and reviewing the decision, neither model capitalizes explicitly on the crew's expertise at recognizing and sizing up the situation, as in NDM. Both imply concurrent weighing of multiple options, which is most suited for complex decisions when time is not limited. Neither is tuned to differences in decision situations that constrain which decision strategies are appropriate (i.e., rule-based, choice, or creative decisions). Essentially, these remain domain-independent general approaches that could be applied in any domain by any decision-maker (see O'Hare, 2003).

Li and colleagues examined the utility of adapting ADM training to various types of decisions described in Section 5.2 (this chapter). A brief ADM training program for Chinese Air Force cadets used two models—SHOR (Stimuli, Hypotheses, Options, and Response) and DESIDE (Detect, Estimate, Set Safety Objectives, Identify, Do, and Evaluate)—and yielded improvements in SA and risk management behaviors, but these have not yet been tested in actual flight simulations (Li & Harris, 2008).

5.5.2 NDM-Based Training

The goal of training within an NDM framework is to help novices learn to "think like an expert" (Ericsson & Charness, 1997; Klein, 2008). NDM-driven training emphasizes opportunities for developing domain-specific rapid pattern recognition, serial consideration of options, use of mental simulation to evaluate options, and metacognitive skills to evaluate and correct one's understanding of the situation and develop a response (Cohen et al., 1996; Klein, 2008; Means et al., 1993). Klein (1998) has pointed out that learning to think like an expert depends on developing deep knowledge as a basis for making decisions.

A unique support for learning to think like an expert is a tool called ShadowBox. Originally conceived by Hintze, a Battalion Chief with the New York City Fire Department (Klein, Hintze, & Saab, 2013), it is a way for trainees to see the world "through the eyes of experts" without the experts having to be present (Klein & Wright, 2016). In response to challenging training scenarios, a panel of domain experts provides their rankings of options at various decision points, plus their rationales. Decision points may concern cues to monitor, information to gather, goals to prioritize, or actions to choose. Then trainees go through the scenarios and do their own option rankings and provide their rationales. After responding, trainees are shown the aggregate expert responses to the same decision questions. This shows them how similar their responses are to the experts', what they may have missed, and the experts' rationales. Providing the expert feedback helps trainees to learn about the experts' mental models and to "see" the scenario through the experts' eyes.

ShadowBox also can be used to train teams. After going through their own rankings/rationales, members can be asked to predict how their team mates would respond. Again, a comparison of predicted and actual responses helps the teams to build team mental models by increasing predictability of each other's behaviors.

Situation Assessment

Training within an NDM framework emphasizes development of SA skills, an element that was totally absent from traditional decision models and decision training. For aviation decisions, rapid pattern recognition, time and risk assessment, diagnostic skills, and knowledge-based reasoning are needed. Recognition of danger cues and generation of appropriate responses to them should become automatic, which requires repeated practice with feedback as recommended by Klein (1998), Phillips, Klein, & Sieck, 2004. Efforts to train pilots to recognize weather cues, for instance, have yielded some success (Endsley & Robertson, 2000; Wiggins & O'Hare, 2003).

As noted in an earlier section, a major contributor to decision difficulty is uncertainty concerning the meaning of cue patterns, which may be incomplete, ambiguous, or misleading. Based on expert reports, Lipshitz and Strauss (1997) developed a framework for coping with uncertainty: RAWFS stands for the tactics of *Reduction, Assumption-based reasoning, Weighing Pros and Cons, Forestalling*, and *Suppression. Reduction*, the most commonly mentioned, involves collecting additional information to reduce uncertainty arising primarily from ambiguity. If additional information is not forthcoming, *assumption-based reasoning* may be used. It involves extrapolation, or using what is known to fill the gaps in information, allowing decision-makers to respond quickly if needed. *Weighing pros and cons* is used when legitimate cues conflict, leading to multiple possible interpretations. *Forestalling* involves acknowledging uncertainty and either taking it into account in making one's decision or preparing to avoid or confront potential risks with various options. *Suppressing* uncertainty involves tactics of denial or rationalization. Training based on the RAWFS strategy has been used for military command and control and firefighting (Lipshitz, Omodei, McClellan, & Wearing, 2007), among others.

Selecting a Course of Action

The second major component of training within an NDM framework is choosing a workable CoA. In the case of a rule-based or RPD decision, the response frequently is prescribed by a procedure or checklist. What pilots need to learn in these cases is to use self-critique skills to ask (1) whether they have correctly interpreted the situation and (2) whether there is any reason they should not apply the prescribed action. Choice decisions involve multiple options rather than a condition—action pairing. Time is required to consider the pros and cons of options, as in the RAWFS strategy. Mental simulation is used to evaluate sequentially the adequacy of each option in meeting the crew's goals until a workable option is identified. However, this process takes time, which may entail adopting a time management strategy such as shedding less critical tasks (Wickens & Raby, 1991) or buying time, for example, by requesting a holding pattern. NDM-based training maintains that generating and evaluating one option at a time is appropriate under many circumstances rather than simultaneously considering all possible options, especially under time-pressure and high risk. Training for ill-structured problems in which the problem is not well understood and no ready solution is at hand is the most challenging. Metacognitive training and use of uncertainty reduction strategies may be the most useful in helping with these difficult problems. New decision aiding tools are being developed that may assist with these challenging problems (e.g., Letsky, Warner, Fiore, & Smith, 2008).

Metacognitive Training

Perhaps the most trainable decision-supporting skill is metacognition, that is, awareness and monitoring of one's own cognitive processes, including limitations. Metacognition includes self-checks such as: Is my understanding of the situation accurate? Are there cues that don't seem to fit? Are there other possible explanations for the pattern I see? How much time do I have to solve this problem? Do I need more time? What could go wrong if I take this CoA? Why? Am I overloaded, fatigued, or anxious? Are my fellow crewmembers?

The point is to evaluate the adequacy of one's own and the crew's understanding of the situation, potential flaws associated with a CoA, and approaches to managing the risks it entails. Nowhere is this process more important than before taking an irrevocable action that has potentially catastrophic consequences if incorrect, like shutting down an engine due to a suspected malfunction (AAIB, 1990).

Cohen, Freeman, and Thompson (1998) developed an NDM decision model that combines recognition and metacognitive elements (R/M). The model describes how decision-makers come to reasonable decisions as they deal with uncertainty and time pressure in many real-world environments. A pattern of event cues retrieves a situation template that is instantiated with the features of the present situation (the recognitional processes). If this process does not lead to understanding and an acceptable response, then metacognitive processes are invoked that combine critiquing and correcting.

Based on the R/M model, Cohen and colleagues developed a training program called STEP that is designed to help decision-makers come to reasonable interpretations of unfamiliar situations and to generate and resolve conflicting interpretations of events (Cohen et al., 1996). STEP stands for building a *Story* that explains one's current understanding of the situation, essentially a causal model; *Testing* the story for conflicts and resolving them, if possible; *Evaluating* the assumptions on which the story is based; and formulating contingency *Plans* for protection. Training aims to sensitize trainees to domain-specific cues including time constraints, stakes, and problem familiarity, as well as conflicts, completeness, and reliability of information.

R/M emphasizes training under realistic practice conditions to promote accurate recognition, and repetition with feedback to facilitate automatic performance. Practice involves making metacognitive processes explicit (i.e., critiquing and correcting), which benefits from a team context. Devil's advocate and crystal ball techniques are used to challenge assumptions and discern weaknesses in SAs and plans. Senders and Moray (1991) noted that pilots often need training in "how to change one's mind" and how to avoid cognitive "lockup," which may play a role in PCEs. STEP has been evaluated in both military and aviation contexts (Freeman, Cohen, & Thompson, 1998) and has been found to significantly improve participants' abilities to cope with challenging uncertain problems.

5.5.3 Monitoring Skills

Effective SA depends on vigilant monitoring of the environment, including aircraft systems, weather, traffic, and fellow crewmembers for potential threats. Sumwalt, Thomas, and Dismukes (2002) recommend training for monitoring that focuses on specific areas of vulnerability, such as top-of-descent or points at which clearances are expected. Noncritical tasks should be accomplished during less critical phases. Monitoring other crewmembers is essential to mutual back-up behaviors.

Effective monitoring depends on effective workload and task management strategies. Overall crew performance depends on the captain's ability to prioritize tasks and allocate duties. Demands can be managed by contingency planning, but this depends on the captain anticipating possible problems, which in turn depends on good situation awareness and metacognitive skill. These are skills that can be developed in low-fidelity simulators that maintain cognitive fidelity to the real environment.

5.5.4 Communication Training

Communication is the medium through which most team decision-making and threat management is accomplished. As Kanki (2010) points out, communication serves multiple functions, often simultaneously. These include (1) conveying information, (2) establishing interpersonal and team relationships, (3) establishing predictable behavior and expectations, (4) maintaining attention to task and situational awareness, and (5) serving as a management tool.

A fundamental feature of communication that supports all the others is closed-loop communication: questions are answered and commands or requests are acknowledged in accord with normative conversational patterns, a pattern that is associated with effective team performance (Kanki, Lozito, & Foushee, 1989). Standardized phraseology and role-specific utterances at specific points in standard procedures also contribute to communication efficiency. Closed-loop communication and standardization are thought to reduce cognitive load by increasing predictability.

Effective and efficient communication is essential in uncertain dynamic conditions, as SA benefits from the contributions of all crewmembers, especially under time pressure, when their models must be updated. Important functions of communication that contribute directly to effective decision-making include building *shared situation models* through explicit communication, establishing a *positive crew climate*, and engaging in successful *monitoring and challenging skills* in order to manage threats and trap errors. Effective communication skills can be modeled and practiced in low- or high-fidelity simulation environments with appropriate feedback.

Build Shared Situation Models

As unexpected dynamic conditions arise, it is essential that team members communicate to build a shared model of the emergent situation and how to cope with it: What is the problem? What is our plan? Who does what and when? What contingencies must be planned for? What cues or conditions must we look out for and what will we do (Orasanu & Salas, 1993)? Only if all participants have a shared model will they be able to contribute efficiently to the shared goal and to update their plans as conditions evolve.

The intent is not simply to encourage crews to talk more. More is not necessarily better: high levels of talk can contribute to crew workload (Dismukes et al., 2007) and may depress performance by interrupting other tasks. What is needed is explicit discussion of the problem: its definition, plans, strategies, and relevant information. Explicit problem-related talk is associated with effective problem management and overall crew performance in simulated flights with commercial air transport pilots (Grote, Kolbe, Zala-Mezo, Bienefeld-Seall, & Kunzle, 2010; Orasanu, 1994).

Current training programs that integrate CRM with technical training encourage crews to use prebriefings to assure that all members know what to do in case of time-critical emergencies, such as how to handle aborted take-offs. In effective crews, the captain usually takes the lead in managing crew discussions that support SA and task management (Flin et al., 2008; Marks et al., 2000).

Establish a Positive Crew Climate Through Briefings

Briefings conducted by the captain go a long way to assure that team members understand their role in crew efforts and feel comfortable offering their contributions, which may be critical to managing threats in challenging situations (Flin et al., 2008; Ginnett, 1993). During effective preflight briefings, decisions on flight path and fuel load are made, and how risks and threats will be managed is discussed (Cahill, McDonald, & Losa, 2013). Briefings set the tone for team climate; team members "follow the leader," adopting the interactional style of the leader (Lingard, Reznick, Espin, Regehr, & DeVito, 2002). A recent meta-analysis of team training research found that training targeted at the interpersonal dynamics of the team, specifically, managing interpersonal conflict and providing social support, contributed to more effective team performance (McEwan et al., 2017). Negative interpersonal relations may prevent team members from fully contributing to team efforts. Salas et al. (2005) point out the importance of mutual trust in supporting mutual performance monitoring essential to flight safety.

Monitor and Challenge Threats and Errors

Crewmembers also must learn appropriate ways to bring problems to the attention of the captain (called *advocacy* and *assertion* in CRM parlance).

These include being as specific as conditions allow, pointing out problems, suggesting solutions, and providing reasons for one's concerns. Strategies identified by Fischer and Orasanu (1999, 2000) to be most effective in correcting crew errors include crew *obligation statements* (such as "We need to deviate right about now"), *preference statements* (e.g., "I think it would be wise to turn left") and *hints* (e.g., "That return at 25 miles looks mean"). In addition, requests that were supported by problem or goal statements (e.g., "We need to bump the airspeed to Vref plus 15. *There's windshear ahead.*") were rated as more effective in lab studies than utterances without supporting statements.

5.5.5   Develop Accurate System Mental Models

Training for future flight operations will need to support the development of accurate system models and strengthen pilots' systems understanding to ensure adequate system monitoring, mode awareness, and information integration for decision-making. As the flight environment becomes more automated, knowledge-driven processes, and thus the quality of an individual's underlying knowledge structures, gain in importance. Training for decision-making needs to include instruction and practice in using appropriate skills to find relevant data and information, assess automated system functions and displays, and develop highly accurate mental models of how the automation works (Mosier & Fischer, 2010).

5.6   CONCLUSIONS: THE FUTURE OF AVIATION DECISION-MAKING

The jobs of pilots and air traffic controllers are constantly evolving. With modern equipment on the flight deck, pilots have more information at their disposal. Designing information displays to support good situation awareness and fast, accurate problem diagnosis is a theme of current research and development efforts. Providing information on risks is more problematic. New systems may be capable of critiquing proposed plans for flaws—essentially, an intelligent automated metacognitive aid. Advances in technology will be accompanied by changes in roles and responsibilities in the not-too-distant future, for example, as next-generation air traffic control technology leads to the transfer of some responsibility for aircraft separation during flight from air traffic controllers to pilots of appropriately equipped aircraft and ground-based airline operations centers. The question will become: how to prepare crews and controllers, with their deep knowledge and adaptability but also with their vulnerabilities, to manage such a system and use it to enhance the effectiveness of their decision-making. Mutual trust, respect, and a positive crew climate will continue to be the foundations for effective crew decision-making in future automated systems.

ACKNOWLEDGMENTS

The first author's research was supported by the National Aeronautical and Space Administration (NASA) Aviation Safety Program and by the FAA. The opinions expressed in this chapter are the authors' and do not represent official views of any federal agency.

REFERENCES

Air Accidents Investigations Branch (AAIB). (1990). *Report on the accident to Boeing 737-400 G-OBME near Kegworth, Leicestershire on 8 January, 1989. (Aircraft Accident Report 4/ 90)*. London: HMSO.

Berman, B. (1995). Flightcrew errors and the contexts in which they occurred: 37 major US air carrier accidents. In *Proceedings of the 8th international symposium on aviation psychology*. Ohio State University: Columbus, OH, pp. 1291–1294.

Billings, C. E. (1991). *Human-centered aircraft automation: A concept and guidelines. (Tech. Mem. No. 103885)*. Moffett Field, CA: NASA-Ames Research Center.

Bourgeon, V., & Navarro, C. (2013). Communication and flexibility in aircrews facing unexpected and risky situations. *International Journal of Aviation Psychology, 23*, 289–305.

Brown, A. L., Armbruster, B. B., & Baker, L. (1986). The role of metacognition in reading and studying. In J. Orasanu (Ed.), *Reading comprehension: From research to practice* (pp. 49–76). Hillsdale, NJ: Erlbaum.

Burian, B.K., Barshi, I., & Dismukes, K. (2005). *The challenge of aviation emergency and abnormal situations, NASA Technical Memorandum 2005-213462*. Moffett Field, CA: National Aeronautics and Space Administration.

Cahill, J., McDonald, N., & Losa, G. (2013). Understanding and improving flight crew performance of the preflight, flight planning, and briefing task. *International Journal of Aviation Psychology, 23*, 27–48.

Cannon-Bowers, J., & Bell, H. H. (1997). Training decision makers for complex environments: Implications of the Naturalistic Decision Making perspective. In C. E. Zsambok, & G. Klein (Eds.), *Naturalistic decision making* (pp. 99–110). Mahwah, NJ: Lawrence Erlbaum Associates.

Cannon-Bowers, J. A., & Salas, E. (1998). Individual and team decision making under stress: Theoretical underpinnings. In J. A. Cannon-Bowers, & E. Salas (Eds.), *Making decisions under stress* (pp. 17–38). Washington, DC: American Psychological Association.

Cannon-Bowers, J. A., Salas, E., & Converse, S. (1990). Cognitive psychology and team training: Training shared mental models of complex systems. *Human Factors Society Bulletin, 33*(12), 1–4.

Cannon-Bowers, J. A., Salas, E., & Pruitt, J. S. (1996). Establishing the boundaries of a paradigm for decision research. *Human Factors, 38*, 193–205.

Chamberlin, R. W. (1991). *Rejected takeoffs: Causes, problems, and consequences. Proceedings of the sixth international symposium on aviation psychology* (pp. 993–998). Columbus, OH: The Ohio State University.

Chase, W. G., & Simon, H. A. (1973). Perception in chess. *Cognitive Psychology, 4*, 55–81.

Chi, M. T. H., Glaser, R., & Farr, M. J. (1988). *The nature of expertise*. Hillsdale, NJ: Erlbaum.

Cohen, M. S., Freeman, J. T., & Thompson, B. (1998). Critical thinking skills in tactical decision making: A model and a training strategy. In J. A. Cannon-Bowers, & E. Salas (Eds.), *Making decisions under stress: Implications for individual and team training* (pp. 155–190). Washington, DC: APA.

Cohen, M. S., Freeman, J. T., & Wolf, S. (1996). Metacognition in time-stressed decision making: Recognizing, critiquing, and correcting. *Human Factors, 38*(2), 206–219.

Comision de Accidentes. (1978). *Colision aeronaves, Boeing 747 PH-BUF de KLM y Boeing 747 N 736 PA de Panam en Los Rodeos (Tenerife), el 27 de Mβarzo de 1977.* Madrid: Ministerio de Transportes y Comunicaciones, Subsecretaria de Aviacion Civil.

Dawes, R. M. (1988). *Rational choice in an uncertain world.* New York: Harcourt Brace Jovanovich.

Degani, A., Barshi, I., & Shafto, J. G. (2013). Information organization in the airline cockpit. *Journal of Cognitive Engineering and Decision Making, 7,* 330–352.

de Boer, R. J., Heems, W., & Hurts, K. (2014). The duration of automation bias in a realistic setting. *International Journal of Aviation Psychology, 24,* 287–299.

Dismukes, R. K., Berman, B. A., & Loukopoulos, L. D. (2007). *The limits of expertise: Rethinking pilot error and the causes of airline accidents.* Aldershot, England: Ashgate Publishing.

Driskill, W. E., Weissmuller, J. J., Quebe, J. C., Hand, D. K., & Hunter, D. R. (1998). *Evaluating the decision-making skills of general aviation pilots (Final Report, DOT/FAA/AM-98/7).* Washington, DC: U.S. Dept. of Transportation, Federal Aviation Administration.

Endsley, M. R. (1995). Toward a theory of situation awareness. *Human Factors, 37.*

Endsley, M. R., & Robertson, M. M. (2000). Training for situation awareness in individuals and teams. In M. R. Endsley, & D. J. Garland (Eds.), *Situation awareness analysis and measurement* (pp. 349–366). Mahwah, NJ: Lawrence Erlbaum Associates.

Ericsson, K. A., & Charness, N. (1997). Cognitive and developmental factors in expert performance. In P. J. Feltovich, K. M. Ford, & R. R. Hoffman (Eds.), *Expertise in context: Human and machine* (pp. 3–41). Cambridge, MA: MIT Press.

Ericsson, K. A., & Smith, J. (1991). Prospects and limits of the empirical study of expertise: An introduction. In K. A. Ericsson, & J. Smith (Eds.), *Toward a general theory of expertise: Prospects and limits.* Cambridge, MA: Cambridge University Press.

Fischer, U., & Orasanu, J. (1999). Say it again, Sam! Effective communication strategies to mitigate pilot error. In R. S. Jensen, & L. A. Rakovan (Eds.), *Proceedings of the 10th international symposium on aviation psychology* (pp. 362–366). Columbus, OH: Ohio State University.

Fischer, U., Davison, J., & Orasanu, J. (2003). What makes flight situations risky? Examining commercial and general aviation pilots' concepts of risk. In *Proceedings of the 12th International Symposium on Aviation Psychology.* Lawrence Erlbaum Associates.

Fischer, U., McDonnell, L., & Orasanu, J. (2007). Linguistic correlates of team performance: Toward a tool for monitoring team functioning during space missions. *Aviation, Space, and Environmental Medicine, 78*(5), B86–B95, II.

Fischer, U., & Orasanu, J. (2000). *Error-challenging strategies: Their role in preventing and correcting errors. Proceedings of the 44th annual meeting of the human factors and ergonomics society* (pp. 30–33). Santa Monica, CA: HFES.

Fischer, U., & Orasanu, J. (2001). *Do you see what I see? Effects of crew position on interpretation of flight problems.* NASA Technical Memorandum (2002-209612).

Fischer, U., Orasanu, J., & Montalvo, M. (1993). Efficient decision strategies on the flight deck. In R. Jensen (Ed.), *Proceedings of the 7th symposium on aviation psychology* (pp. 238–243), April 1993, Columbus, OH.

Fischer, U., Orasanu, J., & Wich, M. (1995). *Expert pilots' perceptions of problem situations. Proceedings of the eighth international symposium on aviation psychology* (pp. 777–782). Columbus, OH: Ohio State University Press.

Fischhoff, B. (1975). Hindsight / = foresight: The effect of outcome knowledge on judgment under uncertainty. *Journal of Experimental Psychology: Human Perception and Performance, 1*, 288–299.

Flanagan, J. C. (1954). The critical incident technique. *Psychological Bulletin, 51*, 327–358.

Flight Safety Foundation. (1998). Approach and Landing Accident Reduction (ALAR) Tool KitUpdate (cd). Available from https://flightsafety.org/toolkits-resources/past-safety-initiatives/approach-and-landing-accident-reduction-alar/alar-tool-kit-update-cd/.

Flin, R., O'Connor, P., & Crichton, M. (2008). *Safety at the sharp end: A guide to non-technical skills.* Farnham: Ashgate.

Freeman, J.T., Cohen, M.S., & Thompson, B. (1998). Time-stressed decision making in the cockpit. In *Americas conference on information systems (AMCIS) 1998 proceedings*, Vol. 85. Available from http://aisel.aisnet.org/amcis1998/85.

Ginnett, R. C. (1993). Crew as groups: Their formation and their leadership. In E. Weiner, B. Kanki, & R. Helmreich (Eds.), *Cockpit resource management* (pp. 71–98). San Diego, CA: Academic Press.

Glaser, R., & Bassok, M. (1989). Learning theory and the study of instruction. *Annual Review of Psychology, 40*, 631–666.

Grote, G., Kolbe, M., Zala-Mezo, E., Bienefeld-Seall, N., & Kunzle, B. (2010). Adaptive coordination and heedfulness make better cockpit crews. *Ergonomics, 53*(2), 211–228.

Hammond, K. R., Hamm, R. M., Grassia, J., & Pearson, T. (1987). Direct comparison of the efficacy of intuitive and analytical cognition in expert judgment. *Proceedings of IEEE Transactions on Systems, Man, and Cybernetics, SMC-17*, 753–770.

Hancock, P. A., & Desmond, P. A. (2001). *Stress, workload and fatigue.* Mahwah, NJ: Erlbaum.

Harville, D., Lopez, N., Elliott, L., & Barnes, C. (2005). *Team communication and performance during sustained working conditions.* Air Force Research Laboratory, Report #AFRL-HE-BR-TR-2005-0085, May, 2005.

Hawkins, S. A., & Hastie, R. (1990). Hindsight: Biased judgments of past events. *Psychological Bulletin, 107*, 311–327.

Helmreich R.L. (2002). Threat and error management: 6th generation CRM training. In *Proceedings of the first TEM workshop (ICAO)* (pp. 1–14). San Salvador, El Salvador, April 30, 2002.

Helmreich, R. L., & Foushee, H. C. (2010). Why CRM? Empirical and theoretical bases of human factors training. In B. G. Kanki, R. L. Helmreich, & J. Anca (Eds.), *Crew resource management* (2nd ed., pp. 3–57). San Diego: Academic Press.

Helmreich, R. L., Klinect, J. R., & Wilhelm, J. A. (1999). Models of threat, error and CRM in flight operations. In R. S. Jensen (Ed.), *Proceedings of the tenth international symposium on aviation psychology* (pp. 677–682). Columbus, OH: Ohio State University.

Helmreich, R. L., Klinect, J. R., & Wilhelm, J. A. (2001). *System safety and threat and error management: The line operational safety audit (LOSA). 11th International symposium on aviation psychology.* Columbus, OH: Ohio State University.

Hockey, G. R. L. (1979). Stress and the cognitive components of skilled performance. In V. Hamilton, & D. M. Warbuton (Eds.), *Human stress and cognition: An information-processing approach.* Chichester: Wiley.

Hoermann, H. J. (1995). FOR-DEC—A prescriptive model for aeronautical decision making. *Human Factors in Aviation Operations*, 17–23.

Hoffman, R. R., Crandall, B. W., & Shadbolt, N. R. (1998). Use of the critical decision method to elicit expert knowledge: A case study in cognitive task analysis methodology. *Human Factors, 40*(2), 254–276.

Hogarth, R. M. (1987). *Judgement and choice: The psychology of decision.* New York: Wiley.

Hollenbeck, J., Ilgen, D., Phillips, J., & Hedlund, J. (1994). Decision risk in dynamic two-stage contexts: Beyond the status-quo. *Journal of Applied Psychology, 79*(4), 592−598.

Hutchins, E. (1995). *Cognition in the wild.* Cambridge, MA: MIT Press.

Johnston, N. (1996). Managing risk in flight operations. In B. J. Hayward, & A. R. Lowe (Eds.), *Applied aviation psychology: Achievement, change and challenge* (pp. 1−19). Brookfield, VT: Ashgate.

Kahneman, D. (2011). *Thinking fast and slow.* New York: Farrar, Straus and Giroux.

Kanki, B. G. (2010). Communication and crew resource management. In B. G. Kanki, R. Helmreich, & J. Anca (Eds.), *Crew resource management* (2nd ed., pp. 111−145). San Diego, CA: Academic Press.

Kanki, B. G., Lozito, S., & Foushee, H. C. (1989). Communication indices of crew coordination. *Aviation, Space, and Environmental Medicine, 60*, 56−60.

Keinan, G. (1988). Training for dangerous task performance: The effects of expectations and feedback. *Journal of Applied Social Psychology, 18*(4, Pt 2), 355−373.

Klein, C., Salas, E., DiazGranados, D., Burke, C.S., Stagl, K.C., Goodwin, G.F., et al. (2008). Do team training interventions enhance valued team outcomes? A meta-analytic initiative. In *Paper presented at the 23rd annual conference of the Society for Industrial and Organizational Psychology,* San Francisco, CA.

Klein, G. (1993b). Sources of error in naturalistic decision making. In *Proceedings of the human factors and ergonomics society 37th annual meeting* (pp. 368−371). HFES: Santa Monica.

Klein, G. (1998). *Sources of power: How people make decisions.* Cambridge: MIT Press.

Klein, G. (2008). Naturalistic decision making. *Human Factors, 50*, 456−460.

Klein, G., Feltovich, P. J., Bradshaw, J. M., & Woods, D. D. (2005). Common ground and coordination in joint activity. In W. R. Rouse, & K. B. Boff (Eds.), *Organizational simulation.* New York: Wiley.

Klein, G., Hintze, N. & Saab, D. (2013). Thinking inside the box: The ShadowBox method for cognitive skill development. In *Proceedings of the11th International Conference on Naturalistic Decision Making (NDM2013).* Paris: Arpege Science Publishing.

Klein, G., Orasanu, J., Calderwood, R., & Zsambok, C. E. (Eds.), (1993). *Decision making in action: Models and methods.* Norwood, NJ: Ablex.

Klein, G., Ross, K. G., Moon, B. M., Klein, D. E., Hoffman, R. R., & Hollnagel, E. (2003). Macrocognition. *IEEE Intelligent Systems, 18*, 81−85.

Klein, G., & Wright, C. (2016). Macrocognition: From theory to toolbox. *Frontiers in Psychology, 7*, Article 54.

Klein, G. A. (1989). Recognition-primed decisions. In W. B. Rouse (Ed.), *Advances in man-machine system research* (Vol. 5, pp. 47−92). Greenwich, CT: JAI Press.

Klein, G. A. (1993a). A recognition-primed decision (RPD) model of rapid decision making. In G. Klein, J. Orasanu, R. Calderwood, & C. Zsambok (Eds.), *Decision making in action: Models and methods* (pp. 138−147). Norwood, NJ: Ablex.

Klein, G. A., Calderwood, R., & Clinton-Cirocco, A. (1986). *Rapid decision making on the fire ground, . Proceedings of the human factors and ergonomics society annual meting* (Vol 30, pp. 576−580). Dayton, OH: Sage Publications.

Klinect, J. R., Wilhelm, J. A., & Helmreich, R. L. (1999). *Threat and error management: Data from line operations safety audits. Tenth International Symposium on Aviation Psychology* (pp. 683−688). Columbus, OH: The Ohio State University.

Larkin, J., McDermott, J., Simon, D. P., & Simon, H. A. (1980). Expert and novice performance in solving physics problems. *Science, 20*, 1335−1342.

Letsky, M. P., Warner, N. W., Fiore, S. M., & Smith, C. A. P. (Eds.), (2008). *Macrocognition in teams: Theories and methodologies*. Aldershot, Hampshire: Ashgate Publishing, Ltd.

Li, W.-C., & Harris, D. (2008). The evaluation of the effect of a short aeronautical decision-making training program for military pilots. *The International Journal of Aviation Psychology, 18*(2), 135−152.

Lingard, L., Reznick, R., Espin, S., Regehr, G., & DeVito, I. (2002). Team communications in the operating room: Talk patterns, sites of tension, and the implications for novices. *Acadamic Medicine, 77*, 232−237.

Lipshitz, R. (1997). Naturalistic decision making perspectives on decision errors. In C. Zsambok, & G. Klein (Eds.), *Naturalistic decision making.* (pp. 151−162). Mahwah, NJ: Erlbaum.

Lipshitz, R., Klein, G., Orasanu, J., & Salas, E. (2001). Taking stock of naturalistic decision making. *Journal of Behavioral Decision Making, 14*, 331−352.

Lipshitz, R., Omodei, M., McClellan, J., & Wearing, A. (2007). What's burning? The RAWFS heuristic on the fire ground. In R. R. Hoffman (Ed.), *Expertise out of context: proceedings of the sixth international conference on naturalistic decision making* (pp. 97−111). New York, NY: Erlbaum.

Lipshitz, R., & Strauss, O. (1997). Coping with uncertainty: A naturalistic decision making analysis. *Organizational Behavior and Human Decision Processes, 66*, 149−163.

Maher, J.W. (1989). Beyond CRM to decisional heuristics: An airline generated model to examine accidents and incidents caused by crew errors in deciding. In R. S. Jensen (Ed.), *Proceedings of the 5th international symposium on aviation psychology*, Columbus, OH.

Marks, M. A., Zaccaro, S. J., & Mathieu, J. E. (2000). Performance implications of leader briefings and team-interaction training for team adaptation to novel environments. *Journal of Applied Psychology, 85*(6), 971−986.

Martin, L., Davison, J., & Orasanu, J. (1999). Identifying error-inducing contexts in aviation. In *SAE conference*, San Francisco, CA, October, 1999.

Maule, A. J. (1997). Strategies for adapting to time pressure. In R. Flin, E. Salas, M. Strub, & L. Martin (Eds.), *Decision making under stress: Emerging themes and applications* (pp. 271−279). Aldershot: Ashgate.

McEwan, D., Ruissen, G. R., Eys, M. A., Zumbo, B. D., & Beauchamp, M. R. (2017). The effectiveness of teamwork training on teamwork behaviors and team performance: A systematic review and meta-analysis of controlled interventions. *PLoS One, 12*(1), e0169604. Available from https://doi.org/10.1371/journal.pone.0169604.

Means, B., Salas, E., Crandall, B., & Jacobs, T. O. (1993). Training decision makers for the real world. In G. Klein, J. Orasanu, R. Calderwood, & C. E. Zsambok (Eds.), *Decision making in action: Models and methods* (pp. 51−99). Norwood, NJ: Ablex.

Militello, L., Wong, W., Kirschenbaum, S., & Patterson, E. (2011). Systematizing discovery in cognitive task analysis. In K. L. Mosier, & U. M. Fischer (Eds.), *Informed by knowledge: Expert performance in complex situations*. New York, NY: Taylor & Francis.

Ministre de l'Equipement, des Transports et du Tourisme. (1993). *Rapport de la Commission d'Enquete sur l'Accident survenu le 20 Janvier 1992 pres du Mont Saite Odile a l/Airbus A320 Immatricule F-GGED Exploite par lay Compagnie Air Inter*. Paris: Author.

Moritz, S., Kerstan, A., Veckenstedt, R., Randjbar, S., Vitzthum, R., Schmidt, C., ... Woodward. (2010). Further evidence for the effectiveness of a metacognitive group training in schizophrenia. *Behaviour Research and Therapy*. Available from https://doi.org/10.1016/j.brat.2010.11.010.

Mosier, K., Fischer, U., Burian, B., & Kochan, J. (2017). *Autonomous, context-sensitive, task management systems and decision support tools I: Contextual constraints and information sources.* NASA/TM-2017-219565. NASA Ames Research Center.

Mosier, K., Fischer, U., Hoffman, R., & Klein, G. (in press). Expert professional judgments and "Naturalistic Decision Making." In K. A. Ericcson, R. Hoffman, A. Kozbelt, & M. Williams (Eds.), *The Cambridge handbook of expertise and expert performance.* Cambridge University Press.

Mosier, K., Sethi, N., McCauley, S., Khoo, L., & Orasanu, J. (2007). What you don't know can hurt you: Factors impacting diagnosis in the automated cockpit. *Human Factors, 49,* 300–310.

Mosier, K. L. (2002). Automation and cognition: Maintaining coherence in the electronic cockpit. In E. Salas (Ed.), *Advances in human performance and cognitive engineering research, volume 2* (pp. 93–121). Elsevier Science Ltd.

Mosier, K. L. (2008). Technology and "naturalistic" decision making: Myths and realities. In J. M. C. Schraagen, L. Militello, T. Ormerod, & R. Lipshitz (Eds.), *Naturalistic decision making and macrocognition.* Aldershot: Ashgate Publishing Limited.

Mosier, K. L., & Fischer, U. M. (2010). Judgment and decision making by individuals and teams: Issues, models and applications. In D. Harris (Ed.), *Reviews of human factors, Volume 6* (pp. 198–256). Santa Monica, CA: Human Factors and Ergonomics Society.

Mosier, K. L., & Skitka, L. J. (1996). Humans and automation: Made for each other? In R. Parasuraman, & M. Mouloua (Eds.), *Automation and human performance: Theory and applications* (pp. 201–220). NJ: Erlbaum.

Mosier, K. L., Skitka, L. J., Heers, S., & Burdick, M. D. (1998). Automation bias: Decision making and performance in high-tech cockpits. *International Journal of Aviation Psychology, 8,* 47–63.

Nagel, D. C. (1989). Human error in aviation operations. In E. L. Wiener, & D. C. Nagel (Eds.), *Human factors in aviation* (pp. 263–304). NY: Academic Press.

National Transportation Safety Board. (1982). *Aircraft accident report: Air Florida, Inc., Boeing 737-222, N62AF, Collision with 14th Street Bridge near Washington National Airport, Washington, DC, January 13, 1982 (NTSB/AAR-82-8).* Washington, DC: NTSB.

National Transportation Safety Board. (1985). *Aircraft accident report: Air Illinois Hawker Siddley, HS 748-2A, N748LL, near Pinckneyville, Illinois, October 11, 1983 (NTSB AAR 85/03).* Washington, DC: NTSB.

National Transportation Safety Board. (1986a). *Aircraft accident report: Delta Air Lines, Inc., Lockheed L-1011-385-1, N726DA, Dallas/Fort Worth International Airport, Texas, August 2, 1985 (NTSB-AAR-86/05).* Washington, DC: NTSB.

National Transportation Safety Board. (1986b). *Aircraft accident report: Galaxy Airlines, Inc., Lockheed Electra-L-188C, N5532, Reno, Nevada, January 21, 1985 (NTSB AAR-86-01).* Washington, DC: NTSB.

National Transportation Safety Board. (1990). *Aircraft accident report: United Airlines Flight 232, McDonnell Douglas DC-10-10, Sioux Gateway Airport, Sioux City, Iowa, July 19, 1989 (NTSB/AAR-91-02).* Washington, DC: NTSB.

National Transportation Safety Board. (1991). *Aircraft accident report: NW Airlines, Inc., Flights 1482 and 299 runway incursion and collision, Detroit Metropolitan-Wayne County Airport, Romulus, Michigan, December 3, 1990 (NTSB AAR 91/05).* Washington, DC: NTSB.

National Transportation Safety Board. (1994). *A review of flightcrew-involved, major accidents of U.S. Air Carriers, 1978 through 1990 (PB94-917001, NTSB/SS-94/01)*. Washington, DC: NTSB.

National Transportation Safety Board. (2008). CHI08IA292.

National Transportation Safety Board. (2010). *Loss of thrust in both engines after encountering a flock of birds and subsequent ditching on the Hudson River, US Airways Flight 1549, Airbus A320-214, N106US, Weehawken, New Jersey, January 15, 2009*. Aircraft Accident Report NTSB/AAR-10 /03. Washington, DC.

National Transportation Safety Board. (2013). *Descent below visual glidepath and impact with Seawall, Asiana Airlines Flight 214, Boeing 777-200ER, HL7742, San Francisco, CA, July6, 2013*. Washington, DC: Author.

Nowinski, J.L., Holbrook, J.B., & Dismukes, R.K. (2003), Human memory and cockpit operations: an ASRS study. In *Proceedings of the international symposium on aviation psychology*.

O'Hare, D., & Smitheram, T. (1995). "Pressing on" into deteriorating conditions: An application of behavioral decision theory to pilot decision making. *International Journal of Aviation Psychology*, 5(4), 351–370.

Orasanu, J. (1994). Shared problem models and flight crew performance. In N. Johnston, N. McDonald, & R. Fuller (Eds.), *Aviation psychology in practice*. (pp. 255–285). Aldershot, UK: Ashgate.

Orasanu, J. (1997). Stress and naturalistic decision making: Strengthening the weak links. In R. Flin, E. Salas, M. Strub, & L. Martin (Eds.), *Decision making under stress: Emerging themes and applications* (pp. 43–66). Aldershot, UK: Ashgate Publishing.

Orasanu, J. (2010). Decision-making in the cockpit. In B. G. Kanki, R. L. Helmreich, & J. Anca (Eds.), *Cockpit resource management* (2nd ed., pp. 147–179). San Diego, CA: Academic Press.

Orasanu, J., & Connolly, T. (1993). The reinvention of decision making. In G. A. Klein, J. Orasanu, R. Calderwood, & C. E. Zsambok (Eds.), *Decision making in action: Models and methods* (pp. 3–20). Norwood, NJ: Ablex Publishers.

Orasanu, J., & Fischer, U. (1992). *Team cognition in the cockpit: Linguistic control of shared problem solving. Proceedings of the 14th annual conference of the cognitive science society* (pp. 272–277). Erlbaum. Columbus, OH: The Ohio State University: Hillsdale, NJ.

Orasanu, J., & Fischer, U. (1997). Finding decisions in natural environments: The view from the cockpit. In C. Zsambok, & G. Klein (Eds.), *Naturalistic decision making* (pp. 343–357). Mahwah, NJ: Erlbaum.

Orasanu, J., Fischer, U., & Davison, J. (2004). Risk perception and risk management in aviation. In R. Dietrich, & K. Jochum (Eds.), *Teaming up: Components of safety under high risk.* (pp. 93–116). Aldershot: Ashgate.

Orasanu, J., Fischer, U., McDonnell, L. K., Davison, J., Haars, K. E., Villeda, E., et al. (1998). *How do flight crews detect and prevent errors? Findings from a flight simulation study. Proceedings of the human factors and ergonomics society 42nd annual meeting* (pp. 191–195). Santa Monica, CA: Human Factors and Ergonomics Society.

Orasanu, J., & Salas, E. (1993). Team decision making in complex environments. In G. A. Klein, J. Orasanu, R. Calderwood, & C. E. Zsambok (Eds.), *Decision making in action: Models and methods* (pp. 327–345). Norwood, NJ: Ablex Publishers.

Orasanu, J., Martin, L., & Davison, J. (2002). Cognitive and contextual factors in aviation accidents. In E. Salas, & G. Klein (Eds.), *Naturalistic decision making.* (pp. 343–358). Mahwah, NJ: Lawrence Erlbaum.

Orasanu, J., & Strauch, B. (1994). Temporal factors in aviation decision making. In L. Smith (Ed.), *Proceedings of the human factors and ergonomics society 38th annual meeting* (Vol. 2, pp. 935−939). Santa Monica, CA: Human Factors and Ergonomics Society.

O'Hare, D. (2003). Aeronautical decision making: Metaphors, models, and methods. In P. S. Tsang, & M. A. Vidulich (Eds.), *Principles and practice of aviation psychology: Human factors in transportation* (pp. 201−237). New Jersey: Lawrence Erlbaum.

O'Hare, D., & Waite, A. (2012). Effects of pilot experience on recall of information from graphical weather displays. *International Journal of Aviation Psychology*, *22*, 1−17.

Paletz, S. B. F., Bearman, C., Orasanu, J., & Holbrook, J. (2009). Socializing the human factors analysis and classification system: Incorporating social psychological phenomena into a human factors error classification system. *Human Factors*, *51*(4), 435.

Parke, B., Kanki, B., Nord, K., & Bianchi, A. (2000). Crew climate and performance: Use of group diagrams based on behavioral ratings. In *44th IEA2000/HFES 2000 Congress* (pp. 3149−3152). San Diego.

Patel, V. L., & Groen, G. J. (1991). The general and specific nature of expertise: A critical look. In K. A. Ericsson, & J. Smith (Eds.), *Toward a general theory of expertise: Prospects and limits.* (pp. 93−125). Cambridge, MA: Cambridge University Press.

Petrilli, R. M., Roach, G. D., Dawson, D., & Lamond, N. (2006). The sleep, subjective fatigue, and sustained attention of commercial airline pilots during an international pattern. *Chronobiology International*, *23*, 1357−1362.

Phillips, J. K., Klein, G., & Sieck, W. R. (2004). Expertise in judgment and decision making: A case for training intuitive decision skills. In D. J. Koehler, & N. Harvey (Eds.), *Blackwell handbook of judgment and decision making.* (pp. 306−315). Oxford: Blackwell Publishing, LTD.

Predmore, S. C. (1991). *Micro-coding of communications in accident analyses: Crew coordination in United 811 and United 232. Proceedings of the sixth international symposium on aviation psychology* (pp. 350−355). Columbus, OH: The Ohio State University.

Rasmussen, J. (1985). The role of hierarchical knowledge representation in decision making and system management. *IEEE Transactions on Systems, Man, and Cybernetics*, *15*(2), 234−243.

Rasmussen, J. (1993). Deciding and doing: Decision making in natural context. In G. Klein, J. Orasanu, R. Calderwood, & C. Zsambok (Eds.), *Decision making in action: Models and methods*. Norwood, NJ: Ablex.

Reason, J. (1990). *Human error*. Cambridge, UK: Cambridge University Press.

Reason, J. (1997). *Managing the risks of organizational accidents*. Brookfield, VT: Ashgate.

Resnick, L. B., Salmon, M., Zeith, C. M., Wathen, S. H., & Holowchak, M. (1993). Reasoning in conversation. *Cognition and Instruction*, *11*(3 & 4), 347−364.

Rhoda, D.A., & Pawlak, M.L. (1999). *An assessment of thunderstorm penetrations and deviations by commercial aircraft in the terminal area.* Project Report #NASA/A2 to NASA Ames Research Center, Moffett Field, CA.

Salas, E., Diaz Granados, D., Klein, C., Burke, C. S., Stagl, K. C., Goodwin, G. F., & Halpin, S. M. (2008). Does team training improve team performance? A meta-analysis. *Human Factors*, *50*(6), 903−933, December.

Salas, E., Nichols, D. R., & Driskell, J. E. (2007). Testing three team training strategies in intact teams: A meta-analysis. *Small Group Research*, *38*, 471−488.

Salas, E., Sims, D. E., & Burke, C. S. (2005). Is there a "big five" in teamwork? *Small Group Research*, *36*(5), 555−599.

Sarter, N. B., & Woods, D. D. (1995). How in the world did we ever get into that mode? Mode error and awareness in supervisory control. *Human Factors*, *37*(1), 5−19.

Schraagen, J. M., Klein, G., & Hoffman, R. R. (2008). Macrocognition framework of naturalistic decision making. In J. M. C. Schraagen, L. Militello, T. Ormerod, & R. Lipshitz (Eds.), *Naturalistic decision making and macrocognition.* (pp. 3−25). Aldershot: Ashgate Publishing Limited.

Senders, J. W., & Moray, N. P. (1991). *Human error: Cause, prediction, and reduction.* Hillsdale, NJ: Lawrence Erlbaum Assoc.

Shappell, S. & Wiegmann, D. (2004). HFACS analysis of military and civilian aviation accidents: A North American comparison. In *Paper presented at the International Society of Air Safety Investigators*, Queensland, Australia, November 2004.

Silva, S., & Hansman, J. (2015). Divergence between flight crew mental model and aircraft system state in auto-throttle mode confusion accident and incident cases. *Journal of Cognitive Engineering and Decision Making, 9*, 312−328.

Simon, H. (1991). Bounded rationality and organizational learning. *Organization Science, 2*(1), 125−134.

Sitkin, S. (1992). Learning through failure: The strategy of small losses. *Research in Organizational Behavior, 14*, 231−266.

Skitka, L. J., Mosier, K. L., & Burdick, M. (1999). Does automation bias decision making? *International Journal of Human-Computer Studies, 50*, 991−1006.

Slovic, P. (1987). Perception of Risk. *Science, 236*(17 April), 280−285.

Stokes, A. F., Kemper, K., & Kite, K. (1997). Aeronautical decision making, cue recognition, and expertise under time pressure. In C. E. Zsambok, & G. Klein (Eds.), *Naturalistic decision making* (pp. 183−196). Mahwah, NJ: Erlbaum.

Strauch, B. (1997). *Automation and decision making—Lessons from the Cali accident. Proceedings of the human factors and ergonomics society 41st annual meeting* (pp. 195−199). Santa Monica, CA: Human Factors and Ergonomics Society.

Sumwalt, R.L., Thomas, R.J., & Dismukes, R.K., 2002. Enhancing flight crew monitoring skills can increase flight safety. In *Proceedings of the 55th international air safety seminar*, Dublin, Ireland, November 4−7, 2002.

Thomas, M. J. W. (2004). Predictors of threat and error management: Identification of core nontechnical skills and implications for training systems design. *International Journal of Aviation Psychology, 14*(2), 207−231.

Tversky, A. (1972). Elimination by aspects: A theory of choice. *Psychological Review, 79*, 281−299.

Tversky, A., & Kahneman, D. (1974). Judgment under uncertainty: Heuristics and biases. *Science, 185*, 1124−1131.

Van den Bossche, P., Gijselaers, W., Segers, M., Woltjer, G., & Kirschner, P. (2011). Team learning: Building shared mental models. *Instructional Science, 39*, 283−301.

Van Lehn, K. (1990). *Mind bugs: The origins of procedural conceptions.* Cambridge, MA: MIT Press.

Walters, A. (2002). *Crew resource management is no accident.* Wallingford: Aries.

Wickens, C., & Raby, M. (1991). *Individual differences in strategic flight management and scheduling. Proceedings of the sixth international symposium on aviation psychology* (pp. 1142−1147). Columbus, OH: The Ohio State University.

Wickens, C. D., Stokes, A., Barnett, B., & Hyman, F. (1993). The effects of stress on pilot judgment in a MIDIS simulator. In O. Svenson, & A. J. Maule (Eds.), *Time pressure and stress in human judgment and decision making* (pp. 271−292). Cambridge: Cambridge University Press.

Wiegmann, D. A., Goh, J., & O'Hare, D. (2002). The role of situation assessment and flight experience in pilots' decisions to continue visual flight rules flight into adverse weather. *Human Factors, 44*(2), 189–197.

Wiener, E. (1998). Cockpit automation. In E. L. Wiener, & D. C. Nagel (Eds.), *Human factors in aviation*. New York: Academic Press.

Wiggins, M., & O'Hare, D. (2003). Weatherwise: Evaluation of a cue-based training approach for the recognition of deteriorating weather conditions during flight. *Human Factors, 45*, 337–345.

Woods D.D., & Sarter N.B. (1998). *Learning from automation surprises and "going sour" accidents: Progress on human-centered automation (NASA report NCC2-592)*. Moffett Field, CA. NASA Ames Research Center.

Yates, J. F., & Stone, E. R. (1992). The risk construct. In J. F. Yates (Ed.), *Risk-taking behavior* (pp. 1–25). Chichester, UK: Wiley.

Zsambok, C., & Klein, G. (Eds.), (1997). *Naturalistic decision making*. Mahwah, NJ: Erlbaum.

Chapter 6

CRM (Nontechnical) Skills: A European Perspective

Rhona Flin

Aberdeen Business School, Robert Gordon University, Aberdeen, Scotland

INTRODUCTION

Crew resource management (CRM) training and nontechnical skills assessment are well-established components of the management of safety in European commercial aviation. Typically CRM is defined as the effective utilization of all available resources (e.g., crewmembers, aircraft systems, supporting facilities and persons) to achieve safe and efficient operations. Its objective is to enhance the flight management skills of crewmembers with an emphasis placed on the nontechnical knowledge, skills, and attitudes of crew performance. The term nontechnical skill has been used by the European aviation regulator for many years as a synonym for CRM skills. Pilots' nontechnical skills have been defined as the cognitive and social skills of flight crewmembers in the cockpit, not directly related to aircraft control, system management, and standard operating procedures. This chapter mainly concerns CRM for flight crew, although regulations on CRM apply also to cabin crew and technical crew.

The current requirements on CRM training and skills assessment from the European regulator (European Aviation Safety Agency: EASA) and their application by the UK Civil Aviation Authority (CAA) are briefly described. Some examples are given of how air operators in Europe are applying these regulatory provisions. Much of the material in this chapter is drawn from documents published by EASA and CAA which are available on their websites. Telephone or face to face interviews were conducted with training captains from five fixed wing operators of different sizes (Aer Lingus, British Airways, Flybe, KLM, and Loganair) and one rotor wing Company (CHC Helicopters), as well as receiving information from EASA, the CAA, a training company (LMQ), the EBT Foundation, and two additional pilots (from other large airlines). There are reams of legislation, guidance, and associated reports covering CRM training and assessment; not all of them easy to

Crew Resource Management. DOI: https://doi.org/10.1016/B978-0-12-812995-1.00006-3

navigate. Recent regulatory changes in Europe and the degree of freedom in meeting the acceptable means of compliance, as well as the current evolution to evidence-based training (EBT), has produced a significant level of variability across operators' practices. So despite the assistance of those mentioned above, this chapter represents only a selective overview of the current landscape for European flight crews' CRM training and assessment, and any errors are entirely of my own making.

In 2012, the European regulator recognized concerns as to whether CRM training was sufficiently practical and effective for current conditions and also, if the regulatory provisions for CRM trainers were adequate (Boettcher, 2016). Internationally at this time, questions had been raised as to whether CRM training was meeting current demands, given changes in operations (e.g., evolving technologies, larger aircraft, new generations of pilots, FDM (flight data monitoring)) and emerging threats (e.g., increasing traffic; the loss of control identified in several accidents). So the suitability and effectiveness of pilot training in general, as well as the existing CRM programs, began to require scrutiny. The view of the European regulator (see Boettcher, 2016) was that any update in the regulatory provisions should consider new developments, accumulated experience from regulators and operators, as well as recent safety recommendations from accident investigations (e.g., the Air France Flight 447 accident in 2009, BEA, 2012; see Law & Chidester, 2014; Chapter 7: Crew Resource Management and Individual Resilience by Martin in this volume).

In 2012, EASA began to work on a review of CRM training and assessment, consulting air operators, regulators, and other experts, as well as conducting a survey of CRM practices, plus examining accident reports and related safety data. In September 2015, two Executive Director Decisions (2015/022/R and 2015/023/R[1]) were published which introduced the new AMC (Acceptable Means of Compliance) and GM (Guidance Material). The changes significantly extended and modernized the existing CRM training scheme and the new requirements came into force on October 1, 2016. These changes relate to the content and conduct of CRM training and skills assessment, as well for qualification of inspectors of competent authorities. They can be found in the operations (PART-ORO, Subpart FC)[2] and flight crew licensing (PART-FCL) sections (see EASA, 2016a,b) relating to the regulations (965/2012 and 1178/2011). In November 2016, EASA organized a 1 day workshop in Cologne, "CRM in Practice," which discussed current issues relating to CRM, followed by a second workshop in August 2017. Key papers from these workshops, explaining the new requirements, giving

---

1. Decision 023/R relates to cabin crew initial CRM.
2. Much of the material in this section is drawn from EASA (2016a) AMC/GM TO ANNEX III (PART-ORO) SUBPART FC − FLIGHT CREW (p107 onwards) AMC1 ORO. FC. 115 Crew resource management (CRM) training. Multipilot operations.

examples of CRM in current practice, and describing the role of the regulators in inspecting the revised CRM activities can be found in EASA (2017).

In the United Kingdom, the EASA aviation regulations and acceptable means of compliance apply and the UK CAA issues related guidance in the form of standards documents (e.g., CAA, 2016 *Standards Doc 29 v, Flightcrew training and testing of Human Factors*) and other advice (e.g., CAA, 2014 CAP 737, *Flight-crew Human Factors Handbook*). Also influential for current CRM developments in Europe, are industry reports from IATA (International Aviation Training Association) and ICAO (International Civil Aviation Organization), especially those on EBT (e.g., IATA, 2013; ICAO, 2013).

6.1   CRM TRAINING

The CRM training for European pilots generally consists of the in-depth, initial operator's CRM training and recurrent training, as well as conversion (operator and type) and command regulatory provisions. Minimum hours of training are specified (e.g., for initial operator's CRM training (multipilot): 18 training hours with a minimum of 12 training hours in classroom training).

Operators have to update their CRM recurrent training program over a period not exceeding 3 years to cover all the stipulated topics (see below). The design of the recurrent program takes into account information (e.g., hazards and risks) from the operator's management system, including the de-identified results of the CRM (nontechnical skills) assessments (for flight crew training). Operators must provide combined training for flight crew, cabin crew, and technical crew during the recurrent CRM training. This should address effective communication, coordination of tasks, and functions of flight crew, cabin crew, and technical crew; and mixed multinational and cross-cultural crewmembers and their interaction, if applicable. This combined CRM training can be conducted by a flight crew CRM trainer or cabin crew CRM trainer. It is also advised that there should be an effective liaison between flight crew, cabin crew, and technical crew training departments, with provision for transfer of relevant knowledge and skills between them. In essence, recurrent CRM training provides an opportunity to share and learn from other crewmembers. Guidance from CAA (2014, p. 166) advises that "experienced crew-members should leave the training feeling motivated to continue or improve their use of non-technical skills and behaviours in line operations. To be effective, recurrent training material should be more carefully researched than other CRM training course material. If there is little material 'in-house' available, then using examples from other operators can be valuable."

The CRM training usually consists of classroom sessions and may also have computer-based components, as well as sessions in simulators (e.g., line oriented flight training) and in aircraft. CRM principles should be integrated into relevant parts of flight crew training and operations including checklists, briefings, abnormal and emergency procedures. In the classroom, tools such as problem-solving exercises, group discussions, scenario analysis, role plays and task simulations, videos, as well as lectures, can be used.

The new requirements state that case studies should be incorporated into the training. These should cover aircraft type-specific case studies, based on the information available within the operator's management system, including: accident and serious incident reviews to analyze and identify any associated nontechnical causal and contributory factors, and instances or examples of lack of CRM; and analysis of occurrences that were well managed. If relevant case studies are not available, (i.e., to the aircraft type or operator), then other case studies relevant to the scale and scope of its operations, should be considered.

6.1.1 Content of CRM Training

In terms of the content of the CRM training, there are two different sets of competency and associated knowledge requirements in EASA (2016b) Part-FCL, AMC1 FCL. 735A (on MCC multicrew cooperation course) and EASA (2016a) Part-ORO, ORO. FC. 115 and ORO. FC. 215 (on CRM) (see section 2.1 of CAA, 2016 on the regulatory framework). However, the main nontechnical skills topics in the different regulations essentially cover similar ground and these are summarized below in Table 6.1 with the newer topics shown in italics.

There is also mention of briefing, monitoring, and cross-checking, as well as the more technical skills relating to flight management, with

---

TABLE 6.1 Main CRM Training Course Topics

- Application of the principles of CRM and threat and error management (TEM)
- Situation awareness
- Problem-solving and decision-making
- Workload management/task sharing
- Communication/assertiveness
- Leadership and teamwork
- Stress and Stress Management
- Fatigue and vigilance
- *Automation*
- *Monitoring and intervention*
- *Resilience development*
- *Surprise and startle effects*
- Operator's safety *culture* and company *culture*

knowledge requirements that include SOPs (standard operating procedures), aircraft systems, undesired aircraft states, emergency and abnormal procedures.

The threat and error management (TEM) model (Helmreich, 1997) has been a core component of CRM training in Europe since the 1990s. From my interviews with airline captains, it appears that TEM remains well ingrained in their CRM training programs and is found to be a valuable framework to discuss error management and the role of nontechnical skills. They also mentioned referring to it when giving feedback during the checking process. As the training content of the original CRM components listed above (e.g., situation awareness) are well established (see other chapters in this volume), only the more recent additions are described below.

Automation

The benefits and challenges of increasingly automated aircraft and the implications for pilots' skill base is a long standing matter of debate in aviation (e.g., Eurocontrol, 2014). A CRM syllabus should include training in the use and knowledge of automation, and in the recognition of systems and human limitations associated with its use. Flight crewmembers should receive training on the application of the operations policy concerning the use of automation (from the operations manual) and system and human limitations related to automation, particularly issues of mode awareness, automation surprises, and overreliance, including false sense of security and complacency. Special attention should be given to how automation increases the need for crews to have a common understanding of the way in which the system performs, and any features of automation that make this understanding difficult.

Monitoring and Intervention

Monitoring can be defined (CAA, 2013b, p. 9) as follows: "The observation and interpretation of the flight path data, configuration status, automation modes and on-board systems appropriate to the phase of flight. It involves a cognitive comparison against the expected values, modes and procedures. It also includes observation of the other crew member and timely intervention in the event of deviation." Flight crew should be trained in CRM-related aspects of operation monitoring before, during, and after flight, together with any associated priorities. This should include guidance to the pilot monitoring on when it would be appropriate to intervene, if felt necessary, and how this should be done in a timely manner. Reference should be made to the operator procedures for structured intervention as specified in the operations manual.

A pilot's ability to monitor the state of the aircraft and the flying environment is not a new topic but monitoring skills have received recent emphasis. This is due to concern about loss of control which has been prioritized as a significant safety issue. For example, between 2000 and 2012, there were at least nine fatal accidents attributed to loss of control which resulted in 1128 fatalities (CAA, 2013a). The CAA (2013b) issued a guidance paper on the development of pilot monitoring skills which provides a very comprehensive explanation of the cognitive components of monitoring with a series of case examples and advice for trainers and assessors. Another useful resource for trainers is the NASA report on the importance of checklists and monitoring in the cockpit (Dismukes & Berman, 2010).

Resilience Development

Again influenced by renewed attention to loss of control events (particularly the Air France 447 accident, BEA, 2012), two related topics which have to be incorporated into CRM training in Europe are the development of resilience and the skills to cope with unexpected events that could produce surprise, or worse, a startle reaction in the pilots. Resilience is a topic that has recently received considerable interest in other industries, relating both to organizational (Hollnagel, Woods, & Leveson, 2006) and individual resilience (Drath, 2017). It can be defined as "the ability of a system to adjust its functioning prior to, during, or following changes and disturbances, so that it can sustain required operations under both expected and unexpected conditions" (EASA, 2017, p. 14). The CRM training in Europe should address the main aspects of resilience development by covering:

1. Mental flexibility—Flight crew should be trained to: (a) understand that mental flexibility is necessary to recognize critical changes (i.e., be prepared to respond to situations for which there is no set procedure); (b) reflect on their judgement and adjust it to the unique situation; (c) avoid fixed prejudices and overreliance on standard solutions (learn to update solutions and standard response sets, which have been formed on prior knowledge); and (d) remain open to changing assumptions and perceptions (constantly monitor the situation, and be prepared to adjust their understanding of the evolving conditions).
2. Performance adaptation—This training is designed to help flight crews to: mitigate frozen behaviors, overreactions, and inappropriate hesitation (i.e., correct improper actions with a balanced response); and adjust actions to current conditions.

From the EASA regulatory guidance, it is explained that the main aspects of resilience development can be described as the ability to: learn ("knowing what has happened"); monitor ("knowing what to look for"); anticipate ("finding out and knowing what to expect"); and respond ("knowing what to do and being capable of doing it"). It states that operational safety is a continuous process of evaluation of and adjustment to existing and future conditions. Therefore, resilience development involves an ongoing and adaptable process including situation assessment, self-review, decision, and action. Training in resilience development enables crewmembers to draw the right conclusions from both positive and negative experiences. Based on those experiences, crewmembers should be better prepared to maintain or create safety margins by adapting to dynamic complex situations.

Surprise and Startle Effects

When an unexpected event occurs, such as an alarm for an equipment malfunction, sudden extreme turbulence, loud noise, or very strong vibration, then a normal human reaction is to experience a mental sense of surprise, which may have physiological aspects. If the sudden event is perceived as very threatening, then a stronger emotional and physical reaction may be experienced known as "startle" (see SKYbrary, 2016). These phenomena have been studied in both animals and humans for many years but there had been less research into the effects on pilots in flight, although studies of acute stress in pilots have been undertaken (Dismukes, Goldsmith, & Kochan, 2015). Wayne Martin, a Virgin Australia captain studied startle effects for his doctoral project (Martin, Murray, Bates, & Lee, 2015; Martin, Murray, Bates, & Lee, 2016; see Chapter 7: Crew Resource Management and Individual Resilience this volume) and as the aviation regulators became more interested in this issue, other studies have been undertaken (e.g., Landman, Groen, van Paassen, Bronkhorst, & Mulder, 2017a,b), although there seems to be some debate as to the differences between surprise and startle effects (Rivera, Talone, Boesser, Jentsch, & Yeh, 2014). A recent EASA funded study on startle effect management conducted by NLR (Netherlands Aerospace Centre) with the help of KLM pilots, suggests a three step method for recovery from "mental upset" which consists of: (1) Unload—to control emotions; (2) Roll—to reestablish cognitive processes; and (3) Power—for projection and foreseeing mitigation measures (EASA, 2017, presentation 15 by Isambert).

The new regulatory provisions state that CRM training should address unexpected, unusual and stressful situations. The training should cover:

1. surprises and startle effects; and
2. management of abnormal and emergency situations, including:
   a. the development and maintenance of the capacity to manage crew resources;
   b. the acquisition and maintenance of adequate automatic behavioral responses; and
   c. recognizing the loss and rebuilding situation awareness and control.

Operator's Safety Culture and Company Culture

The final new topic that CRM training should now include is the operator's safety culture, its company culture, the type of operations, and the associated procedures of the operator. This should include areas of operations that may lead to particular difficulties or involve unusual hazards. The training should also cover cultural differences of multinational and cross-cultural crews. As Helmreich and Merritt (1998) demonstrated, national, organizational, and professional cultural differences can have a significant influence on the behavior of flight crewmembers. Nowadays some airlines have more than 50 nationalities working on their flight decks. Therefore the training should recognize that different cultures may have their own communication styles, ways of understanding, and problem-solving. As has been shown in aviation (Cushing, 1994), fatalities have resulted from crewmembers and controllers communicating in a common language which is not their first language. Moreover, cultural differences may lead to different cognitive approaches to analyzing a situation and problem-solving (Amer, Ngo, & Hasher, 2017; Varnum, Grossmann, Kitayama, & Nisbett, 2010).

Table 6.2 shows which CRM training elements should be covered in each type of training.

"Required" means training that should be instructional or interactive in style to meet the objectives specified in the CRM training program or to refresh and strengthen knowledge gained in a previous training. "In-depth" means training that should be instructional or interactive in style taking full advantage of group discussions, team task analysis, team task simulation, etc., for the acquisition or consolidation of knowledge, skills, and attitudes. The CRM training elements should be tailored to the specific needs of the training phase being undertaken.

6.1.2   CRM Trainers

For the training and assessment of CRM skills, the previous roles of CRMI (Instructors) and CRMIE (Instructor Examiner) no longer exist in the United Kingdom. Instead, CRM training is undertaken by a CRMT (CRM Trainer) (see CAA, 2016). The basic training for a flight crew CRM ground school trainer is 40 training hours (or 24 hours for those holding a specified instructor certificate). Flight crew CRM trainers responsible for classroom CRM training require an adequate knowledge of: (1) the relevant flight operations; and (2) human performance and limitations. They should also: (3) have completed flight crew initial operator's CRM training; (4) have received training in group facilitation skills; (5) have received additional training in the fields of group management, group dynamics and personal awareness; and (6) have demonstrated the knowledge, skills, and credibility required to train the CRM training elements in the nonoperational environment.

Training of flight crew CRM trainers should be both theoretical and practical. Practical elements should include the development of specific trainer skills, particularly the integration of CRM into line operations. The training of flight crew CRM trainers should be conducted by flight crew CRM

TABLE 6.2 Flight Crew CRM Training

CRM Training Elements	Initial Operator's CRM Training	Operator Conversion Course When Changing Aircraft Type	Operator Conversion Course When Changing Operator	Annual Recurrent Training	Command Course
General Principles					
Human factors in aviation; general instructions on CRM principles and objectives; human performance and limitations; threat and error management.	In-depth	Required	Required	Required	Required
Relevant to the Individual Flight Crewmember					
Personality awareness, human error and reliability, attitudes and behaviors, self-assessment and self-critique; Stress and stress management; Fatigue and vigilance; Assertiveness, situation awareness, information acquisition and processing.	In-depth	Not required	Not required	Required	In-depth
Relevant to the Flight Crew					
Automation and philosophy on the use of automation.	Required	In-depth	In-depth	In-depth	In-depth
Specific type-related differences.	Required	In-depth	Not required	Required	Required
Monitoring and intervention.	Required	In-depth	In-depth	Required	Required

(Continued)

TABLE 6.2 (Continued)

CRM Training Elements	Initial Operator's CRM Training	Operator Conversion Course When Changing Aircraft Type	Operator Conversion Course When Changing Operator	Annual Recurrent Training	Command Course
Relevant to the Entire Aircraft Crew					
Shared situation awareness, shared information acquisition and processing; Workload management; Effective communication and coordination inside and outside the flight crew compartment; Leadership, cooperation, synergy, delegation, decision-making, actions; Resilience development; Surprise and startle effect; Cultural differences.	In-depth	Required	Required	Required	In-depth
Relevant to the Operator and the Organization					
Operator's safety culture and company culture, standard operating procedures (SOPs), organizational factors, factors linked to the type of operations; Effective communication and coordination with other operational personnel and ground services.	In-depth	Required	In-depth	In-depth	In-depth
Case studies	In-depth	In-depth	In-depth	In-depth	In-depth

From EASA (2105a, p. 111) Annex II PART-ORO to Decision 2015-022-R-vo21. <https://www.easa.europa.eu/sites/default/files/dfu/Annex%20II%20to%20ED%20Decision%202015-022-R%20(correction%20on%20p.%2026).pdf> Accessed 18.03.18, Table 6.1.

trainers with a minimum of 3 years' experience. Assistance may be provided by experts in order to address specific areas. A flight crew CRM trainer should be assessed by the operator when conducting the first CRM training course. This first assessment should be valid for a period of 3 years. For recency of the 3-year validity period, the flight crew CRM trainer should: (1) conduct at least two CRM training events in any 12-month period; (2) be assessed within the last 12 months of the validity period by the operator; and (3) complete CRM trainer refresher training within the 3-year validity period.

For assessing flight crew CRM trainers, the operator may nominate experienced flight crew CRM trainers who have demonstrated continued compliance with the provisions for a flight crew CRM trainer and capability in that role for at least 3 years. They may be called CRMTE (CRM Trainer Examiner) and specific guidance for this process can be found in CAA (2016).

There are also requirements concerning pilot instructors and examiners involved in flight crew licensing (Part FCL Subpart J (instructors) and K (examiners); EASA, 2016b). For example, all instructors shall be trained to integrate TEM and CRM during any instruction. This training should be both theoretical and practical. The instructor must also be competent in the assessment of trainee performance and observing of CRM behavior. Some recent studies have begun to examine the complexity of the cognitive processes underlying ratings of pilots' nontechnical skills (Roth, 2015) and issues around interrater reliability (Gontar & Hörmann, 2015).

The importance of CRM trainers' and all instructors' facilitation skills is increasingly recognized, especially for the EBT/competence-based systems (see CAA, 2014; Dismukes and Smith (2010) for advice on facilitation skills training). One pilot commented in relation to nontechnical skills, "Not all trainers have the confidence or ability to apply effective learning interventions in the simulator. Those that do, achieve significantly better learning outcomes and are usually well-known and appreciated by the pilot community. The learning value of the [debrief] process is heavily dependent on the ability of the trainer to facilitate the discussion. Some of these debriefs are excellent and others very awkward."

The competence of the trainers and instructors was strongly emphasized by several sources and thus the process for their competence assessment is a key component of an effective CRM program. The new CAA (2017) CRM "Handy Guide" devised by the Flight Crew Human Factors Advisory Panel to help national aviation authority inspectors, managers and examiners evaluate CRM programs provides useful guidance, for example, on "Easy to Spot Markers" of effective CRM training and trainers.

6.1.3 Evidence-Based Training

The traditional compliance-based approach for CRM training may be substituted by a competency-based approach, such as EBT. In a competence-based system, the CRM training should be characterized by a performance orientation, with emphasis on standards of performance and their measurement, and the development of training to the specified performance standards. Where European operators have approval for an ATQP (Alternative Training and Qualification Programme), they can use their own evidence to design their own training syllabus and assessment programs. CRM training is an essential element of this program (EASA - ORO. FC. A. 245).

The movement towards EBT in aviation began a number of years ago as an attempt to anchor pilots' training more firmly against the realities of the current situations and conditions encountered in present day operations. A joint project between ICAO (International Commercial Aviation Organization), the International Air Transport Association (IATA), the International Federation of Air Line Pilots' Associations (IFALPA), and other industry partners, developed a new paradigm for competency-based training and assessment of flight crew, which is based on evidence (EBT) (IATA, 2013; ICAO, 2013). This approach is intended to enhance the confidence and capability of flight crews to operate the aircraft in all flight regimes and to be able to recognize and manage unexpected situations and has now been implemented in the European aviation regulations (EASA, 2015b).

The initial evidence behind this approach was gathered from multiple sources, such as opinion surveys of pilots, accident investigations, airlines' FDM archives, LOSA (line oriented safety audits), and other reporting systems. Part of this work involved "an evaluation of all the systems in use [including NOTECHS] and defined an acceptable industry-wide example framework combining technical and nontechnical competencies, descriptions and behavioral indicators, which are designed to be used according to the methodologies for assessment" (IATA, 2013, p. 10). It was also emphasized that the behavioral indicators are not intended to be used as performance criteria, or as a checklist. The resulting analyses produced a set of eight core competencies. The competencies were not subdivided into elements, but each competency was shown with a set of 6–13 positive "behavioral indicators" (IATA, 2013; ICAO, 2013). There were five typical nontechnical skills competencies of Situation Awareness, Problem-Solving and Decision-Making, Leadership and Teamwork, Communication, and Workload Management. In addition, there were three categories of technical skills, covering Flight Path Management (Manual and Automated), plus Application of Knowledge and Procedures. EASA (2015b, p. 7) advised that "Knowledge" could be distinguished as a ninth competency, with behavioral indicators such as: "Demonstrates practical and applicable knowledge of limitations

TABLE 6.3 Summary of Pilot Competencies in EBT

Competency	Description
APK—Application of procedural knowledge	Identifies and applies procedures in accordance with published operating instructions and applicable regulations using the appropriate knowledge.
COM—Communication	Demonstrates effective use of language, responsiveness to feedback, and that plans are stated and ambiguities resolved.
FPA—Flight path management, automation	Controls the aircraft flight path through automation, including appropriate use of flight management system (s) and guidance.
FPM—Flight path management, manual	Controls the aircraft flight path through manual flight, including appropriate use of flight management system (s) and flight guidance systems.
LTW—Leadership and teamwork	Uses appropriate authority to ensure focus on the task. Supports others in completing tasks.
PSD—Problem-solving and decision-making	Detects deviations from the desired state, evaluates problems, identifies risk, considers alternatives and selects the best course of action. Continuously reviews progress and adjust plans.
SAW—Situation awareness	Has an awareness of the aircraft state in its environment; projects and anticipates changes.
WLM—Workload management	Prioritizes, delegates, and receives assistance to maximize focus on the task. Continuously monitors the flight progress.
KNO—Knowledge*	Demonstrates knowledge and understanding of relevant information, operating instructions, aircraft systems, and the operating environment

From IATA (2013) *Evidence-based training implementation guide.* Montreal: International Air Transport Association; Appendix A, ICAO (2013) *Manual of evidence-based training. DOC 9995.* Montreal: International Civil Aviation Organization; *Appendix 1, EASA (2015b) *ED Decision 2015/027/R Implementation of evidence-based training (EBT) within the European regulatory framework.* <https://www.easa.europa.eu/document-library/agency-decisions/ed-decision-2015027r> Accessed 16.02.18.

and systems and their interaction. Demonstrates required knowledge of published operating instructions." See Table 6.3 for the nine competencies and their definitions.

These nine competencies (or airlines' versions of them) are now used in EBT: the central concept is that a pilot who possesses and can demonstrate the core competencies is more likely to perform to the required standards in the full range of situations that may be encountered during flight, including the unexpected occurrences. In essence, this is to develop individual and crew resilience to manage an evolving range of risks. This contrasts with the traditional method of training pilots to cope with a specified set of situations. No specific distinction is made here between technical and nontechnical skills: they are listed as one set of competencies, and are of course, interdependent. One captain said that he found this type of approach to be more effective and realistic, in essence it specifies "what good looks like," which is more accessible for pilots and their trainers. A recent study of the core competencies from 2560 operator proficiency check (OPC) missions from several fleets in a Middle East airline were analyzed using a principal component analysis to determine their interdependence and they produced a model indicating how the other components could influence the two flight path management scores (Mansikka, Harris, & Virtanen, 2017).

Under EBT, there is a move away from checking performance of a prescribed list of situations towards rating performance in dealing with events that occur during a series of scenarios. As mentioned above, this requires both trainers and examiners to demonstrate facilitation skills, as a more learner-centered approach is introduced (Kearns, Mavin, & Hodge, 2015; Learmout, 2013). One captain commented, "Trainers can now create any number of scenarios by combining different failure combinations. The pilots are less likely to know what is coming up so their NTS responses will be more genuine due to less anticipation and expectation. This should draw out the pilot's actual strengths and weaknesses and create opportunities for individualized learning. It also changes the trainer role from 'instructor' to "teacher and coach", hence the need for extensive trainer CPD [Continuing Professional Development] as the roles are significantly different. This is where I think the biggest problem will lie for a while."

Within Europe, operators are at different stages of applying EBT which can be a lengthy task. British Airways is in the process of implementing EBT, as are Air France and KLM. Iberia will be one of the first airlines in Europe to move to EBT Mixed Implementation in January 2018 (UBF, 2017). According to Read (2017), Lufthansa in Germany began to transition to EBT in 2016 and the process involved training 600 type-rating instructors and type-rating examiners who will then train 6500 pilots. The first Lufthansa Group airlines are expecting to begin implementing EBT in 2018. According to one of the captains I interviewed, the smaller airlines may have more difficulty in accruing sufficient internal information for this approach and may supplement their own data with the more generic evidence sources (e.g., IATA, 2013; ICAO, 2013). The EBT Foundation (www.ebt-foundation. com) and associated company EBT Solutions (www.ebt.solutions) works with Lufthansa and a number of other European airlines on implementation; one of its founders, Captain Michael Varney was the driving force behind EBT and led the IATA ICAO EBT working group. He explained (Varney, personal communication March 18, 2018) that the initial driver for the EBT approach was realizing how much rich data on flight operations were being collected, but those data were not being analyzed to understand which challenges could best be mitigated by simulator training. In addition, he and others had recognized the need to move from a checking regime to a learning culture. The "First Look" element of competency-based training under EBT involves the pilot being observed in the simulator during a routine flight where various events occur. The trainer then assesses on the basis of that performance which of the pilot's competencies would be most beneficial to focus on for the rest of the training process and the rest of the scenarios are tailored accordingly. He also said that the EBT Foundation is continuing to collect and analyze data from accidents and pilot surveys, and data from normal operations monitoring, in this case LOSA (www.loscollaborative.com), to enhance the evidence base.

6.2 NONTECHNICAL (CRM) SKILLS ASSESSMENT

Almost 20 years ago, the aviation regulations in Europe (Joint Aviation Authorities (JAA), 2001, 1.956) introduced a requirement on the assessment of flight crews' CRM skills. According to the latest guidance from EASA (2016a,b), the assessment of CRM skills is the process of observing, recording, interpreting, and debriefing crews and a crewmember's performance using an accepted methodology in the context of the overall performance. It takes place in the operational environment, on an aircraft or in a flight simulator. The assessment of pilots' CRM skills is carried out, along with technical skills, in the routine program of license and OPCs carried out by TRE (Type Rating Examiners) and CRE (Class Rating Examiners).

Some of the current EASA regulatory provisions (see also CAA, 2016) is similar to that issued in the earlier rules. For example, the assessment should be based on the following principles: (1) only observable behaviors are assessed; (2) the assessment should positively reflect any CRM skills that result in enhanced safety; and (3) assessments should include behavior that results in an unacceptable reduction in safety margin. Operators have to establish procedures, including additional training, to be applied in the event that flight crewmembers do not achieve or maintain the required CRM standards.

The assessment of CRM skills should: (1) include debriefing the crew and the individual crewmember; (2) serve to identify additional training, where needed, for the crew or the individual crewmember; and (3) be used to improve the CRM training system by evaluating de-identified summaries of all CRM assessments. A detailed description of the CRM methodology, including the required CRM standards and the terminology used for the assessment, should be published in the operations manual. As with CRM training (which can be prescriptive as per the requirements or evidence-based), skills assessment practices can now either follow: (1) a competency-based approach which combines technical and nontechnical skills into one set of competencies (usually nine) (as in the larger operators I interviewed); or (2) the traditional approach with mandated events for the technical skills and a set of nontechnical skills categories with an approved rating method (e.g., NOTECHS) and two companies were using this approach; or (3) some type of hybrid system. The two principal methods are described below.

6.2.1 Nontechnical Skills Assessment Within Competency Frameworks

Operators who are approved to use EBT, may be working under ATQP and interrogating their own data sets (e.g., from FDM, reporting systems, feedback from assessments, LOSA) to derive the core competencies that have to be checked. Or companies may be using versions of the nine competency set (EASA, 2015b; see Table 7.3) to provide the skill set that will be assessed. As mentioned above, many operators are in the process of moving towards EBT and their nontechnical skills rating systems are being altered accordingly, as they are integrated with the technical competencies.

For example, one company had developed their own set of nine pilot competencies that are now used for training and checking (essentially those in Table 7.3 but with knowledge and procedures combined and professional standards as the ninth). Similarly another airline was using the core set of nine competencies and each had four possible grades (Not acceptable; Acceptable; Standard; Standard +). A third company had developed their own "Pilot Skill List" with nine categories (similar to those above) each of which has four elements. Their categories are: Teamwork; Leadership; Situation Awareness; Decision-Making; Workload Management; Communication; Aircraft Operation (elements: adherence to SOPs, use of automation, manual handling, and checklist discipline); and Briefings and Professional Style. Another operator had more of a hybrid system and was using the nine competencies as the basis of their skills assessment in the line check, along with the set of mandated technical items. In all the systems I saw, there were lists of behavioral markers/performance indicators for good performance of the particular competency and in some cases, examples of poor practice were also provided. There seemed to be little debate about the nontechnical skill categories but there was variability in how the technical categories relating to knowledge, procedures, monitoring, and standards are composed and labeled.

One captain from a large operator discussed the challenges of moving from a well-established and familiar competency framework (with over 20 components) to the nine competency model, as this requires "translating" their present system which had more detail, to a new framework. Another captain, from a different operator felt that hybrid systems might provide an acceptable level of customization. Many of the principles of behavioral rating which were made explicit in the NOTECHS guidance (see below) are still applicable to the newer (nine) competencies approach and featured in the manuals for the new systems.

6.2.2 The Assessment of NTS Using the NOTECHS System

When the assessment of a pilot's nontechnical skills was introduced in Europe (JAA, 2001), there were a number of rating methods already in use (Flin & Martin, 2001) but no particular method was regarded as suitable for adopting as a pan-European method for both large and small carriers. Therefore a new framework and rating system for pilots' nontechnical skills (called NOTECHS) was developed (by a research consortium of pilots and psychologists) as a behavioral rating tool that could be used across European operators. (See Flin et al, 2003; van Avermaete & Kruijsen, 1998 for details of the system and the design process and see Hörmann, 2001; JARTEL, 2002; O'Connor et al, 2002 for a description of how the system was tested.) This was recommended at the time by the European regulator as a suitable method and NOTECHS is the only method named by the regulator (EASA, 2016a GM6 ORO. FC. 115) as one of the validated tools for assessing flight crew CRM skills. Other rating systems may also be acceptable.

The NOTECHS framework consists of four main categories: (1) Cooperation; (2) Leadership and managerial skills; (3) Situation awareness; and (4) Decision-making. Each category is subdivided into elements and each of these has a set of behavioral markers illustrating good and poor performance (see Fig. 6.1). The categories/elements are assessed by a rating scale to be established by the operator.

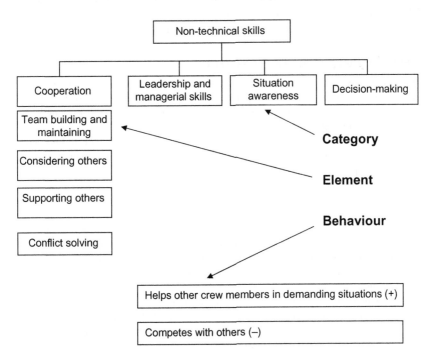

FIGURE 6.1 The NOTECHS system.

In the guidance on the use of NOTECHS (van Avermaete, Kruijsen, 1998), operational principles (Box 6.1) were established to ensure that each crewmember would receive as fair and as objective an assessment as possible with the system.

The NOTECHS system was designed to assess individual pilots and therefore the individual contributions to overall crew performance need to be disentangled. But this difficulty already exists during checks when considering technical performance. It was argued that the NOTECHS system did not solve this problem in some magical fashion. Rather it was suggested that the system should assist the examiners to objectively point to behaviors that are related more to one crewmember than the other, therefore allowing them to differentiate their judgement of the two crewmembers. A second factor related to possible concern that raters might not be judging the nontechnical skills on an appropriate basis. NOTECHS requires the instructor/examiner to justify any criticisms at a professional level, and with a standardized vocabulary. Furthermore, a judgement should not be based on a vague global impression or on an isolated behavior or action. Repetition of the behavior during the flight is usually required to explicitly identify the nature of the problem. In summary, the NOTECHS method was designed to be a guiding tool to look beyond failure during recurrent checks or training, and to help point out possible underlying deficiencies in CRM competence in relation to technical failures.

It was recommended that the basic training period for the use of NOTECHS is 2 full days or longer (depending on the level of previous experience of rating pilots' nontechnical skills) (Klampfer, Flin., & Helmreich,

---

BOX 6.1 Design Principles For NOTECHS

1. *Only observable behavior is to be assessed*—The evaluation must exclude reference to a crewmember's personality or emotional attitude and should be based only on observable behavior. Behavioral markers were designed to support an objective judgement.

2. *Need for technical consequence*—For a pilot's nontechnical skills to be rated as unacceptable, flight safety must be actually (or potentially) compromised. This requires a related objective technical consequence.

3. *Acceptable or unacceptable rating required*—The JAR-OPS requires the airlines to indicate whether the observed nontechnical skills are acceptable or unacceptable.

4. *Repetition required*—Repetition of unacceptable behavior during the check must be observed to conclude that there is a significant problem. If, according to the JAR paragraph concerned, the nature of a technical failure allows for a second attempt, this should be granted, regardless of the nontechnical rating.

5. *Explanation required*—For each Category rated as unacceptable the examiner must: (1) Indicate the Element(s) in that Category where the unacceptable behavior was observed. (2) Explain where the observed NTS (potentially) led to safety consequences. (3) Give a free-text explanation on each of the Categories rated unacceptable, using standard phraseology.

2001). NOTECHS presupposes sufficient knowledge of CRM concepts, as well as the basic material for pilots on human performance and limitations. No additional theoretical knowledge is required. It was recommended that the majority of any training should be devoted to the understanding of the NOTECHS method, the specific use of the rating form, the calibration process of judgement, and the debriefing phase. As the NOTECHS system is primarily used as a tool for debriefing and identification of training needs, then it is important to ensure that in debriefing an emphasis is placed on skill components, rather than more "global" analyses of performance.

In response to the initial regulatory requirements on evaluation of CRM skills, many European airlines developed their own nontechnical skills assessment systems. Some of these predated NOTECHS (e.g., KLM's feedback and appraisal system, Antersijn & Verhoef, 1995), others made use of the basic NOTECHS framework in the design of their own customized systems (e.g., Alitalia's PENTAPERF, Polo, 2002). Some airlines initially used NOTECHS or their own versions of it to complement their proficiency evaluation methods and this still seems to be the case. The original NOTECHS rating scale had five points, but airlines now use a range of scales, with four and five point scales being commonly adopted.

6.2.3 Failing an Assessment of Nontechnical Skills

For the NOTECHS system, it was proposed (see Box 6.1) that the evaluation of nontechnical skills in a check should not provoke a failed (not acceptable) rating without a related objective technical consequence, leading to compromised flight safety in the short or long term. In the event of a crewmember failing a check for any technical reason, NOTECHS could provide useful insights into the contributing individual human factors for the technical failure. Used in this way, the method could provide valuable assistance for debriefing and orienting tailored retraining. In 2018, it appears that in some European airlines, the requirement for an associated technical failure is still the case but in other operators, it is now possible for a pilot's check to be failed on nontechnical grounds alone. According to the pilots I spoke to, this situation is unusual and would only occur when the examiner had sufficient concern that the observed deficiency in nontechnical skills could potentially endanger flight safety. This may be more typically phrased as "if the observed behavior could lead to an unacceptable safety margin."

6.3 CONCLUSION

Since the earlier version of this chapter was written for the second edition of this book, there have been a considerable number of changes in the European regulations governing CRM training and assessment, as well as in the practices of the operating companies. During this time period, the regulator has conducted a major review of CRM and issued new information on the acceptable means of compliance and associated guidance. In essence, the fundamental components of CRM training have been maintained with several new additions to the syllabus, such as resilience development, coping with surprise and startle reactions and increased emphasis on monitoring. The regulatory provisions for the CRM trainers, and for their assessment, have also been updated. One major change which has a global, rather than just a European influence, is the development of EBT and the related competency methods. It appears that many companies are in the process of transitioning towards this approach. The EBT philosophy was generally welcomed by the captains I interviewed, but they recognized that considerable work was required to make this transition. Finally, it was interesting to find that one company (CHC Helicopters) was extending its CRM program to all of its staff currently within UK operations with the intention of introducing it globally due to a belief that everyone was involved in aviation safety and would benefit from the training.

What is notable in the aviation industry is the strong emphasis on maintaining high, measurable standards of nontechnical skills and their increasing integration with technical skills as a means to enhance flight safety. The recognition that professional competencies have to be periodically reviewed in relation to changing working conditions and the operational risk profile, as illustrated by the new CRM regulatory provisions and the option to move to EBT, would be a worthy lesson for other safety-critical industries.

ACKNOWLEDGMENTS

I would like to thank all those who provided the information and advice that enabled the writing of this chapter.

REFERENCES

Amer, T., Ngo, K., & Hasher, L. (2017). Cultural differences in visual attention: Implications for distraction processing. *British Journal of Psychology, 108*, 244–258.

Antersijn, P., & Verhoef, M. (1995). Assessment of non-technical skills. Is it possible?. In N. McDonald, N. Johnston, & R. Fuller (Eds.), *Applications of psychology to the aviation system*. Aldershot: Avebury Aviation.

BEA. (2012). *Final Report. Flight AF 447 on 1st June 2009 A330-203*. Paris: Bureau d'Enquetes and d'Analyses pour la Securite d'Aviation Civile.

Boettcher, J. (2016). Regulatory update. In *Paper presented at the EASA Workshop 'CRM in Practice'*, 8 November, Cologne, Germany. <https://www.easa.europa.eu/newsroom-and-events/events/easa-crm-workshop-%E2%80%9Ccrm-practice%E2%80%9D> Accessed 16.02.18.

CAA. (2013a). *Global fatal accident review 2002-2011 (CAP1036)*. London: Civil Aviation Authority.

CAA. (2013b). *Monitoring matters. Guidance on the development of pilot monitoring skills*. CAA Paper 2013/02. Gatwick: Civil Aviation Authority.

CAA. (2014). Flight-crew human factors handbook. *CAP737 (December 2016 version)*. London: Civil Aviation Authority.

CAA. (2016). Guidance on the requirements that pertain to Flightcrew for the training and testing of Human Factors under EASA Part-ORO and EASA Part-FCL. *Standards Document No.29 Version 7*. London: Civil Aviation Authority.

CAA. (2017). Practical Crew Resource Management (CRM) standards: The handy guide. *CAP 1607*. London: Civil Aviation Authority.

Cushing, S. (1994). *Fatal words. Communication clashes and aircraft crashes*. Chicago: University of Chicago Press.

Dismukes, R.K., & Berman, B. (2010). *Checklists and monitoring in the cockpit: Why crucial defences sometimes fail*. NASA TM 2010-216396.

Dismukes, R.K., Goldsmith, T., & Kochan, J. (2015). *Effects of acute stress on aircrew performance: Literature review and analysis of operational aspects*. NASA TM 2015-218930.

Dismukes, R. K., & Smith, G. (2010). *Facilitation and debriefing in aviation training and operations*. Aldershot: Ashgate.

Drath, K. (2017). *Resilient leaders*. Oxford: Routledge.

EASA. (2105a). *Annex II PART-ORO to Decision 2015-022-R-vo21*, p. 111. <https://www.easa.europa.eu/sites/default/files/dfu/Annex%20II%20to%20ED%20Decision%202015-022-R%20 (correction%20on%20p.%2026).pdf> Accessed 18.03.18.

EASA. (2015b). *ED Decision 2015/027/R Implementation of evidence-based training (EBT) within the European regulatory framework*. <https://www.easa.europa.eu/document-library/agency-decisions/ed-decision-2015027r> Accessed 16.02.18.

EASA. (2016a). *Acceptable means of compliance (AMC) and guidance material (GM) to annex III—Part-ORO*. February. <www.easa.europa.eu/sites/default/files/dfu/Consolidated%20unofficial%20AMC&GM_Annex%20III%20Part-ORO.pdf> Accessed 16.02.18.

EASA. (2016b). *Annex 1-PART FCL [flight crew licensing] (v.1, June) AMC1 FCL. 735. A. Multi-crew cooperation course* (p. 834). <https://www.easa.europa.eu/sites/default/files/dfu/Part-FCL.pdf> Accessed 16.02.18.

EASA. (2017). CRM Training Implementation, December 2017. <https://www.easa.europa.eu/document-library/general-publications/crm-training-implementation> Accessed 26.08.18.

Eurocontrol. (2014). Safety and automation. *HindSight*, 20, Winter. <http://www.eurocontrol.int/publications/hindsight-20-winter-2014> Accessed 15.02.18.

Flin, R., & Martin, L. (2001). Behavioural markers for crew resource management: A review of current practice. *International Journal of Aviation Psychology*, *11*(1), 95−118.

Flin, R., Martin, L., Goeters, K.-M., Hörmann, H.-J., Amalberti, R., Valot, C., & Nijhuis, H. (2003). Development of the NOTECHS (Non-Technical Skills) system for assessing pilots' CRM skills. *Human Factors and Aerospace Safety*, *3*(2), 97−119.

Gontar, P., & Hörmann, H.-J. (2015). Inter-rater reliability at the top end: Measures of pilots' non-technical skills. *International Journal of Aviation Psychology*, *25*, 171−190.

Helmreich, R. (1997). Managing human error in aviation. *Scientific American*, 62−67, May.

Helmreich, R., & Merritt, A. (1998). *Culture at work in aviation and medicine. National, organizational and professional influences*. Aldershot: Ashgate.

Hollnagel, E., Woods, D., & Leveson, N. (Eds.), (2006). *Resilience engineering: Concepts and precepts*. Aldershot: Ashgate.

Hörmann, H.-J. (2001). Cultural variations of the perceptions of crew behaviour in multi-pilot aircraft. *Le Travail Humaine*, *64*, 247−268.

IATA. (2013). *Evidence-based training implementation guide*. Montreal: International Air Transport Association.

ICAO. (2013). *Manual of evidence-based training. DOC 9995*. Montreal: International Civil Aviation Organization.

JARTEL. (2002). *Joint aviation requirements translation and elaboration of legislation (JARTEL). WP5 report. Guidelines for implementation of NOTECHS. April 2002. Implementation guidelines. EC JARTEL project report.*

Joint Aviation Authorities (JAA). (2001). JAR OPS 1.940, 1.945, 1.955 and 1.956. Hoofdorp, Netherlands.

Kearns, S., Mavin, T., & Hodge, S. (2015). *Competency-based education in aviation: Exploring alternate training pathways.* London: Routledge.

Klampfer, B., Flin. R., Helmreich, R., et al. (2001). *Enhancing performance in high risk environments: Recommendations for the use of Behavioural Markers.* Report from the behavioural markers workshop, Zurich, June. Berlin: Daimler Benz Foundation.

Landman, A., Groen, E., van Paassen, M., Bronkhorst, A., & Mulder, M. (2017a). Dealing with unexpected events on the flight deck: A conceptual model of startle and surprise. *Human Factors, 59,* 1161–1172.

Landman, A., Groen, E., van Paassen, M., Bronkhorst, A., & Mulder, M. (2017b). The influence of surprise on upset recovery performance in airline pilots. *International Journal of Aerospace Psychology, 27*(1-2), 2–14.

Law, J. & Chidester, T. (2014). Human factors in challenging environments. In J. Stepanek, R. Johnson & D. Cocco (Eds.), *Mayo Clinic: Medicine in challenging environments.* Available on the Apple App Store.

Learmout, D. (2013). Providing evidence of success. *Flight International,* 9–15, July.

Mansikka, H., Harris, D., & Virtanen, K. (2017). An input-process-output model of pilot core competencies. *Aviation Psychology and Applied Human Factors, 7*(2), 78–85.

Martin, W., Murray, P., Bates, P., & Lee, P. (2015). Fear-potentiated startle: A review from an aviation perspective. *The International Journal of Aviation Psychology, 25*(2), 97–107.

Martin, W., Murray, P., Bates, P., & Lee, P. (2016). A flight simulator study of the impairment effects of startle on pilots during unexpected critical events. *Aviation Psychology and Applied Human Factors, 6,* 24–32.

O'Connor, P., Hörmann, H.-J., Flin, R., Lodge, M., & Goeters, K.-M. (2002). Developing a method for evaluating crew resource management skills, The JARTEL Group *International Journal of Aviation Psychology, 12,* 265–288.

Polo, L. (2002). Evaluation of flight crew members' performance. Is evaluation a product or a tool? In O. Truszczynski (Ed.), Proceedings of the 25th European aviation psychology conference, Warsaw. Warsaw: Polish Airforce.

Read, B. (2017). Training for the new millennium. *Aerospace,* 28–31, December.

Rivera, J., Talone, A., Boesser, C., Jentsch, F., & Yeh, M. (2014). *Startle and surprise on the flight deck: Similarities, differences, and prevalence,* . Proceedings of the human factors and ergonomics society annual meeting (Vol. 58, 1, pp. 1047–1051). Los Angeles, CA: Sage.

Roth, W. (2015). Flight examiners' methods of ascertaining pilot proficiency. *International Journal of Aviation Psychology, 25*(3-4), 209–227.

SKYbrary. (2016). *Startle effect.* <www.skybrary.aero/index.php/Startle_Effect> Accessed 23.02.18.

UBF. (2017). <https://evidencebased.training/blog/2017/03/31/news-and-events/> Accessed 16.02.18.

van Avermaete, J. & Kruijsen, E. (Eds.). (1998). *NOTECHS: Non-technical skill evaluation in JAR-FCL. NLR-TP-98518.* Amsterdam: National Aerospace Laboratory (NLR).

Varnum, M., Grossmann, I., Kitayama, S., & Nisbett, R. (2010). The origin of cultural differences in cognition: The social orientation hypothesis. *Current Directions in Psychological Science, 19*(1), 9–13.

Chapter 7

Crew Resource Management and Individual Resilience

Wayne L. Martin
University of Southern Queensland, Cairns, QLD, Australia

> Resilience implies [being] prepared ... and [being] prepared to be unprepared.
>
> Pariés (2012)

INTRODUCTION

The traditional interpretation of the term *resilience* has widespread applications across a number of domains. Agriculture may use the term to describe crops which are *resilient* to drought or pests; medicine may describe it in terms of patients who were resilient to infection, or diseases which were resilient to treatment; businesses may use the term to describe *resilience* to economic downturns; and macro systems may describe their *resilience* to internal and external errors or failures.

Not all systems, or even elements of those systems, are always resilient however, and may suffer catastrophically when adversity strikes. While post hoc measures may make such systems resilient to future failures of a similar nature, it is the *unknown unknowns* which must be anticipated, and broad strategies for managing adversity need to be developed and practiced at systemic, organizational, individual, and team levels to ensure future resilience.

While *resilience* is often used as a strategic term, including in aviation, a number of aircraft accidents over the last few years have also demonstrated a need for *tactical* resilience, and the industry is slowly starting to move towards training strategies which will make personnel across the aviation system more resilient to unexpected adversity.

In the aviation domain, airline training has only developed incrementally over the last hundred or so years, with training practices being a mix of largely skill and knowledge development, which changes little in real terms from year to year. Despite the ultrareliable aircraft which now seem ubiquitous across the world's airlines, and technology which is already extremely

Crew Resource Management. DOI: https://doi.org/10.1016/B978-0-12-812995-1.00007-5
207

sophisticated, yet still accelerating in its complexity, the human element of the aviation system, and the training of those humans, seems to be based on seemingly perpetually out of date best practice.

The airline industry has not been ignorant of this phenomenon, and resilience training, either through traditional or evidence-based training (EBT) processes, has become a topic of much consideration and interest. However, while the resilience challenges are certainly becoming widely recognized across the world, there is substantial debate on how to implement training which realistically makes pilots more resilient to real-world challenges during line operations.

One could argue that most aviation accidents have been caused by a lack of pilot resilience, simply because something happened which was unexpected and was probably abnormal, yet the flight crew failed to address the changed circumstances adequately. This lack of adaptability to circumstances outside their expectations, has illustrated a major concern for the industry. It almost requires a paradigm shift, but at the least, a concerted refocusing of training, to better equip pilots to deal not just with predictable abnormalities, but with more emphasis on strategies for dealing with unpredictability.

The following chapter will examine the nature of resilience and various examples of both resilience success and resilience failures in aviation. It will also look to tie existing crew resource management (CRM) skill-sets to resilience, and discuss training strategies which could be used to better develop resilience amongst airline crews.

7.1 THE NATURE OF "RESILIENCE"

The Oxford Dictionary (n.d.) defines resilience as "the capacity to recover quickly from difficulties; toughness." In this respect resilience in an aviation context could refer to any abnormal, unexpected, or adverse event which befalls a member of an airline or other aviation system. Furthermore, the concept of resilience could be considered across a broad spectrum of the industry, including individual resilience, team resilience, organizational resilience, and systemic resilience.

Hollnagel, Paries, Woods, and Wreathall (2011) describe system resilience in terms of "the intrinsic ability of a system to adjust its functioning prior to, during, or following changes and disturbances, so that it can sustain required operations under both expected and unexpected conditions." Practically speaking, at an airline level, this means an ability to keep functioning, despite one or more serious adverse events taking place. The literature also describes an ability to *anticipate and circumvent threats* (Woods, Leveson, & Hollnagel, 2012). This definition of systemic resilience would also apply appropriately to a team, such as a flight crew.

At an individual level resilience is often defined in terms of bouncing back from adversity, or of maintaining an even keel during times of stress.

Claesson (2006) describes individual resilience as "the ability to cope well with high levels of ongoing disruptive change; to sustain good health and energy when under constant pressure; to bounce back easily from setbacks; to overcome adversities; or to change to a new way of working and living when an old way is no longer possible."

Regardless of whether it is an individual, a team, an organization, or an entire system, it appears that resilience has common themes: an ability to bounce back from adversity, and an ability to sustain operations regardless of what circumstances arise.

7.2   IS RESILIENCE JUST THREAT AND ERROR MANAGEMENT?

There have been questions raised about the use of the term *resilience* within aviation (e.g., Jarvis, 2017), and especially with regards to comparisons with existing constructs such as threat and error management (TEM). The industry often adopts new buzzwords with gusto, and frenetic activity abounds as operators, academics, and trainers endeavor to understand it and incorporate it into their doctrine. Such was the case with TEM, and it is probably worth considering the commonalities and differences between TEM and the *next big thing*, resilience, (Jarvis, 2017) to better understand the commonalities of the two concepts, and when it is appropriate to use the two terms correctly.

TEM was borne from fifth generation CRM attempts to reduce, or even eliminate, the errors which pilots and other crew members were making. This generation was however short-lived, as it quickly became evident that humans were always going to make errors, and it was far more appropriate therefore to develop systems and processes which were both error tolerant, and able to manage the external threats which also prevailed in airline operations. This focus on the management of both threats and errors, began with the development of the line oriented safety audit in 1995 and then gained international traction in the early 2000s. It became known as TEM, and was ubiquitously adopted as the sixth generation of CRM—a construct which still exists today.

The underlying premise of TEM was that in order to manage risk, crews would avoid, mitigate, and manage the threats and errors which abound (Helmreich, Klinect, & Wilhelm, 1999). Helmreich et al. (1999) further suggested that risk emanates from both expected and unexpected threats, and that CRM behaviors were the last line of defense against such threats.

When examining TEM for comparisons with resilience then, it is easy to identify comparable goals in terms of *strategic* resilience. In this construct, pilots and other crew members are prepared, and have an expectation for, eventualities (threats or errors). This could be termed resilient behavior, because the very act of being prepared makes someone less likely to be put in a position where they will have to recover from an undesired state. This resilient state equates to the *avoid* part of TEM.

There is also a *tactical* side to resilience, where crew members react to events happening in real time. When such events have potentially negative consequences, resilient behavior allows the crew member to recover to a safe state. This could be considered analogous to the mitigate and manage stages of TEM.

It is clear that there are similarities between TEM and resilience, and there are likely elements of crossover between the two concepts, however resilience has much wider and more diverse applications. Resilient behavior can be characterized by an ability to resist impairment from adverse circumstances, or to at least recover from such circumstances. It also has applications at an individual level, a team level, an organizational level, and even at a systemic level.

7.3 THE CONSEQUENCES OF RESILIENCE FAILURES

Aircraft accident data is full of examples of nonresilient pilot behaviors. In fact, almost all accidents which were human-centric in causality, could conceivably be classified as lacking in pilot resilience, because the pilots involved failed to recover from adverse circumstances. In a lot of those cases, the circumstances which arose may even have been predictable, and/or entirely preventable, so the strategic resilience behaviors which could have prevented the undesired state, were either missing, or at least deficient.

Likewise, the tactical resilience which would have enabled pilots to recover from adverse circumstances has been noticeably absent at times. The inability to apply previously learned skills and knowledge to both novel and to well-known adverse events, has illustrated a possible shortcoming in the modern pilot's arsenal. Whether this is a trend which is borne from increasing complexity and sophistication in modern aircraft, which more than ever, removes pilots from the loop in system awareness, or whether the ubiquitous reliability reduces expectation for adverse events to a point where pilots become complacent, is not always clear. However, both of these issues have been identified as problematic, and will likely only become more so in the future, as older generation aircraft are phased out, and even further technological advances are made.

In the face of such advancements, it could be argued that pilots of earlier generation aircraft were more resilient because they needed to be more resilient. Such aircraft were far more prone to failures, had less sophisticated technology, which required pilots to be in the loop more, and were more challenging to fly. Pilots of earlier generation aircraft had a far greater expectation for adverse events, simply because they happened more regularly, and perhaps therefore they were more likely to know their aircraft more intimately, to monitor systems and the aircraft flight path more closely, and to be well practiced in dealing with nonnormal events.

While it is somewhat unfair to look back at previous aircraft accidents and to identify areas where pilot resilience was lacking, there are always useful lessons to be learned. Accident data which shows lapses in resilience enable investigators, regulators, and aircraft operators to identify trends, to determine better practices, and to develop training which addresses these deficiencies going forward. Such EBT is becoming more prevalent around the world, and is endorsed by the International Civil Aviation Organization (ICAO), and a number of regulatory agencies.

If we look at a specific example of such advances, the Air France Flight 447 accident in the Atlantic Ocean in 2009 (BEA, 2012), has led to a far greater transparency and understanding of the alternate law characteristics of some fly-by-wire aircraft, and the inherent challenges associated with high level upset recovery. It also illustrated the concepts of startle and surprise in pilots during critical events, which had received little attention previously.

In the Air France (AF) 447 accident the aircraft suffered a degradation in airspeed indications, caused by high level pitot icing. As a result, the aircraft entered a reduced capability state called alternate law, which afforded the pilots far less envelope protections than they were used to in normal modes. Despite indications of an aircraft stall, the junior First Officer, who was flying the aircraft at the time (pilot flying, PF), chose to pull back on the control stick, which caused the aircraft to climb several thousand feet. This caused further reduction in airspeed and eventually led to a fully developed aerodynamic stall. Despite the fact that the aircraft was at around 38,000 feet and that the Captain and a senior First Officer were on the flight deck for much of the descent, at no stage was an effective stall recovery made, and the aircraft perished with the loss of all lives on board.

How then, can pilots be more resilient, and avoid accidents such as AF 447?

When considering strategic resilience, there are a number of ways that pilots can address this. They can be well rested, be free of additional lifestyle stressors, be technically competent in their role, ideally have previous experience to relate to, and have a high level of knowledge about their aircraft, their SOPs and their nonnormal procedures. While the crew of AF 447 may not have been impaired by fatigue or lifestyle stress, they perhaps lacked sufficient technical knowledge to assimilate and comprehend the cues that were available to them. Whether other pilots in the same situation would have been equally confused is of course unknown, however the lack of understanding of highly complex and sophisticated aircraft is a problem that is perhaps more widespread than we would like it to be.

Breakdowns in strategic resilience also come about by poor judgement and decision-making. Sound naturalistic decision-making comes from sound situational awareness, and experience, but also requires a high level of knowledge, which can be used as a basis for making informed, quality decisions.

Reactive, or tactical resilience is also borne from sound CRM skills. It is unclear how many unexpected critical events have resulted in disaster, which could have been saved by sound leadership and teamwork, by effective communication skills, by sound situational awareness and decision-making, and by effective task assignment and execution (workload management), but it is likely to have been a substantial number.

7.4   RESILIENCE SUCCESS STORIES IN AVIATION

7.4.1   Qantas Flight QF 32

On November 4, 2010, a Qantas Airways A380 was climbing out of Singapore en route to Sydney, Australia, when the number two engine suffered an uncontained engine failure. The failure ejected pieces of engine at high velocity through the engine cowls, through the wing and against the lower and upper fuselage. The projectiles which went through the wing severed a wiring loom, which caused a significant number of system failures, with nearly 60 failure messages appearing on the ECAM (electronic centralized aircraft monitor), 43 of them in the first minute.

The ATSB found that a large fragment of the turbine disc penetrated the left wing leading edge before passing through the front spar into the left inner fuel tank and exiting through the top skin of the wing. The fragment initiated a short duration low intensity flash fire inside the wing fuel tank. The ATSB determined that the conditions within the tank were not suitable to sustain the fire.

Another fire was found to have occurred within the lower cowl of the No. 2 engine as a result of oil leaking into the cowl from the damaged oil supply pipe. The fire lasted for a short time and self-extinguished.

The large fragment of the turbine disc also severed wiring looms inside the wing leading edge that connected to a number of systems.

A separate disc fragment severed a wiring loom located between the lower centre fuselage and body fairing. That loom included wires that provided redundancy (back −up) for some of the systems already affected by the severing of wires in the wing leading edge. This additional damage rendered some of those systems inoperative.

The aircraft's hydraulic and electrical distribution systems were also damaged, which affected other systems not directly impacted by the engine failure. (ATSB, 2013, p. xii)

The extent of this emergency called upon all of the crew's resilience in dealing with the initial issues, and then also with further challenges associated with being unable to shut the number one engine down, once safely on the ground. Both the emergency situation in the air, and the completely unexpected situation on the ground, required the whole crew to work as a coherent team. It required strong leadership from the Captain and senior members of the Flight and Cabin Crews, and effective communication within the flight deck, with the cabin, with ATC, and eventually with the Rescue Fire Crews, in order to have a safe outcome.

7.4.2   US Airways Flight 1549

On January 15, 2009, a US Airways Airbus A320 took off from La Guardia airport in New York and encountered a flock of Canada geese at around 2800 feet. The aircraft sustained multiple bird strikes, including into the engines, and suffered a near total loss of thrust in both engines.

The flight crew immediately went into action to try and restart the engines, multiple times, and to evaluate the safest landing options. In an incredibly stressful situation, the Captain considered a return to La Guardia airport, a diversion to Teterboro airport, and eventually settled on the only achievable outcome, which was a controlled ditching into the Hudson river, between Manhattan Island and New Jersey.

Throughout the emergency, and subsequent successful ditching, the flight and cabin crew displayed immense professionalism. The flight crew showed superb teamwork skills, the Captain showed impressive leadership, the situational awareness and decision-making proved to be spot on, and by and large, the task management was conducted almost perfectly.

The entire crew's resilience was superb, both during the emergency and immediately following the ditching. They used their excellent CRM skills to facilitate a safe outcome for all crew and passengers on board.

7.4.3   United Airlines Flight 232

On July 19, 1989 a United Airlines DC-10 was en route from Denver to Chicago when a stage one fan blade separated, causing an uncontained failure of the number two engine. The disintegration of the fan blade and other engine parts caused the lines of all three aircraft hydraulic systems to be severed, resulting in a total loss of hydraulic pressure. This in turn meant that there was no pressure to power the aircraft flight controls, and while the crew were initially concerned with securing the failed engine, their attention quickly turned to the loss of control which became apparent following the failure.

The Captain demonstrated creditable leadership throughout the remaining flight, utilizing all available resources to try and manage the situation, and to retain control of the aircraft. This included the use of a senior Captain who was a passenger on the flight, who was used to assist with manipulating the thrust levers, in an attempt to use asymmetric thrust to control the aircraft's pitch and roll.

An almost impossible situation was very nearly rescued completely as the crew nursed the crippled aircraft to a nearby airport at Sioux City, however at the last minute a wing dropped and the crew were unable to compensate with thrust quickly enough, resulting in the aircraft striking the runway wing down, and subsequently cart-wheeling into a nearby cornfield.

While the outcome was not perfect, and 111 people onboard died, 185 crew and passengers survived, thanks to an incredible feat of resilience by the flight crew. The CRM skills they exhibited were extraordinary, with the most exemplary teamwork, communication, workload management, decision-making, and judgement imaginable, in what could only have been acutely stressful circumstances.

This accident epitomized the need for sound CRM skills during nonnormal and novel events, and was a constructive exemplar for CRM training for some years afterwards. The tenacity and resolve to overcome adversity shown by the whole crew was commendable, and while not a term in common use back then, it would now be viewed as a shining example of individual, crew, and systemic resilience. While the accident was a long time ago, it still remains one of the best examples of crew resilience in a dire situation.

7.5 STARTLE, SURPRISE, AND RESILIENCE

One of the more common reasons for pilots having their resilience tested, is that they encounter a situation which was unexpected. One of the downsides of ubiquitous reliability and normalcy, is that the expectation levels for nonnormal events may be lower than desirable.

Considerable work has been done since the Air France Flight 447 and Colgan Air Flight 3407 accidents (BEA, 2012; NTSB, 2010b) to understand the effects of startle and surprise on pilots during unexpected critical events (e.g., Gillen, 2016; Martin, 2014; Rivera, Talone, Boesser, Jentsch, & Yeh, 2014). As a result, a greater understanding now exists of the physiological and cognitive effects on the body, and considerable work is still being undertaken to establish training interventions which would better equip pilots to respond in such unexpected situations.

Surprise is a relatively common phenomenon, which occurs when something happens which is outside the expectation set of the pilot(s) concerned. This surprise element can temporarily destroy the situational awareness mental model which pilots maintain, as they try to integrate this new sensory information into their existing understanding of what is going on (Wessel et al., 2016). This process can be relatively quick, as the new cues are easily understood and integrated, or it may take some considerable time to make sense of (Foster & Keane, 2015). During this period of sense making, where new information is trying to be comprehended and integrated, the pilots are vulnerable to breakdowns in situational awareness, and decision-making, and therefore require some level of resilience to ensure the aircraft does not enter an undesired state.

Lanir (1986) differentiates between *fundamental* surprise and *situational* surprise. Fundamental surprise involves events which are completely outside the reasonable expectation set of a person, and therefore have profound effects on their sense making of the situation. Such events in aviation are often referred to as *Black Swan* events (Taleb, 2010), and are difficult to train for because of their scarcity and novelty, requiring sound recovery skills. Situational surprise events are more common, and while they may be unexpected, could be considered to be within the realms of possibility, and it is possible for pilots to be strategically prepared for events which fall into this category, regardless of whether they have experienced such an event personally before, or not.

Startle is less common in aviation, thankfully, however strong startles are potentially quite serious. Whereas surprise is a largely cognitive effect, unexpected startles also have a reflexive physiological effect, with the "fight or flight" reaction (Lang, Bradley, & Cuthbert, 1997; Misslin, 2003) being initiated, in concert with the startle reflex (an aversive action designed to protect the body and to align the attentional resources towards the source of the startling stimulus). In addition, the body's acute stress circuits may be activated, particularly in conditions of real or perceived threat. The acute stress response can have significant impairment effects on the working memory, which further burden the sense making process which goes on following the stimulus onset.

Following a startle, or a significant surprise, it is imperative that pilots endeavor to refocus their attention to flying the aircraft. Where it does enter an undesired state, then sound CRM skills are required to ensure it returns to a safe state as soon as possible, even if the integrated understanding of what has occurred, is not yet fully clear.

Training interventions which assist pilots to recover and to maintain control of the aircraft following startle are in their early stages of testing (e.g., Boland, 2016; Gillen, 2016), however some fundamental processes are important: firstly, it is critical that the pilots continue to fly the aircraft, and deal with immediate actions where necessary. Secondly, where immediate action is not required then pilots should endeavor to not take any impulsive action, but rather take some time to let the fight or flight reaction subside, while they try to make sense of the situation—to regain their situational awareness.

There are relatively few situations which require immediate action, however these are some examples of critical events where it is important to take prompt action:

- EGPWS[1] Terrain Warning
- Aircraft loss of control/upset

---

1. EGPWS – Enhanced Ground Proximity Warning System.

- Reactive windshear
- TCAS[2] Resolution Advisory
- Rejected Takeoff
- Stall Warning
- Cabin Altitude Warning

It is strongly recommended that pilots overlearn the recovery actions for these events, so that they can implement them with relatively little conscious effort. It is also important that pilots have a clear understanding of the cues they will receive for each event, so that they can quickly recognize the situation and implement the overlearned response.

Where events do not require immediate action, then it is worth taking the time to recover from the startle or surprise and to recover a sound level of situational awareness before implementing a new plan. Impulsive behaviors have been shown in a number of accidents to be either ineffective or even counterproductive (e.g., BEA, 2012; NTSB, 2010a).

While these "immediate action required" situations are relatively uncommon, there are a lot of situations which occur which do not require any immediate action, where the situation is better managed by taking the time to carefully consider the actions required. Having a strategy on hand to deal with such events, by the use of sound CRM skills, is likely to facilitate a better opportunity for a successful outcome than impulsive recovery reactions.

While acronyms abound already in aviation, the following set of actions is designed to illustrate an example of the three-step process for recovery from events with a nonimmediate response required:

B   Breathe (pause)
A   Analyze (as a crew)
D   Decide (on the best course of action, once the situation is understood clearly)

By taking the time to manage the fight or flight reaction, by pausing and actively breathing in and out for a few seconds, the crew can start to recover from any initial working memory impairment. By then, through analyzing as a crew what the exact problem is, a shared mental model can be redeveloped, further enabling a sound decision on what action is best to take.

Startle and surprise can be a significant test of pilot resilience and the principal techniques for survival are preparation and rehearsal (strategic resilience), and sound CRM skill-sets for the recovery phase. This equally applies to other crew members, who may also be faced with unexpectedly challenging situations.

---

2. TCAS (or ACAS) – Traffic (or Airborne) Collision Avoidance System.

7.6 INDIVIDUAL VERSUS TEAM RESILIENCE

Individual resilience varies substantially across the population, with some people handling adversity with aplomb, while others crumble. While generally speaking, the pilot population is likely to be nearer the more resilient end of the spectrum, purely because nonresilient types often self-select out during demanding pilot training, there will still be some pilots who are naturally more resilient than others.

Substantial literature exists in the public domain on individual resilience (e.g., Deveson, 2003; Flach, 2004; Greitens, 2015; Reich, Zautra, & Hall, 2012). The vast majority of this work is not aviation related, but is aimed at informing the general public of ways to be more resilient in their everyday lives. Often the work centers around coping skills and positive outlooks, counseling and sharing of problems, and elements of defensive or strategic resilience.

As individuals, pilots can enhance their strategic resilience by being technically competent, by having sound technical knowledge of their aircraft and procedures, and by having a healthy suspicion and expectation for nonnormal events.

Pilots can also become more tactically resilient by using visualization to rehearse their responses to critical events, by having a clear understanding of the cues associated with time critical events, and for having a strategy for managing their emotional state and their recovery, following events where time to recover is available.

Team resilience is a more complex phenomenon because it involves individuals who may not have the same natural level of resilience as other members of the team. Anybody who has seen the Apollo 13 movie, or is familiar with the intense teamwork that went on in the United Flight 232 accident (see Section 7.4.3), will note that the crew resilience was impressive, not only because the individuals concerned were resilient themselves, but because of the leadership and teamwork demonstrated. A strong leader, who is able to resurrect the capabilities of their crew to work effectively as a team, following adversity, is an important conduit for recovery.

Likewise, individual crew members who can compensate for less resilient crew in the postevent phase, are likely to engender a positive outcome, while the impaired crew members recover to a state where they can once again contribute fully.

The literature on team resilience, particularly at a small team level, is relatively limited. Some considerable work has been done in the areas of system and organizational resilience however (e.g., Leflar & Siegel, 2012; Woods et al., 2012), and there are principles which can be taken from both organizational and individual resilience which can still be applied at a dyad or small team level.

7.7 CRM SKILLS AND THEIR RELATIONSHIP TO RESILIENCE

Within the crew environment, considerable work has been done over the last 40 odd years to build capabilities into crew members, which have equipped them to not only be technically competent, but also competent in their nontechnical skills (NTS). These nontechnical skills are at the heart of effective CRM and include elements such as leadership, teamwork, communication, situational awareness, decision-making, workload management, stress management, fatigue management, as well as a number of other competencies.

CRM, NTS, and Human Factors programs across most of the world's airlines, have generally received strong support, and are recognized by ICAO and other regulatory organizations as an intrinsic part of the battle to improve aviation safety. While the very limited nature of accident data makes quantified empirical assessment of the exact nature of safety improvements difficult, the intangible benefits of CRM training are generally well acknowledged (Salas, Burke, Bowers, & Wilson, 2001).

The outcomes of the critical situations in Section 7.4, point to the role of CRM skills as an inherent part of both individual and team resilience, and are no doubt a vehicle for improving pilot capabilities in adverse circumstances. Making the link between resilience and CRM skills will perhaps highlight to crews going forward, how they can best be prepared to manage future critical events.

7.8 DEVELOPING INDIVIDUAL AND CREW RESILIENCE THROUGH EFFECTIVE CRM SKILLS

7.8.1 Situational Awareness

Situational awareness (SA) has been described in various ways, but is commonly conceived as a three-step process: perception of environmental cues; comprehension of their meaning; and projection of the implications of this information into the future (Endsley, 1995). While resilience is not necessarily a direct result of SA, it could be argued that strategic resilience, where adversity is anticipated and prepared for, is dependent on SA.

Hollnagel et al. (2011) describe a form of strategic resilience where people have a readiness to respond to eventualities. They accomplish this by being situationally aware. This means that they have a fundamental understanding of what is going on around them at the moment, and also have an expectation for what is *likely* to happen in the future. They also have an expectation for what *could* happen in the future.

Hollnagel et al. (2011) further describe four cornerstones of resilience: anticipating, monitoring, responding, and learning. These would go hand in hand with Endsley's (1995) interpretation of situational awareness, given that the learning function is more allied to future states of SA.

SA competencies are often assessed in airlines using behavioral marker (BM) assessment systems, such as NOTECHS (Flin et al., 2003). NOTECHS uses a system of four categories, which are further divided into elements, and observable behaviors. For the BM of situational awareness, the elements are divided into awareness of aircraft systems, the external environment, and time, and outline some typical examples of good and bad practice which can be graded on a scale of 1−5. Typical behaviors which are said to exemplify sound SA, and therefore would likely facilitate positive resilience characteristics, include:

- Monitors and reports changes in systems' states
- Acknowledges entries and changes to the systems
- Collects information about environment (position, weather and traffic)
- Shares key information about environment with crew
- Contacts outside resources when needed (to maintain SA)
- Discusses time constraints with crew
- Discusses contingency strategies
- Identifies possible future problems (Flin et al., 2003).

7.8.2   Decision-Making

Sound decision-making, particularly in complex, high risk environments such as aviation, is a strong contributor to resilience, both at a strategic level, and in a recovery period following an adverse critical event. Conversely, resilience could be considered a fundamental requirement when crews are required to make rapid, accurate, safety-critical decisions under stress, such as during an aircraft emergency.

Considerable work has been done on pilot decision-making (e.g., Flin, O'Connor, & Chrichton, 2008; Harris & Li, 2015; Wise, Hopkin, & Garland, 2009; Zsambok & Klein, 2014), however, definitive answers on the relationship between decision-making and resilience have not yet been addressed in great detail.

One of the significant factors affecting decision-making, and therefore resilience in aviation, is uncertainty. Decisions are relatively simple when situations are readily assessed, and there are a limited number of decision options, with clearly associated levels of risk. However, real-world decision-making, particularly during complex safety-critical events, does not always enjoy the benefit of being predictable, or easily understood, which can impact on recovery efforts. While the ideal answer would be that pilots were more "resilient," and therefore better equipped to deal with such events, regrettably such resilience is often tested during novel, safety-critical events.

A resilient flight crew could be considered to be a crew who made decisions commensurate with risk, who were prepared technically for any eventuality, and had on hand a range of preconsidered decision options which could be adapted to suit a range of both known, and novel circumstances. Such crews could be considered to be strategically resilient (i.e., prepared for most eventualities), and tactically resilient (i.e., able to respond with appropriate decisions following an unexpected critical event).

Research has shown that greater exposure to decision-making tasks, and also to novel, unexpected events, can improve future decision-making during such events through the development of decision strategies, and a wider breadth of experience to base such decisions on (Cannon-Bowers & Salas, 1998; Chrichton & Flin, 2001; Zsambok & Klein, 2014). This is one of the premises of EBT and is likely to become more prevalent in the future.

As with SA, decision-making is regularly assessed using behavioral markers. In the NOTECHS system Flin et al. (2003) cite the following exemplary behaviors which would produce sound decision-making, and would be likely as a result to facilitate resilient behaviors:

- Gathers information to identify problem
- Reviews causal factors with other crew members
- States alternative options
- Asks crew members for options
- Considers and shares estimated risk of alternative options
- Talks about possible risks for action in terms of crew limits
- Confirms and states selected option/agreed action
- Checks outcome against plan (Flin et al., 2003).

While these are not necessarily a comprehensive list of behaviors which would enable both strategically and tactically resilient behaviors to flourish, they do represent sound decision-making practices which would be likely to enhance such behaviors.

7.8.3   Communication

One of the common themes in organizational resilience literature is the need for strong, clear, and effective communication skills. These same requirements apply equally to flight and cabin crews in times of adversity. One of the common occurrences under periods of acute stress is a breakdown in communication, sometimes to the point where it stops entirely, or is at least stilted. Contrast this to the measured, clear communication styles exhibited by Captains Haines and Sullenberger in the United 232 and US Airways 1549 accidents (NTSB, 1990, 2010a), respectively, and it becomes clearer what the ideal communication style is under immense adversity.

Communication is an enabling skill for effective situational awareness and for decision-making, and therefore forms an equally important role in strategic resilience as it does in tactical resilience. It is often the basis of a shared mental model (Cannon-Bowers, Salas, & Converse, 1993;

Jonker, van Riemsdijk, & Vermeulen, 2011), which is an effective tool for TEM. Shared mental models can be hard to restore in the initial aftermath of an adverse critical event, particularly where it involves surprise or startle, and therefore ensuring a communication stream which announces the most critical information, will ensure all crew are focused appropriately and as a team.

Effective communication can be a preventive strategy for avoiding critical events, particularly when allied to effective monitoring. It is also fundamental in coping with adversity during the initial onset and recovery from critical events. To develop better communication skills which would make crews more resilient during critical emergencies, more focus could be applied during simulator training events on ensuring that shared mental models were enhanced during emergencies through the greater application of sound team communication processes.

7.8.4   Workload Management

Task management is a critical skill, particularly under periods of high workload. Effective workload management has a very significant role in preventive, or strategic resilience by reducing the chances that crew members will be distracted by tasks, and thereby creating a window for an adverse event to develop.

It is also a tactical resilience skill, allowing crew members to focus on the critical tasks following an adverse nonnormal event. The old adage of *Aviate − Navigate − Communicate* is a prioritization tool which is particularly effective in nonnormal situations, and lends itself to resilient behavior. While there may be a number of attention getters during a critical situation, the onus must always be on flying the aircraft and managing the flight path. This was very effectively done in the three cases looked at in Section 7.4, but has not been well done in a myriad of other cases which ended in negative outcomes.

7.8.5   Stress Management

Significant stress has largely negative effects on information processing. While a moderate level of arousal is useful for keeping focus and vigilance, the impairment effects of acute stress during emergencies or conditions of threat, can have a serious impact on the resilience of crews.

Prior to critical events, high levels of stress can cause decreased or narrowed attention, poor concentration, or concentration on task irrelevant issues (Staal, 2004); a less resilient state because of the impaired awareness.

During and immediately following a critical event, stressed crew members suffer from all of the same issues, but often at a much more heightened level. The results of this can be impairment beyond the point of being able to contribute meaningfully, including episodes of freezing (Martin, 2014). While these are rare, the impairment effects of stress are likely to be exacerbated during conditions of threat, reducing both individual resilience, and therefore overall team resilience.

There are a number of techniques for remediating the effects of stress. Most of these are lifestyle based and involve psychological or actual means of either reframing stressors, or removing them completely (Franklin, Saab, & Mansuy, 2012). Such techniques include social support, counseling, exercise, yoga, meditation, improved diet, and reduction of relationship or financial stressors (Olpin & Hesson, 2016). Such efforts could be considered strategic resilience, designed to alleviate the stress which predisposes crew members to poor performance during stressful events.

Following critical events, where stress levels may spike, the effects of deliberate breathing have been shown to improve recovery time (Boland, 2016; Varvogli & Darviri, 2011). Earlier recovery will likely enhance resilience as more working memory capacity is freed up.

7.8.6 Fatigue Management

Fatigue is an insidious impairment, which is receiving much attention worldwide. While ICAO has published guidelines (ICAO, 2016), individual regulators are quite varied in the way they apply those guidelines. There is also a move towards Fatigue Risk Management Systems, which allow mature operators some leeway to manage their risk exposure based on evidence from their own operation.

The effects of fatigue on crew members has been relatively well studied (e.g., Caldwell, 2005; Goode, 2003; SRG, 2005) however there is still further room for scientific rigor in establishing contemporary empirical bases for fatigue rules across a diverse and complex industry.

At an individual level, fatigue often manifests itself as a reduction in concentration, vigilance, attentional span, and teamwork (Pilcher, Vander Wood, & O'Connell, 2011; Tanaka, Ishii, & Watanabe, 2015). It also adversely impacts on complex mental tasks, such as those that would be required during novel critical events (Burke, Scheer, Ronda, Czeisler, & Wright, 2015; ICAO, 2016; Killgore, Balkin, & Wesensten, 2006).

Fatigue is therefore likely to have a significant impact on an individual's resilience, both strategically and tactically. Where the situation encountered calls for exemplary teamwork, leadership, and higher order thinking skills for successful resolution, then the resilience of the team could also be affected. Managing fatigue through appropriate preduty rest, through inflight naps (where appropriate), and through the appropriate use of caffeine, can enhance individual and therefore team resilience.

7.9   CONCLUSION

Resilience is a term which has become widely used, particularly at an individual level and at an organizational or systemic level. It is however rarely discussed at a small team level, a situation which happens everyday in flight operations. However, the concepts applicable to individual resilience and to larger units, such as organizational resilience, are largely transferable to the small team flight crew environment in the aviation industry.

A concept which contributes to resilience, which generally isn't found in other industries, is TEM. This overarching focus on identification and avoidance of threats, and on the management, or mitigation of threats and errors, supports a resilient team framework, which is enhanced by sound situational awareness.

Resilience in the literature often talks about the ability to recover from some event, and there are certainly some unexpected events that happen in aviation which are challenging and unexpected. Such events often call upon the application of sound CRM skills to enable a safe outcome to be achieved. Such situations require clear communication and sound leadership. They also require coherent teamwork, sound decision-making, and well-prioritized task management.

While the tactical resilience which saves the day is essential, there is also a strong case for CRM skills to be used as a defensive, more strategic tool, utilizing this array of abilities and behaviors to be on top of the TEM challenge, and to avoid situations which would require a recovery using tactical resilience. These skills are appropriate at both an individual and team level.

Training pilots in the future to be resilient will continue to focus on CRM skill development, in both normal and nonnormal situations. It will also focus on exposure to unexpected critical events, in a constructive, learning environment. Better resilience will also be borne from raising the expectation levels for critical events, a battle which will not be easy as aircraft become ever more automated, sophisticated, and reliable.

REFERENCES

Australian Transport Safety Board [ATSB]. (2013). *In-flight uncontained engine failure Airbus A380-842, VH-OQA, overhead Batam Island*, Indonesia, 4 November 2010. Available from http://www.atsb.gov.au/publications/investigation_reports/2010/aair/ao-2010-089.aspx.

Boland, E. (2016). *Managing startle & surprise [Powerpoint presentation]. Proceedings of the PACDEFF CRM and aviation human factors conference* (pp. 7−8). South Australia: Glenelg, November.

Bureau d'Enquêtes et d'Analyses pour la sécurité de l'aviation civile [BEA]. (2012). Final report on the accident on 1st June 2009 to the Airbus A330-203 registered F-GZCP operated by Air France flight AF 447 Rio de Janeiro − Paris. Available from https://www.bea.aero/doc-spa/2009/f-cp090601.en/pdf/f-cp090601.en.pdf.

Burke, T. M., Scheer, F. A. J. L., Ronda, J. M., Czeisler, C. A., & Wright, K. P. (2015). Sleep inertia, sleep homeostatic and circadian influences on higher-order cognitive functions. *Journal of Sleep Research, 24,* 364−371.

Caldwell, J. A. (2005). Fatigue in aviation. *Travel Medicine and Infectious Disease, 3,* 85−96.

Cannon-Bowers, A., Salas, E., & Converse, S. (1993). Shared mental models in expert team decision making. In N. J. Castellan (Ed.), *Individual and group decision making* (pp. 221−245). Mahwah, NJ: Lawrence Erlbaum Associates.

Cannon-Bowers, J. A., & Salas, E. (1998). *Making decisions under stress: Implications for individual and team training.* Washington, DC: American Psychological Association.

Chrichton, M., & Flin, R. (2001). Training for emergency management: Tactical decision games. *Journal of Hazardous Materials, 88*(2-3), 255−266.

Claesson, G. (2006). *What is resilience?* Available from http://www.rico.com.au/resilience/.

Deveson, A. (2003). *Resilience.* Sydney, Australia: Allen Unwin.

Endsley, M. R. (1995). Toward a theory of situation awareness in dynamic systems. *Human Factors, 37*(1), 32−64.

Flach, F. F. (2004). *Resilience: Discovering a new strength at times of stress.* Hobart, NY: Hatherleigh Press.

Flin, R., Martin, L., Goeters, K.-M., Hormann, H.-J., Amalberti, R., Valot, C., & Nijhuis, H. (2003). Development of the NOTECHS (non-technical skills) system for assessing pilot's CRM skills. *Human Factors and Aerospace Safety, 3*(2), 95−117.

Flin, R., O'Connor, P., & Chrichton, M. (2008). *Safety at the sharp end. A guide to non-technical skills.* Aldershot: Ashgate.

Foster, M. I., & Keane, M. T. (2015). Why some surprises are more surprising than others: Surprise as a metacognitive sense of explanatory difficulty. *Cognitive Psychology, 81,* 74−116.

Franklin, T. B., Saab, B. J., & Mansuy, I. M. (2012). Neural mechanisms of stress resilience and vulnerability. *Neuron, 75*(5), 747−761.

Gillen, M. W. (2016). A study evaluating if targeted training for startle effect can improve pilot reactions in handling unexpected situations in a flight simulator *(Doctoral Dissertation).* University of North Dakota.

Goode, J. H. (2003). Are pilots at risk of accidents due to fatigue? *Journal of Safety Research, 34,* 309−313.

Greitens, E. (2015). *Resilience: Hard-won wisdom for living a better life.* Boston, MA: Houghton, Mifflin Harcourt.

Harris, D., & Li, W.-C. (Eds.), (2015). *Decision making in aviation.* Farnham: Ashgate.

Helmreich, R. L., Klinect, J. R., & Wilhelm, J. A. (1999). *Models of threat, error, and CRM in flight operations. Proceedings of the Tenth International Symposium on Aviation Psychology* (pp. 677−682). Columbus, OH: The Ohio State University.

Hollnagel, E., Paries, J., Woods, D. A., & Wreathall, J. (Eds.), (2011). *Resilience engineering in practice: A guidebook.* Farnham, Surrey: Ashgate Publishing Limited.

International Civil Aviation Organization [ICAO]. (2016). *Manual for the oversight of fatigue management approaches (Document 9966)* (2nd ed.). Available from https://www.icao.int/safety/fatiguemanagement/FRMS%20Tools/Doc%209966.FRMS.2016%20Edition.en.pdf.

Jarvis, S. (2017). *Colin 1 and Colin 2: A review of CRM programs.* Paper presented at the PACDEFF CRM Conference, Melbourne, Australia, August 8-10, 2017. Available from http://pacdeff.com/wp-content/uploads/2017/08/PACDEFF-Keynote-2017.pdf.

Jonker, C.M., van Riemsdijk, B.M. & Vermeulen, B. (2011). Shared mental models: A conceptual analysis. In *Proceedings of the 9th international conference on autonomous agents and multiagent systems (AAMAS 2010)*, van der Hoek, Kaminka, Lespérance, Luck and Sen (eds.), May, 10–14, 2010, Toronto, Canada.

Killgore, W. D. S., Balkin, T. J., & Wesensten, N. J. (2006). Impaired decision making following 49 h of sleep deprivation. *Journal of Sleep Research, 15*, 7–13.

Lang, P. J., Bradley, M. M., & Cuthbert, B. N. (1997). Motivated attention: Affect, activation and action. In P. J. Lang, & R. F. Simons (Eds.), *Attention and orienting: Sensory and motivational processes*. Mahwah, NJ: Lawrence Earlbaum & Associates.

Lanir, Z. (1986). *Fundamental surprise: The national intelligence crisis*. Eugene, OR: Decision Research.

Leflar, J. J., & Siegel, M. H. (2012). *Organizational resilience: Managing the risks of disruptive events – A practitioner's guide*. La Baton, FL: CRC Press.

Martin, W. L. (2014). Pathological behaviours in pilots during unexpected critical events: The effect of startle, freeze and denial on situation outcome *(Doctoral Thesis)*. Brisbane, Australia: Griffith University.

Misslin, R. (2003). The defense system of fear: Behavior and neurocircuitry. *Clinical Neurophysiology, 33*(2), 55–66.

National Transportation Safety Board [NTSB]. (1990). *United Airlines Flight 232, McDonnell Douglas DC-10-10, Sioux Gateway Airport, Sioux City, Iowa, July 19, 1989 Report Number NTSB/AAR-90/06*. Available from https://www.faa.gov/about/initiatives/maintenance_hf/library/documents/media/human_factors_maintenance/united_airlines_flight_232.mcdonnell_douglas_dc-10-10.sioux_gateway_airport.sioux_city.lowa.july_19.1989.pdf.

National Transportation Safety Board [NTSB]. (2010a). *Loss of thrust in both engines after encountering a flock of birds and subsequent ditching on the Hudson River – US Airways Flight 1549 Airbus A320-214, N106US*, Weehawken, NJ, January 15, 2009. Available from https://www.ntsb.gov/investigations/AccidentReports/Reports/AAR1003.pdf.

National Transportation Safety Board [NTSB]. (2010b). *Loss of Control on Approach Colgan Air, Inc., Operating as Continental Connection Flight 3407 Bombardier DHC-8-400, N200WQ, Clarence Center, New York, February 12, 2009*. Available from https://www.ntsb.gov/investigations/AccidentReports/Reports/AAR1001.pdf.

Olpin, M., & Hesson, M. (2016). *Stress management for life: A research-based experiential approach*. Boston, MA: Cengage Learning.

Oxford Dictionary. com. (n.d.). *Definition of resilience in English*. Available from https://en.oxforddictionaries.com/definition/resilience.

Pariés, J. (2012). *Resilience in aviation: The challenge of the unexpected*. Paper presented at the IAEA Technical Meeting on managing the unexpected: From the perspective of the interaction between individuals, technology and organization, Vienna, 25 to 29 June 2012. Available from https://gnssn.iaea.org/NSNI/SC/TMMtU/Presentations/Mr%20Paries%27s%20Presentation%201.pdf

Pilcher, J. J., Vander Wood, M. A., & O'Connell, K. L. (2011). The effects of extended work under sleep deprivation conditions on team-based performance. *Ergonomics, 54*(7), 587–596.

Reich, J. W., Zautra, A. J., & Hall, J. S. (Eds.), (2012). *Handbook of adult resilience*. New York: The Guildford Press.

Rivera, J., Talone, A.B., Boesser, C.T., Jentsch, F. & Yeh, M. (2014). Startle and surprise on the flight deck: Similarities, differences and prevalence. In *Proceedings of the 58th annual meeting of the human factors and ergonomics society*, Chicago, IL, 27–31 October.

Safety Regulation Group [SRG]. (2005). *Aircrew fatigue: A review of research undertaken on behalf of the UK Civil Aviation Authority (CAA Paper 2005/04)*. Available from https://publicapps.caa.co.uk/docs/33/CAAPaper2005_04.pdf.

Salas, E., Burke, C.S., Bowers, C.A., & Wilson, K.A. (2001). *Team training in the skies: Does Crew Resource Management (CRM) training work?* Available from http://www.raes-hfg.com/reports/22may01-SitAssessment/240501-salas-ROI.pdf.

Staal, M.A. (2004). Stress, cognition, and human performance: A literature review and conceptual framework (Technical report NASNTM-2004-212824). Available from https://ntrs.nasa.gov/archive/nasa/casi.ntrs.nasa.gov/20060017835.pdf.

Taleb, N. N. (2010). *The black swan: The impact of the highly improbable* (2nd ed.). New York: Random House Trade.

Tanaka, M., Ishii, A., & Watanabe, Y. (2015). Effects of mental fatigue on brain activity and cognitive performance: A magnetoencephalography study. *Anatomy & Physiology: Current Research, 54*(2), 1–5.

Varvogli, L., & Darviri, C. (2011). Stress management techniques: Evidence-based procedures that reduce stress and promote health. *Health Science Journal, 5*(2), 74–89.

Wessel, J. R., Jenkinson, N., Brittain, J.-S., Voets, S. H. E. M., Aziz, T. Z., & Aron, A. R. (2016). Surprise disrupts cognition via a fronto-basal ganglia suppressive mechanism. *Nature Communication, 7*(11195), 1–10.

Wise, J. A., Hopkin, V. D., & Garland, D. J. (Eds.), (2009). *Handbook of aviation human factors* (2nd ed.). Boca Raton, FL: CRC Press.

Woods, D. D., Leveson, N., & Hollnagel, E. (Eds.), (2012). *Resilience engineering: Concepts and precepts.* Aldershot: Ashgate Publishing Ltd.

Zsambok, C. E., & Klein, G. (Eds.), (2014). *Naturalistic decision making* (2nd ed.). New York: Psychology Press.

Chapter 8

Crew Resource Management, Risk, and Safety Management Systems

Thomas R. Chidester[1] and José Anca[2]

[1]*Civil Aerospace Medical Institute, Federal Aviation Administration, Oklahoma City, OK, United States,* [2]*Faculty of Science, Engineering and Technology, Swinburne University of Technology, Hawthorn, VIC, Australia*

8.1 SAFETY MANAGEMENT SYSTEMS

The Federal Aviation Administration (FAA, 2015) defines safety management systems (SMS) as a "comprehensive and preventative approach to managing safety" (p. 1). The International Civil Aviation Organization (ICAO, 2013) uses a similar definition and articulates equivalent processes in a detailed safety management manual. In fact, the ICAO has recommended its member-states to implement SMS (Hollinger, 2013). SMS builds upon the organization's safety culture rooted in safety policy, and emphasizes three fundamental ongoing processes of safety risk management, safety assurance, and safety promotion. This requires some definitions. Antonsen (2009) defined *Safety Culture* as the product of formal measures taken to minimize risk to an acceptable level and to ensure that stakeholders feel secure and in control, and the informal understood priorities of the organization and key subgroups within it. From this perspective, SMS is one of the formal measures, accompanied by procedures, training, and reporting and monitoring systems. But informal measures, the perceptions of frontline workers and supervisors of how work is to be accomplished, are also critical. Culture is an emergent product of both—leaders may influence culture by what they say and write into procedure; employees act upon both what is stated and what they understand. So the SMS Advisory Circular emphasizes that culture cannot be "created or implemented, but [emerges] over time and as a result of experience" (p. 7). *Safety Policy* is often the highest level public statement of that safety culture, wherein senior management clearly articulates its expected standards of performance and how the organization approaches

Crew Resource Management. DOI: https://doi.org/10.1016/B978-0-12-812995-1.00008-7
227

risk. An SMS becomes the formal mechanism by which an airline makes decisions about risk. The Advisory Circular states the following requirements for Safety Policy:

---

§ 5.21 Safety policy.

1. The certificate holder must have a safety policy that includes at least the following:
   a. The safety objectives of the certificate holder.
   b. A commitment of the certificate holder to fulfill the organization's safety objectives.
   c. A clear statement about the provision of the necessary resources for the implementation of the SMS.
   d. A safety reporting policy that defines requirements for employee reporting of safety hazards or issues.
   e. A policy that defines unacceptable behavior and conditions for disciplinary action.
   f. An emergency response plan that provides for the safe transition from normal to emergency operations in accordance with the requirements of § 5.27.
2. The safety policy must be signed by the accountable executive described in § 5.25.
3. The safety policy must be documented and communicated throughout the certificate holder organization.
4. The safety policy must be regularly reviewed by the accountable executive to ensure it remains relevant and appropriate to the certificate holder.

FAA (2015, p. 16).

Safety Risk Management is a formal process of identifying risks faced in an airline's operations, deciding which risks are acceptable and which require mitigation, documenting those decisions, and implementing them in the policies, procedures, training, and infrastructure of the airline. Were an airline built from scratch using this approach, decisions about which aircraft to purchase, what airports to serve, where to perform maintenance, and how to document policy and procedures and accomplish training of various workforces would be included. But, most airlines predate SMS. It may be straightforward to make post-SMS implementation decisions in this manner, but it is challenging to develop an inventory of past decisions and a profile of airline risk. Ideally, SMS would result in a present-state inventory of hazards, the risks they present to the airline, and the mitigations in place. Continued application results in disciplined decisions about revision to operations to conform with the airline's approach to safety management.

Safety Assurance involves the monitoring and measuring of the airline's daily activities to ensure that the level of safety achieved matches expectation and that policy and risk mitigation are functioning as intended. Airlines use flight operations quality assurance (FOQA; FAA, 2004a; monitoring flight performance data downloaded from aircraft), Aviation Safety Action Programs (ASAP; FAA, 2002; reviewing safety concerns and events reported by pilots, dispatchers, mechanics, and other employees), line oriented safety audits (LOSA; FAA, 2006a; collecting standardized observations of samples of flights), training data from Advanced Qualification Programs (AQP; FAA, 2006b; collecting performance data from simulator and line flight evaluations), and other programs to observe and quantify risk. This both feeds back to formal decisions and policy and makes the airline aware of emerging hazards.

Safety Promotion communicates to each employee group its safety functions and how the airline expects them to respond to hazards and approach risks encountered on the job. This includes both training necessary to qualify and maintain qualification and policy, procedure, and *ad hoc* publications. "Because a key component of SMSs is the effective control of risk, every member in your organization must understand and take responsibility for the role they play in controlling risk by their actions and behavior" (FAA, 2015, p. 46).

So, how might this approach be applied? Consider the case of a hypothetical airline that has identified a potentially lucrative market operating from a US hub to a Central American resort destination. While its airport is near sea level and the majority of its days are sunny and clear, the airport is surrounded by mountainous terrain and experiences tropical rainfall and low visibility on occasion. The SMS accountable executive conducting the safety assessment notices that the airport has an instrument landing system (ILS) to approach the single runway from one direction, but a nonprecision approach (no vertical guidance) using only the VOR on the field from the other. However, both a circle-to-land maneuver from the ILS approach and a GPS-based nonprecision area navigation (RNAV) approach overlaid upon the VOR approach have been published. The executive calls together a team of technical, training, and management personnel to assess the hazards. They identify terrain as a hazard to operations during night or low visibility approaches to the non-ILS runway, and determine that the circle-to-land maneuver, backed up by the Ground Proximity Warning System (GPWS), does not provide sufficient mitigation under the airline's safety policy. What mitigations might the airline apply? They might require use of the ILS and prohibit operation to the non-ILS runway during low visibility or night, but this would on some occasions prohibit dispatch to the airport and in others could require diversion to another airport due to a tailwind exceeding limitations at time of the approach. With a nonprecision approach to the other runway, these could be overcome, but nonprecision approaches are empirically more risky than precision approaches (Flight Safety Foundation; FSF, 2000). Our hypothetical airline prefers GPS/RNAV approaches with constant-angle descent guidance where available. Consistent with that, the airline could require that only aircraft also capable of using the GPS overlay of the non-precision approach be dispatched to the airport. This disqualifies aircraft not equipped with GPS receivers and crews not qualified or current on this type of approach. Ultimately, the team chooses this solution, adds a note to its flight manual prohibiting circle-to-land maneuvers and requiring use of the ILS or the GPS overlay to their respective runways during night and instrument meteorological (IMC) conditions. They publish a special note on flight plans to the destination to highlight the requirement, and incorporate the airport into the airline's qualification and continuing qualification simulator training for the coming year.

Notice the assessments conducted, hazards identified, and mitigations selected; these are the essence of the Safety Risk Management process. Notice also that it would be legal to operate into the airport with none of these mitigations in place. Compliance with published circle-to-land maneuvers meets FAA and ICAO requirements for terrain separation. But our hypothetical airline has formalized its safety policy, a process of risk management, and implemented a set of mitigations which set a higher standard of safety. The team's decisions do not preclude the ability to dispatch or operate into the airport. Safety assurance could be applied here by timely review of FOQA data, reminding pilots to report any anomalous conditions encountered at this airport, increasing the frequency of line evaluations on this route, or making it a target of LOSA observations. Safety Promotion was incorporated into the flight plan alerts and manual notes, incorporation of the airport into simulator training, and could be enhanced by *ad hoc* publications discussing the airport or the airline's implementation of SMS. A direct link to crew resource management (CRM) training is possible as well—the airline might choose to emphasize strategies for terrain awareness and avoidance at both the policy and crew level as part of its qualification or continuing qualification CRM training.

How might SMS actions or deficiencies be observed following an accident? On August 14, 2013, UPS Flight 1354, an Airbus A-300-600 crashed short of the runway at Birmingham, Alabama (National Transportation Safety Board; NTSB, 2014). Runway 06/24, the longest available at the airport was noticed to be closed for maintenance at the time of the approach. Weather was overcast with low and variable ceilings in predawn darkness. The open runway 18 had a nonprecision approach using a localizer, and a GPS-based nonprecision area navigation (RNAV) approach. The Captain briefed the RNAV approach to runway 18, to be flown in profile mode—the aircraft autopilot and flight guidance would be coupled to the localizer and would provide a calculated constant descent angle from the final approach fix to the decision altitude of 1200 ft above mean sea level (ft msl), where the crew must decide to continue to land or execute a missed approach. But when cleared for the approach, "the Captain did not request and the First

Officer did not verify that the flight plan [in the Flight Management Computer (FMC)] included only the approach fixes; therefore, the direct-to-KBHM leg that had been set up during the flight from Louisville remained in the FMC. This caused a flight plan discontinuity message to remain in the FMC, which rendered the glideslope generated for the profile approach meaningless" (p. xi). As a result, when the Captain reached the final approach fix, no vertical guidance was provided. Starting the descent late, he attempted to complete (without announcing) the nonprecision approach by switching the autopilot to vertical speed mode and monitoring the published step-down fixes and altitudes. The First Officer, noticing the mode change, made the 1000 ft above field elevation callout, but not the decision altitude callout. Descending at a high rate, the aircraft flew through the decision altitude. A "sink rate" warning was annunciated by the Ground Proximity Warning System (GPWS) and the Captain reduced the descent rate as he reported the runway in sight. However, the descent rate remained at about 1000 ft/min, and the aircraft impacted trees about one mile short of the runway and then the ground, killing both crewmembers.

What were the hazards faced by the crew? Early morning darkness and IMC. A closed runway requiring an approach to a shorter runway with only a nonprecision approach available. Terrain up-sloping to a forested ridgeline north of the airport. An approach time at the window of circadian low for crew alertness, meaning a high potential for fatigue. What would an SMS do with any of these hazards in advance of this accident? The NTSB investigation identified a number of actions by the airline evidencing SMS application to this airport and similar circumstances and mitigating a number of hazards for this flight. For example, nighttime instrument approaches using a nonprecision approach are empirically challenging, but the airline had equipped its aircraft with GPS receivers enabling the crew to fly the RNAV approach to 18 and had trained crews to proficiency on the procedures. (The A-300/600 had been manufactured prior to implementation of these technologies for airline operations but with the ability to add them when certified for use.) Only the Captain's switch, mid-approach, to a more manual operation (vertical speed attempting to honor altitude restrictions) removed that layer of protection. The airline had in place training on the consequences of fatigue, a fitness for duty policy and fatigue risk management plan published in the Flight Manual, and a fatigue event reporting and review process. (The NTSB was critical of how the First Officer used her off-duty time during the trip, failing to take advantage of rest opportunities, as evidenced by her smartphone usage.) The airline had implemented a stabilized approach policy requiring abandonment of an approach if the aircraft were descending at a rate greater than 1000 fpm below 1000 ft above the field. The accident approach exceeded the criterion, but was not abandoned by the crew. The NTSB did note that the aircraft was capable of an automated "minimums" callout that UPS had not implemented and that a software update for the

EGPWS system was available that would have provided an additional, slightly earlier warning of terrain conflict. So, from accident analysis, only three potential SMS additions were identified—a prohibition on changing autopilot modes to continue an approach, consideration of automating available and critical callouts, and consistent updating of TAWS software. Perhaps the latter two could have been identified in Safety Risk Management. The former would likely be identified only through Safety Assurance, if a crew reported a similar error or if FOQA monitoring identified similar autopilot mode usage and accompanying exceedances. Perhaps the mode change issue could be added to the stabilized approach policy, as well.

At least one other airline, years before, identified the up-sloping terrain north of runway 18 as a potential issue though its Safety Assurance processes. A crew was cleared for the approach to runway 18 in early morning visual conditions and noticed the proximity of the trees during their approach. They reported it to their ASAP program. Approaches to this runway are rare for airline crews and the Captain was concerned others needed to be made aware of the terrain. Ultimately, that airline asked their chart vendor to provide an airport familiarization page with color photographs for Birmingham for addition to their flight manual. The vendor continues to offer qualification and familiarization charts for the airport. But, these charts are not required. The NTSB did not discuss this as relevant to the accident. It appears only as a reference in the public docket (NTSB, 2013). Another airline prohibits use of this runway during its operations. So, we are aware that multiple airlines made safety management decisions about operations into the airport. Some consider it relatively benign. Others purchase vendor-published photographic familiarization charts. At least one airline chose not to use the accident runway. In our opening section, we said that an SMS becomes the formal mechanism by which an airline makes decisions about risk. These differing approaches to flight operations at Birmingham reflect differences in risk assessment and experience.

More broadly, what are the implications of an accident for an SMS? Reason (1997) argues for defenses in depth or layers of protection. Despite our best efforts, defenses will fail on occasion. SMS can serve as a method for identifying defenses in infrastructure, policy, procedure, and training and monitoring to assure their effectiveness. The UPS accident illustrates that even when much is in place from an SMS perspective, an accident can still occur. But the accident provides further feedback to prevent future events. Human behavior is probabilistic, rather than deterministic. Unlike physics, we cannot determine with certainty that an action will affect every person in the same way. But, we *can* make desired and undesired actions and consequences more and less likely. As a result, we never know whether mitigations are necessary or sufficient to always prevent incident or accident, but can only judge whether risk is sufficient to offer defenses in depth. And we can commit to continuously improve. The NTSB probable cause statement emphasized CRM-related behaviors:

> *The National Transportation Safety Board determines that the probable cause of this accident was the flight crew's continuation of an unstabilized approach and their failure to monitor the aircraft's altitude during the approach, which led to an inadvertent descent below the minimum approach altitude and subsequently into terrain. Contributing to the accident were (1) the flight crew's failure to properly configure and verify the flight management computer for the profile approach; (2) the captain's failure to communicate his intentions to the first officer once it became apparent the vertical profile was not captured; (3) the flight crew's expectation that they would break out of the clouds at 1000 ft above ground level due to incomplete weather information; (4) the first officer's failure to make the required minimums callouts; (5) the captain's performance deficiencies likely due to factors including, but not limited to, fatigue, distraction, or confusion, consistent with performance deficiencies exhibited during training; and (6) the first officer's fatigue due to acute sleep loss resulting from her ineffective off-duty time management and circadian factors (p. 90).*

In the sections that follow, we explore CRM interfaces with SMS, methods for incorporating risk identification and mitigation into CRM training, and future expectations for collaborative advances in CRM and SMS.

8.2 CRM INTERFACES WITH SMS

CRM has evolved alongside improving information streams about airline operations (Farrow, 2010) and concepts of safety management. Naturally, each of these has become entwined, with a number of benefits. Whilst having its roots in aviation, CRM has coexisted within an SMS especially in the realm of using effective teamwork to produce better quality products, for instance in the automotive industry. In this section, we consider how CRM, construed as a skillset, an approach to flying, and a body of knowledge, can serve an SMS process, and how SMS can improve training and implementation of CRM.

Considering CRM as a skillset reveals how it may both serve safety promotion functions and provide more specific mitigations to some issues. Helmreich and Foushee (1993) discussed behavioral markers of three dimensions which were subsequently codified as skills in the FAA CRM advisory circular (AC120-51e; FAA, 2004b). These dimensions were communication and decision skills, team building and maintenance skills, and workload management and situation awareness skills. As airlines implemented Advanced Qualification Programs (AQP; FAA, 2006b), they were required to integrate these skills into the performance objectives required to operate their aircraft. Most described a high level skillset composed of these dimensions and within phase of flight and abnormal or emergency performance objectives describing how these skills were to be implemented. American Airlines (1996) provides a good summary of phase-independent CRM skills:

41. Maintain Principles of GLOBAL CRM.
    41.01. Captain's Authority/Responsibility (CRM)
        41.01.01. Exercise Pilot in Command Responsibility IAW FAR 1.1, FM Part 1. [CA]
        41.01.02. Maintain the safety of passengers and aircraft [CA]
        41.01.03. Coordinate crew duties within the framework provided by AA [CA]
        41.01.04. Communicate plans and decisions to the crew [CA]
        41.01.05. Enforce standardization, policies, and procedure [CA]
        41.01.06. Respond to any safety-related concern raised by any crewmember [CA]
        41.01.07. Counsel and develop the aviation skill and knowledge of junior crewmembers [CA]
    41.02. FO/FE Responsibility (CRM)
        41.02.01. Comply with Second in Command responsibility IAW FM Part 1. [FO, FE]
        41.02.02. Maintain the safety of passengers and aircraft [FO, FE]
        41.02.03. Support decisions articulated by the Captain within the limits of safety, legality, and procedure. [FO, FE]
        41.02.04. Request a plan or decision if none is articulated by the Captain [FO, FE]
        41.02.05. Follow procedure and techniques requested by the Captain [FO, FE]
        41.02.06. Crosscheck and back the Captain up. This requires maintaining vigilance and proficiency in the aircraft and with procedures. [FO, FE]
        41.02.07. Report to the Captain any safety-related concern and advocate a safe course of action. [FO, FE]
        41.02.08. Develop your proficiency and learn from the Captain [FO, FE]
    41.03. Establish an effective communications process (CRM)
        41.03.01. Conduct effective briefings. [CA]
        41.03.02. Contribute to effective briefings. [FO]
        41.03.03. Establish and maintain a communications "loop." [CA & FO]
        41.03.04. Communicate decisions. [CA]
        41.03.05. Resolve disagreements or conflicts. [CA & FO]
        41.03.06. Debrief critical flight events. [CA]
    41.04. Maintain situation awareness (CRM)
        41.04.01. Prepare, plan and maintain vigilance. [CA] [FO]
        41.04.02. Distribute workload and avoid distractions. [CA]
        41.04.03. Prioritize actions and decisions. [CA]

41.05. Develop and maintain teamwork (CRM)

41.05.01. Establish appropriate duties and responsibilities by crew position.   [CA]

41.05.02. Demonstrate motivation appropriate to the situation.   [CA]

41.05.03. Maintain an effective group climate.   [CA]

41.05.04. Protect crewmembers from the consequences of work overload.   [CA]

41.05.05. Coordinate with other groups: F/A's, gate agents, dispatch, ground crew.   [CA]

41.06. Use judgement in use of automated systems and mode (CRM)

41.06.01. Operate the airplane using different levels of automation as appropriate.   [CA] [FO]

41.06.02. Verify that automation is doing what you expect.   [CA] [FO]

41.06.03. When using automation, back each other up.   [CA] [FO]

41.07. Crew coordination unique to abnormals and emergencies (CRM)

41.07.01. Upon detecting an existing or impending emergency condition, immediately notify the Captain.   [FO]

41.07.02. Acknowledge the emergency and call for the accomplishment of any memory items.   [CA]

41.07.03. In any emergency, designate which pilot is responsible for flying the airplane.   [CA]

41.07.04. Direct attention primarily to the control of the airplane. However, monitor the accomplishment of the procedural items.   [PF]

41.07.05. Read the MFDU (for an alerted procedure) or the Emergency checklist for a nonalerted procedure. Both challenge and response should be read aloud.   [PNF]

41.07.06. The pilot accomplishing each item will repeat the response after assuring the item is accomplished.   [PF] [PNF]

41.07.07. Upon completion of the checklist, announce: "____ checklist complete."   [PNF]

41.07.08. Refer to the expanded information in the OM for additional, supplementary, clean-up action or information, time and conditions permitting. The section and page where the expanded checklist can be found is noted on the checklist.   [PNF]

41.07.09. After completing a procedure in the OM, ensure that all other procedures and checklists are completed as appropriate for the phase of flight.   [CA]

To these core dimensions, airlines have added phase specific skills and actions. Most list skills required by phase of flight (preflight, engine start, taxi-out, takeoff, climb, cruise, descent, precision approach, nonprecision approach, go-around, landing, taxi-in, and aircraft parking). For example at American Airlines (1996), for each phase, a subelement called, "establish and maintain crew coordination during [phase name]" was developed and carried over though proficiency objectives. Here is their nonprecision approach objective:

> 09. Perform NONPRECISION APPROACH.
>> 09.01. Establish and maintain crew coordination during Approach. (CRM)
>>> 09.01.01. Brief the selected approach.   [CA]
>>> 09.01.02. Designate who will fly the approach and who will land the aircraft.   [CA]
>>> 09.01.03. Coordinate duties and responsibilities of crewmembers in case of a "Go Around."   [CA]
>>> 09.01.04. Monitor the approach and use standard callouts as the primary mechanism of crew coordination.   [PF] [PNF]
>>> 09.01.05. Monitor autopilot and instruments throughout approach.   [PF] [PNF]

Revisiting the UPS accident, consider how each of these points might mitigate specific elements of the NTSB probable cause statement. A sufficient briefing might prevent the route discontinuity error that caused the lack of vertical guidance. A focus on criticality of standard callouts might prevent a descent below minimums without required visual reference by alerting the pilot flying of reaching the decision point.

By incorporating CRM elements into its AQP task analysis and carrying them through its proficiency objectives, an airline engages in Safety Promotion. It trains skills and techniques deemed necessary to safe flight, based upon breakdowns observed in previous accidents and incidents and behaviors observed among effective crews confronting similar challenges. By carrying skills to the individual phase of flight, an airline pursues mitigations to characteristics or behaviors observed in previous accidents. For example, the nonprecision approach subtask is at least partially responsive to concerns expressed by FSF (2000). FSF developed an approach and landing accident reduction toolkit in response to the study of an average of 17 accidents during this flight phase each year between 1980 and 1998. Among their recommendations were application of CRM skills, approach briefings, identification of unique approach hazards, and being prepared to go-around. Airlines' carrying of CRM to specific actions by phase of flight evidences use of CRM as mitigation of safety management issues.

Most current CRM programs are based in Threat and Error Management (TEM; Helmreich, Klinect, & Wilhelm, 1999). TEM operationalizes CRM as an approach to daily flying that may be construed as a localized implementation of SMS. TEM suggests that most adverse events can be described in terms of risks or challenges present in an operational environment (threats) and the actions of specific personnel that potentiate or exacerbate those threats (errors). While most accident sequences begin with some provocation in the operating environment, every flight is presented with some number of hazards. Only the risks that the crew recognizes and mitigates separate an accident chain from a routine outcome. Pilots, flight attendants, mechanics, dispatchers, etc., should be alert for developing threats and should position themselves to catch and correct any mistakes. The latter is a secondary function of procedures and checklists—we do and then we review. Importantly, some risks are constant, but many are contingent upon the situation and vary by phases of activity. This regularity may be used to predict and prevent error (Helmreich et al., 1999). Applied to the UPS accident, TEM would urge crewmembers to discuss the threat of the coming phase of flight—a nonprecision approach to an unfamiliar runway in early morning darkness and marginal weather—expecting them to develop and discuss their plan for each. What will be critical to a successful approach? What might we reasonably expect to go wrong? How will we deal with that?

From a TEM perspective, CRM training should be both a vehicle for addressing risks identified through an airline's Safety Management and Feedback systems and make use of its airline's risks and incidents as a vehicle for communicating its core concepts. As TEM argues for individual pilots and crews to identify and mitigate threats in flight, SMS programs identify and mitigate threats to aggregate operations. Because CRM training provides individual pilots skills to mitigate risk to individual flights, its content should be driven by the macro threats faced by the airline. SMS becomes the intel for the substance of CRM. CRM becomes one vehicle for fortifying the workforce against the identified risks.

An example of this grew out of implementation of Enhanced Ground Proximity Warning Systems (EGPWS; or generically Terrain Awareness and Warning Systems, TAWS). These systems took advantage of digitized global satellite-mapped terrain databases enabling much earlier warnings of potential terrain conflict. Previous versions (GPWS) had been based upon the radar altimeter and gave a few seconds of warning of terrain conflict. In those few seconds, an alerted crew had to maneuver their aircraft into a rapid climb, optimizing angle of attack and engine thrust to gain as much clearance from terrain as possible. This is an escape maneuver (similar to what is trained for windshear recovery) and crews were trained in initial/qualification and recurrent/continuing qualification courses to perform these maneuvers since the 1970s. TAWS can give a continuous picture of terrain or can generate cautions 30 seconds or more prior to conflict and alerts as that margin closes. Soon after TAWS implementation, crews reported encountering terrain "cautions" to which they responded with an escape maneuver. Notice that the new system had made available two levels of alert, caution and warning; escape maneuvers were necessary only for the latter. Airlines discovered this through their Safety Assurance processes. A number of CRM programs used such incidents to discuss the philosophy of warnings (TAWS and Traffic Collision Avoidance Systems, TCAS, use caution and alert levels), situations leading to encounters, and crew coordination techniques to avoid and respond to warning level alerts.

Given over 30 years of experience, CRM can be viewed as a body of knowledge of applications to flight operation experience. These are observable in the InfoShare meetings developed by the FAA Flight Standards organization (Huerta, 2014). Most airlines have attempted to adjust at least their recurrent/continuing qualification curricula to respond to the context in which their airlines operate. During the postderegulation growth cycle of the late 1980s, courses focused on defending operations from the risk of rapid transition of crewmembers with resulting low levels of experience in aircraft type. During the recession that followed, courses focused on complacency and maintenance of proficiency as crews stayed in career position for extended periods. With the advent of ASAP programs, many challenges became visible, and CRM classes became an opportunity to introduce issues to be reinforced in simulator training. Terrain awareness became an issue at some airlines, as cases of unexpected terrain conflict gained attention, particularly among pilots operating to newer markets with significant terrain threats.

Two examples of building this kind of knowledge are Key Dismukes' work on pilot monitoring and Immanuel Barshi's work on procedure optimization for crew performance. Both were influenced by precursor research in accident investigation or airline information sharing. Sumwalt (1999) had cited multiple studies finding poor monitoring to have contributed to accidents and incidents, and argued that while most CRM courses enabled and motivated pilots to challenge deviations from intended flight path, few emphasized the skills necessary to reliably *identify* those deviations. Dismukes and Berman (2010) conducted cockpit observational studies and observed that monitoring of data and actions is required constantly, is overwhelmingly successful, but fails with sufficient frequency as to be observable on most flights. Though most monitoring failures were inconsequential, even a 1% failure rate can be devastating at the wrong time. They argued for countermeasures in policy, procedure, training, checking, mentoring, and system design. FSF (2014) pulled together a working group to package this body of knowledge into practical actions recommended for airlines to increase the effectiveness of flight path monitoring by pilots.

Degani and Wiener (1990) observed that while proceduralization has been the bedrock of cockpit safety, few procedures could be described as being optimal for enabling crew performance. They argued for rooting procedures in philosophy of operations and more concrete policy. Loukopoulos, Dismukes, and Barshi (2003) observed that checklist design often requires pilots to perform tasks concurrently and that each flow is frequently interrupted or suspended, making prospective memory errors likely (remembering to take or resume an action at some future point). Barshi engaged airlines in tackling procedures, such as taxi for takeoff, that demand multitasking, to create more intact action sequences and make error less likely. This enabled Barshi, Mauro, Degani, and Loukopoulous (2016) to craft a comprehensive guide to flight deck procedure design. FAA (2017) incorporates these recommendations. Farrow discusses methods to generalize the proceduralization of CRM behaviors in Chapter 17, A Regulatory Perspective II.

To be fair, these examples are not CRM per se, but part of the broader field of human factors. However, airlines have made use of this work in their classroom CRM and simulator LOFT/LOS training and in revision of their procedures to improve safety through improved crew performance. To the extent that CRM programs and SMSs engage the broader literature, they tap into and apply the body of knowledge. This literature is a resource for guidance to safety risk management and responses to findings from safety assurance.

8.3 INCORPORATING RISK AND RESPONSE INTO CRM TRAINING

Because of the SMS commitment to Safety Assurance, new risks are discovered. They were not identified in the Safety Risk Management process and have yet to result in accident, but monitoring data streams allowed identification of unmitigated risk. CRM training is an excellent opportunity to address many of these findings. Considering that most airlines have adopted a career-long approach to emphasize skills necessary to each role (First Officer, Captain) assigned through career progression, CRM can emphasize identified risks at each level. For example, while Captains and First Officers alternate pilot flying and pilot monitoring roles, the captain retains leadership and command responsibility throughout. How do we best train Captains to organize against threats and errors? How do we optimize flying skill, monitoring, and communication among First Officers? We can infuse training materials with their airline's approach to safety risk management and import what we learn during safety assurance. This allows continuous improvement of CRM training. We can also make strategic decisions about what to emphasize in each recurrent/continuing qualification training cycle and link classroom and simulator training curricula. The UPS accident is a good vehicle for introducing these concepts in a CRM classroom, designing simulator scenarios that challenge these skills, and debriefing crews on the effectiveness of their mitigating actions. Pilots hear concepts and see examples in the classroom, then practice and receive feedback in the simulator. In turn, teaching core skills in the context of successful and unsuccessful threat and error management is the best way to make training real. Careful selection of safety reports or FOQA observations, reenacted in the simulator and presented in the classroom, allows the instructor to lead a class through the same conditions that resulted in a report. Pilots in the classroom can be coaxed into similar judgments of a threat, challenged to detect and correct a developing chain of errors, and draw broader lessons from the individual occurrence. Presenting similarly constructed simulator scenarios reinforces those lessons. Using this approach, issues and examples from Safety Assurance programs become the staple for teaching CRM.

Airline industry response to increasing flight path automation represents one good example of this process. Wiener (1993) summarized research identifying concerns and inconsistent performance among initial cadres of pilots operating FMC aircraft and argued this would become a CRM problem. "Not only were the world's airlines facing an industrial revolution in the cockpit, but they were simultaneously witnessing the beginning of the end of the era of the flight engineer and the three-pilot flight deck" (p. 200). "Flightdeck equipment and configuration materially affect the quality and perhaps quantity of communication and crew coordination in the cockpit" (p. 208). Wiener et al. (1991) documented a number of these issues experimentally. Comparing DC-9-30 and MD-88 crews flying an identical scenario, they found higher workload reported on the MD-88 during abnormal flight conditions, longer time to landing following an abnormal event on the MD-88, a doubling of communication acts following an abnormal event on the MD-88, and a change in the dominant form of communication from command/instruction-response on the DC-9-30 to question-response on the MD-88. Research findings were accompanied by airline operating experience—pilots reported examples to their airlines and the Aviation Safety Reporting System (ASRS); airlines observed them in line incidents and flight checks or LOSA. By 1994, Delta Air Lines, American Airlines, and Federal Express had implemented courses on aircraft automation based upon this research. Sarter and Woods (2005) documented a variety of events in which pilots were surprised by actions taken or not taken by autoflight systems and traced them to underlying problems in mode communication by flightdeck systems and mode awareness among pilots. FAA (1996) documented vulnerabilities among FMC-generation aircraft, including understanding the capabilities, limitations, modes, and operating principles of automated flightdeck systems and choosing levels of automation appropriate to flight situations.

In response, the Air Transport Association (now Airlines for America; A4A) tasked its Human Factors committee to review research and member airline experience to make recommendations for policy, procedure, and training. This led to four reports (ATA, 1997, 1998, 1999, 2000) emphasizing review and revision of operating philosophy and training for FMC aircraft, offering more detailed policy than previously published in order to correct specific issues or system misunderstandings, proposing a framework for communicating aircraft differences in performance of standard navigation tasks, and communicating specific issues during introduction of Required Navigation Performance (RNP) aircraft. For example, ATA (1998) offered this draft revision to Automation Policy:

1. Operating Policy

    Pilots will be proficient in operating their aircraft in all levels of automation. However, the level of automation used at any time should be the most appropriate to enhance safety, passenger comfort, schedule, and economy. Pilots are authorized to choose what they believe to be an appropriate level of automation.

2. Choosing among levels

    In general, choices among levels can be guided by their functionality and the demands of the situation.

    a. Where immediate, decisive, and correct control of aircraft path is required, the lowest level of automation—hand-flying without flight director guidance—may be necessary. Such instances would include escape or avoidance maneuvers (excepting aircraft with flight-director windshear guidance) and recovery from upset or unusual attitudes. With the exception of visual approaches and deliberate decisions to maintain flying proficiency, this is essentially a nonnormal operation for flight guidance or FMS-generation aircraft. It should be considered a transitory mode used when the pilot perceives the aircraft is not responding to urgent aircraft demands. The pilot can establish a higher level of automation as soon as conditions permit.

    b. When used with flight director guidance, hand flying is the primary takeoff and departure mode. It is also the primary mode for landings, except for autolands.

    c. Where short-range tactical planning is needed (i.e., radar vectors for separation or course intercept, short-range speed or climb rate control, etc.), Mode Control or Flight Guidance inputs may be most effective. This level should be used predominantly in the terminal environment when responding to clearance changes and restrictions, including in-close approach/runway changes.

    d. Autoflight coupled to the FMS/GPS is the primary mode for nonterminal operations and should be established as soon as "resume own navigation" or similar clearance is received. This level exploits programming accomplished preflight. Where the longer-range strategic plan is changed (i.e., initial approach and runway assignment, direct clearances, etc.), Flight Management inputs remain appropriate. However, when significant modifications to route are issued by ATC, the pilot should revert, at least temporarily, to lower levels of automation.

3. Confirming inputs to autoflight systems

    Pilots must confirm the results of autoflight selections to prevent mode or course surprises and confusion. A selection on the Mode Control or Flight Guidance panel must be checked against its result on the Flight Mode

(Continued)

(Continued)

Annunciator. An input into the FMS/GFMS-CDU must be checked against its resulting course displayed on the Nav Display, and *the pilot making the input must confirm the resulting course with the other pilot prior to executing the change when feasible.* And in all cases, both pilots must continue their scan to ensure the autopilot performs as directed and anticipated.

4. Cross-checking FMS data against charted procedures

For a variety of reasons, displayed FMS legs making up a departure, arrival, or approach procedure may not correspond with charted fix names, bearings, or radials even though the database is designed to follow the same ground track. However, from time to time, pilots have encountered situations where the FMS did not fly a procedure as defined by radio navigation or in compliance with ATC expectations. Therefore, pilots must brief and cross-check charted procedures against FMS data to ensure they have selected the correct procedure and will comply with their clearance.

Before departure, thoroughly review your assigned departure and cross-check the waypoints obtained with your desired course. If you select or build a transition, verify between pilots that it matches your clearance and produces the desired track. Ask ATC for clarification if any conflict exists.

Before arriving in the terminal area, thoroughly brief the arrival and approach you expect to fly and cross-check fixes presented by the FMS against fixes depicted on the approach chart. Should the runway or approach change and you wish to use the FMS for the new approach, that same level of cross-check is essential. If time constraints or circumstances prevent your cross-check, decline the clearance or tune and identify radio aids to navigation and fly the approach in a lower level of automation.

5. Raw data monitoring and cross-check requirements

Except for those aircraft designed to meet Required Navigation Performance (RNP) for the Approach Phase (B-737 or B-777 with Advanced FMS, for example), Flight Management Systems are certified for en route and terminal navigation, but not for approaches. Except where prohibited by bulletin or company-specific pages in the Airway Manual, pilots may accomplish a SID and its transitions, navigate en route, and accomplish a STAR and its transitions to the initial approach fix solely by FMS navigation, *but not approaches.*

Except for published FMS, GPS, and RNAV instrument approach procedures, approaches are flown relative to ground-based NAVAIDs. For all other approaches, prior to the initial approach fix, one pilot must tune, identify, and monitor (on a CDI display, where available) the NAVAIDs that define the approach. These actions are necessary to ensure the path flown by the aircraft complies with the ground track required by the approach procedure. The function of the FMS and Nav display during an approach is to assist your situation awareness—not to fly the approach. Any discrepancy between the Nav Display or Flight Director based on FMS/GFMS guidance and raw data from NAVAIDs defining the approach must be challenged and resolved immediately. Should the ground-based signal be lost, the crew must abandon

(Continued)

(Continued)

that approach if in instrument conditions. On all instrument approaches inside the final approach fix in IMC weather conditions, a go-around is required whenever unreliability or full-scale deflection of the ground-based approach NAVAIDs is encountered. *[Note: this paragraph describes what is necessary for the pilot to comply with FMS certification.]*

Specific autoflight and display modes required for precision and nonprecision approaches are specified in each aircraft flight manual. Requirements to accomplish published FMS, GPS, and RNAV instrument approaches are published in the operating manual of fleets so equipped. In addition, ground-based NAVAIDs defining a course must be tuned, identified, and monitored where specified by bulletin or company-specific pages in the Airway Manual, and when operating in Latin America below FL250. *[Note: this paragraph describes additional, company-specific requirements.]*

6. Dealing with ATC clearance changes

Proper use of automation will reduce your workload, freeing you to complete other tasks. Improper use will do just the opposite. Whenever possible, avoid FMS/GFMS programming during critical phases of flight. Complete as much programming as possible during low workload phases. ATC clearance changes in the terminal area directly challenge this requirement.

A departure change during taxi for takeoff requires review of the assigned departure. If the FMS is to be used for navigation during the departure, pilots must cross-check the waypoints obtained with the desired course. However, pilots may choose to navigate the departure by ground-based NAVAIDs if update and cross-check of FMS moving map displays would distract from primary ground and flight duties.

While pilots must tune, identify, and monitor all applicable approach NAVAIDs for every approach and landing, it is not necessary to update FMS moving map displays close-in to the landing airport where "heads down" data entry would distract from primary flight duties.

Member airlines customized and implemented most of the ATA recommendations over the next few years. CRM courses were often the forum for introducing or reviewing changes documented in Aircraft Operating Manuals and made use of events tied to each issue reported or observed through Safety Assessment processes. Member airlines also challenged pilots to use these new policies or skills in Line Oriented Simulation events.

How successful was this approach? FAA (2013) reported the results of a working group study of worldwide incidents and manufacturer and operator structured interviews. Its findings suggest the threat has evolved, requiring further intervention. Evolution involved "increased aircraft onboard capabilities for flight path management, increased use of FMS functions, transition away from conventional procedures constructed upon ground-based navigation aids to increased use of RNAV-based navigation (RNAV and RNP), reliance on the quality and availability of digital data, increased focus on managing costs, and changes in new hire pilot demographics" (p. 2). They reported new vulnerabilities in knowledge and skill for manual flight operations, including prevention, recognition, and recovery from unusual attitudes, transition from automated control, and energy state management. They were concerned about crew coordination relating to aircraft control and the retention of manual flying skills. And they emphasized:

- Pilots sometimes rely too much on automated systems and may be reluctant to intervene;
- Autoflight mode confusion errors continue to occur;
- The use of information automation is increasing, including implementations that may result in errors and confusion; and
- FMS programming and usage errors continue to occur (p. 3).

These findings indicate that some of the original concerns continue to be present, and that other vulnerabilities have accompanied increasing aircraft capabilities. From an SMS perspective, airlines should treat this report as new feedback from a more global safety assurance process. They should engage in another round of Safety Risk Management, allocating mitigations to various policy, procedure, and training functions, followed by ensuring safety assurance processes can assess effectiveness of their interventions. Expect CRM classroom and Line Oriented Simulation to be called upon again to communicate risk and mitigation strategy, and to practice and receive feedback on the associated skills.

8.4 EXPECTATIONS ABOUT SMS AND CRM IN THE FUTURE

Both SMS and CRM are still evolving (Velasquez & Bier, 2015) with SMS at a faster rate than CRM, largely because of its acceptance by company governance. While SMS progresses through a system safety approach, CRM has had its own evolution from localization in the cockpit; through to "corporate resource management"; and contemporarily, threat and error management. Kern (2001) for instance argues that the next "generation" of CRM will establish its clear operational interfaces with human factors issues such as fatigue, complacency, and automation.

On the other hand, SMS will evolve as risk management, control, and assurance tools become more mature to the extent that such tools are easier to implement. However, some of the inarguable intersections of both SMS and CRM which attract continuous improvement and promise are:

- SMS and CRM are the logical platform for safety culture to be examined and developed;
- As more safety data is collected by an organization, there is greater demand to blend such data (i.e., ASAP, FOQA, CRM training feedback,

LOSA, etc.) in order to gain a better and meaningful understanding of an organization's safety health;

- Like CRM, SMS will have to be endorsed by top management in order to be successfully implemented (Broyhill & Freiwald, 2012); and
- SMS and CRM are in the best position to inform organizations about improving the level of predictive value of the confluence of human and system risk data.

8.5 CONCLUSION

SMS require a disciplined approach to identifying and mitigating hazards and risk within an airline's operations and assessing the adequacy of mitigation. These are enabled by an organization's safety culture and implement processes of safety risk management, safety promotion, and safety assurance. CRM interfaces with these systems in several ways. As a skillset, CRM may both serve safety promotion functions and provide more specific mitigations to some issues. SMS and CRM are complementary in that SMS targets the improvement of the safety system while CRM is intended primarily for the user (Velasquez & Bier, 2015). When organized as threat and error management, CRM serves as an approach to daily flying that may be construed as a localized implementation of SMS. Given over 30 years of experience, CRM can be viewed as a body of knowledge of applications to flight operations experience, setting the stage for effective responses to issues identified through safety assurance functions. CRM training also benefits directly from what an airline learns through its safety monitoring and assurance processes. SMS becomes the intel for the substance of CRM. CRM becomes one vehicle for fortifying the workforce against the identified risks.

REFERENCES

Air Transport Association. (1997). *Towards a model training program for FMS-generation aircraft*. Subcommittee on Automation Human Factors.

Air Transport Association. (1998). *Potential knowledge or policy gaps regarding operation of FMS-generation aircraft*. Subcommittee on Automation Human Factors.

Air Transport Association. (1999). *Performance of standard navigation tasks by FMS-generation aircraft*. Subcommittee on Automation Human Factors.

Air Transport Association. (2000). *Human performance considerations when introducing alerted-RNP aircraft*. Subcommittee on Automation Human Factors.

American Airlines. (1996). *Advanced qualification program supporting analysis*. Dallas, TX: DFW Airport.

Antonsen, S. (2009). *Safety culture: Theory, measurement, and improvement*. Burlington, VT: Ashgate.

Barshi, I., Mauro, R., Degani, A., & Loukopoulous, L. (2016). Designing flightdeck procedures. *(NASA Technical Memorandum 2016-219421)*. Moffett Field, CA: NASA Ames Research Center.

Broyhill, C. & Freiwald, D. (2012). CRM & SMS: Directing the evolution of organizational culture. In *Paper presented at the CASS: 57th Annual Corporate Aviation Safety Seminar,* San Antonio, TX.

Degani, A. S., & Wiener, E. L. (1990). Human factors of flight−deck checklists: The normal checklist. *(NASA Contractor Report 177549).* Moffett Field, CA: NASA Ames Research Center.

Dismukes, R. K., & Berman, B. (2010). Checklists and monitoring in the cockpit: Why crucial defenses sometimes fail. *(NASA Technical Memorandum 2010-216396).* Moffett Field, CA: NASA Ames Research Center.

Farrow, D. R. (2010). A regulatory perspective II. In B. Kanki, R. Helmreich, & J. Anca (Eds.), *Crew resource management* (2nd ed.). San Diego, CA: Academic Press.

Federal Aviation Administration. (1996). *The interface between flightscrews and modern flight deck systems.* Washington, DC. Retrieved from https://www.google.com/url?sa = t&rct = j&q = &esrc = s&source = web&cd = &cad = rja&uact = 8&ved = 0ahUKEwjxrfqXld7RA-hWH2yYKHX-8AYwQFggdMAA&url = http%3A%2F%2Fwww.tc.faa.gov%2Fits%2Fworld pac%2Ftechrpt%2Fhffaces.pdf&usg = AFQjCNExSK6xi0bmAz0AOLIS07-jPaOX6g&bvm = bv.145063293,d.eWE.

Federal Aviation Administration. (2002). *Aviation safety action program (ASAP).* Advisory circular 120-66B. Washington, DC. Retrieved from https://www.faa.gov/regulations_policies/advisory_circulars/index.cfm/go/document.information/documentID/23207.

Federal Aviation Administration. (2004a). *Flight operational quality assurance (FOQA).* Advisory circular 120-82. Washington, DC. Retrieved from https://www.faa.gov/regulations_policies/advisory_circulars/index.cfm/go/document.information/documentID/23227.

Federal Aviation Administration. (2004b). *Crew resource management training.* Advisory circular 120-51e. Washington, DC. Retrieved from http://www.faa.gov/documentLibrary/media/Advisory_Circular/AC120-51e.pdf.

Federal Aviation Administration. (2006a). *Line operations safety audits.* AC-120-90. Washington, DC. Retrieved from http://rgl.faa.gov/Regulatory_and_Guidance_Library/rgAdvisoryCircular.nsf/list/AC%20120-90/$FILE/AC%20120-90.pdf.

Federal Aviation Administration. (2006b). *Advanced qualification program.* AC-120-54A. Washington, DC. Retrieved from https://www.faa.gov/regulations_policies/advisory_circulars/index.cfm/go/document.information/documentID/23190.

Federal Aviation Administration. (2013). *Operational use of flight path management systems: Final Report of the performance-based operations Aviation Rulemaking Committee/Commercial Aviation Safety Team flight deck automation working group.* Washington, DC. Retrieved from https://www.faa.gov/about/office_org/headquarters_offices/avs/offices/afs/afs400/parc/parc_reco/media/2013/130908_parc_fltdawg_final_report_recommendations.pdf.

Federal Aviation Administration. (2015). *Safety management systems for aviation service providers.* Advisory circular 120-92B. Washington, DC. Retrieved from https://www.faa.gov/regulations_policies/advisory_circulars/index.cfm/go/document.information/documentID/1026670.

Federal Aviation Administration. (2017). *Standard operating procedures and pilot monitoring duties for flight deck crewmembers.* Advisory circular 120-71B. Washington, DC. Retrieved from http://www.faa.gov/documentLibrary/media/Advisory_Circular/AC_120-71B.pdf.

Flight Safety Foundation. (2000). Approach and landing accident reduction tool kit. *Flight Safety Digest, 19,* 1−196.

Flight Safety Foundation. (2014). *A practical guide for improving flight path monitoring: Final report of the active pilot monitoring working group.* Washington, DC. Retrieved from https://www.google.com/url?

sa = t&rct = j&q = &esrc = s&source = web&cd = &cad = rja&uact = 8&ved = 0ahUKEwi-ps4zsgd7RAhXD2yYKHUcpBc8QFggaMAA&url = https%3A%2F%2Fwww.flightsafety.org%2Ffiles%2Fflightpath%2FEPMG.pdf&usg = AFQjCNFsJ56a9CvarVu4xAW0MUsZXzF nxw&bvm = bv.145063293,d.eWE.

Helmreich, R. L., & Foushee, H. C. (1993). Why crew resource management? Empirical and theoretical bases of human factors training in aviation. In E. Wiener, B. Kanki, & R. Helmreich (Eds.), *Cockpit resource management*. San Diego, CA: Academic Press.

Helmreich, R. L., Klinect, J. R., & Wilhelm, J. A. (1999). *Models of threat, error, and CRM in flight operations. Proceedings of the 10th international symposium on aviation psychology.* Columbus, OH: The Ohio State University.

Hollinger, K. (2013). *Safety management systems for aviation practitioners: Real world lessons.* Reston, VA: American Institute of Aeronautics & Astronautics.

Huerta, M. (2014). InfoShare works. In *Presentation to 2014 InfoShare meeting*, Baltimore, MD. Retrieved from https://www.faa.gov/news/speeches/news_story.cfm?newsId = 17154&omni Rss = speechesAoc&cid = 104_Speeches.

International Civil Aviation Organization. (2013). *Safety management manual.* Document 9859, AN/474. Montreal, Canada. Retrieved from http://www.icao.int/safety/SafetyManagement/Documents/Doc.9859.3rd%20Edition.alltext.en.pdf.

Kern, T. (2001). *Culture, environment and crew resource management.* Columbus, OH: McGraw-Hill Professional.

Loukopoulos, L. D., Dismukes, R. K., & Barshi, I. B. (2003). *Concurrent task demands in the cockpit: Challenges and vulnerabilities in routine flight operations.* Proceedings of the 12th international symposium on aviation psychology. Dayton, OH: Wright State University.

National Transportation Safety Board. (2013). *Operatons 2 exibit 2-V − attachment 21 − BHM chart information. UPS flight 1354 public docket.* Washington, DC. Retrieved from https://dms.ntsb.gov/pubdms/search/document.cfm?
docID = 409716&docketID = 55307&mkey = 87780.

National Transportation Safety Board. (2014). *Crash during a nighttime nonprecision instrument approach to landing: UPS flight 1354.* Accident report AAR-14/02; PB2014-107898. Washington, DC. Retrieved from https://www.ntsb.gov/investigations/AccidentReports/Reports/AAR1402.pdf.

Reason, J. (1997). *Managing the risks of organizational accidents.* Aldershot, UK: Ashgate.

Sarter, N., & Woods, D. (2005). Pilot interaction with cockpit automation *(Cognitive Systems Engineering Laboratory Report CSEL 91-017).* Columbus: The Ohio State University.

Sumwalt, R. (1999). Enhancing flight-crew monitoring skills can increase flight safety. *Flight Safety Digest, 18*, 1−9.

Velasquez, J., & Bier, N. (2015). SMS and CRM: Parallels and opposites in their evolution. *Journal of Aviation/Aerospace Education & Research, 24*(2), 55−78.

Wiener, E. L., Chidester, T. R., Kanki, B. G., Palmer, E. A., Curry, R. E., & Gregorich, S. E. (1991). The impact of cockpit automation on crew coordination and communication: I. Overview, LOFT evaluations, error severity, and questionnaire data. *(NASA Contractor Report 177587).* Moffett Field, CA: NASA-Ames Research Center.

Wiener, E. L. (1993). Crew coordination and training in the advanced-technology cockpit. In E. B. Wiener, & R. Helmreich (Eds.), *Cockpit resource management*. San Diego, CA: Academic Press.

Part II

CRM Training Applications

Chapter 9

The Design, Delivery, and Evaluation of Crew Resource Management Training

Pamela Farago[1], Marissa L. Shuffler[1] and Eduardo Salas[2]
[1]Psychology Department, College of Behavioral, Social, & Health Sciences, Clemson University, Clemson, SC, United States, [2]Department of Psychological Sciences, Rice University, Houston, TX, United States

INTRODUCTION

Airline pilots, doctors, oil drillers, and railroad operators may not initially seem to have much in common. However, each of these occupations is part of a high reliability organization, where teamwork enables complex work to be completed on an exceptionally consistent basis. In these environments, even the smallest error can cause great harm and far-reaching consequences. In fact, one of the most common human factors contributing to accidents in the airline industry can be attributed to failures in teamwork (Munene, 2016) and communication (Bienefeld & Grote, 2012; Ford, O'Hare, & Henderson, 2013). Therefore, training these workers to perform together consistently is of utmost importance in such industries. Equally important is the evaluation of such trainings, allowing organizations to be sure that what they want to train is actually being trained. What training is available for these high reliability organizations, and how can industries ensure that it actually leads to performance improvement?

One answer to this question is crew resource management (CRM; Gregorich, Helmreich, & Wilhelm, 1990). The need for CRM stemmed from a series of unfortunate events in aviation, whereby subsequent analyses demonstrated that the causes of accidents were unrelated to technical or engineering issues. This research showed that a substantial majority of accidents were related to poor decision-making, loss of situation awareness, and lack of leadership (Jimenez, Kasper, Rivera, Talone, & Jentsch, 2015). Thus, the need for teamwork, communication, and leadership training in this industry was born.

Crew Resource Management. DOI: https://doi.org/10.1016/B978-0-12-812995-1.00009-9

An explosion of CRM training within the aviation industry ensued, and its success led other industries to adopt similar training principles. For example, TeamSTEPPS is a CRM-inspired program that has been implemented in healthcare (Alonso et al., 2006). Bridge resource management (BRM) and maritime resource management (MRM) are two programs employed in the maritime industry, with roots in CRM (Jimenez et al., 2015). Furthermore, the perception of CRM as an effective tool has led to its incorporation into still other industries, including oil, railroad, and general transportation (Salas, Wilson, Burke, Wightman, & Howse, 2006b). Building on the aviation industry's extensive use of CRM, it is clear that other industries are interested in and further implementing team-based training (Buljac-Samardzic, Dekker-van Doorn, van Wijngaarden, & van Wijk, 2010).

However, unanswered questions still surround CRM, even decades after its inception. Is this training program achieving its stated objectives? Do the perceptions of the effectiveness of CRM training match reality? There has been a lack of a systematic approach for assessing CRM training programs, creating confusion over and casting doubt on the effectiveness of such trainings. With that being said, there are several evaluation issues that have specifically plagued CRM. The first is that current CRM training evaluations vary widely in terms of *what* is assessed. The second is that these evaluations vary in terms of *how* competencies are assessed. The third is that there is not a systematic method for using the collected information to improve the delivery of training. Lastly, the sheer complexity of a comprehensive CRM training evaluation can be daunting to many organizations.

Therefore, the purpose of this chapter is to build upon Shuffler, Salas, and Xavier's (2010) earlier review to provide an updated picture of the current state of CRM training evaluation. This will be accomplished through the presentation of a framework of evaluation and discussion of practical guidelines that practitioners can use across diverse organizational industries and contexts. To assist in providing this clarity, the purpose of training evaluation as it applies to CRM will be outlined first. Following this background, current practices in CRM training evaluation will be reviewed. The purpose of this is to highlight the challenges and limitations in current evaluation techniques. Next, the work of Salas et al. (2006b) will be used to inform a discussion of future directions needed to improve CRM evaluation, built around their framework for CRM training design, delivery, and evaluation. This discussion will elucidate a set of practical guidelines that are necessary for an effective CRM training evaluation. Therefore, the goals of this chapter are twofold. The first goal is to advance the science of training design, delivery, and evaluation for CRM. The second goal is to provide a foundation for practitioners to develop cutting-edge assessment strategies that are scientifically sound, functional, and flexible for use in a variety of organizational contexts.

9.1 WHAT IS TRAINING EVALUATION?

The purpose of a training evaluation is to provide a clear picture as to whether or not a training program is, in fact, achieving its goals successfully. Furthermore, since CRM training has been and continues to be an evolving process, evaluation accounts for these changes and determines if such changes are effective. With that being said, assessing training is not a simple process. There are many components to consider in an effective evaluation, including the evaluation of training at individual, team, and organizational levels, and the evaluation of both the outcomes and the program elements themselves (Gregorich & Wilhelm, 1993). These latter two components are perhaps the most critical, as it is important that an evaluation focuses not only on whether learning outcomes were achieved, but also on the elements that make a program more or less successful.

In the training literature, these two facets are separated into training evaluation and training effectiveness. Although training evaluation and effectiveness are often considered to be one and the same, they are in fact two different concepts. According to Alvarez, Salas, and Garofano (2004), training effectiveness is the theoretical approach utilized to understand the success or failure of achieving learning outcomes, whereas training evaluation is focused upon the methodologies designed to measure such outcomes. The following discussion provides a more in-depth explanation of these components and why both are equally valuable in assessing CRM training.

9.1.1 Training Evaluation

Training evaluation can be viewed as serving three purposes: decision-making, feedback, and marketing (Kraiger, 2002). Evaluations provide information regarding the usefulness and appropriateness of a program, as well as identifying the strengths and weaknesses of the program so that improvements can be made (Noe, 2002). Furthermore, evaluation results can be utilized in order to sell the program to potential trainees or other organizations (Kraiger, 2002). As such, training evaluation can be seen as primarily focused upon the learning outcomes and how their measurement can be used to benefit the organization, providing more of a microview for the results of training (Alvarez et al., 2004).

Training evaluation is primarily conducted through the measurement of specific, tangible outcomes that are the desired outputs. Multiple models exist to define the best approach to training evaluation, including the traditional model presented by Kirkpatrick (1976). This model is perhaps the most simplistic, as it highlights four levels of evaluation that should be considered by organizations conducting training evaluations. These levels involve reaction, learning, behavior, and results outcomes, and will be discussed in greater detail later.

While Kirkpatrick's approach is the one most commonly used in CRM evaluations, more recent approaches have attempted to expand beyond Kirkpatrick's original model to further improve training evaluation methods. Kraiger, Ford, and Salas (1993) take Kirkpatrick's model a step further by detailing the outcomes (skill-based, cognitive, affective) that must be evaluated after training. This model takes a multidimensional approach that is designed to provide a more comprehensive view of outcomes in order to best match those outcomes to what is being learned. Ford, Kraiger, and Merritt (2009) provide an additional update to this approach through their review of studies utilizing the Kraiger et al. (1993) model of evaluation. Ford and colleagues highlight the need to include four additional evaluation methodologies that have emerged following the publication of the original model: mental models, metacognition, goal orientation, and attitude strength. Such multidimensional approaches have a distinct advantage over other approaches to training evaluation, as they provide a more in-depth understanding as to the specific effects of training on outcomes.

9.1.2 Training Effectiveness

More formally, training effectiveness can be defined as "the study of the individual, training, and organizational characteristics that influence the training process before, during, and after training" (Alvarez et al., 2004). To determine whether training is or is not effective, training effectiveness takes a much broader view of assessing training and focuses not only on identifying whether training results in learning, but also focuses on identifying whether skills learned in training are used and transferred to the job. Transfer of training is a key component of training effectiveness and consists of determining whether skills learned in training are used on the job and maintained over time (Baldwin & Ford, 1988).

Training effectiveness is assessed not just through learning outcomes, but through an overall review of the training design, development, and delivery process (Buljac-Samardzic et al., 2010; Salas & Cannon-Bowers, 2001). Effective training begins with a needs analysis, conducted to study the individual differences of trainees, the organizational climate, and the characteristics of tasks to be trained (Alvarez et al., 2004). Training will not be effective if it does not account for this spectrum of needs at the individual, organizational, and task levels. In addition to needs, these levels all have unique characteristics that must also be accounted for when assessing training effectiveness. At the individual level, these characteristics involve anything a trainee brings to the training, including his or her personality, motivation, attitude, experience, and expectations. Organizational characteristics involve those characteristics that account for the context of the training, including learning climate, policies, trainee selection, and trainee notification. Finally, task or training characteristics involve the aspects of the training program, such as the instructional style, practice, or feedback (Salas & Cannon-Bowers, 2001).

Much of the training effectiveness literature focuses on how these factors can be assessed before, during, and after training, as well as strategies to remedy factors that may be damaging training effectiveness, such as a lack of organizational support for training (Broad & Newstrom, 1992). Additionally, models of training effectiveness emphasize the particular characteristics that may impact learning and transfer. For example, Mathieu, Martineau, and Tannenbaum (1993) propose in their model that individual and training characteristics are related to cognitive learning and training performance, whereas organizational characteristics are more strongly predictive of transfer performance. These distinctions aid in understanding more precisely how to revise training based on the factors that impact effectiveness.

9.1.3   Merging Training Evaluation & Training Effectiveness

In summary, a successful training evaluation will involve a close look at both evaluation and effectiveness. While these two literatures have often been treated as separate entities, there has been an emerging drive to develop a comprehensive perspective that incorporates both areas. Alvarez et al. (2004) present such an integrated model, as can be seen in Fig. 9.1.

This model depicts both the individual, training, and organizational characteristics necessary for consideration in training effectiveness, as well as the multidimensional aspects of training evaluation that are most common across the varying models of evaluation, and those most consistently linked to influencing training outcomes. While this model may not capture every nuance of the training process, it serves as a representation for how effectiveness and

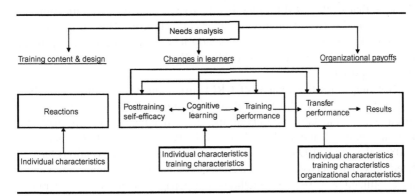

FIGURE 9.1   An integrated model of training effectiveness and evaluation. *Adapted from Alonso, A., Baker, D.P., Holtzman, A., Day, R., King, H., Toomey, L., & Salas, E. (2006). Reducing medical error in the Military Health System: How can team training help? Human Resource Management Review, 16, 396–415.*

evaluation can be integrated to successfully get at the issues critical to proper training evaluation. For simplicity, throughout the remainder of the chapter we will use the term evaluation to refer to both training effectiveness and evaluation.

9.2 WHY IS EVALUATION OF CRM TRAINING NECESSARY?

There are several reasons that evaluation is valuable to CRM training (Goldstein, 1993; Salas & Cannon-Bowers, 2001). First, evaluating CRM training can aid in indicating if the goals of the CRM program are appropriate for achieving the desired outcome. This is especially important for CRM, as CRM has been used as an umbrella term for several training interventions. For example, early CRM training focused on changing attitudes, neglecting the training of behavioral skills (Helmreich, Merritt, & Wilhelm, 1999; Salas, Fowlkes, Stout, Milanovich, & Prince, 1999a). Because of this lack of attention to behavioral skills, these early CRM interventions were not as effective as originally hoped.

More recent CRM training has focused on improving trainees' behaviors and teamwork skills (Helmreich et al., 1999; Salas et al., 1999b). However, even CRM training evaluations that have focused on improving behavioral competencies have been inconsistent. For example, CRM has been used to improve such diverse competencies as communication, situation awareness, decision-making, leadership, preflight briefing, stress awareness, assertiveness, conflict management, and mission analysis, among others (see Table 9.1 for more detail; Salas et al., 2006b).

Second, an evaluation of CRM training can indicate if the content and methods used in the training result in the achievement of the overall program goals. Given the multitude of competencies addressed by CRM, it may be the case that while CRM training is effective at improving certain competencies, it is ineffective at improving other competencies. Thus, it is crucial for training effectiveness endeavors to clearly identify the specific competencies that are trained to determine what skills CRM training is effective or ineffective at improving.

Not only does the content of CRM differ, but the training methods are highly variable as well. Different training programs have utilized lectures, discussions, videotapes, observations, game-playing, classroom role play, mishap analysis, and high and low fidelity simulators (O'Connor et al., 2008; Salas et al., 1999b). Furthermore, some training interventions have utilized only one method, such as lectures, whereas other training interventions have utilized a variety of methods (Littlepage, Hein, Moffett, Craig, & Georgiou, 2016; Salas et al., 1999b; Ritzmann, Kluge, Hagemann, & Tanner, 2011). Thus, an important question that needs to be answered is how much of the CRM training effectiveness is attributable to the training method and how much is attributable to the training content.

TABLE 9.1 Potential CRM Skills to be Trained

CRM Skill	Definition	Alternative Names	References
Communication	Ability of two or more team members to clearly and accurately send and receive information or commands and to provide useful feedback.	*Closed-loop communication*	Cannon-Bowers, Tannenbaum, Salas, and Volpe (1995)
Briefing	Ability of team members to develop plans of action by organizing team resources, activities, and responses to ensure tasks are completed in an integrated and synchronized manner.	*Mission analysis, Planning*	Salas and Cannon-Bowers (2001)
Backup behavior	Ability of team members to anticipate the needs of others through accurate knowledge about each other's responsibilities, including the ability to shift workload between members to create balance during periods of high workload or pressure.	*Advocacy*	Mcintyre and Salas (1995), Porter, Hollenbeck, Ilgen, Ellis, West, and Moon (2003)
Mutual performance monitoring	Ability of team members to accurately monitor other team members' performance, including giving, seeking, and receiving task-clarifying feedback.	*Workload management*	Mcintyre and Salas (1995), Salas and Cannon-Bowers (2001)

(Continued)

TABLE 9.1 (Continued)

CRM Skill	Definition	Alternative Names	References
Team leadership	Ability of a team leader to direct and coordinate the activities of team members, encourage team members to work together; assess performance; assign tasks; develop team knowledge, skills, and abilities; motivate; plan and organize; and establish a positive team atmosphere.	*Management*	Salas and Cannon-Bowers (2001)
Decision-making	Ability of team members to gather and integrate information, make logical and sound judgments, identify alternatives, consider the consequences of each alternative, and select the best one.	*Judgment, problem solving*	Salas and Cannon-Bowers (2001)
Task-related assertiveness	Willingness/readiness of team members to communicate their ideas, opinions, and observations in a way that is persuasive to other team members and to maintain a position until convinced by the facts that other options are better.	*Confidence Aggressiveness Authoritarian*	Salas and Cannon-Bowers (2001)
Team adaptability	Ability of team members to alter a course of action or adjust strategies when new information becomes available.	*Flexibility*	Cannon-Bowers, Salas, Tannenbaum, and Mathieu (1995), Klein and Pierce (2001)

(Continued)

TABLE 9.1 (Continued)

CRM Skill	Definition	Alternative Names	References
Shared situation awareness	Ability of team members to gather and use information to develop a common understanding of the task and team environment.	*Shared mental models, situation assessment*	Salas and Cannon-Bowers (2001)

Source: Adapted from Salas, E., Wilson, K.A., Burke, C.S., & Wightman, D.C. (2006a). Does CRM training work? An update, extension and some critical needs. Human Factors, 48, 392−412.

Finally, evaluation of CRM training programs can aid both in determining how to maximize the transfer of training, and in serving as feedback at the individual and team levels to provide suggested areas of improvement or revision. Clearly, continued evaluation is valuable and necessary for addressing these issues, particularly in terms of determining what aspects of CRM training are successful as-is and which need improvement.

9.3 HOW HAS CRM TRAINING BEEN EVALUATED IN THE PAST?

In order to provide guidelines regarding future training evaluation, it is useful to identify what is already known about CRM evaluation. While most CRM training evaluation studies have been carried out in the aviation community, the popularity and apparent success of CRM has led other industries such as military, offshore oil production, nuclear power, and medical to begin adopting CRM training (Salas, Wilson, Burke, & Wightman, 2006a). Although many organizations believe CRM is effective, a key question remains regarding whether CRM training actually results in learning and transfer of training. In the following section, we will provide a brief review as to what is known regarding CRM training evaluation, primarily through the examination of the components of evaluation and effectiveness. In this discussion, we will highlight both the strengths of prior evaluation research, as well as some of the challenges faced.

9.3.1 CRM Training Evaluation

Several reviews have sought to answer the question of whether CRM is effective in achieving learning objectives (Crichton, 2017; O'Connor et al., 2008; O'Connor, Flin, & Fletcher, 2002; Salas et al., 2006a; Salas, Burke,

Bowers, & Wilson, 2001). As previously discussed, most of the CRM evaluation studies cited in the reviews addressed some aspect of Kirkpatrick's (1976, 1987) training evaluation framework, which identified four levels of training evaluation. The first level, *reactions*, measures trainees' emotional/affective responses and is mainly concerned with whether trainees liked training and/or found it useful. Because of the ease of collection from paper and pencil surveys, reaction data is perhaps the most common form of training evaluation.

The second level, *learning*, is concerned with whether trainees learned/absorbed the content, principles, and facts. The third level, *behaviors*, is concerned with whether trainees can apply/use the skills taught in training on the job. Studies often conceptualize behaviors and transfer of training as the same thing. The last level, *results*, addresses whether training achieves organizationally-relevant goals and objectives, such as increased profit and reduced turnover. In the case of CRM, the desired training result is increased safety and reduced accidents. Research at each of Kirkpatrick's four levels will be reviewed in the following discussion.

9.3.2 Reactions

Reaction data can be thought of as the equivalent of customer satisfaction, with its emphasis on whether trainees liked the training (O'Connor et al., 2008). The rationale behind collecting reaction data is the common assumption that trainees who disliked training are less likely to attend to training and apply trained competencies to their jobs. While those who dislike training are unlikely to apply trained skills, it should be noted that favorable reactions to training do not guarantee learning or positive transfer.

In terms of what is known regarding the effects of CRM on trainee reactions, O'Connor et al. (2002) found reaction data to be the most common measure of CRM training effectiveness, with 69% of studies in their review reporting reaction data. Salas et al. (2001, 2006a) also found several studies reporting reaction data. In a review of the CRM literature between 1983 and 1999, Salas et al. (2001) located 58 studies evaluating the effectiveness of CRM training. Of the 58 studies, 27 collected reaction data. In a follow-up to their 2001 review, Salas et al. (2006b) located 28 studies that examined the effectiveness of CRM training between 2000 and 2006. Of the 28 studies, 13 collected reaction data. Practically all studies measuring trainees' reactions reported positive results (O'Connor et al., 2002, 2008; Salas et al., 2001, 2006a). In terms of measurement approach, almost all studies that assessed participants' reactions collected reaction data via paper and pencil surveys (O'Connor et al., 2002). More recent studies not included in the meta-analyses still place heavy emphasis on reaction measure collection (Buljac-Samardzic et al., 2010; Ford, Henderson, & O'Hare, 2014; Littlepage et al., 2016; Ritzmann et al., 2011; Rottger, Vetter, & Kowalski, 2013).

9.3.3 Learning

While learning as conceptualized by Kirkpatrick focused primarily on the acquisition of factual information (i.e., cognitive learning outcomes), other researchers have proposed learning to be a multidimensional construct that consists of cognitive, skill-based, and affective learning outcomes (Gagne, 1984; Kraiger et al., 1993). Cognitive learning outcomes are most closely aligned with Kirkpatrick's conceptualization of learning outcomes and primarily address whether trainees acquired factual knowledge, as well as cognitive strategies (Kraiger et al., 1993). Skill-based learning outcomes are focused on whether trainees acquired necessary technical or motor skills (Kraiger et al., 1993). Affective learning outcomes are focused on the extent to which trainees develop the attitudes, motivation, and goals targeted by training.

In terms of CRM training, the research literature seems to indicate that CRM may be effective at achieving positive learning outcomes (O'Connor et al., 2008; Salas et al., 2001, 2006a). Studies that have evaluated the effectiveness of CRM training at improving cognitive learning outcomes have typically used paper and pencil measures of declarative knowledge. So far, findings have been mixed. Some studies found that CRM training resulted in improved cognitive learning (Littlepage et al., 2016; Salas et al., 1999b; Stout, Salas, & Fowlkes, 1997), while other studies showed no effects on cognitive learning (Brun et al., 2000). Furthermore, other studies obtained mixed findings, where CRM training resulted in cognitive learning for some people and not others (Howard, Gaba, Fish, Yang, & Samquist, 1992). Recent work has looked to expand the principles that can contribute to positive cognitive competencies and outcomes in a variety of industry settings (Crichton, 2017).

Compared to cognitive and skill-based learning outcomes, affective learning outcomes are perhaps the most common CRM learning outcome assessed. The majority of studies examining attitude change find that CRM training results in positive attitude change (Alkov & Gaynor, 1991; Fonne & Fredriksen, 1995; Gregorich et al., 1990; Gregorich, 1993; Grubb, Morey, & Simon, 1999; Irwin, 1991; Morey, Grubb & Simon, 1997; Morey et al., 2002; Marquardt, Robelski, & Hoeger, 2010; O'Connor et al., 2008). Most studies use the cockpit management attitudes questionnaire (CMAQ; Gregorich et al., 1990; Helmreich, 1984) to measure this attitude change. More specifically, the CMAQ measures people's attitudes toward communication and coordination, command responsibility, and stressor effects (Gregorich et al., 1990). This self-report measure (or a modified version) has often been used to illustrate that trainees like the training they received, and that they found it useful in their jobs. However, there are inconsistencies in terms of the linking of these self-reports to actual learning of trained competencies, as illustrated through the evaluation of behaviors (Salas et al., 2006b).

9.3.4 Behaviors

Behavioral data is another common method of evaluating CRM training. For CRM, this type of data can be collected through the use of the Targeted Acceptable Responses to Generated Events or Tasks (TARGETs) or Line/LOS checklists. TARGETs require trainees to respond to multiple, scripted, simulated events while observers indicate whether trainees did or did not demonstrate targeted behaviors on a behavioral checklist. Studies by Salas and colleagues (Salas et al., 1999a; Stout et al., 1997) have utilized TARGETs to evaluate CRM training outcomes and found that individuals receiving CRM training demonstrated more CRM-related behaviors than individuals placed in a control condition.

The assessment of behavioral outcomes has been mixed. Several studies have reported positive results (Clothier, 1991; Connolly & Blackwell, 1987; Fung et al., 2015; Goeters, 2002; Grubb & Morey, 2003; Grubb, Crossland, & Katz, 2002; Katz, 2003; Morey et al., 2002; Spiker, Wilson, & Deen, 2003). Other studies reported both positive and negative results (Buljac-Samardzic et al., 2010; Gaba et al., 1998; Gaba, Howard, Fish, Smith, & Sowb, 2001; Jacobsen et al., 2001; Marquardt, Robelski, & Jenkins, 2011; Robertson & Taylor, 1995; Taylor & Thomas, 2003; Taylor, Robertson, Peck, & Stelly, 1993). Additionally, a handful of studies reported negative results (Ellis & Hughes, 1999; Howard et al., 1992; O'Connor, 2010).

A limitation of studies gathering behavioral data is that a majority of studies collected behavioral data in simulators immediately after training. While this approach is useful to assess whether trainees can immediately apply trained behaviors, it fails to provide data regarding whether trainees actually use training when back on the job. Another limitation is not knowing the broad competencies that should be used to measure behaviors learned through CRM training (Alavosius, Houmanfar, Anbro, Burleigh, & Hebein, 2017). Different approaches to tackle these limitations will be addressed later in the chapter.

9.3.5 Results

The results level of CRM training evaluation has been the least studied of Kirkpatrick's four levels. However, the value of assessing the costs and benefits of training interventions is highly desirable (Cascio & Boudreau, 2008). Both the complexity of obtaining such data as well as the extensive resources required (as compared to other levels of evaluation) are primarily responsible for this lack of more complete evaluations. This low number is reflected in recent meta-analyses conducted on CRM training evaluation, with Salas et al. (2006b) reporting that only five out of 28 studies collected data at the results level of analysis. Similarly, Salas et al. (2001) reported only six out of 58 studies collected data at the results level of analysis.

Based on this limited sample size, it appears that CRM training produces positive organizational results such as reduced accidents and injuries (Diehl, 1991; Grubb & Morey, 2003; Kayten, 1993; Taylor et al., 1993). For example, one recent study has indicated the positive results outcomes of decreased distractions and decreased medication errors in medical staff as a result of CRM trainings (Fore, Sculli, Albee, & Neily, 2013). Other results include financial outcomes and return on investment, studied using subject matter experts and a utility analysis approach (Arthur, Kyte, Villado, Morgan, & Roop, 2011), However, this method warrants more future testing.

While promising, one should be cautious about generalizing these findings because they are based on only a handful of studies. Furthermore, the challenges of evaluating training at this level (e.g., lack of control over extraneous variables, difficulty identifying criterion measures) provide additional hesitation in concluding that CRM training is, in fact, directly linked to such outcomes.

9.3.6 CRM Training Effectiveness

As illustrated through the lack of evidence for the results stage of Kirkpatrick's (1976) training evaluation model, most CRM studies have focused on training evaluation, while neglecting training effectiveness. Training transfer is a key component of training effectiveness. Unfortunately, few studies have examined whether CRM skills are successfully transferred from training onto the job (O'Connor et al., 2008; Salas et al., 2001, 2006a).

As previously discussed, training effectiveness is also dependent on the individual, training, and organizational characteristics that influence learning and training transfer. Individual characteristics that can affect CRM training effectiveness include intelligence, motivation, self-efficacy, and organizational commitment (Gregorich & Wilhelm, 1993. There are additionally some characteristics that may influence team composition and the subsequent effectiveness of CRM, including hierarchical status and competence (Sauer, Darioly, Mast, Schmid, & Bischof, 2010). However, the specifics of how these characteristics impact CRM training effectiveness, including at what point in the training cycle they are most influential, is currently unknown and in need of future research.

Training characteristics include CRM training design elements that can impact training effectiveness, such as information delivery (i.e., lecture, self-paced readings), practice elements (i.e., role plays and simulations), and training materials (i.e., outlines, handouts; Beard, Salas, & Prince, 1995). Another recent advance in training is the use of online, computer-based platforms for CRM (Kearns, 2011). Although there are several federal regulations regarding the requirements of CRM training, none describe the appropriate design elements such as training methods or strategies.

Therefore, a range of these design elements have been incorporated into CRM training, with some being more successful than others. In particular, evaluations show that low fidelity simulations can be used to effectively train CRM-related skills (Baker, Prince, Shrestha, Oser, & Salas, 1993; Bowers, Salas, Prince, & Brannick, 1992; Cook et al., 2011; Jentsch & Bowers, 1998). Additionally, training evaluations have illustrated the importance of scenario design (Prince & Salas, 1999; Prince, Oser, Salas, & Woodruff, 1993) and scenario debrief and feedback (Crichton, 2017; Prince, Brannick, Prince, & Salas, 1997; Salas, Rhodenizer, & Bowers, 2000). Still another training design that has been developed is the line-oriented flight training (LOFT). This uses a situated approach that combines methods and techniques from human factors and ergonomics, and is supported by social construction theories (de Carvalho, Saldanha, Vidal, & Carvalho, 2016). However, while there is evidence suggesting that these myriad training characteristics may impact CRM effectiveness, much is still to be learned, as there are many other training design aspects of CRM that have not been effectively evaluated.

The final aspect of training effectiveness involves organizational characteristics. Organizational characteristics are concerned with system-wide factors that can affect training effectiveness such as supervisor support, rewards for utilizing trained skills, and organizational climate that values using CRM. Unfortunately, much like assessing training transfer, few studies have gathered and/or reported data regarding individual, training, and organizational characteristics that affect training effectiveness.

A primary issue that has been noted, however, is the effect of organizational culture on CRM training. Evaluations of the first several iterations of CRM training found that those designed for specific organizations did not transfer well to other organizations, emphasizing the need to develop CRM that meets organizational needs (Dawson, Cleggett, Thompson, & Thomas, 2017; Helmreich et al., 1999). Future research is needed to further explore additional organizational characteristics such as these, as they may have a significant impact on the effectiveness of CRM training.

9.4 SUMMARY

A summary of this prior research on CRM training evaluation and effectiveness can be found in Table 9.2. After almost three decades of research, much remains unknown regarding the evaluation of CRM training. What is known, however, is that CRM seems to produce positive reactions, learning outcomes (both knowledge and attitude change), and behavior change.

However, it remains unknown if CRM achieves organizational-level results, such as improved safety. Furthermore, less is known regarding the effectiveness of CRM training, as few studies have been conducted to specifically examine the individual, training, and organizational characteristics that impact CRM outcomes. Since the primary goal of CRM is to improve safety

TABLE 9.2 Summary of CRM Training Evaluation

Evaluation Criteria	Key Findings	Example Sources
Reactions	• Reaction data is the most common measure of CRM training evaluation • Majority of studies assess reactions using paper and pencil surveys • Practically all studies measuring trainee reactions to training reported positive results	Brun et al. (2000), Ford et al. (2014), Littlepage et al. (2016), O'Connor et al. (2002), O'Connor et al. (2008), Ritzmann et al. (2011), Rottger et al. (2013), Salas et al. (2001), Salas et al. (2006b), Sauer et al. (2010), Taylor (1998)
Learning	• Cognitive, skill, and affective learning outcomes are all evaluated in CRM training, with affective being the most common • Majority of studies involve assessing learning through declarative knowledge tests for cognitive and skill learning outcomes, CMAQ for affective learning outcomes • Generally, CRM training results in positive attitude change • Findings for cognitive and skill learning are more mixed, as some studies found that CRM training improved cognitive learning, while others found no effects	Alkov and Gaynor (1991), Fonne and Fredriksen (1995), Gregorich et al. (1990), Gregorich (1993), Grubb et al. (1999), Irwin (1991), Morey et al. (1997), Crichton (2017), Fung et al. (2015), Marquardt et al. (2010), Morey et al. (2002), O'Connor et al. (2008)
Behaviors	• Behavioral data is collected through the use of TARGETS or Line/LOS checklists • Behavioral outcomes are mixed, with studies reporting positive results, a mix of negative and positive results, or just negative results • A limitation of behavioral data is that it is often collected in simulators immediately after training, which fails to capture long term impacts on transfer of training	Clothier (1991), Connolly and Blackwell (1987), Goeters (2002), Grubb and Morey (2003), Grubb et al. (2002), Jacobsen et al. (2001), Katz (2003), Morey et al. (2002), Robertson and Taylor (1995), Spiker et al. (2003), Alavosius et al. (2017), Ellis and Hughes (1999), Howard et al. (1992), Littlepage et al. (2016), Marquardt et al. (2011), Taylor and Thomas (2003), Taylor et al. (1993)

(Continued)

TABLE 9.2 (Continued)

Evaluation Criteria	Key Findings	Example Sources
Results	• Results data is the least studied of the four levels of evaluation • CRM training has been shown to reduced accidents and injuries, but the limited sample size provides caution in interpreting these results • Challenges of collecting data at this level include the lack of control over extraneous variables and difficulty identifying criterion measures	Arthur et al. (2011), Diehl (1991), Fore et al. (2013), Grubb and Morey (2003), Kayten (1993), Salas et al. (2006b), Taylor et al. (1993)
Training Transfer	• Few studies have focused on the transfer of CRM training onto the job • Transfer of CRM training has primarily been assessed through simulations and videotaped observations of participants engaged in scenarios • Mixed results have been found when assessing training transfer	O'Connor et al. (2008), Salas et al. (2001, 2006a), Spiker, Tourville, Bragger, Dowdy, and Nullmeyer (1999), Verbeek-van Noord et al. (2014)
Individual Characteristics	• Individual characteristics that affect CRM training effectiveness include motivation, intelligence, self-efficacy, organizational commitment, and personality • However, the specifics as to how these characteristics impact CRM training have not been studied	Gregorich and Wilhelm (1993), Gregorich et al. (1990), Gregorich, Helmriech, Wilhelm, and Chidester (1989), Sauer et al. (2010)
Training Characteristics	• Training characteristics that impact CRM training include information delivery, practice elements, and training materials • Low fidelity simulations have been found to effectively train CRM skills • Scenario design and feedback are also an important consideration for CRM training effectiveness	Alonso et al. (2006), Baker et al. (1993), Beard et al. (1995), Bowers et al. (1992), Buljac-Samardzic et al. (2010), Cook et al. (2011), Crichton (2017), de Carvalho et al. (2016), Jentsch and Bowers (1998), Kearns (2011), Prince and Salas (1999), Prince et al. (1993)

(Continued)

TABLE 9.2 (Continued)

Evaluation Criteria	Key Findings	Example Sources
Organizational Characteristics	• The impact of organizational characteristics on CRM training effectiveness is rarely assessed • Organizational and national culture has been shown to impact CRM training, with organization-specific trainings not transferring well to other organizations	Gregorich and Wilhelm (1993), Helmreich et al. (1999), Helmreich et al. (1999), Dawson et al. (2017), O'Connor (2010)

and reduce error, it remains imperative for evaluation of such programs to continue, especially to more clearly link CRM to such outcomes and address potential characteristics that may detract from training effectiveness.

9.5   HOW SHOULD CRM TRAINING BE ASSESSED IN THE FUTURE?

As the previous section highlights, there are multiple challenges to the effective evaluation of CRM training. However, successful evaluation can still be accomplished if the proper procedures are followed. In the following section, these proper procedures will be discussed, using the past challenges of CRM evaluation in conjunction with the current knowledge about the science of training. The goal is to provide a clear discussion about considerations that must be made when developing a CRM evaluation. To provide a framework for this discussion, a model of CRM training design, implementation, evaluation, and transfer (see Fig. 9.2; Salas et al., 2006b) will be used to identify the areas in need of future evaluation attention.

It is not enough for this section to merely identify these areas, however. It is crucial that guidelines are also provided here for practitioners to reflect on and to inform their future endeavors in training teamwork within their unique organizational contexts. It is hoped that this combination of information will serve to better inform both the science and practice of CRM training and evaluation moving forward.

9.5.1   A Framework for CRM Training Design, Development, & Evaluation

As previously discussed, there are several areas in need of attention regarding CRM evaluation. First and foremost, however, is the need for a

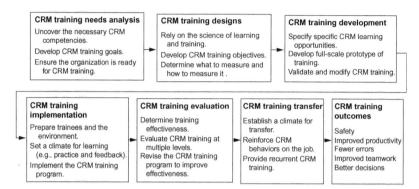

FIGURE 9.2 The progression of CRM training design, development, and evaluation. *Adapted from Salas, E., Wilson, K.A., Burke, C.S., Wightman, D.C., & Howse, W.R. (2006b). Crew resource management training research, practice, and lessons learned. In R.C.Williges (Ed),* Review of human factors and ergonomics *(Vol. 2, pp. 35–73). Santa Monica, CA: Human Factors and Ergonomics Society.*

systematic tool to assess CRM training. While previous models have been developed to address this issue (e.g., Gregorich & Wilhelm, 1993), recent advances in the science of training have led to the need for a revised approach. Of particular interest is the progression of CRM training and its related checklist, as provided by Salas et al. (2006b).

Recognizing the overall lack of consistency in CRM trainings, Salas et al. (2006b) identified both a scientifically-based progression of CRM training (see Fig. 9.2) and an in-depth checklist (see Table 9.3 for an abbreviated version) that can be used to guide CRM training developers throughout the entire process, from design to evaluation. As a detailed explanation of the entire progression and checklist is beyond the scope of this chapter, we highlight the components of each that are relevant to the future of CRM evaluation in the following discussion, paired with recommended guidelines for each component.

9.5.2 Guidelines for CRM Training Evaluation

In terms of the progression of CRM training as recommended by Salas et al. (2006b), it is important to note that CRM training evaluation actually begins before the training evaluation. The first step in successful evaluation is conducting an initial training needs analysis. As previously discussed, to thoroughly assess the effectiveness of an organization, it is important that the individual, training, and organizational needs are identified and addressed throughout the training design and development process. A needs assessment is not a new concept, but it is one that organizations rarely take the time to perform (Arthur, Bennett, Edens, & Bell, 2003). The needs assessment itself has three essential components: task, person, and organizational analysis

TABLE 9.3 CRM Training Assessment Checklist

Step	Considerations	Outcome
V. CRM Training Evaluation		
• **Evaluate CRM training program.**	Have both utility and affective reaction data (i.e., attitudes) been collected? Has learning been assessed at multiple levels? Has behavior been assessed in a transfer situation? Has the impact of training on the organization been evaluated at multiple time intervals (e.g., immediately, 3 months after; 6 months after)? Have the data been analyzed to determine instructional effectiveness?	Data on CRM training's effectiveness are collected at four levels. Data on job performance are collected.
• **Revise CRM training program.**	Are any revisions needed based on the empirical data? How will the revisions be implemented? What impact will the revisions have? Are the revisions cost-effective? How long will the revisions take? How will it affect upcoming training sessions?	CRM training is revised on the basis of empirical data.
VI. CRM Training Transfer		
• **Establish the climate for transfer.**	Is there supervisor support? Are the resources available to support the transfer of knowledge and skills? What rewards system is in place? Are trainees encouraged to learn from mistakes?	Supervisors support CRM competencies on the job. Organization supports CRM competencies on the job. Continuous learning climate is established.
• **Reinforce CRM behaviors.**	Are trainees being rewarded to encourage the transfer of the trained CRM competencies? Are behaviors that contradict what was taught in CRM training discouraged?	Trainees are rewarded. Behaviors that contradict CRM are discouraged.

(Continued)

TABLE 9.3 (Continued)

Step	Considerations	Outcome
• **Provide recurrent CRM training.**	How often does training need to be offered?	CRM competencies remain stable over time.

Source: Adapted from Salas, E., Wilson, K.A., Burke, C.S., Wightman, D.C., & Howse, W.R. (2006b). Crew resource management training research, practice, and lessons learned. In R.C. Williges (Ed), Review of human factors and ergonomics (Vol. 2, pp. 35-73). Santa Monica, CA: Human Factors and Ergonomics Society.

(Goldstein & Ford, 2002). Task analysis provides information regarding task duties and level of task difficulty. Person analysis gathers information regarding the personality characteristics, adaptability, tolerance for ambiguity, and strengths and weaknesses of individual employees. Organizational analysis provides information regarding organizational level factors that can affect training effectiveness, such as organizational culture, social support, and strategic objectives. The needs analysis serves as the critical foundation upon which a successful training evaluation can be built, and the error of not conducting a needs analysis may lead to adverse outcomes for a CRM training (O'Connor, 2010).

> Guideline 1: While not a new concept, a needs analysis should always be conducted prior to training implementation to ensure successful outcomes.

The completion of the needs analysis phase leads directly to the next phase of articulating appropriate learning outcomes. As mentioned previously, CRM has been used as an umbrella term to cover a range of competencies and training methods. Several studies fail to mention the competencies targeted by their CRM intervention, while others fail to mention the specific methods used to train CRM competencies. In both of these cases, in order to properly assess training effectiveness, both the training content and methods must be clearly operationalized. By doing so, evaluation criteria can be derived from and built upon the specific training objectives, content, and methods, ensuring that what is evaluated is relevant to the originally-stated objectives and goals of the training program. Furthermore, this will allow other trainers and researchers to more accurately compare the effectiveness of CRM training programs based on the similarity of the target competencies and training methods.

> Guideline 2: Document the content, objectives, and methods of a training program to foster greater standardization and successful completion of CRM-based learning outcomes.

The next phase of Salas et al.'s (2006b) progression of CRM training that is relevant to assessment involves training evaluation. As discussed previously, several training researchers have recognized the limitations of Kirkpatrick's four levels of training evaluation (Alliger & Janak, 1989; Alliger, Tannenbaum, Bennett, Traver, & Shotland, 1997; Alvarez et al., 2004; Holton, 1996; Kraiger et al., 1993). Despite frequent calls for trainers to move away from Kirkpatrick's four levels, this model of training evaluation continues to be the most frequently used approach. While the intuitive appeal and substantial body of research on Kirkpatrick's levels make it difficult to cut ties with completely, at the very least, trainers should be aware of the limitations associated with this training evaluation model so they can take steps to remedy its shortcomings. More specific issues associated with Kirkpatrick's model and more detailed recommendations to overcome those issues will be discussed in guidelines 4−9.

Guideline 3: Acknowledge the shortcomings of Kirkpatrick's levels of evaluation in CRM assessment in order to remedy them moving forward.

The overreliance on reaction data as the primary form of CRM training effectiveness is problematic because reaction data has been found to be either unrelated or minimally related to Kirkpatrick's other levels of learning, behaviors, and results (Alliger et al., 1997). What this means is that if CRM training is evaluated solely at the reaction level, training practitioners and researchers cannot be confident that the training program is effective at meeting longer-term organizational goals. With that being said, the collection of reaction data should not be abandoned completely. If trainees feel that a training program is useless, reaction measures can help inform modification of the training to make it more impactful. However, it is important for evaluators to recognize the limitations of reaction data. Additionally, if reaction data is collected, gathering utility reactions (i.e., how useful was training) is more informative than gathering affective reactions (i.e., how enjoyable was training). Utility reactions have been found to be related to the levels of learning and transfer, which may overcome some limitations associated with reaction measures (Alliger et al., 1997).

Guideline 4: Utility reactions should be gathered to supplement training evaluations, but not serve as a cornerstone for basing all assessments.

Salas and colleagues (Alvarez et al., 2004; Kraiger et al., 1993) argue for a multidimensional view of learning that consists of affective/attitudinal, behavioral/skill-based, and cognitive learning. Training evaluators must be aware of the importance of collecting measures of different learning outcomes because each aspect of learning may contribute to the successful enactment of CRM behaviors. To date, CRM training assessment studies have done a good job of measuring attitude change through self-report responses to the CMAQ and skill-based learning through trainee's performance in simulator exercises. However, more studies need to include measures of cognitive learning. For example, this can easily be accomplished by including a paper and pencil measure of declarative knowledge administered after training completion.

Guideline 5: When evaluating learning, measure multidimensional outcomes.

The third level of Kirkpatrick's model, behaviors (i.e., transfer of training), is viewed as one of the primary goals of training, but few CRM training assessment studies have evaluated training transfer. However, some methods of collecting behavioral outcomes of training have been around for decades, and include the Advanced Qualification Program (AQP), Airlines Safety Action Partnership (ASAP), and Flight Operations Quality Assurance (FOQA) (Orlady & Orlady, 1999). While these are well-known techniques within aviation, they have not made their way into CRM training assessment studies. Moving forward, the agencies that collect such behavioral data should make that accumulated information more broadly available to enable greater understanding of how training is tied to behavioral outcomes. The resulting best practices can then be more widely published, so researchers and practitioners can use this knowledge moving forward.

However, there are several recent, formalized techniques that show promise in assessing the behavioral outcomes of training. The first is the Line Operations Safety Audit (LOSA), which involves having trained observers ride in cockpits and observe pilots in action. The second is the explicit professional oral communication observation form (EPOC), which can be used in healthcare to observe key work dimensions (Verbeek-van Noord, de Bruijne, Twisk, van Dyck, & Wagner, 2014). The third is Team Strategies and Tools to Enhance Performance and Patient Safety (TeamSTEPPS), which teaches specific tools and principles to improve teamwork performance in the military medical profession (Alonso et al., 2006).

In addition to these formal techniques, there are other, more flexible, methods that can also be used to assess behavioral outcomes. For example, observers can interview employees during and after a given situation to gather additional, behavioral information. Alternatively, trainees can be asked to complete simulator exercises, knowledge tests, or report on how often they utilized trained skills on the job after the passage of sufficient time (i.e., 6–12 months) to see if training is retained and used by trainees. Unfortunately, transfer of training is often left out of evaluation since its collection involves more extensive, longitudinal assessment. However, it is critical to truly understanding the effectiveness of a CRM training program back on the job. Organizations should treat this level as one of paramount importance for incorporation into existing training evaluation schemes.

Guideline 6: Training transfer is a valuable measure of training used on the job, and should always be measured to ensure success.

In Kirkpatrick's model, behaviors are seen as primarily determined by learning. However, extensive research on training transfer has revealed that transfer is influenced by a wide range of variables besides learning, such as organizational/environmental characteristics, individual characteristics, and training design characteristics (Baldwin & Ford, 1988). In order to predict training transfer, training evaluators must collect organizational/environmental, individual, and training design data in addition to learning data. By collecting this diversity of information, training evaluators can better identify factors that may impede or facilitate the effectiveness of training.

Guideline 7: Be sure to measure individual, training, and organizational characteristics to inform how behaviors are transferred from training to the job.

Despite its limitations, one key takeaway from Kirkpatrick's model is the recognition of the importance of collecting multiple measures of training effectiveness at multiple levels. Additionally, several calls have been made for the use of multiple measures of training effectiveness when evaluating CRM training (Salas et al., 1999b, 2006a). Recent studies have heeded these calls (Hughes et al., 2016). A meta-analysis of team training in healthcare sought to quantify the effectiveness of CRM-inspired trainings. It was found that team training improved reaction, learning, transfer, and results outcomes. This points to the generalizability of team training interventions to diverse contexts, and the increase in studies looking at multiple measures of effectiveness is promising. However, while this demonstrates some improvement in recent years in terms of collecting multiple measures of effectiveness, there is still much work to be done (Buljac-Samardzic et al., 2010; Littlepage et al., 2016; Marquardt et al., 2011; Marquardt et al., 2010; Sauer et al., 2010).

Through a clear focus on collecting these diverse measures prior to training implementation, effectiveness can be easily evaluated at multiple levels. For example, when collecting reaction measures of effectiveness, trainees should be asked if they find training useful. When collecting learning measures of effectiveness, multiple assessments should be included to measure both interpersonal and cognitive attitudes. Additionally, evaluators should make more attempts to measure cognitive learning to ensure that trainees absorbed key training concepts. When collecting behavioral measures of effectiveness, simulators can be used as a measure of training transfer. This wide range of collected data can inform a more holistic picture of training effectiveness moving forward.

Guideline 8: Collect multiple measures of training effectiveness at multiple levels.

Moving on to the training outcomes phase of the Salas et al. (2006b) model, an important facet of outcome data is assessing the effects of training on different outcomes over time. To address this concern, several calls have been made for evaluators to collect longitudinal data (Brannick, Prince, & Salas, 2005; Salas et al., 2006a). Collecting longitudinal data is important because training skills have been found to decay with the passage of time. Understanding this decay may be critical to ensure that training prevents this from happening. With the majority of studies measuring behaviors in simulations, more field observations are needed in order to determine if CRM skills are being used by pilots during actual flights (Sauer et al., 2010). At the very least, pilots should participate in simulators several months after training to determine if trained skills are maintained over time.

Behavioral outcomes are not the only ones that can be measured longitudinally. Assessing knowledge and attitudes over time should also be implemented, and this is comparatively much easier than measuring behaviors. Former trainees can be given a short knowledge test, as well as the CMAQ, at a specified interval of time after training. Ensuring that attitudes, knowledge, and behaviors are stable after training can enable greater training effectiveness and minimize the need for future refresher courses.

Assessing knowledge, attitudes, and behaviors longitudinally can also lead to the important outcome of an accurate measure of shifts in safety culture within an organization. A culture of safety encompasses the key features of acknowledging the high-risk nature of an organization's activities and determining safe operations, creating a blame-free environment, encouraging collaboration across disciplines to seek solutions to safety problems, and addressing safety concerns through organizational commitment of resources (Chidester, 2016). If CRM training is successful, greater transfer of these principles back to the work context should impact how all employees view the safety culture of their organization. Ideally, this safety culture can lead to further increases in safe behaviors and decreases in workplace accidents.

Guideline 9: Collect longitudinal data at the individual and organizational levels to assess effects of training over time.

Organizations as a whole are integral to ensuring the implementation, evaluation, and ultimate effectiveness of a training program. To do this, organizations can provide both resources and support to encourage successful training. In terms of resources, organizations must be prepared to devote them to the entire training design, delivery, and assessment process. In order to properly assess the effectiveness of CRM training, organizations must acknowledge the importance of using their resources to gather training effectiveness data. For example, this may involve providing trainers with the necessary resources (i.e., funding and time) to carry out a well-designed training assessment (Salas et al., 2006b). Resources are especially needed if trainers attempt to evaluate training at multiple levels and/or longitudinally.

In addition to providing trainers the necessary resources, organizations must support the evaluation of training. A supportive organizational climate that recognizes the benefits of both training and its assessment is critical. In order to encourage employees, managers and supervisors must publicly support training evaluation efforts. If supervisors and managers do not support assessing training effectiveness, trainers may have considerable difficulty convincing people to participate and report their training outcomes accurately.

> Guideline 10: As an organization seeking to implement CRM training, devote adequate resources and support to training assessment.

The final guideline moves the discussion into the broader context where CRM operates in today's world. While CRM was initially developed and studied within the aviation industry, there are countless other high reliability organizations that have advanced the modern science and practice of CRM. For example, healthcare systems routinely use integrative CRM training to align surgical teams (Jimenez et al., 2015). This allows many diverse workers and their unique skill sets to be trained together, providing a more accurate workplace simulation and more seamless transfer of learned skills back to the job (Blum et al., 2004). Another example of best practices moving CRM forward can be found in the realm of military healthcare. TeamSTEPPS was developed in this context, and its strength comes from evaluating training effectiveness at all levels of Kirkpatrick's evaluation model (Alonso et al., 2006). Finally, the maritime domain developed extensive standardization of training, including training methods, assessment techniques, and trainers' certification. This can allow training to be more effective and consistently delivered (Jimenez et al., 2015). These diverse contexts provide meaningful best practices that other organizations can benefit from using.

> Guideline 11: Look beyond the aviation industry when considering best practices in training implementation and evaluation.

9.6 SUMMARY

The aforementioned guidelines contribute to conversations related to practical, research, and organizational considerations. From a practical perspective, these guidelines are provided so practitioners can inform their future endeavors in training teamwork within unique organizational contexts. While these guidelines are not exhaustive, they do capture the most critical areas in need of attention for evaluation to be effective. From a methodological and research perspective, these guidelines allow comparisons across training programs to be more effective, since the same types of data should be available across assessments (e.g., multiple source, multiple level, longitudinal). From an organizational perspective, it is hoped that these guidelines will aid in improving the process of implementing CRM training so that critical error management goals can be reached and sustained over time.

9.7 CONCLUDING REMARKS

CRM training has come a long way since its inception in the aviation industry. Today, it is used in high reliability organizations around the globe and continues to evolve. With this rapid evolution, however, has come concerns regarding a systematic approach to assessment and evaluation. Proactive steps must be taken to ensure that CRM is, and continues to be, effective.

The current chapter sought to illustrate the present state of CRM training evaluation. The first part of this chapter highlighted training evaluation's history, generally, and the past challenges of CRM evaluation, specifically. The second part of this chapter described practical guidelines for conducting an effective CRM training evaluation in the future, as a counterpoint to those challenges. Therefore, the goals of this chapter were twofold. The first goal was to advance the science of training design, delivery, and evaluation for CRM. The second goal was to provide a foundation for practitioners to develop cutting-edge assessment strategies that are scientifically sound, functional, and flexible. This can enable CRM to continue to save lives today and in the future.

ACKNOWLEDGEMENT

This work was supported by both the NASA grant (NNX14AK54G) to Dr. Shawn Burke, Principal Investigator, Dr. Eduardo Salas and Dr. Marissa Shuffler, Co-Principal Investigators and the NSF CAREER grant (1654054) to Dr. Marissa Shuffler, Principal Investigator. The views expressed in this work are those of the authors and do not necessarily reflect the organizations with which they are affiliated or their sponsoring institutions or agencies. An additional thanks to Luiz Xavier for his work on an earlier version of this chapter.

REFERENCES

Alavosius, M. P., Houmanfar, R. A., Anbro, S. J., Burleigh, D., & Hebein, C. (2017). Leadership and crew resource management in high-reliability organizations: A competency framework for measuring behaviors. *Journal of Organizational Behavior Management, 37*, 142–170.

Alkov, R. A., & Gaynor, J. A. (1991). Attitude changes in navy/ marine flight instructors following an aircrew coordination training course. *International Journal of Aviation Psychology, 1*, 245–253.

Alliger, G. A., & Janak, E. A. (1989). Kirkpatrick's levels of training criteria: Thirty years later. *Personnel Psychology, 42*, 331–342.

Alliger, G. A., Tannenbaum, S. I., Bennett, W., Traver, H., & Shotland, A. (1997). A meta-analysis of the relations among training criteria. *Personnel Psychology, 50*, 341–358.

Alonso, A., Baker, D. P., Holtzman, A., Day, R., King, H., Toomey, L., & Salas, E. (2006). Reducing medical error in the Military Health System: How can team training help? *Human Resource Management Review, 16*, 396–415.

Alvarez, K., Salas, E., & Garofano, C. M. (2004). An integrated model of training evaluation and effectiveness. *Human Resources Development Review, 3*, 385–416.

Arthur, W., Bennett, W., Edens, P. S., & Bell, S. T. (2003). Effectiveness of training in organizations: A meta-analysis of design and evaluation features. *Journal of Applied Psychology*, *88*(2), 234−245.

Arthur, W., Kyte, T. B., Villado, A. J., Morgan, C. A., & Roop, S. S. (2011). Introducing a subject matter expert-based utility analysis approach to assessing the utility of organizational interventions such as crew resource management training. *The International Journal of Aviation Psychology*, *21*, 191−215.

Baker, D., Prince, C., Shrestha, L., Oser, R., & Salas, E. (1993). Aviation computer games for CRM skills training. *The International Journal of Aviation Psychology*, *3*, 143−155.

Baldwin, T. T., & Ford, J. K. (1988). Transfer of training: A review and directions for future research. *Personnel Psychology*, *41*, 63−105.

Beard, R. L., Salas, E., & Prince, C. (1995). Enhancing transfer of training: Using role-play to foster teamwork in the cockpit. *International Journal of Aviation Psychology*, *5*(2), 131−143.

Bienefeld, N., & Grote, G. (2012). Silence that may kill: When aircrew members don't speak up and why. *Aviation Psychology and Applied Human Factors*, *2*(1), 1−10.

Blum, R. H., Raemer, D. B., Carroll, J. S., Sunder, N., Felstein, D. M., & Cooper, J. B. (2004). Crisis resource management training for an anaesthesia faculty: A new approach to continuing education. *Medical Education*, *38*(1), 45−55.

Bowers, C., Salas, E., Prince, C., & Brannick, M. (1992). Games teams play: A method for investigating team coordination and performance. *Behavior Research Methods, Instruments, and Computers*, *24*, 503−506.

Brannick, M. T., Prince, C., & Salas, E. (2005). Can PC-based systems enhance teamwork in the cockpit?. *The International Journal of Aviation Psychology*, *15*, 173−188.

Broad, M. L., & Newstrom, J. W. (1992). *Transfer of training: Action-packed strategies to ensure high payoff from training investments*. Reading MA: Addison Wesley.

Brun, W., Eid, J., Jihnsen, B. H., Ekornas, B., Laberg, J. C., & Kobbeltvedt, T. (2000). Shared mental models and task performance: Studying the effects of a crew and bridge resource management training program *(Project Report: 1 2001)*. Bergen, Norway: Militaer Psykologi og Ledelse.

Buljac-Samardzic, M., Dekker-van Doorn, C. M., van Wijngaarden, J. D., & van Wijk, K. P. (2010). Interventions to improve team effectiveness: A systematic review. *Health Policy*, *94*, 183−195.

Cannon-Bowers, J. A., Salas, E., Tannenbaum, S. I., & Mathieu, J. E. (1995). Toward theoretically based principles of trainee effectiveness: A model and initial empirical investigation. *Military Psychology*, *7*, 141−164.

Cannon-Bowers, J. A., Tannenbaum, S. I., Salas, E., & Volpe, C. E. (1995). Defining team competencies and establishing team training requirements. In R. Guzzo, & E. Salas (Eds.), *Team effectiveness and decision making in organizations* (pp. 333−380). San Francisco, CA: Jossey-Bass.

Cascio, W. F., & Boudreau, J. W. (2008). *Investing in people: Financial impact of human resource initiatives*. Upper Saddle River, NJ: FT Press.

Chidester, T. (2016). Creating a culture of safety. In K. J. Ruskin, M. P. Stigler, & S. H. Rosenbaum (Eds.), *Quality and safety in anesthesia and perioperative care*. London: Oxford University Press.

Clothier, C. C. (1991). Behavioral interactions across various aircraft types: Results of systematic observations of line operations and simulations. In R. S. Jensen (Ed.), *Proceedings of the 6th International Symposium on Aviation Psychology* (pp. 332−337). Columbus: Ohio State University.

Connolly, T. J., & Blackwell, B. B. (1987). A simulator approach to training in aeronautical decision making. In R. S. Jensen (Ed.), *Proceedings of the 4th International Symposium on Aviation Psychology* (pp. 251−258). Columbus: Ohio State University.

Cook, D. A., Hatala, R., Brydges, R., Zendejas, B., Szostek, J. H., Wang, A. T., & Hamstra, S. J. (2011). Technology-enhanced simulation for health professions education. *The Journal of the American Medical Association, 306*, 978−988.

Crichton, M. T. (2017). From cockpit to operating theatre to drilling rig floor: Five principles for improving safety using simulator-based exercises to enhance team cognition. *Cognition, Technology & Work, 19*, 73−84.

Dawson, D., Cleggett, C., Thompson, K., & Thomas, M. J. W. (2017). Fatigue proofing: The role of protective behaviours in mediating fatigue-related risk in a defense aviation environment. *Accident Analysis and Prevention, 99*, 465−468.

de Carvalho, R. J. M., Saldanha, M. C. W., Vidal, M. C. R., & Carvalho, P. V. R. (2016). Situated design of line-oriented flight training (LOFT): A case study in a Brazilian airline. *Cognition, Technology & Work, 18*, 403−422.

Diehl, A. (1991). The effectiveness of training programs for preventing aircrew "error". In R. S. Jensen (Ed.), *Proceedings of the 6th International Symposium on Aviation Psychology* (pp. 640−655). Columbus: Ohio State University.

Ellis, C., & Hughes, G. (1999). Use of human patient simulation to teach emergency medicine trainees advanced airway skills. *Journal of Accident Emergency Medicine, 16*, 395−399.

Fonne, V. M., & Fredriksen, O. K. (1995). Resource management and crew training for HSV-navigators. In R. S. Jensen, & L. A. Rakovan (Eds.), *Proceedings of the 8th International Symposium on Aviation Psychology* (pp. 585−590). Columbus: Ohio State University.

Ford, J., Henderson, R., & O'Hare, D. (2014). The effects of Crew Resource Management (CRM) training on flight attendants' safety attitudes. *Journal of Safety Research, 48*, 49−56.

Ford, J., O'Hare, D., & Henderson, R. (2013). Putting the "we" into teamwork: Effects of priming personal or social identity on flight attendants' perceptions of teamwork and communication. *Human Factors, 55*(3), 499−508.

Ford, J. K., Kraiger, K., & Merritt, S. M. (2009). *An updated review of the multidimensionality of training outcomes: New direction for training evaluation research. Learning, Training, and Development in Organizations* (pp. 135−165). Routledge Taylor & Francis Group.

Fore, A. M., Sculli, G. L., Albee, D., & Neily, J. (2013). Improving patient safety using the sterile cockpit principle during medication administration: A collaborative, unit-based project. *Journal of Nursing Management, 21*, 106−111.

Fung, L., Soet, S., Bould, M. D., Qosa, H., Perrier, L., Tricco, A., ... Reeves, S. (2015). Impact of crisis resource management simulation-based training for interprofessional and interdisciplinary teams: A systematic review. *Journal of Interprofessional Care, 29*, 433−444.

Gaba, D. M., Howard, S. K., Fish, K. J., Smith, B. E., & Sowb, Y. A. (2001). Simulation-based training in anesthesia crisis resource management (ACRM): A decade of experience. *Simulation and Gaming, 32*, 175−193.

Gaba, D. M., Howard, S. K., Flanagan, B., Smith, B. E., Fish, K. J., & Botney, R. (1998). Assessment of clinical performance during simulated crises using both technical and behavioral ratings. *Anesthesiology, 89*, 8−18.

Gagne, R. M. (1984). Learning outcomes and their effects: Useful categories of human performance. *American Psychologist, 39*, 377−385.

Goeters, K. M. (2002). Evaluation of the effects of CRM training by the assessment of nontechnical skills under LOFT. *Human Factors and Aerospace Safety, 2*, 71−86.

Goldstein, I. L. (1993). *Training in organizations: Needs assessment, development, evaluation.* Monterey: Brooks-Cole.

Goldstein, I. L., & Ford, K. (2002). *Training in organizations: Needs assessment. Development and Evaluation* (4th Edn). Belmont: Wadsworth.

Gregorich, S. E. (1993). *The dynamics of CRM attitude change: Attitude stability. Proceedings of the 7th International Symposium on Aviation Psychology* (pp. 509–512). Columbus: Ohio State University.

Gregorich, S. E., Helmreich, R. L., & Wilhelm, J. A. (1990). Structure of cockpit management attitudes. *Journal of Applied Psychology, 75*, 682–690.

Gregorich, S. E., Helmreich, R. L., Wilhelm, J. A., & Chidester, T. (1989). Personality based clusters as predictors of aviator attitudes and performance. *NTRS, 2*.

Gregorich, S. E., & Wilhelm, J. A. (1993). Crew resource management training assessment. In E. L. Wiener, B. G. Kanki, & R. L. Helmreich (Eds.), *Cockpit resource management* (pp. 173–198). San Diego, CA: Academic Press.

Grubb, G., Crossland, N., & Katz, L. (2002). *Evaluating and delivering the U.S. Army aircrew coordination training enhancement (ACTE) program. Proceedings of the Interservice/IndustryTraining, Simulation and Education Conference* (pp. 1143–1149). Arlington, VA: National Training Systems Association.

Grubb, G., & Morey, J. C. (2003). Enhancement of the U.S. Army aircrew coordination training (ACT) program. In R. S. Jensen (Ed.), *Proceedings of the 12th International Symposium on Aviation Psychology* (pp. 446–452). Columbus: Ohio State University.

Grubb, G., Morey, J. C., & Simon, R. (1999). Applications of the theory of reasoned action model of attitude assessment in the air force CRM program. In R. S. Jensen, & L. A. Rakovan (Eds.), *Proceedings of the Tenth International Symposium on Aviation Psychology* (pp. 298–301). Columbus OH: Aviation Psychology Laboratory of the Ohio State University.

Helmreich, R. L. (1984). Cockpit management attitudes. *Human Factors, 26*, 583–589.

Helmreich, R. L., Merritt, A. C., & Wilhelm, J. A. (1999). The evolution of crew resource management training in commercial aviation. *The International Journal of Aviation Psychology, 9*, 19–32.

Holton, E. F. (1996). The flawed four-level evaluation model. *Human Resource Development Quarterly, 7*, 5–21.

Howard, S., Gaba, D., Fish, K., Yang, G., & Samquist, F. (1992). Anesthesia crisis resource management training: Teaching anethesiologists to handle critical incidents. *Aviation, Space, and Environmental Medicine, 63*, 763–770.

Hughes, A. M., Gregory, M. E., Joseph, D. L., Sonesh, S. C., Marlow, S. L., Lacerenza, C. N., ... Salas, E. (2016). Saving lives: A meta-analysis of team training in healthcare. *Journal of Applied Psychology, 101*(9), 1266–1304.

Irwin, C. M. (1991). The impact of initial and recurrent cockpit resource management training on attitudes. In R. S. Jensen (Ed.), *Proceedings of the 6th International Symposium on Aviation Psychology* (pp. 344–349). Columbus: Ohio State University.

Jacobsen, J., Lindekaer, A. L., Ostergaard, H. T., Nielsen, K., Ostergaard, D., Laub, M., et al. (2001). Management of anaphylactic shock evaluated using a full-scale anaesthesia simulator. *Acta Anaesthesiologica Scandinavica, 45*, 315–319.

Jentsch, F., & Bowers, C. A. (1998). Evidence for the validity of PC-based simulations in studying aircrew coordination. *International Journal of Aviation Psychology, 8*, 243–260.

Jimenez, C., Kasper, K., Rivera, J., Talone, A. B., & Jentsch, F. (2015). Crew resource management (CRM): What aviation can learn from the application of CRM in other domains.

Proceedings of the Human Factors and Ergonomics Society 59th Annual Meeting, 59(1), 946–950.

Katz, L. (2003). *Army CRM training: Demonstration of a prototype computer-based program. Proceedings of the 12th International Symposium on Aviation Psychology* (pp. 648–650). Columbus: Ohio State University.

Kayten, P. J. (1993). The accident investigator's perspective. In E. L. Wiener, B. G. Kanki, & R. L. Helmreich (Eds.), *Cockpit resource management* (pp. 283–314). San Diego, CA: Academic.

Kearns, S. (2011). Online single-pilot resource management: Assessing the feasibility of computer-based safety training. *The International Journal of Aviation Psychology, 21,* 175–190.

Kirkpatrick, D. L. (1976). Evaluation. In R. L. Craig (Ed.), *Training and development handbook: A guide to human resource development* (2nd ed.). New York: McGraw-Hill, 18-1-18-27.

Kirkpatrick, D. L. (1987). Evaluation of training. In R. L. Craig (Ed.), *Training and development handbook: A guide to human resource development* (3rd ed, pp. 301–319). New York: McGraw-Hill.

Klein, G., & Pierce, L.G. (2001). Adaptive teams. Proceedings of the 6th ICCRTS Collaboration in the Information Age Track 4.

Kraiger, K., Ford, J. K., & Salas, E. (1993). Application of cognitive, skill-based, and affective theories of learning outcomes to new methods of training evaluation [Monograph]. *Journal of Applied Psychology, 78,* 311–328.

Kraiger, K. (2002). Decision-based evaluation. In K. Kraiger (Ed.), *Creating, implementing, and maintaining effective training and development: State-of-the-art lessons for practice* (pp. 331–375). San Francisco, CA: Jossey-Bass.

Littlepage, G. E., Hein, M. B., Moffett, R. G., III, Craig, P. A., & Georgiou, A. M. (2016). Team training for dynamic cross-functional teams in aviation: Behavioral, cognitive, and performance outcomes. *Human Factors, 58,* 1275–1288.

Marquardt, N., Robelski, S., & Hoeger, R. (2010). Crew resource management training within the automotive industry: Does it work? *Human Factors, 52,* 308–315.

Marquardt, N., Robelski, S., & Jenkins, G. G. (2011). Designing and evaluating a crew resource management training for manufacturing industries. *Human Factors and Ergonomics in Manufacturing & Service Industries, 21,* 287–304.

Mathieu, J. E., Martineau, J. W., & Tannenbaum, S. I. (1993). Individual and situational influences on the development of self-efficacy: Implications for training effectiveness. *Personnel Psychology, 46*(1), 125–147.

Mcintyre, R. M., & Salas, E. (1995). Measuring and managing for team performance: emerging principles from complex environments. In R. Guzzo, & E. Salas (Eds.), *Team effectiveness and decision making in organizations.* Jossey-Bass: San Francisco.

Morey, J. C., Grubb, G., & Simon, R. (1997). Towards a new measurement approach for cockpit resource management attitudes. In R. S. Jensen, & L. A. Rakovan (Eds.), Proceedings of the 9th International Symposium on Aviation Psychology (pp. 478–483). Columbus: Ohio State University.

Morey, J. C., Simon, R., Jay, G. D., Wears, R. L., Salisbury, M., Dukes, K. A., et al. (2002). Error reduction and performance improvement in the emergency department through formal teamwork training: Evaluation results of the MedTeams project. *Health Services Research, 37,* 1553–1581.

Munene, I. (2016). An application of the HFACS method to aviation accidents in Africa. *Aviation Psychology and Applied Human Factors, 6*(1), 33–38.

Noe, R. A. (2002). *Employee Training and Development*. McGraw-Hill/Irwin.

O'Connor, P. (2010). Assessing the effectiveness of bridge resource management training. *The International Journal of Aviation Psychology*, *21*, 357–374.

O'Connor, P., Campbell, J., Newon, J., Melton, J., Salas, E., & Wilson, K. A. (2008). Crew resource management training effectiveness: A meta-analysis and some critical needs. *The International Journal of Aviation Psychology*, *18*, 353–368.

O'Connor, P., Flin, R., & Fletcher, G. (2002). Methods used to evaluate the effectiveness of CRM training: A literature review. *Journal of Human Factors and Aerospace Safety*, *2*, 217–234.

Orlady, H. W., & Orlady, L. M. (1999). *Human factors in multi-crew flight operations*. Aldershot, Hants: Ashgate.

Porter, C. O., Hollenbeck, J. R., Ilgen, D. R., Ellis, A. P., West, B. J., & Moon, H. (2003). Backing up behaviors in teams: the role of personality and legitimacy of need. *Journal of Applied Psychology*, *88*(3), 391–403.

Prince, A., Brannick, M. T., Prince, C., & Salas, E. (1997). The measurement of team process behaviors in the cockpit: Lessons learned. In M. T. Brannick, E. Salas, & C. Prince (Eds.), *Team performance assessment and measurement: Theory, methods, and applications* (pp. 289–310). Hillsdale, NJ: Lawrence Erlbaum Associates, Inc.

Prince, C., Oser, R., Salas, E., & Woodruff, W. (1993). Increasing hits and reducing misses in CRM/LOS scenarios: Guidelines for simulator scenario development. *International Journal of Aviation Psychology*, *3*, 69–82.

Prince, C., & Salas, E. (1999). Team processes and their training in aviation. In D. Garland, J. Wise, & D. Hopkins (Eds.), *Handbook of aviation human factors* (pp. 193–213). Mahwah, NJ: Erlbaum.

Ritzmann, S., Kluge, A., Hagemann, V., & Tanner, M. (2011). Integrating safety and crew resource management (CRM) aspects in the recurrent training of cabin crew members. *Aviation Psychology and Applied Human Factors*, *1*, 45–51.

Robertson, M. M., & Taylor, J. C. (1995). Team training in aviation maintenance settings: A systematic evaluation. In B. J. Hayward, & A. R. Lowe (Eds.), *Applied aviation psychology: Achievement, change, and challenge*. *Proceedings of the Third Australian Aviation Psychology Symposium* (pp. 373–383). Aldershot, UK: Avebury Aviation.

Rottger, S., Vetter, S., & Kowalski, J. T. (2013). Ship management attitudes and their relation to behavior and performance. *Human Factors*, *55*(3), 659–671.

Salas, E., Burke, C. S., Bowers, C. A., & Wilson, K. (2001). Team training in the skies: Does CRM training work? *Human Factors*, *43*, 641–674.

Salas, E., & Cannon-Bowers, J. A. (2001). The science of training: A decade of progress. *Annual Review of Psychology*, *52*, 471–499.

Salas, E., Fowlkes, J., Stout, R. J., Milanovich, D. M., & Prince, C. (1999a). Does CRM training enhances teamwork skills in the cockpit?: Two evaluation studies. *Human Factors*, *41*, 326–343.

Salas, E., Prince, C., Bowers, C. A., Stout, R., Oser, R. L., & Cannon-Bowers, J. A. (1999b). A methodology to enhance crew resource management training. *Human Factors*, *41*, 161–172.

Salas, E., Rhodenizer, L., & Bowers, C. A. (2000). The design and delivery of crew resource management training: Exploiting available resources. *Human Factors*, *42*(3), 490–511.

Salas, E., Wilson, K. A., Burke, C. S., & Wightman, D. C. (2006a). Does CRM training work? An update, extension and some critical needs. *Human Factors*, *48*, 392–412.

Salas, E., Wilson, K. A., Burke, C. S., Wightman, D. C., & Howse, W. R. (2006b). Crew resource management training research, practice, and lessons learned. In R. C. Williges

(Ed.), *Review of human factors and ergonomics* (Vol. 2, pp. 35–73). Santa Monica, CA: Human Factors and Ergonomics Society.

Sauer, J., Darioly, A., Mast, M. S., Schmid, P. C., & Bischof, N. (2010). A multi-level approach of evaluating crew resource management training: A laboratory-based study examining communication skills as a function of team congruence. *Ergonomics, 53,* 1311–1324.

Shuffler, M. L., Salas, E., & Xavier, L. F. (2010). The design, delivery and evaluation of crew resource management training. In B. Kanki, R. Helmreich, & J. Anca (Eds.), *Crew resource management* (pp. 205–232). Oxford, UK: Elsevier Inc.

Spiker, V. A., Tourville, S. J., Bragger, J., Dowdy, D., & Nullmeyer, R. T. (1999). *Measuring C-5 crew coordination proficiency in an operational wing. Proceedings of the Interservice/ Industry Training, Simulation and Education Conference [CD-ROM].* Arlington, VA: National Training Systems Association.

Spiker, V. A., Wilson, D. D., & Deen, G. C. (2003). CRM and mission performance during C-130 mission-oriented simulator training. In R. S. Jensen (Ed.), *Proceedings of the 12th International Symposium on Aviation Psychology* (pp. 1108–1114). Columbus: Ohio State University.

Stout, R. J., Salas, E., & Fowlkes, J. E. (1997). Enhancing teamwork in complex environments through team training. *Group Dynamics, 1,* 169–182.

Taylor, J.C. (1998, August). *Evaluating the effectiveness of maintenance resource management (MRM).* Paper presented at the 12th International Symposium on Human Factors in Aviation Maintenance, Washington, DC.

Taylor, J. C., Robertson, M. M., Peck, R., & Stelly, J. W. (1993). Validating the impact of maintenance CRM training. In R. S. Jensen (Ed.), *Proceedings of the 7th International Symposium on Aviation Psychology* (pp. 538–542). Columbus: Ohio State University.

Taylor, J. C., & Thomas, R. L. (2003). Written communication practices as impacted by a maintenance resource management training intervention. *Journal of Air Transportation, 8,* 69–90.

Verbeek-van Noord, I., de Bruijne, M. C., Twisk, J. W. R., van Dyck, C., & Wagner, C. (2014). More explicit communication after classroom-based crew resource management training: Results of a pragmatic trial. *Journal of Evaluation in Clinical Practice, 21,* 137–144.

Chapter 10

Line Oriented Flight Training: A Practical Guide for Developers

Robert W. Koteskey[1], Charles Hagan[2] and Eric T. Lish[3]
[1]San Jose State University Research Foundation, NASA Ames Research Center, Mountain View, CA, United States, [2]Flight Training International, Denver, CO, United States, [3]Private Consultant, Denver, CO, United States

INTRODUCTION

Line oriented flight training (LOFT) is a key vehicle for training crew resource management (CRM). It is the primary means for providing crewmembers the opportunity to practice skills and to receive feedback on their performance in a crew setting. This chapter will provide a practical guide for construction and implementation of LOFT as it is used for training and evaluation purposes. It is particularly aimed at the airline or aviation training designer who is new to working under the FAA Advanced Qualification Program (AQP). We hope that developers of human factors research simulations and those from non-AQP organizations may find the discussion on production of LOFT materials valuable as well.

The authors' experience includes aviation human factors research, as well as the development of training for major airlines, regional and supplemental carriers, and the Department of Defense. We'll try to paint as broad a picture as possible and will rely heavily on guidance from the FAA Advisory Circulars on AQP, line oriented simulation (LOS), and CRM.

"LOFT" was a term coined in the 1970s to describe any simulation set in a realistic, mission-based environment. It continues today as a generic term widely used to describe all LOS activity. Indeed, this chapter is titled using this common style. But, it is perhaps important to realize that the current governing literature defines LOFT as the smaller, training oriented, subset of LOS. Our discussion will concentrate on production of this training subset and on line oriented evaluation (LOE). One other form of LOS, special purpose operational training (SPOT) is used narrowly by most operators and is beyond the scope of our discussion.

Crew Resource Management. DOI: https://doi.org/10.1016/B978-0-12-812995-1.00010-5

10.1 BASIC DEFINITIONS

Line Oriented—the type of experiential learning where the crew is allowed to perform in an environment that is as close as possible to the environment in which they fly.

LOS—any simulation of the line environment for the purpose of training or evaluating a flight crew. Emphasis is on a combination of technical and CRM skills. Types of LOS include LOFT, LOE, and SPOT.

LOFT—the subset of LOS that refers purely to training activity in a full mission setting (as opposed to evaluation).

LOE—the subset of LOS that is used to evaluate and qualify flight crews.

SPOT—a simulator session similar to LOFT in that it is line oriented, but geared towards training specific procedures or experiences. It is typically not a full flight segment. Examples might include windshear avoidance and recovery training or RNAV-RNP approach procedures.

AQP—the FAA program that allows the development of customized curriculum and the use of LOS to qualify and maintain currency for flight crews. It can be used to replace the historical method of qualifying crews and allows for individualized airman qualification standards to be created for a specific airline, fleet, and seat.

ISD—Instructional Systems Development is the FAA recommended process for construction and implementation of an AQP. It is, therefore, also pertinent to any LOS construction.

10.2 HISTORY AND CONTEXT: SIMULATION AND CRM COME OF AGE AT THE SAME TIME

(Fig. 10.1)

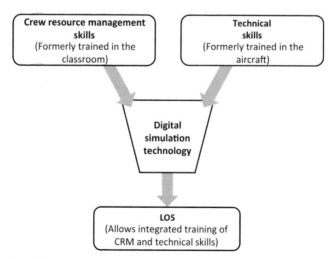

FIGURE 10.1 The Confluence of advanced simulation technology and CRM.

10.2.1 Simulation

The full motion, high fidelity, digital flight simulators that we take for granted today are the result of several complimentary technologies that came together from the late 1940s through the mid 1960s. Evolved from early analog simulators and part task trainers, these revolutionary devices enabled even the most demanding training to be moved out of the aircraft to a safer and more efficient environment (Page, 2000, p. 11).

Before the advent of this technology, training for transport crews was carried out in actual aircraft. An instructor pilot or evaluator was responsible for the safety and efficiency of the flight in addition to trying to teach and evaluate flight deck crews. At the airlines and in the military, instructor pilots, instructor flight engineers, and check airman were run through an extensive syllabus of their own that ensured they could present training while always maintaining the safety of the aircraft they were using as a training platform. Engine failures on takeoff, no flap landings, engine out landings, and other pretty hazardous maneuvers were all carried out in an actual aircraft. The very nature of any training was necessarily limited by what could be safely presented. In addition to these fairly obvious safety concerns, economics were a factor as well. The expense of operating a jet transport is extreme. When that jet is used as a training platform and is also taken out of revenue service, the expense is multiplied.

These limits on the scope of training that could be conducted in the aircraft produced an environment that was quite unlike the actual line operation. It was impractical to burn fuel and add cycles to a ship for any purpose other than the most salient to actually controlling the aircraft. Increasingly, technical skills were emphasized in isolation from any training on managing the flight operation. This isolation of individual technical skills in training was not ideal, but the trend progressed naturally in this environment. Reinforcing this effect was the fact that ground trainer technology was initially limited to trainers with part task capability. So, the culture became used to training this way, in bits and pieces, literally part-task training. One possible consequence was unintended negative effects in what we now know as CRM skills. Let's examine the crew setup on one of those presimulation training flights and see how this could be the case.

The flight deck complement on these training flights might consist of a trainee pilot, a trainee flight engineer, an instructor pilot, and an instructor flight engineer. The trainees would occupy the control seats for which they were being trained. The instructor pilot would occupy the vacant pilot seat, and the instructor flight engineer would occupy a jump seat. There were many connections between each of these people that could be considered a "team," but none of them resembled the actual team that the trainee would become part of in line operations.

The prime team connection was between the instructor pilot and instructor flight engineer. Their task was to present failure modes for the trainees while retaining responsibility for safely flying the aircraft. Another team would be the trainee pilot with the trainee flight engineer and perhaps the instructor pilot who would sometimes play a role. This made for interesting undercurrents and barriers to open communication between the occupants of the flight deck—the very condition CRM seeks to avoid. This situation in no way resembled an actual mission segment where two or three crewmembers are expected to form a cohesive team to plan a flight and fly an aircraft safely from point to point. It was, however, the best the technology and concepts of the time had to offer.

Both safety and economics made moving training from the aircraft to the simulator fairly easy. Aircraft were damaged and pilots killed doing inherently risky maneuvers in training aircraft (NTSB, 1973). By the late 1970s most major airlines either owned or had access to simulation devices that very accurately modeled the aircraft that they operated (Page, 2000).

Modern digital flight simulators relieved flight instructors from the underlying and simultaneous necessity of managing actual safety of flight in the training environment. Accurate modeling of flight characteristics of virtually any transport category aircraft became possible. The supporting systems, engines, hydraulics, electrical, pneumatics, etc. along with their associated indicators and controls could all be modeled with great accuracy as well. Out the window visuals became highly realistic as displays gained better definition. Digital models of airports, weather, and terrain became the accepted standard and norm. In addition, they allowed all control seats to be occupied by a team composed exactly as the one that would fly the aircraft in line operations. At the same time that digital technology was revolutionizing transport flight training, CRM was gaining acceptance and growing up. CRM training began to move onto the flight deck.

10.2.2 CRM Is Integrated With Technical Skills

Evolving from what had been solely classroom seminars, emphasis was now being placed on developing specific CRM behavioral tools and techniques that could be used effectively on the flight deck to foster collaborative decision-making and communication. This presented an opportunity to combine the new discipline of CRM with the advances in simulation technology (Lauber & Foushee, 1981a,b).

FAA Advisory Circular 120-35D on LOS from 2015 describes this history:

The use of gate-to-gate flight simulator scenarios, known as LOFT, began in the mid-1970s as a means to provide pilot training that is more representative of actual flight operations than maneuver-based training alone. LOFT was soon recognized as a highly effective means of developing and practicing CRM skills. Due to the role of CRM issues in accident causation, it has become evident that training curriculums must develop pilot proficiency in both technical and CRM skills. While LOFT is designed to include all phases of flight, scenario-based training may also include limited portions of flight designed to focus on specific operational training needs, known as SPOT. Air carriers with an approved AQP must also conduct evaluated LOFTs, known as LOE, for jeopardy grading purposes. These three methodologies, LOFT, SPOT, and LOE, are now grouped under the general heading of flightcrew member LOS.

FAA (2015, p. 4).

As LOS evolved, training began to focus on concrete tools that could be used for effective teaming and mitigation of errors. Instruction was delivered on topics such as formalized crew briefings, communication strategies, and creating assertive statements. Later, threat and error management (TEM) and verbalize verify monitor (VVM) techniques would be introduced. These new skills are now practiced in the simulator alongside, and concurrent with, the technical skills that had previously been the only focus of training.

10.2.3   A Standardized Approach

So, perhaps you are intrigued, and would like to build LOS scenarios into your organization's training program. How are you going to go about making viable LOFT and LOE scenarios happen in your organization? And how do you use them for training and certification that the FAA will approve?

The AQP codifies this process as described below:

The Federal Aviation Administration introduced a major change in the training and qualification of flight crews in 1990 with the initiation of its Advanced Qualification Program (AQP: Birnbach & Longridge, 1993). AQP is a voluntary program that allows air carriers to develop innovative training that fits the needs of the specific organization. In exchange for this greater flexibility in training, carriers are required to provide both CRM and LOFT for all flight crews and to integrate CRM concepts into technical training. Most of the major U.S. airlines and several regional carriers are transitioning into AQP from the older model expressed in Federal Aviation Regulations, Parts 121 and 135. To complete the shift to AQP, carriers are required to complete detailed analyses of training requirements for each aircraft and to develop programs that address the human factors (CRM) issues in each aspect of training. In addition, special training for those charged with certification of crews and formal evaluation of crews in full mission simulation is required (Line Operational Evaluation or LOE).

Helmreich, Merritt, and Wilhelm (1999, p. 20)

AQP is a voluntary program which emphasizes CRM, crew performance, and scenario based training that allows realistic exposure to events and errors that build over the course of a flight, much as in the actual operation. It is data-driven, and based in a systematic approach to development, delivery, and evaluation:

> *Instead of basing curriculums on prescribed generic maneuvers, procedures and knowledge items, AQP curriculums are based on a detailed analysis of the specific job tasks, knowledge, and skill requirements of each duty position for the individual airline [or your organization]. Compared to traditional training programs, the AQP process provides a systematic basis for establishing an audit trail between training requirements and training methodologies.*
>
> *AQPs are systematically developed, continuously maintained, and empirically validated, proficiency-based training systems. They allow for the systematic analysis, design, development, implementation, progressive evaluation, and maintenance of self-correcting training programs that include integrated Crew Resource Management (CRM), improved instructor/evaluator standardization, scenario-based evaluation, and a comprehensive data-driven quality assurance system.*
>
> FAA (2017, p. 2)

While LOS may be pursued without AQP, it has shaped and improved the construction of LOS scenarios. AQP suggests an approach to designing and implementing LOS called instructional systems development (ISD). Under ISD, a systematic approach is emphasized. A step-by-step process is defined for the production of LOS events and for the training programs in which they occur. Individual organizations and groups can tailor their product to their own specific needs and still be assured that they will have relevant flight standards and be in compliance with regulation.

10.3 PRACTICAL GUIDE TO LOFT AND LOE DEVELOPMENT USING THE INSTRUCTIONAL SYSTEMS DEVELOPMENT PROCESS

ISD is the underlying approach that governs LOS design under AQP programs, and can be useful for traditional Part 121 programs. It emerged in the mid 1970s as an outgrowth of the larger general systems approach used during and after World War II to deal with complex problems ranging from logistics to strategy. A popular acronym used to describe the process is "ADDIE," which stands for: Analysis, Design, Development, Implementation, and Evaluation (Molenda, 2003, p. 35).

The components of the acronym could be defined as follows, to describe a process that can produce a LOS event.

- *Analyze*—Define the training or evaluation need.

  What is the gap between existing student capability and the desired capability? This question is revisited throughout the training cycle to ensure training is correctly targeted, and as new LOS scenarios are produced.
- *Design*—Write the proposed scenario down on paper. Create instructional objectives using regulatory and organizational resources, and build a scenario that fits the defined need.
- *Develop*—Identify and use training devices, software tools, and other instructional and authoring resources to turn the scenario script into a tested and well supported LOS session. This includes authoring of support material (instructor guides, student materials, simulator presets, etc.), and beta testing.
- *Implement*—Bring the LOS to the organization. This includes project management, scheduling, instructor training, and further beta testing.
- *Evaluate*—Continue data driven evaluation and improvement of the scenario during production and after it is live. This involves mining of the data to identify improvements to the training, to discover existing procedural flaws, to highlight safety issues, and to identify the next training need.

This process can best be envisioned as a continuing cycle of improvement in both the training and the organization, with evaluation occurring throughout (see Fig. 10.2).

Let's explore how ISD might be used to produce a LOS event for a typical airline organization.

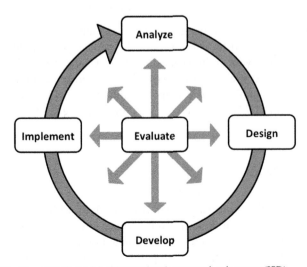

FIGURE 10.2   The ADDIE model of instructional systems development (ISD).

10.3.1   Analysis

(Fig. 10.3)

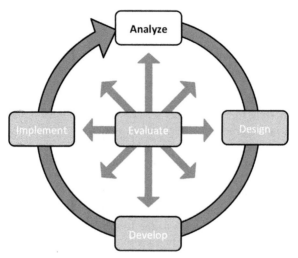

FIGURE 10.3   Analysis.

> *The moral of this fable is that if you're not sure where you're going, you're liable to end up someplace else. Before you prepare instruction, before you select instructional procedures or subject matter or material, it is important to be able to state clearly just what you intend the results of that instruction to be.*
> [emphasis added] (Mager, 1984, pp. v−vi).

Analysis involves determining the current capability of your students, and what you want them to be able to do at the end of your training. The gap between the two is your training need (Dick & Carey, 1990). It will define the overall goal and specific objectives of your entire program and the LOS scenarios that fit within it. The output of this phase will be a clear set of *prerequisite entry skills* and a clear set of *learning goals and training objectives.*

Prerequisite Skills

What can the students *do* already?

Entry capabilities will vary from fleet to fleet, airline to airline, and student to student but can be fairly well defined. FAA certification standards and airline hiring criteria ensure that even new hire airline pilots will have a minimum level of knowledge. It is important to realize that your trainees are not completely homogeneous in their skills, however.

At a large air carrier, aircraft fleet type has an impact. There are subtle differences in courses for different fleets and for different seats within those fleets. Will the captain in a 747 transition course need the same amount of help as a young first officer in the 737 who is just starting his or her airline career? The type of operation that a specific fleet performs will impact the type of training required for the pilots. These are important questions to answer before training is produced. If you're unsure of entry knowledge level, do a quick review of student training records, or give the exit survey in the beginning. You can think of other methods that might fit your own situation.

Learning Goals and Objectives

What do I want the students to be able to *do* after training?

Now that you've researched what your students can do before you've trained them, it is time to define what you want the students to be able to do after your training.

Learning Goals

The broad goal of your LOS must be defined to keep your design focused. You may get to suggest a goal, or management and the FAA may set them. In any case, goals will probably be defined by the analysis of some type of data.

Keeping in mind that LOFT is realistic experiential learning, your best bet for finding subject matter is in the real world. Flight operations quality assurance (FOQA) reports, line operations safety audits (LOSA), existing AQP grades and trends, NASA's aviation safety reporting system (ASRS), and industry publications are all great data sources. While your company might not have a full-blown AQP, FOQA, or integrated ASRS reporting program, line-check airmen, principle operations inspector (POI), and dispatchers are great sources of trend data, too. Data regarding incidents at other carriers that operate your aircraft and regarding incidents of a more generic nature like turbulence injuries can also be searched.

A typical airline will have at least three courses running for any given fleet. These might include, but aren't limited to the following: an Initial Qualification Course, a Requalification Course, a Recurrent Training Course, and an Instructor Training Course. LOFT and LOE design goals should vary depending the course. For an early LOFT event during the qualification course, your goal might be introductory, with less complexity and lower completion standards than later in the course when final preparation for the LOE is desired.

Goals can modify your thinking about entry skills, too. For instance, little or no CRM credit may typically be given for a pilot's prior experience when entering initial or qualification training for a particular fleet. One goal for those courses is that the pilots be molded into the specific fleets' culture, making the operation safer and more efficient.

If you are designing for a non-AQP organization, or are a one-person shop, you may have to dig into the regulations or a procedures manual to determine what is relevant to flight crews and then build your own goals. In any case, you will either have outside direction, or build these broad goals on your own using the sources above and some of your own specific methods. LOFT goals will come from organizational guidance and needs defined by real-world events and resources.

While LOFT goals may vary, for LOE, there are always two consistent goals:

1. Determine whether the students met the goals and objectives of the training course.
2. Assess whether the training is effective in helping the students meet the stated goals and objectives.

Learning Objectives

If goals are general, then these are the specifics of what you want the students to be able to do after training or during evaluation. One useful way to think of this part of analysis is that you are attempting to write your "exit quiz" first, before anything else (Kemp, 1985, p. 161). For a LOFT, this means that you should end up with a list of behaviors that you would like to see your students exhibit during, and as a result of, the training:

Objectives ... are useful in providing a sound basis (1) for the selection and designing of instructional content and procedures, (2) for evaluating or assessing the success of the instruction, and (3) for organizing the students' own efforts and activities...

Mager (1984, p. 6).

In an AQP airline, there is already a master list of these objectives in the form of a Job Task Analysis (JTA). A JTA exhaustively describes and catalogs the individual components of the job that a pilot does in his or her crew position. It lists the entire spectrum of behaviors that a qualified pilot should display while doing their job. This includes not only physical and technical skills, but also cognitive abilities like problem-solving and CRM skills. To the LOS developer, the JTA is a palette of observable behaviors from which to draw. Not all behaviors need be observed; you can pick the ones you feel are important for a particular training session (LOFT), or that represent a common set of skills that need to be evaluated (LOE), and plug them into the list.

If you are a small shop, and don't have the luxury of having a JTA already built for you, you might consider compiling one of your own to use as you begin building the objectives for each of your individual LOS projects. You'll need to identify those objectives anyway, so you might as well organize them into a JTA as you go.

As you analyze tasks, keep in mind how you will grade the event, what the requirements are for later data analysis, what your capabilities will be, and what you hope to hope to gain from the JTA. Here's an example for the task "Perform a nonprecision approach":

Which includes the following behaviors:

- Tune a navaid
- Correctly identify the navaid
- Install the approach in the FMC
- Brief the approach
  - Course
  - Altitudes
  - Minimums
    - Differentiate MDA from DDA
  - Missed approach
  - Runway Exit Plan
  - MSA/Terrain
  - Weather
- Select appropriate MCP modes
  - Pitch modes
  - Roll modes
- Comply with autoflight requirements
  - Autopilot on/off altitudes

The behaviors listed in the JTA are commonly categorized into terminal proficiency objectives (TPOs), supporting proficiency objectives (SPOs), and enabling objectives (EOs). There is a standard outline format used to document them. Here's an example of one small portion of what that might look in its common layout:

12 CREW RESOURCE MANAGEMENT/THREAT AND ERROR MANAGEMENT SKILLS

    12.1 Demonstrate Crew Resource Management/Threat and Error Management skills

        12.1.1 Demonstrate Effective Communication Skills

            12.1.1.1 Effectively exchange information in a timely manner

            12.1.1.2 Effectively exchange ideas

            12.1.1.3 Effectively exchange instructions

        12.1.2 Identify ... etc.

This excerpt describes part of a TPO called: "Demonstrate Crew Resource Management/Threat and Error Management Skills" along with some of the associated Supporting Proficiency Objectives and Enabling Objectives. In this example, the task is numbered as 12, the TPO as 12.1, an SPO is 12.1.1, and some enabling objectives are 12.1.1.1 through 12.1.1.3.

Here is a more extensive second excerpt with the TPO: "Perform Special Qualifications Operations," which is a Technical TPO. "Perform International Operations Procedures" is listed as an SPO, as are further applicable Enabling Objectives.

11 SPECIAL QUALIFICATION OPERATIONS

    11.1 Perform Special Qualification Operations

        11.11.1 Perform Regional Operational Procedures

        11.11.2 Perform International Operations Procedures

            11.11.2.1 Perform Preflight Planning and Dispatch procedures

            11.11.2.2 Perform Flight deck Preparation procedures

            11.11.2.3 Perform Enroute and Enroute prior to ETOPS entry procedures, as required

            11.11.2.4 Perform Enroute ETOPS procedures, if applicable

            11.11.2.5 Perform Waypoint Procedures, as required

            11.11.2.6 Perform Re-Dispatch procedures, if required

            11.11.2.7 Perform North Atlantic Track Change Procedures, if applicable

            11.11.2.8 Perform Enroute and Enroute prior to ETOPS exit procedures, as required

            11.11.2.9 Perform Coast In and Arrival Procedures

            11.11.2.10 Perform Track/Airway Diversion, if required

The idea is to pull from these TPO/SPO/EOs as building blocks to construct your LOS. Once you have a goal for the training, you select the objectives from the JTA that meet your needs.

Let's try an example "pull" from our abridged lists above. We'll assume you want to create a LOS event training extended-range twin-engine operational performance standards (ETOPS) Procedures. Let's also assume that there is a desire to train TEM. In this case you might pull the entire TPO (#12) for TEM with its associated SPOs and EOs, and a selection of SPOs and EOs (11.11.2.2, 11.11.2.3, ... etc.) that would apply to your goal of ETOPS training. As you continue through the design process you may find that you need to pull more and return others. For example, is it possible to train ETOPS procedures without also putting the students into the international environment? The answer will depend on your situation, but this the kind of thing that you'll consider as you compile your list of objectives.

Once you've defined a goal or goals for the LOS, and referenced your JTA to compile some objectives (or defined your own set if your organization has no JTA), you should have a comprehensive list of the things that your students will now be able to do as a result of their LOS experience.

You're almost ready to move on to the next step. Before proceeding much further, though, it might be time to consider another question: perhaps you should still revisit the question of why are you conducting a LOS in the first place? Is LOFT or LOE really the right format? Can you meet your goals and objectives without LOS? As an example, a new procedure or change to a maneuver might best be introduced first as a series of maneuvers within a non-LOFT simulator session, or even in the classroom. A developer might then choose to test these same procedures as part of a later LOFT.

To Summarize

The analysis phase defines the gap between existing skills and those desired after the event is complete. For both LOFT and LOE, this means defining prerequisite skills, and the training goal and objectives. Goals can be generated by organizational guidance (LOSA, FOQA, and safety programs), regulatory guidance, and other sources. For an LOE the goal is to evaluate the students' level of performance and the effectiveness of the course. Training objectives, backed by the JTA, are selected to support the goals of the LOFT or LOE. Finally, ask yourself if LOFT is really appropriate before moving on to the Design phase.

10.3.2   Design

(Fig. 10.4)

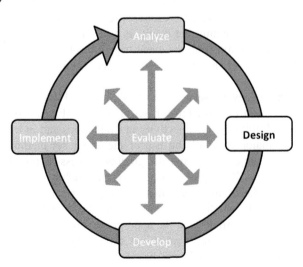

FIGURE 10.4   Design.

At this point, you've defined entry-level knowledge, goals, and objectives. Now, you'll write the simulation scenario.

You will devise experiences to enable your students to master those objectives and create the simulated world that your students will live inside for two to four hours. What needs to exist in that world? Where will it be? What kind of weather will exist? Are there aircraft systems malfunctions? Do we need NOTAMS that will impact the experience? You will write your answers in the form of a script containing a series of events and all the window dressing that will make the experience seem real. The creative process and design methodology will be consistent for building both LOFT and LOE scenarios. You'll need to determine content, subject matter, and success criteria. This process should be logical, orderly, and repeatable. The first concept to master in order to begin the design process is the Event Set.

Event Sets

The real-world flight scenarios you are designing are built using a standard concept known as the Event Set, which presents the scenario in a conceptual manner that is often based on phase-of-flight. An individual event set is constructed around selected CRM and technical objectives that are derived from your list pulled from the JTA.

The event set includes an event trigger, supporting conditions, and optional distracters. The event trigger is the condition which fully activates the event set and provides the instructor/evaluator with a specific time segment to focus the assessment process. Supporting conditions are other events taking place within the event set designed to further CRM and technical training objectives and to increase event set realism. The optional distracters are conditions inserted within the event set time frame that are designed to divert the crew's attention from the event trigger or other events taking place within the timeframe of the event set (Seamster, Hamman, & Edens, 1995, p. 664).

The concept of event sets is endorsed by the FAA LOFT Advisory Circular as the preferred structure for Scripting LOS (FAA, 2015). This disciplined approach minimizes subjectivity in evaluations and in training:

One of the major goals of the use of the event set methodology is to remove as much subjectivity from the grading process as possible, particularly for CRM skills. By engineering the event in such a way that there is a clear indicator of the desired performance, the performance issue is focused down to, for example, whether the copilot either did or did not communicate weight and balance information at the appropriate time and in the appropriate manner. That is what is being graded, not some subjective notion of "communication." The assessment is not based on the general adequacy of the copilot's communication skills, but instead on the adequacy of a very specific behavior. This technique has allowed evaluators to be trained to grade CRM skills with the same consistency with which they grade technical skills (FAA, 2015, p. 34).

The event trigger initiates the event. It may be as simple as a call from ATC or may be a technical failure. If your event has a CRM TPO for irregular procedure management and communications, and a technical one for ETOPS procedures, a pretty nice trigger to the event might be a flameout of the right engine at cruise over the middle of the ocean.

The distracters may be created conditions within an event set or they may be carried from previous event sets that continue to distract the crew. Distracters for our ETOPS engine failure scenario could be many things. Perhaps there is a communications panel failure left over from a previous event set. Or, if a new distracter is needed, maybe it is time to have the flight attendant, ATC, or Dispatch call with an unrelated communication. It might be something as simple as a routine call about passing traffic.

Supporting events are sometimes included to enhance the training objectives within the event set. An example of a supporting event might be a related system failure, or perhaps a traffic or weather conflict that would not have occurred unless caused by the triggering event.

Other Characteristics of Event Sets

It is important to remember that event sets are built around both the CRM and the technical training objectives you have selected. They need not be overly elaborate as long as they allow the students the opportunity to practice, or be evaluated on, the TPOs, SPOs, and EOs that you selected. They may contain more than one CRM objective, which may carry into the next event set. A particular CRM objective may be the priority in one event set, but become secondary in the follow-on event set, serving there as a distracter or supporting event.

Typically, event sets are broken down with respect to phase of flight as follows:

1. Preflight setup to pushback
2. Engine start and taxi
3. Takeoff and departure
4. Top of climb
5. Descent and arrival
6. Approach and landing
7. Taxi in and secure

Each event set within the LOFT should allow the crew time to assess the realism of the situation. Some phases naturally move from one to the other; however, there should be sufficient time to complete any cockpit flows, procedures, checklists, etc.

General Scripting Considerations

Now that we've introduced the Event Set, which is the basic building block of LOS script writing, let's look at some other things that you will need to consider as you design the simulation.

How Many Event Sets in a LOS?

For an LOE event, coordinate in advance with your FAA Principal Operator Inspector to determine what the required passing score will be for the final exam (the LOE). It is typically 75%. With this knowledge, develop enough event sets to allow for optimum success but not too many, which increases the threat. The goal here is to afford ample opportunity to be successful but not with such restrictive parameters that success is limited. For example, a crew would fail their LOE if they received below passing grades on two event sets in a scenario with only seven event sets (71%), but they would pass that same situation if the scenario had eight event sets (75%).

Conversely, the number of event sets within a training LOFT typically does not have an impact on success since the purpose of the LOFT is to train. The goal and objective of the particular LOFT event will drive the number of event sets. The general rule of thumb here is that less is more, however. There is always a realistic limit to the number of events that can be presented in a given time. Remember too, that in LOFT events, the instructor quite often interjects to ensure the learning objectives are met, which further limits the available time.

Recurrent Training Versus Qualification Training

Scenario-based recurrent training assumes that the students have a foundation; therefore, the training here has reduced guidance and much less interaction with the instructor as compared to qualification training for a new fleet. Recurrent training focuses on refreshing technical skills, realigning the students' CRM behavior, or at the least, to reassure the students that they comply with corporate or fleet expectations. This type of cyclic training is critical to CRM longevity, and recurrent training is the prime opportunity to reinforce these skills.

If resources allow, multiday recurrent training affords opportunity to present a mini-LOFT in addition to the typical critical maneuvers' training. This mini-LOFT is presented under the premise of training and helps to prepare students for the LOE. Poor performance during the mini-LOFT can be extensively debriefed to help prepare the students for LOE.

Qualification training programs will generally contain more than one LOFT. Succeeding LOFTs should build on the foundation of the preceding LOFTs. Technical objectives can be concentrated early in the sequence where instructor intervention and guidance is more common. The final LOFT should culminate in a foundation of CRM objectives, and its complexity should vastly exceed the challenges of the LOE. Instructors may interject or guide during the LOFT if the crew does not perform as expected during a particular phase as previously addressed within the classroom. The objective is to afford opportunity for the crew to have positive learning and to communicate with one another. All crewmembers should feel compelled to actively contribute to the resolution at hand regardless of the seriousness of the scenario.

Regardless of whether the LOFT is for Recurrent or Qualification training, at least one in the series should include all phases from preflight paperwork through debrief after parking. An LOE would definitely have event sets for each phase. Including the flight papers puts the crew into the planning mindset. This should stimulate conversations regarding individual crew duty expectations. During the training, classroom time may be used to set the expectations of the crew's behavior for each phase.

The LOE at the end of either qualification or recurrent training is an evaluation and is not train-to-proficiency. Debriefing the LOE should highlight improvements or degradations of the students' CRM skills. Severe degradations may result in either a failure or a requirement for the student to return for training at a reduced cyclic time period

Level of Difficulty

A series of Event Sets must afford sufficient challenges for the crew's technical and CRM skills. However, the LOS must be constructed so that it will not adversely increase the crew's workload to the point that they are overloaded. While a line flight may actually experience a multifaceted, unbelievable event, the training program needs to employ a systematic approach to teach and solidify (or evaluate) each of your selected CRM and technical skills

LOS scenarios and individual events sets should receive difficulty ratings. LOS does not have to be particularly difficult; the goal is to present realistic training and evaluation scenarios. The level of difficulty should simply match the level of complexity of the problem selected. When multiple scenarios are available, scenarios should be designed so that all students receive problems of similar difficulty even if the problems are totally different:

> It is important to control the level of difficulty for all LOS scenarios, but it is imperative for the LOE. Students should not have to struggle because their evaluation is more difficult than another student's evaluation. The most common methodology used in AQPs is to develop a difficulty scale for each task, subtask, and element (if necessary) on the job task list. Operators training using traditional means can develop a similar inventory of flight elements to rate. These values vary from aircraft type to aircraft type, so separate analyses must be conducted for each fleet. One carrier uses a 5-point scale, where noncritical events are scored 1−3 and critical events 4−5. For example:

- 5—Wind shear, ditching, evacuation, emergency descent, landing with flaps or slats jammed, etc.
- 4—Bomb on board, incapacitation, manual Nonprecision Approach (NPA), rejected takeoff below 100 knots, etc.

- 3—Manual precision approach, manual holding, instrument meteorological conditions (IMC) takeoff, runway change, operations out of limits, unreliable speed indication, etc.
- 2—Visual meteorological conditions (VMC) takeoff, abnormal descent, two-engine manual landing, missing documentation during ground operations, etc.
- 1—Normal descent, two-engine auto landing, FMS normal workload, normal after landing operations, etc.

NOTE: Most event set worksheets have a field for the event set trigger, the distractor(s), the supporting event(s), and the difficulty rating for each particular event set. Once the scenario is drafted all of the difficulty values for all of the events are added together. This number is then compared to what is considered an acceptable range of difficulty such as 35–45. If the scenario is out of range, events may be switched out to bring the overall scenario within range (FAA, 2015, p. 43).

Multiple Branches for Each Scenario

In addition to a trigger, distracter, and supporting events, each event set has its own prospective set of outcomes. You will not be able to envision the entire set of possible crew actions, but you should map out some of the alternatives that would be considered good, bad, and ugly. This will also help with developing grading criteria.

Inevitably, word will begin to get out as to what the new scenarios are. Part of the impact of any LOS is that it should be a somewhat novel experience, with challenges coming unexpectedly as they do on the line. Consider creating multiple main events for each event set that could be interchangeable. The design process remains virtually identical up to the decision tree for each event, and this process provides flexibility once the training is implemented. With a variety of events, each designed to meet the same objectives, you can still provide some element of the desired novelty. Multiple scripted scenarios can also serve as a back-up training or evaluating products for crewmembers who were unsuccessful.

The only caveat to this approach is that, after the decision point, different major system degradations will begin to present different application of CRM skills. In addition, details like scripted divert fields may have to change. Airports accessible during one scenario may not be accessible for the other scenario. So, you'll have to be careful to make sure you really are meeting or evaluating the same training objectives with parallel events.

Available Resources and Limitations

Another component of the Design phase is to consider what resources are available to you. At one end of the spectrum will be the major air carrier or military unit that has several full flight simulators available on demand, each configured to match its fleet. All displays, components, and communications systems will be identical to what the crew experiences on the line. Simulating contact with dispatch or other company resources will be realistic and transparent.

At the other end of the spectrum are smaller operators that lease simulator time at one or more location. These simulators may have capabilities or configurations that differ from the operator's aircraft in minor or major ways. In all cases, there are limits to how realistic simulator training can be. Smaller operators may have limited communications capabilities in leased simulators which are unlikely to support details like custom datacomm message printouts.

Even at major carriers, you are unable to simulate a 14-hour flight from Chicago to Beijing. You'll have to use repositioning at some point. You will not be able to anticipate every piece of information a crew may ask for while attempting to problem solve, you'll never be able to accurately replicate the accents of foreign controllers, the static of HF radios, or the feeling of flying into the sun for 9 hours. You're also unlikely to have every airport in the world available in your simulator database, and even if you did, several of them would be generic visual models. You must identify as many of these limitations as you can and design your scenarios around them.

Fortunately, most of these issues are relatively easy to solve. ACARS messages can be printed in advance and handed to crews as though they were printed in the cockpit and unavailable airports can be closed for weather or due to NOTAMS. Spending some time on identifying and mitigating these issues when selecting city pairs for training can also help with many issues surrounding simulator limitations. For example, while you might want to train crews to operate at Kabul, Afghanistan, you might end up settling for Reno, Salt Lake City, or Denver as an alternative.

Documenting Event Sets, Objectives, and Observable Behaviors

At this point you might have some initial ideas on how to proceed with writing your scenario. Fig. 10.5 shows how you might begin to script an RNAV departure from a special qualification airport with mountainous terrain, an inflight

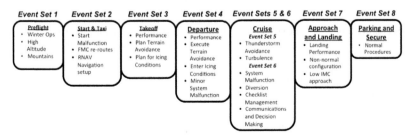

FIGURE 10.5   Sample of LOFT event sets.

problem such as a fire or passenger medical emergency, and a return to an RNAV RNP approach all during winter ops or thunderstorm season.

This sort of whiteboard exercise is effective for brainstorming initial ideas and can get you started. As your ideas begin to take more specific form, a matrix of some kind can be helpful for tracking where and how event sets and training objectives are included in the scenario. This matrix (or set of matrices) will be useful for tracking required training items and for presenting your scenario to the FAA for approval. The matrix can be used to categorize the various problems and learning objectives from simple to complex and for documenting required CRM skills. It will also provide a good source for summarizing your training later, and for developing grade sheets. Here is an example of a LOS scripting matrix with desired technical proficiency objectives categorized by event set and phase of flight (Tables 10.1 and 10.2):

TABLE 10.1 Selected Scenario Event Set Index With Phases of Flight and (Technical) Proficiency Objectives

Scenario Event Set Number	Phases of Flight	Terminal Proficiency Objectives
Scenario Event Set One	Predeparture and Pushback	Dispatch–Winter Preflight–with Malfunctions Start and Pretaxi–Hung Start
Scenario Event Set Two	Taxi	Taxi–Low Visibility Taxi–Winter Conditions Deicing
Scenario Event Set Three	Takeoff	Takeoff–Winter Conditions Climb to Cruise Altitude–Winter Conditions
Scenario Event Set Four	Climb	Climb to Cruise Altitude–Winter Conditions
Scenario Event Set Five	Cruise	En Route Cruise–Winter Conditions, with Malfunctions–Severe Compressor Stall
Scenario Event Set Six	Descent	Descent from Cruise–Winter Conditions, with Malfunction Engine Out Driftdown–Winter Conditions
Scenario Event Set Seven	Approach and Landing	Engine-Out Instrument Landing System (ILS)–Winter Conditions Engine-Out Landing–Winter Conditions Taxi In–Winter Conditions
Scenario Event Set Eight	Taxi/Parking	Parking–Winter Conditions Shutdown–with Auxiliary Power Unit (APU) Postshutdown

Source: FAA. (2015). *FAA Advisory Circular 120-35D, Flightcrew Member Line Operational Simulations: Line-Oriented Flight Training, Special Purpose Operational Training, Line Operational Evaluation.* USGPO, p. 42.

TABLE 10.2 Sample Scenario Event Set Index With Phases of Flight and Crew Resource Management Behaviors (Objectives)

Scenario Event Set Number	Situational Awareness	Workload Management	Planning	Decision-Making
Event Set One-Predeparture			Pilot Flying (PF) planned deice for winter operations standard operating procedure (SOP) PF briefed rising terrain	PF analyzed departure weather radar (WX) and requests takeoff alternate
Event Set Two-Taxi	Crew discussed route and holdover times		Taxi—Low Visibility Deicing pad	Surface Movement Guidance and Control System (SMGCS) plan Pad coordination
Event Set Three-Takeoff	Crew discussed icing issue before it could become a problem	Crew set clear priorities for tasks and their order		
Event Set Four-Climb	PF requested higher altitude			
Event Set Five-Cruise		PF directed pilot monitoring (PM) to deal with engine problem PM performed needed checklists and announced compliance	Crew assessed one engine landing with WX at diversion field PF calculated time and distance to Mahlon Sweet Field Airport (EUG)	PF stated that they cannot go back to Seattle-Tacoma International Airport (SEA)

(Continued)

TABLE 10.2 (Continued)

Scenario Event Set Number	Situational Awareness	Workload Management	Planning	Decision-Making
Event Set Six-Descent		PF prioritized tasks and got ready for approach	PF reviewed single engine approach procedures and aircraft evacuation	
Event Set Seven-Approach and Landing		PF properly prioritized PM provides backup for PF on all his tasks	PF briefed cabin crew PF planed and briefed Safety Enhancement (SE) instrument landing system (ILS)	
Event Set Eight-Taxi In				

NOTE: The four CRM challenges are spread across the eight event sets, such that only two of the eight event sets presents more than two CRM challenges. One of the strengths of the event set methodology is that it allows the facilitator to focus on a limited set of CRM issues at a time.
Source: FAA. (2015). *FAA Advisory Circular 120-35D, Flightcrew Member Line Operational Simulations: Line-Oriented Flight Training, Special Purpose Operational Training, Line Operational Evaluation.* USGPO, p. 45.

This example provides a matrix of observable CRM behaviors categorized by type of behavior, event set, and phase of flight:

> With the event sets defined, the proficiency objectives assigned, and the CRM objectives validated, the design team is now ready to develop the scripts and [test] fly the scenarios.

FAA (2015, p. 44).

10.3.3 Development

(Fig. 10.6)

Development is the process of taking the scenarios you've just scripted during the design phase and producing the materials needed to execute a viable LOS session. The training resources you thought about during design now need to be positively identified and vetted (e.g., Will our only available simulator be able to model the malfunction I have selected as a trigger for my TPO in the cruise Event Set?).

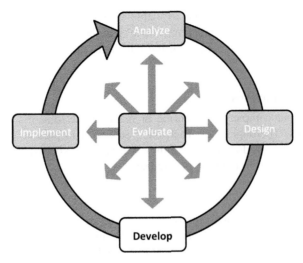

FIGURE 10.6 Development.

Resources are selected (briefing room, simulator, etc.) and materials are created (flight plans, aircraft maintenance history, weather, instructor guides, etc.). All the elements that are required to carry out the actual instruction are produced during this phase. Your scenarios will reflect reality, including communications to ATC, the company, flight attendants, and ground personnel. The greater the fidelity of the products the better the end result. You may be surprised by the length of time it takes to properly produce and assess your materials.

Training Device Considerations

You'll need to carefully evaluate each of the simulators that you intend to use during development in order to shake out any potential problems they may pose to the completion of your scenario. Here are just a few of the things you'll need to consider:

Preposition, Reposition, and Repeat Points

A simulator with preprogrammed reposition capability enables the instructor to focus on the crew rather than on the device. Scrub the scripts for flow and logical breaks to determine repeat and reposition points. These are the points the instructor will use to stop and restart a LOFT scenario. For example, consider a script that has a distractor within the "go" phase of a takeoff. The script will have had the crew taxi from the gate through the proper takeoff flow. If the crew needs to repeat the takeoff event, the reposition point might be at the takeoff position on the runway. Similarly, an international scenario may take more hours than the available training time. After the crew is trained or evaluated on departure, there will be a need to assess them near destination or in an area requiring mid-flight diversion. Where will that point be?

Systems Malfunctions

Talk with your company engineering or maintenance to assess modeling of malfunctions. Thoroughly test each one you intend to present. Just because they are on a menu does not mean they will work as you expect. Determine if they can be reset in the case of a repeat.

Weather

You'll need to assess what kind of weather can be simulated, the fidelity of that display, and how it is called up by the instructor. You may have to search National Weather Service or NOAA databases for examples of realistic wide area weather effects on multiple stations. Radar images and photographs of archived storms can be helpful to simulator engineers who may have to model your desired weather.

Communications

Most voice communications will require a script for the instructor or at least a cue. You may want to gather actual samples of the types of printout formats as well as screen presentations in the airplane. Is it possible to create messages within the device, or must you have the instructor simulate these? For data link, paper tear-offs will have to be included as part of the instructor materials if the simulator printer is not interfaced. Are these communication modes realistic, allowing the crew to use headsets (and smoke masks)? Or, do they require instructors to simulate using a particular mode? Having the crew use the communications panel adds realism but it also increases workload on both the instructor and students.

ATC Modeling

Contact appropriate and local ATC for correct primary and secondary frequencies and proper verbiage in accordance with the ATC handbook. Request a point of contact for resolution to real-world scenarios: speed, holding, approaches, local area operations, or anything else that may be impacted by your scenarios. Consider utilizing the company's ATC coordinator.

Preprogramming Triggers

If possible, you'll coordinate with the simulator engineers to preprogram weather, weights, fuels, malfunctions, and visual effects. Preprogramming nearly always works best because it keeps the instructor focused on the students. Additionally, it retains continuity within the scripts. For instance, you might ensure a weather cell is anchored so that it does not drift since crews may arrive to that area sooner or later, depending on their performance. Even a wind shear event on takeoff may require preprogramming or at least a scripted note to tell you when to activate the trigger.

The same applies to malfunctions designed to occur at a specified condition (speed, heading, altitude, etc.). For example, a takeoff go/no-go decision may require a distractor at a certain speed but must account for different flap selections and for the pilot who is slow on his callouts. In cases when the instructor must activate the malfunction, preprogramming on the instructor panel allows the push of a single button instead of searching. If there is no preprogramming available, ensure specific, detailed instructions are listed in the instructor's materials in order to minimize the time their focus is away from the crew.

Flight Papers and Documents to Support the Simulated World

Dispatchers and Performance groups can help create realistic products for your training. Request complete flight paper packages that include what a flight crew would normally receive. Consider leaving enough room for the crewmembers to add/remove fuel. Review all the NOTAMs for applicability to the objectives—modify and/or delete them as necessary. Determine whether the extensive list of NOTAMs is required. Modify the weather at the divert airfields to meet the objectives.

Review the takeoff, inflight, landing, and go-around performance data. Assess whether the data meets the needs of the objectives to include intersection takeoff, other runways, clutter, wet runway, flap selection, etc. Review the go-around performance for all the applicable airports and any optional runways. Assess special go-around procedures and performance as required. The training team should calculate landing distance for applicable varying airplane weights for the nonnormal landing conditions. Consider having the data arrive via simulated data communication or readily available from the instructor group, as a tear-off or via radio communications with the Dispatcher.

For smaller operators, simply generating a flight plan can be a major undertaking. There are several companies that may be willing to generate flight papers for training purposes. Developers may also use open source web applications to create flight plans themselves. Weather and NOTAM information can be obtained from NOAA sources and modified to match the LOFT scripting. Weight and balance information and maintenance logs can be generated for an actual aircraft, or perhaps simply created at a word processor using correct formats for the operator. Performance data will normally be generated in accordance with the operator's procedures, either from a manual or via a computerized system. When manuals are used, be sure to provide correct information to the facilitators so that they can verify the crew's answers.

Real World Changes That May Impact Your Scenario

Developers must also keep in mind that airspace, regulations, procedures, and policy change regularly. You will have to update routes of flight, flight plans, and supporting paperwork. Generating documents in a format that allows for easy editing after the fact can provide significant time savings. Alternatively, scripting the scenario to allow for changes to routes of flight can be an excellent solution when flight planning systems don't generate flexible formats.

A Note About LOE Versus LOFT

LOFT scenarios typically do not require the same length of time to develop as those for LOE. An LOE scenario may require a full year from initial determination/development thru activation date.

LOEs should have two or more script options. This allows for crewmembers who fail an evaluation to complete a second attempt without already having seen the scenario. This second option typically parallels the first script in its objectives and event sets, but would differ in the major technical event trigger and possibly involve different divert airfields. As with LOFT events, you may want to design your LOE scripts so that they are identical with the exception of the specific technical trigger. Employing this design returns more consistent data regarding crewmembers' actions and performance, at least up to the trigger. Identical scripting also reduces duplicate efforts of development compared to multiple different scripts that do not parallel one another.

Instructor Materials

Clear and easily navigable instructor guides make presenting the LOS and training the instructors much easier. The instructor material should be laid out so that it can be easily referenced in the dimly lit cab of a moving simulator. Ensure the print, font, and sentence structure is adequate for this setting. Clearly identify instructor actions as unique from ATC communications. Incorporating different font sizes, italics, color, heading styles, bookmarks, and hyperlinks will pay huge dividends in terms of making the LOS effective. Present any dialog that needs to be spoken in a clear readable manner and add phonetics if applicable. Try to standardize your approach to using these tools so that any future LOS events are more easily facilitated by the instructor group.

Developing Grade Forms

If you spent some time defining objectives and determining what data you want to collect during the analysis and design phases, grade forms should be easy to develop. The objectives you pulled from the JTA, which you are building your training around, are essentially the list of what should be on your grade sheet. Often, company documents will specify formats to be used and there is little to be done beyond inserting learning objectives into preformatted forms. In other cases, you'll have to develop the forms on your own. In any case, keep the end user in mind.

In addition to generating a list of what will be graded (the objectives), grading standards must also be established. What will be your range of performance? What will be a passing grade? When can a crew simply repeat a portion of the LOS, or when do they need additional training? The answers to these questions must account for a wide array of outcomes from the crew. Evaluators and management should be in on this discussion.

You'll have to develop separate grade sheets for each LOFT and for each LOE scenario option. Definitions must be provided for end-level proficiency, conceptual proficiency (cognitive skills), and for what constitutes completion of the flight segment. Additionally, it is probably wise to have leadership predetermine grading standards under certain conditions within specific event sets. You'll likely want to ask for guidance on defining things like what constitutes a "failure," a "repeat," or a "debrief-to-standards," among others.

You may want to create a supplement for the grade sheets that delineates and expounds the parameters used for specific grades. Grades are applied in different capacities to the event set: as an overall crew outcome, individual CRM, and technical objectives. These are assessed for the pilot flying and for the pilot monitoring (nonflying pilot). For event sets that were not performed to standards, you will need to have predetermined criteria that would result in a "Repeat" of the event set or criteria that requires a "Debriefing-to-standards" for each event.

Grade Forms Assist in Data Mining and Analysis

If forms are presented in a logical and easy to read format, you are likely to get good data back. If the forms are laid out poorly, or if you require the same information in multiple places, you are likely to get useless and conflicting information back.

As an example, one major carrier developed a form that required the user to fill out more than 100 lines of data. The form required use of a Likert Scale where events were graded from 1 to 5 with 1 being excellent and 5 being unsatisfactory. The form also required the user to indicate the number of times a particular item was scripted and the number of times the item was accomplished even though the answer was always once. Not surprisingly, the instructors quickly discovered that the quickest way to fill out this form was to mark every square on the form with a 1. One scripted attempt, 1 actual attempt, and a grade of 1 (excellent). Thus the norm became excellent when it should have been 3 (average). Try it for yourself, build a table with 100 rows and three columns and see how quickly you get tired.

Electronic Forms

Electronic grade sheets are a great product but only if the hosting device allows for easy input. One advantage of electronic grade sheets is that you don't have to employ data entry personnel. Additionally, the electronic device should also have some functionality built in that helps the team receive augmented input. For example, a grade of excellent should create a pop-up box for instructor comments; however, you want the instructor to also be able to not make a comment if he chooses. This would possibly encourage more accurate grading. For an unsatisfactory grade, you would want to force the instructor to input comments. Using the aforementioned 1 through 5 grading scale, a "5" would require comment, "1" would strongly desire (nearly require) comment, "2" and "4"desire comment, and "3" comment only if it would augment training or aid a follow-on training event.

If you want good data, you need to provide instructors and evaluators with good tools. This includes well laid out forms that flow in the same order as the event (by event set) are easy to understand and use, uncluttered, and offer reasonable space for adding comments. These rules will apply equally as well to electronic forms as they do to paper forms, however with electronic forms you may be more limited in design options depending on the program being used.

Beta Testing: Evaluate and Revise

Extensive testing produces a better product. This should involve Subject Matter Experts (SMEs), the development team, the instructor and evaluator cadre, fleet and or corporate leadership, line pilots, the FAA principal operations inspector (POI), engineers, and possibly any outsourced, sim-leasing groups.

Scripts will remain in a state of flux until all devices are tested with all scenarios and options. The development team should run the whole script in each of the devices, operating the device as an instructor or evaluator would. Each decision choice must be run to its conclusion. Record the elapsed time adjacent to the event sets. Annotate device quirks and record applicable lat/longs for repositions. Recording the process with a personal device may aid in later development. Once the scripts have all been run, coordinate with the Simulator Engineers to determine automation processes, as previously discussed.

Try to predict the timing of the students as they progress through the script. Remember that the line pilots are not prebiased and will require more time to complete a task than the development team or the instructor cadre. This timing could be significantly different from trial runs with SMEs and other beta testers. Time planned in the device must account for these differences.

You'll probably test fly your scenario multiple times. In the beginning, you'll want to verify that the airports are present in the simulator and that the visual depictions and navigation databases meet your needs. As you firm up the script, you'll want to test fly the scenario again. Using seasoned instructors or evaluators as a crew can be a good technique to get a set of fresh eyes on the scenario and identify any weaknesses or errors. Frequently, these crews will come up with solutions that you had not anticipated necessitating development of additional scripting and documentation. Both the operators of the devices and the pilots should contribute to the improvements of the scripts and the operations of the devices as well as critique the grade sheets. At some point, invite the FAA, they are the approving authority and must feel confident in the product.

You'll look for design flaws such as errors in the scripting, gaps in initial instructor training, or areas where the simulators do not support the scenario. You'll also determine the corrective action to be taken. Perhaps your organization will eventually have instructors and evaluators receive some of their annual training using a new scenario. This process allows this group to get training that they have not previously seen while at the same time providing a small group trial for the LOS to ensure that it works well.

The point of beta testing is to find the flaws that inevitably exist no matter how diligent you have been. Let's say you found (or produced) and modified a great set of flight papers. You rewrote the NOTAMs and deleted all the unnecessary and superfluous material. Then, just before turning on your script, you and the team conclude that a different divert airfield is better. So, you obtain new flight papers realizing all the meticulous work won't be used this time.

Or, perhaps you'll find that one particular device is a limiting factor. For example, scripted ATC progressive taxiing could be required because a particular device's visual system does not have the fidelity to allow the student to reliably taxi. You might have to increase the simulator's displayed runway visual range (RVR), while still reporting it as a lower value that is in keeping with your script. This kind of modification would propagate to all devices so that continuity is retained for all students. Maybe, too, that limiting device would need to be restricted from certain training so that the other devices are optimized.

Paperwork Delivery

The materials all have to be delivered to their various destinations. You'll have to ensure crewmember paperwork prints correctly on all printers or personal devices. Email the products via both work and personal email accounts to varying computers to ensure all files correctly open and present. Download your products from a server and open them on the destination sources, confirming that the sources have the same security and profile as the line pilot.

Consider FAA and Management Requirements

Once the Development team is satisfied with the review, complete a run through of the script with management. Modify the scripts as necessary per management's request. Repeat the entire processes as necessary to account for the changes to the scripts. Once the final review is completed, coordinate with the management to arrange a meeting and presentation with the FAA. You will present, as a minimum, an overview of the Event Sets, the Triggers, main CRM objective per event set, expected Crewmember and ATC communications, distractors, and the main training objective of the script. You will present and discuss the technical trigger that will instigate the main CRM objective. Be prepared to address successful and unsuccessful criteria and how those repeats/debriefs will be addressed.

Line Pilot Review

Once the instructor and evaluator cadre expresses their confidence in the product, the time has come to test the scripts with regular, nonbriefed line pilots. The FAA will be invited and expected to ride along on at least one line pilot review. Distribute validation assessment forms to both the instructor and line pilots. This form delineates the objectives of the review flights and requires all members to submit their assessment, input, and suggestions. The line pilots are assessing realism as it applies to city-pairs, divert airfields, weather forecasts, line operation flow, etc. Each script scenario must be tested a minimum of two times with a separate line paired crew; do not use the same line crew members for more than one scripted scenario—they would have biases. These tests do not require a review of each divert option, rather a review of each scenario option. The goal here is to finalize the scripts for realism and for accuracy. At some time during the review process, the development team submits to the FAA POI a request to approve the scripts or at least any script that is fully functional.

10.3.4   Implementation

(Fig. 10.7)

This is the phase where you take your neatly produced materials, schedules, and plans and make it a daily reality. You're now going to take it live to your students, your instructors, your management, and the FAA on a daily and continuing basis. You'll mass produce the course materials and build the

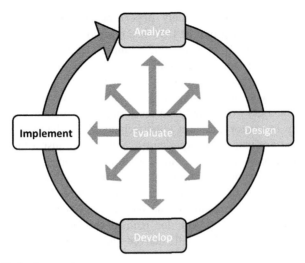

FIGURE 10.7   Implementation.

organization that will sustain the project in the long term. This is where you'll train the trainer, and ensure that the course is delivering what you intended.

Organizational Expectations

As the developer, you'll be responsible for ensuring that your LOS program is meeting the expectations of stakeholders. Continuous communication and status reporting will most likely be required regarding instructor and evaluator training and currency, simulator functionality, and classroom resources and courseware. Again, a checklist can be helpful here and you can provide regular status updates to stakeholders who are likely to include instructors, evaluators, management, FAA POI, simulator techs, classroom resource managers, union representatives, and line pilots.

Train the Trainer

Don't be fooled into thinking that just because you scripted it, everyone will understand what you are trying to achieve. You will likely need to bring instructors and evaluators in for a classroom session where you step them through the scenario and the likely solutions. You'll want to ensure that instructors and evaluators understand the learning objectives of the scenario as well as how to present the scenario.

Having a checklist available can be helpful because the procedures for training the trainer are likely to be the same each time you roll out a new scenario and you'll want to keep track of lessons learned. The degree of training required will vary widely depending on the experience of the instructor and evaluator group. If LOS is a new concept within the organization, then you will likely need to conduct more classroom training and provide some simulator training sessions where the instructors and evaluators can participate either as an observer or crewmember.

Similarly, if you are training a new instructor, having that individual observe several LOS events and then teach under instruction with an experienced backup instructor can be a good technique. On the other hand, if the instructors and evaluators are experienced, and you are just rolling out a new LOS, you be able to simply provide a briefing to them to get them ready. Some carriers will time the rollout of continuing training to coincide with required annual training for instructors and evaluators. This allows instructors to get a recurrent training profile they haven't seen before, creates an opportunity to check the profile for realism and errors, and provides an opportunity for those who will deliver the profile to actually fly it themselves.

The overview of the LOS is discussed and each Event Set is reviewed to ensure there are no misunderstandings over the goals and objectives. The grade sheets and accompanying supplement are explained in detail; evaluators are reminded that they must comply with the agreed upon standards. Discuss in detail the criteria for success and the required processes for unsatisfactory event sets and for an overall unsatisfactory evaluation. Pay particular attention to any limitations associated with the simulators and how you want the instructors to work around those limitations. You'll also want to ensure instructors and evaluators understand the observable behaviors that should be displayed and what the completion standards are for the LOS. Consider recording this training so that future instructors can watch the training rather than repeating it.

In addition to covering the learning objectives of the LOS, there are some general topics that will be always appropriate for additional conversation with instructors. These basically revolve around the fundamentals of LOS:

- LOS events should be conducted in real time. Avoid using speed multipliers or position freeze. The exception here is when simulating long haul flights.
- For LOE make the event as realistic as possible. Don't interject yourself. You aren't really there. Use headsets, radios, proper ATC communication procedures and full taxi routes. You can answer questions when queried as ATC, Dispatch, Maintenance Control, etc. but don't offer solutions. Role play realistically. Try to provide the information and ask the questions that flight attendants and ATC would really require. Be professional and avoid shortcuts. If a procedure is required in the airplane, then do it in the LOE.

- In LOFT the instructor may provide input to the crew, but most learning is intended to occur via facilitated debrief after the event has concluded as opposed to on the spot via immediate debriefings.

Training the Debrief

After the event, instructors and evaluators will provide a facilitated debrief. Ensure instructors and evaluators are comfortable with the concept that in LOS there is no right solution, the crew determines the outcome and the debrief focuses on the process. Crews should be helped to reconstruct the event, noting what worked well and what did not. The instructor or evaluator should primarily ask questions rather than provide answers. For example, "What happened to the engine during start? What is the SOP for that condition? What did the PF/PM do there?" Instructors and evaluators should always attempt to depersonalize the debrief. This can be accomplished by talking in the third person. A debrief form can help instructors to provide some structure here.

Training the Grade Forms

You'll want to review your LOFT grading forms with instructors under training. Your goal here is to ensure the instructors and evaluators provide feedback in a format that is consistent with your grading scales and that the comments are relevant and usable. Generally, comments will hold far more value than actual grades. Ensure instructors and evaluators understand this. For example, a crew who fails to run a certain checklist might reasonably have this error graded as a problem with checklists, situational awareness, workload management, or some combination of the three depending on who views the event. In this scenario, the comments will ultimately be far more useful to the person who later analyzes grade forms than the specific grades.

LOS Development as a Driver for Procedural Quality

As you were producing the LOS, it is likely that you reviewed the specific technical objectives in the aircraft flight manual (AFM) and sought guidance from the airline's flight operations manual (FOM). You will likely find errors and room for improvement in both those documents. Is there a procedure that all your colleagues think is unnecessarily complex? Your review provides a good opportunity for the organization to improve. Compare and contrast the company's FOM against the AFM. Assess whether the two manuals conflict with one another or with the training objectives. This may be an opportunity to update manuals as a by-product of the LOFT and LOE development process.

10.3.5   Evaluation

(Fig. 10.8)

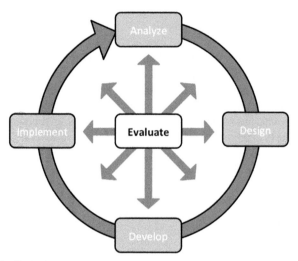

FIGURE 10.8   Evaluation.

AQP is a data-driven process and the Evaluation phase is where you will find out if your ISD model is working or not. The entire purpose of your effort to this point has been to build a process that attempts to meet a training need. The purpose of evaluation is to objectively determine whether or not that need is being met. Objective determinations require data collection and data analysis. That is what we'll tackle next.

With good data you can assess effectiveness of the training, the performance of individual students, and the effectiveness of instructors and evaluators. It can also be used to refine and modify the training so that it continues to meet changing needs.

Data Collection

LOS events provide an opportunity to collect a lot of data on your crews, training programs, and procedures. However, collecting data takes time away from the instructor and evaluator's monitoring time. When the instructor or evaluator is taking notes, he's not watching the crew or running the simulator scenario. As you think about what data you want to collect, you need to decide what you want to do with the data and what you are capable of analyzing. If your goal is simply to document completion of training, you don't need to grade every aspect of a flight. On the other hand, if your organization has robust capabilities for data analysis and you can collect the information electronically to ensure clean data, then you may want to collect more information.

You should decide early on what you intend to do with the data you collect. If you plan to revise your scenarios based on feedback from the facilitators and evaluators, then you will want enough information to update the scenario and possibly the training program that precedes the scenario. On the other hand, if you simply want to expose your crews to a new procedure, then your needs can be limited to determining whether or not the demonstration was complete.

A common methodology for LOS data collection is to utilize Likert Scales in combination with reason codes and comments to grade each event set. There is no set standard for a Likert Scale, however a minimum of 5 grades is considered preferable and scales with more than 7 grades have been shown to be unreliable. Thus your scale could be 1 through 5 or A through F or Well Above Average to Well Below Average. The important thing here is that instructors and evaluators understand the scales and apply them consistently. Each event set should include both a technical grade on this scale and a CRM grade on this scale. Commonly used reason codes for technical grades include Procedural Knowledge, Aircraft Control, and Autoflight. You can add more as needed, but try to keep them consistent over time. CRM codes will usually address the CRM skills used within your organizational CRM model such as Leadership, Communication, Resource Management, Workload Management, Situational Awareness, and Decision-Making. You should also include a place for instructors and evaluators to provide feedback on the LOFT itself, this will help you maintain the LOFT over time as departures and arrivals change names and airways are modified. You may also wish to subcategorize crews based on time in type, base, time of day the event was conducted, simulator used, or a variety of other factors that would help isolate trends, which ultimately makes it easier to address them.

Data Analysis

The basis for sound evaluation is accurate collection and analysis of training data and line operational safety data. It is possible to collect large volumes of data, or relatively little data. In the design phase you hopefully gave some thought to your data collection and analysis methodologies. Now, you have to dig into the data and do your analysis. Your data analyst (possibly you) should be trained at this point and you should have a good software package in place. Modern statistical software is not particularly expensive and is well within reach for even the smallest organizations.

Proper training for your analyst is important. A flawed methodology for analyzing data can result in misinterpreting your data and mislead you to taking incorrect actions regarding your training programs. For example, when event sets are graded with a Likert Scale that has a range of 1 through 5 it can be tempting to treat the data as a collection of integers and find a mean grade for the event set, say 2.5, and then compare this average over time. However, when you consider that this scale is really just ordinal and could equally have been Well Above Average through Well Below Average you'll see that the data does not represent integers at all and that a mean is the wrong statistical tool to use. As an extreme example, imagine an event set where half the pilots were graded well below average and the other half were graded well above average. Clearly there is a problem for one half of the pilots, but the mean for this event set is average and no problem is indicated using this tool. For the same reason, standard deviations and any parametric analysis based on the normal distribution will also be invalid approaches.

A better approach might involve one where you compare the change in the distribution of grades over time to determine performance levels and changes in performance levels. This is accomplished with non parametric procedures based on rank, median, or range. Tabulations, frequencies, contingency tables, and chi-squared statistics are also valid methodologies for analyzing Likert Scale data. (Allen & Seaman, 2007) There are many open source resources available for help with selecting appropriate statistical analysis of your data. Time spent learning the ins and outs of what you really want to do with the numbers you'll be harvesting, is well spent and pays dividends in streamlining your process.

For those organizations that lack the capability to analyze data, local universities frequently have graduate students who need a real-world project to work on. Graduate students are typically free and come with the added benefit of supervision from a faculty member. Alternatively, developers or managers can often audit a statistics class at a local junior college, university, graduate school, or even online and obtain the necessary skills to do data analysis in just a few months. Sadly, while most aviation organizations collect huge amounts of data, the ability to effectively analyze data is a skill that is lacking.

Let's assume you're trained. So what do you look at? Start with summarizing the available data. You know what type of data you have and your first task is to look for changes and trends. Is any event set performing exceptionally well or poorly? If so, has this change persisted over time or is it a relatively new event? You'll also want to check that any changes you observe are statistically significant. Keep in mind that minor changes may just be due to statistical noise or the result of taking different samples from quarter to quarter and you don't want to look for problems where none exist.

If you believe you've identified an issue your next task is to look at individual grade forms, comments, and reason codes. These may be presented in a report from a grading database or you may have to read the actual forms depending on how your organization collects data. If your data analyst is not a pilot, you'll want to have a pilot participate in the process at this point. As you review the comments you'll notice trends that appear. In our example earlier regarding completing a checklist, we noted that one instructor may categorize this as an issue related to checklist management, while another may identify it as workload management and still another as situational awareness. In reading comments you'll discover if there is a common theme such as crews consistently missing the same checklist. It is here that your knowledge of the operation comes into play. You'll have to asses why this is happening. Some reasons could include poor training regarding checklist use, poorly designed or labeled checklists, or higher priorities within the scenario that preclude the checklist being run at that time. You'll also want to recommend corrective actions. These might include rewording the checklist, additional training regarding checklist procedures, or adding CRM tools that help crews review what has happened in the flight to that point.

After repeating this process for each event set you'll want to put your results in writing. A short report with a consistent format will be useful for analyzing your LOS over time. As changes occur within your organization you'll want to review performance from previous periods relative to what is currently happening. You'll also need to document this analysis as part of most quality control programs. Reviewing these reports with the FAA or other oversight authorities on a regular basis will satisfy regulatory requirements but also help you to improve your training programs over time.

10.4 CUSTOMIZING LOS PRODUCTION FOR DIFFERENT ORGANIZATIONS

Now that we have described a complete process for developing LOS, you may be wishing, for instance, that we had put Beta Testing under Development or Design, rather than inside Implementation. Or perhaps you'd prefer to be in contact with resource providers as you are defining objectives, rather than waiting. Well, that's completely fine! The order of these steps isn't really as important as making sure you have a process for your organization that ensures that they get done or are at least considered.

In the research arena, for example, grade sheets aren't necessarily needed because the students aren't really even students. They are test subjects who are being observed. But, this means that instead of grading criteria, you are now designing the LOS scenario to produce experimental conditions that need to be consistently replicated. So, an observation guide for researchers replaces the grade sheet, and grading standards are replaced by adherence to experimental conditions. You'll still gather data and try to define interrater reliability as you might in a training environment, but now it is used to report experimental findings. The system for constructing the LOS still holds true. Try to follow or consider using the ADDIE model, and you shouldn't go too far wrong.

For the developer in a small organization, you may not have some of the resources we have described. At a major airline you can call dispatch and ask them to generate a fictitious flight plan for you and then deliver 10 copies. When you are a one-person shop, you will spend some time searching for resources or advocating for subscriptions to flight planning services. You may spend an afternoon on the web researching preferred routing on an FAA website, then populating a flight log that you find in another web tool with fuel burns and times between fixes. When you go on line flights, your flight papers (maintenance, weather, and flight plan) will be valuable relics you'll want to save. You'll refer to them for formatting and content as you produce your own facsimiles of the real thing. Your timeline will be longer than a large organization's as well, because you wont have large numbers of people to throw at some of the problems. Some steps in the process wont be possible due to lack of resources. That's when you look at the ideal process, and make the best educated guess that you can, taking your experience and the outcome into account.

10.5   AN ARGUMENT IN FAVOR OF LOS AS A CONTINUED, VALUABLE TRAINING STRATEGY

There is certainly an economic and a safety argument for high fidelity simulation in flight training, but simulation does not necessarily need to incorporate a realistic mission environment. LOS has been voluntary. Are there still training advantages to LOS over the former, part-task, "dial-a-disaster" approach that had a narrow focus on technical skills?

Without the context of the complete mission, leadership, goal setting, decision-making, and other important team skills cannot be trained. By setting training in a real-world flight situation, crews can practice the actual team skills they will need and use on the line. The technical skills that need to be trained and evaluated are still present, but are now practiced in the fluid, complex setting where they will be used instead of an artificially narrow environment.

In this way, LOS continues to emphasize training of both team and technical skills simultaneously, because these skills must also be used concurrently in the actual work that pilots do. CRM skills are practiced and evaluated concurrently with requisite technical skills rather than performing each in isolation. A presented problem does not simply go away, it must be worked in sequence and in parallel with other challenges, as in actual flight. LOS becomes a true compliment to, and allows reinforcement of, the CRM skills that are now part of the airline pilot's toolbox.

10.5.1   The Paradox of Success

Today, CRM has become imbedded in, and is a seamless part of, training and aviation culture. We must remember though, that team training like

CRM works best when it is theory driven and focused on teaching core competencies with realistic practice opportunities (Salas & Cannon-Bowers, 2001). Indeed, LOS is a proven way to provide that practice, and to help transfer these skills to actual line operation (Helmreich et al., 1999).

The very success of LOS and CRM has perhaps begun to promote the assumption that these team skills were simply always there without the training and enculturation of a generation of pilots who are now passing those gains along. Proper LOS design and implementation is a labor-intensive process. It requires valuable resources, and it may be tempting for new designers to discount the relevance of LOS in contemporary training programs.

Recent high-profile accidents and incidents support the opposite view: that CRM team skills and LOS are as relevant now as in the past. The research indicates that these skills and attitudes are indeed perishable (Helmreich et al., 1999). LOS is necessary to maintain the current high state of competency in both team and technical skills and to combat natural cognitive biases.

The very essence of LOS is the opportunity for combined practice of CRM and technical skills. Crews that train to only solve a very specific set of problems associated with old-style, "dial-a-disaster" simulator training will likely not have the flexibility required to solve complex problems. As part of the academic training associated with the LOS, either in a prebrief or during classroom training, crews are given tools to help them solve problems in flight. The LOS then affords them real-world practice in using these tools. TEM and VVM are two of the fairly recent CRM concepts that can have been largely introduced and put into practice through briefing and training during LOS opportunities.

The specifics of any tool or model are less important than the idea that crews need to learn processes for handling inflight problems. These processes can then be applied to a wide range of issues they may encounter. Examples of the success of this approach are many, but it might be instructive to review two of them as CRM and LOS success case studies.

Consider UAL 232, the now famous case of Captain Al Haynes' DC-10 which suffered a catastrophic, uncontained engine failure and lost all hydraulics in 1989. Because McDonnell Douglas considered this malfunction impossible, there was no procedure for it. Captain Haynes utilized all his available resources including a deadheading pilot to wrestle the uncontrollable airplane to the airport at Sioux City, Iowa. One hundred eighty-five of the 296 people on board survived what was deemed by most experts to be a completely unsurvivable situation.

More recently, Captain Chesley Sullenberger landed his A320 on the Hudson River after a series of bird strikes crippled both engines over the middle of one of the most densely populated places on the planet. This "Miracle on the Hudson," as it is now known, is directly attributable to the exemplary teamwork and sound decision-making of Captain Sullenberger, his First Officer Jeff Skiles, and the rest of their crew. Had the leadership, decision-making, situation awareness, and other CRM skills exhibited that day not been present on that flight, the aircraft may never have had a chance to reach the point over the Hudson where superior airmanship could then be utilized to save the day.

Neither of these scenarios were part of the air carrier's qualification course. These pilots utilized the CRM and technical skills they practiced in LOS events to solve problems they'd never even considered before they were faced with them in the real world.

REFERENCES

Allen, I. E., & Seaman, C. A. (2007). Likert scales and data analyses. *Quality Progress, 40*(7), 64.

Dick, W., & Carey, L. (1990). *The systematic design of instruction (3rd ed.).* Glenview, IL: Scott, Foresman; Harper Collins.

FAA. (2015). *FAA Advisory Circular 120-35D, Flightcrew Member Line Operational Simulations: Line-Oriented Flight Training, Special Purpose Operational Training, Line Operational Evaluation.* USGPO.

FAA. (2017). *FAA Advisory Circular 120-54A, Advanced Qualification Program.* USGPO.

Helmreich, R., Merritt, A., & Wilhelm, J. (1999). The evolution of crew resource management training in commercial aviation. *International Journal of Aviation Psychology, 9*(1), 19−32.

Kemp, J. E. (1985). *The instructional design process.* New York: Harper & Row.

Lauber, J., & Foushee, H. (1981a). *Guidelines for line-oriented flight training, Vol. 1.* Moffett Field, California: NASA: NASA Ames Research Center.

Lauber, J. K., & Foushee, H. C. (1981b). *Guidelines for line-oriented flight training, Vol. 2.* Moffett Field, California: NASA: NASA Ames Research Center.

Mager, R. (1984). *Preparing instructional objectives, revised 2nd ed.* Belmont, CA: Lake Publishing Company.

Molenda, M. (2003). In search of the elusive ADDIE model. *Performance Improvement, 42*(5), 34−36.

NTSB. (1973). *Aircraft Accident Report NTSB - AAR - 73 - 3 Delta Air Lines, Inc., McDonnell Douglas, Dc-9-14, March 13, 1973.* Washington, DC: National Transportation Safety Board.

Page, R. (2000). *A brief history of flight simulation.* SimTecT 2000 Proceedings (pp. 11−17). Lindfield, Australia: Simulation Industry Association of Australia.

Salas, E., & Cannon-Bowers, J. (2001). The science of training: A decade of progress. *Annual Review of Psychology, 52*(1), 471−499.

Seamster, T., Hamman, W., & Edens, E. (1995). Specification of observable behaviors within LOE/LOFT event sets. In R. Jensen (Ed.), *Proceedings of the 8th International Symposium on Aviation Psychology* (pp. 663−668). Columbus, OH: The Ohio State University Press.

FURTHER READING

FAA. (2004). *FAA Advisory Circular 120-51E, Crew Resource Management Training.* USGPO.

George, F. (2016, 03 24). Cockpit Cognitive Biases Can Cause Real Trouble. Retrieved 08 06, 2017, from BCA Business & Commercial Aviation, AviationWeek. com.: http://aviation-week.com/bca/cockpit-cognitive-biases-can-cause-real-trouble.

Chapter 11

Line Operations Simulation Development Tools

Michael Curtis and Florian Jentsch
University of Central Florida, Orlando, FL, United States

INTRODUCTION

On February 12, 2009, Colgan Air flight 3407 crashed into a residential neighborhood in Buffalo, New York, killing all passengers aboard and one person on the ground. By any measure of flight experience, the crew involved was new to their respective flight roles. Given this, the accident is no less tragic, but it is logical that difficult flight conditions might hinder an inexperienced crew. On June 1, 1999, American Airlines flight 1420 touched down in Little Rock, Arkansas, fast and long on the runway. This subsequently resulted in the aircraft leaving the paved landing surface, crashing into nearby approach lights. The crash and resulting fire caused 11 casualties including the captain, and numerous additional injuries. In contrast to the Colgan tragedy, the crew involved in this accident included one of the most senior pilots at the airline's Chicago O'Hare hub (Dismukes, Berman, & Loukopoulos, 2007). The circumstances leading up to both of these catastrophic outcomes were very different, but based on National Transportation Safety Board (NTSB) investigations they are bound by a common thread, insufficient training.

To categorize one of the mitigating factors in these accidents as insufficient training could be misleading, however. The knee jerk reaction to these reports is to add a component to training that specifically addresses the problem. For example, in response to the Little Rock accident, a specific flight training module focused on reverse thrust settings in slippery runway conditions might be the resulting recommendation. This, however, does not account for the myriad of other, very specific, aircraft settings that differ in conditions that may also be inadequately addressed in training. In a perfect world there would be unlimited time and money to dedicate to providing pilots with the most comprehensive training that exposes each trainee to every known pilot error imaginable. However, in reality, training time is

Crew Resource Management. DOI: https://doi.org/10.1016/B978-0-12-812995-1.00011-7

limited. In practice, the solution seems simple; improve pilot training and assessment—problem solved. Unfortunately, given the complexity of aircraft operation, the solution is more complex.

Current training methods, such as crew resource management (CRM[1]) training, in combination with some more traditional methods have been found to produce exceedingly positive training outcomes for pilots. The problem with these training methods is not that they do not cover every maneuver in flight, no training program can. Instead, the issue is the complexity of designing such a training program, which makes it difficult for airlines to keep current reliable training programs going. This is not a commentary on either airline mentioned in the above examples, but instead, these examples serve to emphasize the importance of developing a comprehensive training program that continues throughout a pilot's career.

The objectives of flight training can be separated into two general functions. These are (1) to provide sufficient skill to successfully execute all phases of flight and (2) to prepare pilots to adapt to the dynamic and sometimes unexpected nature of flight. Although this is a simplistic breakdown of what comprises aviation training, it encompasses everything from the technical skill required to operate the aircraft to the interpersonal CRM skills that improve team communication, leadership, and decision-making. Line operations simulations (LOS) provide the most effective, currently available, platform for this in aviation training.

Due to the fact that LOS development is a challenging task for airline training departments, we will focus on areas where the process can be made more efficient. In the following chapter we will discuss the process of LOS development and illustrate how specific tools can be used to supplement the development process. Before discussing development, we will first provide a brief introduction on flight training, and more specifically, discuss the use of LOS to accomplish flight training goals.

11.1 FLIGHT TRAINING

Although pilots are heavily trained on both normal and abnormal flight conditions in initial training, throughout a pilot's career flight experience will vary. These experiences will shape how an individual reacts in certain situations. In some cases, this may result in the development of behaviors that do not work in all flight conditions. This could be related to weather conditions, aircraft functionality, or even occurrences in the cabin. For example, the highly experienced

---

1. In this chapter, we use CRM as the general representation of a number of teamwork related training and evaluation concepts in aviation, such as threat and error management (TEM) and risk & resource management (see FAA Advisory Circular AC 120-35D, 2015a, for further definitions).

flight crew, in the Little Rock accident discussed earlier, faced a combination of several conditions resulting in a fast, long landing onto a slippery runway. Improper reverse thrust settings led to loss of control and subsequent crash. The NTSB suggested that despite the flight crew's extensive experience, they may not have received adequate training on reverse thrust on a wet landing surface (Dismukes et al., 2007). This helps illustrate the importance of varied and continuous training throughout a pilot's career.

A majority of the flights that a pilot will experience over their career fall into the category of routine flight, where practiced procedure will be sufficient for safe operations. This, unfortunately, does not adequately prepare a pilot to react to ambiguous and dynamic situations which infrequently arise in the cockpit. It is impractical to try to train individuals to learn every possible known combination of events that could occur due to the sheer volume of training that would be required. In most cases, in less than a year's time, training decrement begins to occur especially for rarely used flight skills (Arthur, Bennett, Stanush, & McNelly, 1998; Childs & Spears, 1986). This is not to mention the propensity for new, previously unexperienced (or unreported), events to occur. In addition to varying flight experience, technological advances and organizational shifts will result in changes over the course of a pilot's career which also will require training. As a result, aviation requires continual training to maintain operational know-how in less frequently occurring situations.

Currently used experience-based training methods have been widely accepted and generally found to enhance previous training techniques. The intention of these methodologies is to provide pilots with simulated experience that would closely match what is required on the line. The idea is based on research in recognition-primed decision-making (Klein, 2008) which suggests that varying experiences drive mastery of complex skills. That is, the more experiences from which an individual has to draw from memory, the better equipped they are for completion of a task in a variety of situations. In many cases, pilots encounter similar flight conditions on a daily basis. This helps reinforcement of general flight skill, but does little for infrequently occurring events.

11.1.1   Line Operational Simulations

Although there is still a substantial class lecture aspect to flight training, the most important learning is gained through flight experience. In practice, actually flying an aircraft is logically the best way to achieve this. Unfortunately, it is impractical to provide extensive in-flight training to pilots. Operation cost, increasingly congested airspace and safety are among the primary reasons why in-flight training is limited to the final phase of training before pilots join line operations. Because of this, the next best option is using computer-generated simulations of flight, which consist primarily of simulated flight in high-fidelity motion simulations housed at specific training facilities. Since the cost for these types of simulations is still relatively high, there are a limited number of available simulators running nearly continuously to accommodate the high volume of training sessions needed. As a result, it is imperative that simulator sessions provide maximal flight realism and optimized experience. Simply providing operators with free flight simulator sessions does not ensure exposure to all relevant training goals and is subsequently inefficient use of simulator time. Instead, sessions should incorporate preplanned scenarios that build from what was learned in classroom lectures and provide practice executing important operations in a realistic cockpit environment. The most practical form of training currently in use which provides a platform for what is described above is accomplished through the development of LOS.

LOS has been used to describe the development of realistic flight scenarios for use in any simulator training event (Chidester, 1993). More specifically, LOS refers to a number of similar methods of flight training and evaluation that reproduce gate-to-gate operations in a simulated environment (FAA, 2015a). Unlike part-task trainers, the main purpose of LOS-based training is not to provide specific instruction on an individual aspect of flight, but instead to provide experience with combining technical and CRM skills into line operations. Beyond the logistical aspects, such as technological requirements, supplemental material (i.e., preflight paperwork, checklists, etc.), and training department involvement, the driving force in LOS effectiveness is scenario development.

The scenario- or simulation-based training (SBT) method that LOS utilizes is widely used in a number of domains including military, medicine, and aviation applications (Salas et al., 2008; Salas, Priest, Wilson, & Burke, 2006a). The crux of SBT is in providing a platform for trainees to gain experience through realistic task environment simulation. Instead of isolating individual skill sets, SBT provides a training context where an individual must integrate skills to achieve a realistic simulation of the real-world task. This is accomplished through the use of embedded events, within a scenario, that are designed to specifically elicit certain behaviors (Salas et al., 2006a). Beyond the experiential learning benefits associated with SBT, it also provides an effective means for observation and evaluation of target skills.

Primarily, LOS-based programs are focused on one of two things, training or evaluation. In the following sections we will briefly describe the main ways that LOS is used in an aviation setting. This will provide context for discussion on the critical features that must be focused on in the LOS development process.

11.1.2 Types of LOS

Historically, the Federal Aviation Administration (FAA) Advanced Qualification Program (AQP) was the program where several training and evaluation programs characterized as LOS gained support (Birnbach & Longridge, 1993). Two of them, line oriented flight training (LOFT) and specific operational training (SPOT), are methods of training, while a third, line operation evaluation (LOE), is used to assess pilot mastery of training objectives (FAA, 2015a). Although each is based on the developmental ideals behind SBT, the intended purpose of each differs slightly.

LOS for Training

Both LOFT and SPOT are methods intended to provide a training platform in which individuals can practice technical and CRM skills without fear of negative consequences, especially in the event of a failure to complete a flight within acceptable safety parameters. LOFT is a full gate-to-gate simulator scenario intended to provide flight experience including simulation of all preflight, in-flight, and postflight events. It is used both for qualification and recurrent training purposes. This includes everything from completion of preparations, paperwork, communication with air traffic control and company facilities, and performing routine procedures for a normal flight (Chidester, 1993). LOFT training is regarded as one of the most effective forms of incorporating technical and CRM skills in training (e.g., Barshi, 2015; Helmreich, Wilhelm, Kello, Taggart, & Butler, 1991; Jensen, 1989). The inclusion of CRM in training has been found to elicit a positive change in attitude and behavior (Helmreich & Foushee, 1993).

SPOT is intended to address more specific training objectives. Although in some cases this involves full flight simulation similar to LOFT, more often SPOT is made up of partial flight segments. This provides trainers with the flexibility to attend to areas of specific training needs, efficiently. This is especially useful when new technologies are introduced in the cockpit. For instance, if a new glideslope indication display is being introduced into a cockpit, that technology is really only useful in approach and landing phases. SPOT is also useful if a trainee needs remediation on CRM skill in a specific phase of flight. Because time is often a constraint for pilots and trainers alike, it is more efficient to provide abbreviated flight simulations to address these specific areas.

Although similar, SPOT and LOFT are not interchangeable training methods (Butler, 1993). Outside of the obvious potential differences in length and depth of scenarios, training personnel involvement also varies. The role of the instructor in LOFT is to take on the role of noncockpit personnel during the flight, providing radio calls or cabin crew interactions throughout the flight. In fact, FAA advisory circular 120-35D (FAA, 2015a) recommends that instructors avoid interrupting LOFT scenarios to provide instruction. By withholding instructional feedback in flight, LOFT scenarios can capitalize on the benefits of pilot self-realization through decision-making and crew coordination (Helmreich & Foushee, 1993). In contrast, SPOT is more dependent on the objectives of the specific training. In some cases this allows for instructors to intervene in a scenario and provide feedback.

Depending on the objective of training, LOFT and SPOT both can provide beneficial training outcomes. Whether geared toward a specific training goal or to overall flight proficiency training, these methods provide a platform in which simulated flight is optimized to most closely mimic flight conditions. By providing a no jeopardy exposure to full flight scenarios, these types of training allow for flight crews to test out numerous strategies for both technical and CRM skill in the cockpit. All in all, both of these methods rely on the development of scenarios that give practice in both normal and abnormal flight conditions. In addition to being used for training purposes, LOS can also effectively be used as an evaluation tool. In the following section, we will briefly describe the LOE before further discussing LOS development in general.

LOS for Performance Evaluation

Another similar application of LOS is through performance evaluation. LOEs assess pilot proficiency on targeted skills deemed relevant to overall flight safety. In execution, LOE is very similar to LOFT. Instructors do not interfere with the flight crew as they conduct a realistic gate-to-gate simulation. Where LOE differs is that the observation and assessment of performance can influence pilot career advancement. As well as developing scenarios that address specific skills, for LOE valid evaluation of those skills is very important. Due to the safety concerns in aviation, there is low tolerance for inconsistent measures of performance, to be used to help dictate a pilot's fate. In light of this, additional care must be taken to ensure that assessment is consistent and fair across flight crews being evaluated.

Summary of LOS Types

As illustrated above and documented in FAA AC 120-35D (FAA, 2015a), LOS has become a standard methodology for training and evaluation in aviation. LOFT and SPOT are both training implementations that are heavily dependent on scenarios that provide flight experience as close to what one would experience on the line without being in the aircraft. The goal of these is to provide a means of practicing both technical and CRM skills in observable event sets. Similar to these two training methods, LOE is the evaluation version of LOS. Instead of providing a platform for practice, the LOE is intended to evaluate performance on technical and CRM skills. Since the LOE is used to make decisions on whether or not a trainee is capable of safely operating an aircraft, it is important to develop consistent measures of performance from scenarios. As AQP becomes more widespread among airlines, the demand for these types of LOS applications will increase. Although we outlined the primary applications of LOS, improving the development process may lend LOS to additional applications beneficial for training and evaluation. In the next section we will discuss the process of developing scenarios, including discussion on the numerous ways that make LOS development challenging without the aid of development tools.

11.2 DEVELOPING LOS SCENARIOS

Developing LOS scenarios requires a thorough process in which attention to detail is crucial to achieving training or evaluation goals. The success of LOS development is contingent on construction of scenarios that fulfill these training or evaluation goals. Due to the range of technical and CRM skills that occur in various phases of flight, it is not sufficient to develop a general scenario where behaviors might be observed. Instead, since the scenario is generally comprised of an entire flight from cockpit entry to cockpit exit, simply dictating a handful of malfunctions during the course of the flight does not guarantee practice with specific skills. For LOS to be effective, the wide variety of tasks, environmental variables, and possible interactions in a given flight should be considered. In order to accomplish this, LOS developers break the overall scenario into smaller parts or events. Event sets are smaller segments of the scenario in which a specific event is triggered to elicit target behaviors. The event-based approach to training (EBAT) is intended to initiate opportunities for practice or evaluation of target skill sets (Fowlkes, Dwyer, Oser, & Salas, 1998). By using event sets, LOS developers can build larger scenarios that target multiple skill sets in different phases of flight.

The LOS development process has been described in a number of ways. The first step in this process is identifying the technical and CRM skills that need to be addressed and identifying aviation events that occur which can elicit demonstrations of these skills. Following the identification step, the information gathered must be formulated into logical event sequences and evaluated by subject matter experts for accuracy and effectiveness. After this has been accomplished and all required approvals have been acquired, instructor preparation documents and LOS materials can be developed. Prior to widespread use, the final product LOS should be assessed to ensure the scenario is a valid and reliable rendition of the objectives outlined for the LOS. FAA advisory circular 120-35D (FAA, 2015a) outlines the process of scenario development in multiple steps. For the purposes of this chapter, we have collapsed these steps into three categories of action, for discussion. These are (1) identification of training objectives, (2) scenario building, and (3) assessment. In the following sections we will further describe how each is accomplished and the challenges associated with each.

11.2.1 Objective Identification

The primary step in LOS scenario development is the identification of the objectives for training or evaluation. This step is similar to what would be recommended in any training/evaluation development process. Logically, before any event sets are developed, one must determine what is important for training or assessment. In aviation, this is an especially challenging task. The complexity of flying an aircraft does not lend itself to an easy isolation of target objectives. The variation of possible aircraft, phases of flight, events, behaviors, environmental conditions, and organizational structure are an oversimplification of the categories of difference that can occur in aviation. As a result, no generic scenarios can be built for all pilots or all airlines. Each circumstance calls for variations.

The identification of objectives in LOS is driven by the need for event sets to realistically populate scenarios (Prince, Oser, Salas, & Woodruff, 1993). To do this effectively, scenario designers have to identify objective skills to target in the LOS scenario in addition to identifying cockpit events that will elicit these skill behaviors.

Identifying Target Skills

The multitudes of complex technical, interpersonal and environmental interactions that make up each flight make it difficult to cover all flight scenarios in training. Instead, as mentioned earlier in this chapter, training relies on building a solid foundation of skills that can be applied in a variety of circumstances. In order to do this successfully, designers have to identify both technical and CRM skills that will best equip trainees to react in the dynamic environment of the cockpit. Identification of technical skills from a designer's standpoint is a relatively straightforward task. Technical skills involve those specific to flying an aircraft. This includes proficiency with tasks that would fall under the label of "normal" flight in addition to less frequently occurring tasks such as adverse weather or flight plan revision. Until the genesis of CRM, technical skill development was the focus of training. Since technical skill is defined by the technology present in the cockpit, training objectives can be determined by the procedural steps that are required to accomplish a task. Technical skills are driven by the aircraft itself. Although much of flying is based on the general principle of lift and drag, the function of the system that is used can vary between aircraft and flight route. As a result, identifying the range of technical skill that will most adequately address the range of technical demands on the pilot is most useful.

As evidenced by other chapters in this book, the use of CRM training has become an important feature in the aviation industry. It has also been utilized successfully in other domains such as military and medicine (Helmreich, 2000). Despite the success with CRM, there is not a blanket CRM training methodology that can be applied in all circumstances. In line with this, it is important to identify the specific CRM skills that need to be developed and observed for success in aviation. Unlike technical skills, CRM skills do not have as direct an operational counterpart. There have been a number of skills that have been identified under the label of CRM. These include but are not limited to such skills as communication, planning, leadership, decision-making, assertiveness, and adaptability (Salas, Wilson, Burke, Wightman, & Howse, 2006b). Designers should have more than a passing understanding of what each CRM skill involves. That is, simply saying pilots should display communication ability is not sufficient to identifying a CRM objective. Instead, LOS designers should keep the individual crew member roles in mind when selecting the appropriate CRM skills to focus on. Assertiveness, for example, is a critical skill in the cockpit. The need to observe or train this skill may differ between crewmembers. A new hire first officer may not be immediately willing to offer their opinions on how to proceed. This would obviously warrant focus in training. On the other hand, a captain that has had years of experience with crew interaction both as a captain and as a first officer may not need as much attention on how to be assertive, but may not know how to receive assertive behavior from their first officer. After all, a captain who does not recognize and accept assertive behavior from their crew may put crew and passengers in an unnecessarily dangerous situation if the first officer recognizes a threat to safety that is disregarded by the captain. By identifying this as a target training objective, an LOS can be developed to address important skill development at different phases in a pilot's career. Unfortunately, the nature of CRM skill makes it such that there is no one-stop resource for designers to reference in terms of what CRM behaviors are critical.

Identifying Aviation Events

In unison with identifying the target skill objectives of training or evaluation, LOS designers must also identify flight events that coincide with these skills. Since a major part of LOS is contingent upon the ability to observe technical and CRM behaviors, just putting a generic flight scenario together and waiting for the behaviors to surface is not an efficient method. Instead, identifying specific events that elicit behaviors is necessary. This can be accomplished by identifying the operational equivalent, in the aircraft, to the technical skill. For instance, if revision of flight path is one of the target technical behaviors, a flight event that would elicit this skill would best be served in a phase of flight, where individuals may have difficulty making the necessary flight changes. For flight path revision this would be most likely to occur in the approach and landing phases of flight. Unfortunately, defining CRM skill objectives for training is not as easily categorized as technical skill. Overall, CRM-related skills, such as leadership or decision-making, may be easy to identify but more difficult to match with events that would trigger the behavior in the cockpit. Automation failure by itself does not automatically elicit leadership behavior. Instead, the context in which system failures, unexpected weather changes, or other events occur will influence the propensity for a CRM skill to occur. Whereas technical skill can sometimes be observed as simple when considering whether or not the pilot flipped the appropriate switch, CRM skill observation is a much more complex undertaking.

In the past decade, in particular, a number of new and emerging safety issues have been incorporated as objectives into the LOS development. These include Controlled Flight into Terrain (CFIT), loss of control (LOC) in flight and upset prevention (FAA, 2015b), and training for pilots in attention management (Stephens et al., 2017) and to reduce the negative effects of startle and surprise on the flight deck (Casner, Geven, & Williams, 2013; FAA, 2015b; Landman, Groen, van Paassen, Bronkhorst, & Mulder, 2017; Rivera, Talone, Boesser, Jentsch, & Yeh, 2014).

Summary

For the objective identification phase of scenario development, LOS designers have to be careful not to fall into the trap of relying on the same objectives year after year. As cockpit technology is evolving, the nature of pilot tasking is changing as well. This means that objective identification cannot satisfactorily be accomplished by going through flight procedure once, then relying on it to guide future scenario development. Instead, developers have to stay current with the evolution of the aviation industry and allow that to help guide the development of scenarios. As a result, a scenario that was developed several years ago may have a focus on aviation events that are now outdated. Due to this, the task of objective identification is an ongoing process for LOS designers. Individuals should stress the importance of monitoring industry changes and current trends that can indicate where there may be training needs. In addition, the increased availability and analysis of data provided by aviation safety programs, such as flight operational quality assurance (FOQA) and Aviation Safety Action Program (FAA, 2015a), can provide LOS developers with valuable information to identify the target knowledges and skills for their LOS scenario development.

11.2.2 Scenario Building

After identifying target skills and aviation events that coincide with them, the next step is to combine all of these objectives into full flight scenarios. Scenarios should be operationally relevant and believable while testing crew skill (Butler, 1993). Taking the training objectives and flight events that coincide with them, designers have to combine these parts into a coherent whole. Due to the complexity of an entire flight, and the number of individual events that can influence how a flight transpires, scenario building can quickly turn into an arduous process. In order to build a scenario effectively, the identified training objectives and corresponding events have to be further developed into event sets. These event sets then must be organized into the structure of a flight to create a realistic full flight mission.

Combining Events

Events are the basic building block of scenario design which are then compiled into event sets. Each event set is comprised of an event trigger, which initiates the action on the specific event (Johnston, Smith-Jentsch, & Cannon-Bowers, 1997). Additionally, events can contain distracters and supporting events to enhance the realism of the event and help promote specific technical or CRM behaviors (FAA, 2015a).

Event sets are classified as either simple events or complex events depending on how each can be resolved. A simple event, once addressed, requires no further action. Many simple events may be addressed by referring to procedural manuals. For example, a TCAS warning alert may trigger action of an avoidance maneuver; once this is completed, there is no further action required. Conversely, complex events do not have a well-defined solution and can have a continuous effect over the duration of the flight. The failure of any flight system can have more complex corrective action. Failure of an automated system, for example, in the flight deck will result in the crew having to adapt from monitoring the state of the automated system, to manually taking over the function that the automation drove. In order to get the most realistic scenarios, a mix of simple and complex problems should be included in the overall scenario. Too many of either of these can detract from realism though. As a result, designers have to find an appropriate balance of event sets, dispersed throughout the flight.

In addition to balancing simple and complex events, designers also have to find a good mix of both proceduralized and nonproceduralized event sets. Proceduralized event sets follow specific rules for resolution, which can often be addressed by referencing to procedural manuals and generally require very little observable CRM behavior to rectify. Nonproceduralized event sets, in contrast, cannot be addressed by following an established corrective procedure. Instead, nonproceduralized events require the flight crew to use knowledge-based solution management to address the problem. In many cases, nonproceduralized events will elicit more CRM behaviors. In order to effectively resolve an issue, the flight crew will have to engage in a process that may include brainstorming solutions, making the decision of which alternative is the best course of action, and then executing the action. By providing a nonproceduralized event, success hinges on whether the crew effectively utilizes both technical and CRM skills to address a unique flight occurrence.

Instructor Workload

For training, one misconception is that scenarios should progressively increase in workload until the trainee experiences overload (FAA, 2015a). This, however, is not the case. Instead, scenario development should reflect the normal progression of events in a flight. Not only is trainee workload important, but design with instructor workload in mind is also critical. If the instructor is not able to keep up with all of the activities in the LOS, the gains from feedback and evaluation will be lost (Beaubien, Baker, & Salvaggio, 2004). Considering this, scenario design should make sure that there is not an overload of target skills per event set, that event sets are not too short, and that the crew gets multiple opportunities to demonstrate the target skills. These will improve the quality of the observations being made, and also will help maintain appropriate workload of both instructor and crew.

Summary

Although it is impossible to predict and account for every possible incident that can occur, it is important to provide continuous training on both routine and less frequently occurring conditions. In order to effectively accomplish this, a variety of event sets and subsequent scenarios have to be developed for use. To do this, designers have to be sure to include enough event sets that address skill needs, while at the same time maintaining a realistic flight. Training value may be lost if the pilot does not believe the scenario could really occur. As a result, in addition to finding the appropriate training objectives, designers also have to be sure that the progression of events makes sense from an operational, environmental, and common sense point of view.

11.2.3   Scenario Assessment

The final and perhaps most important phase of LOS development is the assessment phase. Because providing a variety of scenarios is critical to the success of an LOS program, it is important that scenarios are generated to produce consistent experiences from scenario to scenario. Producing a consistent scenario result is critical to providing equal training opportunities, and is even more important when the LOS is used for performance evaluation (Dismukes, 1999). Designers have to come up with an effective way to assess the scenario for difficulty and operational relevance to the training or evaluation goals (Birnbach & Longridge, 1993). The goal is not to produce scenarios that are so difficult that failure is likely, but to find an acceptable range of performance from which performance evaluation is valid and reliable.

Assessment of LOS

Since different scenarios can result in differing CRM and technical skill, difficulty of problem resolution and workload imposed, there is no clear cut method of making comparisons between each (Chidester, 1993). Developing a rating system seems most logical, but LOS is made up of multiple layers of events and objectives. Since raters tend to underestimate overall difficulty as they rate smaller parts of the scenario, it is challenging to come up with the most accurate measure of performance (Jentsch, Abbott, & Bowers, 1999).

LOS designers are challenged to develop scenarios to make sure that they are not too broad or too focused. Jentsch et al. (1999) investigated a number of ways in which to achieve accurate difficulty ratings of the scenarios. They found that difficulty ratings derived by simply adding or averaging task component ratings did not result in accurate difficulty scores. Instead, they found that averaging the task difficulty within the phase and averaging the phase-based ratings into an overall difficulty rating preserved the relative differences in difficulty scores. This gives the best estimate of overall difficulty. Since these difficulty scores are component based, they are narrower than those based on overall LOE, which suggests that one would have to set cutoff scores for too easy or too hard items. They suggested that this method of evaluation makes it tough to find a balance between a narrow band for consistent experience and allowing a wide range of combinations of events.

Assessment of Performance

In addition to assessing LOS scenarios for consistency, scenario designers also have to consider how trainees will be evaluated in the process. In any case, LOS effectiveness hinges on the ability to provide useful feedback to trainees and a valid measure of performance in evaluations. Developing performance assessments for proceduralized events can be organized into a checklist of actions that should occur to successfully address the event. Developing checklists of action for nonproceduralized events that are intended to elicit CRM behavior is not as easily accomplished. If the target behavior is communication, simply checking a box if the crew communicates will not be sufficient. Instead, developers have to find specific communication behaviors that would signify success in the event.

Summary

In order to fully realize the potential of LOS training and evaluation, the assessment of scenarios, in addition to the assessment of trainee performance, has to be included. Development of event sets should be built for easy examination of crew action, especially for CRM skills where performance is ill-defined. Ultimately, designers have to consider that assessment is going to involve a subjective human component, and that there are subsequent shortcomings that result.

11.3   NEED FOR DEVELOPMENTAL TOOLS

Currently, LOS development is not a flawless process. The aviation industry is largely driven by monetary and time cost influences. For LOS development, this presents some challenges. The development process, described above, from conception to implementation can be a lengthy and involved endeavor, just to develop one scenario. Without the benefit of developmental aids, costs can begin to soar to keep up with industry demands. To be effective, LOS programs have to be comprised of multiple scenarios. Otherwise a limited number of scenarios to use for LOS can result in limitations to the scope of what can be trained. For evaluation purposes, a limited number of scenarios also run the risk of becoming known to trainees prior to the evaluation. This has serious implications for the validity of measuring performance. In order to combat this, it is important to have a satisfactory pool of scenarios from which to choose. In order to produce a more efficient scenario development cycle, there are a number of tools have been developed to address important needs. In this section we will describe the tools that can be used in each phase of development.

11.3.1 Safety Report Databases

In order to effectively identify objectives, LOS designers need a solid understanding of the types of skills that go into flight, and how and where these skills fit into different phases of flight.

In addition, they need to be aware of new cockpit instrumentation, overall aircraft advances and organizational changes to be sure that the objectives they are identifying link up with current needs. When identifying training objectives, LOS designers should consider frequently misunderstood parts of the flight manual, recently reported flight incidents, and observed poor performance areas that need specific attention. Although direct observation from training personnel about issues that they are observing in training and practice can help guide this step of design, by itself this method of objective identification could lead to an unnecessary narrowing of the objectives of training. If one pilot at an airline is having difficulty remembering to raise the gear in a timely fashion after takeoff, although the LOS developers observe this, it would not be practical to expand training on gear procedure to accommodate everyone based on this individual. In order to get a broader picture of the issues that are occurring, there are additional safety reporting tools that can help to more thoroughly inform this process.

Safety reporting systems are an excellent resource for extracting data of current trends in incidents that occur in flight, especially if they are part of a larger system that also collects and analyzes FOQA data, line check observations, data from LOSA safety audits, and maintenance feedback. Industry sponsored programs such as the Aviation Safety Reporting System (ASRS) and Aviation Safety Action Program (ASAP) provide safety reporting programs where flight crewmembers voluntarily report safety issues they encounter. Since participation is the critical driver of the success of these programs, it is important to understand that this method will not capture all incidents that occur. Safety reporting systems do provide a broader representation of aviation issues than individual training department personnel observations. Other sources of information such as NTSB accident report databases and internal airline databases can also be helpful in identifying industry trends.

Safety reporting tools are beneficial in informing the objective identification aspect of LOS design, but should be noted as not being an automated system. That is, safety reporting systems are databases of information that can be used to assess current trends, but there is no current tool that keeps real-time information on the issues occurring. The availability of this information still must be met with a critical eye to identify relevant and irrelevant trends in the data.

11.3.2 RRLOS

As outlined in the previous sections, the process required to build a scenario even after the pieces are assembled is still no small task for developers. Developers must balance realism of events with objective goals, and generate useful supporting materials for LOS sessions. Provided that each scenario must go through this process, in addition to an approval process prior to implementation, the amount of time can become an issue for airline training departments.

The cost and difficulty of creating LOS scenarios has always been a limiting factor to the number of scenarios a carrier could use. Others have been instructor workload, the availability and commonality of flight training devices (FTDs) and full flight simulators (FFSs). Thus, scenarios are frequently only changed once a year, and especially evaluation scenarios in LOEs become quickly known to pilots. This is not necessarily a bad thing, as the preparation pilots undergo for a scenario can be an important part of training. That said, it is also important to appropriately incorporate startle and surprise into scenarios (Casner et al., 2013; FAA, 2015b; Rivera et al., 2014). Thus, it would be desirable to reduce the overall cost and time required for the creation of a large number of LOS scenarios.

Rapidly reconfigurable line operations simulation (RRLOS; aka RRLOE) was one attempt to respond to this need: RRLOS was a freely distributed program designed to automate the event set pairing process to provide quick, valid LOS scenarios (Bowers, Jentsch, Baker, Prince, & Salas, 1997; Jentsch, Bowers, Berry, Dougherty, & Hitt, 2001). RRLOS generated either full or partial flight LOS scenarios (i.e., LOFT, SPOT) from a database of existing event sets. The notion is that if individual event sets can be approved by the FAA (or other international governing bodies), these events can then be combined to form full sets of preapproved LOS flight scenarios (Hitt, Jentsch, Bowers, Salas, & Edens, 2000). To do this, RRLOS took advantage of algorithmic calculations that provide both useful and realistic combinations of event sets. By creating a program that was sensitive to aircraft variation, weather patterns, and general flight characteristics, RRLOS aimed to avoid producing random but unrealistic scenarios. RRLOS generated a phase-by-phase log of realistic flight events that link up with a scripted series of preflight paperwork, air traffic clearances, and evaluation forms for the trainer (Prince & Jentsch, 2001).

RRLOS was a powerful tool that provided the potential of flexibility to generate random scenarios, or specify precise event sets. In addition, RRLOS was built to utilize a difficulty rating system similar to what was described previously to aid development of scenarios that did not differ in difficulty, but provided variation in the types of events that occur. This method was intended to make it easier for LOE developers to maintain consistency between LOS sessions without the risk of information breach which can occur if only one scenario is available for use.

Although RRLOS was an effective tool for working towards reducing the amount of time required to develop individual LOS scenarios, the program's flexibility and complexity was also a stumbling block for its widespread adoption. Many air carriers evaluated and partially implemented RRLOS, but especially during and immediately following the great recession of 2008−12, many air carriers found the upfront time and effort to fully populate, implement, and update RRLOS unaffordable. Since RRLOS was only useful if it was continually updated to account for new challenges that arise in the area of aviation training, many organizations eventually abandoned its use, and continued to use a relatively small number of LOS scenarios each year. However, many of the principles and findings from the research underlying the development of RRLOS have found widespread adoption in carriers, including the use of limited branching (which help in reducing predictability), of difficulty estimation for event sets and overall scenarios, and regarding the importance of targeted, yet realistic weather patterns and radio communications.

11.4 CONCLUSION

This chapter was intended to provide a brief discussion on the process of developing LOS for aviation training and performance evaluation. Currently, LOS-based methods (i.e., LOFT, SPOT, and LOE) have been found to be effective alternatives to live flight missions for training and evaluation. Unfortunately, the process of developing these has so far been an expensive and timely venture. As a result, training departments may settle for creating fewer scenarios to save money. Since the continued effectiveness of an LOS-based program is contingent upon providing varied and relevant experiences to trainees, if a training department is forced to reduce the number of available LOS scenarios to draw from, they run the risk of providing inadequately diverse training or evaluation programs. This is why the utilization of current development tools and the development of additional tools are important to fully realize the benefits of the LOS methodology.

To say that the accidents outlined at the beginning of this chapter were solely a result of poor training design would be inaccurate. The countless factors that can cause an accident to occur are too numerous to pinpoint the lack of training as the cause (cf. BEA, 2012). What those examples do provide is an illustration that despite improvements in training methodologies, errors can occur at any stage of a pilot's career and that methods of improving the development process can only serve to benefit pilots, airlines, and the safety of the general public.

Given the dramatic restructuring of the current landscape of aviation, through the future generation of industry-supported programs, the need for efficient training is becoming increasingly important. LOS provides an effective means to do that, even if the development process can be time- and resource-consuming. That said, LOS is now recommended to train pilots for a number of current and continuing safety-related concerns, such as startle and surprise and upset prevention.

REFERENCES

Arthur, W., Bennett, W., Stanush, P. L., & McNelly, T. L. (1998). Factors that influence skill decay and retention: A quantitative review and analysis. *Human Performance*, *11*(1), 57−101.

Barshi, I. (2015). From Healy's training principles to training specifications: The case of the comprehensive LOFT. *American Journal of Psychology*, *128*(2), 219−227.

Beaubien, J. M., Baker, D. P., & Salvaggio, A. N. (2004). Improving the construct validity of line operational simulation ratings: Lessons learned from the assessment center. *The International Journal of Aviation Psychology*, *14*(1), 1−17.

Birnbach, R., & Longridge, T. (1993). The regulatory perspective. In E. Wiener, B. Kanki, & R. Helmreich (Eds.), *Cockpit resource management*. (pp. 263−282). San Diego, CA: Academic Press.

Bowers, C., Jentsch, F., Baker, D., Prince, C., & Salas, E. (1997). Rapidly reconfigurable event-set based line operational evaluation scenarios. In *Proceeding of the human factors and ergonomics society 41st annual meeting* (pp. 912−915). Albuquerque, NM.

Bureau d'Enquêtes et d'Analyses [BEA]. (2012). *Pour la Sécurité de l'Aviation Civile. Final report on the accident on 1st June 2009 to the Airbus A330-203 registered F-GZCP operated by Air France, flight AF 447 Rio de Janeiro−Paris*. Paris: BEA.

Butler, R. (1993). LOFT: Full-mission simulation as crew resource management training. In E. Wiener, B. Kanki, & R. Helmreich (Eds.), *Cockpit resource management*. (pp. 231−263). San Diego, CA: Academic Press.

Casner, S. M., Geven, R. W., & Williams, K. T. (2013). *The effectiveness of airline pilot training for abnormal events, Human Factors* (55, pp. 477−485).

Chidester, T. (1993). Critical issues for CRM. In E. Weiner, B. Kanki, & R. Helmreich (Eds.), *Cockpit resource management* (pp. 315−336). San Diego, CA: Academic Press.

Childs, J. M., & Spears, W. D. (1986). Flight-skill decay and recurrent training. *Perceptual Motor Skills*, *62*(1), 235−242.

Dismukes, R., Berman, B., & Loukopoulos, L. (2007). *The limits of expertise: Rethinking pilot error and the causes of airline accidents*. Burlington, VT: Ashgate.

Dismukes, R.K. (1999). Discussion: Issues in evaluating crew performance in line oriented evaluation. In *Proceedings for the 10th International Symposium on Aviation Psychology* (pp. 329−331). Columbus, OH.

FAA. (2015a). *Line operational simulations: Line oriented flight training, special purpose operational training, line operational evaluation.* (AC120-35D). US Department of Transportation: Federal Aviation Administration: Author.

FAA. (2015b). *Upset Prevention and Recovery Training.* (AC120-111). US Department of Transportation: Federal Aviation Administration: Author.

Fowlkes, J., Dwyer, D., Oser, R., & Salas, E. (1998). Event-based approach to training. *International Journal of Aviation Psychology, 8*(3), 209−221.

Helmreich, R., & Foushee, H. (1993). Why crew resource management? In E. Wiener, B. Kanki, & R. Helmreich (Eds.), *Cockpit resource management.* (pp. 1−45). San Diego, CA: Academic Press.

Helmreich, R., Wilhelm, J., Kello, J., Taggart, W., & Butler, R. (1991). *Reinforcing and evaluating crew resource management: Evaluator/LOS instructor reference manual.* Austin: University of Texas.

Helmreich, R. L. (2000). On error management: Lessons from aviation. *British Medical Journal, 320,* 781−785.

Hitt, J.M., Jentsch, F., Bowers, C.A., Salas, E., & Edens, E.S. (2000). Scenario-based training for autoflight skills. In *Paper presented at the Australian Aviation Psychology Association Conference,* Sydney, Australia.

Jensen, R. (1989). *Aeronautical decision making—Cockpit resource management.* Washington, DC: Federal Aviation Administration.

Jentsch, F., Abbott, D., & Bowers, C. (1999). Do three easy tasks make one difficult one? Studying the perceived difficulty of simuation scenarios. In *Proceedings of the tenth international symposium on aviation psychology.* The Ohio State University, Columbus, OH.

Jentsch, F., Bowers, C., Berry, D., Dougherty, W., & Hitt, J.M. (2001). Generating line-oriented flight simulation scenarios with the RRLOE computerized tool set. In *Proceedings for the 45th annual meeting of the human factors and ergonomics society.* Minneapolis, MN, p. 749.

Johnston, J., Smith-Jentsch, K., & Cannon-Bowers, J. (1997). Performance measurement tools for enhancing team decision-making training. In M. Brannick, E. Salas, & C. Prince (Eds.), *Team performance assessment and measurement.* (pp. 311−330). Mahwah, NJ: Lawrence Erlbaum Associates.

Klein, G. (2008). Naturalistic decision making. *Human Factors, 50*(3), 456−460.

Landman, A., Groen, E. L., van Paassen, M. M., Bronkhorst, A. W., & Mulder, M. (2017). Dealing with unexpected events on the flight deck: A conceptual model of startle and surprise. *Human Factors, 59*(8), 1161−1172. Available from https://doi.org/10.1177/0018720817723428.

Prince, C., & Jentsch, F. (2001). Aviation crew resource management training with low-fidelity devices. In E. Salas, C. Bowers, & E. Edens (Eds.), *Improving teamwork in organizations.* (pp. 147−164). Mahwah, NJ: Lawrence Erlbaum Associates.

Prince, C., Oser, R., Salas, E., & Woodruff, W. (1993). Increasing hits and reducing misses in CRM/LOS scenarios: Guidelines for simulator scenario development. *International Journal of Aviation Psychology, 3*(1), 69−82.

Rivera, J., Talone, A. B., Boesser, C. T., Jentsch, F., & Yeh, M. (2014). *Startle and surprise on the flight deck similarities, differences, and prevalence. Proceedings of the Human Factors and Ergonomics Society 58th Annual Meeting* (pp. 1047−1051). Santa Monica, CA: Human Factors and ErgonomicsSociety.

Salas, E., Priest, H., Wilson, K., & Burke, C. (2006a). Scenario-based training: Improving military mission performance and adaptability. In T. Britt, A. Adler, & C. Castro (Eds.),

Military life: The psychology of serving in peace and combat. (Vol. 2, pp. 32−53). Westport: Praeger.

Salas, E., Wilson, K., Burke, C. S., Wightman, D. C., & Howse, W. R. (2006b). A checklist for crew resource management training. *Ergonomics in Design: The Quarterly of Human Factors Applications, 14*(2), 6−15.

Salas, E., Wilson, K. L., King, H., Augenstein, J., Robinson, D., & Birnbach, D. (2008). Simulation-based training for patient safety: 10 principles that matter. *Patient Safety, 4*(1), 3−8.

Stephens, C., Harrivel, A., Prinzel, L., Comstock, R., Abraham, N., Pope, A. & Kiggins, D. (2017). Crew state monitoring and line-oriented flight training for attention monitoring. In *Proceedings of the international symposium on aviation psychology (ISAP 2017)*. Dayton, OH.

Chapter 12

Crew Resource Management and Line Operations Safety Audit*

Bruce A. Tesmer[†]

INTRODUCTION

This chapter begins with a one paragraph general description of crew resource management (CRM), and then defines the term "company operations plan" as the plan flight crews' execute to fly every flight to a safe conclusion. When flight crews use their CRM skills to execute their flight plan, it is intended to result in a safe operation. Measuring the variance in the safety margin, based on flight crew performance, during that flight is what a Line Operations Safety Audit (LOSA) observation does. The aim of this chapter is to provide a working understanding of CRM and LOSA: how both programs integrate and support safety goals in aviation.

12.1 CRM DESCRIPTION

CRM covers a wide range of knowledge, skills, and abilities including communications, teamwork, situational awareness (SA), decision-making, and leadership. CRM is the management of all resources—hardware, software, and human-ware—to maximize safety and efficiency in flight operations.

---

* Editors' note: *Crew Resource Management and Line Operations Safety Audit* has been preserved intact from the previous edition of this book as we honor the excellent work Bruce Tesmer accomplished in his aviation life. A retired US Air Force commander and Continental Airlines captain, Bruce spent many years in the flight safety department at Continental Airlines and worked collaboratively with Dr. Robert Helmreich in the early years of the LOSA program. The chapter provides both historical narrative as well as an operational, practical approach to implementing LOSA. Bruce passed away in late 2016.
† Deceased November, 2016.

Crew Resource Management. DOI: https://doi.org/10.1016/B978-0-12-812995-1.00012-9

12.2 COMPANY OPERATIONS PLAN

Commercial air carriers in the United States plan each of their flights to be in compliance with their Federal Aviation Administration (FAA)-approved Operations Specifications. This ensures the flight is planned to the minimum compliant safety level. Air carriers then add tasks, decision aids, policies, procedures, and other requirements, based on risk assessment and risk reductions, to improve the safety of every flight plan. The object of these additions is to account for all known system threats (weather, airport conditions, air traffic control delays, etc.) and prevent these threats from affecting the safety of each flight. The best operations plan is one where all threats are known and accounted for before the flight crew starts executing the plan.

12.3 LOSA DEFINITION

LOSA is a *safety* data collection program that gathers *frontline employee* (flight crew) performance data during *normal* operations. It is designed to identify *system* safety issues, not to identify individual pilots or crews as being safe or not safe. It is used to diagnose the relative health of an air carrier's level of safety in frontline normal operations.

12.4 LINE OPERATIONS SAFETY AUDIT

12.4.1 The LOSA History

The development of LOSA started with a desire by industry and the aviation research community to find better sources of safety data in normal flight operations. The standard safety data used prior to LOSA came from accident investigation and individual carrier-required incident/event flight crew reporting. Commercial aviation accidents are rare, but often catastrophic with no survivors, making postaccident investigation difficult, at best. Required event reporting systems can put pilots in jeopardy and are historically underreported. It would be far better to find ways to evaluate the flight crew's performance in normal operations, before an accident happens, to gain insight concerning commercial aviation accident precursors.

The University of Texas Human Factors Research Project (UTHF), headed by Professor Robert Helmreich, began normal flight operations monitoring in the early 1980s. The project's observations worked to evaluate CRM, behaviors, skills, and attitudes of flight crews as they flew their normal flights (Klinect et al., 2003).

To ensure that flight crews are relaxed and that the observers would be unobtrusive, the pilots were told by a signed letter of agreement that all data would be de-identified, sent directly to the researchers at UTHF, and that there would be no jeopardy to the flight crews from the data.

In 1995, Continental Airlines expanded their safety department, and being aware of Professor Helmreich's work using normal operations monitoring, began contemplating a normal operations safety audit program. Continental wanted a program that would include collecting safety data on technical issues as well as CRM. A meeting was set between Continental Safety and Professor Helmreich in February 1996. The day before that meeting, Continental experienced a landing-gear up, landing accident at Houston Intercontinental Airport (NTSB, 1996).

While there were no fatalities and everyone walked away from the aircraft at ground level, the question was asked: how could a qualified flight crew land a perfectly good aircraft, with the landing-gear up, on a clear day, with very low air traffic volume? Before waiting for the answer, in the form of the NTSB Accident Report, Continental and UTHF came to agreement on a normal operations audit program. The program was favorably viewed by the FAA which approved FAA research grant funding to UTHF for the project.

The program would use the UTHF methodology for normal operations monitoring which had previously been effective on CRM focused programs at Delta and other carriers. However, it would be expanded to include data collection on flight crew performance concerning crew execution of the plan for their flight, and any errors the crew made in standard operating procedures (SOP), especially, if the flight environment became more difficult.

The 1996 audit at Continental Airlines used 30 Continental instructor line captains and five UTHF researchers as observers. The audit collected data on all fleet type aircraft, over the entire route structure of the airline, in a 3-month period. Eight hundred thirty-six flight segments were observed. The data took 7 months to enter, collate, and structure. Data analysis took an additional 3 months. The results were extremely illuminating.

The data and analysis showed the good, the bad, and the ugly. The good flights were flights where crew performance was excellent even when the operating environment got rough. Pilots on good crews did make errors but the crew discovered their errors and mitigated the consequences of those errors. They also stepped up to the challenges when the environment became nasty and good crews were proactive in their handling of system threats.

The bad flights were flights with more prevalent errors that generally increased as the environment deteriorated. On these flights, the flight crew did not detect all their errors. Some of those errors may have led to a negative event except that some external system threats just went away (the weather cleared, or air traffic control provided a less difficult route, there was extra fuel on board, etc.).

The ugly flights were flights where crews did not comply with procedures, made their own policies, and disregarded rules and regulations, some vowing that they had a better way of accomplishing the plan. None of these flights operated below the minimum safety level, but the flight crews did not take advantage of the added safety provided by SOP and good CRM. Intentional noncompliance would become a large safety target highlighted from the data.

The 1996 audit at Continental stimulated other carriers, worldwide, to conduct similar audits partnered with UTHF and advanced the science of the normal operations monitoring process. Continental was the first repeat audit partner with UTHF, accomplishing partial-system focused audits in 1997, 1998, and 1999. All of which led to the data and analysis structure of threat and error management (TEM), which will be discussed later.

With the TEM data taxonomy in place, the UTHF normal operations monitoring audit took the name of "LOSA." The first LOSA audit took place at Continental Airlines in 2000. After that LOSA project, the FAA would only fund the research regarding the data and analysis, with no more funding for conducting LOSA projects at individual air carriers.

The funding of future LOSA projects would have to come from the carriers themselves. The growth of LOSA projects continued and required a separate entity to manage both the projects themselves and the continually growing archive database. The entity that evolved was The LOSA Collaborative (TLC) whose CEO was, and is, Dr. James Klinect. Dr. Klinect was the lead doctoral candidate under Dr. Helmreich in 1996 when the Continental Airlines project first began and was the first to propose the TEM structure from the data.

The agreement between UT and TLC ensures the openness of the normal operations monitoring program and data collection forms developed under FAA funded research. This has allowed carriers the ability to derive their own normal flight operations monitoring programs, which some have done. Eight normal flight operations monitoring audits (fewer than 4000 observations) used the FAA research grant funded forms for data collection. Data collection forms and the data that were funded through the individual air carriers, remain the property of those individual carriers through TLC.

In 2005, LOSA was recognized as an FAA Voluntary Safety Program, with a FAA LOSA Advisory Circular, AC 120-90, following on April 27, 2006. As of November 2006, TEM and LOSA concepts were added to several of the Annexes to the Convention on International Civil Aviation (Chicago Convention). In Annex 1 (Personnel Licensing), TEM is now a requirement for all pilot and ATCO licenses (standard). Annex 6 was amended to require TEM for all initial and recurrent flight crew training. In Annex 14 (Aerodromes), the new Safety Management System standards highlight LOSA as a recommended practice for normal operations monitoring (www.icao.int).

To date, the LOSA archive database contains over 10,000 observed flight segments from over 50 audits and 35 different worldwide air carriers. The LOSA data have been used to identify many issues, from checklist misuse and unstable landing approaches, to poorly designed operating procedures and outdated checklists/briefing guides/callouts. LOSA has also highlighted favorable and ineffective use of CRM behaviors/skills and attributes in all phases of flight.

Significant changes to operations philosophies, policies, and procedures have been driven by LOSA data in its TEM form. The data have spawned a new focus in training which is based on eliminating the consequences of threats and errors by using TEM countermeasures, CRM attributes and tools that bind human factors to specific task completion.

The history of LOSA also shows the new emphasis that has been placed on safety change processes and safety management systems that involve everyone in the organization, at all levels, to work towards reducing the difficulty in the flight crew's operating environment (Helmreich, 2002).

12.4.2   The LOSA Process

The LOSA process begins with an air carrier's desire to obtain data on the crew performance as it applies to the execution of the flight plan in normal everyday operations. That desire has to manifest itself at a vice president level, or higher, for the project to take hold. Without support for the LOSA at that level, there is often too much resistance for project responsibility and funding or competition for control. Competition can exist between the functional areas of flight operations, flight standards, and training and flight safety, fearing that any negative safety data will reflect poorly on any one of those areas of the organization.

The difference between fear and anxiety is preparation. The fear of negative data turns to anxiety for the valid data, as the carrier prepares to conduct its first LOSA and begins to understand that there will be as much positive data as negative data resulting from the LOSA observations.

There is a requirement to have both a LOSA oversight committee and a LOSA manager in place early in the project due to the preplanning required. The oversight committee will determine the size of the LOSA in terms of how many dataset comparisons are desired, by aircraft fleet type, by crew base, geographical operations, or other comparisons. The committee will also select the observers and how they will be scheduled and compensated. The selection process chooses observers that have both the company's recommendation and the pilot's union recommendation from lists supplied by both the company and union. Committee coordination with the union will be similar to the departmental coordination between all other members of the oversight committee. The chairperson of the committee normally is from the sponsoring department. The committee's decisions and tasking will become the focus of the LOSA manager for preobservation requirement completion. The LOSA manager becomes the point of contact throughout the LOSA project including coordination with TLC.

The last requirement prior to the start of observations is observer training and calibration; both accomplished by TLC. The most important training requirement is to ensure observers can write a complete narrative. The narrative describes how the crew performs in terms of executing the operations plan (flight plan) and how they handle external system threats and internally generated crew errors.

How observers describe crew performance in terms of identifying system threats and internal crew errors, the responses that crews use after discovering threats and errors, and threat and error outcomes are the basis for observer calibration. These criteria will also be used to recalibrate the observers after their first few observations. Observers are scheduled to begin line observations immediately after training and calibration are completed.

The time period for conducting line observations varies depending on the number of segments required for data comparisons and the number of observers used. The observation period normally runs from 1 to 4 months. The data validation process begins as soon as the first data are received. The validation is completed after the data are reviewed and certified as accurate by the carrier. Data certification by the carrier is normally accomplished by members of flight operations and flight standards.

Data analysis begins after certification. The analysis is accomplished using the structure of TEM, developed by the University of Texas Human Factors Research Project in 2001. TLC maintains the LOSA archive database which is used by carriers as a comparison to their data analysis results. The archive dataset currently contains more than 10,000 observed flight segments.

In addition to the TEM structured observation data, LOSA also includes data from crew interviews regarding safety issues and/or survey data on pilot attitudes concerning organizational and safety culture, and resource management. All these data and analyses can be used to diagnostically uncover crew performance safety issues that currently exist. LOSA provides these as a snapshot of operations safety.

12.4.3 Synthesis of the TEM Framework from the LOSA Data Tsunami

The 836 flight observations from the 1996 Continental line audit used a data collection tool from UTHF named the Line/LOS Checklist, which effectively looked at CRM behaviors by phase of flight (Helmreich, 1995). The data collected described the effectiveness of crew performance in completing the required tasks of that flight's operations plan. Added to the Line/LOS checklist was a Continental data collection form developed by Flight Standards and Training that collected crew error data relating to technical tasks such as handling performance (takeoff rotation angle and rate; climb profile; lateral, vertical, and speed adherence; cruise altitude selection; the accuracy of the descent; arrival and approach handling to achieve a stabilized approach; and landing accuracy in terms of the landing touchdown zone). Also included were data on checklist accomplishment, briefing thoroughness, required altitude callouts, and any limitations that were exceeded.

The result of collecting all this information was a data tsunami. Both the Line/LOS data and the company technical data were analyzed. The analysis of the CRM behaviors data showed where flight crews had performed well, identifying issues that could or did impact the flight and how crews worked to reduce the difficulty back to normal through effective teamwork. The analysis also showed where an increase in the difficulty of the system environment resulted in more errors, concerning technical task completions required during flight. All flight crew errors were captured in the analysis.

Upon review, the data showed that crews with good CRM behaviors outperformed crews with poor CRM behaviors, especially when the system environment became more difficult. When the going got tough the good crews got going but the poor CRM crews got worse. The focus on correction for this finding was to develop tools that could help the crew determine when the system environment was moving to an "off normal" environment and how to bring it back to a normal state.

Not until the Error Management Training for flight crews started, did the concept "there is no such thing as a *normal* environment," come to light. Most everyone these days has flown a commercial flight to get somewhere. Our experiences range from flights that were on time, smooth, in good weather with our bags and dog waiting at baggage claim, to flights where the aircraft was late getting in, required maintenance to fix something, had to be de-iced because of the heavy snow falling, was so turbulent that the flight attendants never got up, had to hold over the destination but never got in due to heavy air traffic, and was diverted to an alternate airport, where the landing was firm and the airplane sat for 3 hours until an ATC clearance could be obtained to get back to our destination.

So, which one is the "normal" flight? The answer is that there is no *normal*. There are flights with more or fewer threats that pop up during the flight, and there are flights with more or fewer crew errors made during the flight, but there is no normal! Therefore, flight crews can't just accept the flight, thinking that what they get is the luck of the draw. They have to use their senses for the entire flight looking for threats and looking to trap their own errors when they occur, in order to manage those threats and errors to a safe conclusion without allowing the combinations of threats and errors to form an undesired state.

The datasets from the Continental audits of 1997, 1998, and 1999, along with several foreign audits, clearly showed that the crew performance could be defined through the numbers of threats and errors experienced, and how those threats and errors were managed. The structure of the accident precursors and how they relate to each other and to accidents can be seen by reviewing Fig. 12.1, UTHF Framework for TEM. Of particular concern were

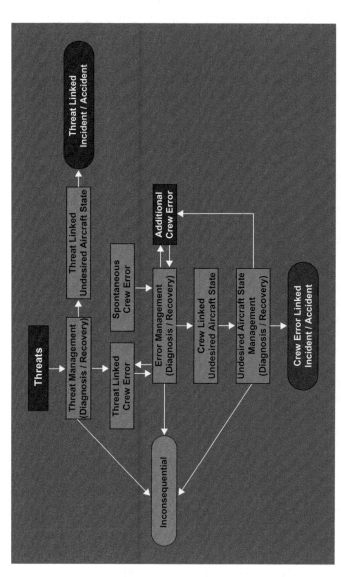

FIGURE 12.1 University of Texas Human Factors Research Project—Framework for threat and error management. This structure was developed by organizing the empirical LOSA observation data.

the threats and errors that resulted in the formation of an Undesired State. An Undesired State is defined as a state where the aircraft is in the wrong position or at the wrong speed or in a wrong configuration. Examples include wrong heading set for takeoff, wrong altitude set during descent, the landing gear not extended for landing, no flaps set for takeoff, or incorrect speed set for final approach. The list is extensive. Undesired states are to be avoided since they are the last state before an accident.

Every accident has a preceding undesired state; however, every undesired state does not result in an accident. The structure of the diagram in Fig. 12.1 shows how threats can induce errors and how human errors can occur without a threat, but both threats and errors have to be managed before they become an undesired state or the undesired state is likely to become an accident. Undesired states are difficult to detect and can have a very short life cycle before they manifest into an accident.

It was the first few audits that provided the datasets that allowed the TEM framework to precipitate from the empirical data. The use of LOSA has brought about the focus for applying CRM. While developing training for TEM, countermeasures were explored as a proactive intervention to deal with threats and errors. Many CRM behaviors were considered but the basic TEM countermeasures that resulted came from defining the errors flight crews made when dealing with automation.

Automation provides crews with the ability to be more precise and to work long calculations with ease. However, as powerful as the flight management computer (FMC) is, it lacks one very important feature: it does not know flight crew intent! Because of that fact, the FMC is considered the dumbest crewmember of the flight crew. The countermeasures developed for interfacing and using the FMC are simple. First, when asking the FMC to accomplish a task, verbalize to the other pilot the exact task you want the automation to perform. Then have the other pilot verify the question is correct. After verification, the execute function can be activated and then the last countermeasure, monitoring, can be used to ensure the desired intent is achieved.

The most basic TEM countermeasures, VVM (verbalize, verify, and monitor), developed for use with the dumbest flight crewmember, happen to work well with the smarter crewmembers, the humans, too. By verbalizing, we start to build the CRM attribute of Communications. It is critical to verbalize the exact information of concern to the appropriate flight crewmembers or outside agencies. That is what builds the second CRM attribute of Coordination/Teamwork. The information passed by verbalization updates the crewmember(s) to ensure their individual mental models are equal to the shared mental model and that the shared model is equal to reality. This defines SA as the third CRM attribute, and is required if flight crews are to make good and safe decisions. For safety in line operations, good decision-making is the fourth CRM attribute and safety goal. See Fig. 12.2 (Threat & Error Management Hierarchy of CRM attributes ...). Higher level CRM

FIGURE 12.2   Threat and error management hierarchy of CRM attributes and TEM counter-measures that build to safe decision-making.

behaviors of leadership, modeling, mentoring, and others are designed to bring improvement to VVM skills and to foster crew learning.

The last group of countermeasures includes the tools used to marry human factors knowledge and performance with specific technical task accomplishment. These tools are briefings, callouts, bottom lines, checklists, criteria matrices, and SOP. If you want to communicate the plan you use a briefing, if you want to verify that your altitude for climb or descent is near you use a callout, if you want to ensure all required tasks are completed before takeoff you design a checklist. The tools are as important as the CRM skills or the technical skills of task accomplishment. Tools are used to reduce the difficulty of the frontline employees' work environment, which increases the ability of the crew to avoid and manage the accident precursors. The entire organization wants to reduce environmental difficulties since the frontline is doing the work at the sharp end of the spear.

12.5   FLIGHT CREW PERFORMANCE AND PROCEDURAL DRIFT

CRM and TEM data from the LOSA observations, along with data from the crew interviews and surveys, showed that there is a crew performance negative drift component that affects compliance with the company's guidance, policies, and procedures. Drift is related to the time between currency events and also to the time between training and checking events. The more recent the experience and training for that event, the closer the performance was to standard.

Flight crew performance relative to SOP appeared to decline with time (drift) for three reasons. First, is unintentional drift, where deviations are generally minor. When the flight crews unintentionally drift, and they identify the drift, they immediately self-correct. The second form of drift concerns following the "norm" instead of the standard procedure. It is equivalent to driving a motor vehicle over the posted speed limit to keep up with traffic because everyone else is speeding. The correction for drift due to a norm is training to show why the speed limit is there and practice in obeying that limit. Training corrects this form of drift because those involved want to comply with the standards. The third form of drift is intentional noncompliance. It is the worst and most insidious.

Intentional noncompliance is reckless behavior. It stems from a belief that guidance, policy, and procedures were meant for the weakest individual and not a skilled professional like me. "I have a better, faster, smoother way of doing things." "I liked the way we did it at XYZ, so I'm doing it that way." "I have more experience than the people who wrote these procedures and I know best."

Intentional noncompliance cannot be tolerated by anyone, especially other crewmembers. Discipline is required and appropriate, within a just culture, to deal with intentional noncompliance. The only requirement before applying discipline is to answer the question: is the guidance, policy, or procedure reasonable? When intentional noncompliance occurs on a frequent basis it tends to show an unrealistic, hard to comply with procedure or that the entire operation is too procedural and does not allow enough crew flexibility that is reasonable and safe. All three forms of drift were observed in the LOSA observations and became even clearer in the crew interviews.

The disturbing findings from the LOSA archive database show that crews observed in one or more intentional noncompliance errors had three times the number of mismanaged threats and errors and also a higher number of undesired states than crews without intentional noncompliance errors. This is another reason why intentional noncompliance cannot be tolerated.

12.6 THE SAFETY CHANGE PROCESS AND SAFETY MANAGEMENT SYSTEMS

As mentioned earlier, LOSA is a recommended voluntary safety project approved by the FAA and ICAO. It provides a detailed look at flight crew performance in normal operations. But data and analysis aside, there will be no reduction in the number or severity of the LOSA detected accident precursors without action to develop safety changes. Every organization needs a safety change process that functions in a continuous cycle beginning with measurement of safety, where valid data are collected and starts again with measurement of the changes implemented from the last measurement. The entire cycle consists of safety measurement, data analysis, safety target identification, proposed changes to reduce the risk of the safety target, prioritization of risk reductions, funding of the changes, and implementation of the approved and funded changes. Since auditing of the results is a function of the next LOSA, the audit process is already in place. Auditing of TEM is also in place since any level can ask levels below what threats they are working to reduce and a response of "I don't know" means a process breakdown at the lower level. Change is inevitable and safety change in normal operations is no exception.

Safety management systems (SMS) provide a means of conducting operations risk assessment, operations task risk reduction, and ongoing risk management through programs like LOSA. SMS involves every level of the company by placing requirements for safety processes that keep all levels of the organization aware of and involved in safety management. SMS keeps the middle management zone from spinning the direction from the top and blocking information from the frontlines on the way to the top, and truly holds everyone in the organization accountable for safety change and awareness. It makes the regulator's task of ensuring regulatory compliance easier because the company's focus is on safety change; being better tomorrow than you were today and having the data to prove it. It is no longer a business of avoiding regulatory fines for violations to the regulations; it is process management for safety improvement.

LOSA and CRM are integral parts of safety improvement within SMS and continue to be linked together.

12.7 SUMMARY

- CRM is defined as the use of all hardware, software, and human-ware to manage all resources and achieve a safe flight.
- LOSA is a safety data collection program based on observations from the cockpit jump-seat by trained pilot observers on normal flight operations.
- The LOSA observations are at no jeopardy to the flight crew as the project looks at how well flight crews perform in managing the system threats and flight crew errors that are present on almost every flight.
- The history of LOSA starts with the Line/LOS−CRM behavioral marker data collection by observation, first accomplished by the University of Texas Human Factors Research Project.
- The TEM framework came together from the precipitation of empirical LOSA data.
- The LOSA Archive database is continuously updated with the finish of each LOSA project (10,000 + flight segments from 50 + separate audits for 35 + worldwide air carriers). The database is maintained by TLC.
- TEM data provide a focus for application of CRM.
- TEM and CRM countermeasures provide a hierarchy of attributes that when achieved simplify and are a catalyst to successfully managing the accident precursors.

- Tools that marry CRM skills to operations plan task accomplishment are critical in managing accident precursors.
- Intentional noncompliance is the most serious form of performance drift and data show three times the number of mismanaged threats and errors for crews that participate in intentional noncompliance. CRM and LOSA are forever strongly linked in the TEM taxonomy.

12.8   QUESTIONS AND ANSWERS

1. What is CRM? It is the management of all hardware, software, and people-ware to achieve a safe and efficient flight.
2. What is LOSA? It is a safety data collection program for normal operations monitoring, looking for system problems that the crews must manage.
3. Is LOSA recognized by the FAA? LOSA is recognized by the FAA as a Voluntary Safety Project and is also recommended as an ICAO best practice.
4. What data collection types are used in LOSA? LOSA uses nonjeopardy observations, crew interviews, and crew surveys as data collection types.
5. What constitutes a "normal" flight? There is no such thing as a normal flight.
6. What defines the dumbest crewmember on the flight? The dumb automation, because it cannot know the crew's intent.
7. What is the highest level CRM attribute that TEM looks for in safe operations? Building on Communications, Coordination/Teamwork, and SA is the focus CRM attribute of decision-making.
8. What is used to ensure good CRM behavior skills are directly tied to operations plan technical task accomplishment? Tools such as briefings, callouts, checklists, limitations, bottom lines, and SOP.
9. What is the worst form of performance drift? Intentional noncompliance; it is reckless behavior.
10. What is the historical data supported risk if you choose to intentionally noncomply? A three times higher rate of threat and errors mismanagement.

AUTHOR'S PERSPECTIVE (2010)

This chapter references only materials from the members of the University of Texas Human Factors Research Project, the FAA, the NTSB, and ICAO. The reason for this is because the actual LOSA data, that includes CRM data and technical data, are proprietary to the individual air carriers that participated in LOSA audits. My involvement in developing LOSA, Threat & Error Management, and CRM was to assist those conducting research by providing a test bed in actual operations, then using the results to stimulate safety changes by the organizations conducting the LOSA audits.

All six of the LOSA audits that I managed and the seventh that I consulted on at Continental Airlines were different. The time span for those seven LOSA audits ran from 1996 through 2008 in which time there were numerous changes in personnel at all levels of the organization. I want to thank all the Flight Operation's, Flight Standards & Training, and Safety & Regulatory Compliance Directors and Vice Presidents for their support and belief in the LOSA and Safety Change Process, especially during the ups and downs of the business cycle. While the structure of funding the LOSA changed with every audit, there was never a question of if the LOSA was going to happen; just a question of how it would be accomplished. From my communications with LOSA managers at other air carriers, I find the same flexibility is required by every air carrier. The data and analysis from LOSA can be obtained in no other way than by normal operations monitoring.

I encourage all who read this chapter to contact the LOSA managers of all LOSA accomplished air carriers to validate and update the perspective I have given in this text. Most carriers are willing to openly share their findings because they feel a commitment to aviation safety in general. To obtain the latest information concerning LOSA, TEM and their relationship with CRM, contact Dr. James Klinect, CEO of TLC, through his website. He has been involved with LOSA and TEM from the beginning and has a perspective supported by past and current data that no one else has.

REFERENCES

FAA Advisory Circular, AC 120-90-LOSA, April 27th, 2006, www.faa.gov.
Helmreich, R. FAA Technical Reports 95-1, NASA/University of Texas Aerospace FAA Crew Research Report, March 1995.
Helmreich, R. (2002). Crew performance monitoring program. *ICAO Journal, 57*, 6—7.
Klinect, J. R., Murray, P., Merritt, A., & Helmreich, R. (2003). *Line operations safety audit (LOSA): Definition and operating characteristics. Proceedings for the 12th International Symposium on Aviation Psychology* (pp. 663—668). Columbus, OH, Dayton: The Ohio State University.
NTSB Identification: FTW96FA118, Probable Cause; accident on February 19, 1996 in HOUSTON, TX, www.ntsb.gov.

FURTHER READING

ICAO Annexes ICAO Annexes 1, 6 & 14; www.icao.int.

Chapter 13

Maintenance Resource Management for Technical Operations

Manoj S. Patankar
School of Aviation and Transportation Technology, Purdue University, West Lafayette, IN, United States

INTRODUCTION

On April 28, 1988, a Boeing 737-200 operated by Aloha Airlines experienced explosive decompression and structural failure at 24,000 ft. It resulted in a dramatic separation of the fuselage upper lobe and made startling headlines like, "And Then, Whoosh! She was Gone" (Wright & Tanji, 1988). The accompanying photos showed evidence of what might have been considered impossible in the past. The National Transportation Safety Board (NTSB) noted that the probable cause of the accident was "the failure of the Aloha Airlines maintenance program to detect the presence of significant disbonding and fatigue damage which ultimately led to...the separation of the fuselage upper lobe" (NTSB, 1989, p. v). Almost a year later, on March 10, 1989, Air Ontario accident in Dryden, Canada, also revealed a number of systemic factors, including maintenance failures (Commission of Inquiry, 1992a). On June 10, 1990, a British Airways BAC 1-11 experienced explosive decompression when the captain's window blew out (King, 1992). These three accidents resulted in both an intense focus on maintenance-related accidents as well as a unique, multiparty collaboration between the United States Federal Aviation Administration (FAA), the United States National Aeronautics and Space Administration (NASA), Transport Canada (TC), and the United Kingdom's Civil Aviation Authority (UK CAA), as well as partnerships across airlines, maintenance repair and overhaul facilities, and universities.

Early efforts to assess safety-related issues in maintenance and develop appropriate intervention programs relied heavily on the success of the cockpit resource management (CRM) program among the flight crew during

Crew Resource Management. DOI: https://doi.org/10.1016/B978-0-12-812995-1.00013-0

357

the decade of the 1980s, which was focused on crew communication and teamwork. Thus, the early maintenance resource management (MRM) programs, which were essentially CRM principles applied to the maintenance environment, also focused on communication and teamwork among the maintenance personnel (Fotos, 1991; Taggart, 1990). Pre/post training evaluation tools developed by Gregorich, Helmreich, and Wilhelm (1990) were modified from CRM to MRM to suit the audience while maintaining their psychometric integrity and applied to the assessment of MRM programs (Taylor, Robertson, Peck, & Stelly, 1993). Similarly, much of the style and content of the MRM training intervention was borrowed from the successful CRM programs as studied by Helmreich, Foushee, Benson, and Russini (1986).

Concurrent with the emerging research in MRM, three other major accidents drew attention to safety in maintenance operations: June 1995 Valujet accident in Atlanta, Georgia; August 1995 Atlantic Southeast Airlines accident in Carrollton, Georgia; and 1996 Valujet accident in Miami, Florida. Reviews of these three accident cases, along with the knowledge from previous accidents and effects of early MRM training interventions resulted in improved understanding of the maintenance environment, resulted in the beginning of a shift from individual-level blame to system-level responsibility, and led to both conceptual as well as psychometric separation of MRM from CRM. For example, in 1994, Gordon Dupont from TC identified twelve overarching issues in aviation maintenance, which were later known as the "dirty dozen": lack of communication, complacency, lack of knowledge, distraction, lack of teamwork, fatigue, lack of resources, pressure, lack of assertiveness, stress, lack of awareness, and norms (CAA, 2002, p. 20). Concurrently, Dr. James Taylor from Santa Clara University built a robust survey instrument to study the pre/post effects of MRM training programs (Taylor, 1998, 2000a). Through such efforts of various scientists and practitioners, MRM matured beyond a CRM application to the maintenance environment and a clear definition of MRM emerged: MRM is "... an *interactive* [emphasis added] process focused upon improving the opportunity for the maintenance technician to perform work more safely and effectively" (ATA, 2002, p. 5).

Typical MRM programs were dominated by awareness-level training with the following components (Patankar & Taylor, 2004a, 2004b):

1. *Dirty Dozen elements*: Lack of communication, complacency, lack of knowledge, distraction, lack of teamwork, fatigue, lack of resources, pressure, lack of assertiveness, stress, lack of awareness, and norms. Safety nets associated with each of these elements were also discussed.

2. *Accident case analysis*: One or more exercises were designed to illustrate how a chain of events (at times each event is a minor deviance) can lead to disastrous consequences.

3. *Organization-specific problem*: Focus was placed on a particular problem that the organization wants to rectify immediately. Examples of such problems include shift turnovers, logbook errors, ground damage, or lost-time injuries.

4. *Interactive exercises*: Typically, the training also included at least one interactive exercise to illustrate concepts such as the value of teamwork or hazards of verbal turnovers.

In the subsequent decade, collaborations across government agencies (FAA, NASA Ames Research Center, UK CAA, and TC), airlines (e.g., Continental, United, US Airways, and Southwest), repair stations (e.g., AAR, TIMCO, and BF Goodrich), major manufacturers (Boeing and Airbus), and universities (e.g., Santa Clara University, San Jose State University, Purdue University, University of Buffalo, and Clemson University) resulted in a number of research projects, design of practical training interventions, and assessment of those interventions. Concurrently, the aviation industry also suffered a number of serious public health, security, and economic challenges like the Asian economic crisis of 1997, terrorist attacks of September 11, 2001, the Severe Acute Respiratory Syndrome (SARS) epidemic in 2003, the US financial crisis of 2007−08, and the H1N1 Swine Flu pandemic of 2009. These challenges had substantial impact on MRM programs: the initial efforts to build and sustain MRM programs had to be redesigned, updated, and regrouped into different other programs in order to cope with the decline in available resources, as well as retirements or transfers of many committed champions of the MRM programs. Awareness of these external factors provides valuable insight into the need to stay true to the core value of safety in the aviation industry and to remain resilient to external challenges.

This chapter starts with a brief historical overview of the MRM program; next, it presents some of the most commonly used incident review tools and the associated taxonomies. Finally, it reviews the influence of MRM programs on the safety culture in technical operations and identifies emerging opportunities for continued research and development.

13.1   HISTORICAL OVERVIEW

Taylor and Patankar (2001) presented the evolution of MRM programs across four generations:

1. CRM-based training in communication skills and awareness;
2. Behavior-focused MRM training in interpersonal communication and error causation;
3. Individual awareness and readiness for behavioral change; and
4. A systemic approach to behavioral change in maintenance.

As mentioned in the Introduction section of this chapter, three maintenance-related aviation accidents led to an intense focus on the maintenance environment and the human factors associated with errors in maintenance. For example, the NTSB investigation report (NTSB, 1989) regarding the Aloha Airlines accident cited the failure of Aloha's maintenance program—specifically, inspection and quality control, as well as the FAA's surveillance of those programs, and the human factors associated with maintenance and inspection of transport category aircraft. For the first time, the actual environment in which maintenance personnel carry out their assigned tasks, as well as the human factors associated with repetitive inspection tasks and circadian rhythms, were considered. Of particular note is Dr. Colin Drury's (a professor at the State University of New York at Buffalo at that time) testimony noted in the investigation report:

> He (Dr. Drury) indicated that in the inspection process, it is not easy for the human being to perform a consistent visual search because (1) the area the searchers can concentrate on at any one time is limited by the conspicuity or size of the defect to be looked for and (2) the search process may not be systematic enough; therefore, the searcher is prone to miss areas that were thought to have been covered. Further, there is the vigilance decrement during long inspection periods that have low event rates and to some extent involve social isolation. . .such vigilance decrements occur during very long and isolated inspection duty times in which there is a low probability of finding a defect. In such cases, the human being tends to proceed through the task by saying no when a decision is to be made.
>
> NTSB (1989, p. 55)

This testimony and the NTSB's recommendations were particularly influential in (1) raising the awareness about the conditions under which maintenance personnel perform critical tasks and are thereby susceptible to errors due to human factors issues; (2) acknowledging that the aviation maintenance sector is complex—it has several interacting parties with sometimes conflicting goals or priorities—and errors made at a given time may not result in serious consequences in the immediate future, but lay dormant for a long time before manifesting themselves; and (3) shaping the investigation and reporting of subsequent NTSB investigations—for example, in the case of the Aloha investigation, Dr. John K. Lauber, a renowned scientist and developer of CRM programs, served as one of the Board Members and later John Goglia, an aircraft mechanic, served as a Board Member.

13.1.1   First Generation

Taylor and Patankar (2001) reported three cases that illustrate the purpose, content, and outcomes of the first generation MRM programs. These programs were in effect from 1989 through 1995. Early on, the purpose of the

MRM programs was similar to that of the company's CRM program—to improve safety through improved awareness, interpersonal communication, and teamwork. For example, Taggart (1990) reported the following topics in one of the training programs:

1. Interpersonal communication;
2. Assertion and conflict management;
3. Stress awareness and management;
4. Value of shift-turnover briefings;
5. Situational awareness;
6. Leadership behavior; and
7. Case studies.

These training programs were very practical—they had specific case studies woven across the instruction program as well as individual and team exercises to raise awareness about human fallibility in communication, conflict management, and shift-turnover briefings. The programs were conducted in small group sessions over several weeks and the early sessions included mostly management personnel. Posttraining feedback indicated that over 80% of the participants would expect at least a moderate change in their on-the-job behavior. However, the program was suspended shortly after completion of the first round of training because the company was liquidated.

Another program, started in 1991 and emphasized open and assertive communication (Fotos, 1991). In this program, the training topics included the following:

1. Organizational "norms" and their effect on safety;
2. Assertiveness;
3. Individual leadership styles;
4. Stress awareness and management;
5. Problem solving and decision-making skills; and
6. Interpersonal communication skills.

The delivery of the training program included interactive exercises, role play, and team exercises (Stelly & Taylor, 1992; Taylor & Robertson, 1995, p. 49). Over 2000 management and professional engineering staff were trained through this program. Enthusiasm for this program was higher than for the previous case—nearly 90% of the participants said there would be at least a moderate change in their on-the-job behavior (Taylor & Robertson, 1995, p. 15). Over a 26-month period, the program participants reported a gradual improvement in attitude toward change and moved from passive practices (like being a better listener) to active practices (like will not hesitate to speak up) (Taylor & Christensen, 1998; Taylor & Robertson, 1995; Robertson, Taylor, Stelly, & Wagner, 1995). During the same time frame, lost-time injuries and ground damage incidents decreased (Taylor & Robertson, 1995). Thus, there were three levels of improvements: enthusiasm about the training content, individual attitude toward safety, and safety outcomes. Unfortunately, even this program did not continue past the initial 26-month run and it had to be put on hold as the management's attention shifted toward economic priorities such as station closures and cost-cutting; soon the excellent results of their MRM program began to reverse (Taylor & Christensen, 1998, pp. 128−129).

The third case reported by Taylor and Patankar (2001), under the first generation of MRM programs, illustrates the beginning of training for the actual aviation maintenance technicians (rather than just managers and engineers). Although only 450 personnel (about 300 technicians) were reported to have completed this training, 80% of them reported that they expected moderate to large changes in their behavior as a result of the MRM training (Taylor, Robertson, & Choi, 1997). With respect to behavioral changes, 40% committed to active behavioral changes as a result of the MRM training and about 45% committed to passive behavioral changes. Furthermore, there was even stronger (compared to the previous case) improvement in lost-time injuries and ground damage incidents. Thus, this case also proved that MRM programs can be effective in improving attitudes, behaviors, and performance outcomes. More importantly, the frontline personnel are more responsive to the training as evidenced in the higher level of improvement in performance outcomes. Again, this program did not continue past the initial phase due to resource constraints.

13.1.2   Second Generation

During 1992−94, while the first generation MRM programs were being implemented, an example of a second generation program emerged. The content of this program was differentiated from the first generation programs in two ways: (1) it emphasized behavioral change rather than just an attitudinal change that was emphasized in the first generation programs and (2) it included company-specific cases from maintenance and was directed at maintenance technicians rather than managers and/or engineers. Additionally, there was a strategic differentiation: this program was built on an informal agreement between the company, the FAA, and the maintenance technicians' union. The agreement was that the union would encourage their members to participate in the training program and be forthcoming in their errors so that the company could focus on systemic issues and implement changes that would minimize the opportunity for similar errors in the future. In exchange for such cooperation from the union, the company promised to address the broad systemic issues rather than just individual-level corporate disciplinary action (assuming the error was inadvertent) and the FAA Flight Standards District Office also adopted a broader, collaborative stand recognizing that individual-level disciplinary actions were not effective in long-term improvements in safety. Moreover, all the parties recognized the importance of engaging the erring technician in the safety conversation in order to minimize recurrence of similar errors. The agreement between the FAA, company, and the union was built on the trust among the three individuals (John Goglia, Joe Kania, and Jim Ballough) representing the three parties and their respective credibility among their affiliate groups. This critical risk taken by the three individuals and the subsequent success of the second generation MRM programs was foundational to the modern-day Aviation Safety Action Program (ASAP) and the Safety Management System (SMS) Program.

The purpose of this second generation program was much more focused: reduce the number of maintenance documentation errors. The overall program lasted two years and was spread over three phases: focus group discussion and data collection, implementation of the first-order changes, and implementation of the second-order changes. The initial focus group discussions and data collection efforts led to specific recommendations to management that could reduce the documentation errors. Examples of such recommendations included formal training in documentation for all maintenance technicians. The result of this training was immediate and the errors decreased, but it did not last long (Taylor & Christensen, 1998; Taylor, 1995). The second-order changes included more structured efforts, but in the form of a control group and an experimental group. As part of the MRM training, the experimental group/station received specific content (awareness, role-playing, group exercises, and tutorials) on how to reduce documentation errors. All other stations formed the control group. The experimental group's errors declined and stayed lower than the control group (Taylor, 1994, 1995).

By 1995, the experimental group of second generation programs concluded as the managers and supervisors who supported the training left the station/company. Their successors were encouraged to continue support the MRM program and the company-FAA-union relationship continued until the airline economic crisis following the terrorist attacks of September 11, 2001.

13.1.3 Third Generation

About the same time as the second generation program was being launched in the United States, the report of the Canadian Commission of Inquiry into the Air Ontario accident of March 1989 was released. In this report, the Honorable Commissioner Moshansky took a very broad, systemic stand on the investigation and noted several limitations of the aviation system that allowed the accident to occur. This philosophical shift—from individual blame to systemic responsibility—and review of the specific role of air carrier management, practical recommendations for the airline, the regulator, and the global aviation industry laid the foundation for broader systemic changes across the global aviation industry. Similar to the value of

Dr. Drury's testimony in the case of the Aloha Airlines accident, in the case of the Air Ontario accident, Dr. Robert Helmreich was invited to review the investigative data and make his recommendation. Dr. Helmreich, a professor at the University of Texas at Austin, was funded by the NASA Ames Research Center to conduct this study. Based on his study, Dr. Helmreich claimed the following:

> The results of this analysis suggest that the concatenation of multiple factors from each category allowed the crew to decide to take off with contaminated wings. According to this view, no single factor taken in isolation would have triggered the crew's behaviour prior to and during take-off, but in combination they provided an environment in which a serious procedural error could occur. This array of contributory influences without a single, proximal cause warrants classification of the accident as a system failure.
>
> Commission of Inquiry (1992b, Appendix 7, p. 322)

In 1994, TC developed a different kind of MRM program called, Human Performance in Maintenance (HPIM), which was based on a 2-day program developed specifically for maintenance technicians. One of the striking and most impactful features of this program was the introduction of the "Dirty Dozen." Gordon Dupont was at TC at that time and he analyzed a number of accidents and created the list of 12 most common maintenance-related causes: (1) lack of communication, (2) complacency, (3) lack of knowledge, (4) distraction, (5) lack of teamwork, (6) fatigue, (7) lack of resources, (8) time pressure, (9) lack of assertiveness, (10) stress, (11) lack of awareness, and (12) norms. He had these illustrated in the form of memorable posters and they became an integral part of most MRM programs throughout North America (Taylor & Christensen, 1998, pp. 145−146).

The HPIM program was different from the previous generation MRM programs in two important ways: first, it focused on awareness and coping mechanisms or safeguards and second, it focused on the individual technician rather than the broader system. Although the HPIM program was developed for the Canadian audience, and the first two generation of MRM programs were a mix of awareness and behavior programs, thereafter, the majority of the North American MRM programs developed during 1994−98 focused on awareness and individual coping. For example, in 1996 a major US airline developed its MRM program to create an awareness of the impact of human performance on maintenance-related errors and personal safety. The Dirty Dozen were thoroughly integrated in this program. This program was developed by a team of technicians, supervisors, and the company's training department. Thus, it had broad support and had good instructional design. As a result of this training, over 60% of the participants said there would be a moderate or large change in their on-the-job behavior (Taylor & Christensen, 1998), which is substantially lower than that claimed by the first generation MRM programs. In terms of behavioral intentions, about 46% of the participants committed to passive changes and 27% committed to active changes. This outcome is also substantially different from that reported in the third case of first generation MRM programs. Given that the training focused on awareness rather than behavior, such intentions were not surprising. On the other hand, statistically significant improvements were found in attitudes about sharing responsibility, communication, and stress management immediately following the training sessions, and they remained stable for several months after the training (Taylor & Christensen, 1998, pp. 154–155).

Furthermore, a strong correlation was noted between improvement in attitude about stress management and improvements in both loss time injuries and ground damage (Taylor, 1998a). Thus, the training was causing the intended improvement in attitude, and the change in attitude must have translated into a change in behavior which resulted in reduced rate of injuries and ground damage.

In spite of the success of this third generation MRM program, the focus on individual-level awareness and coping resulted in "bridge to nowhere" scenarios. The original enthusiasm of the participants started to decay as they felt alone or unsupported in their quest for safety improvements, and eventually, they became frustrated and angry at their managers and co-workers for failing to fulfill the promise of the MRM program (Taylor, 1998), concluding in lost hope for the usefulness of the MRM program in the future (Taylor & Christensen, 1998, pp. 152–160).

In another example of a third generation MRM program, the training was divided into two days, but the two days were separated by several months. This airline worked with its union and the local FAA to develop the MRM training program based on the Canadian HPIM model, but decided to split it into two days that were separated by several months. The separation of the training days enabled the trainers to introduce the various topics on the first day, allow the participants to return to work and reflect on the training content, and return to the training topics for a more applied approach on the second day, when the emphasis was on how to manage errors through practiced assertiveness and awareness of risk factors. Thus, this approach seemed to be a bridge between the behavioral focus of the first two generations and the purely awareness-level focus of the third generation MRM programs. Most of this training was accomplished in one city during 1998 and in another city in 1999. In 1998, the likelihood for voluntary change increased from 60% to about 65% from phase 1 to phase 2 of the training program, while in 1999, the likelihood for such a change increased from 69% to 85%. Similarly, attitude and opinion changes after the two training days/phases showed significant improvement. However, in 1998, field interviews several months after phase 2 of the training revealed that the safety standards and MRM program implementation were deteriorating due to lack of management follow-through. The intentions to change at both cities were largely passive (between 44% and 61%), while the active change responses ranged between 8% and 14%. With respect to performance changes, both cities showed a significant decline in ground damage incidents following the start of the MRM program and the decline continued for about 16 months after the second phase of the training. (Taylor & Robertson, 1995; Taylor et al., 1997). Again, the third generation MRM programs showed an improvement in participant attitudes, commitment to change their behaviors (mostly passive behaviors, but some active behaviors as well), and a sustained improvement in performance outcomes. Thus, by all measures these training programs were successful. Nonetheless, they lacked continued support and follow-through from management (Taylor, 1998) and they remained focused on improving awareness and passive influence over behaviors (Taylor & Patankar, 2001). They also did not have clear safety performance goals, rapid feedback of results, and appropriate reinforcement for those who demonstrated the desired safety behaviors.

13.1.4 Fourth Generation

Around 1999, a fourth generation of MRM programs began to differentiate itself in two important ways: (1) these programs took a systems perspective and expected the entire aviation maintenance system to change and not just the individual technician and (2) these programs had very clear objectives—to raise awareness, change behavior, and impact specific performance outcomes. While these programs continued to build upon the best practices from previous generations, like including the Dirty Dozen topics and incorporating role-playing and interactive exercises, they started incorporating cases involving internal maintenance error investigations. The management and the technicians knew from previous experience and research findings that employee–management trust was low and improved transparency with data-sharing and open communication would help strengthen the employee–management trust. Also, one critical investigative lesson learned through the Aloha Airlines accident, the Air Ontario Accident, and the BAC 1-11 accident was that the underlying systemic causes of human errors must be investigated thoroughly in order to develop meaningful, comprehensive preventive solutions for the future. Thus, the fourth generation programs included specific tools for human factors investigations of maintenance errors, thereby translating the awareness of elements like the Dirty Dozen into practical, actionable tools (Allen & Marx, 1994; FAA, 1997). However, the fundamental challenge of interpersonal trust between technicians and managers, as well as between technicians and the local FAA inspectors continued to challenge the continuation of MRM programs. As a result, the efforts to advance MRM program development and implementation kept returning to the notion that technicians, management, and the FAA must uphold their commitment to certain fundamental tenets: focus on systemic issues rather than individual blame; implement nonpunitive error-reporting system; and follow-through on their commitments. It was known from previous studies that the technicians did not tend to trust others very easily because they tend to be more individualistic (Taylor & Patankar, 1999; Taylor, 1999) and self-reliant (Taylor & Christensen, 1998). Thus, the fourth generation programs not only addressed individual awareness and behavioral issues, but also gradually shifted toward seeking a deeper, cultural change (Taylor & Patankar, 2001).

Taylor and Patankar (2001) presented two cases that illustrate the transition of the fourth generation MRM programs toward cultural change. In the first case, the emphasis was on individual behavior, regardless of the attitudinal readiness. This approach was quite the opposite of previous attempts to seek attitudinal change first and hope for a behavioral change to follow. In this case, certain behaviors were expected from the maintenance, flight, management, and dispatch personnel. Their emphasis was on a structured communication protocol, called the Concept Alignment Process (Lynch, 1996; Patankar & Taylor, 1999), which was specifically designed to expect procedural compliance, integration of risk analysis in tactical decision-making, vigilance and safeguard against individual complacency, and question another team member's decision in a safe and respectful environment (Lynch, 1996). The key to the success of this program was a reinforcement cycle: prescribed behavior led to procedural changes for flight, maintenance, as well as management; these procedural changes were supported and implemented; the participants' acceptance of the new communication protocol increased and their attitude toward the protocol improved; and improved attitude led to improved adoption and more consistent adherence to the prescribed behavioral protocol, which led to further organizational changes (Patankar & Taylor, 1999). One of the key performance outcomes of this program was that it not only resulted in changes to internal organizational procedures, but it also impacted the FAA's approved procedures and manufacturer's service bulletins. While the internal impact was not surprising, the external impact brought to light the potential for a broader influence of MRM programs.

In the second case of a fourth generation MRM program, Taylor and Patankar (2001) presented an airline's MRM program that involved both awareness training, which was based on the Dirty Dozen, as well as behavioral training related to improved decision-making and human error incident investigation. This program was representative of the state-of-the-art at that time. It utilized the available training materials and past practice in terms of the Dirty Dozen topics and the associated case examples, but it also incorporated behavioral aspects such as the Concept Alignment Process and known tools and techniques associated with the investigation of human error in maintenance. Additional information available through the FAA, NASA, and other public domain web sites was also made available. Thus, the expectation was that the participants would continue to build their awareness after the training and practice their behavioral skills taught in the course. Furthermore, the company was also better prepared to act on the systemic improvement ideas that might arise from the training participants. The company management was open to making the necessary changes and keeping everyone informed of the changes as well as rationale for adopting or not adopting the suggested changes.

13.1.5 Fifth Generation

After the terrorist attack of the World Trade Center in New York, on September 11, 2001, the aviation industry went into a tailspin: financial losses followed by cost-cutting measures, retirements, employment changes, and redirection of resources. As a result, most companies in the United States suspended their MRM programs. In 2003, the FAA funded a different type of project. Instead of continuing to fund research related to traditional MRM programs, they funded a project related the Aviation Safety Action Program (ASAP) in maintenance. This change in research focus was consistent with the internal shift the airline industry had made—it had shifted from the traditional CRM/MRM programs to ASAP programs, which were consistent with the core concept over which MRM programs were built. As presented in the discussion about the second generation MRM programs, the core concept was that three parties—company, labor, and regulator—need to come together and focus on systemic improvement rather than individual blame. Also, by that time, there was sufficient awareness regarding the human factors principles and so the MRM training could focus on event investigation and classification of human error. Thus, the fifth generation MRM programs were in fact, Maintenance ASAP programs, which continued to use the basic MRM concepts (like the Dirty Dozen and case studies), but focused more on the integration of human factors in event investigation methods. However, since the adoption of ASAP programs was much slower in the maintenance community (in 2003, there were only six programs in maintenance; whereas, there were 28 programs in flight), the FAA was interested in learning about the barriers to adoption, particularly if the barriers were related to the FAA's ASAP policy (FAA, 1997, 2002).

The purpose of a Maintenance ASAP agreement between the FAA, air carrier, and the labor union is to provide a nonpunitive forum for technicians to come forward and disclose their errors to the FAA and the air carrier so that systemic solutions could be implemented and similar errors, due to similar causes, could be minimized. Since the advisory circular pertaining to Maintenance ASAPs used language similar to the flight domain, it was hypothesized that it would be difficult to apply the same circular in the maintenance domain. Patankar and Driscoll (2005) conducted an extensive field study and reported eight best practices across successful Maintenance ASAP programs; of those, five are presented here:

1. Use the template MOU provided by the FAA, but create an addendum to provide maintenance-specific details about the specific program: The original template MOU was based on the needs of the flight crew. It was incredibly difficult to create an entirely new MOU for maintenance; thus, it was recommended that the maintenance community try to accept the flight MOU and add a separate document to provide details about the maintenance ASAP program.

2. Try to keep an open mind and accept as many ASAP reports as possible: In the beginning, the Maintenance ASAP program suffered from the same interpersonal trust issues as those discovered during the early generation MRM programs. Since the intent of the Maintenance ASAP program was to provide a nonpunitive pathway to report errors and implement systemic solutions, it was recommended that the ASAP program's Event Review Committee (ERC) accept as many reports as possible.

3. Consider a report as "sole source" if it is from anyone within the company: In the early stages of the Maintenance ASAP program, there was much debate about what would be considered a "sole source" report because if it was not a sole source report, it could be subject to company and/or FAA action. To simplify matters, the recommendation from the industry was to consider all reports from within the company to be sole source reports.

4. Try to link ASAP reports from different professional communities to leverage the overall benefits: In some companies, there were separate ASAP programs and ERCs for each professional community—flight, maintenance, and dispatch. While there were several reasons to keep these reports and programs separate, the industry also noted potential to link the reports so that comprehensive solutions could be developed.

5. Follow through on labor, management, and FAA commitments: Since an ASAP program is a tripartite agreement, all three members must honor their commitments, regardless of the political pressures or cost of the corrective actions. Thus, the industry strongly advocated for consistent commitment from all parties.

Concurrent with the challenges associated with policy guidance, procedures, and consistent implementation, the Maintenance ASAP program also faced the challenge of developing, enforcing, and updating its own "community standard" for unacceptable behavior. Taylor (2004) focused on this issue and reported on his findings regarding acceptance criteria for maintenance ASAP events. Taylor noted that for the maintenance community, the notion of "intentional disregard for safety" was a difficult concept to define, but could be approached with a risk-based philosophy of error management, and decisions could be made on a case-by-case basis. Taylor concluded that the regulators, union representatives, and air carrier representatives responded similarly to the accept/reject decision with respect to the ASAP cases provided to them. Thus, the community standard approach could be used in Maintenance ASAP programs to detect intentional disregard for safety, without having to explicitly define it.

In a parallel development, the flight community had been working with the FAA and hosting Information Sharing meetings (called the FAA InfoShare). Until about 2004, the maintenance community did not have a strong presence at these meetings, but some of the attendees thought that it was time for the community to come together and start presenting their experiences with MRM and M-ASAP programs to the broader audience, much like the flight community was doing. So, members from American Airlines, Southwest Airlines, AAR Corporation, United Airlines, Continental Airlines, Delta Airlines, International Association of Machinists (IAM), Aircraft Mechanics Fraternal Association (AMFA), FAA, NASA Ames Research Center, and Saint Louis University started organizing and holding separate Maintenance InfoShare meetings. Until about 2008, these meetings were held separately, but thereafter, there was sufficient momentum and interest that they could be integrated in the national InfoShare meetings, along with flight and dispatch communities. Today, these meetings are robust and are attended by over 1000 participants from a variety of professional communities (flight, maintenance, dispatch, cabin, regional airlines, universities, etc.) and there is a broader exchange of lessons learned and informal consultation with the FAA representatives.

As a result of all of the above concurrent developments and substantial efforts on the part of hundreds of safety champions in the aviation maintenance industry, the number of Maintenance ASAP agreements has grown exponentially from just six in 2003 to 168 as of August 31, 2017; in the same period, the Flight ASAP agreements have grown from 28 to 188 (FAA, 2017a). This growth and overall success of the program is a true testimonial to the cultural change in aviation maintenance—now, it would be fair to say that the maintenance industry has moved from a blame culture to a just culture (Marx, 1998, 2001; Reason, 1997); however, there continue to be some exceptional cases where a person experiences a punitive treatment either from the company or from the FAA. Also, although the fifth generation of MRM programs provided a stronger integration of attitudinal and behavioral approaches to training and strengthened employee—management—regulator trust, they remained largely reactive safety programs.

13.1.6   Sixth Generation

Regular participation in the InfoShare meetings led the maintenance community to consider some of the other programs that were successful in flight operations and air traffic control communities, particularly the ones that would be proactive, continue to foster a just culture, and provide sufficient protection of data. Thus, toward the end of 2008, the maintenance community's attention turned toward the line oriented safety audit (LOSA) program that had been operational in the flight community since the 1990s (Klinect, Wilhelm, & Helmreich, 1999; Klinect, Murray, Merritt, & Helmreich, 2003). The LOSA name was changed to Line Operations Safety *Assessment* (rather than Audit) to make it more consistent with the nonpunitive intent of the program (Ma & Rankin, 2012). It was based on a strong theoretical model of Threat and Error Management (Klinect et al. 1999), and it had proven to be successful in improving safety in the United States as well as abroad (ICAO, 2002). Ma et al. (2011) reported the early rationale for the exploration of LOSA programs in maintenance as follows:

1. Implementation of a LOSA program in Maintenance and Ramp operations would enable proactive identification of threats and errors before they lead to an incident or accident, thereby reducing ground damage and personal injuries.
2. Early success with Maintenance and Ramp LOSA programs demonstrates their ability to not only reduce ground damage (decline in ground damage attributable to human error ranged from 43% to 73%), but also their ability to improve efficiencies and reduce potential for human error by simplifying procedures like the lock-out and tag-out procedure for B767 leading edge devices at one of the partner air carriers.
3. Improved communication and coordination of safety expectations with airport officials and external contractors working on air carrier aircraft.

There are two fundamental principles behind successful LOSA programs:

1. The root causes of fatal accidents are similar to those of events involving substantive damage and injuries as well as unreported errors that did not result in any harm. This principle is based on the Heinrich ratio (Heinrich, 1941), which states that for every fatal outcome, there are about 30 major harm outcomes and about 300 unreported or no harm outcome scenarios. Thus, the assumption is that if one increases the vigilance regarding routine threats and errors, the operator(s) will be able to stop the error trajectory from manifesting itself in harm (this is the proactive aspect of this approach), and if the operator(s) is mindful of the systemic causes for such errors, he/she could enhance the safety even further by implementing systemic solutions (this is the predictive aspect of this approach).
2. The data from LOSA observations are collected anonymously and are maintained entirely within the organization; therefore, there is no need for an approval from the FAA/regulator. While the anonymity and lack of formal agreement with the FAA may create a certain degree of separation from punitive action, the company is still expected to honor its nonpunitive policy for data collected under the LOSA program.

The move toward a Maintenance LOSA program is also an attempt to centralize all safety programs under the programmatic umbrella of an SMS Program (FAA, 2013). This integrated approach allows for education and voluntary reporting programs from all employee groups to be managed under a cohesive programmatic umbrella, which not only improves administrative efficiency, but also improves the potential for cross-program leveraging of data and predictive analytics. Furthermore, if all the employee groups receive similar treatment regarding anonymity, confidentiality, nonpunitive report handling, there is a greater likelihood of improved interpersonal trust among the employees, management, and the regulator.

CAUTION: Most organizations with fifth or sixth generation MRM programs have built a robust awareness of the fundamentals of maintenance human factors (MHF) and they tend to assume that maintenance and ramp personnel are familiar with topics like the Dirty Dozen. Therefore, fundamentals of MHF are not included in the 11 major steps to LOSA implementation, as suggested by Ma and Rankin (2012). The organizations that have not incorporated such fundamental human factors training in their maintenance programs, would find it useful to incorporate at least the following presentation provided by the FAA: https://www.faa.gov/about/initiatives/maintenance_hf/training_tools/.

13.2   MRM RESEARCH PROGRAM

13.2.1   FAA–TC–UK CAA

As presented earlier in this chapter, the 1988 Aloha Airlines accident was the first airliner accident publicly acknowledged as one caused by maintenance errors. Recognizing that much of the transport aircraft fleet across the nation was aging, and similar challenges could be lying dormant at other companies, in June 1989, Dr. William Shepherd, from the Biomedical and Behavioral Sciences Division of the FAA, called the first meeting on human factors issues in aircraft maintenance and inspection (Shepherd & Parker, 1989). The objective of this meeting was to identify key human factors issues that impact maintenance and inspection actions, and Dr. Shepherd sought to both raise the awareness of the conditions under which an aircraft maintenance technician performs his/her job, as well as to identify research efforts necessary to improve safety in aviation maintenance and, if necessary, make appropriate recommendations for regulatory changes. The recommendations arising out of this initial meeting could be categorized as follows:

1. Modernize technical training: It was widely recognized that the extant technical training and performance requirements in the FAA Part 147 curriculum are inadequate for the modern aircraft technology that is in

use. The participants recommended a thorough review and rewrite of the regulatory requirements so that both technical requirements as well as instructional technologies could be enhanced. It was also noted that the supply of trained aircraft maintenance technicians was inadequate to meet the future demand; therefore, enhanced marketing efforts were recommended.

2. Add soft skills training: The need for supplementing technical training with soft skills focused on the need for training in interpersonal communication and management of stress and time pressures in the work environment.

3. Create means for ongoing research on aviation MHF: There was a need for ongoing research in aviation MHF ranging from task analysis of actual technician and inspector jobs to improvement in maintenance instruction and data as reported in various technical publications and manuals. Also, the participants expressed the need for a centralized database of industry information concerning maintenance technologies, procedures, and problems.

Overall, the participants encouraged Dr. Shepherd to continue with such meetings on a regular basis and engage the industry, academic researchers, consultants, and FAA representatives in a collaborative dialog. Thus, in response to the above recommendations and overwhelming support from the aviation maintenance industry, the Human Factors in Maintenance Research Program was born, and it was housed under the Office of Aviation Medicine. Ms. Jean Watson was appointed the Program Manager. From then on, the FAA followed a structured process of engaging the aviation maintenance industry in identifying research requirements, identifying and selecting appropriate researchers (both academic and nonacademic), leveraging resources from other federal agencies, and disseminating results through annual conferences, published reports and proceedings, as well as journal articles, books, book chapters, software, website archives, and videos. Today, most of the training materials and research reports are available at the following site: https://www.faa.gov/about/initiatives/maintenance_hf/.

Just months before Dr. Shepherd organized the first Human Factors in Aviation Maintenance and Inspection meeting, in March 1989, Air Ontario's Fokker F28 crashed in Dryden, Ontario, Canada. The subsequent investigation resulted in almost 200 recommendations, including those related to aviation MHF. Thus, Transport Canada (TC) was also highly motivated to develop stronger awareness regarding human factors in aviation maintenance. The year 1990 onward, representatives from TC started to participate in the FAA's Human Factors in Aviation Maintenance and Inspection meetings. In 1993, TC hired Gordon Dupont to develop their HPIM training program and released the program in 1994 (as previously discussed in Section 13.1.3 under Third Generation MRM Programs). Almost concurrent with this development in Canada, and triggered by the 1990 BAC 1-11 accident in the United Kingdom, the UK CAA's interest in MHF also began to grow. The participation of representatives from both TC and the UK CAA, as well as airlines and maintenance organizations from Canada and Europe continued throughout the 1990s. Ultimately, the FAA, TC, and the UK CAA decided to take turns hosting the meetings. The first international meeting was in fact the Twelfth Human Factors in Aviation Maintenance and Inspection Symposium, which was hosted by the UK CAA in 1998 and held at Gatwick Airport. In 1999, the 13th symposium was in Daytona Beach, FL; in 2000, the 14th symposium was in Vancouver, BC; in 2001, the 15th symposium was in London, UK; in 2002, the 16th symposium was in San Francisco, CA; and in 2003, the 17th (and final) symposium was in Toronto, ON.

There are numerous outcomes that could be linked with this series of seventeen symposia that lasted for 14 years. Some of the key outcomes are as follows:

1. Built the legitimacy of Maintenance Human Factors (MHF): Through numerous funded research projects, many serious academics from a variety of universities, as well as the NASA Ames Research Center, were drawn to research opportunities. They developed a substantive scholarly body of knowledge and built the foundation upon which text books and training materials could be developed. The applied nature of research in this field enabled the industry partners to fully participate in the research studies and not only appreciate the value of academic research, but also strengthen it by providing practical guidance and validation. Thus, the research outcomes had both practical significance as well as substantive contributions to the advancement of the state of knowledge in the field of MHF. Additionally, two of the most critical appointments that could be directly attributed to the success of the MHF program were as follows:
   a. In 1995, Mr. John Goglia was appointed to the Board of the NTSB and he served till 2004. He was the first aircraft mechanic to ever serve on the NTSB Board and throughout his term, he was the most effective champion of human factors in maintenance.
   b. In 2002, Mr. James "Jim" Ballough, an early believer in human factors created the position of the Chief Scientist and Technical Advisor for Human Factors in Aviation Maintenance with the FAA. He selected Dr. William "Bill" Johnson for that position and brought MHF on equal footing with flight deck human factors and other technical disciplines.
2. Created foundational materials and ready-to-use products for training: The FAA, TC, and the UK CAA used results of research projects and

industry best practices derived from various generations of implementation to develop foundational materials such as the PEAR Model, the SHEL(L) Model, Reason's Swiss Cheese Model, the Dirty Dozen, and various role-playing exercises, case studies, and videos that are commonly used in MHF courses across the western world. Such widespread shared use led to the development of a common body of knowledge, including shared understanding of terminology such as fatigue, sleep deprivation, closed-loop communication, and safety nets. The impact and dissemination of research results is demonstrated by the depth and breadth of outcomes posted on the following websites:

   a. Most of the FAA-funded research products, including reports, tools, and training materials are available at https://www.faa.gov/about/ initiatives/maintenance_hf/

   b. Ashgate Publishing, Ltd., which was recently acquired by Taylor & Francis, has built up a niche in aviation human factors and published a number of seminal works. Their catalog of current publications is available at https://www.routledge.com

   c. TC's publications and videos are available at http://www.tc.gc.ca/eng/ civilaviation/publications/menu.htm

   d. The UK CAA has published guidance material to help approved maintenance organizations comply with the EASA Part-145 requirements. This document is available at http://publicapps.caa.co.uk/docs/ 33/CAP716.PDF

3. Contributed toward regulatory guidance materials and requirements: The various MRM programs implemented at the participating airlines and repair stations achieved numerous changes to maintenance tasks, organizational procedures (like maintenance manuals updates), and industry-wide best practices (like nonpunitive error-reporting policies). At the national and international levels, the reports and recommendations from various research projects and conversations at the symposia contributed toward the development of the following legislative changes:

   a. Canadian Aviation Regulations, Subpart 7: SMSs. In 1999, TC began its journey toward system-wide implementation of SMS programs by first developing an overall framework for the entire Canadian aviation industry. It was published as, *Flight 2005: A Civil Aviation Safety Framework for Canada* (Transport Canada, 1999). Canada became the first country in the world to regulate the implementation of SMS in the aviation industry, but took a phased approach to building awareness through guidance materials and progressive phase-in requirements across all the industry sectors (flight operations, maintenance, design, airports, etc.). Subsequently, in *Flight 2010*, TC increased the emphasis on risk-based decision-making (Transport Canada, 2006). Today, Subpart 7 of the Canadian Aviation

Regulations delineates the general requirements of SMS programs at all approved, certificate-holding organizations. Advisory Circular 107-001 provides guidance regarding development and maintenance of a Safety Management Program at large or complex organizations (Transport Canada, 2015).

b. **International Civil Aviation Organization (ICAO).** In 1986, the ICAO Assembly adopted Resolution A26-9 regarding flight safety and human factors, and the Air Navigation Commission formulated the subsequent objectives. Among those objectives was the development of training materials to raise awareness regarding how human factors issues impact safety in every aspect of the aviation industry—design, operation, navigation, air traffic control, and maintenance. ICAO began with the publication of a series of *Human Factors Digests* (earliest guidance material on Human Factors in Aircraft Maintenance and Inspection dates back to 1995, Circular 253), but subsequently integrated their content into a two-part training manual: *Human Factors Training Manual*, Doc 9683-AN/950 (ICAO, 1998). With respect to the handling of MRM in this Manual, the following topics were included: contemporary maintenance problems; human errors in maintenance; organizational perspective on human errors in the maintenance and inspection environment; illustration of various cases of maintenance errors; human factors issues such as interpersonal communication and shift turnovers; variations in technical training methodologies and tools; teamwork and organizational factors; and job design. In 2003, ICAO published the *Human Factors Guidelines for Aircraft Maintenance Manual* (ICAO, 2003). Many of the outcomes from the Human Factors in Aviation Maintenance and Inspection Research Program were incorporated in this document: general background on human factors in aviation maintenance; key issues in maintenance error; countermeasures to maintenance errors; skills training in shift turnover/handover, task turnover/handover, and planning and recording of nonscheduled maintenance; environmental factors impacting maintenance actions and errors; ergonomic audit programs; document design for aircraft maintenance; and fatigue management. In 2008, ICAO published amendments to Annex 6, which included the requirement for all operators of international general aviation operations with certificated maximum take-off weight exceeding 5700 kg or those equipped with turbojet engines, to establish and maintain a SMS (ICAO, 2008, section 3.3.2), In February 2013, ICAO developed the new Annex 19, dedicated to safety management, and adopted it in November 2013—this annex provides comprehensive guidance on SMS implementation requirements and timelines for both operators and regulators (ICAO, 2013).

c. European Aviation Safety Agency (EASA) and UK CAA. EASA incorporated the human factors training requirements under Joint Airworthiness Requirements (JAR) Part-145. The deadline to comply with this requirement was July 1, 2005 and for alternate means of compliance, the deadline was September 28, 2006 (CAA, 2003, Chapter 11, p. 1). All approved maintenance organizations were expected to have in place a process for initial and recurrent human factors training. The guidance material, with respect to interpretation and compliance with the JAR-145 requirements, from UK CAA (CAA, 2003) began with the discussion of safety culture and organizational factors leading to maintenance errors; thereafter, it continued with focus on error management, individual-level human factors issues such as fatigue, environmental factors, maintenance procedures and documentation, communication, planning, professionalism, event reporting systems, and concluded with human factors training for maintenance professionals.

d. FAA. While ICAO, TC, EASA, and UK CAA took the compliance-based approach to implementation of MRM and SMS programs, the FAA took a voluntary approach to MRM and SMS adoption and produced numerous materials that could be used for awareness training. The FAA also updated its Aviation Maintenance Technician Handbook (General) by adding Chapter 14 on Human Factors (FAA, 2008), and further revised it in 2011. In recent years, the FAA has committed to comply with the ICAO requirements and is making efforts to make the appropriate regulatory changes (FAA, 2016). For example, in 2015, the FAA issued the final rule requiring all air carriers operating under Part 121 to develop and implement an SMS program; it also indicated that a similar requirement might be extended to Part-145 operators (approved repair stations) through the corresponding Part 121 air carriers. The requirements for human factors training are not specifically listed in the final rule, but under Subpart E (Safety Promotion), it is expected that the workforce will "attain and maintain the competencies necessary to perform their duties relevant to the operation and performance of the SMS" (FAA, 2015, §5.91, p. 1328). Also, according to the latest Notice of Proposed Rulemaking regarding the implementation of SMS programs at certificated airports, the requirement for an SMS program will only apply to small, medium, or large hub airports—the comments in response to this NPRM are under review (FAA, 2016). Thus, the US aviation industry is on a good path to sustainable implementation and continuous improvement of MRM and SMS programs.

13.2.2 Government–Academia–Industry

The majority of the research related to MHF was carried out in the United States. It was funded by the FAA and/or the NASA; conducted by academic researchers (faculty and students) or consultants; and supported by industry partners. Some of the key advantages of this government–academia–industry partnership were as follows:

1. Government funding allowed for the research products to be available to the broader aviation industry rather than specific consulting clients, advance the body of knowledge and produce numerous academic publications, and provide content and recommendations for the production of numerous policy documents.
2. The academic partners served as trusted agents between the government agencies and the industry partners. The participating faculty and students brought a high degree of rigor, neutral assessment and objective guidance, and consistency in reporting results from several years of sustained efforts.
3. The industry partners not only provided access to their personnel and facilities, but actively engaged in the research projects—they developed the initial research requirements, appointed internal liaison personnel to help the research teams with project logistics, provided matching support in terms of personnel time, and complimentary air tickets. They also tested, critiqued, and used the products arising from the research projects. Some partners also hired the students who participated in the research projects.

Overall, the impact of the MRM research program was global in scope. For example, the ICAO, FAA, TC, and UK CAA guidance materials were developed from the results of the MRM research efforts. Similarly, a broad range of training materials and handbooks were also developed from the MRM research efforts:

1. Human Factors Guide for Aviation Maintenance and Inspection. Available at https://www.faa.gov/about/initiatives/maintenance_hf/training_tools/media/HF_Guide.pdf
2. MHF Presentation System (consisting of Powerpoint slides). Available at https://www.faa.gov/about/initiatives/maintenance_hf/training_tools/
3. Aviation MHF (CAP 716): Guidance material on the UK CAA interpretation of Part-145 Human Factors and Error Management Requirements. Available at https://www.faa.gov/about/initiatives/maintenance_hf/training_tools/
4. TC videos, posters, and guidance material. Available at http://www.tc.gc.ca/eng/civilaviation/publications/menu.htm

13.3 MRM TRAINING CONTENT AND DELIVERY

13.3.1 MRM Training Content

The target population for MRM training has varied over the years, but it is now generally believed that such training should be aimed at field personnel as well as the full line of supervisory and management personnel (Aircraft Maintenance Technicians/Engineers, quality assurance/control personnel, ramp personnel, incident/accident investigators, maintenance supervisors and managers, planning and maintenance program engineers, as well as technical training instructors). Generally, a broad overview of the fundamental human factors topics is recommended for all, but focused behavioral training and skills exercises are recommended based on the job categories and level of oversight responsibilities. For example, all personnel may receive a 4-hour general introductory course, and the different professional groups may receive a follow-on series of 8-hour workshops to build their proficiency in applying the general concepts to their routine job duties.

The *ICAO Human Factors Training Manual* (ICAO, 1998) recommended several training syllabus objectives (see Table 13.1). Available at https://www.globalairtraining.com/resources/DOC-9683.pdf.

The following training syllabus objectives were recommended. Each objective is further designated as either skill (S), knowledge (K), or attitude (A). Also, each objective could be taught at one of three levels of proficiency:

1. Level 1: Familiarization (be able to describe in simple terms, give examples, and use typical Human Factors terms).
2. Level 2: Basic Theory and Application (be familiar with the fundamental theoretical constructs underlying the Human Factors issues, familiar with the current literature, and apply the Human Factors knowledge to practical situations).
3. Level 3: Advanced Understanding of Theory and Applications (understand the underlying theoretical concepts and their interrelationships, give detailed examples, combine knowledge of multiple concepts in a logical, comprehensive and practical manner, and interpret results from various sources to apply corrective actions as appropriate).

By the time the ICAO manual was published, MRM programs in North America were in their third generation of evolution; however, they were largely focused on raising awareness. This emphasis on awareness was consistent with the fact that the large majority of training objectives listed in Table 13.1 were intended to raise either the knowledge level (awareness) or improve attitude (as a result of improved awareness). The introduction of the

TABLE 13.1 ICAO Recommended Training Syllabus Objectives

Training Objectives	Knowledge (K); Skill (S); or Attitude (A)
1. General Introduction to Human Factors	
a. Understand the basic concepts of human factors, recognize human factors contributions to aircraft accidents, and understand the goal of human factors training.	K
b. Appreciate the need to address human factors in aviation maintenance	A
2. Safety Culture and Organizational Factors	
a. Understand the concepts of a good safety culture and organizational aspects of human factors	K
b. Appreciate the importance of a good safety culture	A
3. Human Error	
a. Understand key error models and theories, recognize different types of errors and know the techniques used to avoid or recover from them, understand the difference between errors and violations, apply risk assessment methods to proactively manage error-inducing conditions, Appreciate that human error cannot be totally eliminated; it must be controlled.	K
b. Demonstrate a proactive attitude toward procedural compliance, avoidance of rule violations, and vigilance toward errors and error-inducing conditions.	A
4. Human Performance and Work Environment	
a. Recognize the effect of physical limitations and work environment on human performance, and be aware of various safety practices to guard against human physical, psychological, and physiological limitations.	K
b. Appreciate that humans are susceptible to environmental, physical, psychological, and physiological conditions, as well as effects of alcohol, drugs, and medications, and there is a tendency to take shortcuts.	A
c. Develop ways to improve situational awareness, cope with stress and fatigue, manage workload, stay motivated, and avoid complacency.	S

(Continued)

TABLE 13.1 (Continued)

Training Objectives	Knowledge (K); Skill (S); or Attitude (A)
5. The Maintenance Organization's own Human Factors Program	K
a. Achieve an in-depth understanding of the structure and aims of the company's own Human Factors program, including error-reporting programs, error/ event investigation process, and disciplinary policies.	
b. Appreciate the importance of reporting incidents, errors, and problems.	A

Dirty Dozen by TC led to accelerated adoption of a number of knowledge- and attitude- level ICAO training objectives in a simplistic, but memorable manner across the world. As the MRM programs continued to mature, particularly in the fifth and sixth generation programs, the emphasis shifted toward application and synthesis of basic Human Factors knowledge, incorporating increased Level 3 proficiency. Table 13.1 summarizes the training objectives and their knowledge/skill/attitude designations as recommended by (ICAO, 1998, pp. 2-1-19-22).

The UK CAA recommends the following topics in order to comply with the above ICAO requirements:

1. Safety Culture and Organizational Factors;
2. Errors, Violations, and Noncompliance with Procedures;
3. Factors Associated with the Individual (fatigue, shiftwork, stress, etc.);
4. Environmental Factors (includes tooling and ergonomic audit programs);
5. Procedures, Documentation, and Maintenance Data;
6. Communication, Handover, and Sign-offs;
7. Planning, Preparation, and Teamwork;
8. Professionalism and Integrity; and
9. Organization's Error Management Program (including error-reporting polices, investigation process, and solutions tracking process).

The FAA's recommendations for current generation MRM programs also include Fatigue Risk Management and Return on Investment Analysis. Both these topics have been particularly salient in the United States because the continuous duty-time for maintenance technicians can be extended beyond reasonable limits, and since the MRM programs are voluntary, they need to demonstrate a positive return-on-investment.

13.3.2 Delivery Options

Most airlines and repair stations (Maintenance, Repair, and Overhaul facilities) offer their own MRM training. A typical distribution of emphasis, and awareness (knowledge and attitudinal change) versus behavioral (skills change) training is presented in Table 13.2. Generally, the Phase 1 awareness training is a 16-hour program; whereas, the rest of the training programs tend to be offered as 8-hour recurrent training programs. As illustrated in Table 13.2, each phase builds upon the awareness developed in the preceding phase and adds a behavioral or skill development component to it. While the broad categories of emphasis remain fairly stable, the specific topics, exercises, case studies, etc. vary. However, they all strive to achieve the learning objectives stated by ICAO (see Table 13.1).

Three delivery styles have been used:

1. Half-Day Introductory Seminar: a 4-hour introductory seminar is typically aimed at senior management to get their support for the full training program.
2. Seminar/Workshops: 1-day or 2-day events.
3. Seminars Spaced 3–6 months apart: A series of 1-day progressive training events separated by 3–6 months.

13.4 RESULTS OF MRM TRAINING

13.4.1 Key Findings Across all Generations of this Research Program

MRM Training Programs, in General, Are Effective in Raising Awareness About Human Performance Limitations and Have Been Correlated With Improvements in Safety Performance Outcomes

In the United States, MRM training programs were received very well by the frontline maintenance personnel. The general pattern of scores on attitudinal survey items indicated an improvement soon after training, stable scores even one year after the training, but a decline thereafter and a shift toward negative scores thereafter. Subsequent interviews with the participating personnel indicated that while they were enthused during the training and remained optimistic that their colleagues and supervisors would implement appropriate changes to their work environment (consistent with the human factors elements discussed in the MRM training), they were disappointed because they did not see significant follow-through from their management. After sustained periods of nonimprovement in management follow-through, their initial enthusiasm turned from disappointment to frustration and finally to anger. Thus, the attitudinal scores declined and turned negative (Taylor, 1998).

TABLE 13.2 Phased Approach to MRM Training Implementation

Emphasis Area	Type of Training (Awareness/Behavioral)				
	Phase 1	Phase 2	Phase 3	Phase 4	Phase 5
Dirty Dozen	Awareness				
Individual and Team Skill Development	Awareness	Behavioral			
Individual and Organizational Error Mitigation Strategies	Awareness	Awareness	Behavioral		
Error Investigation and Analysis	Awareness		Awareness	Behavioral	
Proactive and Predictive Analysis and Systemic Improvements				Awareness	Behavioral

Although the emphasis of the MRM training was on raising the overall foundational knowledge about human factors issues and improving the participants' attitude toward human factors, the enthusiastic response to MRM training was correlated with improvements in work performance. For example, stress management was a key topic in these MRM programs—the participants must have taken most positively to this aspect of the training because they showed the greatest improvement in attitude toward stress management and this improvement was most positively correlated with decline in lost-time injuries as well as ground damage (Taylor, 1998). Based on a number of longitudinal studies, Taylor & Christensen (1998) reported that the MRM training programs resulted in an improved attitude toward safety, and this attitudinal improvement correlated with parallel and subsequent performance improvements such as reduction in lost-time injuries, ground damage, and logbook errors.

In search of a theoretical explanation for these observed effects of training, it seems Alvarez, Salas, and Garfano (2004) might offer valuable insight. They attribute transfer performance (the degree to which what is learned results in a measurable change in performance) to individual characteristics (mostly motivation to learn and transfer), training characteristics (content and delivery mechanisms most likely to support transfer), and organizational characteristics (generally termed as organizational climate conducive to transfer of training). With respect to the MRM programs, the participants seemed to be very motivated to learn and transfer (as indicated by the posttraining attitudinal scores), but the organizational climate for transfer of training was not always conducive to realize the full potential of the MRM training (as evidenced by the interview data that claimed lack of management follow-through). Thus, future implementation of MRM programs might benefit from Sitzman and Weinhardt's (2015) training engagement theory, which advocates for continuous assessment of engagement and commitment from multiple levels of the organization so that there is an ongoing attention to the training and multilevel vested interest in the training program's success.

Individual Professionalism and Interpersonal Trust Are Two Key Indicators of Safety Climate/Culture in Aviation Maintenance

MRM training programs, throughout all six generations, tend to emphasize the role of the individual maintenance technician in reducing errors, as evidenced by individual-level procedural compliance, stress management, situational awareness, fatigue management, workload management, and complacency, as well as interpersonal communication. It is not surprising that this increased emphasis on individual-level accountability, as a part of professionalism, has given rise to the importance of interpersonal trust as a matter of mutual accountability. Thus, individual professionalism and interpersonal trust have emerged as the most consistent indicators of safety attitudes and behaviors, as well as the resultant safety climate/culture in aviation maintenance (Taylor & Patankar, 2001).

Individual professionalism is found to be comprised of two key factors: stress management and assertiveness (Patankar & Taylor, 1999, 2001; Taylor & Christensen, 1998). Stress management is not only about self-awareness of environmental, operational, and personal factors that lead to increased stress, but also about being able to manage that stress and being able to prevent such stress from manifesting itself into human error. Assertiveness, on the other hand, refers to one's commitment to respectfully speak up in support of safety, regardless of labor-management challenges, social pressure, or personal risk, as well as to be able to receive input from others.

Interpersonal trust, in the context of aviation maintenance, is defined as willingness of maintenance personnel to trust their co-workers on matters of professionalism and safety—they should be able to rely on one another to carry out their commitments and to protect each other from hazards. Thus, interpersonal trust and open communication tend to be mutually-supportive properties. Patankar, Taylor, and Goglia (2002) studied interpersonal trust across five maintenance organizations and discovered that one-third of the mechanics did not trust that their supervisor would act in the interest of safety. The significance of interpersonal trust began to emerge in fourth generation MRM programs and grew stronger in the fifth and sixth generation programs. In the early stages (fourth generation), the realization of the significance of interpersonal trust was limited to co-workers and employee—management relationship. As the MRM programs continued to mature through the fifth generation, the notion of interpersonal trust became foundational to the sustainability of MRM programs, and in the sixth generation programs, the level of trust expected from co-workers, managers, regulators, and industry-wide colleagues has set a new high standard without which incorporation of programs like ASAP and LOSA, and predictive analytics available due to sharing of safety data, would be impossible.

Aircraft Maintenance Engineers/Technicians Are Among the Most Individualistic People in Aviation

Hofstede (1984), through his landmark study of IBM workers around world, classified work values of different people. Those who were more inclined to value group harmony or community goals over individual autonomy were classified as "collectivistic," and those that valued individual autonomy over group or community harmony were classified as "individualistic." Hofstede noted that the individualistic versus collectivistic differentiation mapped very well across national boundaries—people from western countries were more individualistic than those from eastern or South American countries. This study laid the foundation for classification of cultures based on national boundaries. Helmreich and Merritt (1998) called such differentiation "national culture" and built on the underlying concepts across professional and organizational boundaries to define "professional culture" and "organizational culture." Helmreich and Merritt applied Hofstede's individualistic versus collectivistic measure to airline pilots and surgeons and discovered that the surgeons were more individualistic than Hofstede's original sample of IBM workers and that the pilots were more individualistic than the surgeons. When Taylor (1999) conducted a similar study of aircraft maintenance technicians, he discovered that the technicians were more individualistic than pilots. Thus, on the continuum of individualism-through-collectivism, aircraft maintenance technicians tend to be the most individualistic, which is quite the opposite of the goals of MRM programs. Therefore, in order for MRM programs to be effective in improving interpersonal communication and teamwork, they must place greater emphasis on behavior modeling and skills training. In terms of cross-national implications, subsequent studies (Patankar & Taylor, 2001; Patankar, 1999; Taylor & Patankar, 1999) have noted that while the North American MRM training transitions well to Asian audiences, the assertiveness scores increased more significantly in Taiwan and India. Therefore, a typical North American MRM training could be used in more collectivistic national cultures, but certain populations may respond differently to the modules related to assertiveness.

Return-On-Investment (ROI) for MRM Training Can Be Demonstrated

In the United States, the implementation of MRM training has been voluntary. Thus, most companies needed to demonstrate a positive return-on-investment in order to offer such programs and make them part of the broader safety strategy. The FAA has provided a basic return-on-investment calculator tool (FAA, 2017b). This tool provides a good way to generate an initial estimate of the ROI to be expected from an MRM program. However, while it accommodates for a less than 100% probability of success with the MRM program (training may not achieve 100% of its goals), it does not accommodate for other concurrent or recently completed safety initiatives that might influence the overall safety performance outcome. In order to objectively measure the financial impact of MRM training, while giving credit to non-MRM safety initiatives that might have been concurrently or previously supported, Taylor (2000b) presented a formula that distills the effects of MRM instruction for a realistic assessment of return-on-investment from MRM training alone. In this formula, a "causal operator" is used as a multiplier (between 0 and 1) to appropriately right-size the estimated ROI. The actual value of this causal operator is based on the pre/post comparison of change in participant attitudes resulting from an MRM training program. Thus, if there was a 30% improvement in participant attitudes after the

MRM training, the training program could take credit for only 30% of the total ROI. Patankar and Taylor (2004a) presented two examples to illustrate that substantial positive ROI is possible from expensive MRM programs that affect "high value" outcomes (such as the lost-time injuries example). Also, at times, MRM programs may be successful at improving safety outcomes, but not result in a positive ROI. Therefore, it is important to plan and design one's MRM program to impact the specific targets and their associated ROI.

Lercel, Steckel, Mondello, Carr, and Patankar (2011) classify ROI analysis in terms of three levels: micro, mid, and macro. According to this classification, the type of analysis suggested by the FAA and Taylor (as discussed in the preceding paragraph), would be regarded as micro-level analysis. At the next higher level, the analysis shifts to company-wide safety programs. Thus, the analysis of a company-wide SMS program, which may include programs like MRM, CRM, and LOSA, as well as implementation across number of locations, would be considered a mid-level tier of ROI analysis. Although Lercel et al. did not report any mid-level examples from the aviation industry, they presented compelling examples from construction and pharmaceutical industries to illustrate both company-wide benefits of safety programs as well as risks of a safety-related failure. At the macro level of analysis, Lercel et al. illustrated the devastating effects of safety incidents (even those with a relatively benign or positively heroic outcome) on company stock prices—essentially, companies could lose substantial market value as a result of a safety incident, regardless of the actual outcome (in terms of loss of life/property).

Since safety programs are rarely implemented in isolation, Taylor (2000b) introduced the concept of causal operator to right-size the impact of a particular safety program such as the MRM training. Lercel et al. (2011) acknowledged the same fact, but presented the "Safety Investment Combination Matrix" as a way to compound the financial impact of multiple safety programs. This approach presents all the safety programs combined into one, comprehensive investment, much like a mutual fund with respect to financial investments. Such a portfolio-based approach fundamentally shifts the notion of safety programs from "costs" to "investments"; brings top management interest by connecting safety program success with corporate financial success; enables longer-term outlook by considering the overall impact of all safety programs rather than financial benefits of discrete programs; leverages the benefits of multiple, concurrent programs; and accommodates short-term negative returns from one or two individual programs.

MRM Programs Have Had a Profound Impact on the Safety Culture Across the Global Aviation Maintenance Community

According to Schein's (1988) model of organizational culture, shared values are the essence of any group's collective culture, and such values are formed based on shared experiences of the individuals in that group. One could argue that in the early years of MRM programs, the shared experience of aircraft maintenance engineers/technicians revolved around blame. Accident/incident investigations focused on "who" made the mistake and the corrective actions were largely punitive to the individual responsible for the mistake. Thus, theoretically, if one had to change this blame-oriented culture in aviation maintenance, it was essential to create a different shared experience. While they may not have realized it at the time, the founders of the second generation MRM programs—John Goglia, Jim Ballough, and Joe Kania—knew from personal experience that the technician who made the mistake was most knowledgeable about the circumstances leading up to the mistake and therefore needed some degree of protection from disciplinary action so that he/she could help prevent similar errors in the future. As the second generation programs went through implementation and the three parties—company, FAA, and the union—demonstrated that they could uphold their mutual agreement, all three parties created a new shared experience. Over time, repeated and consistent emphasis on nonpunitive error management helped move the aviation maintenance community away from blame-oriented culture. However, it took almost a decade for this cultural shift to be institutionalized as a formal, replicable process: it came in the form of ASAP programs as part of the fifth generation MRM programs. Thus, today, the artifact that illustrates the shift from a blame culture to a reporting or just culture within a particular organization is the ASAP agreement between labor, management, and the regulator. The claim that such cultural shift is a national phenomenon is supported by the rise in Maintenance ASAP programs from 6 to 168 from 2003 to 2017.

On a global scale, the collaboration between the FAA, TC, and UK CAA resulted in specific requirements and guidance materials from ICAO, and many of the member States have ratified these requirements and customized the ICAO guidance materials to meet their needs. The recommended training syllabi as well as supporting materials such as posters, books, and videos have helped institutionalize a common body of knowledge expected from all aviation maintenance technicians. Also, the Aviation Accreditation Board International (AABI; the accrediting body of collegiate aviation programs) has included the requirement for a robust safety management program in all AABI-accredited aviation colleges/universities. Thus, the MRM research efforts that were initiated in the United States have contributed toward a policy- and practice-level impact across the globe, and they have penetrated many of the premier collegiate programs so that the future maintenance technicians will enter the industry with sufficient knowledge, appropriate attitude, and essential skills to practice behaviors consistent with the expectations of a just safety culture.

13.4.2 Implications for the Future

The story of MRM programs makes for an interesting case study in large-scale culture change. Trigger events like the three seminal accident cases— Aloha Airlines, Air Ontario, and British Airways BAC 1-11—challenged the prevailing unquestioned assumptions about the maintenance environment, practices, and personal vulnerabilities. The resultant accident investigations also played a critical role in shifting the mindset from individual-level blame to system-level responsibility. Thus, when MRM programs were created and implemented, they offered an alternate shared experience to the maintenance personnel, management, and regulators. As each party learned from the new experience and held steadfast on their mutual commitment, the old assumptions melted away, interpersonal trust improved, shared values changed, and workplace performance outcomes improved. Both internal and external leaders (people who held formal positions) and influencers (people who did not hold direct operational responsibilities) played their part in shaping the interventions, providing objective feedback from the success and challenges in implementing the interventions, and developing reports and training materials. Holistically, an intricate web of social systems, comprising of individuals, corporations, labor unions, universities, and government agencies, achieved a fundamental shift in shared values across the global aviation industry. This is not to say that the process was flawless or the experience was without challenges and setbacks; nonetheless, people persevered, adapted to the changing fiscal, geopolitical, and regulatory constraints, and in some cases passed on the responsibilities to their successors to continue the core pursuit.

Looking forward, future opportunities for large-scale cultural change should bear in mind the following observations: (1) large-scale, industry-wide, and global cultural change could take decades, but it is possible; (2) development of both awareness and behavioral change programs is essential, and such programs should be implemented across the entire workforce vertical (from preemployment academic programs to executive level seminars); (3) leaders and influencers must stay committed to the core cause, but be willing to adapt to the changing external and internal conditions; (4) positive financial returns can be achieved, but they need not be preconditions for starting modest efforts; (5) government, industry, and academia can partner very effectively in leveraging each other's strengths; and (6) once there is sufficient political support, legislative changes at the national and international levels are most effective in institutionalizing the cultural change.

To build on the Information Sharing meetings hosted by the FAA, and the ongoing efforts to share safety data across air carriers, the next level of improvement in safety culture calls for research projects that leverage the power of integrating data regarding normal operations, lessons learned, best practices, and impact achieved across the flight, maintenance, cabin, and dispatch siloes. Such studies need to be funded by government agencies like the FAA, TC and the UK CAA so that the reports are publicly available and usable across the industry. Aviation is a global industry and multinational collaborations are essential to foster continued improvements in the industry's safety culture.

13.5 INCIDENT REVIEW TOOLS AND TAXONOMIES

13.5.1 Maintenance Error Decision Aid

The maintenance error decision aid (MEDA) was developed by the Boeing Company (Rankin, 2007). This tool was developed during 1992−95 and coincided with the parallel development of second and third generation MRM programs. With the growing adoption of MRM programs across major air carriers in the early 1990s, and the concurrent push toward identification of broader systemic and human factors related root causes of airliner accidents, the aviation industry wanted a practical tool that they could use to investigate maintenance-related errors. Once the MEDA tool was developed, field-tested, and ready for broad distribution, the Boeing Company started providing the tool and the accompanying training on how to use it to all its customer airlines. Thus, the tool as well as the basic concepts of human factors in maintenance, nonpunitive reporting systems, and emphasis on systemic solutions were promulgated across the international air carrier community.

The MEDA process involves five steps: event, decision, investigation, prevention strategies, and feedback. By setting the trigger on an "event" rather than an accident or incident, the MEDA process encouraged review of all undesirable outcomes. Also, it allowed the operators to track events that were important to them. Examples of such events included flight cancellation, gate return, and inflight engine shut-down. All the events were associated with actual cost incurred by the air carrier (although the cost varied by company), and therefore the process encouraged the users to consider financial implications of both the errors as well as the solutions. In the decision phase, the operator is expected to determine whether or not the event was maintenance-related; only if it was maintenance-related, the operator would use the MEDA process further to conduct the investigation. The predeveloped MEDA form guided the investigators in determining the underlying causes of the event and enabled them to determine whether the event occurred due to an error or a violation. According to MEDA, an error is an unintentional human error and a violation is an intentional human action; maintenance-related events can be caused by either errors, violations, or a combination of the two. MEDA also allowed the investigators to consider appropriate prevention strategies. Finally, the feedback phase was intended to communicate back to the workforce the nature of the event, results of the investigation, and strategies to be employed to prevent similar events in the future. As of 2007, Boeing claimed that over 500 of its customer organizations have used MEDA training, and the outcomes ranged from a 16% reduction in delays due to maintenance to 48% reduction in operationally significant events. Thus, MEDA has proven to be an effective tool to mitigate lower-level events and thereby reduce the risk of higher-consequence events (assuming that the contributing factors for both levels of consequences are similar or the same).

According to the MEDA taxonomy, maintenance errors are classified into the following categories (Boeing, 2001):

1. installation error;
2. servicing error;
3. repair error;
4. fault isolation, test, or inspection error;
5. foreign object damage error;
6. airplane/equipment damage error;
7. personal injury error; and
8. other.

Next, the MEDA process calls for the identification of various contributing factors:

1. information;
2. equipment, tools, and safety equipment;
3. aircraft design, configuration, and parts;
4. the job or task;
5. technical knowledge and skills;
6. individual factors;
7. environment and facility;
8. organizational factors;
9. leadership and supervision; and
10. communication.

The MEDA Guide (Boeing, 2001) provides additional guidance on what the investigator should consider in responding to the various contributing factors. Using the MEDA Guide could help improve consistency in the interpretation of contributing factors and the information collected by the organization is more likely to be reliable.

With respect to the error prevention strategies, the MEDA process first calls to review the existing strategies that may not have been effective in the given instant. If so, rather than creating a new strategy, it might be wise to review the factors that make the existing strategy ineffective, and then consider a new strategy, if one is needed.

13.5.2   HFACS for Maintenance

The Human Factors Analysis and Classification System (HFACS) was developed by the Naval Safety Center and subsequently extended to include maintenance-related events (called the HFACS−Maintenance Extension or HFACS-ME) (Schmidt, Lawson, & Figlock, 2001). One of the core principles of the HFACS-ME model is that accidents are a combination of latent conditions and active failures; thus, in order to develop long-term preventive measures, one should address the latent conditions. Latent conditions and active failures are classified into four broad categories: unsafe management conditions, unsafe maintainer conditions, unsafe working conditions, and unsafe acts of the maintainer. As a result of this approach, it is likely that any given investigation will reveal latent conditions that could contribute to other undesirable events in the future. Schmidt et al. (2001) analyzed 15 NTSB accident reports and discovered that 100% of them reported unsafe management conditions, 73% reported unsafe maintainer conditions, 67% reported unsafe working conditions, and with respect to unsafe maintainer acts, 87% reported errors (unintentional human error) and 47% reported violations (intentional risky or illegal actions).

13.5.3   LOSA in Maintenance and Ramp Operations

While both MEDA and HFACS-ME are both excellent tools, they are designed to be used to investigate events that have already occurred; hence, they are reactive. On the other hand, the line oriented safety assessment (LOSA) observations are intended to actively intercept errors as they happen and identify potential problems; hence, data from such observations can be used proactively (Crayton, Hackworth, Roberts, & King, 2017). The foundational taxonomy for Maintenance LOSA is quite similar to MEDA; just the trigger point is not an actual event, but a routine observation of normal operations. For example, the first contributing factor listed in MEDA is "Information." While filling out a MEDA report, the investigator must consider various questions related to information and then fill out a narrative response. On the other hand, in the case of a LOSA observation, the observer can select from a drop-down list of options and report whether the information is not understandable, unavailable, incorrect, etc. (FAA, 2017c).

It is important to note that LOSA observations are a combination of understanding the safety risk and threats, as well as how the threats are being managed. Thus, when there is an eminent safety risk and a threat, but the threat is not managed effectively to contain the risk, it will result in an undesirable event. If the threat is managed within acceptable limits, the underlying data will provide some opportunities for analysis regarding whether or not broader risk management strategies need to be developed.

13.6 INFLUENCE ON SAFETY CULTURE IN TECHNICAL OPERATIONS

Ployhart, Hale, and Campion (2014) reviewed a number of definitions of culture and concluded that they converge on three dimensions: (1) artifacts, (2) values and beliefs, and (3) underlying assumptions, which are consistent with Schein's theory of organizational culture (1988, 2010, 2015). Hofstede's (1984) work focuses on shared values and has been used most commonly for studies involving cultural comparisons. Helmreich and Merritt (1998) extended the use of values-based differentiation to categorize groups of people in accordance with national boundaries (national culture), organizational boundaries (organizational culture), and professional boundaries (professional culture). Thus, Hofstede's comparative scales such as individualism versus collectivism or power distance could be used in the context of different national groups, organizational groups, or professional groups. With respect to safety culture, the key shared value is safety. Thus, safety culture is a focused study of organizational culture. Therefore, in order to examine the influence of MRM programs *on* the safety culture in technical operations, one needs to focus on how the shared values and beliefs were influenced, how the underlying assumptions might have changed as a result of the MRM programs, and what specific artifacts were created to memorialize the changes in shared values and beliefs.

13.6.1 Shared Values, Beliefs, and Assumptions

Schein (2015) claims that over a period of time, assuming that the group membership remains fairly stable, most groups go through certain experiences and learn not only how to avoid mistakes, but also what behaviors are rewarded, thereby forming their shared values and beliefs. In the case of technical operations, maintenance personnel had experienced a blame-oriented culture wherein it was common for error investigations to focus on the person who might have committed the error rather than addressing latent issues in the system. Thus, the maintenance community had learned to not speak up or maintain their personal notes on how to prevent errors. However, certain key leaders knew that in order to address the challenge of maintenance errors, they needed to earn the trust of their maintenance personnel and engage them in solving the system problems. Therefore, when John Goglia, Joe Kania, and Jim Ballough decided to work together to address this issue, they took the foundational step toward changing the shared experiences of maintenance personnel and thereby setting in motion the long journey toward a sustainable cultural change in aviation maintenance. At that time, a deeper, underlying assumption in the maintenance community was that if the technician was forthright in admitting his/her mistake, he/she would be subject to not only corporate disciplinary action, but also to a certificate action by the FAA. Thus, it was essential for both the company and the FAA to provide the technician with consistent protection while not making the protection serve like a "get out of jail free" card (full amnesty). This approach was also foundational to today's notion of a just culture, wherein there is a clear separation between inadvertent errors and intentional disregard for safety; the latter is punishable. Reflecting on how the culture in technical operations matured over the six generations of MRM programs, it is clear that the shared experience of the technicians, managers, and the regulators must have changed, which eventually led to the development of formal tripartite agreements among company, union and the FAA. Once these agreements started to be formalized and supported, the subsequent shared experiences served to reinforce the shared organizational values regarding safety, nonpunitive reporting, and just culture.

13.6.2 Role of Leaders and Influencers

For the purpose of this section, leaders are defined as persons holding formal positions of leadership in labor unions, companies, or regulatory agencies. On the other hand, influencers are defined as persons who do not hold any formal positions like the leaders, but they are generally well-regarded by their professional communities and can influence attitudinal and behavioral changes. In the case of MRM programs, there has been a robust coalition of leaders and influencers, and some have trades places as well. For example, pioneers like John Goglia, Joe Kania, and Jim Ballough started off as influencers (although they had formal roles, their authority was limited), and subsequently secured high-profile formal leadership roles and continued to "transform their individual drive into collective purpose and commitment" (Pettigrew, 1979).

At this point, it is important to acknowledge the role of all the major labor unions:

- IAM and Aerospace Workers;
- AMFA;
- International Brotherhood of Teamsters;

Representatives from these organizations played a critical role in protecting the rights of the individual maintenance technician and advancing the overall safety agenda, as well as serving as role models for higher standards of professional behavior. For example, they worked with their membership to develop key behaviors that would form the baseline expectations of professionalism from their members. Violation of any one of these behaviors constituted negligent behavior and hence the individual did not receive amnesty, bringing about a balance between accountability and benevolence (Patankar and Baines, 2003). Numerous individuals across all the labor unions served as role models and champions of just culture, thereby routinely reinforcing the shared safety values.

Similarly, US air carriers like American, Continental, Delta, Northwest, Southwest, United Airlines, and US Airways offered their staff and facilities to help collect data, participate in research studies, and test prototype training materials. The in-kind contribution of their employees' time and access to physical resources could easily be measured in millions of dollars. Also, many of the large repair stations like AAR, B.F. Goodrich Aerospace, Lufthansa Technic, and TIMCO contributed their resources to support MRM research. More importantly, each of these partners used research results to improve their internal MRM training programs, safety policies, and consistent practice of desired behaviors by the frontline personnel as well as senior management. They also supported participation in regular information sharing meetings across the industry so that the best practices and lessons learned could be available for customization and adoption by other companies.

Academic and federal researchers were key influencers of safety culture in technical operations. Some of the most notable contributions, in the area of MRM/MHF research, came from Clemson University, FAA Civil Aero Medical Institute, NASA Ames Research Center, Purdue University, Saint Louis University, San Jose State University, Santa Clara University, and the University of Buffalo. Faculty researchers and their students worked with practically all the US air carriers and most of the repair stations, as well as some foreign air carriers, to develop robust research tools, analytical techniques, datasets, and results. Outcomes from these research projects as well as testimonials from key faculty members served as external influencers of training materials, guidance documents, policies, and regulations.

Several leaders in the FAA, TC, UK CAA, and the ICAO have also made an incredible impact on the safety culture in technical operations. While they helped build awareness, hosted training programs and conferences, funded research, and hosted information sharing events, their most critical contribution has been in the area of legislative influence—they were influential in developing and approving regulations that require MHF training and specify the topics that must be covered in such training programs. This level of direction and specificity created regulations, policies, and guidance materials as significant artifacts of cultural change in technical operations and enabled consistent adoption of safety values across the global aviation industry.

13.6.3   MRM as a Planned Intervention

There is a long history in training research that delineates the role of training as a planned intervention (Alvarez et al., 2004). As noted in the preceding sections, the various generations of MRM programs have aimed at both improving awareness and changing individual behavior. While some programs had specific behavioral change goals directed at addressing problems like documentation errors, others simply assumed that a change in awareness would translate into change in behaviors and ultimately into change in performance outcomes such as reduction in ground damage or lost-time injuries. For the most part, however, the *planned* aspect of the program was limited to individual-level awareness or individual-level change in behavior. Furthermore, most programs were successful in achieving passive behavioral changes suggested by their increased self-awareness regarding human performance issues, but not active changes in the sense that the participants were not overtly committed to *doing* anything different such as implementing mitigation measures to counter fatigue, distractions, stress, etc. In the future, interventions involving training programs could consider comprehensive models of training evaluation like Alvarez et al.'s (2004) integrated model of training evaluation and training effectiveness as well as Spitzer's (2005) Learning Effectiveness Measurement (LEM) methodology, which take a more active stance on transfer of learning into workplace behaviors and incorporate the role of extant organizational culture. Such an approach would not only make MRM-like training interventions more effective in achieving their outcomes, but also enable the managers (frontline through senior management) to be better prepared to support the organizational changes emanating from the implementation of the training intervention.

Another observation regarding the MRM programs is that the early generation programs were rooted in the corresponding CRM programs and customized for the maintenance application. Also, the early FAA InfoShare meetings were focused almost exclusively on flight-related issues and had no formal representation of the maintenance community. Over the years, both these conditions changed: the MRM training became more independent of CRM training and the InfoShare meetings had strong representation from the maintenance community. Thus, although one cannot claim that MRM was planned as a training intervention to influence safety culture in technical operations, it has certainly served that purpose. Learning from this experience, and drawing on relevant literature on training effectiveness, future interventions can be even more successful at achieving a large-scale cultural change.

13.6.4 Performance Outcomes

It has already been reported in this chapter that MRM training programs were effective in improving participant attitudes toward safety and there was a positive correlation between improvement in safety attitudes and improvement in safety performance related to ground damage and lost-time injuries. Also, these programs have achieved significant return-on-investment through cost savings associated with safety performance improvements. Thus, performance improvements have been noted at the individual and unit levels.

Theoretically, however, transfer of training into workplace behavioral change is a function of the extant organizational climate (Birdi, 2007;

Holton, 2005), and a shift in participants' behaviors, supported by feedback focused on task performance (Senge, 1990), can bring about a change in organizational climate and culture. Thus, one could argue that the training intervention serves as a specially designed shared experience, which could employ Spitzer's LEM, with specific operational goals as well as value-based goals. Birdi and Reid's (2013) Taxonomy of Training and Development Outcomes would be particularly helpful in formulating training outcome goals at the individual-, group-, organization-, as well as the entire aviation industry-level.

13.6.5   Artifacts

Schein (1988) defines artifacts as manifestations of the underlying culture and hence they can take the form of language, symbols, stories, as well as implementation mechanisms like policies and procedures. Since artifacts are *products* of culture, Patankar (2017) proposes the study of artifacts as outcomes or manifestations of culture rather than the culture itself. Vilnai-Yavetz and Rafaeli (2012) argue that artifacts are much more than evidence of organizational culture. They incorporate relevant literature and provide an expansive definition of artifacts:

> *Artificial products, something made by human beings and thus any element of a work environment…perceived by senses and that they have certain intentions, aiming to satisfy a need or a goal…include intangible notions such as names, language, and contracts, as well as tangible notions such as inanimate objects introduced by organizational members into their organizations. (p. 10)*

Considering the broad range of tangible and intangible items that could be included within the scope of an artifact, Vilnai-Yavetz and Rafaeli present three dimensions from which artifacts should be analyzed: instrumentality, esthetics, and symbolism. Instrumentality refers to the utility (or lack thereof) of the artifact—many physical artifacts such as tools, checklists, policies and procedures would have a positive influence on the outcomes and hence would be considered to have positive instrumentality. Esthetics refers to the sensory reaction to the artifact—is it pleasing, is it appropriately used (graphic or symbolism in the context of local customs and traditions), or does it evoke generally positive emotional reactions? Symbolism refers to the meaning of the artifact—it could mean something entirely different to the ones that create the artifact versus those that see it or observe it. Thus, "artifacts can have both intended and unintended symbolic consequences" (p. 14).

In the case of MRM programs in technical operations, numerous items could be considered cultural artifacts. Some examples of such artifacts are as follows:

- The Dirty Dozen posters (available at http://aviationknowledge.wikidot. com/aviation:dirty-dozen)
- The ASAP Advisory Circular (AC 120-66B) (available at https://www. faa.gov/documentLibrary/media/Advisory_Circular/AC120-66B.pdf)
- MEDA Form (available at https://www.faa.gov/about/initiatives/mainte-nance_hf/library/documents/media/media/meda_results_form_revl.pdf)
- Fundamentals of SMSs Video (available at https://www.youtube.com/watch?v = IdRwNZ-7s4Y)
- ASAP Memorandum of Understanding (available at http://www. iamdl142.org/wp-content/uploads/2017/09/127-AA_2017a.pdf)
- Safety Awards (e.g., available at https://www.tn.gov/workforce/news/5552)

Most of these artifacts have a very high level of instrumentality—they were designed to be used to convey a message or used as references/tools for specific tasks. Some of them, like the Fundamental of SMSs video, have a good esthetic appeal as well. Other artifacts like the ASAP MOU have a very high degree utility as well as symbolism. The public display of names and signatures on the MOU have a very high symbolic value, expressing the joint commitment toward the shared value of safety and the operating princi-ples agreed upon in the document. Such documents serve as authoritative license for frontline personnel to hold each other accountable for agreed upon behaviors. Finally, safety awards, as symbolic artifacts, play a critical role in recognizing individual and group-level achievements as well as in encouraging others to engage in similar behaviors. Overall, all these artifacts seek to reinforce shared values and beliefs regarding safety.

13.7 CONCLUSIONS

The story of MRM for technical operations provides an interesting roadmap for a large-scale cultural change. In the case of MRM programs, three cata-strophic maintenance-related accidents (Aloha Airlines, Air Ontario, and British Airways BAC 1-11) served as the defining moments or trigger events. In response to these events, there was a flurry of responses. First, there was an organized series of symposia to gather industry-wide input in determining the nature of the work environment and general challenges like aging air-craft, workforce development, and human fallibility. Almost concurrent with these symposia the previously successful CRM training was adapted to the maintenance environment and the first generation of MRM training program was launched. Over the years, both the series of industry symposia and the MRM training programs evolved through six generations, they survived mul-tiple economic challenges, and adapted to meet the emerging regulatory and economic needs. Thus, today's MRM programs tend to be embedded in the broader SMS program.

In response to the needs identified by the industry symposia, and in partial support of the ongoing MRM training programs, the FAA funded a number of research programs that enabled serious action research in collaboration with aviation companies and labor unions. This research program is also possibly the only example of large, industry-wide collaboration across the US FAA, NASA, TC, and UK CAA. Such multinational collaboration allowed for many of the research results to be translated into guidance materials, policies, and regulations in the United States, Canada, and the United Kingdom, as well as on a global scale through the International Civil Aviation Organization. Thus, it helped infuse a common language across the world's leading regulators and create a shared platform for long-term, cultural change. The findings from these research projects clearly demonstrate that the training programs were effective in improving participant attitudes toward safety and those attitudinal improvements were positively correlated with improvements in safety performance outcomes like ground damage and lost-time injuries.

In addition to the training programs and tangible artifacts like policies and regulations, the MRM program also reinforced the importance to interpersonal trust. In the early years, it was acknowledged that trust among technicians, company management, and the regulatory representative was critical to the success of MRM programs. This recognition served as the key to the subsequent success of ASAPs, the development of just culture, and it is well-integrated in the expectations of the current SMS program as well as maintenance and ramp LOSA programs.

Moving forward, there is growing interest in preventive and predictive measures. Thus, there is no doubt that MRM programs will continue to evolve and their impact will also grow. The adoption and use of an MRM program could be viewed along a maturity continuum with reactive programs on one end and predictive programs on the other. As aviation organizations become comfortable with one generation of MRM programs, they may move to the next generation along the continuum toward predictive programs. The ability to move along the maturity continuum will likely be a function of interpersonal trust, management commitment, availability of fiscal and human resources, and the overall state of the industry.

REFERENCES

Allen, J., & Marx, D. (1994). *Maintenance error decision aid project. Proceedings of the Eighth International Symposium on Human Factors in Aircraft Maintenance and Inspection* (pp. 101–115). Washington, DC: Federal Aviation Administration.

Alvarez, K., Salas, E., & Garofano, C. (2004). An integrated model of training evaluation and effectiveness. *Human Resource Development Review*, 3(4), 385–416. Available from https://doi.org/10.1177/1534484304270820.

ATA. (2002). *SPEC 113: Maintenance human factors program guidelines.* Washington, DC: Air Transport Association of America. Retrieved on October 18, 2017 from https://www.faa. gov/about/initiatives/maintenance_hf/library/documents/media/support_documentation/ata_ spec_113_hf_guidelines.pdf.

Birdi, K. (2007). A lighthouse in the desert? Evaluating the effects of creativity training on employee innovation. *Journal of Creative Behavior, 41*(4), 249–270. Available from https:// doi.org/10.1002/j.2162-6057.2007.tb01073.x.

Birdi, K., & Reid, T. (2013). Training. In R. Lewis, & L. Zibarras (Eds.), *Work and occupational psychology: Integrating theory and practice.* London: Sage.

Boeing. (2001). *Maintenance error decision aid (MEDA) users guide.* Seattle, WA: The Boeing Company. Retrieved on September 29, 2017 from https://omnisms.aero/wp-content/uploads/ 2016/12/Boeing-MEDA-Users-Guide.pdf.

CAA. (2002). *An introduction to aircraft maintenance engineering human factors for JAR 66.* Safety Regulation Group, Civil Aviation Authority. Retrieved on September 9, 2017 from http://www.skybrary.aero/bookshelf/books/2036.pdf.

CAA. (2003). *Aviation maintenance human factors: Guidance material on the UK CAA interpretation of part-145 human factors and error management requirements,* CAP 716. Retrieved on September 9, 2017 from http://www.air.flyingway.com/books/hf-boock.pdf.

Commission of Inquiry. (1992a). *Commission of inquiry into the Air Ontario Crash at Dryden, Ontario (Canada).* Final Report. Retrieved on September 9, 2017 from http://lessonslearned. faa.gov/Fokker/000347.pdf.

Commission of Inquiry. (1992b). *Commission of inquiry into the Air Ontario Crash at Dryden, Ontario (Canada).* Final Report Appendix 7. Retrieved on September 10, 2017 from http:// lessonslearned.faa.gov/Fokker/000001.pdf.

Crayton, L., Hackworth, C., Roberts, C., & King, S. (2017). Line operations safety assessments (LOSA) in maintenance and ramp environments. *Report DOT/FAA/AM-17/7.* Washington, DC: Federal Aviation Administration, Office of Aviation Medicine.

FAA. (1997). *Advisory circular no. 120-66A, aviation safety action programs (ASAP).* Washington, DC. Retrieved on October 18, 2017 from https://www.faa.gov/ documentLibrary/media/Advisory_Circular/AC120-66.pdf.

FAA. (2002). *Aviation safety action programs.* Advisory Circular AC 120-66B. Federal Aviation Administration. Retrieved on February 21, 2006 from http://www.faa.gov/safety/programs_i-nitiatives/aircraft_aviation/asap/policy/.

FAA. (2008). *Aviation maintenance technician handbook—General,* H-8083-30. Federal Aviation Administration. Retrieved on September 19, 2017 from https://www.faa.gov/regula-tions_policies/handbooks_manuals/aircraft/media/AMT_Handbook_Addendum_Human_ Factors.pdf.

FAA. (2013). *Safety management system,* Executive Order 8000.369B. Washington, DC: Federal Aviation Administration. Retrieved on September 19, 2017 from https://www.faa.gov/ documentLibrary/media/Order/FAA_Order_8000.369B.pdf.

FAA. (2015). *Safety management systems for domestic, flag, and supplemental operations certif-icate holders, final rule 14 CFR parts 5 and 119.* Washington, DC: Federal Aviation Administration. Retrieved on September 19, 2017 from https://www.gpo.gov/fdsys/pkg/FR-2015-01-08/pdf/2015-00143.pdf.

FAA. (2016). *Supplemental notice of proposed rulemaking. 14 CFR Part 139.* Washington, DC: Federal Aviation Administration. Retrieved on September 19, 2017 from https://www.federal-register.gov/documents/2016/07/14/2016-16596/safety-management-system-for-certificated-airports.

FAA. (2017a). *ASAP participants*. Retrieved on September 29, 2017 from https://www.faa.gov/about/initiatives/asap/media/asap_participants.pdf.

FAA. (2017b). *Training and tools*. Retrieved on September 29, 2017 from https://www.faa.gov/about/initiatives/maintenance_hf/training_tools/.

FAA. (2017c). *Training, LOSA software, and forms*. Retrieved on September 29, 2017 from https://www.faa.gov/about/initiatives/maintenance_hf/losa/training/.

Fotos, C. P. (1991). *Continental applies CRM concepts to technical, maintenance corps, and Training stresses teamwork, self-assessment techniques* (pp. 32−35). Aviation Week & Space Technology, August 26th.

Gregorich, S. E., Helmreich, R. L., & Wilhelm, J. A. (1990). The structure of cockpit management attitudes. *Journal of Applied Psychology, 75*, 682−690.

Heinrich, H. W. (1941). *Industrial accident prevention* (2nd ed.). New York, NY: McGraw-Hill Book Company, Inc.

Helmreich, R. L., Foushee, H. C., Benson, R., & Russini, R. (1986). Cockpit management attitudes: Exploring the attitude-performance linkage. *Aviation, Space and Environmental Medicine, 57*, 1198−1200.

Helmreich, R. L., & Merritt, A. C. (1998). *Culture at work in aviation and medicine*. Aldershot, UK: Ashgate Publishing.

Hofstede, G. (1984). Culture's consequences: International differences in work-related values *(Abridged Edition)*. Beverly hills, CA: Sage.

Holton, E. (2005). Holton's evaluation model: New evidence and construct elaborations. *Advances in Developing Human Resources, 7*(1), 37−54. Available from https://doi.org/10.1177/1523422304272080.

ICAO. (1998). *Human factors training manual*, Doc 9683 AN/950: International Civil Aviation Organization. Retrieved on September 19, 2017 from https://www.globalairtraining.com/resources/DOC-9683.pdf.

ICAO. (2002). *Line operations safety audit*, Doc 9803 AN/761: International Civil Aviation Organization. Retrieved on September 19, 2017 from https://www.tc.gc.ca/media/documents/ca-standards/losa.pdf.

ICAO. (2003). *Human factors guidelines for aircraft maintenance manual*, Doc 9824 AN/450: International Civil Aviation Organization. Retrieved on September 19, 2017 from https://www.faa.gov/about/initiatives/maintenance_hf/library/documents/media/support_documentation/icao_hf_guidelines_2003.pdf.

ICAO. (2008). *Operation of aircraft*, Annex 6 to the Convention on International CivilAviation. Part II. International General Aviation Aeroplanes. International Civil Aviation Organization. Retrieved on September 19, 2017 from https://www.iaopa.eu/static/CKFinderJava/userfiles/files/news/2014/beijing2014/ANNEX6partII,%207th%20Edition.pdf.

ICAO. (2013). *Safety management*, Annex 19 to the Convention on International Civil Aviation. International Civil Aviation Organization. Retrieved on September 19, 2017 from http://cockpitdata.com/Software/ICAO%20Annex%2019.

King, D.F. (1992). *BAC one-eleven, G-BJRT: The main document*. Air Accidents Investigation Branch Retrieved on September 9, 2017 from https://www.fss.aero/accident-reports/dvdfiles/GB/1990-06-10-UK.pdf.

Klinect, J., Murray, P., Merritt, A., & Helmreich, R. (2003). Line operations safety audit (LOSA): Definition and operating characteristics. *Paper presented at the 12th International Symposium on Aviation Psychology*, Dayton, Ohio.

Klinect, J., Wilhelm, J., & Helmreich, R. (1999). Threat and error management -- Data from line operations safety audits. *Paper presented at the 10th International Symposium on Aviation Psychology*, Columbus, Ohio.

Lercel, D., Steckel, R., Mondello, S., Carr, E., & Patankar, M. (2011). *Aviation safety management systems: Return on investment study*. Saint Louis, MO: Center for Aviation Safety Research, Saint Louis University. Retrieved on September 27, 2017 from http://citeseerx.ist.psu.edu/viewdoc/download?doi = 10.1.1.461.9123&rep = rep1&type = pdf.

Lynch, K. P. (1996). *Management systems: A positive, practical method of cockpit resource management*. Proceedings of the 41st Corporate Aviation Safety Seminar (pp. 244−254). Orlando, FL: The Flight Safety Foundation.

Ma, J., Pedigo, M., Blackwell, L., Gildea, K., Holcomb, K., Hackworth, C., & Hiles, J. (2011). The line operations safety audit program: Transitioning from flight operations to maintenance and ramp operations. *Report DOT/FAA/AM-11/15*. Washington, DC: Federal Aviation Administration, Office of Aviation Medicine.

Ma, J., & Rankin, W. (2012). Implementation guideline for maintenance line operations safety assessment (M-LOSA) and ramp LOSA (R-LOSA) programs. *Report DOT/FAA/AM-12/9*. Washington, D.C: Federal Aviation Administration, Office of Aviation Medicine.

Marx, D. (2001). *Patient safety and the "just culture": A primer for health care executives*. Retrieved from http://www.mers-tm.net/support/Marx_Primer.pdf on October 11, 2004.

Marx, D.A. (1998) *Learning from our mistakes: A review of maintenance error investigation and analysis systems (with recommendations to the FAA)*. Available electronically at http://hfskyway.faa.gov, and on the FAA distributed CD-ROM, *Human factors in Aviation Maintenance and Inspection*, 1999.

NTSB. (1989). *Aloha Airlines, Flight 243, Boeing 737-200, N73711, near Maui, Hawaii, April 28, 1988*. National Transportation Safety Board Report Number AAR89-03. Retrieved on September 9, 2017 from https://www.ntsb.gov/investigations/AccidentReports/Reports/AAR8903.pdf.

Patankar, M., & Baines, K. (2003). Establishing effective error-reporting programs: A cross-cultural comparison of lessons learned. In: *Proceedings of the 17th Annual FAA / CAA / Transport Canada Safety Management in Aviation Maintenance Symposium: Integrating Human Factors Principles*, Toronto, Canada. September 16−18.

Patankar, M., & Driscoll, D. (2005). Factors affecting the success or failure of Aviation Safety Action Programs in aviation maintenance organizations. In W. Krebs (Ed.), *Aviation Maintenance Human Factors Program Review FY04*, p. 9−14. Retrieved on September 1, 2005 from http://www.hf.faa.gov/docs/508/docs/AvMaint04.pdf.

Patankar, M., & Taylor, J. (1999). *Corporate aviation on the leading edge: Systemic implementation of macro-human factors in aviation maintenance* (SAE Technical Paper No. 1999-01-1596). SAE General, Corporate & Regional Aviation Meeting & Exposition, Wichita, KS.

Patankar, M., & Taylor, J. (2001). Effects of MRM programs on the evolution of a safer culture in aviation maintenance. In R. Jensen (Ed.), *Proceedings of The Eleventh International Symposium on Aviation Psychology*. The Ohio State University.

Patankar, M., Taylor, J., & Goglia, J. (2002). *Individual professionalism and mutual trust are key to minimizing the probability of maintenance errors*. Proceedings of the 1st Aviation Safety & Security Symposium. George Washington University.

Patankar, M.S. (1999). *Professional and organizational barriers in implementing MRM programs: Differences between airlines in the U.S. and India*. SAE Technical Paper No. 1999-01-2979. SAE Airframe/Engine Maintenance and Repair Conference, Vancouver, BC.

Patankar, M. S. (2017). An integrated model of organizational culture and climate: A case study in obstetrics practice in Ontario. *Doctor of Philosophy degree in Management*. Sheffield, UK: Institute for Work Psychology, University of Sheffield.

Patankar, M. S., & Taylor, J. C. (2004a). *Risk management and error reduction in aviation maintenance.* Aldershot, UK: Ashgate Publishing.

Patankar, M. S., & Taylor, J. C. (2004b). *Applied human factors in aviation maintenance.* Aldershot, UK: Ashgate Publishing.

Pettigrew, A. M. (1979). On studying organizational cultures. *Administrative Science Quarterly, 24,* 570−581.

Ployhart, R. E., Hale, D., & Campion, M. (2014). Staffing within the social context. In B. Schneider, & K. M. Barbera (Eds.), *The Oxford handbook of organizational climate and culture.* Oxford, England: Oxford University Press.

Rankin, W. (2007). MEDA Investigation process. *Aero Magazine.* Seattle, WA: The Boeing Company. Retrieved on September 29, 2017 from http://www.boeing.com/commercial/aero-magazine/articles/qtr_2_07/AERO_Q207_article3.pdf.

Reason, J. (1997). *Managing the risk of organizational accidents.* Aldershot, UK: Ashgate Publishing Limited.

Robertson, M. M., Taylor, J. C., Stelly, J. W., & Wagner, R. (1995). *A systematic training evaluation model applied to measure the effectiveness of an aviation maintenance team training program. Proceedings of the Eighth International Symposium on Aviation Psychology* (pp. 631−636). Columbus, Ohio: The Ohio State University.

Schein, E. (1988). *Organizational culture and leadership.* San Francisco: Jossey-Bass.

Schein, E. (2010). *Organizational culture and leadership* (4th ed.). San Francisco, CA: Jossey-Bass.

Schein, E. (2015). Corporate culture. *International Encyclopedia of the Social & Behavioral Sciences, 4*(2), 923−926. Available from https://doi.org/10.1016/9978-0-08-097086-8.73014-5.

Schmidt, J.K., Lawson, D., & Figlock, R. (2001). *Human factors analysis and classification system—Maintenance extension (FHACS-ME). Review of select NTSB maintenance mishaps, an update.* Retrieved on September 29, 2017 from https://www.faa.gov/about/initiatives/maintenance_hf/library/documents/media/human_factors_maintenance/hfacs_me.pdf.

Senge, P. (1990). *The fifth discipline: The art and practice of the learning organization.* New York, NY: DoubleDay.

Shepherd, W.T., & Parker, J.F. (1989). *Proceedings of the first meeting on human factors issues in aircraft maintenance and inspection.* Accessed on September 17, 2017 from https://www.faa.gov/about/initiatives/maintenance_hf/library/documents/media/human_factors_maintenance/human_factors_issues_in_aircraft_maintenance_and_inspection.pdf.

Sitzman, T., & Weinhardt, J. (2015). Training engagement theory: A multilevel perspective on the effectiveness of work-related training. *Journal of Management,* 1−25. Available from https://doi.org/10.1177/0149206315574596.

Spitzer, D. R. (2005). Learning effectiveness measurement: A new approach for measuring and managing learning to achieve business results. *Advances in Developing Human Resources, 7* (1), 55−70. Available from https://doi.org/10.1177/1523422304272167.

Stelly, J., Jr., & Taylor, J. (1992). *Crew coordination concepts for maintenance teams. Proceedings of the Seventh International Symposium on Human Factors in Aircraft Maintenance and Inspection -- Science Technology and Management: A Program Review.* Washington, D.C: Federal Aviation Administration.

Taggart, W. (1990). *Introducing CRM into maintenance training. Proceedings of the Third International Symposium on Human Factors in Aircraft Maintenance and Inspection* (pp. 93−110). Washington, D.C: Federal Aviation Administration.

Taylor, J., & Patankar, M. (2001). Four generations of Maintenance Resource Management programs in the United States: An analysis of the past, present, and future. *The Journal of Air Transportation World Wide*, 6(2), 3–32.

Taylor, J., & Patankar, M. (1999). Cultural factors contributing to the success of macro human factors in aviation maintenance. In R. Jensen (Ed.), *Proceedings of the Tenth International Symposium on Aviation Psychology*. Columbus, Ohio: The Ohio State University.

Taylor, J., & Robertson, M. (1995). *The effects of Crew Resource Management (CRM) training in airline maintenance: Results following three years experience*. Washington, DC: National Aeronautics and Space Administration (NASA). Available electronically at http://hfskyway. faa.gov, and on the FAA distributed CD-ROM, *Human factors in Aviation Maintenance and Inspection*.

Taylor, J.C. (1994). Using Focus Groups to Reduce Errors in Aviation Maintenance (Original title: Maintenance Resource Management [MRM] in Commercial Aviation: Reducing Errors in Aircraft Maintenance Documentation, Technical Report -- 10/31/94) Los Angeles: Institute of Safety & Systems Management, University of Southern California. Retrieved on September 29, 2017 from http://hfskyway.faa.gov.

Taylor, J.C. (1998). Evaluating the effectiveness of Maintenance Resource Management (MRM). In *Proceedings of the 12th International Symposium on Human Factors in Aircraft Maintenance and Inspection*, Gatwick, UK, pp. 85-99.

Taylor, J. C. (1995). Effects of communication & participation in aviation maintenance. In R. Jensen (Ed.), *Proceedings of the Eighth International Symposium on Aviation Psychology* (pp. 472–477). Columbus, Ohio: The Ohio State University.

Taylor, J.C. (1999). *Some effects of national culture in aviation maintenance* (SAE Technical Paper No. 1999-01-2980). SAE Airframe/Engine Maintenance and Repair Conference, Vancouver, B.C.

Taylor, J. C. (2000a). Reliability and validity of the maintenance resource management, technical operations questionnaire (MRM/TOQ). *International Journal of Industrial Ergonomics*, 26(2), 217–230.

Taylor, J.C. (2000b). *A new model for measuring return on investment (ROI) for safety programs in aviation: An example from airline maintenance resource management (MRM)*. (SAE Technical Paper No. 2000-01-2090). SAE Advances in Aviation Safety Conference & Exposition, Daytona Beach, FL.

Taylor, J.C. (2004). *Prototype Training Materials for Acceptance Criteria of Maintenance ASAP Events Occurring within Social Context*. Report submitted to QSS/NASA Ames Research Center, Moffett Field, CA. Retrieved on September 16, 2017 from https://ntrs.nasa.gov/archive/nasa/casi.ntrs.nasa.gov/20050168086.pdf.

Taylor, J. C., & Christensen, T. D. (1998). *Airline maintenance resource management: Improving communication*. Warrendale, PA: SAE Press.

Taylor, J. C., Robertson, M. M., & Choi, S. (1997). *Empirical results of maintenance resource management training for aviation maintenance technicians. Proceedings of the Ninth International Symposium on Aviation Psychology* (pp. 1020–1025). Columbus, Ohio: The Ohio State University.

Taylor, J. C., Robertson, M. M., Peck, R., & Stelly, J. W. (1993). Validating the impact of maintenance CRM training. In R. Jensen (Ed.), *Proceedings of the Seventh International Symposium on Aviation Psychology* (pp. 538–542). Columbus, Ohio: The Ohio State University.

Transport Canada. (1999). *Flight 2005: A civil aviation safety framework for Canada (TP13521)*. Ottawa, ON: Transport Canada.

Transport Canada. (2006). *Flight 2010: A strategic plan for civil aviation (TP14469)*. Ottawa, ON: Transport Canada.

Transport Canada. (2015). *Guidance on safety management systems development*. Retrieved on September 9, 2017 from https://www.tc.gc.ca/eng/civilaviation/opssvs/managementservices-referencecentre-acs-100-107-001-5-457.htm.

Vilnai-Yavetz, I., & Rafaeli, A. (2012). Managing artifacts to avoid artifact myopia. In A. Rafaeli, & M. Pratt (Eds.), *Artifacts and organizations: Beyond mere symbolism* (pp. 9–21). New York, NY: Psychology Press.

Wright, W., & Tanji, E. (April 30, 1988). And then, whoosh! She was gone. *The Washington Post*. Retrieved on September 9, 2017 from https://www.washingtonpost.com/archive/politics/1988/04/30/and-then-whoosh-she-was-gone/a4da02d6-c8c3-47f7-a4e4-da2097a73b2a/?utm_term = .4c43b3f6f9e1.

Chapter 14

Flight and Cabin Crew Teamwork: Improving Safety in Aviation

Candace K. Kolander

Formerly with the Association of Flight Attendants-CWA, Washington, DC, United States

14.1 CRM IN THE CABIN

The first courses in crew resource management (CRM) were in "cockpit" resource management. Early accident trends were on the rise until around the 1960s when we then saw accident rates leveling off from the 1970s onward. Part of the accident rate decline was attributed to better equipment and better training on the technical aspects of flying. These two things were not enough though, as crew-related actions such as poor decision-making, ineffective communication, and inadequate leadership and task management were contributing factors in 60%−80% of accidents and incidents, according to advisory circular (AC) 120-51E (FAA, 2014). Therefore, in the mid-1980s, we saw "Cockpit" Resource Management training adopted at some airlines.

Eventually deficient crew communications between the cabin and the flight deck were cited as contributing factors in accidents and incidents and "Cockpit" Resource Management expanded into the cabin and other operational areas. It is now appropriately termed CRM.

One accident example was the March 1989 Air Ontario Fokker F-28 which crashed on takeoff in Dryden, Ontario, resulting in 24 fatalities. The accident investigation found that the cabin crew did not tell the pilots that there was wet snow building upon the wing. The cabin crewmember had been reluctant to report, because in the past when she had related safety concerns to pilots, they did not welcome the information (Commission of Inquiry, 1992). She also assumed that the pilots were aware of exactly what was happening and that she should not second guess that they had all the information.

A similar failure of the cabin crew to communicate safety information was also evident in the January 1989 British Midlands Boeing 737 accident

Crew Resource Management. DOI: https://doi.org/10.1016/B978-0-12-812995-1.00014-2

407

in which a fan blade fractured in the No. 1 engine (left). The pilots, however, thought that the No. 2 engine (right) had been damaged. The cabin crew and passengers could see fire on the left engine but the pilots were never informed. The error went uncorrected and the only good engine was subsequently shut down. Forty-seven of the 126 occupants died (AAIB, 1990).

A primary focus of CRM is effective team coordination and communication. Although individual performance is still important, cabin crew personnel offer an important information resource; thereby expanding the eyes and ears of the pilots. The more the two crew components act as a team, the more likely crew effectiveness will be increased, and error management decreased. The two accident recaps above clearly showed that the "team" philosophy had broken down.

14.2 TWO CULTURAL AND GEOGRAPHICAL ENVIRONMENTS

CRM training is a major contributor to safety by building on teamwork between the cabin and flight deck crews, during both normal and emergency operations. The international civil aviation authority (ICAO) notes that there are four types of cultures that can influence CRM intracrew communication: the national culture of the crewmember, professional culture, organizational culture, and the organization's safety culture (ICAO, 2003).

Individuals from homogenous cultures tend to have positive influences especially when communicating with each other. On the other hand, when varying cultures interact especially in problem-solving situations, negative outcomes including communication errors may occur (Chute & Weiner, 2009). Adding to the cultural differences, the commercial aircraft environment is further divided into two geographical environments: the flight deck and the cabin.

My US predecessors were "skygirls" who had to be registered nurses, single, childless females under the age of 25, and under the weight of 115 pounds. They were hired to quell the nervousness of new fliers on those long, arduous journeys that sometimes took between 18 and 24 hours to complete, in an airplane that was not pressurized, heated, or air-conditioned. They were onboard the aircraft for practical reasons, but marketing played a large role also. Compliance and sociability in the 1930s were important attributes of skygirls. Pilots by contrast evolved from the 1920s stunt pilots and aerialists. These "barnstormers" performed almost any trick or feat with an airplane that people could imagine. They also took the role of ensuring that the coast-to-coast airmail flights of the 1920s were successful. In subsequent years, the commercial aviation pilot stream came from military pilots.

These cultural differences, one dedicated to public service and trained to be marketing driven and the other dedicated to the operation of machinery and proficient in technical matters, have been imbued by tradition and airline management and are still somewhat present today.

In addition to the cultural barriers between cabin and flight deck, there is also the physical barrier that has been there for years, the flight deck door. The cabin crew can be even further divided themselves by the class in the cabin they are working, either first class, business, or coach. In a sense, there may be two or more teams in the cabin; with the pilots behind the flight deck door the potential for a fragmented onboard crew is high.

Duty time and rest regulations are strategic tools put in place to combat fatigue for safety reasons. Yet, if the administrative rostering or scheduling of pilots and cabin crew do not follow the same pattern, the team culture can again be disrupted. Many regulatory authorities have developed regulations and guidance around duty time and rest requirements that treat these two working groups the same, with some minor variances, recognizing that the body's biological needs for sleep to combat fatigue are the same for both work groups. However, if the regulatory requirements treat the two groups differently related to flight and duty time, another barrier can be put in place, this one by the regulatory authority treating them as two groups. There is no sound scientific basis for these differences. Pilots and cabin crew are affected at least equally by the core contributors to fatigue—time of day relative to one's home time zone, time on task, time since awakening, and any previously accumulated sleep debt.

When the administrative rostering or scheduling between the two groups differs significantly, another layer of separation, or barrier to cohesiveness, can be created. For example, cabin and flight deck crews could fly together for a series of flights, then head in different directions. In the US, some of our pilot and cabin crewmembers don't even stay in the same hotel, which is another factor that separates the two teams. While these are not the specific areas of concern addressed in this paper, they are worth thinking about in relation to barriers to effective CRM.

Effective CRM training can help overcome some of the cultural, geographical, and regulatory practices.

14.3 SEPTEMBER 11 SECURITY MEASURES ADDED

CRM teaches crewmembers to utilize all resources available to the crew (e.g., hardware, software, and other individuals) to achieve a safe flight. But what if one of the pieces of hardware has an adverse effect on communications with the flight deck? In the interests of reducing incident and accident rates, we would be remiss if we did not assess this risk.

After September 11, 2001 the United States and other countries responded to the aviation threat that aircraft could be used as weapons. Aviation security needed to be revised and strengthened to meet the newest threats. In the area of airport security the screening of passengers and belongings needed to be improved. Identification and validation of persons having access to secured areas of the airport and to aircraft needed to be updated and strengthened; and more effective security measures need to be included in any future airport construction, to name a few.

Inside the aircraft, training was redesigned to address the new threat and incorporate a new philosophy in the way a crew was to respond to a terrorist attack. In terms of physical infrastructure, new reinforced flight deck doors were also mandated. There have always been doors that could be used to separate the flight deck and cabin crews, but the reinforced door is a much more substantial barrier than the old door. The reinforced doors are designed to stop, or at least delay, forced intrusions and to resist ballistic penetrations and small cabin explosions. No longer can cabin crewmembers use a key to enter the flight deck because the doors have hardened locks. Those old keys have been destroyed with the intent to keep terrorists out; unfortunately, cabin crew are also kept out. Furthermore, in addition to being a physical barrier, the locked door is also a psychological barrier that discourages an open stream of communication.

The locked door also forces cabin crew to handle more issues and make more decisions on their own. No longer does an additional flight deck crewmember come out of the flight deck and assist in the cabin. Even with the emergence of the two-pilot crew, one of the pilots would typically come into the cabin to help handle a situation if they felt it necessary. That is, prior to September 11.

Operational changes restricting access to the flight deck during flight were also required to strengthen security. The basic philosophy is that the flight deck, and its pilot occupants, need to be protected at all times, by prohibiting unauthorized individuals from gaining entry to the flight deck. This means limiting the number of times crew enter or exit the flight deck, with the entry and exit process done as quickly as possible. Additionally, before even opening the door, the cabin crew needs to ensure there is a clear zone in the cabin sections adjacent to the door.

Prior to this operational change due to security, the cabin crew may have gone up to the flight deck several times to give a status report on a situation in the cabin or to let them know about something odd happening in the cabin even though it was not a concern yet. Or they could simply have gone to the flight deck to talk during a low workload cabin service period. Such informal bonding has been a significant part of CRM; unfortunately, the new operational changes have discouraged such activities, creating another psychological barrier.

The method of communication with the pilots after September 11 is now limited to the interphone system. Entering the flight deck to have a face-to-face conversation with the pilots to tell them about a possible problem passenger is no longer an acceptable practice.

Direct interaction with pilots is now reduced to merely fulfilling specific requests such as delivering food and drinks, and minimal contact when they need to exit and reenter the flight deck for physiological breaks. And that interaction is usually only performed by the cabin crewmember stationed closest to the door. On a given long haul flight, cabin crew may only see the pilots twice, when delivering meals or picking them up. On short haul flights the communication may be even more limited, because of the need to maintain sterile cockpits and the fact that cabin crew are not necessarily delivering any meals up front.

Communicating with the interphone can sometimes be problematic due to static on the line making understanding difficult. In situations like this, face-to-face conversation could help alleviate any miscommunication.

These security factors designed to mitigate one hazard, can in fact, affect the relationship between the cabin crew and the pilots and can affect the overall performance of the crew as a team. The front-end crew/back-end crew mentality is returning, further undermining the benefits of CRM. The strides that have been made in the past relative to ensuring the "team" mentality between the flight deck and cabin crew are in jeopardy of being lost if we don't proactively look at the issue.

14.4 TRAINING TRENDS

To understand how we can begin to make improvements to CRM, especially strengthening communication and coordination in emergency situations, we need to look at some of the current training methods.

Internationally, aviation authorities have treated human factors as a multidisciplinary field, including but not limited to: engineering, psychology, physiology, medicine, sociology, and anthropometry (ICAO, 2003). The concept of CRM is one component of the larger concept of human factors and line-oriented flight training (LOFT) is used to facilitate practice and feedback in crew coordination and CRM.

Although the high-level guidance and approaches by these organizations on CRM may vary, their training course structure is generally the same and is comprised of three training components:

- Initial indoctrination/awareness;
- Recurrent practice and feedback; and
- Continual reinforcement.

Training can be delivered via classroom instruction and can be followed by some type of scenario-based training where the crewmember's performance skills can be evaluated as a whole. However, that traditional classroom training methodology is slowly being transitioned into computer-based training (CBT) to capture some of the changing technology available to instructors, and to reduce the classroom training footprint which can be expensive. Other terms for the online or CBT methodology are distance education (DE), distance learning (DL), or even self-guided training. Whatever the reader chooses to call it, one thing remains important when evaluating this delivery method, the limitations of the delivery method must be assessed. That is, whether the training outcome is to deliver knowledge, cognitive or performance skill.

All three of these are important training components. Knowledge is the ability to identify facts or know rules and how to apply them. Skill is an individual's ability to take their knowledge and put it together to perform an action. Skill is further broken into cognitive and psychomotor skills. Finally, there is performance. Performance is the ability of the individual to combine knowledge, skill, and intangibles, such as inference and judgement (sometimes called "soft skills"). Performance objectives are typically validated through performance of multiple related tasks, sometimes grouped together in event sets, like an evacuation drill in training (ACT ARC, 2016 a,b).

When it comes to the delivery of CRM specific training, there are some limits on how much of the overall concept can be delivered and evaluated in a CBT format. The format can be extremely beneficial for knowledge delivery, the recalling of facts, components, or suggested procedures related to CRM. While the trend may be to deliver more and more training via CBT, the reality is that there is still a need for classroom instruction related to CRM. The complexities of CRM training do not make it applicable to be delivered via CBT as a stand-alone training method, but may be conducted as a complimentary training method to other classroom or performance drills—in this specific case, joint CRM training between the pilots and the cabin crew.

14.5   JOINT CRM TRAINING

Over the years, many organizations have implemented working groups to review, evaluate, and revise their CRM documents and trainings. The European Aviation Safety Agency (EASA) published Notice of Proposed Amendment (NPA) 2014−17, CRM Training seeking comments on their recommendations. The recommendations in the NPA were drafted to incorporate new items for training to provide operators with more reliable tools to mitigate further CRM-related risks and hazards.

In 2014, the US Federal Aviation Administration (FAA) established the Air Carrier Training Aviation Rulemaking Committee (ACT ARC) to provide a forum for the US aviation community to discuss, prioritize, and provide recommendations to the FAA concerning air carrier training. One of the four initial work groups was the CRM Enhancement Workgroup (CRM WG). The CRM WG was tasked with making recommendations to update the FAA's CRM guidance to enhance crews' CRM skillsets, including skills related to Threat and Error Management (TEM) and Risk and Resource

Management (RRM). Finally, the CRM WG was tasked with providing recommendations related to enhancing CRM training between multiple working employees to improve the effectiveness and safety of the entire operations team.

Part of the reason for the formation of the CRM WG was driven by US cabin crew organizations in that they were concerned with some of the communication breakdowns between the pilots and cabin crew. Of no less concern was the anecdotal information that the cultural barriers, the enhanced locked flight deck door and procedures, and the lack of "together" time that used to be shared during some layovers was having a negative effect on the cohesiveness between the flight deck and cabin of the aircraft.

The CRM WG suggested that FAA guidance consider ICAO and EASA guidance, which promotes joint (combined) CRM training exercises between pilots, flight attendants, and technical crew. In the course of the CRM WG meetings it was noted that many international air carriers were in fact conducting joint training.

Some of the reasons cited by US air carriers as to why conducting joint pilot and cabin crew training was not feasible included difficulty in scheduling of the two types of crews and the economic costs involved. In addition, some participants mentioned the negative impact of joint training. That discussion seemed to mirror a 1988 FAA report titled "Cockpit and Cabin Crew Coordination" (DOT/FAA/FS-88/1 February 1988) in which five airlines reported conducting joint pilot and cabin crew training, with two of the five airlines reporting a negative experience with their program. For these two airlines, the report stated, joint training "inhibited a free and open exchange of ideas and, in some cases, intimidated the participants and inhibited their performance."

While we should be aware of negative effects of training, we should also be cognizant that sometimes a negative training experience can be due to a lack of effective instructional skills. The US CRM WG held lengthy discussions related to CRM trainers and submitted a recommendation to the US FAA related to specific trainer requirements to deliver and/or facilitate CRM training, specifically when designing or conducting joint training. The WG noted that the success of an effective joint training depended on the skill of proficient facilitators "(1) to help the CRM trainee understand the roles and responsibilities of others and (2) to further facilitate discussions which may be more complex and context based than relaying technical knowledge" (ACT ARC, 2016a,b). EASA in NPA, 2014–17 came to a similar conclusion, the recommendation noted the need for more defined criteria for the CRM trainer qualification, training, assessment, and recency.

Similarly, the US AC 120-51E on CRM (FAA, 2014) references the critical role and necessary skills for people who administer CRM training and measure its effectiveness. The AC also notes that instructors, supervisors, check pilots, and course designers require an additional level of training related to the practice and assessment of CRM, as well as special training to calibrate and standardize their own skills. Gaining proficiency and confidence in CRM instruction, observation, and measurement requires specialized training for instructors, supervisors, and check pilots in many CRM training processes.

Acknowledging there is a need for joint training, should also lead regulators and air carriers to acknowledge there is a need for specialized skills for the CRM trainer, especially when contemplating joint training.

Effective CRM skills require active participation of all crewmembers, which cannot be attained from passive classroom lectures alone; rather, active participation and practice are required. In fact, the negative experiences reported in the 1988 FAA report by the two carriers who chose to discontinue the joint training represent perfectly the reason why hands-on CRM training is essential. The best training methods emphasize practicing desirable behaviors during times of low stress, which will increase the likelihood that emergencies are handled effectively. This is borne out by the comments from the other three airlines that reported positive experiences with joint training; the FAA report stated that their training "increased the understanding of the other crew's duties, ensured that the two crew's instructions were compatible and enhanced the working relationship (Cardosi & Huntley, 1988)."

When the US FAA AC 120-51 on CRM was first promulgated in 1993 the focus was on the pilot. In 1998 the AC was updated to include the concept of joint training between pilots and cabin crew. The change was to incorporate the evolving concept of CRM with the objective to improve the effectiveness and safety of the entire operations team. Other FAA guidance documents specific for their inspectors, aviation safety inspectors (ASI) in FAA Order 8900.1, also discuss joint CRM training and encourages joint training and other activities to improve crewmember communication and coordination in emergency situations (FAA 8900.1).

EASA has suggested more firm CRM training requirements. Specifically, there should be a combined CRM training component for flight crew, cabin crew, and other technical crew in the recurrent training. The Agency recognized that annual training may not work so allowed the combined training hours to be spread out over a 3-year period. But the requirement for combined training in recurrent was a major step in enhancing precise and accurate communication between the different groups to enhance safety.

While the FAA has not gone as far as requiring joint training on an annual basis, the agency recognized the need to update their guidance on joint training when they created the CRM WG in 2014. Joint training is still being "encouraged" but the guidance material, when revised and published, should contain more suggestions for attaining the joint training mentality, or cross-functional training, of the multiple work groups, that is, pilots, cabin crew, and other technical crew.

Additional specifics on designing and conducting joint training are needed now more than ever as more and more hours of training are being pushed into the CBT delivery format. Some air carriers also noted that CRM concepts are routinely getting merged with other training subjects (ACT ARC 2016a,b). This can result in CRM no longer being provided as a stand-alone subject specifically in recurrent training. As an example, CRM time management and communication skills may be rolled into emergency response training.

During the CRM WG air carriers noted that many of their training programs already provide varying levels of cross-functional CRM training and suggested that air carriers would support the cross-functional CRM training concept as appropriate and as needed. They noted that it should be based on its current learning objectives or safety needs as dictated by the air carrier's safety management system (SMS). For example, while one air carrier may need to conduct cross-functional CRM training on an annual basis, another air carrier may not have that same training need based on their SMS. The CRM WG recognized that air carriers should have some flexibility related to the need for periodic cross-functional CRM training. However, there was concern that too much flexibility also could result in an unexpected situation where an air carrier provides joint training, or cross-functional CRM training, only once in a long-term employee's work history.

While quantity of hours spent in training do not necessarily guarantee quality, the setting of a minimum number of hours for subjects like CRM training would help to prevent rolling the subject in with other training subjects. Likewise, setting a minimum periodic training schedule may be important. For that reason, the CRM WG researched how other authorities or agencies address joint or cross-functional CRM training. An air carrier may need to consider if any of its training requirements are subject to review and approval by other authorities or agencies. For example, the EASA standard on recurrent CRM training recommends combined CRM training for flight crew and cabin crew during annual recurrent training and further states the combined training should be a minimum of 6 hours over a period of 3 years.

Further, in the United States air carriers doing business with specific US government agencies must follow those agencies regulations which require crew coordination training that facilitates full cockpit crews training and full crew interaction using standardized procedures including the principles of CRM. An air carrier must provide appropriate emergency procedures training (e.g., evacuation procedures) to flight deck and flight attendant personnel as a total crew whenever possible to ensure they can function as a coordinated team during emergencies.

Joint CRM training is an important and effective tool for improving crew coordination and should therefore be implemented at all airlines as one means of ensuring maximum levels of safety throughout the aviation system. And while frequent, at least annual training is desirable, the reality is that biennial or even triennial training can be effective if done properly.

14.6   A CAVEAT TO JOINT TRAINING

The benefits of joint training should not be underestimated as a way to build upon the core knowledge of CRM general philosophies and skills—communication; leadership and teamwork; problem-solving and decision-making; situation awareness; and task/workload management. However, before progressing to a joint or cross-functional type training outside of the individual's specific workgroup, it is imperative that the trainee understands the core CRM behaviors and skills targeted for their workgroup which should have been delivered during that workgroup's new hire or initial training at the air carrier.

That base workgroup understanding of CRM is to help ensure that joint training is effective by creating compatible foundational assumptions, that is, a shared understanding of the goal/outcome of CRM. Individual work groups learn CRM through their own operational experience. That previous operational experience in their own workgroup will also likely allow them to be better suited and understanding of some of the complexities of a joint training with a workgroup outside of their own. This workgroup operational experience and core understanding of CRM skills should also allow for the complexity of the joint or cross-functional training can be increased.

14.7   DELIVERY OF JOINT TRAINING

There is no one size fits all solution for joint or cross-functional CRM training because trainings should be tailored to an individual air carrier's operational or SMS needs. However, whatever the training/learning objectives, the joint CRM training is best presented with rich context and in a highly operationalized way. That is, the joint training is best delivered combined with case examples, scenarios, or live simulator training.

Joint CRM training should focus on the functioning of the crew as an intact team providing crewmembers opportunities to practice their skills together in the roles that they would normally be performing during the operation. This allows the trainee to have a personal understanding of their own behavior during normal or emergency situations. These similar situations, or scenario-based trainings, increase the probability that the crew will handle actual emergency situations more competently.

Therefore, there are some limits on how much of the overall concept and delivery of CRM specific training can be transmitted and evaluated in a CBT format. This is especially true when putting two or more different work groups together for training.

14.8   OTHER JOINT TEAM CRM BUILDING CONCEPTS

There are other approaches or tools that can enhance the idea of joint training or understanding of other work groups as a part of continued aviation safety. Although there are likely more, only two are mentioned here, namely, observation flights and preflight briefings.

14.8.1   Observation Flights

Prior to 9/11 some air carriers permitted new hire cabin crew to observe an actual ride in the flight deck as part of the crewmember's new hire training requirement. The ride could consist of one takeoff and landing or multiple takeoffs and landing. The training experience was to familiarize the new cabin crew with the pilot work environment and help them get a better understanding and awareness of the pilots' duties. This effective tool for developing CRM situational awareness was unfortunately stopped with the restriction of access to the flight deck following the events of September 11.

In the United States, aircraft dispatchers are required under the Aircraft Dispatcher Qualifications (2017) to complete familiarization flights on the flight deck or in a simulator annually. Although these familiarization type rides for cabin crew are not required, it is a worthwhile joint training type tool for air carriers to pursue if the regulatory environment permits that access to the flight deck during an active flight. This author had the benefit of having this invaluable vicarious experience as a new hire. Newer cabin crewmembers have not had the opportunity to experience an observation ride in the flight deck.

Recognizing that an observation ride on an actual flight may not be possible, there is another possible option. As a part of joint training, the observation flight could be conducted during a pilot simulator training session, with the caveat that it is not during a pilot's proficiency check session. While this may not allow all the cabin crew access to the simulator session, the session could be offered at a minimum to those cabin crew that are considered pursers or leads at the air carrier. As the lead in the cabin, this observation interaction could allow for better, clearer, and more concise discussions related to cabin flight issues. Specifically, the cabin crew lead discussing and conferring with the pilot lead on a course of action necessary to mitigate a situation in the cabin.

This is just one more example of something that can be done to support the necessary concept of joint pilot and cabin crew training. Pilots and cabin crew have different cultures and often react to situations in very different ways, so good communications between the groups is vital (ACT ARC 2016 a,b).

14.8.2   Preflight Briefings

One of the reasons for CRM training is to reduce the frequency and severity of crew-based errors. It is not just about "getting along." Flight deck and cabin crewmembers need to know precisely what information the other needs to help enhance the safe operation of the flight. Our cultural and professional differences, our relative positions within the carrier's organizational hierarchy, and the ways our two groups approach training may lead each group to respond to an incident in completely different ways.

One of the single most important practices for effective communication and crew coordination is the preflight briefing. This is even more important now that security enhancements have limited the communication pathways that have existed between flight deck and cabin crews. Preflight briefings from the pilots to the cabin crew set the tone for crew interactions. Briefings also allow each crewmember to solicit information from the other crewmember that they feel is necessary for performing their specific job, be it the pilot role or the cabin crew role.

If there is no briefing, the cabin crew may feel that the flight deck crew are not interested in open communications, or perhaps that they would rather not entertain any future requests or consider any opinions put forward by the cabin crew. This could lead to another situation similar to the 1989 Air Ontario crash in Dryden, Ontario in which the cabin crew failed to report the snow build up on the wings to the pilots.

And then there is the most basic reason for a preflight briefing, namely, introducing oneself to the other crewmember. This simple action can go a long way in opening the lines of communication. Interactions between the cabin and flight deck crewmembers need to be just as well scripted as those that occur between the crewmembers on the flight deck.

The FAA AC 120-51E (FAA, 2014) on CRM includes many references to topics that are important to include when evaluating the training program's effectiveness. One note states that the "captain's briefing establishes an environment for open/interactive communications." Yet, despite the obvious importance attached to open intracrew communications, preflight briefings are not required by US FAA regulations. A simple yet effective tool to enhancing crew interaction is that a preflight briefing between the flight deck and cabin crews occur on all flights.

14.9 CONCLUSION

CRM philosophy and training will continue to evolve to ensure crewmembers and other essential aviation employees have the toolsets to ensure a continued safe operation of aircraft. As part of that growth, the aviation community must also continue to assess any impediments to that effective team recognition of errors and mitigation of those concerns. That means continuing to look at areas like cultural differences that can affect the interaction of multiple work groups during problem-solving. The physical barriers, like the enhanced flight deck doors and differing rostering schedules, can also create a feeling of isolation, both real and emotional. Instead, crewmembers are now sharing only technical or need-to-know information. Communication is more than facts, especially when relevant to CRM philosophies.

Finally, there is the training aspect of CRM. Joint CRM training is not a new concept, it is just one that still needs more development and refinement as a way to enhance the CRM. The lack of interaction between the differing work groups, specifically in this case the pilots and cabin crew, can have a negative effect on crew coordination in normal operations as well as emergencies. The training interaction also allows for a continued understanding and appreciation of the other crewmember's role.

To continue to foster the sense of working as a cohesive team, with collective responsibility between the flight deck and cabin crewmembers to share necessary safety information, we need to reevaluate the available CRM tools. Aviation authorities and air carriers should require that pilots and cabin crew attend joint training sessions regularly—this will facilitate open communications and coordination between the flight deck and cabin crew so that procedural errors during incidents and accidents can be minimized.

It is imperative that we, the aviation safety community, address these communications concerns before they lead to an incident or accident, if they haven't already. Addressing these concerns will help facilitate and ensure an effective coordinated team effort when responding to an emergency, and quite probably save lives.

REFERENCES

Air Accidents Investigations Branch (AAIB). (1990). *Report on the accident to Boeing 737-400 G-OBME near Kegworth, Leicestershire on 8 January, 1989.* (Aircraft Accident Report 4/90). London: HMSO.

Air Carrier Training Aviation Rulemaking Committee (ACT ARC). (2016a). *Recommendation 16-2, Facilitator Training to Deliver Cross-Functional CRM Training.* Washington, DC. Available from https://www.faa.gov/about/office_org/headquarters_offices/avs/offices/afx/afs/afs200/afs280/act_arc/act_arc_reco/.

Air Carrier Training Aviation Rulemaking Committee (ACT ARC). (2016b). *Recommendation 16-6, Delivery of Cross-Functional Crew Resource Management (CRM) Training.* Washington, DC. Available from https://www.faa.gov/about/office_org/headquarters_offices/avs/offices/afx/afs/afs200/afs280/act_arc/act_arc_reco/.

Aircraft Dispatcher Qualifications, 14 C.F.R. § 121.463. (2017).

Cardosi, Kim., & Huntley Jr, Stephen. (1988). DOT/FAA Report, Cockpit and Cabin Crew Coordination (DOT/FAA/FS-88/1), Cambridge, Massachusetts. February 1988.

Chute, R., & Weiner, E. L. (2009). Cockpit-cabin communication: I. A tale of two cultures. *The International Journal of Aviation Psychology, 5*(3), 257−276. Available from https://doi.org/10.1207/s15327108ijap0503_2.

Commission of Inquiry Into the Air Ontario Crash at Dryden, Ontario, 1989-1992. Four Volumes, Volume III specific to page 1075. Canada.

European Aviation Safety Agency (EASA) published Notice of Proposed Amendment (NPA) 2014-17, Crew Resource Management (CRM).

Federal Aviation Administration. (2014). *Crew resource management training* (Advisory Circular 120-51E), Washington, DC.

Federal Aviation Administration (FAA) Order 8900.1, Flight Standards Information Management System (FSIMS), Aviation Safety Inspectors (ASI) Guide. FAA Order 8900.1, Volume 3, Chapter 19, Section 4, paragraph 3 1167.B, Policy, and FAA Order 8900.1, Volume 3, Chapter 23, Section 4, paragraph 3 1792.B, Policy.

International Civil Aviation Organization (ICAO). (2003). Human Factors Digest No. 15 AN/173 Cir 300, Reference 1.21, 2003.

Chapter 15

The Migration of Crew Resource Management Training

Brenton J.H. Hayward[1], Andrew R. Lowe[1] and Matthew J.W. Thomas[2]
[1]*Dédale Asia Pacific, Albert Park, VIC, Australia,* [2]*Westwood-Thomas Associates, Adelaide, SA, Australia*

In the aviation industry, crew resource management (CRM) training has become the accepted model for developing applied human factors skills amongst front-line employees. In contrast to purely or predominantly knowledge-based human factors courses, CRM training typically uses an experiential, adult learning approach to provide operational personnel with the understanding and nontechnical skills required to manage themselves and all available resources safely and effectively. The CRM training model, initially developed for flight deck crew, has subsequently been adapted and successfully applied beyond the cockpit within aviation, and to a range of other safety critical domains, to enhance the performance of individuals and teams in both routine and emergency situations. These include the maritime and rail industries, health care, and the offshore oil and gas industry. This chapter will examine the migration of the CRM philosophy and training methods to these other domains.

15.1 BEYOND THE FLIGHT DECK

Since its inception as *cockpit* resource management in the late 1970s, CRM has extended well beyond the flight deck and has been embraced by many groups across the commercial aviation industry. As has been discussed extensively elsewhere, the focus of CRM quickly extended outside the cockpit to include cabin crew as critical elements of operational safety (Chute & Wiener, 1994, 1995, 1996; Vandermark, 1991). Today, joint CRM training with both flight deck and cabin crew is relatively commonplace, and specific programs for training and assessing the applied human factors competencies of cabin crew have been established (cf. Simpson, Owens, & Edkins, 2004).

Crew Resource Management. DOI: https://doi.org/10.1016/B978-0-12-812995-1.00015-4
421

In a similar fashion to flight crew, many regulatory regimes now require aviation maintenance technicians and engineers to undertake regular training in human factors principles and human performance issues in a manner consistent with flight deck CRM programs. In the aviation maintenance domain, applied human factors training has been dubbed Maintenance Resource Management (MRM[1]; Stelly & Taylor, 1992; Taylor, 2000a, 2000b). MRM evolved as a direct response to several aviation accidents where human factors issues had impacted on the performance of aircraft maintenance and resulted in catastrophic outcomes. Most MRM training programs share a common structure with their traditional CRM origins, and cover a range of topics from communication, workload management through to human error and its management (Patankar & Taylor, 2004; Reason & Hobbs, 2003).

MRM programs have evolved considerably over the years and studies have demonstrated their potential to reduce aircraft ground damage events, enhance worker safety, and provide a positive return on investment (Patankar & Taylor, 2004, 2008; Taylor, 2000a, 2000b).

Air Traffic Control is another aviation discipline that has embraced human factors training in a similar way to flight operations (Andersen & Bove, 2000; EUROCONTROL, 1996; Härtel & Härtel, 1995). Referred to as either controller resource management (another "CRM") or team resource management (TRM), more recent versions of such training have focused on Threat and Error Management (TEM) as an effective way to structure the content of training around applied human factors principles (Kontogiannis & Malakis, 2009).

EUROCONTROL (1996) has been instrumental in funding the development and implementation of TRM training within Europe and elsewhere, and in 2002 formed a TRM User Group (now the TRM Working Group) that meets regularly to support and promote the use and development of TRM in Europe. The group consists mainly of operational air traffic controllers who also work as TRM facilitators (EUROCONTROL, 2004).

EUROCONTROL also provides TRM Awareness and TRM Facilitator training courses at their Institute for Air Navigation Services in Luxembourg. Air Navigation Service Providers (ANSPs) from many countries have recognized the potential benefits of TRM training, and the results of a TRM implementation survey conducted by EUROCONTROL in 2017 indicate that about 70% of ANSP respondents had implemented TRM training, while 44% of ANSPs yet to implement TRM were planning to do so "in the near future" (EUROCONTROL, 2018). In most cases, respondents indicated that their organizations found TRM training to be effective, with

---

1. The acronym "MRM" is also used in this chapter to pertain to Maritime Resource Management, the CRM variant used in the maritime industry.

some ANSPs rating TRM as highly effective (EUROCONTROL, 2018). In some European states TRM training has been introduced by both civilian and military ATM organizations, and more broadly EUROCONTROL TRM training materials and support have also been provided to nonmember states such as Israel, Thailand, Brazil, and Japan.

15.2   THE MARITIME INDUSTRY

The first proliferation of CRM principles beyond the aviation industry occurred in the early 1990s, when elements of the international maritime industry became aware of the evolution and apparent impact of CRM training within the airline community.

15.2.1   Rationale for CRM Training in the Maritime Industry

Maritime and aviation resource management training have their origins in very similar occurrences: serious accidents involving the ineffective use of available resources on the ship's bridge or the airliner flight deck (see Barnett, Gatfield, & Pekcan, 2004; Helmreich & Foushee, 1993; Lauber, 1979, 1987, 1993; National Transportation Safety Board, 1979). The need for maritime CRM is highlighted by evidence from investigations into maritime accidents that reveal critical inadequacies in the ability of individuals to manage both resources and emergency situations effectively (e.g., Marine Accident Investigation Branch, 1994, 1996, 1999). In particular, the grounding of the QE2 at Martha's Vineyard, Massachusetts in 1992 prompted the US NTSB to recommend that pilots, masters, and bridge personnel be trained in Bridge Resource Management (National Transportation Safety Board, 1993). Specifically, the report cited failures by the vessel's pilot and master to exchange critical information and a failure to maintain situational awareness as probable causes of the accident.

The requirement for maritime CRM was further confirmed by British and American studies that identified human error as a causal factor in a large proportion of the shipping incidents and accidents examined. A study by the shipping insurance industry in the UK found that human error accounted for 90% of collision accidents and 50% of cargo damage (UK P&I Club, 1997). The United States Coastguard estimated that 70% of shipping incidents were due to human error (United States Coastguard, 1995; cited in Barnett, et al., 2004). These figures fit with broadly accepted views on the contribution of human action and/or inaction to the vast majority of industrial safety occurrences (see, e.g., Hollnagel, 2004; Reason & Hobbs, 2003; Reason, 1990, 1997, 2008).

The results of these various studies and investigations revealed a notable gap in maritime training and an opportunity to improve understanding about error prevention, detection, and management as a means of promoting safety through human behavior. As in other transport industries, training for maritime officers had traditionally focused on developing individual technical skills rather than addressing the team management, communication, and coordination issues that are critical for safe operations.

15.2.2 Development of Maritime CRM

In the early 1970s the Warshash Maritime Centre in Southampton, UK developed Bridge Operations and Teamwork simulator-based training for ships' masters and officers employed by large oil companies (Haberley, Barnett, Gatfield, Musselwhite, & McNeil, 2001). The course included training on passage planning and the importance of the relationship between ships' masters and maritime pilots. This course later evolved into what became known as the Bridge Team Management (BTM) course. While differing somewhat in philosophy and approach, the BTM course comprised many of the topics contained in CRM courses in aviation and other industries (Barnett et al., 2004).

More widely known throughout the maritime industry today is the concept of Bridge Resource Management (BRM) training, which first emerged in the early 1990s. In 1992, seven major maritime industry bodies[2] collaborated with the Scandinavian Airlines System (SAS) Flight Academy to establish a global Bridge Resource Management training initiative (Deboo, n.d.; Wahren, 2007). This initiative was based on the premise that the CRM knowledge and expertise, already developed and becoming embedded within the aviation industry, could be beneficially transferred to the maritime sector.

This assumption proved to be correct. The first BRM course was launched in June 1993, and in subsequent years BRM training, founded on the principles of aviation CRM programs, became well established across the global maritime industry, delivered principally by The Swedish Club (a large marine mutual insurer) and a number of regional licensees.

In a parallel development, the Danish company Maersk implemented CRM training for maritime crews in 1994. Byrdorf (1998) describes the successful adaptation of aviation CRM principles to their commercial shipping environment, citing decreases in incident and accident rates and lowering of company insurance premiums as a direct result.

---

2. Collaborators with SAS Flight Academy on the initial BRM training initiative included the Dutch Maritime Pilots' Corporation, Finnish Maritime Administration, National Maritime Administration Sweden, Norwegian Shipowners' Association, Silja Line, the Swedish Shipowners' Association, and The Swedish Club.

15.2.3 Aim of Bridge Resource Management Training

BRM, as originally developed by the SAS Flight Academy and their maritime industry partners, was defined by Deboo (n.d.) as "the use and coordination of all the skills, knowledge, experience and resources available to the bridge team to accomplish or achieve the established goals of safety and efficiency of the passage." This definition obviously draws much from the origins of CRM in aviation.

The aim of BRM was to minimize the risk of incidents by encouraging safe and responsible behavior, and to ensure that sound resource management principles underpin everyday maritime operations. BRM aimed to foster positive attitudes favoring good personal communication, excellence in leadership, and compliance with operating procedures. Although BRM training remained focused primarily on senior bridge crew, some courses included engine room personnel and shore-based marine administrators (Deboo, n.d.).

15.2.4 Maritime Resource Management (MRM) Training

After almost a decade of delivering BRM training in many locations around the world, a decision was taken to revise and expand the BRM training program. In 2003 the organizations involved in the global delivery of BRM training (The Swedish Club and BRM licensees) decided to rebrand the course from BRM to MRM (Maritime Resource Management) to more accurately reflect the contents and objectives of the recently revised training program. The Swedish Club (TSC) currently oversees the delivery of MRM training by about 40 training providers across Europe, Asia, the Americas, and Australia. The target audience for MRM training now includes ships' officers, engineers, maritime pilots, and shore-based personnel. The stated objective of TSC MRM training is to establish genuine safety cultures in shipping companies with the ultimate goal of combating the human errors contributing to accidents at sea.

In 2006 one large Dubai-based global shipping operator commissioned the development of a fully customized, in-house Maritime Resource Management training program. The specific aims of this program were to include contemporary aviation CRM concepts and principles such as TEM, and to extend training beyond the bridge to include all elements of ships' crews. The courses conducted involved bridge, engine room, and other deck personnel, and included all Junior and Senior Officers and ratings, together with some shore-based personnel, and were successful in further integrating these sometimes-disparate groups (Dédale Asia Pacific & Vela International Marine, 2006).

15.2.5 MRM Training Delivery

While techniques vary, the typical 4-day TSC MRM training program includes multimedia teaching methods and consists of a series of lectures and workshops supported by computer-based training (CBT) modules. The original BRM concept had each course participant complete a series of CBT modules, exploring maritime accidents and incidents from a BRM perspective, with each module reflecting a different aspect of the training. At the end of the course, a role-play exercise simulating the pressure of a demanding situation allowed participants to practice newly acquired BRM-related skills. Current TSC MRM courses also employ CBT and some MRM providers use "Group-CBT" to deliver the training.

The Vela MRM course (Dédale Asia Pacific & Vela International Marine, 2006) employed more traditional CRM training methods, using peer facilitated classroom presentations, case studies and skill-development exercises to convey MRM training concepts and techniques across a 3-day in-house course.

Ship's Bridge Simulators are today available in a variety of locations around the world and many mariners have participated in multiple BTM and/or BRM/MRM simulator training sessions. While stand-alone bridge simulators were used initially for BRM training courses, the development of facilities with networked bridge and tug simulators has provided opportunities for more sophisticated forms of training. Indeed, joint training between where there is a focus on interactions between the bridge team and multiple tugs provides innovative opportunities for a more interactive and collaborative "systems-based" approach to CRM training (Havinga, Boer, Rae, & Dekker, 2017; Wang et al., 2014).

15.2.6 Competency Standards for Nontechnical Skills

The International Maritime Organization's (IMO) Seafarer's Training, Certification, and Watchkeeping (STCW) Code (International Maritime Organization, 1995) specifies mandatory nontechnical skills requirements for senior officers with responsibility for passenger safety in emergency situations. This minimum standard of competence includes organizing emergency procedures, optimizing the use of resources, controlling passengers and other personnel during emergency situations, and maintaining effective communications. However, the assessment criteria for this standard are based on generalized statements of performance outputs as opposed to specific demonstrable behaviors and are thus largely subjective (Barnett et al., 2004).

Although the IMO recognizes the requirement for nontechnical skills in resource management, the competency standards and assessment criteria need further improvement to be on a par with aviation standards (Barnett et al., 2004). However, in recent years considerable efforts have been made in developing and validating behavioral marker systems for assessing nontechnical performance in the maritime environment (e.g., Conceição, Basso, Lopes, & Dahlman, 2017; O'Connor & Long, 2011).

15.3 CRM IN HEALTH CARE

Anaesthesiologists initiated the first adaptations of CRM philosophy and principles to health care in the early 1990s. CRM principles are now quite widely discussed and practiced within anaesthesia and in recent years have begun to infiltrate other areas of health care (see Helmreich, 1995, 2000; Pizzi, Goldfarb, & Nash, 2001), as described below. Indeed, the early adaptation of CRM for anaesthesia, alongside the development of operating room simulators specifically designed for team training, has given rise to a considerable body of work in applied human factors across a wide range of health care disciplines today. Elements of the health care industry now set high standards for many aspects of training of nontechnical skills, and have developed a considerable evidence base for what constitutes best practice that many other industries can now draw upon.

15.3.1 Rationale for CRM in Health Care

The delivery of health care occurs in a dynamic, complex environment. This makes it a routinely high-risk activity further complicated by the potential for life-threatening emergency situations. Effective teamwork and crisis management are essential in many areas of health care, including emergency care, anaesthesiology, intensive care, and the operating room. As in aviation, these specialities require individual health care professionals with diverse roles and responsibilities to work as an effective, coordinated team in preventing, recognizing, and managing adverse events.

Over the last 20 years there has been increasing interest in analyzing and understanding errors made by health care workers in handling emergency situations. Studies in the late 1980s (see DeAnda & Gaba, 1990; Gaba & DeAnda, 1989) examined the responses of anaesthesiologists of different levels of experience to simulated crisis situations in the operating room. Findings suggested that anaesthesiologists lacked systematic training in nontechnical skills for critical situations, and that their training was also deficient in important aspects of decision-making and crisis management (Gaba, Howard, Fish, Smith, & Sowb, 2001).

Studies have also indicated that similar "false beliefs" or negative CRM-related beliefs and behaviors observed in the aviation domain also exist in health care. A study reported by Sexton, Thomas, and Helmreich (2000) measured attitudes to teamwork, stress, and error in operating room personnel using an adapted version of a questionnaire developed for use in aviation, the Cockpit Management Attitudes Questionnaire (CMAQ; Helmreich, 1984).

Results showed that junior operating room staff rated teamwork as less effective than their senior counterparts, and that surgeons displayed "authoritarian attitudes." Only about half of those sampled agreed that junior team members should question the decisions of senior staff. Some 70% of surgeons reported a belief that even when fatigued they could perform effectively at critical times. As noted by Merritt (1996) and Helmreich and Merritt (1998), very similar beliefs regarding "infallibility" can be found in comparable surveys of airline pilots across many different national and organizational cultures.

Observations of deficiencies in training of medical personnel and a greater awareness of the need for effective teamwork and communication have led to a growing consensus in health care of the potential benefits of CRM-style training.

15.3.2 Anaesthesia Crisis Resource Management (ACRM)

CRM was first introduced in the health care domain in the form of Anaesthesia Crisis Resource Management training (ACRM; Howard, Gaba, Fish, Yang, & Sarnquist, 1992; Kurrek & Fish, 1996). ACRM was developed in response to the fact that 65%−70% of threats to safety in anaesthesiology were found to be caused in part by human error, and the fact that anaesthetists had little practice in managing crises situations (Howard et al., 1992).

ACRM courses aim to provide trainees with a range of responses to manage critical situations including the ability to coordinate effectively as a team and use all available resources in a crisis (Howard et al., 1992).

One now widely-used ACRM curriculum was developed by Gaba and his colleagues at Stanford University. The program includes three full-day simulation-based courses with increasingly advanced training objectives and goals (Gaba et al., 2001). Each ACRM course begins with an introduction to or review of conceptual material, followed by group exercises in which participants discuss and analyze presented cases of anaesthetic "mishaps" or critical situations. The main part of the course is the simulator training in which participants manage a number of different crisis scenarios. Participants typically play one of three roles in each scenario: the primary anaesthesiologist, the first responder (with no knowledge of the scenario) who can be called into help the primary anaesthesiologist, or an observer.

Each scenario is followed immediately by an extensive debriefing session in which the management of the crisis is critiqued and analyzed. Debriefings follow comprehensive guidelines originally developed for debriefing line-oriented simulation exercises in aviation settings (McDonnell, Jobe, & Dismukes, 1997) and data gathered from trainees has shown that debriefing sessions are considered the most important part of the ACRM course (Gaba et al., 2001).

15.3.3 Effectiveness of Anaesthesia Crisis Resource Management

ACRM training is conducted at a number of major teaching institutions and is now mandatory on an annual basis for anaesthesia trainees at several of these. The effectiveness of ACRM training at various centers has been evaluated with different methods including questionnaires (e.g., Holzman et al., 1995; Howard et al., 1992) and structured interviews (Small, 1998). These evaluation studies show that trainees have found their ACRM experience to be very positive, and most believe that it contributes to their safe practice of anaesthesia (Gaba et al., 2001). For example, trainees "uniformly felt that the ACRM course was an intense, superior form of training related to an important, but inadequately taught, component of anaesthesia practice" (Howard et al., 1992).

To establish whether it might be feasible to measure the impact of ACRM training on performance, Gaba et al. (1998) conducted a study to measure anaesthesiologists' technical and behavioral management of simulated crisis situations. To assess behaviors in crisis management, 12 markers of CRM were adapted from sets previously developed for the evaluation of commercial aviation crews (Helmreich, Wilhelm, Kello, Taggart, & Butler, 1991). The markers included behaviors such as communication, leadership and followership, distribution of workload, and "overall CRM performance."

The study revealed many factors that complicate the assessment of the effectiveness of simulator-based ACRM training, including high interrater variability, the need for a large number of subjects, and biases involved in simulator-based testing of simulation-based learning. The results suggested that measuring ACRM performance was possible, albeit challenging, and that any such evaluations would be complex and expensive (Gaba et al., 2001).

Nonetheless, simulation training for anaesthesia trainees based on CRM principles has developed rapidly in recent years and is expected to become routine in many other health care settings in the future (Gaba et al., 2001).

15.3.4 Other Adaptations of CRM in Health Care

The ACRM approach has been adapted to a variety of other health care areas with a requirement for effective team performance, including emergency and trauma medicine, intensive care, and cardiac arrest response teams. An overview of some of the approaches used is provided further.

15.3.5 Emergency Team Coordination Course

The MedTeams Emergency Team Coordination Course (ETCC) was adapted from ACRM and CRM for Emergency Department care and delivery units

(Risser et al., 1999). The ETCC curriculum covers the five main areas of team structure and climate, problem-solving, enhancing communication, workload management, and team building. Like error management training in aviation CRM, the ETCC approach is based on improving team performance by avoiding errors, trapping them as they occur, and mitigating the consequences of errors that do occur (Morey et al., 2002; Shapiro et al., 2004).

15.3.6 NeoSim

ACRM has recently been adapted as the basis of a 1-day neonatal resuscitation training course for neonatologists and pediatricians called "NeoSim" (Halamek et al., 2000). The NeoSim course is delivered via didactic instruction with simulation and aims to teach behavioral teamwork skills along with some technical content. The Simulated Delivery Room places participants in realistic, dynamic crisis situations requiring the application of effective technical and behavioral skills in a coordinated team response. The training provides delivery room personnel with the opportunity to practice the skills necessary to better prepare for, and effectively respond to, crisis situations.

15.3.7 Team Resource Management

TRM and Operating Room Crisis Training are two versions of CRM customized for the operating room. These courses aim to improve the teamwork and error management skills of operating room personnel and focus on topics including authority, leadership, communication, decision-making, situation awareness, and workload management.

15.3.8 Other Developments in Health Care

An interesting adaptation of CRM to the health care domain was implemented at the Geneva University Hospital in Switzerland (Haller et al., 2008). The objective of this project was to assess the effect of a CRM intervention designed to improve teamwork and communication skills in a multidisciplinary obstetric setting.

The results of the project were evaluated using a pre- and posttraining cross-sectional study designed to assess participants' satisfaction, learning, and behavioral change according to Kirkpatrick's four-level training evaluation framework: reactions, learning, behavior, and organizational impact (Kirkpatrick, 1976, 1994). The project was conducted in the labor and delivery units of a large university-affiliated hospital, and participants included 239 midwives, nurses, physicians, and technicians.

Following completion of the CRM training program the results indicated that most participants valued the experience highly, there was significant participant learning, and there was a positive change in the team and safety climate in the hospital. The authors concluded that implementing CRM training in the multidisciplinary obstetrics setting was well accepted by participants and contributed to a significant improvement in interprofessional teamwork (Haller et al., 2008).

Across health care, many disciplines, from urology to pediatrics and from obstetrics to paramedics are currently embracing nontechnical skills training (Thomas, 2017).

15.3.9   The Use of Behavioral Markers in Health Care

A literature review conducted by Fletcher, Flin, and McGeorge (2000) indicated that nontechnical skills checklists and behavioral marker systems are being used quite widely in health care and that some of these are being used for training, most notably for ACRM. Some of these marker systems, including the Operating Room Checklist (Helmreich, Butler, Taggart, & Wilhelm, 1995), are actually checklists developed to guide performance and actions during training.

Fletcher, Flin, and McGeorge (2003) reviewed a number of behavioral marker systems and checklists used in anaesthesia, and went on to develop a taxonomy of behavioral markers for anaesthesia based on the existing marker systems and extensive consultation with subject matter experts (Fletcher et al., 2004). The resulting markers were published in the form of the Anaesthetists' Nontechnical Skills (ANTS) Handbook (University of Aberdeen & Scottish Clinical Simulation Centre, 2004). The markers cover four main areas important to effective performance in anaesthesia: team working, task management, decision-making, and situational awareness.

The initial development of ANTS has spawned the development of similar behavioral marker systems in other medical domains, from surgery to nursing. Of these the Nontechnical Skills for Surgeons (NOTSS) system has been the subject of extensive validation (Gostlow et al., 2017; Yule et al., 2008). One of the more curious findings of such research has demonstrated that there is not necessarily any relationship between a surgeon's perceived self-efficacy and their performance, suggesting that some new surgeons and trainees have poor insight into their own nontechnical skills (Pena et al., 2015).

This lack of direct relationship between an operator's perception of their nontechnical skills, and their actual performance has significant implications for the training of nontechnical skills, and the creation of strategies for individuals to develop better insight into their performance.

15.4   THE RAIL INDUSTRY

While CRM principles began to appear in isolated outposts of the rail industry in the 1990s, the international rail community was comparatively slow to formally adopt applied human factors training. Only in the past 5 years have any coordinated efforts been made to adapt CRM principles to rail operations.

15.4.1   Rationale for CRM in the Rail Industry

Rail safety workers face the same challenges as front-line operators in other high-risk industries — to ensure safety in a dynamic, demanding operational environment by managing threats and errors effectively. Just as other industries have recognized the need for specialized training to complement comprehensive technical knowledge and skills, in recent years the rail industry in various parts of the world has started to appreciate that CRM skills in the areas of communication, coordination, situational awareness, decision-making, and TEM are essential in preventing accidents and incidents.

Accident investigation and research provide strong support for the view that CRM training can be of potential benefit for the rail industry. For example, the US Federal Railroad Administration (FRA; Federal Railroad Administration, 2002) found that human factors issues accounted for approximately one-third of all rail accidents and half of all rail yard accidents in the United States. More specifically, human error was indicated as a causal factor in up to 37% of all train accidents not related to highway rail grade (level) crossings (Federal Railroad Administration, 1999). Further, ineffective CRM-related behaviors were identified as a contributing factor in a number of major rail accidents (e.g., National Transportation Safety Board, 1999a, 1999b; Office of Transport Safety Investigation, 2004; Transportation Safety Board, 1998), confirming a significant link between CRM behaviors and safety within the industry.

The NTSB investigation report into a 1998 train collision in the US state of Indiana (National Transportation Safety Board, 1999b) concluded that railroad safety would be enhanced if rail safety workers received "Train Crew Resource Management" training (TCRM) and recommended that such training be developed for all train crew members. The recommendation stipulated that TCRM training should at a minimum address: *crewmember proficiency, situational awareness, effective communication and teamwork,* and *strategies for appropriately challenging and questioning authority.*

The report of a Special Commission of Inquiry into a prominent fatal Australian rail accident at Waterfall, NSW in January 2003 included the recommendation that "Train driver and guard training should encourage teamwork and discourage authority gradients" (McInerney, 2005a). A subsequent review of safety management systems within the rail operator involved in the Waterfall accident was even more prescriptive, recommending "customized human factors training for rail safety workers and management/supervisory level staff based on contemporary CRM principles" (McInerney, 2005b).

The need for CRM training within the Australian rail industry had been identified prior to the Waterfall accident. The investigation of an August 2002 collision between a passenger train and a derailed ballast train near Bargo, NSW identified deficiencies in post-accident communication and emergency management, and attributed these to "inadequate resource management" (Transport NSW, 2002). The resulting investigation report included a recommendation that "all Rail Safety Workers undertake CRM training to increase their competence in the use of all resources."

15.4.2   Development of CRM in the Rail Industry

Despite almost two decades passing since the NTSB's 1999 recommendation for the introduction of Train CRM training, research and observation suggests that the adaptation and implementation of CRM principles to the rail industry globally has been patchy (Dédale Asia Pacific, 2006; Morgan, 2005; Morgan, Kyte, Olson, & Roop, 2003). During the 2000s, some CRM-related activities were undertaken in parts of Europe, for example, training in communication skills and teamwork in the UK (Mills, 2003; Rail Safety & Standards Board, 2004). Until 2007 however, CRM had only been formally adapted to significant components of the rail industry in North America, where interest in CRM training principles remains sporadic.

For example, the NTSB reported that in the mid-1990s they became aware of a CRM program implemented by the former Southern Pacific Railroad (now Union Pacific) that was apparently based on the training provided to flight crew at American Airlines (National Transportation Safety Board, 1999b). It is believed that this program was established in the late 1980s (Federal Railroad Administration, 2004b). While the NTSB reported that Union Pacific has required all new employees to undertake this training since 1998, it is difficult to obtain any further details on the actual activities being conducted.

Canadian Pacific Railway (CPR) has conducted a 2-day CRM training program oriented at new-hire conductors and trainmen since 1999 (Ackerman, 2005). In 2000 the FRA Railroad Safety Advisory Committee reported that a combined project between the AAR and Canadian Pacific had begun developing a generic CRM program based on existing CPR materials that could be customized for each individual railroad (Federal Railroad Administration, 2000). Deliverables from this program, however, could not be located.

In 2003, the Texas Transportation Institute (TTI), based at Texas A&M University, conducted a study to collect information about the extent of

CRM activities in the North American rail industry (Morgan et al., 2003). Following an extensive consultation process with a cross-section of railroads, Morgan and colleagues reported the following:

- Seven out of ten railroads evaluated had formal CRM programs in place in 2003.
- Those railroads with active CRM programs generally limited CRM training to engineers and/or conductors, although one also provided CRM training to dispatchers.
- At several of the rail companies, CRM training was included in initial training for new employees, with less emphasis on a broader program to address recurrent training or training for current employees.
- While some railroads had no formal CRM program, they did have specific programs that taught topics related to key elements of CRM such as situational awareness, communication, and/or teamwork.
- Most training programs were classroom-based, with material delivered via PowerPoint and lecture, using videos, group exercises, and role-plays to consolidate learning.
- The length of CRM training courses varied from a half-day to two full days, with the training sometimes presented in four to five segments over a 4–6 week period.
- Refresher training frequently did not entail additional classroom instruction, but was computer-based or accomplished through supervisor "ride-alongs" which allow a supervisor an opportunity to give specific CRM behavioral feedback.
- CRM program content tended to include the broad topics of situational awareness, teamwork, communication and technical proficiency, as well as information on human error, safety culture, avoiding distractions, planning, fatigue management, assertiveness, briefings, conflict resolution, and task prioritization.

The Texas Transportation Institute, working with the FRA's Office of Railroad Development, Office of Safety, and Burlington Northern Santa Fe Railway (BNSF) used this research as the basis for development of a pilot CRM training program for the American rail industry (Federal Railroad Administration, 2004a).

15.4.3 Current Adaptations of CRM in the Rail Industry

Canadian Pacific Railway

As detailed above, since 1999 CPR have conducted a 2-day CRM training program oriented at their new-hire conductors and trainmen. The course was developed by a local community college in Calgary. It is run during the final week of a 13-week training program for entry-level employees and focuses on human error, teamwork, and communication. The course emphasizes the importance of teamwork, communication, and briefings as countermeasures against human error (Ackerman, 2005).

A working group of rail representatives (including representatives from the Association of American Railroads and Norfolk and Southern Railroad) developed a short video based on Canadian Pacific's CRM materials that other railroads then customized with their own logos. A number of these railroads subsequently used the 30–45 minute training video in safety-related training.

Federal Railroad Administration

The FRA railroad industry Task Force created a generic CRM program for train and engine employees. The main topics covered in the program include decision-making, assertiveness, crew coordination, leadership, teamwork, situational awareness, and active practice and feedback (Federal Railroad Administration, 2004a). In June 2000, this CRM program was made available to the railroad industry. The course syllabus contains 10 lesson plans with a coordinating videotape that provides opportunities for role-playing, discussion of textbook examples, classroom style instruction, and opportunities for group participation. The program has three phases: awareness, practice and feedback, and reinforcement (Federal Railroad Administration, 2004a).

Texas Transportation Institute

Following their evaluation of the status of CRM activities in the North American rail industry (see above), TTI has developed a pilot CRM training course which has been tested at several sites on the BNSF Railway (Morgan, 2005). The introductory pilot course has three "tracks":

- transportation (locomotive engineers, conductors, dispatchers, etc.);
- engineering (maintenance-of-way, signaling, electrical catenary workers[3], etc.); and
- maintenance (locomotive and rolling stock service technicians, mechanical shop workers, in-yard train inspectors, etc.).

The same CRM materials are used for all three "tracks" but the scenarios used as examples throughout the course (taken from NTSB or FRA Fatality Reports) are varied dependent on the "track" in order to be operationally relevant to the trainees in each class. Along with presentation materials, detailed scenario handbooks for trainees and scripted instructor guides have been developed for each "track."

---

3. The catenary is the system of wires suspended above the rail track, which supply power to electrically powered trains.

TTI have subsequently been involved in further research and development of rail CRM training practices and materials (Morgan, Olson, Kyte, Roop, & Carlisle, 2006; Olsen, 2005). They have also contributed to the development of a business case which demonstrates the potential monetary value of CRM training in contributing to safety enhancement within the North American rail industry (Federal Railroad Administration, 2007; Roop et al., 2007).

15.4.4   Developments in the Australian Rail Industry

The Australian National Rail Resource Management Project

In 2005 The NSW Independent Transport Safety and Reliability Regulator (ITSRR), and Public Transport Safety Victoria (PTSV), with the endorsement of the Rail Safety Regulators Panel of Australia and New Zealand (RSRP), initiated a national project to develop generic applied human factors training guidelines and materials for the Australian rail industry. A consultant was appointed and ITSRR and PTSV, in partnership with the rail industry, embarked on a project aimed to improve awareness and understanding of the potential benefits of applied human factors training and provide the rail industry with practical guidance and resources to assist with the implementation of such training.

The resulting reports and materials formed the core deliverables of the National Rail Resource Management Project (Dédale Asia Pacific, 2006; Lowe, Hayward, & Dalton, 2007), which were completed and launched in December 2007 (Klampfer, Walsh, Quinn, Hayward, & Pelecanos, 2007). Since that time, the project sponsors have been actively encouraging the rail industry to introduce RRM in some form, drawing on the guidelines and training materials provided. While uptake has been slow, a number of rail transport operators have used the materials selectively to enhance and supplement preexisting operational and safety and human factors training programs.

The RSRP was further involved in part-funding an RRM pilot program conducted by a major Australian rail operator (Klampfer, Grey, Lowe, Hayward, & Branford, 2009). In 2009 the operator conducted three RRM pilot courses to test the concept and some customized training materials. An interesting feature of the training strategy was that mixed groups of rail safety workers attended each course (including train drivers, conductors, train controllers, signalers, shunters, and station staff). The training was well received by participants, and following several protracted delays the operator recently approved the resources to implement a dedicated RRM/Operational Awareness training program (Branford, 2017).

The National RRM Project generated significant interest in RRM and human factors within the Australian rail industry and within New Zealand,

Europe, and the United Kingdom. The size and scope of the project inevitably led to many insights and opportunities to improve the implementation and integration of human factors programs and principles into the rail industry (Alcock, Grey, Klampfer, Raggett, & Rowland, 2013; Klampfer et al., 2009).

Queensland Rail's Confidential Observations of Rail Safety (CORS) Program

Queensland Rail (QR) Passenger Services have conducted introductory human factors training for train drivers since 2003, using a mix of PowerPoint presentations, case studies, and facilitated discussions to cover typical human factors topics in a half-day course. The latest iteration of the course includes scenario-based simulator practice and feedback and a focus on TEM using the results of an adapted rail version of aviation's Line Operations Safety Audit (LOSA) technique (Federal Aviation Administration, 2005). McDonald, Garrigan, and Kanse (2006) provide detail on QR's Confidential Observations of Rail Safety (CORS) program. QR reported promising results from an evaluation of the utility of their RRM program, with results suggesting that RRM training can help improve safe train driving performance (Queensland Rail, 2011).

Developments in the UK

Following on from the Australian National RRM Project the UK Rail Safety and Standards Board (RSSB) investigated the potential utility of implementing RRM-style training to the UK rail industry. A briefing document was produced which concluded that "the delivery of Rail Resource Management training in the GB rail industry has the potential to improve the skills of operational staff, reducing the number and severity of accidents and incidents, and bringing financial benefits" (Rail Safety & Standards Board, 2009). Since that time the RSSB has adopted the Nontechnical Skills (NTS) moniker for applied human factors training and developed, piloted, and evaluated an NTS training course for safety critical staff. The RSSB has also produced a suite of guidance materials and documents to support rail operator development and implementation of NTS training (Rail Safety & Standards Board, 2012, 2016).

15.5 OFFSHORE INDUSTRY

15.5.1 Rationale for CRM in the Offshore Industry

The offshore oil and gas industry has a strong teamwork culture and different crews, shifts, and groups working together typically manage day-to-day operations. Studies of accidents and incidents in the offshore industry have found that, as in other high-risk industries, human error is frequently identified as a contributing factor (e.g., Flin, Mearns, Fleming, & Gordon, 1996; Mearns, Flin, Fleming, & Gordon, 1997).

Closer examination of incidents with human factors causes has demonstrated that a high proportion of these are the result of a failure of specific aspects of CRM (Mearns et al., 1997). When incidents with human factors causes over a 2-year period at seven offshore companies were coded into human factors categories, it was found that 46% fell within one of the broad CRM topics of teamwork, leadership, situation awareness, decision-making, communication, or personal limitations.

With human error and CRM-related failures apparent as frequent contributors to safety events in the offshore environment, it is to be expected that CRM training could lead to long-term improvements in the safety performance of the industry.

15.5.2 Adaptations of CRM to the Offshore Industry

CRM for Offshore Control Room Operators

CRM was first introduced to the offshore industry when it was adapted for offshore control room operators in 1992 (Flin & O'Connor, 2001; Flin, 1997). Elements of CRM from the aviation domain were incorporated into a training program focusing on emergency response training and competence assessment for offshore control room operators.

The course covered four standard CRM topics adapted for control room operations: decision-making, communication, stress, and assertiveness. Modules used by commercial airlines were modified to suit the specific needs of the domain by drawing on psychological research and the expertise of control room operations trainers.

Course delivery included lectures as well as exercises and discussion of personal experiences relating to the topic areas. Four principal modules were developed: *decision-making, communication, assertiveness*, and *stress*.

CRM for Offshore Installation Managers and Emergency Response Teams

CRM has also been developed for Offshore Installation Managers (OIMs) and their teams undergoing emergency response training in control room simulators (Flin, 1997; O'Connor & Flin, 2003). The course was designed around elements that were critical for effective team performance in emergency command centers, including understanding of team roles, communication, group decision-making, assertiveness, team attitudes, stress management, and shared mental models. The aim of the course was to improve team performance in the emergency control center.

Emergency Resource Management—Elf Norge

CRM training has also been used with Norwegian offshore crews, in the form of Emergency Resource Management training at Elf Petroleum Norge (Flin, O'Connor, Mearns, Gordon, & Whitaker, 2000; Grinde, 1994). The overall aim of the course is to provide operators with a comprehensive understanding of the resources available during an emergency. The training program includes elements of decision-making, task allocation, situation assessment, and communication. The initial 3-day course is delivered by lectures, supported by practical scenarios run in an onshore simulator.

CRM for Offshore Production Installation Crews

The first prototype CRM program for offshore production installation crews was run in 1999 (Flin et al., 2000; O'Connor & Flin, 2003). This 2-day course was designed to improve safety and productivity for production and maintenance crews, as well as to reduce down time for these two groups. Course content included modules on fatigue and shiftwork, stress, team coordination, communication, decision-making, situation awareness, and an understanding of human error and the origins of CRM. Evaluation of the eight courses completed suggested that this type of CRM training could have benefits for the offshore oil and gas industry.

The Use of Behavioral Markers

The prototype CRM for offshore production installation crews described above aimed to provide participants with an increased awareness of a set of nontechnical skills. The nontechnical skills framework was based on research and the NOTECHS framework developed for aviation (Flin et al., 2003). Specific objectives were written for each module around the nontechnical skills framework in the early stages of course development (Flin et al., 2000).

15.6   FUTURE MIGRATION

As discussed above, the philosophy and principles of CRM training have been successfully adapted to several other safety critical work domains. Those not discussed in detail here include the Nuclear Power Production industry (e.g., Belton, 2001; Gaddy & Wachtel, 1992), the US Space Program (e.g., see Rogers, 2002, 2010), the mining industry (e.g., Thomas, 2017), and others.

So, what does the future hold for resource management training outside the aviation domain? This chapter has discussed how CRM has migrated successfully from the aviation flight deck to other components of the aviation system, to the bridges and engine rooms of merchant vessels, to hospital emergency departments and operating theaters, offshore oil platforms, and rail transport systems.

Indeed, the recent decades of development have demonstrated the benefits of nontechnical skills training is almost any domain where performance and safety depend on the interaction between people, technology, and complex work environments (Thomas, 2017).

CRM in aviation has evolved considerably in the decades since its inception in the 1970s, with airline operators frequently leading the way, followed by regulators who have in many cases enshrined CRM training principles in regulatory requirements and guidelines (e.g., Civil Aviation Authority, 2003, 2016; Civil Aviation Safety Authority, 2011; European Aviation Safety Agency, 2015a, 2015b, 2017; Federal Aviation Administration, 2004).

However, during the last decade most innovation has occurred outside the aviation industry, and examples of best practice are now to be found in settings such as health care, maritime, and mining. Often these innovations have involved an increased focus on the practical skills involved in CRM, and have turned away from the classroom sessions found in more traditional models (Pena et al., 2015). Further, recent innovations have also focused on enhanced instructional design and educational techniques, such as scenario design and debriefing, rehearsal and assessment techniques to ensure these training programs lead to demonstrated performance outcomes at the individual, team, and organizational level (Thomas, 2017).

Most importantly, many industries are building stronger links between their Safety Management Systems (SMS) and their nontechnical skills training programs in order to identify areas of NTS deficiency and focus training delivery on specific organizational-based needs. The International Air Transport Association (IATA) Training and Qualification Initiative (ITQI), a keystone program of which is Evidence-Based Training (EBT), is one such program that utilized a range of data-sources to produce training programs that target more closely actual industry and organizational needs in nontechnical skills (International Civil Aviation Organization, 2013).

Overall, the scientific and empirical evidence of recent decades has highlighted that nontechnical skills play a critical role in operator performance across a wide range of industrial contexts. Indeed, for all intents and purposes, if an organization today does not have a formal program for nontechnical skill development, it could be regarded as failing to invest in a critical component of operator competency.

REFERENCES

Ackerman, F. (2005). CRM training at Canadian Pacific Railway. *Personal Communication*, December 2005.

Alcock, J., Grey, E., Klampfer, B., Raggett, L., & Rowland, A. (2013). *Rail Resource Management (RRM): Post-implementation review and future directions.* Presentation at the 3rd International Rail Human Factors Conference, London, UK, March 2013.

Andersen, V., & Bove, T. (2000). A feasibility study of the use of incidents and accidents reports to evaluate effects of team resource management in air traffic control. *Safety Science, 35*(1), 87−94.

Barnett, M., Gatfield, D., & Pekcan, C. (2004). A research agenda in Maritime Crew Resource Management. In *Paper presented at the National Maritime Museum Conference on 'Safer Ships, Safer Lives'*, London, March 2004.

Belton, S. (2001). CRM training in the nuclear industry. *Paper presented at the Third CRM Users Group Workshop*, University of Aberdeen, October 2001. Cited in R. Flin, P. O'Connor, & K. Mearns, (2002). Crew resource management: Improving safety in high reliability industries. *Team Performance Management, 8*, 68−78.

Branford, K. (2017). Update on RRM/Operational Awareness Training at V/Line. *Personal communication*, December 2017.

Byrdorf, P. (1998). Human factors and crew resource management: An example of successfully applying the experience from CRM programmes in the aviation world to the maritime world. In *Paper presented at the 23rd Conference of the European Association for Aviation Psychology*, Vienna, September 1998.

Chute, R. D., & Wiener, E. L. (1994). Cockpit and cabin crews: Do conflicting mandates put them on a collision course? *Flight Safety Foundation Cabin Crew Safety, 29*(2), Reprinted in Airline Pilot, March, 1995.

Chute, R. D., & Wiener, E. L. (1995). Cockpit/cabin communication: I. A tale of two cultures. *International Journal of Aviation Psychology, 5*(3), 257−276.

Chute, R. D., & Wiener, E. L. (1996). Cockpit/cabin communication: II. Shall we tell the pilots? *International Journal of Aviation Psychology, 6*(3), 211−231.

Civil Aviation Authority. (2003). *CAP 737: Crew Resource Management (CRM) Training. Guidance for Flight Crew, CRM Instructors and CRM Instructor-Examiners*. London: CAA Safety Regulation Group.

Civil Aviation Authority. (2016). *CAP 737: Flight Crew Human Factors Handbook. December 2016*. Crawley, West Sussex, UK: Author.

Civil Aviation Safety Authority. (2011). *Non-technical skills training and assessment for regular public transport (RPT) operations: Civil Aviation Advisory Publication (CAAP) SMS-3(1), April 2011*. Canberra: Author.

Conceição, V. P., Basso, J. C., Lopes, C. F., & Dahlman, J. (2017). Development of a behavioural marker system for rating cadet's non-technical skills. *TransNav: International Journal on Marine Navigation and Safety of Sea Transportation, 11*.

DeAnda, A., & Gaba, D. (1990). Unplanned incidents during comprehensive anesthesia simulation. *Anesthesia & Analgesia, 71*(1), 77−82.

Deboo, K. N. (n.d.). *Maritime resource management*. Mumbai: Anglo-Eastern Maritime Training Centre.

Dédale Asia Pacific. (2006). *Interim Report, National Rail Resource Management Project: Review of Best Practice, Implementation Issues and Task Analysis*. Melbourne/Sydney: PTSV/ITSRR.

Dédale Asia Pacific & Vela International Marine. (2006). *Maritime resource management (MRM) training course*. Melbourne: Authors.

EUROCONTROL. (1996). *Guidelines for developing and implementing team resource management* (Edition 1.0). Brussels: Author, HUM. ET1. ST10. 1000-GUI-01.

EUROCONTROL. (2004). *Team resource management: A promising future?* Brussels: Author.

EUROCONTROL. (2018). *TRM implementation: Survey report 2017*. Brussels: Author.

European Aviation Safety Agency. (2015a). *Executive Director Decision 2015/022/R amending the acceptable means of compliance and guidance material to commission regulation (EU) No 965/2012*. Retrieved from: https://www.easa.europa.eu/newsroom-and-events/news/crew-resource-management-crm-training.

European Aviation Safety Agency. (2015b). *Executive Director Decision 2015/023/R amending the acceptable means of compliance and guidance material to commission regulation (EU) No 965/2012*. Retrieved from: https://www.easa.europa.eu/newsroom-and-events/news/crew-resource-management-crm-training.

European Aviation Safety Agency. (2017). *Crew resource management in practice*. Cologne: Author.

Federal Aviation Administration. (2004). *Crew resource management training. AC120-51E*. Washington, DC: US Department of Transportation.

Federal Aviation Administration. (2005). *Line operations safety audit (LOSA). Draft advisory circular*. Washington, DC: US Department of Transportation.

Federal Railroad Administration. (1999). *Railroad Safety Statistics Annual Report*. Washington, DC: United States Department of Transportation, Office of Public Affairs.

Federal Railroad Administration (2000). *Minutes of the Railroad Safety Advisory Committee Meeting, 28 January 2000*. United States Department of Transportation, Office of Public Affairs, Washington, DC: Author.

Federal Railroad Administration (2002). *Five-Year Strategic Plan for Railroad Research, Development, and Demonstrations*. United States Department of Transportation, Office of Public Affairs, Washington, DC: Author.

Federal Railroad Administration (2004a). *Safety Assurance and Compliance Program (SACP). Year 2003 accomplishments*. U.S. Department of Transportation Federal Railroad Administration. Office of Safety, June 2004. Washington, DC: Author.

Federal Railroad Administration (2004b). Switching Operations Fatality Analysis. Findings and recommendations of the SOFA working group. August 2004 Update. United States Department of Transportation, Office of Public Affairs, Washington, DC: Author.

Federal Railroad Administration. (2007). *Rail Crew Resource Management (CRM): The Business Case for CRM Training in the Railroad Industry. (DOT/FRA/ORD-07/21)*. United States Department of Transportation, Office of Public Affairs, Washington, DC: Author.

Fletcher, G., Flin, R., & McGeorge, P. (2000). *WP1 Report: Review of Human Factors Research in Anaesthesia. Version 1*. Interim Report on SCPMDE Research Grant RDNES/991/C.

Fletcher, G., Flin, R., & McGeorge, P. (2003). *WP2 Report: Review of Behavioural Marker Systems in Anaesthesia. Version 1.1*. Work package 2 Report on SCPMDE Research Grant RDNES/991/C.

Fletcher, G., Flin, R., McGeorge, P., Glavin, R., Maran, N., & Patey, R. (2004). Rating non-technical skills: Developing a behavioural marker system for use in anaesthesia. *Cognition, Technology and Work, 6*, 165–171.

Flin, R. (1997). Crew resource management for teams in the offshore oil industry. *Team Performance Management, 3*(2), 121–129.

Flin, R., Martin, L., Goeters, K.-M., Hörman, H.-J., Amalberti, A., Valot, C., & Nijhuis, H. (2003). Development of the NOTECHS (non-technical skills) system for assessing pilots' CRM skills. *Human Factors and Aerospace Safety, 3*(2), 97–119.

Flin, R., Mearns, K., Fleming, M. & Gordon, R. (1996). Risk Perception and Safety in the Offshore Oil and Gas Industry. Report (OTH 94454). Suffolk: HSE Books.

Flin, R., & O'Connor, P. (2001). Crew Resource Management in the offshore oil industry. In E. Salas, C. Bowers, & E. Edens (Eds.), *Improving teamwork in organizations*. New Jersey: LEA.

Flin, R., O'Connor, P., Mearns, K., Gordon, R. & Whitaker, S. (2000). *Factoring the Human into Safety: Translating Research into Practice. Vol. 3 - Crew Resource Management Training for Offshore Operations.* OTO 2000 063. Sudbury: HSE Books.

Gaba, D., Howard, S., Flanagan, B., Smith, B., Fish, K., & Botney, R. (1998). Assessment of clinical performance during simulated crises using both technical and behavioral ratings. *Anesthesiology, 89*(3), 8–18.

Gaba, D. M., & DeAnda, A. (1989). The response of anesthesia trainees to simulated critical incidents. *Anesthesia & Analgesia, 68*(4), 444–451.

Gaba, D. M., Howard, S. K., Fish, K. J., Smith, B. E., & Sowb, Y. A. (2001). Simulation-based training in anesthesia crisis resource management (ACRM): A decade of experience. *Simulation & Gaming, 32*(2), 175–193.

Gaddy, C., & Wachtel, J. (1992). Team skills training in nuclear power plant operations. In R. Swezey, & E. Salas (Eds.), *Teams: Their training and performance.* New Jersey: Ablex.

Gostlow, H., Marlow, N., Thomas, M. J. W., Hewett, P., Kermeier, A., Babidge, W., ... Maddern, G. (2017). A study of the non-technical skills of surgical trainees and experienced surgeons. *British Journal of Surgery, 104*(6), 777–785.

Grinde, T. A. (1994) Emergency Resource Management training. In Proceedings of the Second International Conference on Health, Safety, & the Environment in Oil and Gas Exploration and Production (Vol 2, 413-417). Jakarta, Indonesia. Richardson, Texas: Society of Petroleum Engineers.

Haberley, J. S., Barnett, M. L., Gatfield, D., Musselwhite, C., & McNeil, G. (2001). *Simulator Training for Handling Escalated Emergencies. MCA Project RP 467.* Southampton: Warshash Maritime Centre.

Halamek, L. P., Kaegi, D. M., Gaba, D. M., Sowb, Y. A., Smith, B. C., Smith, B. E., & Howard, S. K. (2000). Time for a new paradigm in pediatric medical education: Teaching neonatal resuscitation in a simulated delivery room environment. *Pediatrics, 106*, E45.

Haller, G., Garnerin, P., Morales, M.-A., Pfister, R., Berner, M., Irion, O. & Kern, K. (2008). Effect of crew resource management training in a multidisciplinary obstetrical setting. *International Journal for Quality in Health Care, Advance Access, published May 6, 2008.*

Härtel, C. E. J., & Härtel, G. F. (1995). Controller Resource Management – What can we learn from aircrews? *(Vol. DOT/FAA/AM-95/21).* Washington: US Department of Transportation.

Havinga, J., Boer, R. J. D., Rae, A., & Dekker, S. W. (2017). How Did Crew Resource Management Take-Off Outside of the Cockpit? A Systematic Review of How Crew Resource Management Training Is Conceptualised and Evaluated for Non-Pilots. *Safety, 3* (4), 26.

Helmreich, R., Wilhelm, J., Kello, J., Taggart, W., & Butler, R. (1991). *Reinforcing and evaluating crew resource management: Evaluator/LOS instructor reference manual (NASA/UT Technical Manual 90-2, Revision 1).* Austin: NASA/University of Texas Aerospace Crew Performance Project.

Helmreich, R. L. (1984). Cockpit management attitudes. *Human Factors, 26*, 583–589.

Helmreich, R.L. (1995). Interpersonal Human Factors in the Operating Theater. *Paper presented at the Danish Anaesthesia Simulator Conference, Copenhagen.*

Helmreich, R. L. (2000). On error management: Lessons from aviation. *British Medical Journal, 320*, 781–785.

Helmreich, R. L., Butler, R. E., Taggart, W. R., & Wilhelm, J. A. (1995). *Behavioural markers in accidents and incidents: Reference list. (NASA/UT/FAA Technical Report 95-1).* Austin, TX: The University of Texas.

Helmreich, R. L., & Foushee, H. C. (1993). Why crew resource management? Empirical and theoretical bases of human factors training in aviation. In E. L. Wiener, B. G. Kanki, & R. L. Helmreich (Eds.), *Cockpit resource management* (pp. 3−45). San Diego, CA: Academic Press.

Helmreich, R. L., & Merritt, A. C. (1998). *Culture at work in aviation and medicine: National, organisational and professional influences*. Aldershot, UK: Ashgate.

Hollnagel, E. (2004). *Barriers and accident prevention*. Aldershot, UK: Ashgate.

Holzman, R. S., Cooper, J. B., Gaba, D. M., Philip, J. H., Small, S. D., & Feinstein, D. (1995). Anesthesia crisis resource management: Real-life simulation training in operating room crises. *Journal of Clinical Anesthesia, 7*(8), 675−687.

Howard, S. K., Gaba, D. M., Fish, K. J., Yang, G., & Sarnquist, F. H. (1992). Anesthesia crisis resource management training: Teaching anesthesiologists to handle critical incidents. *Aviation Space & Environ Med, 63*, 763−770.

International Civil Aviation Organization. (2013). *Manual of Evidence-based Training: Doc 9995 AN/497*. Montreal, Canada: ICAO.

International Maritime Organization. (1995). *Seafarer's Training, Certification and Watchkeeping Code (STCW Code)*. London: IMO.

Kirkpatrick, D. L. (1994). *Evaluating training programs: The four levels*. San Francisco, CA: Berrett-Koehler.

Kirkpatrick, D. L. (1976). Evaluation of training. In R. L. Craig (Ed.), *Training and development handbook: A guide to human resources development*. New York: McGraw-Hill.

Klampfer, B., Grey, E., Lowe, A., Hayward, B., & Branford, K. (2009). Reaping the benefits: How railways can build on lessons learned from crew resource management. *Proceedings of the Third International Conference on Rail Human Factors*, Lille, France, March 2009.

Klampfer, B., Walsh, C., Quinn, M., Hayward, B., & Pelecanos, S. (2007). *The national rail resource management (RRM) project. Launch presentation*, Sydney, December 2007.

Kontogiannis, T., & Malakis, S. (2009). A proactive approach to human error detection and identification in aviation and air traffic control. *Safety Science, 47*(5), 693−706.

Kurrek, M. M., & Fish, K. J. (1996). Anesthesia crisis resource management training: An intimidating concept, a rewarding experience. *Canadian Journal of Anesthesia, 43*, 430−434.

Lauber, J. K. (1993). Foreword. In E. L. Wiener, B. G. Kanki, & R. L. Helmreich (Eds.), *Cockpit resource management* (pp. xv−xviii). San Diego, CA: Academic Press.

Lauber, J. K. (1979). Resource management on the flight deck: Background and statement of the problem. In G. E. Cooper, M. D. White, & J. K. Lauber (Eds.), *Resource management on the flight deck: Proceedings of a NASA/Industry Workshop, San Francisco, June 1979. (NASA Conference Publication 2120)*. Moffet Field, CA: NASA Ames Research Center.

Lauber, J. K. (1987). Cockpit resource management: Background and overview. In H. W. Orlady, & H. C. Foushee (Eds.), *Cockpit resource management training: Proceedings of the NASA/MAC Workshop. (NASA Conference Publication CP-2455)* (pp. 5−14). Moffet Field, CA: NASA Ames Research Center.

Lowe, A. R., Hayward, B. J., & Dalton, A. L. (2007). *Guidelines for rail resource management. Report prepared by Dédale Asia Pacific for Public Transport Safety Victoria and Independent Transport Safety and Reliability Regulator, NSW*. Melbourne/Sydney: PTSV/ ITSRR.

Marine Accident Investigation Branch. (1994). *Report of the Chief Inspector of Marine Accidents into the engine failure and subsequent grounding of the Motor Tanker Braer*. Southampton: MAIB.

Marine Accident Investigation Branch. (1996). *Report of the Investigation into the Power Failure on Canberra*. Southampton: MAIB.

Marine Accident Investigation Branch. (1999). *Marine Accident Report 5/99. Report of the Inspector's Inquiry into the loss of MV Green Lily*. Southampton: MAIB.

McDonald, A., Garrigan, B., & Kanse, L. (2006). Confidential Observations of Rail Safety: An adaptation of Line Operations Safety Audit (LOSA). *Paper presented at the Multimodal Symposium on Safety Management and Human Factors*, Swinburne University, Australia, February 2006.

McDonnell, L., Jobe, K., & Dismukes, R. (1997). *Facilitating LOS debriefings: A training manual (NASA Technical Memorandum 112192)*. Moffett Field, CA: NASA Ames Research Center.

McInerney, P. A. (2005a). *Special Commission of Inquiry into the Waterfall Rail Accident. Final Report, Vol. 1*. Sydney: NSW Government.

McInerney, P. A. (2005b). *Special Commission of Inquiry into the Waterfall Rail Accident. Final Report, Vol. 2*. Sydney: NSW Government.

Mearns, K., Flin, R., Fleming, M., & Gordon, R. (1997). Human and Organisational Factors in Offshore Safety.*(OTH 543)*. Suffolk, UK: HSE Books.

Merritt, A. C. (1996). *National culture and work attitudes in commercial aviation: A cross-cultural investigation*. The University of Texas at Austin, Unpublished doctoral dissertation.

Mills, A. (2003). The growth of human factors as a discipline in the UK rail industry. *Paper presented at the Fifth Australian Aviation Psychology Symposium, Sydney, Australia, 1-5 December 2003*.

Morey, J. C., Simon, R., Jay, G. D., Wears, R. L., Salisbury, M., Dukes, K. A., & Berns, S. D. (2002). Error reduction and performance improvement in the emergency department through formal team work training: Evaluation results of the MedTeams project. *Health Services Research, 37*, 1553−1581.

Morgan, C., Olson, L. E., Kyte, T. B., Roop, S., & Carlisle, T. D. (2006). Railroad Crew Resource Management (CRM): Survey of Teams in the Railroad Operating Environment and Identification of Available CRM Training Methods. *Report produced by Texas Transportation Institute for the U.S. Department of Transportation, Federal Railroad Administration*.

Morgan, C. A. (2005). Texas Transportation Institute CRM pilot project. *Personal Communication*. December 2005.

Morgan, C. A., Kyte, T. B., Olson, L. E., & Roop, S. S. (2003). *Assessment of Existing Teams and Crew Resource Management (CRM) Training within the Rail Industry*. Texas Transportation Institute. November 15, 2003. Presented at Transportation Research Board 2004 Annual Meeting.

National Transportation Safety Board. (1979). *Aircraft Accident Report. United Airlines, Inc., DC-8-61, N8082U, Portland, Oregon, December 28, 1978. (Report No NTSB AAR-79-7)*. Washington, DC: Author.

National Transportation Safety Board. (1993). *The grounding of the UK Passenger vessel RMS Queen Elizabeth 2 near Cuttyhunk Island, Vineyard Sound Massachusetts, August 7th 1992. NTSB Report Number: MAR-93-01*. Washington, DC: Author.

National Transportation Safety Board (1999a). *Railroad Accident Report. Collision between Union Pacific Freight Trains MKSNP-01 and ZSEME-29 near Delia, Kansas. July 2, 1997. (Report No NTSB/RAR-99/04)*. Washington, DC: Author.

National Transportation Safety Board (1999b). *Railroad Accident Report. Collision of Norfolk Southern Corporation Train 255L5 with Consolidated Rail Corporation Train TV 220 in*

Butler, Indiana, on March 25, 1998. (Report No. NTSB/RAR-99/02). Washington, DC: Author.

O'Connor, P., & Flin, R. (2003). Crew resource management training for offshore oil production teams. *Safety Science, 41*, 111–129.

O'Connor, P., & Long, W. M. (2011). The development of a prototype behavioral marker system for US Navy officers of the deck. *Safety Science, 49*(10), 1381–1387.

Office of Transport Safety Investigation (2004). *Rail Safety Investigation Report. Unanderra. Signal passed at danger resulting in derailment of Pacific National Service B9162, 20 June 2003.* Reference number 00041. Sydney: Author.

Olsen, L. E. (2005). CRM training in rail. *Personal communication*, December 2005.

Patankar, M. J., & Taylor, J. C. (2004). *Risk management and error reduction in aviation maintenance.* Aldershot, UK: Ashgate.

Patankar, M. J., & Taylor, J. C. (2008). MRM training, evaluation, and safety management. *International Journal of Aviation Psychology, 18*(1), 61–71.

Pena, G., Altree, M., Field, J., Thomas, M., Hewett, P., Babidge, W., & Maddern, G. (2015). Surgeons' and trainees' perceived self-efficacy in operating theatre non-technical skills. *British Journal of Surgery, 102*(6), 708–715.

Pizzi, L., Goldfarb, N., & Nash, D. (2001). Crew Resource Management and its Applications in Medicine. In Making Health Care Safer: A Critical Analysis of Patient Safety Practices. Evidence Report/Technology Assessment, No. 43. Chapter 44CA: University of California at San Francisco, Stanford University Evidence-based Practice Center.

Queensland Rail. (2011). *Rail Resource Management Evaluation Report.* Brisbane: Author.

Rail Safety and Standards Board. (2004). *Teamworking in the railway industry. The Journey Guide, V1.1.* London: Author.

Rail Safety and Standards Board. (2009). *Rail resource management training: A guide for the UK rail industry.* RSSB Briefing Document, May 2009. London: Author.

Rail Safety and Standards Board. (2012). *Non-technical skills required in train driver role: Developing an integrated approach to NTS training and investment.* London: Author.

Rail Safety and Standards Board. (2016). *A Summary Guide to Integrating Non-Technical Skills into Rail Safety Critical Roles.* London: Author.

Reason, J. (1990). *Human error.* Cambridge: Cambridge University Press.

Reason, J. (1997). *Managing the risk of organisational accidents.* Aldershot, UK: Ashgate.

Reason, J. (2008). *The human contribution: Unsafe acts, accidents and heroic recoveries.* Aldershot, UK: Ashgate.

Reason, J., & Hobbs, A. (2003). *Managing maintenance error. A practical guide.* Aldershot, UK: Ashgate.

Risser, D. T., Rice, M. M., Salisbury, M. L., Simon, R., Jay, G. D., & Berns, S. D. (1999). The potential for improved teamwork to reduce medical errors in the emergency department. The MedTeams Research Consortium. *Annals of Emergency Medicine, 34*, 373–383.

Rogers, D. G. (2002). *NASA's Space Flight Resource Management Program: A Successful Human Performance Error Management Program.* Paper presented at Space Ops Conference, 2002.

Rogers, D. G. (2010). Crew resource management: Spaceflight resource management. In B. G. Kanki, R. L. Helmreich, & J. Anca (Eds.), *Crew resource management* (2nd ed.). San Diego: Academic Press.

Roop, S. S., Morgan, C. A., Kyte, T. B., Arthur, Jr., W., Villado, A. J., & Beneigh, T. (2007). Rail crew resource management (CRM): The business case for CRM training in the railroad industry. *Report produced by Texas Transportation Institute for the U.S. Department of Transportation, Federal Railroad Administration.*

Sexton, J. B., Thomas, E. J., & Helmreich, R. L. (2000). Error, stress, and teamwork in medicine and aviation: Cross sectional surveys. *British Medical Journal, 320*, 745−749.

Shapiro, M. J., Morey, J. C., Small, S. D., Langford, V., Kaylor, C. J., Jagminas, L., ... Jay, G. D. (2004). Simulation based teamwork training for emergency department staff: Does it improve clinical team performance when added to an existing didactic teamwork curriculum? *Quality & safety in health care, 13*(6), 417−421.

Simpson, P., Owens, C., & Edkins, G. (2004). Cabin crew expected safety behaviours. *Human Factors and Aerospace Safety, 4*(3), 153−167.

Small, S. (1998). What participants learn from Anesthesia crisis resource management training. *Anesthesiology, 89*(3A), A71.

Stelly, J., & Taylor, J. (1992). Crew coordination concepts for maintenance teams. Continental Airlines, Inc., paper and presentation, August 1992.

Taylor, J. C. (2000a). *Evaluating the effects of maintenance resource management in (MRM) in air safety. Report of Research Conducted under NASA-Ames Cooperative Agreement No. NCC2-1025 (SCU Project # NAR003).* Washington, DC: FAA.

Taylor, J. C. (2000b). The evolution and effectiveness of Maintenance Resource Management (MRM). *International Journal of Industrial Ergonomics, 26*, 201−215.

Thomas, M. J. W. (2017). *Training and assessing Non-Technical Skills: A practical guide.* Boca Raton, FL: CRC Press.

Transport NSW. (2002). *Bargo-Yerrinbool Derailment and Collision, 1 August 2002. Final report.* Sydney: Author.

Transportation Safety Board. (1998). *Railway Investigation Report. Rear-end Train Collision, 11 August, 1998. (Report number R98V0148).* Quebec, Canada: Author.

UK P&I Club. (1997). *Analysis of major claims − ten-year trends in maritime risk.* London: Thomas Miller P&I Ltd.

United States Coastguard. (1995). *Prevention Through People, Quality Action Team Report.* Washington, DC: USCG.

University of Aberdeen and Scottish Clinical Simulation Centre. (2004). Anaesthetists' Non-Technical Skills Handbook, V1.0. Aberdeen: Authors.

Vandermark, M. J. (1991). Should flight attendants be included in CRM training? A discussion of a major air carrier's approach to total crew training. *International Journal of Aviation Psychology, 1*(1), 87−94.

Wahren, E. (2007). Development of BRM training at SAS Flight Academy. *Personal communication,* June 2007.

Wang, A. M., Yuan, R., Li, H., Xie, W., Bakker, J. S., & Pinkster, J. (2014). *Virtual simulation program and its application for challenging floatover installation of Liwan 3-1 Mega topsides in South China Sea. The Twenty-fourth International Ocean and Polar Engineering Conference.* International Society of Offshore and Polar Engineers.

Yule, S., Flin, R., Maran, N., Rowley, D., Youngson, G., & Paterson-Brown, S. (2008). Surgeons' non-technical skills in the operating room: Reliability testing of the NOTSS behavior rating system. *World Journal of Surgery, 32*(4), 548−556.

FURTHER READING

Flin, R., O'Connor, P., & Mearns, K. (2002). Crew resource management: Improving safety in high reliability industries. *Team Performance Management, 8*, 68−78.

Part III

CRM Perspectives

Chapter 16

A Regulatory Perspective*

Kathy H. Abbott
United States Federal Aviation Administration, Washington, DC, United States

INTRODUCTION

This chapter presents crew resource management (CRM), primarily from the perspective of the United States (US) regulatory system, administered by the Federal Aviation Administration (FAA). The chapter begins with a brief primer of the underlying philosophy of US aviation regulation as a form of risk management. It then describes the history and philosophical basis of some of the key aviation regulations in the US system.

The chapter will then focus on specific aspects of CRM: crew coordination and communication, threat and error management, and flight crew monitoring. The chapter will then discuss how these aspects of CRM fit into the regulatory structure for equipment design, flight crew training, and flight crew procedures. The chapter will present a discussion of future examples where implementation of CRM is important and will conclude with a description of where regulatory material for resource management is applied to other areas besides flight crews.

16.1 AVIATION REGULATION—A BRIEF PRIMER[1]

One way to look at regulation is to consider it as a form of risk management, and to consider where a society places certain activities on a notional continuum of risk. Fig. 16.1 shows such a continuum, which describes private risk at one end and public risk at the other. It depicts different activities and

---

* The views represented in this chapter are those of the author and do not represent an official position of the Federal Aviation Administration.

1. The material in this section is based on the regulatory primer perspective from the RTCA Task Force on Certification (RTCA, 1999). In particular, the contributions of several members of RTCA Task Force 4 on Certification were instrumental in developing the material for the regulatory primer, including John Ackland, Tony Broderick, and Tom Imrich.

Crew Resource Management. DOI: https://doi.org/10.1016/B978-0-12-812995-1.00016-6
2019 Published by Elsevier Inc.

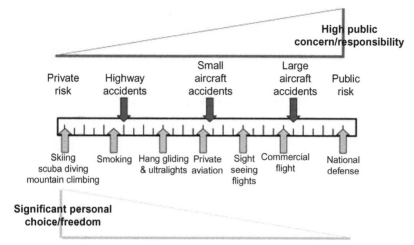

FIGURE 16.1 "Personal" versus "public" risk assumption.

where they may be placed by a society. In the continuum shown in the figure, the left end of the continuum represents private risk, with activities such as scuba diving, mountain climbing, and skiing as examples of items that a society might place on this end. These activities at this end correspond to significant personal choice and freedom, with low public concern and responsibility.

Activities considered to be of high public concern and responsibility are represented on the right end of the continuum, and examples include commercial flights and national defense. In the United States (and many other societies), large aircraft accidents are placed to the right end of the continuum, because they are considered to be of high public concern and responsibility. Highway accidents and small airplane accidents are further to the left on the scale, since this is the choice of the society.

Another society may choose to place these activities and safety-related events at different points on the continuum. For example, another society may choose to place private aviation at the same "risk" point (and therefore the same level of public concern) as commercial aviation.

Society also determines the role of the government in managing or mitigating risk. Consider the continuum shown in Fig. 16.2, which illustrates where the potential government role may be. The leftmost end is intended to represent activities or concerns that are primarily personal and commercial. At this end, the society chooses to limit the government's role—possibly in a role to simply enable the activity. At the rightmost end, one can find activities or concerns that are inherently governmental, such as national defense. At this end, the government actually conducts or controls the activity.

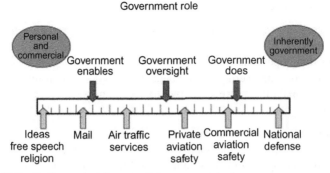

FIGURE 16.2   Continuum depicting potential governmental role.

The location of any particular activity on the continuum is driven by the will of the society for which the government works. In the United States, for example, private aviation is considered to be less of a public concern, and therefore less of a public responsibility by the government. Commercial aviation is much more a public concern, and is expected to have the highest level of safety. Therefore, legislation requires that government oversight and standards are more stringent for commercial aviation than for private aviation.

US aviation regulations were initiated through the Air Commerce Act of 1926, which assigned responsibility and regulatory authority for aviation to the Aeronautics Branch of the Department of Commerce. This branch had the following objectives:

1. establish airworthiness standards and associated system of aircraft registration;
2. administer examination and licensing procedures for aviation personnel and facilities;
3. establish uniform rules for air navigation;
4. establish new airports; and
5. encourage the development of civil aviation.

Basically, the fundamental governmental responsibilities are to assure:

1. that aircraft don't fall on the public (assure the airworthiness of the aircraft);
2. the "highest level of safety" for public transportation;
3. at least a basic level of safety for other "certificated aircraft" passengers; and
4. that aircraft can satisfy safety-related interaircraft responsibilities for mutual separation (e.g., the requirement for altitude-encoding transponders in certain airspace).

The means used to accomplish these responsibilities are:

1. certifying air vehicles and supporting ground elements—if and as necessary;
2. establishing operating rules—"rules of the road"; and
3. providing or empowering certain capabilities (e.g., certain services, facilities, or capabilities agreed to by the aviation system users, or by the public).

In part, these functions are accomplished via some type of "certification." Here, certification means the approval and authorization for aircraft; personnel (e.g., pilots); operations; procedures; facilities; and equipment.

The legal origin for the FAA's regulatory activities is founded in the US Constitution and is generally considered to have begun with the Air Commerce Act, enacted in 1926. This act commissioned by the Secretary of the Department of Commerce is responsible for fostering air commerce, issuing and enforcing air traffic rules, certifying pilots and aircraft, and operating and maintaining air navigation aids (NAVAID). Birnbach and Longridge (1993) provided both a historical perspective on the FAA and a more detailed history of the evolution of the legal structure.

The current regulations that the FAA administers are contained in the US Code, specifically Title 14—Code of Federal Regulations (CFR), Aeronautics and Space Chapter I—FAA, Department of Transportation. Three subchapters of particular interest to this discussion are Subchapter C, Aircraft, Subchapter F, Air Traffic and General Operating Rules, and Subchapter G, Air Carriers and Operators for Compensation or Hire: Certification and Operations. Subchapter C includes the Airworthiness Standards for various categories of aircraft (including Part 25 for Transport Category Airplanes). Subchapter F contains the general operating and flight rules (Part 91) and Subchapter G contains Part 121 Operating Requirements: Domestic, Flag and Supplemental Operations, and Part 135—Operating Requirements: Commuter and On-Demand Operations and Rules Governing Persons on Board Such Aircraft.

Part 25 and several other parts in Subchapter C contain airworthiness standards for aircraft. These requirements are considered to be *point in time* regulations, because once compliance is found with one of these regulations (such as issuance of a Type Certificate for an airplane type design) it is not revisited unless the type design of the airplane changes (e.g., adding equipment or systems not part of the original type design). Therefore, any change in any of the regulations in Part 25 does not result in the change of existing certificated aircraft type designs.

In contrast, the operating rules (Parts 91, 121, 135, etc.) are *continuous applicability* rules, and therefore, when a regulation is changed, the operators certificated under that operating rule must comply according to the date the rule is effective. Crew training requirements fall under the operating regulations, allowing changes to be made continuously as our understanding of good practices in such training improves.

The discussion above describes the underlying philosophy of the regulations, which represents requirements. But regulatory material can have one or more motivations, as discussed below:

- Minimum standards. The regulations might describe the minimum standards for a required characteristic, such as the performance of a system on an aircraft.
- Protection, such as 14 CFR Part 193. This part describes when and how the FAA protects from disclosure safety and security information that is submitted voluntarily to the FAA.
- Incentives for equipage by giving operational credit. For example, aircraft with autoland capability (and corresponding pilot qualification) have the potential to fly to lower visibilities than aircraft without such capability.

The FAA publishes several other types of documents, in addition to regulations. One such type of document is an advisory circular (AC), which provides guidance from the FAA to the external community. An AC may contain guidance on means of compliance with particular regulations, or may provide other information of interest to the aviation community (e.g., one AC lists all the published ACs).

ACs are numbered using a system that corresponds to the regulations for which it provides information. For example, AC 25.1329 Approval of Flight Guidance Systems (FAA, 2006b) provides a means of compliance with 14 CFR 25.1329 (FAA, 2006a). Another example of an AC is AC 120-76D for Authorization for Use of Electronic Flight Bags (FAA, 2017b). This includes approval guidance for approving a technology or type of system, rather than a specific regulation.

The material below discusses both regulations and ACs related to CRM, in airworthiness of equipment design, flight crew training, and operational approval requirements and guidance.

16.2 REGULATORY REQUIREMENTS AND GUIDANCE FOR CREW RESOURCE MANAGEMENT—FLIGHT DECK

The following important aspects of CRM (among others) are addressed in the regulatory material and will be described in the following sections:

1. Crew coordination and communication;
2. Risk, Threat, and Error management; and
3. Flight crew monitoring.

For each of these aspects, this chapter will describe how it is addressed in regulatory material for equipment design, flight crew training, and flight crew procedures.

16.2.1 Airworthiness Requirements for Equipment Design— Examples

Two regulations will be discussed below to illustrate how considerations for CRM are incorporated into the airworthiness requirements for equipment design:

1. 14 CFR Part 25 Section 25.1329 Flight Guidance Systems

    This regulation describes the airworthiness requirements for Flight Guidance Systems (FGS), including autopilots, autothrust systems, flight directors, and associated flight crew interfaces (FAA, 2006a). Operational experience showed that flight crew errors and confusion were occurring when operating the FGS and its subsystems (FAA, 1996), including vulnerabilities that can be mitigated in the equipment design. Therefore, the airworthiness requirements were updated to address these issues, and to address changes in technology and capabilities of FGS.

    As one example of how the equipment design requirements were updated to support crew coordination, paragraph (j) requires that the alert for autopilot disengagement must be done in a way to assure that the information is available to each pilot:

    (j) Following disengagement of the autopilot, a warning (visual and auditory) must be provided to each pilot and be timely and distinct from all other cockpit warnings.

    FAA (2006a).

    The AC for this regulation makes it clear that the intent is that the alert associated with disengagement of the autopilot(s) must be implemented in a way to support flight crew coordination:

    It should sound long enough to ensure that it is heard and recognized by the pilot and other flight crewmembers, but not so long that it adversely affects communication between crewmembers or is a distraction.

    FAA (2006b), p. 25.

    Paragraph (i) explicitly addresses the need to support error management through preventing errors, and through the equipment design providing feedback on current modes of operation:

    (i) The flight guidance system functions, controls, indications, and alerts must be designed to minimize flightcrew errors and confusion concerning the behavior and operation of the flight guidance system.

    FAA (2006a).

    Paragraph (i) also says: "Means must be provided to indicate the current mode of operation, including any armed modes, transitions, and reversions. Selector switch position is not an acceptable means of indication. The controls and indications must be grouped and presented in a logical and consistent manner. The indications must be visible to each pilot under all expected lighting conditions" (FAA, 2006a). This portion of the regulation supports the requirement for equipment design to support crew monitoring of the status of the FGS.

2. European Aviation Safety Agency (EASA) Certification Specification 25.1302 Installed Systems for use by the Flight Crew (EASA, 2007a) and FAA 14 Code of Federal Regulations 25.1302 Installed Systems and Equipment for Use by the Flight crew (FAA, 2013)[2]

Another airworthiness regulation was developed jointly by the FAA, the Joint Aviation Authorities (JAA), the EASA, North and South American industry, and European industry to address the need for the equipment design to support error management by the pilots. This regulation was written to require the equipment design to have characteristics that are known to avoid error. Specifically, the equipment must provide the information and controls necessary for the pilots to do the tasks associated with the intended function of the equipment, and the controls and information must be in a usable form.

In addition, the regulation was written based on the understanding that even well-qualified pilots using well-designed systems will make errors. Therefore, the equipment design must support detection and recovery aspects of error management. The first sentence of paragraph (d) explicitly addresses this:

(d) To the extent practicable, installed equipment must enable the flight crew to manage errors resulting from the kinds of flight crew interactions with the equipment that can be reasonably expected in service, assuming the flight crew is acting in good faith.

EASA (2007a)[3]

With respect to crew monitoring, CS 25.1302 requires that the equipment design provide the information needed to perform the tasks associated with the intended function of the equipment—and this includes monitoring of the equipment—and that the equipment provide information about its operationally relevant behavior. The FAA plans to harmonize with the requirements in CS 25.1302, which will result in the United States and Europe having consistent requirements for this aspect of equipment design.

---

2. The FAA and EASA versions of 25.1302 are harmonized. Although the wording of the regulations may not be identical, the meaning is intended to be the same.

3. As with all regulations, the regulatory material should be read and considered in its entirety, together with other applicable regulations.

The airworthiness regulations described above are "point in time" regulations, as discussed earlier. Therefore, any new airplane type must meet the requirements, but existing airplanes do not, unless the airplane type is changed significantly.

Since there are many aircraft that received their aircraft certification approval before these regulations were implemented, such aircraft do not necessarily meet the requirements for the equipment design to support crew coordination, error management, and crew monitoring. Thus, the mitigations required in the flight crew training and procedures are especially important for such aircraft.

16.2.2 Flight Crew Training and Qualification Requirements

The US regulations include a requirement for training of CRM principles and topics for pilots and dispatchers. These requirements for CRM are codified into 14 CFR Part 121 Section 121.404, Compliance dates: Crew and dispatcher resource management training, which states:

> After March 19, 1998, no certificate holder may use a person as a flight crew-member, and after March 19, 1999, no certificate holder may use a person as a flight attendant or aircraft dispatcher unless that person has completed approved crew resource management (CRM) or dispatcher resource management (DRM) initial training, as applicable, with that certificate holder or with another certificate holder.

FAA (1996).

The Part 121 regulation itself does not specify the content of the training, but AC 120-51E (FAA, 2003b) provides guidance for the content of US operator training programs to address CRM. Subjects such as crew coordination and communication, error management, and flight crew monitoring are specifically described in the AC. This AC also discusses the importance of pre- and posttraining session briefings, and ways to evaluate the pilots' performance as a result of the training, among other topics. As an example of related guidance outside the United States, CAA UK (2006) provides guidance for the content of CRM training.

The requirement extends beyond air carriers operating under Part 121. Effective March 22, 2013, no certificate holder conducting operations under Part 135 may use a person as a flight crewmember or flight attendant unless that person has completed approved CRM initial training with that certificate holder (FAA, 2011). Unlike Part 121, the requirement under Part 135 does specify a minimum set of topics that must be addressed in the training:

1. Authority of the pilot in command;
2. Communication processes, decisions, and coordination, to include communication with Air Traffic Control, personnel performing flight locating and other operational functions, and passengers;

3. Building and maintenance of a flight team;
4. Workload and time management;
5. Situational awareness;
6. Effects of fatigue on performance, avoidance strategies, and countermeasures;
7. Effects of stress and stress reduction strategies; and
8. Aeronautical decision-making and judgment training tailored to the operator's flight operations and aviation environment.

As with all the operating regulations, the requirement for CRM training for flight crews is a continuous applicability requirement. Thus, improvements to the guidance can be made and applied as more is learned about effective implementation of training for CRM.

16.2.3 Flight Crew Procedures

The FAA recognizes that flight crews should use procedures that embody the coordination and communication intended by CRM. The design of procedures should embody that coordination. Degani and Wiener (1994) describe that there are several aspects to the design of the procedures that can promote crew coordination:

1. *Reduced variance*. The procedure triggers a predetermined and expected set of actions.
2. *Feedback*. Procedures specify expected feedback to other crew members (e.g., callouts). This feedback can detail (1) the current, and/or expected system state; (2) the actions that are currently being conducted; (3) the system outcome; and (4) an indication of task completion. There are several ways in which this feedback is provided: (1) verbally (callouts, callback, etc.); (2) nonverbally (gestures, manual operation—such as pulling down the gear lever); (3) via the interface (when the configuration of the system is significantly changed, for example, all displays are momentarily blank when power is switched from APU to engine-driven generators, this provides clear feedback to the other pilot); and (4) via the operating environment (when slats/flaps are extended during approach, there is a clear aerodynamic feedback—pitch change).
3. *Information transfer*. Procedures convey, or transfer, information from one agent to others (e.g., *the after takeoff checklist is complete*).

Another area that is important to consider for crew coordination is the delineation of duties among the pilot flying (PF), the pilot not flying (PNF)/pilot monitoring (PM), and the flight engineer (if present). This includes the identification of who does which tasks, which pilot calls for particular procedures, which pilot reads them, and which one responds.

The FAA has published an AC that provides guidance for implementation of Standard Operating Procedures (SOPs) that address how to design procedures to address these concerns (FAA, 2017a). This AC points out that effective crew coordination and communication depend on the crews having a shared mental model of each task, and that mental model is founded on SOPs.

This AC specifically highlights the need for pilots to perform monitoring tasks, based on recognition of the role that inadequate monitoring played in previous accidents. For example, the National Transportation Safety Board has identified that inadequate crew monitoring or challenging was involved in 84% of crew-involved accidents (NTSB, 1994; Sumwalt, 2004).

The AC also discusses the role and tasks of the pilot monitoring (PM), and emphasizes the importance of the monitoring task. This emphasis must be part of the philosophy that forms the foundation of the SOPs.

An example that illustrates the performance improvement that can result from modifications to procedures to support crew coordination is the Altitude Awareness Programs implemented by several airlines (Sumwalt, 1995). In this example, airlines were experiencing altitude deviations, or altitude "busts"—cases where the pilots were not leveling off at the cleared altitude or were going to different altitudes than the one to which they were cleared. The formal Altitude Awareness Program implemented at these airlines was based on recognition that it is essential that a crew cross-check each other, and challenge each other when there is a doubt about the air traffic clearance. Key elements of the procedures for changing the altitude in the flight deck include setting the altitude alerter and making callouts.

This program provides an example where delineating pilot duties is very important. The successful program at US Air, with a reduction in altitude busts of approximately 75% as compared to preprogram figures (Sumwalt, 1995), illustrates that significant improvement in performance can result from appropriate crew coordination and explicit delineation of duties, with crew monitoring as a key task among those duties.[4]

16.3 FUTURE CONSIDERATIONS

Aviation has always been about change. As civil aviation moves to improved future airspace operations, successful implementation of new technology and new operational concepts will need to include the basic aspects of CRM discussed above—coordination and communication (among all the participants); error management; and monitoring. The discussion below will highlight two areas where these aspects must be implemented for safe, effective, and

---

4. See Sumwalt (1995) for detailed discussion of the characteristics of the procedures and for lessons learned from operational experience.

efficient operations. These two areas are: Electronic Flight Bags (EFBs) and the integration of the flight deck operations as part of new airspace operations.

Although laptop computers have been in use for many years in the flight deck, as computer technology gets smaller, more powerful, and more affordable, their use in the flight deck is expanding—as are the variety of applications for which they are being used. These devices can range from installed systems to portable, handheld systems. The different devices are described in AC 120-76D (FAA, 2017b) and EASA Acceptable Means of Compliance (AMC) 20-25 Airworthiness and Operational Considerations for Electronic Flight Bags (EASA, 2014). These devices are being used for an increasing variety of applications, including such tasks as performance calculations, moving map displays for surface operations, and many others.

Several sources have identified human factors issues (including CRM, among many others) related to EFBs and their use (see Allen, 2003 and Chandra et al., 2003 for detailed discussions). Accordingly, the approval guidance from the FAA and EASA identify assessment of CRM as part of the training and system evaluation (FAA, 2017b; EASA, 2014). This may be especially important because use of EFBs can change the flight crew's way of interacting and communicating, especially if the EFB is located such that cross-flight deck viewing is difficult. If the pilots cannot see each other's EFBs, then explicit coordination and communication must be done to mitigate the lack of visibility into each other's actions. In addition, crew procedures must be carefully defined to include error management (including, specifically, cross verification of data entry and computed information).

The use of EFBs in the flight deck is still evolving, and it will be important to continue to address the role of CRM in this use—and in the integration of EFBs with use of paper. According to Nomura et al. (2006):

> The complex, high-stakes, high-tempo nature of the pilots' work requires careful planning of information access and the management of attention. The fact that shared understandings are essential to safe flight means that whatever the representations are, they must not only be available to both pilots, but available to the pilots jointly in interaction with one another. While engaging in a briefing preceding a high-workload maneuver such as a takeoff, pilots want to locate themselves bodily in an environment that is rich in tangible representations of the parameters relevant to upcoming events. Currently they do this by reading across many disparate documents and displays. A better understanding of how this is done could contribute to the next generation of display design.

According to this work, paper is an integral feature of using new technologies and plays important social interaction roles in crew coordination, message confirmation, note-taking, and information affordance.

This is just one example that illustrates that the introduction of new technologies into the flight deck must consider crew coordination and communication, and the support of pilot tasks and interactions. Training and flight crew procedure design often do consider these aspects of CRM, but the equipment design must support these tasks as well.

The second example expands consideration of the CRM concepts to the interaction between the flight crew and the air traffic personnel, as a key part of integration of aircraft operations in the airspace. Communication and coordination between pilots and air traffic services personnel has been done successfully in operations for many years. However, new airspace operations are expected to make significant changes in operations, with corresponding benefit.

One change that is under way right now is the move towards a performance-based navigation system in both the United States and around the world. Performance-based navigation incorporates the use of Area Navigation (RNAV) equipment that is not reliant on the location of ground-based navigation aids. In addition to the point-to-point capabilities offered by RNAV, new procedures are also being implemented that incorporate Required Navigation Performance (RNP) (Barhydt and Adams, 2006).

RNAV and RNP procedures offer significant benefits to both operators and air traffic managers. These benefits include better access to terrain-limited airports, more environmentally friendly flight paths, and significant gains in airspace efficiency. Performance-based operations are being implemented in both the terminal area and en route environments. The implementation of these procedures has already produced tangible benefits at a number of different airports.

One of the benefits of new RNAV procedures in the terminal area is reduced air/ground communications (Barhydt and Adams, 2006). But the reduction in communications raises potential concerns about the quality of the communication and coordination between air and ground, and the management of errors—preventing, detecting, and correcting them. Therefore, the CRM concepts should be applied within the flight deck, between air traffic personnel, and between the pilots and air traffic services. As new regulatory and policy material is developed to enable these new operations, such material should specifically include the CRM concepts.

16.4   CONCLUDING REMARKS

This chapter has presented a regulatory perspective on CRM, given primarily from a US point of view. It is not comprehensive, since CRM considerations can be found throughout the regulatory material related to flight deck airworthiness, flight crew training, and flight crew procedures—among other application areas. Nor are the examples for future operations a comprehensive set. Rather, they are just intended to illustrate examples of future needs.

The FAA and other regulatory authorities around the world recognize the importance of CRM as a necessary and significant contributor to aviation safety. Although most of this chapter has focused on the pilots, the regulatory system is recognizing the importance of resource management for other personnel in the aviation system, including dispatchers (as evidenced by the requirement for dispatcher resource management training), stated above, and guidance for training of maintenance personnel.

This propagation of resource management considerations throughout the regulatory material reflects the growing understanding of the importance of this area—but it needs to be even more widespread. Application of CRM concepts to air traffic personnel, to the communication and coordination between pilots and ATS, among pilots, maintenance, dispatchers, cabin crew, and others remain important and can be improved even further.

REFERENCES

Allen, D. (2003). Electronic flight bag. *Boeing Aero, 23,* 16–27, July.

Barhydt, R., & Adams, C. (2006). Human factors considerations for performance-based navigation. *National Aeronautics and Space Administration Technical Memorandum,* 2006-214531.

Birnbach, R. A., & Longridge, T. M. (1993). The regulatory perspective. In E. L. Wiener, B. G. Kanki, & R. L. Helmreich (Eds.), *Cockpit resource management.* (pp. 263–281). New York: Academic Press.

Chandra, D.C., Yeh, M., Riley, V., & Mangold, S.J. (2003). Human factors considerations in the design and evaluation of Electronic Flight Bags (EFBs), Version 2. DOT-VNTSC-FAA-03-07. USDOT Volpe Center: Cambridge, MA.

Civil Aviation Authority United Kingdom. (2006). Crew Resource Management (CRM) Training: Guidance for Flight Crew, CRM Instructors (CRMIS) and CRM Instructor-Examiners (CRMIES). (CAP 737). UK Civil Aviation Authority, Gatwick Airport South: West Sussex, United Kingdom.

Degani, A., & Wiener, E. (1994). *On the design of flight-deck procedures. NASA Contractor Report.* Moffet Field, CA: National Aeronautics and Space Administration, June 1994.

European Aviation Safety Agency. (2007a). Certification Specifications for Large Aeroplanes CS-25 Amendment-3, Book 1, Airworthiness Code, Subpart F Equipment, General, CS-25.1302 Installed systems and equipment for use by the flight crew, September 19, 2007.

European Aviation Safety Agency. (2014). Amendment-, ED Decision 2014/001/R 09/02/2014 Annex II, Acceptable Means of Compliance, AMC 20-25, Airworthiness and operational consideration for Electronic Flight Bags (EFBs) January 29, 2014.

Federal Aviation Administration. (1996). *Human factors team report on: The interfaces between flightcrews and modern flight deck systems.* Washington, DC: Federal Aviation Administration, June 18, 1996.

Federal Aviation Administration. (2003b). *Crew resource management training (FAA Advisory Circular 120-51E).* Washington, DC: Department of Transportation, January 22, 2004.

Federal Aviation Administration. (2006a). *Title 14 United States Code of Federal Regulations Part 25, Section 25.1329 (Flight Guidance Systems).* Washington, DC: Department of Transportation, July 2006.

Federal Aviation Administration (2006b). Advisory Circular 25.1329-1B, Approval of Flight Guidance Systems, July 17, 2006.

Federal Aviation Administration. (2011). *Title 14 United States Code of Federal Regulations Part 135, Section 135.330 (Crew resource management training).* Washington, DC: Department of Transportation, January 21, 2011.

Federal Aviation Administration. (2013). *Title 14 United States Code of Federal Regulations Part 25, Section 25.1302 (Installed systems and equipment for use by the flightcrew).* Washington, DC: Department of Transportation, May 3, 2013.

Federal Aviation Administration. (2017a). *Standard Operating Procedures and Pilot Monitoring Duties for Flight Deck Crewmembers (FAA Advisory Circular AC 120-71B).* Washington, DC: Department of Transportation, January 10, 2017.

Federal Aviation Administration. (2017b). *Authorization for Use of Electronic Flight Bags (FAA Advisory Circular 120-76D).* Washington, DC: Department of Transportation, October 27, 2017.

National Transportation Safety Board. (1994). Safety Study: A Review of Flightcrew-Involved, Major Accidents of U.S. Air Carriers, 1978 through 1990. Report no. NTSB/SS-94/01. Washington, DC, United States: NTSB, 1994.

Nomura, S., Hutchins, E., & Holder, B. (2006). The uses of paper in commercial airline flight operations. In Proceedings of Computer Supported Cooperative Work 2006, (CSCW 2006), pp. 249–258.

RTCA (1999). Final Report of Task Force 4, Certification. Washington, DC.

Sumwalt, R.L. (1995). Altitude Awareness Programs Can Reduce Altitude Deviations. In Flight Safety Foundation Flight Safety Digest, December 1995.

Sumwalt, R.L. (2004). Enhancing Flight Crew Monitoring Skills Can Increase Corporate Aviation Safety. 49th Corporate Aviation Safety Seminar. Flight Safety Foundation: Tucson, AZ. April 27–29 (2004).

Chapter 17

A Regulatory Perspective II*

Douglas R. Farrow
Federal Aviation Administration (retired), Washington, DC, United States

INTRODUCTION

This chapter takes the regulatory perspective from the view of the Air Carrier Training and Voluntary Safety Programs Branch at Federal Aviation Administration (FAA) Headquarters. As the policy office for air carrier training this office has been the primary sponsor of most of the crew resource management (CRM) Research and Development for air transport category aircraft that has been supported by the agency over the last 25 years. As such it has shaped, and its policies have been shaped by, the ever increasing body of scientific knowledge accumulated regarding the best methods for training and evaluating CRM behaviors. The three primary FAA guidance documents that have flowed from this research have been the CRM Advisory Circular 120-51, (FAA, 1989), the Line Operational Simulations (LOSs) Advisory Circular 120-35 (FAA, 1978), and the Advanced Qualification Program Advisory Circular 120-54 (FAA, 1991). The LOS Advisory Circular was updated in 2015, while the other two circulars are being updated as this chapter is being written. This chapter will cover the major themes and challenges of this 20-year research program. It will also address the major changes that have occurred since the last edition of this textbook in 2010.

17.1 HISTORICAL PERSPECTIVE

The history of the FAA's evolving understanding of and guidance for CRM may be traced through the evolution of the three Advisory Circulars itemized above, and the many revisions they have undergone. Tracing the historical arc of these guidance materials shows a steady progression from abstract concepts to concrete examples, from issues of attitude to issues of behavior,

---

* The views represented in this chapter are those of the author and do not represent an official position of the FAA.

Crew Resource Management. DOI: https://doi.org/10.1016/B978-0-12-812995-1.00017-8

from nonjeopardy assessment to pass-fail evaluation, from observable behaviors to learned competencies, and from managing people to managing errors to managing risk.

The initial FAA guidance on LOFT, both AC 120-35 and AC 120-35A, (FAA, 1978, 1981) preceded the initial FAA guidance on CRM by several years. While this first guidance lacked detail, it indicated the desire of the FAA to recognize and endorse the approach, and encourage certificate holders to explore the concept in their training programs. On the one hand, the original primary aim of LOFT was not so much the development of CRM skills, as those skills were understood at the time, but the rehearsal of operational procedures in an operational setting (Butler, 1993). On the other hand, one of the goals of LOFT was to expose flight crews to an error chain in a nonjeopardy environment to see how they would manage it, which is entirely consistent with contemporary understandings of CRM.

LOFT subsequently expanded into LOS, which later became the primary vehicle for training and evaluating CRM skills at all large US air carriers. The publication of AC 120-35B (FAA, 1990) expanded the concept of LOFT to LOS, to include LOFT, special purpose operations training (SPOT), and eventually line operational evaluation (LOE). The treatment of SPOT and LOE was, again, relatively conceptual, with a single page dedicated to each. But the goal of the FAA was, again, to recognize and endorse newly emerging training concepts and to encourage the operators to work them into practical procedures. The current version, AC 120-35D (FAA, 2015), incorporates considerable detail based on recommendations from the Airline Transport Association (ATA) ((now Airlines for America (A4A)) Advanced Qualification Program (AQP) working group (ATA, 1995), which has come to be known as the event set methodology for scenario development. This approach was subsequently adopted by the FAA as a recommended procedure for all LOS development, both for training and for evaluation. Thus, the FAA again followed the pattern of introducing general concepts, encouraging the operators to explore those concepts and make them operational, and then folding that operational guidance back into its own guidance documents.

The various revisions to the CRM advisory circular followed a similar pattern. The FAA was quick to adopt concepts in large part from the research community, but conservative in providing procedures or mandates until industry experience could be coalesced into a concrete method or process. Initial CRM training, at first optional but recommended, would later be mandated for 14 CFR Part 121 crews (121.404), followed by a mandate for recurrent training (14 CFR, part 121.427). But these requirements were mandated only after close to a decade of FAA guidance that was purely advisory in nature

17.2   FROM ASSESSMENT TO EVALUATION

In the first edition of this volume, Birnbach and Longridge (1993) introduced the Advanced Qualification Program, a voluntary training program that today is the program of choice for 90% of airline pilots and 70% of flight attendants in the United States, and described its potential impacts of CRM training. They proposed that by measuring CRM at the task level, as opposed to measurement at a more global level, it might be feasible to measure CRM skills with levels of validity and reliability that would enable pass/fail grading of CRM skills with the same level of confidence that check airmen were currently expressing about making pass/fail decisions when grading technical skills. They proposed a 5-year trial period, during which CRM skills would be assessed on a nonjeopardy basis.

This approach involved some parsing of the exact wording of the AQP Special Federal Aviation Regulation (14 CRF 121, SFAR-58, (7)(b)), (FAA, 1990) which required not only teaching CRM, but "evaluation" (jeopardy) rather than "assessment" (nonjeopardy) of "cockpit resource management skills." Outside of AQP CRM was only recommended, but within AQP it was now mandated. Although the FAA hoped to move to jeopardy evaluation of CRM within AQP at some point in the future, neither the science nor the politics of the time—1991—could support such a move. But the agency did telegraph its intended direction in the initial AQP Advisory Circular, AC 120-54: "Collection and analysis of anonymous data (not identified with a named individual) will validate the CRM factors as well as overall crew performance. Until CRM performance factors can be validated, data should be collected without pass/fail considerations" (AC 120-54, Advanced Qualification Program, 1991, pp. 2−1). It went on to indicate that "Final written approval of a program which does not include pass/fail CRM criteria will include a statement that final [meaning Phase V] approval is contingent on eventual compliance with this condition" (AC 120-54, pp. 8−2). But by the time of the first Phase V application for the first AQP fleet, the United Airlines 737, the agency had soften its position ambitions goal and approved the program without addressing pass/fail evaluation. The 5-year goal proved much too ambitious.

The FAA's desire to advance the knowledge of CRM skills to the point where the industry would be willing to apply pass/fail grading of CRM within the context of a voluntary program drove the initiation of an extensive human factors research and development program, sponsored by the FAA AQP program office. This effort sponsored dozens of projects, a sample of which are addressed in this chapter. In the meantime, the FAA agreed that until new methodologies could be developed and tested, CRM would be treated as a contributing factor to a training failure rather than a primary cause. The rationale supporting this agreement was the assumption that if a pilot's CRM skills are poor enough to drive a failure, then they are bound to drive a technical failure at some point in the evaluation. The pilot will fail the evaluation based on that technical issue, with CRM listed as a contributing factor. In this way, data on poor CRM performance could still be collected and analyzed in an effort to better understand CRM skills and their interaction with technical skills, but without the jeopardy of a failed check.

17.3 MEASURING AND GRADING CRM

In cooperation with the FAA and the ATA AQP Working Group and its member airlines, the research community worked to develop a number of human factors tools to support the AQP community. Researchers from George Mason University supported the efforts to develop the event set methodology that the FAA would later recommend for all LOS development (ATA WG, 1995; Seamster, Edens, & Holt, 1995). In cooperation with the University of New Mexico, NASA, the University of Central Florida, and several other research institutions, researchers worked with both major and regional carriers to develop processes for interrater reliability (Holt, Boehm-Davis, & Hansberger, 2001), for referent rater reliability (Goldsmith & Johnson, 2002), for the establishment of gold standards in pilot evaluation (Baker & Dismukes, 2003), and for grade scales and benchmarks for their measurement (Holt, Hansberger, & Boehm-Davis, 2002; Williams, Holt, & Boehm-Davis, 1997).

By 2001, 10 years after the issuing of SFAR 58 and AC 120-54, the agency felt that it had developed CRM evaluation tools to the point that it could begin to require pass/fail grading of CRM skills. At the conclusion of a 3-year effort at a regional carrier, the George Mason University research team prepared a report of their findings for FAA internal consumption (GMU, 2001). It included several measures of both reliability and validity applied to both technical and CRM grading. The report concludes as follows:

> *The basic point that the table makes is that some values of the reliability of measures of CRM performance are as good as the reliability values for measuring technical performance. For example, the agreement on overall CRM for five event sets is .86 for the regional carrier, which is as good as the agreement index obtained for the overall technical performance for the same five event sets of .85. Similarly, the internal consistency estimate for CRM for 11 event sets (.75) is slightly higher than for the consistency of overall technical ratings on those event sets (.66). These data suggest that we can measure CRM performance with at least the same degree of consistency as we can measure technical performance.*

These data provided the FAA with confidence in the toolsets that were now in place for developing, training, conducting, and evaluating event-based scenarios in which CRM skills could be measured on a pass/fail basis: grade sheets, grade scales, the event set methodology, evaluator calibration tools, and best practices for teaching and testing CRM skills, either as isolated or integrated components of a training event.

Although this entire research program had been conducted at participating carriers with actual pilots, instructors, and evaluators, neither the labor unions nor airline management were convinced that the technology was mature enough to fail a pilot on an evaluation based on CRM alone. The agency decided to continue to delay a CRM evaluation mandate and allow the operators sufficient time to become comfortable with the toolsets they had helped to develop. This process took several years, but then it happened. The FAA AQP Program Office received a call from one of the lead AQP operators that they had just failed a captain for his CRM skills alone. He had passed his maneuvers validation with flying colors, but had failed his LOE for lack of leadership and teamwork. A precedent had been set, and slowly but surely other AQP air carriers followed suit. Over time all the airlines in the AQP community transitioned from assessing CRM to evaluating it on a pass/fail basis. The original goal of the AQP rule had at last been realized.

17.4   THE ROLE OF THE REGULATOR

This chapter addresses the role of the FAA in the history of the development of CRM as falling into three broad categories: the enforcement of minimal regulatory requirements, the encouragement of practices that exceed the regulatory minimums, and the funding of research programs, which in part allow the agency to draw the line between what will be strictly mandated and what will be strongly encouraged.

17.4.1   Regulatory Flexibility

The primary vehicle traditionally used by the FAA to maintain safety standards is the establishment, oversight, and enforcement of mandatory requirements, and the publication of those standards as rules, regulations, and policies. The guidance is developed by specialized policy offices at FAA Headquarters in Washington, DC. The FAA routinely coordinates these rules with industry representatives, often forming an aviation rule-making committee (ARC) consisting primarily of industry representatives who advise the agency on the contents of proposed rules. The agency, of course, has the final say. The FAA also considers ICAO regulations and aims for harmony with international guidelines. As a member of ICAO, the FAA must file differences with ICAO in those cases where FAA rules do not meet ICAO requirements. Once rules are issued, field FAA personnel are not permitted to authorize exemptions or deviations, as that is the purview of FAA Headquarters.

One feature that makes the Advanced Qualification Program different from traditional training programs is that it is overseen by an FAA Extended

Review Team (ERT) consisting of both field and headquarters personnel. This team is authorized to approve alternative methods of qualifying, training, and certifying crewmembers and dispatchers without the necessity of involving the FAA exemption process or office. Thus the process of approving unique training and checking solutions is quite nimble from an administrative perspective, encouraging AQP carriers to be innovative and creative with their approaches to addressing emerging training challenges. Under this model the transfer of new human factors and CRM knowledge migrates from the university to the airline in record time.

17.4.2 Rules

The rules for training and evaluating pilots, flight engineers, flight attendants, and dispatchers are contained in 14 CFR Parts 121 and 135. The requirement for CRM training began with an NTSB recommendation resulting from the crash of United Airlines Flight 173 in 1978 (NTSB, 1978). A DC-8 crew ran out of fuel while circling over Portland, Oregon because the captain was preoccupied with clearing a landing gear malfunction. Both the first officer and flight engineer kept hinting to the captain that the aircraft was running low on fuel, but neither was sufficiently assertive to alter the captain's behavior. Although United Airlines introduced the first CRM training in 1981, the FAA did not mandate this training for over a decade. In 1990, the FAA established AQP as a voluntary training option, but mandated CRM training for all those who volunteered for the program (FAA, 1990). CRM training was mandated for all Part 121 operators in 1995 and for all Part 135 operators in 2011.

17.4.3 Policy

While rules are developed at a high level of generality in order to provide a stable, long-term foundation for safety, the specific means of compliance with those rules is detailed in policy. The issuance of a rule is, for example, routinely accompanied by the issuance of two companion documents, an advisory circular for industry guidance, and an entry into FAA Order 890001, which is guidance to the FAA inspector workforce as how to provide oversight of the contents of the rule and advisory circular. Some programs are based on both rules and policy, such as AQP and Flight Operations Quality Assurance (FOQA), while others are based on policy alone, such as the Aviation Safety Action Program (ASAP) and the Line Operational Safety Audit (LOSA). While not every policy has an accompanying rule, all rules have accompanying policy.

Prior to 2013 the AQP and LOS advisory circulars (AC 120-54 and AC 120-35) were not maintained by the same branch that maintained the CRM advisory circular (AC 120-51), making harmonization within the agency slightly more challenging. Since then, all three primary CRM policy documents have been maintained by a single office of primary responsibility (OPR), the Air Carrier Training and Voluntary Safety Programs Branch. Now both industry and FAA field personnel have a single point of contact for all CRM related issues.

17.4.4   Rewarding Best Practices

While statutes, rules, regulations, and policy are the bedrock of safety, from a regulatory perspective, such mandates have their own natural limitations. Not all problems are solved by prescriptive rule-making. The more rules the FAA publishes, the more complex, difficult, and expensive the tasks of both company compliance and FAA surveillance become. The unintended consequence of promulgating more and more rules and restrictions is that it leads to shortcuts, errors, and an increase in violations (Reason, 1995).

The FAA cannot write a rule for every possible contingency, nor are the most challenging safety concerns necessarily addressed by prescriptive procedures. Reason (1997) dedicates an entire chapter to the various dilemmas and double binds the regulators find themselves in when developing guidance. The underspecification of guidance increases errors while the overspecification of guidance increases violations. The balance between too much and too little guidance is based on complex factors whose cause and effect relationships are poorly understood, even today.

In order to increase aviation safety, the FAA has introduced a series of creative voluntary programs that add to aviation safety without providing an undue burden of extra mandatory rules for operators to follow or for the FAA to enforce. These programs provide regulatory incentives to operators to collect safety data above and beyond rule compliance, and to act on that safety data to improve their operations. Because the programs are voluntary, operators that find their requirements too burdensome need not participate. These programs have developed into a major source of CRM data for both the industry and the FAA. They have also become important fuel sources for the industry's various engines of safety, including the operator's safety management system (SMS).

Voluntary Safety Programs

The FAA offers voluntary safety programs to the air carrier industry in two formats: as an early opportunity to adopt a program before it becomes mandatory, or as a program intended to remain voluntary for the foreseeable future. The agency's introduction of the safety management (SMS) system rule is a recent example of a voluntary program that fits into both categories. The rule was introduced to the Part 121 community with a 5-year implementation deadline. But the FAA offered to work with the Part 121 operators to develop an SMS on a voluntary basis prior to the date of the rule's mandate. In addition, it would offer support to other certificates, such as Part 135, who were not required by regulation to develop an SMS for their organizations but elected to do so for their own reasons.

The six voluntary safety programs meant to remain voluntary on a permanent basis are, again, managed by the Air Carrier Training and Voluntary Safety Programs Branch. These programs are considered to be too complex and expensive to mandate for all certificate holders, and are therefore encouraged but not required. These programs fall into two broad categories, reporting programs and auditing programs. The reporting programs allow for personnel who detect safety concerns during the course of performing their duties to report these concerns with a minimum of jeopardy to themselves. The auditing programs are designed for purposeful examination of safety systems and practices by individuals specifically trained for and assigned to perform those duties.

Reporting Programs
    Aviation Safety Reporting System (ASRS)
    Aviation Safety Action Program (ASAP)
    Flight Operations Qualify Assurance (FOQA)
    Voluntary Disclosure Reporting Program (VDRP)
Auditing Programs
    Internal Evaluation Program (IEP)
    Line Operational Safety Audit (LOSA)

Because of the expense and complexity of some of these programs, only the largest operators participate in all of them. What they all have in common is that they are voluntary in nature, provide some mechanism for collecting and analyzing safety data, and provide some process whereby the safety issues that are identified are addressed. Beyond that, each program has its own unique features. The ASRS is funded by the FAA, managed by NASA, and provides a free safety reporting system and safety data repository for all participants in the aviation community. It was established in 1976 as the original voluntary safety program and has been in some ways a template for many of those that followed. Of the three primary purposes for which the ASRS program was founded, one is "Strengthen the foundation of aviation human factors safety research" (NASA ASRS, 2017).

VDRP is funded and managed by the FAA and is available to any certificate holding organization that is willing to report safety violations to the FAA on a voluntary basis prior to FAA discovery. IEP is simply guidance provided to the operator community by the FAA to assist them in developing an internal auditing system. FOQA is available to any aircraft operator willing to install the required equipment. ASAP was originally developed for Part 121 air carriers and Part 142 repair stations only, but has since been expanded to include a wide range of FAR Parts, to include 91, 91K, 135, and 141.

What role does CRM play in these various programs? CRM events, issues, and performance problems are reported to NASA/FAA through ASRS, to the operator/FAA through ASAP, to the operator (and in some cases the FAA) through LOSA and IEP, and to a much lesser extent to the operator/FAA through FOQA and to the FAA through VDRP. These latter programs are not as rich in CRM findings as are the former programs, but some issues do surface through follow-on investigations of reported events. These voluntary programs supplement the traditional data sources, such as accident reports, incident reports, and captain's reports. Most of these programs include taxonomies specifically designed to organize and process human factors and CRM data

In the early days of AQP the most data-rich of these voluntary programs (ASAP, FOQA, and LOSA) did not exist. Those operators who taught CRM at all often addressed the subject in the classroom only, and selected each year's recurrent training topics by cycling through the clusters of CRM behavioral markers in AC 120-51, CRM. One year would be Communications and Decision-Making, the next year would be Team Building and Maintenance, and the third year would be Workload Management and Situational Awareness. Today AQP carriers develop new line operational scenarios every training cycle and base the contents on the risk profile generated by their analysis of relevant safety data from accidents, incidents, safety recommendations, and safety events and concerns generated by the voluntary safety programs. Thus the air carrier community has a method of continuously identifying risks, determining which of those are best mitigated through training interventions, and quickly modifying training as necessary with a minimum of regulatory constraint.

Since its inception in 1990 the Advanced Qualification Program has morphed through three generations, based on the training and operational data available to nourish it. During the decade of the 1990s it was viewed as an alternative training program, informed primarily by its own training data and by whatever operational data an individual operator was able to provide to it. But by the year 2000 the FAA had stood up, and the industry had embraced, the voluntary safety programs. The industry was already experimenting with injecting operational data from these programs into their AQP curriculums, and solicited FAA assistance in moving their efforts forward. For most of the next decade the regular annual industry AQP conferences were held on the odd years only, while on the even years the FAA sponsored what it referred to as Shared Vision of Safety conferences. The focus of these efforts was to determine the best methods for allowing the AQP curriculums to be responsive to the data from the voluntary safety programs. This decade prepared the AQP community for the next step in their evolution, which was the advent of SMS. From roughly 2010 on the AQP was morphing into the training component of the operator's SMS. All current AQP carriers are part 121 Operators and were thus required to have an FAA approved SMS operating by March 9, 2018.

17.5 FUNDING RESEARCH

One of the most important contributions the FAA has made to CRM over the last few decades has been to fund teams of researchers at universities, researcher centers, and private institutions to further the understanding and operationalization of CRM. While most of this research was targeted to the support of specific program requirements, in particular AQP, some of it was also dedicated to supporting promising efforts to explore the fundamental elements of CRM. Some of the problems the researchers were asked to solve were identified by the FAA while others were identified by industry groups or, in some cases, specific airlines. In those cases, where individual airlines had specific issues, the FAA agreed to provide research support when (1) the issues were applicable to other certificate holders as well, (2) the carrier agreed to provide sufficient personnel resources to support the project, and (3) the solution toolsets would be placed in the public domain and made available to all potential users.

17.5.1 Human Factors Research

By the mid-1980s the FAA, NASA, and NTSB all came to the conclusion that the primary cause of crew-caused accidents was not insufficient technical skills but a lack of cockpit management skills. Pilots were much better at flying the aircraft than at managing the overall flight. In some cases, alpha male pilots were attempting to save a troubled flight through individual heroics rather than teamwork and coordination. The diagnosis was a lack of human factors skill and knowledge; consequently the FAA funded a line of human factors research aimed at understanding cockpit resource management and determining the best way to teach and assess it in pilots. While most research at the time was conducted at the FAA Technical Center in Atlantic City, New Jersey or the Mike Monroney Aeronautical Center in Oklahoma City, Oklahoma, this research was to be funded out of FAA Headquarters and sponsored by the policy making branches that resided there.

17.5.2 Crew Resource Management

For the last two decades the FAA Office of the Chief Scientist for Flight Deck Human Factors has advised the agency on its human factors research. Central to this work has been the study of CRM and its supporting training programs. It is telling that the FAA does not have an advisory circular for CRM itself but instead has one for CRM training, as CRM has always been viewed primarily as an issue for training. While considerable CRM research was conducted prior to the birth of AQP, the AQP Program Office was the first Washington policy organization to take full advantage of the ability to sponsor this type of research. The office was led by the only person within the entire Air Transportation Division who had a PhD in human factors as well as a previous career as a human factors researcher. A sudden increase in human factors research funding intersected with professional leadership and a training program aimed specifically at improving the training and assessment of CRM capabilities. Although general CRM concepts were widely accepted by the aviation community by the time of the introduction AQP in 1990, there were no agreed upon tools or best practices for the effective training and valid and reliable assessment of the type of training programs called for in the AQP regulation: fully integrated technical and CRM training and evaluation.

The general philosophy guiding this research was that the pilots, the instructors, the evaluators, and the curriculum developers all had separate needs that would have to be addressed in turn. For the pilots the challenge would be to determine the best type of training and checking events to maximize crew performance. For the instructors the challenge would be to specify a new range of competencies beyond those traditionally applied for stick and rudder training. For the evaluators the challenge would be to develop grade scales that would allow them to accurately capture the full range of both technical and human factors skills and calibration events that would assure standardization across evaluators and events. For the course developers the challenge would be to develop scenario-generation methods that integrated CRM and technical skills for both teaching and testing.

Over two decades this research explored the use of lower fidelity training devices for teaching and evaluating soft skills (Burki-Cohen, Go, & Longridge, 2001: Burki-Cohen and Go, 2005; Burki-Cohen, Sparko, & Go, 2007), tools and methods for the rapid development of training and testing scenarios, methods for providing realistic radio communications in the simulator (Burki-Cohen & Kendra, 2000), tools for calibrating instructors and evaluators both to each other and to a referent "gold standard" (Baker & Dismukes, 2002, 2003), tools for improving training data quality (Johnson & Goldsmith, 1999a, 1999b, 1999c), a model AQP database (Mangold & Neumeister, 1995, 1997), a study to correlate pilot grades to FOQA data, the development of leader and followership training (Dunlap & Mangold, 1998a, 1998b), interruptions and distractions in the cockpit, cognitive task analysis techniques, NOTAM modernization (Hoeft, Kochan, & Jentsch, 2002), mixed fleet flying, pilot selection techniques, the effects of stress on pilot performance, concept mapping (Harper, Evans, Dew, Jentsch, & Bowers, 2002), team mental models, startle and surprise (Rivera, Jentsch, Talone, & Bosser, 2014), pilot monitoring, a training survey that returned over 10,000 questionnaires and a skill decay study that analyzed over 2 million pilot performance grades from 25 fleets at eight airlines, interruptions and distractions in the cockpit, and a project to measure the effects of CRM training in the cockpit that evolved into the LOSA program. The following paragraphs highlight a few of those projects.

Evaluator Calibration

The joint government-industry team that established AQP did not anticipate a need to calibrate check airmen or FAA inspectors. The validity and reliability of their pilot evaluations were simply not in question. It was only after several AQP curriculums had been implemented and monthly submissions of de-identified pilot performance data were being submitted to the agency that the statistician assigned to the AQP Program Office became concerned. The data from virtually all of the participating air carriers had way too much variance. Expert performance tends to be relatively consistent across time and evaluators and this data did not fit the anticipated pattern. The FAA dispatched a researcher to spend a month at a midsized operator watching evaluations and interviewing pilots and check airmen and looking for something out of the ordinary. He returned to report that he had become quite proficient at predicting student grades simply by focusing on a single variable...the name of the check airman giving the check. When the check airmen transitioned from the pass/fail grading of maneuvers under traditional training to the scalar grading of both CRM and technical skills under AQP, they were required to make much more precise judgments than in their previous lives, and the subjectivity of those judgments was skewing the data.

The FAA dispatched teams of researchers to work with two operators, one major carrier and one regional carrier. The team ended up developing enhanced grade scales, new grade sheets, cockpit videos to provide standard input to the evaluators, enhanced training on the importance of data quality, collection and analysis of calibration data, and improved formats for reporting calibration data. The basic approach was to provide each check airman with a grade sheet, have them all watch a video of a crew's performance, and then score the performance and complete their grade sheets. The calibration came from the follow-on discussions of why each check airman gave the grade he or she did (GMU, 1996: Holt & Johnson, 1997; Shultz, Seamster, & Edens, 1997).

Years of data collection and analysis have revealed three "characters" who account for almost all of the error variance in the scores awarded by check airmen and inspectors. They would include the Axe Man (systematic severity error), Santa Claus (systematic leniency error), and Mr. Average (systematic central tendency error). The agency was originally concerned about systematic differences, congruity, consistency, and sensitivity, but it turned out to be adequate to focus only on the first two concerns. The FAA's current AQP data analysis software, AQP VUE, focuses those two measures.

Leadership/Followership

By the mid-1990s industry data were showing that the CRM element leadership was weak within some flight crews, possibly compromising safety of flight. So the question became how best to train this skill. In some academic areas leadership was viewed as a linear, one-way (i.e., downward) action with the primary aim of task accomplishment. Another approach viewed leadership as an activity that involved both leaders and followers as the interaction to accomplish goals. Followership skills, in this view, were as important as leadership skills to the safe and efficient performance of flight crews. In this view the challenge was to train both leadership and followership skills to improve flight crew performance. In order to design an effective training program, background work required the development of a model of cockpit leadership in order to identify the critical skills necessary for safe operations. The next step was to develop a training program to address those skills.

The authors of this study analyzed the cockpit performance of multiple crews to determine the behavioral components of leadership/followership skills appropriate for commercial flight operations. The model developed from this analysis suggested that effective and efficient crew interactions resulted from utilizing the skills of envisioning, modeling, reception, influence, adaptability, and initiative. These six skill sets were common to both leadership and followership performance. The initial analysis also suggested that in order to maintain safe flight the individuals were required to constantly oscillate between the leader and the follower roles, and that weak leader or follower skills were usually compensated for by the other crewmember (Mangold & Neumeister, 2001).

Subsequent data from a line audit at a large US carrier revealed that the components described in the model were useful in analyzing overall crew performance. The data showed, in general, that in more severely abnormal situations, crews tended to be less effective in exhibiting leadership/followership skills, consistent with the issues that initiated this research development in the first place. Under stress, captains were less likely to articulate a vision for the flight, meet company standards, obtain commitment from other crewmembers, or display sufficient adaptability. Both first officers and captains were less likely to initiate actions in response to an operational deficiency when the severity of the situation was high. Yet when handling complex normal situations, these same crews displayed "outstanding" leadership/followership skills. When captains exhibited good conduct and high standards, first officers modeled their behavior. When captains were receptive to first office input, those first officers were likewise receptive.

Maintaining vigilance during the flight seemed to be dependent on the leadership of each crewmember during different phases of flight. During predeparture, takeoff, climb, and cruise, vigilance was related to the captain's envisioning, modeling, and receptiveness. However, during the descent and approach phases, vigilance was related more to the first officer's conduct and standards.

Workload and task distribution was dependent on the captain's conduct, standards, and receptiveness. Establishing guidelines for automated systems in all phases of flight was related to the captain's articulating a vision, modeling exemplary conduct and standards, receptiveness, and the use of interpersonal skills to obtain commitment from others.

Based on the skill analysis model and this line data, the requirements for a leadership/followership curriculum were identified. This included the development of classroom exercises that extended beyond role play, the creation of event sets that addressed critical leadership/followership skills, and addressing company philosophy and policy issues. A training package was developed that included a student manual, instructor manual, and training videos (Dunlap & Mangold, 1998a, 1998b).

Advanced Crew Resource Management (ACRM)

The FAA observed that while high level categories of CRM behavior, such as Communication, are often viewed as too broad and subjective to measure, more specific applications of those broad concepts, such as Conducts Preflight Briefing, rarely caused the same level of concern among the check airman workforce. Playing off this observation, this next set of studies examined ways to proceduralize CRM and integrate those new procedures into existing crew documentation, such as checklists and quick reference handbooks. The goal was to reduce the amount of CRM that needed to be trained by integrating it into operational guidance. What could not be proceduralized would still need to be trained (Seamster, Boehm-Davis, Holt, & Schultz, 1998). It was anticipated that this would increase the range of CRM skills the check airman community felt comfortable grading.

This research was conducted at a regional air carrier. For this study, procedural CRM meant the implementation of specific calls, checks, and/or guidance into one or more of the following documents: normal checklists, quick reference handbooks, abnormal/emergency procedures, the flight standards manual, and any additional job aids. The goal was to translate critical CRM principles into specific CRM procedures. This project focused on proceduralizing four specific CRM skill sets: team management, crew communication, decision-making, and situation awareness.

The study involved two groups of pilots flying different fleets at the same airline. The experimental group received training in the new proceduralized documents and used those documents in training and then on the line. The control group used the standard documents in training and then on the line. The final evaluation of the ACRM modifications and training employed several data sources: simulator and line evaluations from check airmen, subjective evaluations by the pilots and check airmen, and nonjeopardy jumpseat observations. Data from all sources indicated that the combination of specific CRM procedures that were both trained and incorporated into fleet SOP were effective in producing specific changes in crew performance. Combined data showed that the performance of the ACRM-trained fleet was consistently and significantly better than the traditional CRM-trained fleet both in the simulator and on the line in all phases of flight. This also demonstrated the positive effects of ACRM transfer from the training environment to the operational environment. This project produced an extensive ACRM manual to aid in the development of proceduralized CRM as well as the organization, conduct, and assessment of evaluator calibration training (Seamster et al., 1998).

Facilitated Debriefing Techniques

Debriefing after a LOFT or LOE session has been widely accepted as a valuable learning tool. The debriefing is a window into the entire CRM process. Because LOFT and especially LOE simulations are busy, intense, and often stressful experiences, a thoughtful discussion after the experience is necessary in order for the crew to sort out and interpret exactly what they were exposed to, how they responded, and what they might do to improve their performance in the future. This discussion allows the crews to consolidate their lessons learned into long-term memory in a form and format that increases the probability that these lessons will be applied out on the line. These discussions reveal to the check airman how well the crews are able to analyze their own performance and what insight they have into their own levels of CRM effectiveness.

The FAA assumed that if crews were to implement CRM effectively on a day-to-day basis that they should have practice in analyzing their own performance in terms of CRM, and that the debrief was the ideal teaching/learning opportunity. Subsequently the FAA teamed with NASA to provide a guidance document for check airmen (McDonnell, Jobe, & Dismukes, 1997). The goal of the research was to survey the techniques that were in use at the time, how effective the various techniques seemed to be, how consistent they were with FAA guidance, what materials were already available and what obstacles instructors encountered in complying with FAA guidance. The researchers reviewed the activities of the field, identified the best practices, integrated them into a comprehensive process, and developed a manual to teach those best practices to the check airman workforce.

17.6   THE CRM FRAMEWORKS

For over 20 years the agency funded the CRM research of the late Dr. Robert Helmreich of the University of Texas at Austin, often referred to as the Father of CRM. One of his many contributions to the field was to frame the history of the development of CRM within the United States as a series of six successive generations (Helmreich, Merritt, & Wilhelm, 1999). One option the agency has considered in updating its CRM guidance is to reimagine his six generations into six frameworks. The term generations may be seen to imply that each generation flowed from the previous one, and perhaps superseded them, as when an older generation of software is no longer supported by the manufacturer. And while threat and error management (TEM, generation 6) did in fact flow directly from error management (generation 5), the same cannot be said of the other generations. The idea of frameworks, to some readers, suggested a series of perspectives on the subject. Each framework adds new tools to the toolbox of the CRM practitioner, and even the oldest tools are useful in some contexts. Many of the tools of framework 1, Individual Management Styles, while of little use in cultures with a low power distance, such as the United States, are still relevant in cultures with a high power distance (Gladwell, 2008; Helmreich & Merritt, 2001).

Another limitation of the idea of the generations is that they end with generation 6, which dates back to the year 2000. Helmreich identified six separate generations within the 20-year period 1980−2000. Does risk and resource management (RRM) then become generation 7, and resilience training (RT) generation 8, and so on? Teaching the history of the golden age of CRM development (1980−2000) can certainly benefit from so fine a taxonomy, but moving forward as a mature area of study CRM frameworks can probably be more broadly defined. Hence generation 6, TEM, becomes framework 6, risk management. This allows TEM, RRM, RT, and whatever follows to fit within its broad scope.

17.6.1   The Six CRM Frameworks

Building the CRM toolbox

#1.   Individual Management Styles (1980)
      Cockpit resource management
      Psychological testing
      Teamwork exercises
      Line operational flight training (LOFT)
#2.   Improving Crew Performance (1986)
      Behavioral markers
      Subjective grading
      Focus on breaking error chains
#3.   Organizational Inclusion and Culture (1993)
      Crew resource management
      CRM beyond aviation
      Corporate resource management

#4. Integration and Proceduralization (1994)
   Integration of CRM and technical training
   Advanced crew resource management (ACRM)
   Line operational evaluation
   Event-based training and checking
   Evaluator calibration
#5. Error Management (1996)
   From error avoidance to error management
   Reverse debrief
   Error as an effect as well as a cause
#6. Risk Management (2000)
   CRM as a risk management strategy
   Threat and error management (TEM)
   Risk and resource management (RRM)
   Resilience training (RT)

The worldwide aviation safety community is moving from a focus on accident prevention to a focus on risk management. Safety Management Systems (SMS) have been adopted by ICAO. The FAA has mandated SMS for all Part 121 air carriers and has modified its internal oversight system, the safety assurance system (SAS) specifically to provide oversight of each operator's SMS (FAA, 2006b).

One limitation of the current SMS approach is that it is primarily a top-down model with significantly less structure for bottom-up feedback. The US Navy has addressed this by integrating top-down operational risk management with bottom-up CRM activities through their time-critical risk management model (U.S. Navy, 2010). The Navy identifies three levels of operational risk management, based upon the amount of time available to address the risk. The In-depth level provides adequate time for thorough research and analysis of available data regarding the risk to be managed. The Deliberate level provides adequate time to thoroughly plan a mission or flight. The Time-critical level provides only enough time to address pressing problems at hand. The typical preflight briefing would represent a Deliberate level of risk management, while addressing abnormal and emergency events in flight would represent the Time-critical level of risk management.

The SMS approaches recommended by ICAO and the FAA represent primarily In-depth or Deliberate levels of risk management, while the application of real-time CRM skills in flight would represent the Time-critical level. In the case of the Navy, they had adopted a portion of the risk and resource management model as the backbone of their time-critical risk management. They refer to this "tool" in their "toolbox" with the mnemonic ABCD (Department of the Navy, 2010, Naval Safety Center, 2017). The A is for Assess the situation, the B is for balancing resources and options, the C is for communication, and the D is for do and debrief. Because the threat and error management model is relatively simple, it is always used in its entirety. But because of the complexity of the risk and resource management model, it is not at all uncommon to see air carriers and other organizations using only a portion, or module, of the overall model. Several US carriers have used the red-yellow-green visuals and/or the associated grade scales in their AQP curriculums. Southwest Airlines was the first to fully integrate the risk and resource model across its entire training and safety network.

17.6.2   The Air Carrier Training Aviation Rule-making Committee (ACT-ARC)

Following the release of the updated rules for traditional training for Parts 121 and 135 operators, the FAA decided that it would benefit from a standing committee of industry representatives that could not only respond to the laundry list of useful training ARC recommendations that the agency was unable to roll into the most recent training rule, but that could act as a semi-permanent industry brain trust on industry training views and recommendations moving forward.

ARCs consist primarily of industry personnel, as their goal is to make recommendations to the FAA for new or modified rules and other guidance. There are two leads, one from industry and one from the FAA, that head up a high level steering committee. Individual working groups under the direction of the steering committee tackle areas of focus. These working groups usually consist of industry representative with one or more FAA personnel assigned as subject matter experts in the committee's area of focus. The subject matter experts serve the committee rather than lead it. The ACT-ARC formed a working group to focus on cross-functional CRM training. This is training on those tasks that require interaction between two or more work groups. The areas of focus for this working group included pilots, flight attendants, and dispatchers.

Beginning in the early 1990s (CRM Framework #3) the industry recognized the benefits of teaching subjects common to both pilots and flight attendants to a mixed class that included both work groups. This model was very popular but over time proved to be increasingly difficult as air carriers became larger, their operations more complex, and their course delivery methods less reliant on classroom training. The goal of the working group was to explore all of the ways that cross-functional training could be delivered not only in a classroom setting but using other creative approaches.

In particular, the advent of new training technologies has greatly expanded the portfolio of options for cross-functional training, way beyond the simple combination of multiple work groups attending the same classes in the same room. The goal of the workgroup evolved over time but in the end was to explore and organize the full range of possible cross-functional CRM learning opportunities that could be provided to pilots, flight engineers, flight attendants, and dispatchers. Although the scope of the mission of this work group was limited to those job categories, the resulting taxonomy would apply to virtually any work groups. Regardless of what the FAA or the participating operators eventually do with this classification scheme, it is a significant forward step in the development of CRM training.

The taxonomy of cross-functional training methodologies proposed by the working group first divides the schemes into two broad categories: facilitated and nonfacilitated. The facilitated methods are subdivided into four broad categories: joint, separate, hybrid, and distance learning. Joint is defined as having multiple employee groups participating in a facilitated training event or environment (flight simulation training device). Joint training assumes physical proximity of the trainees. Separate is defined as one individual employee group training only to his or her specific employee group about cross-functional CRM topics. Hybrid is defined as members of one employee group in a class with a facilitator(s) from a different employee group(s), including co-facilitation. Distance learning is a situation where a cross-functional facilitator is live (remote), students are training in a different location(s), and there is real-time interaction with the instructor.

The other broad category is nonfacilitated, or e-learning. This category is not divided into subcategories but instead into levels, depending on the level of interaction. Level 1, the lowest level, involves no interaction. The curriculum is linear and the method is used for basic training. Level 2 involves limited interaction and, like level one, is used for knowledge transfer only. At this level, interactions may include interaction with clickable animated graphics, the navigation may include menus, glossaries, and links to external resources, there may be simple drag and drop, matching or identification exercise, along with audio and video. Most currently available course materials are level 1 or 2.

Level 3, moderate interaction, includes case scenarios and decision-point branching. This represents a high degree of complexity and customization with multiple branches, multiple outcomes, and feedback tailored to the individual student. Level 4, simulation and game-based learning, represents the highest level of interaction available from current technology. This level involves the elements of the first three levels with greater sophistication and interactivity, to include elements such as avatars, 3D simulations, and real-time learning.

17.6.3   The State-of-the-Art Study (1999−2014)

In preparation for updating the CRM Advisory Circular 120-51E, the FAA sponsored a research project through the University of Central Florida to investigate the state-of-the-art in CRM outside the aviation domain (Jimenez, Rivera, Talone, Kasper, & Jentsch, 2015). The study covered the 15-year period 1999−2014 and included not only aviation, but also the domains of health care, the US military, maritime, nuclear power, and offshore oil and gas production. It was the hope of the agency that having initiated CRM and seen its widespread adoption in other domains that the FAA could now benefit from new tools and techniques developed by these other domains. Unfortunately, for the most part, these other domains continue to lag behind US air carrier aviation and the researchers were only able to find two relatively novel applications that seemed to have real promise for transfer to airline training. One was the SPOTLITE method employed in the military domain (MacMillan, Entin, Morley, & Bennett, 2013) and the other was the TeamSTEPPS program from the health care domain (Department of Defense, 2017).

17.7 FUTURE TRENDS

As for the FAA CRM Advisory Circular, the agency has gone back to the future. For the first time in almost 20 years the latest version of the document was developed by a team consisting primarily of industry personnel (rather than FAA inspectors) and led by an FAA specialist with a PhD in Human Factors. As for the industry, the larger air carriers now have enough training and safety data to customize their CRM training programs to their own unique requirements. The convergence of approaches from two decades ago has been replaced with a divergence of approaches today. For the first time operators are investing in complex cognitive task analysis methods, although this trend is just emerging. Separate CRM-only job task listings are becoming more common. Carriers are also looking to the ICAO Evidence-Based Training CRM competencies to inform their programs and often to structure their CRM data collection tools to include them. While core CRM competencies are common across most US operators, more and more air carriers are adding unique features based in large part on changing pilot demographics at each operator.

REFERENCES

ATA Working Group. (1995). *LOFT/LOE design*. Washington, DC: Airline Transport Association.

Baker, D. P., & Dismukes, R. K. (2002). A framework for understanding crew performance assessment issues. *International Journal of Aviation Psychology*, *12*(3), 205–222.

Baker, D. P., & Dismukes, R. K. (2003). *A gold standards approach to training instructors to evaluate crew performance. NASA/TM-2003-212809*. Moffett Field, CA: NASA.

Birnbach, R. A., & Longridge, T. M. (1993). The regulatory perspective. In E. L. Weiner, B. G. Kanki, & R. L. Helmreich (Eds.), *Cockpit resource management* (pp. 263–282). New York: Academic Press, Inc.

Burki-Cohen, J., & Go, T.H. (2005). The effect of simulator motion cues on initial training of airline pilots. In AIAA Modeling and Simulation Technologies Conference. American Institute of Aeronautics and Astronautics, AIAA-2005-6109.

Burki-Cohen, J., Go, T.H., & Longridge, T.M. (2001). Flight simulator fidelity considerations for total airline training and evaluation. In AIAA Modeling and Simulation Technologies Conference. American Institute of Aeronautics and Astronautics, AIAA-2001-4425.

Burki-Cohen, J., & Kendra, A. (2000). Realistic radio communications simulation. In Presentation to the Airline Transport Association Advanced Qualification Program Instructor/Evaluator and Line Operational Simulation Focus Group. San Diego, CA.

Burki-Cohen, J., Sparko, A.L., & Go, T.H. (2007). Training value of a fixed-base flight simulator with a dynamic seat. In AIAA Modeling and Simulation Technologies Conference. American Institute of Aeronautics and Astronautics, AIAA-2007-6564.

Butler, R. E. (1993). LOFT: Full mission simulation as crew resource management training. In E. L. Weiner, B. G. Kanki, & R. L. Helmreich (Eds.), *Cockpit resource management* (pp. 231−259). New York: Academic Press, Inc.

Department of Defense. (2017). TeamSTEPPS 2.0. Retrieved November 2017 from <https://www.health.mil/military-health-topics/access-cost-quality-and-safety-of-healthcare/patient-safety/patient-safety-products-and-services/TeamSTEPPS>.

Department of the Navy. (2010). *Operational Risk Management (ORM) Fundamentals, Enclosure (2) Time Critical Risk Management (TCRM). OPNAVINST 3500.39C.* Washington, DC: Author.

Dunlap, J. H., & Mangold, S. J. (1998a). *Leadership/Followership recurrent training. Instructor Manual.* Washington, DC: Federal Aviation Administration.

Dunlap, J. H., & Mangold, S. J. (1998b). *Leadership/Followership recurrent training. Student Manual.* Washington, DC: Federal Aviation Administration.

Federal Aviation Administration. (1990). *Special Federal Aviation Regulation No. 58, Advanced Qualification Program (SFAR 58).* Washington, DC: Author.

Federal Aviation Administration. (1978). *Line Oriented flight training Advisory Circular (AC) 12035.* Washington, DC: Author.

Federal Aviation Administration. (1981). *Line oriented flight training Advisory Circular (AC) 12035A.* Washington, DC: Author.

Federal Aviation Administration. (1989). *Cockpit resource management (Advisory Circular AC120-51).* Washington, DC: Author.

Federal Aviation Administration. (1990). *Line operational simulations (Advisory Circular AC120-35B).* Washington, DC: Author.

Federal Aviation Administration. (1991). *Advanced qualification program (Advisory Circular AC120-54).* Washington, DC: Author.

Federal Aviation Administration. (2006b). *Introduction to safety management systems for air operators (Advisory Circular AC120-92).* Washington, DC: Author.

Federal Aviation Administration. (2015). *Line operational simulations (Advisory Circular AC120-35D).* Washington, DC: Author.

George Mason University. (1996). *Developing and evaluating CRM procedures for a regional carrier: Phase I Report.* Washington, DC: Federal Aviation Administration.

George Mason University. (2001). *Scientific evaluation of aircrew performance.* Washington, DC: Federal Aviation Administration.

Gladwell, M. (2008). *Outliers: The story of success.* New York, New York: Little, Brown and Company.

Goldsmith, T. E., & Johnson, P. J. (2002). Assessing and improving evaluation of aircrew performance. *International Journal of Aviation Psychology, 12*(3), 223−240.

Harper, M.E., Evans, A.W. III, Dew, R., Jentsch, F., & Bowers, C. (2002). Computerized concept mapping validation: Is computerized concept mapping comparable to manual concept mapping? In Poster session presented at the meeting of the American Psychological Association, Chicago, IL.

Helmreich, R. L., & Merritt, A. C. (2001). *Culture at work in aviation and medicine: National, organizational and professional influences.* Aldershot, UK: Ashgate.

Helmreich, R. L., Merritt, A. C., & Wilhelm, J. A. (1999). The evolution of crew resource management training in commercial aviation training. *International Journal of Aviation Psychology, 9,* 19–32.

Hoeft, R., Kochan, J., & Jentsch, F. (2002). *Human factors aspects of notices to airmen (NOTAMs).* Washington, DC: Federal Aviation Administration.

Holt, R. W., Boehm-Davis, D. A., & Hansberger, J. T. (2001). *Evaluation of proceduralized CRM at a regional and major carrier. Technical Report TR-GMU-01-P01.* Fairfax, VA: George Mason University.

Holt, R. W., Hansberger, J. T., & Boehm-Davis, D. A. (2002). Improving rater calibration in aviation: A case study. *International Journal of Aviation Psychology, 12*(3), 305–330.

Holt, R.W., & Johnson, P.J. (1997). Application of psychometrics to the calibration of air carrier evaluators. In Paper presented at the 41st meeting of the Human Factors and Ergonomics Society, Albuquerque, NM.

Jimenez, C., Rivera, J., Talone, A., Kasper, K., & Jentsch, F. (2015). A State-of-the-Art Technical Review to Support the Revision of AC 120-51E, Crew Resource Management Training. Federal Aviation Administration, Washington, DC.

Johnson, P. J., & Goldsmith, T. E. (1999a). *The importance of quality data in evaluating aircrew performance.* Washington, DC: Federal Aviation Administration.

Johnson, P. J., & Goldsmith, T. E. (1999b). *A guide to the evaluation aspects of entering AQP.* Washington, DC: Federal Aviation Administration.

Johnson, P. J., & Goldsmith, T. E. (1999c). *Questions your performance database should address.* Washington, DC: Federal Aviation Administration.

MacMillan, J., Entin, E. B., Morley, R., & Bennett, W., Jr. (2013). Measuring team performance in complex and dynamic military environments: The SPOTLITE method. *Military Psychology, 25*(3), 266–279.

Mangold, S. J., & Neumeister, D. M. (1995). CRM in the model AQP: A preview. In R. S. Jensen (Ed.), *Proceedings of the eighth international symposium of aviation psychology.* Columbus, OH: The Ohio State University.

Mangold, S. J., & Neumeister, D. M. (1997). *Model AQP database training guide.* Columbus, OH: Battle Memorial Institute.

Mangold, S. J., & Neumeister, D. M. (2001). Reconceptualizing leadership and followership for event based training. In R. S. Jensen (Ed.), *Proceedings of the eleventh international symposium of aviation psychology.* Columbus, OH: The Ohio State University.

McDonnell, L. K., Jobe, K. K., & Dismukes, R. K. (1997). *Facilitating LOS debriefings: A training manual. NASA Technical Memorandum 112192.* Moffitt Field, CA: NASA Ames Research Center.

National Aeronautics and Space Administration. (2017). Aviation Safety Reporting Program. Purpose. Retrieved September 2017 from <https://asrs.arc.nasa.gov/overview/summary. html>.

National Transportation Safety Board. (1978). Aircraft accident report: United Airlines, Inc. McDonnell-Douglas, DC-8-1, N8082U, Portland, Oregon, December 28, 1978. NTSB-AAR-79-7.

Naval Safety Center. (2017). ORM...We don't have time for ORM, we have work to do. Heads Up. Safety Topics for Supervisors. Retrieved September 2017 from <www.safetycenter. navy.gov>.

Reason, J. (1995). A systems approach to organizational errors. *Ergonomics, 38,* 1708–1721.

Reason, J. (1997). *Managing the risks of organizational accidents.* Aldershot, UK: Ashgate.

Rivera, J., Jentsch, F., Talone, A., & Bosser, C. T. (2014). *Defining startle, surprise, and distraction: A state-of-the-art technical review to support the development of FAA technical and advisory guidance. Technical Report.* Orlando, FL: University of Central Florida.

Seamster, T. L., Boehm-Davis, D. A., Holt, R. W., & Schultz, K. (1998). *Developing advanced crew resource management (ACRM) training: A training manual.* Washington, DC: Federal Aviation Administration.

Seamster, T. L., Edens, E. S., & Holt, R. W. (1995). *Scenario event sets and the reliability of CRM assessment. Proceedings on the eighth annual international symposium on aviation psychology.* Columbus, OH: Ohio State University.

Shultz, K., Seamster, T. L., & Edens, E. S. (1997). *Inter-rater reliability tool development and validation. Proceedings on the ninth annual international symposium on aviation psychology.* Columbus, OH: Ohio State University.

Williams, D. M., Holt, R. W., & Boehm-Davis, D. A. (1997). *Training for inter-rater reliability: Baselines and benchmarks. Proceedings on the ninth annual international symposium on aviation psychology.* Columbus, OH: Ohio State University.

FURTHER READING

Federal Aviation Administration. (2004). *Crew resource management (Advisory Circular AC120-51E).* Washington, DC: Author.

Federal Aviation Administration. (2006a). *Advanced qualification program (Advisory Circular AC120-54A).* Washington, DC: Author.

Holt, R. W. (2001). *Scientific information systems.* Burlington, VT: Ashgate Publishing Company.

Chapter 18

The Accident Investigator's Perspective

Robert L. Sumwalt*, Katherine A. Lemos, Ph.D and
Ryan McKendrick, Ph.D

The sole objective of the investigation of an accident or incident investigation shall be the prevention of accidents and incidents. It is not the purpose of this activity to apportion blame or liability.

— ICAO Annex 13, Paragraph 3.1 (ICAO, 2016)

18.1 INTRODUCTION AND BACKGROUND INFORMATION

As with accident investigation, the ultimate objective of crew resource management (CRM) is to prevent accidents. According to the US Federal Aviation Administration (FAA) Advisory Circular (AC) 120-51, *Crew Resource Management Training*, first published in 1989, CRM contributes to accident prevention through improved crew performance, including team management, the use of all available resources, and through addressing the challenges of human computer interaction and workload[1] (FAA, 2004). To improve the outcomes intended by this guidance, it is not sufficient to simply state that the crew did not use good CRM. Instead, accident investigators must identify specific aspects of CRM that were lacking. Only by properly identifying those failures can safety truly be improved. This chapter will highlight aspects of CRM that continue to play a role in aviation accidents,

---

* The views expressed by the authors in this chapter do not represent the perspective of their respective employers.

1. FAA AC 120-51E (2004) is the most recent version, and suggests two main areas for training curriculum: Communications Processes and Decision Behavior, which includes briefings, inquiry/advocacy/assertion, crew self-critique, conflict resolution, and communications and decision-making; and Team-Building and Maintenance, which includes leadership/followership/concern for task, interpersonal relationships/group climate, workload management and situation awareness, and individual factors/stress reduction.

Crew Resource Management. DOI: https://doi.org/10.1016/B978-0-12-812995-1.00018-X
2019 Published by Elsevier Inc.

providing operational examples of how the principles of CRM, when not properly applied, can manifest themselves as accident-provoking conditions.

18.1.1   Background Information

Accident investigation has played a significant role in the development and adoption of CRM in the aviation industry. The concept of CRM gained momentum following the 1978 United Airlines' fuel starvation accident at Portland, OR (NTSB, 1979). As a result of the findings of this investigation, the National Transportation Safety Board (NTSB), FAA, and the National Aeronautics and Space Administration (NASA) all responded with action.[2] However, it wasn't until 1997 that FAA regulations actually required[3] CRM training for scheduled air carriers (FAR[4] Part 121 operators), followed by fractional ownership operations (FAR Part 91 Sub-Part K) in 2003, FAR Part 121 Advanced Qualifications Programs (AQP) in 2005, and for FAR Part 135 operators in 2013.[5]

Since 1979, the industry has made significant progress in instituting CRM concepts as a core component of training, to include integration of the concept through both ground courses and simulator sessions, including scenario-based training. In 2015, the FAA published an update to AC 120-35D guidance regarding line operational simulations (LOS) and line-oriented flight training (LOFT) (FAA, 2015). That document provides guidelines for how to best create and carry out training scenarios that will improve total flight crew performance by integrating CRM and technical skills.

Years of collective efforts to improve crew interactions and functionality by incorporating CRM have had a decidedly positive effect on safety. The Sioux City, Iowa accident involving United Airlines Flight 232, which suffered loss of an engine and hydraulic power, is only one example of effective teamwork in which the NTSB lauded the crew's performance (NTSB, 1990). "The Safety Board views the interaction of the pilots, including the check

---

2. In response to NTSB Safety recommendation A-79-047, in November 1979 the FAA issued an operations bulletin to all air carrier operations inspectors to urge operators to indoctrinate flight crews on flight deck resource management.
3. CRM was a component of the FAA knowledge requirements for airman and aircraft dispatcher certification in earlier years (see Title 14 of the Code of Federal Regulation (CFR) Part 61, Section 61.155 and 61.65, and Part 121 Section C141.1).
4. FAR is the abbreviation for Federal Aviation Regulation. Officially, FARs are codified in the United States Code of Federal Regulations (CFR) as Title 14 CFR, and then the related section number. For example, FAR Part 121 could also be referred to as 14 CFR 121. Both conventions will be used in this chapter.
5. Part 121 flight crewmember since March 1998 (14 CFR Section 121.404); Part 121 flight attendant or aircraft dispatcher since March 1999 (14 CFR Section 121.404); Part 91 Sub-Part K since 2003 (14 CFR Section 91.1073); and Part 121 (under AQP) since November 2005 (14 CFR Section 121.907). Note: A Special Federal Aviation Regulation (SFAR No. 58) for AQP was first issued in 1990, which is a voluntary program for Part 121 operators.

airman, during the emergency as indicative of the values of cockpit resource management" (NTSB, 1990, p. 76). The NTSB also stated that, "under the circumstances, the [United Flight 232] flight crew performance was highly commendable and greatly exceeded reasonable expectations" (NTSB, 1990, p. 76).

A modern-day version of positive CRM performance was evidenced in the well-known successful forced landing on the Hudson River, NJ, of US Airways Flight 1549 on January 15, 2009.[6] In this accident, the plane suffered the loss of both engines shortly after departure from New York's LaGuardia Airport, and despite landing in the Hudson River, there were no fatalities. In postaccident interviews, the captain credited the CRM training provided at US Airways that gave them the skills and tools they needed to build a team quickly and open lines of communication to share common goals and work together. The NTSB's final report attests to this positive teamwork: "The professionalism of the flight crewmembers and their excellent CRM during the accident sequence contributed to their ability to maintain control of the airplane, configure it to the extent possible under the circumstances, and fly an approach that increased the survivability of the impact" (NTSB, 2010a, p. 120). The NTSB's probable cause statement highlighted the crew's performance: "Contributing to the survivability of the accident was the... decision-making of the flight crewmembers and their CRM during the accident sequence" (NTSB, 2010a, p. 120).

18.1.2 The Accident Investigator's Perspective

It's important to document and learn from both "what goes right" as well as "what goes wrong" (Reason, 2008). The NASA Aviation Safety Reporting System (ASRS) database includes numerous examples of the mitigating effects of CRM in situations that may easily have led to serious incidents or accidents without this type of intervention. However, the accident investigator's perspective is mostly one of hindsight following a major event with adverse outcomes, of identifying the causal factors, and, knowing that there is always room for improvement when it comes to human lives. Our goal is to learn from these tragedies so we can prevent future accidents.

Since the previous version of this chapter was published, CRM training has become a requirement for Part 135 (charter) operations. A key accident highlighting this need occurred in October 2002, and claimed the life of a US Senator and members of his family. The NTSB found that the flight crew was not utilizing good CRM during the final stages of the approach (NTSB, 2003); they allowed the airspeed to decrease to a dangerously slow speed,

---

6. Reference NTSB public hearing regarding flight 1549 with Captain Sullenberger on June 9, 2009. Access interview with captain in the NTSB Group Chairman's Factual Report: Operations/Human Performance, May 15, 2009, Docket # SA-532, Exhibit #2-A, p. 30.

leading to an aerodynamic stall at low altitude. Unfortunately, the company was not providing their flight crews with CRM training, nor was it required at that time for charter operators. This led to the NTSB's recommendation that the FAA require CRM training for Part 135 charter operators, a requirement which was finalized by the FAA in 2011.[7]

In the Notice of Proposed Rulemaking in 2009, the FAA confirmed that the FAA, NTSB, and industry stakeholders "have consistently recognized the problems associated with poor decision making, ineffective communication, inadequate leadership, and poor task or resource management as major contributors to accidents and incidents within the aviation industry" (NARA, 2009, p. 20264). However, through this rulemaking effort, the FAA's analysis revealed an even stronger impact of CRM in Part 135 charter operations than had been previously documented. [8] Of 268 Part 135 accidents between 1998 and 2008, 24 were directly related to ineffective CRM and resulted in 83 fatalities and 12 serious injuries.

Despite requirements for CRM training across the industry, accidents suggest that, in some cases, we're still struggling with how to execute this training and help flight crews adopt and maintain the attitudes and behaviors that constitute effective CRM. These are complex and challenging concepts to define, to instill, and to measure. In this chapter, we'll review some of the key aspects of CRM that continue to play a vital role in aviation accidents, and that we believe warrant special or renewed attention in both training and investigations moving forward.

Although the scope of this chapter is limited to the aviation industry, and focuses on flight crews, these principles apply equally to other industries, especially other modes of transportation and high reliability organizations operating in high-risk environments. For example, the NTSB (which, in addition to investigating aviation accidents, also investigates maritime casualties) determined that poor use of bridge resource management (BRM) was a factor in the sinking of a 790-foot cargo vessel that claimed 33 lives in 2015 (NTSB, 2017). Modeled after CRM, BRM was developed to ensure

---

7. In 2003 the NTSB issued Safety Recommendation A-03-52 (2003) for the FAA to require CRM for part 135 operators, which was added in 2008 to the NTSB Most Wanted List of Transportation Safety Improvements. The FAA responded and agreed with the NTSB and Aviation Rulemaking Committee's recommendations that "all pilots in part 135 operations be proficient at mastering the resources available to them while managing many operational factors." In finalizing the CRM rule for charter operators, the FAA stated: "CRM training is the incorporation of team management concepts in flight operations. This training focuses on communication and interactions among pilots, flight attendants, operations personnel, maintenance personnel, air traffic controllers, flight service stations, and others. CRM also focuses on single pilot communications, decision making and situational awareness" (NARA, 2011, p. 3831).

8. Between 1979 and 2009, the NTSB specifically cited lack of effective CRM in probable cause and contributing factor analysis in 20 accidents operated under FAR Part 121, and six under Part 135 operations.

crewmembers operating on the bridge of a ship use all available resources to safely operate the vessel. As with CRM, an objective of BRM is to ensure that those in command have accurate, unfiltered information that could affect safety. "As an element of BRM, officers have a duty to speak up if they believe the vessel is at risk" (NTSB, 2017, p. 209).

18.2 LEADERSHIP, COMMUNICATIONS, AND FOLLOWING SOPS

This section is devoted to several elements traditionally considered to be core to CRM, and include leadership, communication, and adherence to standard operating procedures (SOPs). Throughout this section we will highlight the importance of individual accountability within the context of crew performance.

Historically, in "promoting the use of all resources on the flight deck," the focus of CRM has been to ensure that subordinate crewmembers felt empowered to speak up when they believed something was unsafe or unwise. Likewise, it was to actively encourage those in positions of command to seek such input. Early accidents highlighted this critical need, such as the accident in Portland, OR mentioned earlier (NTSB, 1979). In fact, the NTSB's initial recommendation on CRM in 1979 (A-79-047) called for, "particular emphasis on the merits of participative management for captains and assertiveness training for other cockpit crewmembers."

Crew performance profits from increased synergy and increased opportunity to prevent errors, and continual reinforcement of inquiry, advocacy, and assertion is still important.[9] However, acting as a team does not relinquish crew members of their individual roles and responsibilities and accountability. Whether the captain or first officer, pilot flying (PF), or pilot monitoring (PM), effective CRM involves not only inquiry, advocacy, and assertion, but the overlapping components of leadership, communication, and adherence to SOPs.

18.2.1 Leadership

Being pilot-in-command (PIC) of an aircraft centers on leadership, and it embodies a host of behaviors and attitudes. Leadership is not simply having responsibility for the outcome of the flight, but for taking the authority to make the difficult and final decisions, and when the situation requires, making a command decision.[10] As in the case of US Airways flight 1549, the captain testified to the importance of command authority and its role in

---

9. See NTSB (2001), in which a new-hire first officer failed to assert himself appropriately with a senior management captain.
10. According to 14 CFR 91.3, "The pilot-in-command of an aircraft is directly responsible for, and is the final authority as to, the operation of that aircraft," and "In an in-flight emergency requiring immediate action, the pilot in command may deviate from any rule of this part to the extent required to meet that emergency."

effective CRM (NTSB, 2010a). During the event sequence, upon the loss of both engines and the crew's inability to restart the engines, the captain made a command decision regarding the landing location.

The reason to highlight the value of the PIC's strong leadership is that some have erroneously believed or have misinterpreted CRM to mean, "Leadership by Committee." Nothing could be further from the truth. What CRM does do, when properly practiced, is ensure that everyone is on the same page and that information is freely shared so that the PIC can make an informed decision. However, there were early concerns that CRM might be an attempt to diminish the PIC's authority or there may be cases of captains ceding their authority. The FAA voiced concern about this in a response letter to the NTSB regarding Safety Recommendation A-86-019.[11]

> *An over-riding concern of the FAA's efforts in this program is to underscore the role and ultimate responsibility of the captain in a practical manner. The pilot-in-command of an aircraft has a very significant responsibility and must retain unchallenged authority for the conduct of a flight. Certainly the pilot-in-command must integrate the other flightcrew members in the cockpit procedures and decision-making processes. However, the teamwork concept must always stress the role of and authority of the pilot-in-command, and conversely, educate the pilot-in-command of the need to encourage and receive feedback from other flightcrew members... The consequences of an ill-conceived cockpit resource management program could very well be a captain who does not command properly or an overly assertive or dominant first officer who contributes to the problem and not the solution.*
>
> FAA (1986)

Although perhaps isolated instances, accident investigations have revealed reluctance on the part of the captain to assert his/her authority. One example is the December 2005 accident involving Southwest Airlines Flight 1248 in Chicago, IL. On this winter evening, a B-737-700 overran the runway at Chicago Midway Airport (NTSB, 2007c). During the en route phase of the flight, the captain indicated his reluctance to land with the minimal runway stopping margins presented by the onboard performance computer, and checked into the various options for diverting. The captain also stated

---

11. NTSB Safety Recommendation A-86-019 was issued to FAA following the crash of a Lockheed Electra in 1985 at Reno, NV. In the recommendation letter to FAA, NTSB, commented that "The Board believes that this accident again demonstrates the need for training in crew coordination or cockpit resource management, a need that has been identified in past accidents" (NTSB, 1986, p. 34). Safety Recommendation A-86-019 recommended that FAA "Provide, to all operators, guidance on topics and training in cockpit resource management so that operators can provide such training to their flightcrew members, until such time as the FAA's formal study of the topic is completed" (NTSB, 1986, p. 43).

discomfort in using the autobrakes for the first time for this landing,[12] and later stated his decision to use the manual brakes instead. The first officer provided indirect pressure to continue with the landing, reiterating several times that the flight operations manual authorized the landing based on the calculations, as well as the use of autobrakes. Instead of following through with his initial impressions of what was most appropriate or safe, the captain allowed the first officer to convince him otherwise, stating: "Well, keep talkin', I, I, I guess we could do it. Let's, let's see what the conditions are up there. We'll do it. If you're comfortable with that, I am too" (NTSB, 2007c, p. 142).

AC 120-51E states that, as a part of the captain's preflight briefing, "bottom lines for safety are established and communicated." In this case, the captain failed to establish acceptable minimums for safety with the first officer. He stated his level of discomfort, yet still allowed the first officer to talk him into conducting an unsafe operation, as if the decision-making process required consensus. He had the authority to carry out the actions that seemed more sensible and safe, but he did not act upon on it. The NTSB's accident report cited the contributing role of the crew's failure to divert to another airport.

Research in the area of decision-making indicates a tendency for more risky decisions among groups than among individuals. When reaching consensus, the final decision polarizes towards the most risky attitudes among the various group members (Moscovici & Zavalloni, 1969), regardless of whether the leader or another group member is the one with the most risky attitude (Hoyt & Stoner, 1968). This research highlights the need for the captain to be cognizant of, and counteract, this tendency by exercising his/her leadership role as the final authority for setting the safety minimums for each flight, and to use information from others to increase safety margins, versus decrease them. This tendency towards risky decisions in groups should be a special consideration when investigating events for long-endurance international flights that require additional flight crew. The social dynamics of decision-making with one captain and three captain-rated first officers are unique, and would make it even more challenging for a captain who didn't exhibit strong leadership skills. Again, the intention is not for group consensus on the flight deck, which may tend toward a more risky option, but for the PIC to take authority in reaching the safest decision given all available information.

The accident involving Shuttle America Flight 6448, operating as a Delta Connection, is another example of ceding leadership responsibility (NTSB, 2008). This accident, which also involved a runway overrun in winter conditions, occurred in February 2007 at Cleveland Hopkins International Airport,

---

12. The use of autobrakes was a new company procedure that had not previously been used by this crew.

OH. Fortunately, there were only minor injuries. Heavy snow was falling at the airport which reduced visibility to between ¼ and ½ mile. The captain, as the PM, was clearly uncomfortable with the approach. Weather was reported at minimums, and the glideslope unusable, and he was concerned about their rate of descent. "This is just, feels wrong," he stated. After passing the final approach fix, the crew received an updated report that weather conditions were below that required for the approach.[13] As they continued the approach, the captain stated, "This is # up," followed by, "I'm gonna go ahead and ... tell 'em I missed up here," referring to his desire to execute a missed approach (go-around). In spite of the captain's statement and concern, he allowed the first officer, the PF, to continue the approach.

The crew was unable to obtain the required visuals until the moment after they received the "two hundred, minimums" electronic callout. At this point, the captain confirmed having the runway lights in sight, although immediately afterwards stated that he couldn't see the runway and called for a "go-around." The first officer responded that he had the end of the runway in sight and elected to continue with the landing. The captain questioned the first officer's ability to see the runway, but allowed the landing to continue. Both pilots later admitted that they lost visual contact after descending below decision altitude.[14] Given their inability to determine the aircraft's location over the runway, the landing flare was unduly extended, resulting in the aircraft landing approximately halfway down the runway. By this time, there was insufficient runway remaining and the aircraft departed the runway's end.

In this case, the first officer was responsible for responding to the captain's command by immediate initiation of missed approach or "go-around" procedures. Unfortunately, the captain's call for a missed approach was less than assertive,[15] and he made no attempt to reconfirm this decision, nor did he take command of the aircraft when the first officer failed to respond. The captain is responsible for using his authority and leadership role to ensure the safety of the flight, which involves making command decisions that err on the side of safety, versus conceding to the most risky attitudes or behaviors among crew members (Fig. 18.1).

---

13. The crew confirmed with one another that they were legal to land once past the final approach fix, as long as the weather conditions reported prior to this point met the approach requirements. This is consistent with FAA and Shuttle America guidance.
14. According to FAA requirements (14 CFR 91.175) and company procedures, if sufficient visual references are not distinctly visible at or below the decision altitude (DA) or minimum descent altitude (MDA), execution of a missed approach is required.
15. According to the CVR, the captain stated, "I can't see the runway, dude, let's go [around]." This is not in accordance with AC 120-51E, which states that crewmembers must advocate in a clear, unambiguous terms, the course of action they feel is best, even when it involves conflict with others. This callout also did not comply with standard terminology for a missed approach.

FIGURE 18.1 Shuttle America at Cleveland, Ohio. *Credit: NTSB.*

In establishing the leadership role, the captain has the responsibility to set the tone for how the flight will be conducted. AC 120-51E states that the tone in the cockpit should be "friendly, relaxed, and supportive" (FAA, 2004, p. 11). But it also points out that the crew must ensure that cockpit discipline is maintained, crew vigilance is not reduced, and critical items are not missed. This is an important balance to achieve.

In August 2006, 49 people lost their lives in Lexington, KY because of the crew's overly relaxed conduct and lack of vigilance to critical items (NTSB, 2007a). At six minutes after six in the morning, the captain of the Comair Flight 5191 aligned the Bombardier Regional Jet onto a runway at Lexington, KY and turned control over to the first officer. As the first officer advanced thrust for takeoff, neither pilot was aware they were initiating the takeoff roll on the wrong runway—a runway that lacked sufficient length for the aircraft to safely depart.

As they began their take-off role, the first officer sensed something was not right, commenting that the runway was not lighted. "[That] is weird with no lights." "Yeah," responded the captain. The takeoff roll continued and the aircraft was rapidly approaching the end of the runway. With urgency in his voice, the captain called that the aircraft had reached flying speed, but he did so several knots early, "V1 Rotate, Whooo." The jet plowed through an open field at the runway end, and careened into a rising hillside. An immediate and devastating fire erupted, and of 50 passengers and crew onboard, only one survived. The investigation revealed that, from the time they recognized the absence of lights, the crew still had eight seconds during which they could have safely rejected the takeoff and remained on the runway.

The NTSB determined that the casual cockpit atmosphere, created by the captain, contributed to a reduced vigilance for the crew in conducting the preflight tasks. The captain told the first officer several times, "at your leisure," or "finish it up at your leisure," with regard to his performing checklists. The casual tone began prior to engine start and continued throughout the preflight and taxi phases of flight, with continual nonpertinent conversation during the entire preflight check. In setting an overly casual and relaxed tone in the cockpit, the captain set the stage for relaxed standards, and a lack of vigilance to their position on the airport.

Years ago, then-NTSB Board Member John Lauber (a true pioneer in CRM development) put this in perspective: "There is a fine line separating a relaxed and easy atmosphere in a cockpit from a lax one where distractions can result in critical failures. Professionalism may be described as knowing the difference between the two" (Lauber, 1989). It is the captain's leadership responsibility to maintain the proper balance in setting the tone, with the goal of achieving only the highest level of safety standard.

18.2.2 Communication

Effective communications are crucial in safety-critical operations, such as piloting an aircraft, manning the bridge of a ship, or performing surgery. Because communications are the means by which individuals share information about their intentions, expectations, and instructions, when breakdowns in communications occur, it can have deadly consequences.

The most deadly aircraft accident in history, the runway collision between two jumbo jets at Tenerife, Canary Islands, stemmed from ineffective communications on several fronts (Comisión de Investigación de Accidentes e Incidentes de Aviación Civil, 1978). The captain of the KLM Boeing 747 thought he was cleared for takeoff, when in actuality, the air traffic controller had only issued instructions for what the KLM flight should do *after* receiving takeoff clearance—which had not been issued because another aircraft was taxiing on the same runway. Believing his aircraft was cleared for takeoff, the captain shoved the throttles forward to commence takeoff roll. The two jumbo jets collided on the fog-shrouded runway and 583 lives were lost. But, not only was there ineffective communications between the air traffic controller and the KLM cockpit, but breakdowns in communications also existed within the cockpit of the KLM 747, as well. The first officer and flight engineer both had doubts about whether they were cleared for takeoff (they weren't), but they failed to effectively communicate their concerns to the captain. The NTSB describes this tendency to not speak in clear, unambiguous terms when attempting to voice concerns as *mitigated speech.*

Mitigated speech is when a person speaks in a deferential way either to be polite or to show deference to authority. Junior officers would be more likely to make suggestive remarks to the captain or to speak in the form of questions rather than make actionable statements. They would defer to the person in authority to decide instead of proposing an action themselves.

NTSB (2017, p. 210)

The tendency to use mitigated speech has been seen in accident after accident, and attempting to overcome this tendency was one of the primary forces that led to the initial development of CRM. In the 1978 crash of the United Airlines DC-8 in Portland, OR, as with the Tenerife accident, the first officer and flight engineer used mitigated speech, offering only subtle hints to the captain that their airplane was critically low on fuel (NTSB, 1979). Ten lives were lost when the aircraft exhausted its fuel supply and crashed into a wooded area.

An analysis of communication between crew members can play a valuable role in accident investigation, keeping in mind that not all communication is verbal. In the case of US Airways Flight 1549, with a successful landing on the Hudson River, much of their communication was nonverbal, and involved only limited discussion late in the event sequence regarding the best path forward. The only nonessential verbal communication between the captain and first officer was captured by the cockpit voice recorder (CVR) at 22 seconds prior to touchdown on the river: "Do you have any good ideas?" Many other nonverbal cues would have had to occur for this successful outcome, such as listening to and watching each other carry out interactions with ATC and completing checklists.

A wealth of research has been conducted regarding flight crew communication and team functioning (Foushee & Manos, 1981; Kanki & Palmer, 1993), to include information from CVRs of commercial air transport accidents (Goguen, Linde, & Murphy, 1986), some with a specific focus on catastrophic events and communication during high workload conditions (Kanki, 1996; Predmore, 1991). "Because verbal communication is so often the means by which flight crews perform their tasks, patterns of speech are potential indicators of how crewmembers coordinate their work, how they relate to each other and others in the system" (Kanki, 1996).

Research conducted by Foushee and Manos (1981) found that improved performance was associated with crews who utilized patterns of communication that lead to a shared mental model, to include verbal observations about flight status, acknowledgments of messages received from other crewmembers, requests and sequence for information and verification, and verbal agreements. The most effective captains clearly articulate their plans and strategies (Foushee & Manos, 1981). "This articulation helps to build a shared mental model for the situation. It enables the first officer to make suggestions, coordinate actions, and offer information that contributes to solving the problem and making decisions" (Orasanu, 1990). According to Orasanu, shared mental models assures that all participants are solving the same problem, and create a context in which all can contribute efficiently.

One particular analysis that highlights the distinct, yet critical, elements of communication between flight crew was conducted on the accident of US Air Flight 427. The cause of the accident was a malfunction of the Boeing 737 rudder, which resulted in an uncontrolled nose-down descent into terrain near Aliquippa, PA in 1994. At the request of the NTSB, Kanki (1996) examined three aspects of speech acts: (1) task-related speech, which describes crew coordination during routine flight conditions, as well as problem-solving during the emergency conditions; (2) procedural speech, which describes adherence to regulations, policies, and protocol; and (3) nontask-related speech, which describes general cockpit atmosphere and interpersonal relationships among crewmembers. She concluded that "there is casual, friendly interaction among both pilots and flight attendant, implying that, at least on a professional level, there is no particular social barrier or problem that would impede their working together during the emergency" (Kanki, 1996, p. 1). This was just another piece of the puzzle that helped investigators determine how the crew was functioning as a team prior to the upset event.

Just as Kanki did, analysis of these three aspects may be a useful tool for accident investigations, as well as those involved in training and evaluating of CRM performance.

18.2.3 Adherence to Standard Operating Procedures

Another integral component of CRM is adhering to SOPs. According to AC 120-51E, "CRM training is most effective within a training program centered on clear, comprehensive SOPs" (FAA, 2004, p. 6). Further, "A captain's briefing should reaffirm established SOPs" (p. 10) and "sets expectations for handling deviations from SOPs" (FAA, 2004, p. 1). Therefore, each crew member is responsible for carrying out the procedures and guidelines set by the company in a routine and professional manner, and any exceptions to this guidance should be discussed, or, at a minimum, acknowledged and articulated.

The tendency to disregard company guidance has a quantifiable impact on the safety of operations. In 1993, Boeing analyzed 138 airline accidents that claimed over 5600 lives over a 10-year period. The highest accident causal factor (48%) was failure of the PF to follow SOPs (Weener, 1993). In another study, intentional crew noncompliance was a factor in 39.5% of accidents reviewed by researchers using a global fatal accident database (Khatwa & Helmreich, 1999). Furthermore, data from the line operations safety audit (LOSA) Collaborative shows the importance of following SOPs (NTSB, 2007a): Specifically, analysis of LOSA data from over 20,000 line flights, where trained observers rode in cockpit jump seats and performed audits, revealed that flight crewmembers that intentionally deviated from SOPs were three times more likely to commit other types of errors, mismanage more errors, and find themselves in more undesired aircraft situations, compared with those flight crewmembers that did not intentionally deviate from procedures.[16]

The failure to adhere to SOPs is seen all too frequently in aircraft accidents. In the Comair accident mentioned previously, the investigation revealed that the captain failed to follow company procedures for performing taxi briefings, calling for checklists, and in respecting the "sterile cockpit" rules prohibiting extraneous activities (e.g., conversation) during critical phases of flight.[17] The NTSB concluded that "the flight crew's noncompliance with SOPs, including the captain's abbreviated taxi briefing and both pilots' nonpertinent conversation, most likely created an atmosphere in the cockpit that enabled the crew's errors" (NTSB, 2007a, p. 73).

Adherence to SOP continues to be identified in accidents. In May 2014, a Gulfstream G4 crashed after overrunning the runway during a takeoff attempt—as a result of the crew's failure to follow checklists and SOPs. The flight crew attempted to depart without disengaging the flight control gust lock, a key element of preflight checklists for any airplane. After discovering that the gust lock was on, instead of rejecting the takeoff, the crew continued to troubleshoot the issue while accelerating down the runway. The delayed and poorly executed rejected takeoff led to a high-speed overrun, decelerating from around 90 knots to a complete standstill almost instantaneously. The aircraft was immediately consumed in fire, costing the lives of all seven onboard (NTSB, 2015).

Releasing the gust lock was the fourth item on both the G4 Starting Engines checklist contained in the airplane flight manual, and the checklist used by the pilots in training. The CVR revealed that not only was this checklist not verbalized, but neither were any of the four remaining checklists. Although it is possible the checklists were accomplished silently, this would have been contrary to their training, which called for "challenge-response" checklist execution. The NTSB noted there was no discussion of checklists before, during, or after engine start or throughout taxi, and there were no statements to denote the checklists were completed. The NTSB concluded "the crewmembers' lack of adherence to industry best practices involving the execution of normal checklists eliminated the opportunity for them to recognize that the gust lock handle was in the ON position and delayed their detection of this error" (NTSB, 2015, p. 38).

---

16. See page 73 of the Lexington, KY, Comair Accident Report: NTSB (2007a).
17. Federal Aviation Regulation 121.542 prohibits flight crews from engaging in nonessential activities, including conversation, during critical phases of flight. Critical phase of flight includes taxi and operations conducted below 10,000 feet msl.

FIGURE 18.2 Gulfstream G4 at Bedford. *Credit: NTSB.*

Based on information from the flight data recorder, investigators learned that the crew did not accomplish a flight control check to check for freedom of movement of the controls. An even more troubling discovery was made by the NTSB: of the 175 previous flights for this crew, a complete flight control check was skipped on all but two flights.[18] "Given that the flight crew neglected to perform complete flight control checks in 98% of the crewmembers' previous 175 takeoffs in the airplane, the flight crew's omission of a flight control check before the accident takeoff indicates intentional, habitual noncompliance with SOPs" (NTSB, 2015, p. 34) (Fig. 18.2).

In the Shuttle America Flight 6448 mentioned earlier, the crew failed to observe sterile cockpit procedures during the descent, elected to ignore reports of the unusable glideslope, and continued the approach to the lower ILS minimum decision altitude. Had they flown to the higher Localizer minimum descent altitude, as was required, the reduced visibility at that altitude would have required them to initiate a missed approach.[19]

---

18. In addition to a FDR which stored the last 25 hours of flight data, the accident aircraft was also equipped with a Quick Access Recorder (QAR) which stored flight data for the past 303 flight hours and 176 takeoff events, including the attempted accident flight. QARs often are used in flight data monitoring programs such as Flight Operational Quality Assurance (FOQA) programs.
19. According to the NTSB report, the flight crew would have been required to execute a missed approach if they had been using the localizer MDA of 429' agl, as there was no evidence from the CVR or postaccident interviews that either crewmember had the runway environment in sight by that altitude. The decision to continue the landing was made after the electronic callout "two hundred — minimums" based on the MDA of 227' agl for the ILS approach.

The crews in these examples committed multiple deviations from SOPs, further supporting the premise that SOP deviations decrease safety margins and increase opportunities for an accident.

An accident involving a charter flight operated by Execuflight provides a final example of an accident combining failures in leadership and lack of adherence to SOPs. This accident occurred in 2015, when a Hawker 700A crashed into a neighborhood in Akron, OH (NTSB, 2016). The lives of the nine passengers and crew were lost. The investigation found multiple deviations from SOPs, including continuing the instrument approach despite the approach being unstabilized. The entire approach was flown well below the reference approach speed. Upon reaching the minimum descent altitude, when the pitch attitude was increased to arrest the descent, the aircraft stalled and aircraft control was lost. Investigators noted that the captain should have called for a missed approach, but failed to do so. "The repeated deviations from sound operational practices identified in this investigation indicate a culture of complacency and disregard for rules, signifying the need for strong leadership" (NTSB, 2016, p. 52).

As mentioned earlier, the investigation must not stop at simply finding that CRM and procedural compliance were lacking. That finding, in itself, does not accomplish the goal of trying to learn from the mishap so similar events can be prevented. Investigators must go the additional steps of trying to understand why these aspects were insufficient. For the Akron crash, the NTSB found the Execuflight crew's poor CRM was, in part, due to the charter operator's poor CRM training program: "Deficiencies in Execuflight's CRM training program, including the cursory review of CRM topics, the lack of appropriate evaluation of CRM examinations, and the lack of continual reinforcement of CRM principles, resulted in the flight crew receiving inadequate CRM training" (NTSB, 2016, p. 49). They also noted that "Execuflight's management had multiple opportunities to identify and correct the flight crew's routine disregard for SOPs regarding preflight planning but failed to do so" (NTSB, 2016, p. 51). This accident highlights the role of both the individual and the organization in developing and reinforcing strong and consistent attitudes and behaviors towards following procedures.

A government/industry working group attributed the following four factors that can contribute to crew's failure to follow SOPs: (1) procedures misaligned to operational situations; (2) workload preventing completion of the procedures; (3) procedures that are too prescriptive or detailed; and (4) no adverse consequences associated with not following the SOP (PARC/CAST, 2013).

Investigators found evidence of some of these factors in the accident involving Southwest Flight 1248. Conflicting procedures were identified across sections of the flight manual, and this guidance did not match the operational situation. To advise crews to land with a mere calculated 50' runway distance remaining when using maximum autobrakes puts the flight deck leadership at odds with the guidance to make responsible and safe decisions.

18.3 SITUATION AWARENESS

Situation awareness (SA) is a term that is perhaps overused and likely means different things to different people. For purposes of discussion in this chapter, it simply means having an accurate, clear understanding of what is going on around you, and being able to reasonably project that understanding to know what will likely happen in the future. To increase likelihood of increased levels of SA, a person must acquire information, process it, and then decide what to do with it. Factors that can affect flight crew SA are discussed in this section, including monitoring of the aircraft flight path, workload management, and managing flight deck automation. To be clear, however, the items discussed in the previous section (leadership, communications, and adherence to SOPs) are also essential components of maintaining SA. Each of these items are interrelated. For example, poor leadership could lead to an overrelaxed cockpit environment, which results in not following SOPs. This could result in delaying doing a checklist until a high workload period, which leads to the pilot becoming task saturated. In the haste to accomplish the checklist with increased workload, the pilot relaxes his scan of flight instruments and missed the fact that the autothrottles are in an inactive mode and don't increase thrust, as expected. Airspeed rapidly decays and the aircraft stalls at low altitude. These are not just abstract concepts—the above scenario blends together several actual accident scenarios.

18.3.1 Monitoring of the Aircraft Flight Path

An important element of SA is knowing the current state of the aircraft flight path and energy state, and being able to project that into the future. To do that, it is essential that pilots monitor the aircraft flight path by scanning the flight instruments and comprehending their meaning. AC 120-51E considers the monitoring function an essential primary flight duty:

> *To ensure the highest levels of safety, each flight crewmember must carefully monitor the aircraft's flight path and systems and actively cross-check the actions of other crewmembers. Effective monitoring and cross-checking can be the last line of defense that prevents an accident because detecting an error or unsafe situation may break the chain of events leading to an accident.*
>
> FAA (2004, p. 14)

Accident investigations have long identified ineffective flight crew monitoring of the aircraft flight path to be problematic. A seminal accident occurred in December 1972, when the flight crew of an Eastern Airlines

Lockheed 1011 crashed into the Florida Everglades. According to the NTSB (1973), while attempting to replace a faulty landing gear indicator light, one of the flight crewmembers inadvertently bumped the control column, forcing the autopilot out of the altitude hold mode and placing it into a gradual descent. Because of their preoccupation with replacing the jammed light assembly for over 4 minutes, the crew did not notice the descent into the dark, featureless terrain. The aircraft careened into the Everglades, claiming 99 lives (NTSB, 1973). The NTSB determined the probable cause of the accident was: "The failure of the flight crew to monitor the flight instruments during the final 4 minutes of flight; and, to detect an unexpected descent soon enough to prevent impact with the ground. Preoccupation with a malfunction of the nose landing gear position indicating system distracted the crew's attention from the instruments and allowed the descent to go unnoticed" (NTSB, 1973, pp. 23−24).

Ineffective flight path monitoring has continued to be a factor in accidents. In a study of crew-involved air carrier accidents, NTSB (1994b) determined that inadequate monitoring and challenging was a factor in 31 of the 37 (84%) accidents reviewed. Since that study, there have been at least 10 high-profile accidents attributed to inadequate flight path monitoring (Sumwalt, 2014).

Once such crash was the 2013 Asiana Airlines Boeing 777 accident at San Francisco International Airport, CA (NTSB, 2014a). Poor monitoring of airspeed was found to be a factor in that crash. Six weeks after the Asiana crash, an Airbus A-300-600, operated by United Parcel Service (UPS), crashed at Birmingham, AL. Investigators determined that "the flightcrew did not sufficiently monitor the airplane's altitude during the approach and subsequently allowed the airplane to descend below the minimum altitude without having the runway environment in sight" (NTSB, 2014b, p. 87). The airplane impacted the ground, claiming the lives of both crewmembers.

In 2003, the FAA published AC 120-71A, *Standard Operating Procedures for Flight Deck Crewmembers*, where they recognized the wisdom of changing the title of "pilot-not-flying" to "PM."

It is increasingly acknowledged that it makes better sense to characterize pilots by what they are doing rather than by what they are not doing. Hence, PF remains an appropriate term and is unchanged in this AC. But the term pilot not flying misses the point. Studies of crew performance, accident data, and pilots' own experiences all point to the vital role of the nonflying pilot as a monitor. Hence, the term PM is now widely viewed as a better term to describe that pilot. (FAA, 2003, p. 1)

There have also been updates to guidance focusing on improving scenario-based training. Following a 2005 accident involving a Cessna Citation 560 at Pueblo, CO (NTSB, 2007b), in which the crew failed to monitor the approach speed in icing conditions and allowed the aircraft to slow to a speed below the normal approach speed,[20] NTSB issued Safety Recommendation A-07-13 to the FAA. That recommendation called for all pilot training programs to be modified to contain modules that teach and emphasize monitoring skills and workload management and include opportunities to practice and demonstrate proficiency in these areas. Following the 2009 crash of Colgan Air near Buffalo, NY, where investigators determined the crew failed to monitor airspeed (NTSB, 2010b),[21] in 2013 the FAA published a final training rule that will require air carriers to incorporate explicit training pertaining to improving monitoring (NARA, 2013). This training must be incorporated into airline training programs by March 2019 (NARA, 2013).

18.3.2 Workload Management

CRM training should emphasize workload management, vigilance, and distraction avoidance (FAA, 2004). Numerous accident investigations have found that poor workload management can set the stage for accidents, primarily because the crew's attention is diverted from accomplishing safety critical functions, including monitoring the aircraft flight path (NTSB, 1973, 1979, 1986, 1994a, 1994b, 2003, 2006, 2007b, 2010b, 2011). Raby and Wickens (1994) examined how pilots strategically planned workload and allocated tasks to accommodate increasing workload. They noted that crews who experienced highest workload were those who had the greatest tendency to delay critical tasks until later in the flight. In similar manner, the higher performing crews were those who performed tasks earlier.

In the Colgan Air crash investigation, NTSB noted that the crew did not accomplish the descent checklist at an optimal time. Thus, late in the approach, the crew's workload increased as they attempted to cram in doing this checklist along with other tasks. Their workload was further exacerbated by their decision to engage in nonpertinent conversation at an inopportune time. "As part of his overall workload management responsibilities, the captain should have been cognizant of the tasks that he requested the first officer to perform and their effect on her ability to reliably provide the expected monitoring and cross-check" (NTSB, 2010b, p. 92). "Because of their conversation, the flight crewmembers squandered time and their attention, which were limited resources that should have been used for attending to

---

20. Given the icing conditions, the crew should have maintained an even higher approach speed.
21. NTSB determined that "the failure of both pilots to detect [the low speed situation] was the result of a significant breakdown in their monitoring responsibilities and workload management" (NTSB, 2010b, p. 151). NTSB stated: "The monitoring errors made by the accident flight crew demonstrate the continuing need for specific pilot training on active monitoring skills" (NTSB, 2010b, p. 152) and reiterated Safety Recommendation A-07-13.

operational tasks, monitoring, maintaining situational awareness, managing possible threats, and preventing potential errors" (NTSB, 2010b, p. 93).

High workload can lead to increased dwelling on a particular task and postponing the initiation of other critical tasks (Raby & Wickens, 1994) and in multitasking, high levels of workload can lead to task shedding. This can lead to the abandonment of one task, to focus on the task inducing the high workload. In the wake of their investigation of the Colgan Air crash, NASA scientist Key Dismukes testified before the NTSB:

> If we're in the middle of a task and something interrupts us, and the interruption is typically very salient, very abrupt, so we turn our attention to this interruption, take care of the interruption, but then after we're finished with that, it is very, very easy to get sucked into the next task in the queue, forgetting that we didn't finish that task that was interrupted.
>
> NTSB (2009, p. 580)

Sumwalt (2014) found that even necessary flight-related functions such as programming Flight Management Systems (FMS), radio calls, and accomplishing checklists, can detract from flight path monitoring. "While conduct of these duties is necessary, in several [studied incident reports] it appears that pilots became consumed in these activities and allowed scan of flight instruments to drop. They must not be done at the expense of monitoring" (Sumwalt, 2014, p. 50). Although there are numerous examples, the following two accidents provide vivid illustrations of this point.

In December 1993, a Jetstream 31 crashed at Hibbing, MN. This air carrier flight was operated by Express II Airlines/Northwest Airlink (NTSB, 1994a). During a nighttime localizer back-course instrument approach to Runway 13, the captain became involved in directing the first officer to select the common traffic advisory frequency (CTAF) and to illuminate the runway lights by clicking the aircraft microphone seven times. While being distracted by this discussion, the crew allowed the aircraft to be flown into the ground 2.8 miles from the runway threshold. All 18 occupants perished. The captain was busy instructing the first officer how to carry out this task, a task which he already knew how to do. Further, when already under high workload, the addition of another perceptual task, even in a different modality, can increase workload higher and lead to shedding of tasks altogether (McKendrick et al., 2016). In this case, the task of monitoring instruments was shed.

The second example is the 2004 accident of a Sikorsky S-76A operated under Part 135 operations. During an over-water flight in the Gulf of Mexico, the crew established a rate of descent appropriate for a planned stop at an oil platform for fuel. Given the favorable wind conditions, they opted instead to fly directly to their destination platform. The crew changed their heading and began to discuss details associated with the change in route, during which time the rotorcraft slowly descended to the water at cruise airspeed. All 10 on board perished. As so many accident reports before had concluded, this investigation ended with the words: "The Safety Board concludes that the flight crew was not adequately monitoring the helicopter's altitude and missed numerous cues to indicate that the helicopter was inadvertently descending toward the water" (NTSB, 2006, p. 45).

Sumwalt (2014) found that in a quarter of the accidents he studied which involved inadequate monitoring, the pilots were dealing with resolving an aircraft abnormality or malfunction when a significant flight path deviation occurred that led to the crash. Evidence of such was particularly noted in the 1972 Eastern Airlines crash into the Florida Everglades. Recall that in that crash, the pilots were involved with attempting to replace a faulty landing gear indicator light (NTSB, 1973). Likewise, the NTSB stated the following in completing their investigation of an ATR-42 crash at Lubbock, TX:

> Previous accidents have shown that pilots can become distracted from flying duties when an emergency or abnormal situation occurs, and literature suggests that one of the biggest hazards of "abnormals" is becoming distracted from other cockpit duties. While flying the approach, the first officer was likely distracted from monitoring the instruments by the flap anomaly, the captain's nonstandard actions involving the circuit breakers, and the control force inputs needed to maintain control of the airplane because of the flap asymmetry. Further, for the captain to check circuit breakers behind the first officer's seat, he would need to turn away from the instrument panel, a position from which monitoring the instruments was not possible.
>
> NTSB (2011, pp. 57–58)

18.3.3 Managing Flight Deck Automation

In testimony to the NTSB regarding the Colgan Air crash, Dismukes referred to automation as being a "double-edge sword" (NTSB, 2009, p. 579). "It gives us lots of advantages. It can reduce workload. It can fly the plane more precisely, but it puts us a step away from the system, and that makes monitoring even more challenging" (NTSB, 2009, p. 579).

Poor monitoring of automation can be related to overtrust of automation (Parasuraman, 2000). "This result of overtrust or 'complacency' is greatest when the operator is engaged in multiple tasks and less apparent when monitoring the automated system is the only task that the operator has to perform" (Parasuraman, Sheridan, & Wickens, 2000, p. 291).

In the Asiana Boeing 777 crash mentioned earlier, investigators concluded that overreliance in automation contributed to inadequate monitoring of the airspeed (NTSB, 2014a) (Fig. 18.3).

> Human factors research has demonstrated that system operators often become complacent about monitoring highly reliable automated systems when they

FIGURE 18.3   Asiana crash at San Francisco International Airport. *Credit: NTSB.*

> *develop a high degree of trust in those systems and when manual tasks compete with automated tasks for operator attention.... Attentional resources are limited, so shifting them away from automated tasks and toward manually controlled tasks during periods of increased workload can be viewed as adaptive because one of the functions of automation is to ease operator workload. However, the use of such systems has predictable adverse consequences on human performance. Specifically, it reduces monitoring and decreases the likelihood that a human operator will detect signs of anomalous or unexpected system behavior involving the processes under automatic control. In this case, the PF, PM, and observer believed the [autothrottle] system was controlling speed with thrust, they had a high degree of trust in the automated system, and they did not closely monitor these parameters during a period of elevated workload. Thus, the flight crew's inadequate monitoring of airspeed and thrust indications appears to fit this pattern involving automation overreliance.*
>
> (NTSB, 2014a, p. 90)

18.4   MORE TO BE DONE

In 2014, the Commercial Aviation Safety Team (CAST) of aviation industry stakeholders, comprised of 16 agencies and corporations worldwide, published a report of findings and recommendations after intense study of factors that contribute to effective Airplane State Awareness (ASA). As a subset of Loss of Inflight Control, the 18 ASA events (accidents and incidents) were limited to those in which the flight crew lost awareness of their airplane state, defined as attitude (pitch or bank angle or rate) or energy (the combination of airspeed, altitude, vertical speed, thrust, and airplane configuration).

CRM was determined to play a role in 16 of the 18 accidents, and flight crew distraction in 16 of the 18. Recommendations were issued that impact CRM training overall and its subelements.

One such recommendation called for enhanced CRM training, whereby air carriers and other training providers, as well as regulators, enhance acceptance, utilization, and effectiveness of CRM principles by revising curriculum content and delivery. These principles should provide clear, unambiguous roles for the PF and PM in normal and nonnormal operations (CAST, 2014).

Another recommendation stressed the need for air carriers to develop and implement improved SOPs, as well as taking measures to increase flight crew adherence to SOPs (CAST, 2014). The CAST also called for further research on flight crew performance. According to the CAST recommendation, government, industry, and academia should perform research to enhance tools and methods for collecting and analyzing flight crew performance data in situations associated with loss of energy and/or attitude state awareness, suitable for use in the design process. Finally, given that attention management, workload management, and interruptions appears to be factors prevalent in accidents, the CAST called for research into how to improve training for attention management (CAST, 2014).

18.5 SUMMARY

The very need for CRM grew, in part, from accident investigations. No doubt, aviation safety has greatly benefitted from the incorporation of CRM. However, as evidenced by cases profiled in this chapter, breakdowns in principles of CRM can lead to bad outcomes. The perspective of the accident investigator is to identify these breakdowns and make recommendations to improve safety. In some ways, it may seem ironic that safety has improved because of accidents. But, that is precisely the objective of accident investigations—to learn these hard lessons so future accidents are prevented. A saying that is attributed to many sources, says it well: "Learn from the mistakes of others. You won't live long enough to make them all yourself." We hope the lessons presented in this chapter can be used to keep others from making the same mistakes.

REFERENCES

CAST. (2014). Airplane state awareness joint safety implementation team final report. *Commercial Aviation Safety Team (CAST)*. Washington, DC.

Comisión de Investigación de Accidentes e Incidentes de Aviación Civil [CIAIAC]. (1978). *Joint Report: K.L. M. − P.A.A. Collision Aeronaves, Boeing 747 PH-BUF DE, K.L.M. Y Boeing 747, N737 PA de PANAM, en Los Rodeos (Tenerife). El 27 de Marzo de 1.977.*

FAA. (1986). *Correspondence from Honorable Jim Burnett to the Chairman of the NTSB concerning recommendations A-86-14 through -19, March 26, 1986.* Washington, DC: Federal Aviation Administration.

FAA. (2003). Standard operating procedures for flight deck crewmembers, *Advisory Circular 120-71A.* Washington, DC: Federal Aviation Administration.

FAA. (2004). Crew resource management training, *Advisory Circular 120-51E.* Washington, DC: Federal Aviation Administration.

FAA. (2015). Flightcrew member line operational simulations: Line-oriented flight training, special purpose operational training, line operational evaluation, *Advisory Circular 120-35D.* Washington, DC: Federal Aviation Administration.

Foushee, C. H., & Manos, K. L. (1981). Information transfer within the cockpit: Problems in intracockpit communications. In C. E. Billings, & E. S. Cheaney (Eds.), *Information transfer problems in the aviation system.* Moffett Field, CA: NASA, NASA Technical Paper 1875.

Goguen, J., Linde, C., & Murphy, M. (1986). Crew communication as a factor in aciation accidents. *(NASA Technical Report 88254).* Moffett Field, CA: NASA.

Hoyt, G., & Stoner, J. (1968). Leadership and group decisions involving risk. *Journal of Experimental Social Psychology, Vol. 4*(3), 275−284.

ICAO. (2016). *Annex 13: Aircraft Accident and Incident Investigation,* Eleventh Edition, July 2016, Montreal, Quebec, Canada: International Civil Aviation Organization.

Kanki, B.G. (1996). *Untitled report prepared at the request of the NTSB.* December 2, 1996.

Kanki, B. G., & Palmer, M. T. (1993). Communication and crew resource management. In E. L. Wiener, B. G. Kanki, & R. L. Helmreich (Eds.), *Cockpit resource management* (pp. 99−136). San Diego, CA: Academic Press.

Khatwa, R., & Helmreich, R. (1999). Killers in aviation: FSF task force presents facts about approach-and-landing and controlled-flight-into-terrain accidents. *Flight Safety Digest.* November 1998 − February, 1999. 17(11−12). pp. 1−77. Retrieved from http://flightsafety.org/fsd/fsd_nov-feb99.pdf.

Lauber, J. (1989). *Managing human error in flight operations. Proceedings from second conference of human error avoidance techniques, of SAE advances in aviation safety conference.* Warrendale, PA: Herndon, VA, Society of Automotive Engineers, September 18−19, 1989.

McKendrick, R., Parasuraman, R., Murtza, R., Formwalt, A., Baccus, W., Paczynski, M., & Ayaz, H. (2016). Into the wild: neuroergonomic differentiation of hand-held and augmented reality wearable displays during outdoor navigation with functional near infrared spectroscopy. *Frontiers in Human Neuroscience*, 10.

Moscovici, S., & Zavalloni, M. (1969). The group as a polarizer of attitudes. *Journal of Personality and Social Psychology, 12*(2), 125−135.

NARA. (2009, May 1). Department of Transportation, Federal Aviation Administration, Crew Resource Management Training for Crewmembers in Part 135 Operations; proposed rule. *Federal Register, 74*, 83.

NARA. (2011, January 21). Department of Transportation, Federal Aviation Administration, Crew Resource Management Training for Crewmembers in Part 135 Operations; final rule. *Federal Register, 76*, 14.

NARA. (2013, November 12). Department of Transportation, Federal Aviation Administration, 14 CFR Part 121 Qualification, service, and use of crewmembers and aircraft dispatchers; final rule. *Federal Register, 78*, 218.

NTSB. (1973). Eastern Air Lines, Inc., L-1011, N310EA, Miami, FL., December 29, 1972. *NTSB Report No. NTSB/AAR-73/14.* Washington, DC: National Transportation Safety Board.

NTSB. (1979). United Airlines, Inc., McDonnell- Douglas, DC-8-61, N8082U, Portland, Oregon, December 28, 1978, *NTSB Report Number: AAR-79-07*. Washington, DC: National Transportation Safety Board.

NTSB. (1986). Galaxy Airlines, Inc., Lockheed Electra L-188, N5532, Reno, Nevada, January 21, 1985. *Report Number: AAR-86-01*. Washington, DC: National Transportation Safety Board.

NTSB. (1990). United Airlines Flight 232 McDonnell Douglas DC-10-10 Sioux Gateway Airport, Sioux City, Iowa, July 19, 1989. *NTSB Report Number: AAR-90-06*. Washington, DC: National Transportation Safety Board.

NTSB. (1994a). Controlled Collision with Terrain Express II Airlines, Inc./ Northwest Airlink Flight 5719 Jetstream BA-3100, N334PX Hibbing, Minnesota, December 1, 1993, *NTSB Report Number: AAR-94-05*. Washington, DC: National Transportation Safety Board.

NTSB. (1994b). Safety Study: A Review of Flightcrew-Involved, Major Accidents of U.S. Air Carriers, 1978 through 1990, *NTSB Report Number: NTSB/SS-94/01*. Washington, DC: National Transportation Safety Board.

NTSB. (2001). Runway Overrun During Landing, American Airlines Flight 1420, McDonnell Douglas MD-82, N215AA, Little Rock, Arkansas, June 1, 1999, *NTSB Report Number: NTSB/AAR-01/02*. Washington, DC: National Transportation Safety Board.

NTSB. (2003). Loss of Control and Impact With Terrain Aviation Charter, Inc., Raytheon (Beechcraft) King Air A100, N41BE, Eveleth, Minnesota, October 25, 2002, *NTSB Report Number: AAR-03-03*. Washington, DC: National Transportation Safety Board.

NTSB. (2006). Controlled Flight into Terrain, Era Aviation, Sikorsky S-76A++, N579EH, Gulf of Mexico About 70 Nautical Miles South-Southeast of Scholes International Airport, Galveston, Texas, March 23, 2004, *NTSB Report Number: AAR-06-02*. Washington, DC: National Transportation Safety Board.

NTSB. (2007a). Attempted Takeoff From Wrong Runway Comair Flight 5191 Bombardier CL-600-2B19, N431CA Lexington, Kentucky, August 27, 2006, *NTSB Report Number: AAR-07-05*. Washington, DC: National Transportation Safety Board.

NTSB. (2007b). Crash During Approach to Landing, Circuit City Stores, Inc., Cessna Citation 560, N500AT, Pueblo, Colorado, February 16, 2005, *NTSB Report Number: AAR-07-02*. Washington, DC: National Transportation Safety Board.

NTSB. (2007c). Runway Overrun and Collision Southwest Airlines Flight 1248 Boeing 737-74H, N471WN Midway Airport Chicago, Illinois, December 8, 2005, *NTSB Report Number AAR-07-06*. Washington, DC: National Transportation Safety Board.

NTSB. (2008). Runway Overrun During Landing Shuttle America, Inc. Doing Business as Delta Connection Flight 6448 Embraer ERJ-170, N862RW Cleveland, Ohio, February 18, 2007, *NTSB Report Number AAR-08-01*. Washington, DC: National Transportation Safety Board.

NTSB. (2009). *Public hearing in the matter of: Colgan Air, Inc. Flight 3407, Bombardier DHC-400, N200WQ, Clarence Center, New York, February 12, 2009. Thursday, May 14, 2009.*

NTSB. (2010a). Loss of Thrust in Both Engines After Encountering a Flock of Birds and Subsequent Ditching on the Hudson River, US Airways Flight 1549, Airbus A320-214, N106US, Weehawken, New Jersey, January 15, 2009. *NTSB Report Number: AAR-10-03*. Washington, DC: National Transportation Safety Board.

NTSB. (2010b). Loss of Control on Approach Colgan Air, Inc. Operating as Continental Connection Flight 3407 Bombardier DHC-8-400, N200WQ, Clarence Center, New York, February 12, 2009, *NTSB Report Number: AAR-10-01*. Washington, DC: National Transportation Safety Board.

NTSB. (2011). Aircraft accident report: Crash during approach to landing, Empire Airlines flight 8284, Avions de Transport Régional Aerospatiale Alenia ATR 42-320, N902FX, Lubbock, Texas, January 27, 2009. *(NTSB Report No. NTSB/AAR-11/02)*. Washington, DC: Author.

NTSB. (2014a). Descent below visual glidepath and impact with seawall, Asiana Airlines flight 214, Boeing 777-200ER, HL7742, San Francisco International Airport, California, July 6, 2013. *NTSB Report No. NTSB/AAR-14/01*. Washington, DC: National Transportation Safety Board.

NTSB. (2014b). Crash During a Nighttime Nonprecision Instrument Approach to Landing, UPS Flight 1354, Airbus A300-600, N155UP, Birmingham, Alabama. August 14, 2013. *NTSB Report Number: AAR-14-02*. Washington, DC: National Transportation Safety Board.

NTSB. (2015). Runway Overrun During Rejected Takeoff Gulfstream Aerospace Corporation G-IV, N121JM, Bedford, Massachusetts, May 31, 2014. *NTSB Report Number: AAR-15-03*. Washington, DC: National Transportation Safety Board.

NTSB. (2016). Crash During Nonprecision Instrument Approach to Landing, Execuflight Flight 1526, British Aerospace HS 125-700A, N237WR. Akron, Ohio, November 10, 2015. *NTSB Accident Report Number AAR-16-03*. Washington, DC: National Transportation Safety Board.

NTSB. (2017). Sinking of US Cargo Vessel SS El Faro, Atlantic Ocean, Northeast of Acklins and Crooked Island, Bahamas, October 1, 2015. *NTSB Accident Report Number MAR-17-01*. Washington, DC: National Transportation Safety Board.

Orasanu, J. M. (1990). Shared Mental Models and Crew Decision Making *(Cognitive Science Laboratory Report #46)*. Princeton, NJ: Princeton University.

Parasuraman, R. (2000). Designing automation for human use: empirical studies and quantitative models. *Ergonomics, 43*(7), 931−951.

Parasuraman, R., Sheridan, T., & Wickens, C. (2000). A model for types and levels of human interaction with automation. *IEEE Transactions on Systems, Man, and Cybernetics − Part A: Systems and Humans, 30*(3), 286−297.

PARC/CAST. (2013). Operational use of flight path management systems. In *Final Report of the Performance-based operations Aviation Rulemaking Committee (PARC)/Commercial Aviation Safety Team (CAST) Flight Deck Automation Working Group*. Washington, DC.

Predmore, S. C. (1991). *Microcoding of communications in accident investigations: Crew coordination in United 811 and United 232. Proceedings of the sixth international symposium on aviation psychology*. Columbus, OH: Ohio State University.

Raby, M., & Wickens, C. (1994). Strategic workload management and decision biases in aviation. *International Journal of Aviation Psychology, 4*(3), 211−240.

Reason, J. (2008). *The human contribution: Unsafe acts, accidents and heroic recoveries*. Farnham, Surrey, United Kingdom: Ashgate.

Sumwalt, R. (2014). *Examining How Breakdowns in Pilot Monitoring of the Aircraft Flight Path can Lead to Flight Path Deviations*. Unpublished thesis submitted in partial fulfillment of the requirements of the Degree of Master of Aeronautical Science, Embry-Riddle Aeronautical University.

Weener, E. (1993). Accident prevention strategies. In *Proceedings of 46ᵗʰ Flight Safety Foundation International Air Safety Seminar*, November 9−11, 1993, Kuala Lampu, Malaysia.

Chapter 19

The Military Perspective

Paul O'Connor[1], Robert G. Hahn[2], Robert Nullmeyer[3] and Gregg Montijo[4]

[1]*National University of Ireland, Galway, Ireland,* [2]*US Navy School of Aviation Safety, Pensacola, FL, United States,* [3]*Aviation Programs, Arizona State University, Mesa, AZ, United States,* [4]*Crew Training International, Inc., Memphis, TN, United States*

INTRODUCTION

Crew resource management (CRM) training was first introduced in the US military in the late 1980s (Prince & Salas, 1993). The impetus for CRM training in the US military came directly from commercial aviation. Based upon civil aviation models, early CRM courses were not well received by all military aviators. However, in the early 1990s the US Army, Navy, and Air Force began funding CRM-related research, and great advances were made in terms of developing a research-based model for delivering effective military CRM training (see Prince & Salas, 1993 for a review). Researchers and military aviators developed a CRM program that consisted of basic concepts, academics, and skill sets relevant to the demands of military flight operations. In the US military, this model has remained largely unchanged for several decades. This research served as the basis for CRM training in many military services throughout the world. As the technology and complexity of military aircraft changed in the late 1980s and into the 1990s, the services each took different approaches for CRM training.

The purpose of this chapter is to update O'Connor, Hahn, and Nullmeyer's (2010) review of military CRM training, highlighting changes in Air Force CRM training over the past decade. The earlier chapter identified unique challenges encountered in military training, provided examples of how CRM training is currently being used in the world's militaries, and reviewed the evidence supporting the effectiveness of military CRM training.

19.1 CIVILIAN VERSUS MILITARY CRM TRAINING

Table 19.1 summarizes findings in seven studies of civilian and military mishaps where CRM failures were specifically categorized as causal factors. All

Crew Resource Management. DOI: https://doi.org/10.1016/B978-0-12-812995-1.00019-1

TABLE 19.1 A Comparison Between the Frequency With Which CRM Failures Are Identified in Aviation Mishaps Between Military and Civilian Organizations

Study	Domain Analyzed	CRM (Teamwork) Failure Cited	%
Hooper and O'Hare (2013)	193 Australian military fixed wing incidents 2001–08	46	23.8
	93 Australian military fixed wing incidents 2001–08	10	10.5
Li and Harris (2006)	523 Chinese military accidents/incidents	146	27.9
Gibb and Olson (2008)	124 US Air Force Class A accidents 1992–2005	56	45.2
Wiegmann and Shappell (1999)	226 US Navy Class A flight mishaps 1990–96	90	39.8
Total Military	**1159**	**348**	**30.0**
Shappell, et al. (2007)	181 US air carrier accidents 1990–2002	34	18.8
	839 commuter accidents 1990–2002	75	8.9
Gaur (2005)	48 Indian civil aircraft accidents	6	12.5
Shappell and Wiegmann (2001)	164 US general aviation accidents 1990–98	23	14
Total Civilian	**1232**	**138**	**11.2**

seven used a common classification system called the Human Factors Analysis and Classification System (HFACS). See Wiegmann and Shappell (2003) for more information. It should be noted that the HFACS structure used in each of these studies defined the term "CRM" in terms of crew coordination and communication (Gibb & Olson, 2008). Other common CRM-related elements such as decision-making errors and mental awareness are addressed in other parts of the HFACS taxonomy. The Department of Defense HFACS (DoD HFACS) structure now used by all United States military services renamed this topic area "Teamwork" rather than "CRM" (Naval Safety Center, 2014).

From Table 19.1, we see that teamwork failures tend to be identified more often in military as compared to civil aviation accident or incident reports. This may lead to the conclusion that CRM training in commercial aviation is more effective than military aviation. However, this is a vast oversimplification of the issue. One explanation for the differences in the proportion of teamwork-related mishaps may be the stark differences between the air carrier industry and military operations (see Prince & Salas, 1993 for a detailed discussion of these differences). One of the easiest differences to identify is the difference in age, maturity, and experience of the two pilot populations: military aviators are usually younger and less experienced compared to their civilian counterparts. Up until the proliferation of the two-pilot cockpit, many commercial pilots had to work their way up the seniority ranks as a second officer or flight engineer before moving into the right seat as a copilot. Military pilots progress from formal education to flight school, then operational flying assignments before leaving early or retiring from the service.

Given the complexity of modern military operations, there is a considerably smaller margin for error compared to civilian aviation. Military flight operations are extremely complex as aircrew utilize aircraft weapons and various sensor systems while at the same time executing all the requirements that go with flying an aircraft, often in challenging terrain under appalling weather conditions. Due to factors such as the operational environment, mission timing constraints, multiple unit coordination, and workload, it may be more difficult for military aviators to trap and mitigate errors than civilian aviators. It is also possible, that due to the awareness of teamwork skills and concepts that accrues from an effective CRM training program, perhaps military mishap investigators today are keen to list "breakdown in leadership," or "communication failure" to explain the mishap. Dekker (2005) noted that mishap investigators are often driven to find an underlying failure (or failures) that ultimately led up to and caused the mishap.

In addition to the differences described by Prince and Salas (1993), there are also programmatic challenges in the military that may not exist in commercial organizations. For one, *the primary concern of the military is mission accomplishment.* There is arguably a different philosophical approach to CRM training in the military as compared to civilian applications. In most military settings, CRM training can be considered an operational training program. In the past, safety was not always a prioritized goal in military flight operations. To illustrate, the goal of US Naval CRM training is to "improve mission effectiveness by minimizing crew preventable errors, maximizing crew coordination, and optimizing risk management" (Chief of Naval Operations, 2001). While safety is of great importance to military flight operations, it is not the purpose, or primary aim, of flight missions.

Secondly, *military personnel frequently change jobs.* Military CRM trainers do not remain in their posts, or assignments, for very long. This may sometimes lead to shortfalls in continuity and "corporate memory" of the organization's (squadron's) CRM and safety training programs. Again, taking the US Navy as an example, naval aviators will generally only spend 2−3 years in a particular squadron before they move on to a different squadron or other nonflying assignment (e.g., staff job, higher education). The US Air Force follows this personnel assignment practice as well. Further, even when at a squadron, the nonflying duties aviators perform also change regularly. In the US Navy it is likely that the squadron CRM facilitator may only perform that role for as little as a year before it is passed to another individual. The rationale for this practice is to provide officers exposure to a broad base of squadron operations and leadership.

The military is not a homogenous organization. Throughout military aviation, there are great variations in the type of aircraft (e.g., fighter, heavy, rotary wing, and even tilt-rotor), missions performed (e.g., transportation, bombing, surveillance, special operations), operating environment (e.g., airfield, forward deployed, carrier based), number of crew (one to more than 20), and levels of automation (very little, to fully glass cockpit). As variable as the number and types of aircraft in the military aviation organization are the number and "type" of personnel flying these aircraft. In commercial aviation, most pilots are hired on to an airline after they have achieved significant aviation milestones. In military aviation, most "new hires" are college graduates with no previous flight experience. For these "nuggets," experience and proficiency are gained on the job. That is not to say there is a dearth of experience in military aviation. On the contrary, a large number of senior pilots and aircrew garner substantial experience in their careers. This gives rise to the rank and experience gradient in military pilots and aircrew. Rank is important in the military organization. In a given squadron, there is usually a fair number of lower ranking officers with lesser experience mixed with middle and senior ranking officers with greater levels of experience. Given the variety of missions, type of aircraft, and personnel in military aviation, there is a need to balance the goal of having a common overarching program that is also tailored to the needs of the individual operators and specific aircraft. As was found with the early US Navy CRM training, a one-size fits all approach can become a one-size fits nobody.

The military is a multidisciplinary organization, with many different cultures in terms of *acceptance of CRM principles*. Deal and Kennedy (2000) pointed out that most organizations possess a corporate culture. The same can be said of military organizations. Although military services each have their own traditions and "corporate" culture, within each service, individual units acquire their own "subcultures." This stems in large part from their environment. Depending on type of aircraft and mission, military aviation squadrons operate in different locations under different circumstances. In short, they have different operating environments that produce different requirements for success in that situation. This in turn gives rise to the culture, or climate unique to a given squadron, or aircraft community within military aviation. "The way we do things here" describes the effect of organizational culture on local practices within an organization (Bower, 1966).

Sometimes this produces behaviors that are slow to change. This may partially explain why CRM was not widely embraced in its introduction to military flight operations, and why even today, despite widespread integration and acceptance, there are varying degrees of qualitative implementation of CRM programs throughout military aviation.

19.2   CURRENT MILITARY APPROACHES TO CRM TRAINING

For all the research on military CRM in the past two decades, there is certainly no surfeit of literature or studies of military CRM programs. Further, what has been written is almost exclusively from a US military perspective. In an attempt to gather knowledge of the present state of CRM programs in military services worldwide, we contacted mid-grade officers, many of them in safety or CRM program billets, and queried them as to how their service is applying CRM training. Here the authors annotate a short summary of information obtained from their correspondence, interviews, in addition to published material.

19.2.1   United States Navy-Marine Corps

The US Navy and Marine Corps (collectively, the *naval* services) instituted CRM in the early 1990s (for a detailed discussion see O'Connor, Hahn, & Salas, 2009). The program was developed on the basis of a substantial research program carried out at the Naval Air Warfare Center Training Systems Division (NAWCTSD). This led to the identification of seven CRM critical skills (decision-making, adaptability/flexibility, situational awareness, mission analysis, communication, assertiveness, and leadership), and a theoretically grounded method for how to train these skills (for a more detailed discussion of the research used to develop the program, see Oser, Salas, Merket, & Bowers, 2001; Oser, Salas, Merket, Walwanis, & Bergondy, 2000; Prince & Salas, 1993).

The Navy's CRM program is governed by a Chief of Naval Operations (CNO) Instruction—OPNAVINSTR 1542.7C. This instruction sets the basic administrative organization of the CRM program, and outlines a basic framework for CRM in the US Navy and Marine Corps.

The architecture of the CRM program is centrally controlled by the program model manager, but each aviation platform is given the latitude to administer its own CRM program tailored for its particular aircraft and mission. In a sense, the Navy and Marine Corps have 48 separate CRM programs (one for each type and model of aircraft the Navy and Marine Corps flies) each with a Curriculum Model Manager that ensures adherence to basic naval CRM academic principles, skills, and program standardization. The Curriculum Model Managers attend 5 days of training to prepare them for the role of both managing the program for their particular aircraft type, as well as training the CRM facilitators at each squadron.

Although the last comprehensive update of the training curriculum was in 1999 by NAWCTSD (Oser et al., 2001), some Curriculum Program Managers have made exhaustive efforts to improve CRM in their communities. To illustrate, some of the commands that are responsible for training new aviators have drawn extensively on airline models for multiplace CRM training, while the MV-22 Osprey (a tilt-rotor aircraft that can land and take-off like a helicopter and fly like a fixed wing airplane) program has developed robust CRM courseware and models for their CRM program. The CRM curriculum in these communities greatly exceeds the basic minimum requirement in the CNO instruction. However, these exemplar programs are generally the exception. Most Curriculum Program Managers' CRM programs reflect the basic academics required by the CNO instruction. Promulgating the latest academic themes in a "train the trainer" system is sometimes a challenge in a large organization.

Although many high-risk civilian industries have embraced CRM (see Flin, O'Connor, & Mearns, 2002) the same is not true of the nonaviation communities in the US Navy. Bridge Resource Management (BRM) was introduced into the curriculum of the Surface Warfare Officers School (the command that trains officers who will work on ships) in 2006. However, it is still in the process of becoming properly established. The only other isolated examples of the use of CRM training by nonaviation personnel are naval medicine and navy diving (O'Connor & Muller, 2006).

19.2.2 United States Air Force

The Military Airlift Command (now Air Mobility Command) was the first military organization to formally embrace CRM training, implementing CRM instruction in 1985 and co-sponsoring the pivotal Cockpit Resource Management Training Conference with NASA-Ames in 1986 (Orlady & Foushee, 1987).

The Air Force Inspection and Safety Center developed a prototype course for single-seat fighters in 1990. In 1994, the Air Force formally mandated CRM training and assessment for all Air Force flight crew members. Air Force Instruction (AFI) 11-290 is the current document that formalizes the Air Force's CRM program (Department of the Air Force, 2017). This Instruction was formally adopted in 1998 and has remained essentially unchanged since undergoing a major revision and update in 2012. It requires major commands to develop and manage tailored, mission-specific CRM training programs and mandates CRM training for all Air Force aircrew members. The stated goals are to:

- Maximize operational effectiveness.
- Preserve personnel and material resources.
- Ensure the safety of noncombatant civilians.

- Facilitate mishap reduction by providing skills, processes, tools and techniques to aircrew members to effectively identify threats and mitigate errors in aviation operations.

Six core CRM skill and knowledge areas have not changed since the original operating instruction:

- Communication
- Crew/Flight Coordination
- Mission Analysis (mission planning, briefing, and debriefing)
- Risk Management/Decision-Making
- Situational Awareness
- Task Management

While broad requirements are established in AFI 11-290, implementation is the responsibility of major commands, and these organizations have considerable flexibility regarding how these requirements will be met. As a result, the nature of CRM training varies considerably across commands, and even across specific airframes within a command. For example, formal CRM instruction in Air Mobility Command during initial qualification training varies from 2.75 to 16 hours depending upon aircraft type (Fisher, 2007). Most CRM instruction for aircrews in operational commands is delivered by contractor instructors, either as part of a contractor-provided integrated aircrew training system or as stand-alone CRM instruction. CRM training programs typically involve instructor-based ground training as a baseline while some commands allow for computer-based CRM training to fulfill requirements. Classroom instruction may also include the use of workbooks, hands-on experience in various types of training devices, or facilitated integrated combat and training scenarios.

CRM training developers and Air Force program managers often use mishap human factors trend data along with experiences to help focus CRM training on areas of greatest need. For example, crews from several aircraft were observed during challenging simulator scenarios, and strengths and weaknesses were captured and then analyzed to identify CRM behaviors that are correlated with mission performance (e.g., Nullmeyer, Spiker, Wilson, & Deen, 2003; Povenmire, Rockway, Bunecke, & Patton, 1989; Spiker, Tourville, Bragger, Dowdy, & Nullmeyer, 1999; Thompson, Tourville, Spiker, & Nullmeyer, 1999). These studies validated the importance of all six Air Force CRM skill areas in multicrewmember aircraft operations (B-52, C-5, HH-53, and C-130 respectively).

As formal CRM training courses were implemented across the Air Force, they seemed to be more readily embraced by aviators flying crew aircraft than by single-seat fighter and attack aircraft pilots (Karp, Condit, & Nullmeyer, 1999). Nullmeyer, Stella, Harden, and Montijo (2005) found that, while C-130 Class A mishap reports tended to cite problems in all six CRM skill areas, human factors cited in F-16 and A-10 mishap reports were heavily skewed toward situation awareness and task management problems (see Fig. 19.1). Coordination, communication, and mission planning problems are rarely mentioned in Air Force single-seat aircraft mishap reports.

Unmanned aircraft system (UAS) operations are rapidly increasing worldwide and the United States military services are on the forefront of this technology transition. Air Force experiences with larger UASs (e.g., Predators, Reapers, and Global Hawks) may be helpful as larger UASs become more common in civil aviation. High mishap numbers accompanied the introduction of remotely piloted aircraft into military operations based on a comprehensive review of early UAS accident rates across Military Services (Tvaryanas, Thompson, & Constable, 2006). As one example, they reported that the first decade of Predator operations—1996 through 2005—yielded a Class A mishap rate of 32 per 100,000 flying hours. The mishap rate for other Air Force aircraft was approximately two per 100,000 flying hours. It should be noted that most manned aircraft are mature systems, while most UAS platforms were relatively early in their life cycles, and mishap rates tend improve with system maturity. Nullmeyer, Herz, Montijo, and Leonik (2007) found that mishap rates for unmanned systems steadily improved as lessons learned were incorporated into equipment design, operations, and training. Air Force Safety Center (2018) mishap statistical summaries indicate that Predator Class A mishap rates dropped to 4.33 per 100,000 flying hours in 2015−17. Nullmeyer, et al. (2007) analyzed the specific human

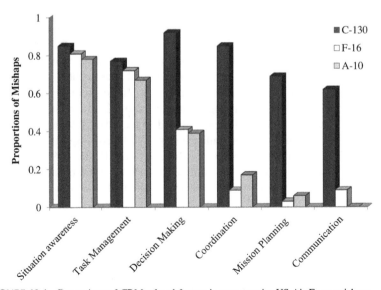

FIGURE 19.1 Proportions of CRM-related factors in recent major US Air Force mishaps.

factors cited in Predator Class A mishap reports from 1997 through 2006. Thirty Class A Predator mishap reports were available over that span of time. Of these, 63% were attributed primarily to operator error and an additional 13% were attributed to maintenance issues. The 10 human factors cited most frequently in these Predator Class A mishap reports are summarized in Table 19.2.

While Predator flight crew errors are frequently cited, other threats to safety also appear. Most of the human factors cited could be accommodated using seven higher-order categories: (1) documentation such as technical orders and written procedures; (2) equipment-related issues related to the operator interface and automation; (3) attention management; (4) crew coordination/teamwork; (5) skills and knowledge-based errors; (6) decision-making; and (7) task management. Many of these remained frequently cited human factors for the next several years (US Air Force Safety Human Factors Team, 2009). Several traditional CRM topic areas dominate the list of crew errors cited. Attention management issues (channelized attention and inattention) were cited most often, followed by teamwork (crew coordination), task management (task misprioritization), and decision-making (course of action selected). While Predator operations involve a flight crew, the types and proportions of CRM issues cited in Predator accidents seem to resemble the patterns of issues seen in Air Force fighter and attack aircraft mishap reports shown above in Fig. 19.1.

Working with the Predator MQ-1 community, Kaiser, et al. (2010) conducted an in-depth CRM training needs analysis, and then developed and evaluated four CRM training interventions for pilots and sensor operators in

TABLE 19.2 Top Ten Detailed Predator Mishap Human Factors 1996–2006 (30 Class A Mishaps) from Nullmeyer et al. (2007)

Human Factor	Crew Error Area	Causal	Contributing
Written Procedures		5	6
Channelized Attention	Attention Management	4	5
Functional System Design		4	4
Checklist Error	Skill/Knowledge	3	3
Crew Coordination	Teamwork	2	4
Course of Action Selected	Decision-Making	4	1
No Training for Task		1	4
Inattention	Attention Management	2	3
Task Misprioritization	Task Management	1	4
Automation		2	2

initial qualification training: (1) academic training focused on predator-specific error patterns; (2) web-based interactive mishap case histories; (3) a game-based multitask skills trainer; and (4) a laptop-based team trainer. Student reactions to the new types of training were consistently positive, and there was consistent evidence of learning. Students preferred the laptop-based team trainer the most followed by academic training focused on Predator-specific CRM issues.

When AFI 11-290 was written in 1995, fourth generation CRM (as defined by Helmreich, Merritt, & Wilhelm, 1999) represented the state-of-the-art in CRM instruction. Aspects of Helmreich's fifth generation (error management) and sixth generation (threat and error management) CRM training entered the commercial aviation industry starting in 2000, but were not formally adopted by the USAF until the AFI 11-290 rewrite in 2012.

The data used for decades by the commercial aviation industry to shape threat and error management training content were not available for Air Force CRM program managers or courseware developers in 2000, but as the USAF has updated their aircraft, more digital information became available. As of 2017, the USAF has a formal MFOQA (Military Flight Operations Quality Assurance) program patterned after that of the airline industry. MFOQA data is produced and distributed by the Air Force Safety Center monthly for the B-1, C-5M, C-17, C-32, C-37, C-40, C-130J, F-16, KC-135, MQ-9, RC-135, and T-6.

As is the case in the commercial industry organizations that have Safety Reporting Systems in place, the USAF has recently implemented an Aviation Safety Action Program (ASAP) where aircrew can report any incident for investigation without repercussion.

While there is still no requirement in AFI 11-290 to conduct a Line Oriented Safety Audit (LOSA), the Air Mobility Command (flying transport aircraft most similar in mission for commercial aviation operations), has a formal program to audit line crews flying operational missions. Continuing combat operations combined with a shrinking force structure has prevented other USAF commands from implementing LOSA programs. Since 2001, the USAF has made a significant effort to bring their CRM programs closer to the practices used in the commercial aviation industry despite the disparate nature of their flying operations.

19.2.3 United States Army

The US Army introduced its CRM training program, called Aircrew Coordination Training (ACT), in the early 1990s. The Army was the first US service to achieve a service-wide standardized CRM program. Since the inception of ACT, the US Army has invested significant resources to update its program, and in 2006 implemented ACT-E (Aircrew Coordination Training—Enhanced).

In the US Army, all aviators are given initial ACT-E training during their primary flight training to become aviators. This training is broad, and covers the core academics and concepts of the ACT-E program. Once the aviator is assigned to an operational aviation unit, he or she then receives annual ACT-E training in the form of a blended presentation by the unit designated ACT-E Instructor.

The CRM skills of aviators are evaluated during every check flight (e.g., annual instrument check, annual aircraft proficiency checkride). Advanced ACT-E training is provided to the unit ACT-E instructors by the US Army ACT-E program manager. This two and a half day training teaches the ACT-E Instructors how to access training media, deliver it to aircrew for aircrew recurrency ground training, and ensure its implementation in all checkrides.

Central to the administration of the US Army ACT-E program is its program manager. The program manager maintains a great deal of standardization throughout Army aviation. Much of the program manager's duties are outsourced to commercial vendors, but uniformed Army personnel occupy key positions in administration of the program, and generally have the final say on programmatic and academic decisions. Under the program manager, Army ACT-E branches to six "subprograms," one for each of the primary type aircraft in Army aviation (heavy attack; reconnaissance; cargo; utility; fixed wing; and unmanned aerial systems).

All operational units send an aviator to receive the ACT-E Instructor training. Once back in the field, the instructor retrieves the curriculum material (learning objectives, lesson plans, and electronic media) from the program manager. ACT-E instructors are provided with the material for recurrent training by the program manager (unlike the U.S Air Force, or Navy, where the onus is not on the Instructor to develop the materials). The training materials consist of electronic media, video case studies, and slide presentations, to guide the aviators through a relevant discussion of ACT-E as it relates to the type aircraft and mission. This ensures new case studies for a given aviator every time he or she participates in annual ACT-E training.

19.2.4 United States Coast Guard

As part of a program started in 2003, all pilots and aircrew are required to participate in initial and annual Coast Guard CRM training (Commandant US Coastguard, 2005). Coast Guard CRM training is very similar to that of the US Navy, addressing the same seven skills. However, as with the Air Force, the Coast Guard has also been looking to "best practices" from the commercial CRM industry, and recently started to incorporate them into their aviation CRM training.

The Coast Guard also delivers CRM training to boat personnel, called Team Coordination Training (TCT). This was first introduced in 1991 and was revised on the basis of an analysis of mishaps in 1994 (see Hanson, 1996 for details). The most recent iteration of TCT is designed to increase team effectiveness and minimize human error in cutter, boat, and command/control operations and activities (Commandant US Coastguard, 1998). The curriculum of the TCT course also consists of the same seven skills taught in the US Navy CRM program. The training is given by Coast Guard personnel, tailored towards personnel fulfilling particular roles within the Coastguard, and varies in length and delivery method depending on who is receiving the training (see Commandant U.S. Coastguard, 1998 for details). Hanson (1996) reported a reduction in minor navigational errors as a result of the first generation of TCT training.

19.2.5   Non-US Military

Most of the worlds' military services have a CRM program. As noted above, the authors contacted mid-grade officers, many of them in safety or CRM program billets, and queried them as to how their service is applying CRM training. In response to research requests, communications were received from: Royal Air Force (United Kingdom); Royal Australian Air Force; Royal Australian Navy; Italian Navy; Dutch Navy; Spanish Navy; South African Air Force (SAAF); Taiwan Navy; and the Finnish Air Force. Most of the contacts here are officers who have attended US military training courses for CRM and safety programs.

The influence of United States military CRM programs, curricula, and research can be seen in all the services above. In some cases however, such as the United Kingdom, there is substantial independent research and subsequently a distinct CRM program is emerging. In the United Kingdom, study is underway to modify its CRM training. The aim is to shift the focus from error reduction and flight safety to human factors training that improves individual and team performance. In the Netherlands, the basic academic curriculum for military CRM programs is administered by the Netherlands Defense Academy (NLDA). Dedicated staff have imported much of the US Navy and Marine Corps CRM tenets, but have molded an implementation scheme that is highly integrated into the NLDA's curriculum for its students.

It was noted that all the services reviewed possess a basic CRM curriculum that is centered upon key academic topics and skill sets. Unsurprisingly, these topics and skills are very similar to those taught by the US military services.

Most countries have a Ministry of Defense order or instruction that governs their CRM program. The Dutch military CRM program subscribes extensively to civilian CRM program governance promulgated by Dutch civil aviation authorities. In the case of the Australian military services, there is an Australian government Department of Defense instruction (DI-G OPS 40-4) that governs military CRM programs. Each military service has adopted this instruction as the service's CRM governing order. The result is continuity in CRM programs throughout the organization.

There is considerable variability in CRM programs as regards recurrent training. Some services such as the Italian and South African CRM programs do not have prescribed recurrent requirements. In several services, recurrency consists merely of a ground training session; and in services that do conduct recurrent training, periodicity requirements range from annual to once every 4 years. In most services, CRM training is conducted by service members. In the SAAF, efforts are underway to implement a CRM program taught by uniformed personnel.

For all the services above, CRM programs were implemented in the 1990s. Once the United States military adopted CRM programs, it appears many non-US militaries followed suit. As was the case in the civilian world, the military is beginning to recognize the relevance of CRM training beyond aviation. In the SAAF, there is an initiative to provide CRM to ground crews and Air Traffic Controllers. The NLDA has integrated CRM training into the curriculum for its midshipmen. This is significant because not all midshipmen will go on to become aviators. The NLDA expects these young officers in the making to take these skills with them to their warfare areas wherever they may be—submarines, engineering offices, or surface ships. Another initiative in the Netherlands Navy is the implementation of Bridge Resource Management for officers on ships. Therefore, as CRM training is widely used by the militaries around the world, what evidence is there that they are getting a good return on the investment of time, money, and personnel?

19.3   THE EFFECTIVENESS OF MILITARY CRM TRAINING

The Federal Aviation Administration (2004) states that for CRM training "it is vital that each training program be assessed to determine if CRM training is achieving its goals. Each organization should have a systematic assessment process. Assessment should track the effects of the training program so that critical topics for recurrent training may be identified and continuous improvements may be made in all other respects" (Federal Aviation Administration, 2004, p. 12). This is also true for military CRM training.

Table 19.3 lists 27 studies the authors have found in the literature reporting an evaluation of the effectiveness of CRM training in military organizations, and the type of evaluation that has been carried out (for a more detailed summary of these studies see O'Connor et al., 2008; O'Connor, Flin, & Fletcher, 2002; Salas, Burke, Bowers, & Wilson, 2001; Salas, Wilson, Burke, & Wightman, 2006). The evaluation methods were categorized in accordance with Kirkpatrick's (1976) training evaluation hierarchy. Evaluating reactions are the equivalent to measuring satisfaction. For example, did the participants like the training? Learning is the second level in the hierarchy, and refers to "the principles, facts, and skills which were

TABLE 19.3 Evaluations of the Effectiveness of Military CRM Programs (√ Indicates a Positive Finding, X a Negative or Nonsignificant Finding)

Author	Participants	Reactions	Learning			Organization
			Attitudes	Knowledge	Behavior	
US Navy						
Alkov (1991)	90 air crew		√			√
Baker et al. (1991)	41 helicopter pilots	√				
Brannick et al (1995)	51 air crew				√	
Salas et al. (1999)	35 pilots and 34 enlisted helicopter air crew	√	×	√	√	
Stout et al. (1997)	27 helicopter pilots	√	×	√	√	
Stout et al. (1996)	42 student aviators	√	√	√	√	
	12 helicopter pilots	√	×	×	√	
Wiegmann and Shappell (1999)	290 naval aviation mishap (1990–96)					×
US Air Force						
Chidester et al. (1991)	531 USAF military airlift command pilots		√			

Reference	Sample					
Grubb (2001)	US Air Force crew	√	√			√
Grubb et al. (1999)	2,659 Air Force crews		√			√
Karp et al. (1999)	36 F-16 pilots	✗				
Morey et al. (1997)	188 fighter, 198 transport and 77 bomber pilots		√			√
Nullmeyer et al. (2003)	20 C-130 crews					√
Povenmire et al. (1999)	Unknown number of B-52 pilots					√
Spiker et al. (1999)	16 C-5 air crews					√
Thompson et al. (1999)	16 helicopter crews		√			√
US Army						
Geis (1987)	Pre-test 838 US Army pilots, post-training 163, and 142 responses from a survey 3 months after the course	√	√			√
Grubb et al. (2001)	Air crew	√	√			√
Katz (2003)	18 helicopter personnel					√
Leedom and Simon (1995)	32 military helicopter pilots				√	√
	30 helicopter crew personnel				✗	

(Continued)

TABLE 19.3 (Continued)

Author	Participants	Learning			Behavior	Organization
		Reactions	Attitudes	Knowledge		
US Coast Guard						
Hanson (1996)	Ship navigational mishaps					√
Other US—branch not specified						
Baker et al. (1993)	112 US military aviators	√				
Dwyer et al. (1997)	19 military participants from close air support				√	
Royal Air Force (United Kingdom)						
Elliott-Mabey (1999)	3,212 air crew	√	√			
French Air Force						
Grau and Valot (1997)	172 air crew	√			√	

understood and absorbed by the participants" (Kirkpatrick, 1976, p. 18.11). Learning is made up of two components: attitudinal change and knowledge gains. Evaluation of behavioral changes is the assessment of whether knowledge learned in training actually transfers to behaviors on the job, or a similar simulated environment. The organizational level is the highest in Kirkpatrick's (1976) hierarchy. The ultimate aim of any training program is to produce tangible evidence at an organizational level, such as an improvement in safety and productivity.

It can be seen from Table 19.3 that on the whole, military CRM training seems to be having a positive effect at each of Kirkpatrick's (1976) levels of training evaluation. However, a number of caveats need to be made regarding the evaluation data.

1. *The evaluations lack currency.* These studies were carried out well over two decades ago, with none carried out in the last 5 years. Therefore, there is little to guide thinking on the current state of military CRM training beyond anecdotal evidence.
2. *The evaluations are heavily US centric.* Apart from four studies, the evaluations were exclusively carried out within the US military.
3. *The evaluations are generally of specific populations of small number of aviators.* The majority of the studies report evaluations of small numbers of participants from a specific aviation community, who all attended the same training course (e.g., Salas, Fowlkes, Stout, Milanovich, & Prince, 1999; Stout, Salas, & Kraiger, 1996). Thus, the findings may not be generalizable to the military organization as a whole, and may partially be a reflection of the tutors' teaching abilities, rather than the actual content of the training.

Therefore, although these findings are encouraging, there is a need for military organizations to conduct large-scale evaluations of the current effectiveness of their CRM training program. Without this information it is impossible to assess the effectiveness of the program, and identify whether the organization is obtaining an acceptable return-on-investment. Further, just because a program was successful a decade ago, does not mean this continues to be the case. There is a great deal of information available on how CRM training can be evaluated (e.g., Flin, O'Connor, & Crichton, 2008). It is suggested that the world's militaries should use this information to evaluate the effectiveness at as many levels of Kirkpatrick's evaluation hierarchy as is feasible.

19.4 THE FUTURE OF CRM TRAINING IN THE MILITARY

The authors have no doubt that military aviators will continue to receive CRM training for a long time to come. However, the training will have to adapt to address the automation issues associated with the new advanced aircraft (e.g., Joint Strike Fighter, Euro Fighter, F-22 Raptor, and V-22 Osprey). CRM in highly automated aircraft presents special challenges for aviators. Just as has been the case with CRM training in commercial aviation, there is a need to address the change in crew coordination dynamics that can result from a more automated aircraft. The other big area to which it is suggested that CRM should be applied is nonaviation military communities.

Given the almost two decades that have passed since it was first used in military aviation, the dearth of nonaviation applications in the world's militaries is surprising. In high-risk civilian industries, those that adopted it first were, unsurprisingly, involved in the aviation business (e.g., aviation maintenance, air traffic control). However, CRM training has also begun to be used in a number of other high-reliability industries unrelated to aviation such as nuclear power generation, anesthetics, the maritime industry, and offshore oil and gas production (see Flin et al, 2002 for a review). It is suggested that given the experience with delivery of CRM training in aviation, and the range of other high-risk military occupation, the military is well placed to introduce CRM into other domains.

One particular domain in which CRM training should be more widely used in all services is for the training of UAS operators. UASs have become an indispensible asset in military operations. A seemingly insatiable demand for the capabilities that UASs bring to the battlefield have all the US services struggling to train enough operators to keep pace with rapidly growing demand. A number of new human factors issues accompany this major move toward remotely piloted aerial vehicles including many pertaining to resource management. McCarley and Wickens (2005) identified some of the more salient emerging human factors challenges including the loss of sensory cues such as ambient visual information, kinesthetic/vestibular inputs, and sound. Second, UASs differ dramatically in the degree to which flight control is automated. An emerging challenge is to develop and optimize procedures for responding to automation failures, including common expectations among UAS operators and air traffic controllers. A third set of issues pertains to the selection, composition, and training of UAS flight crews. The steepness of demand for UAS operators is forcing the services to think beyond the traditional approach of assigning experienced pilots to the task of controlling UASs. All the US services are either using nonpilots as UAS controller trainees or are actively considering that option.

In the past, mishap rates were much higher for UASs than for manned military aviation. To illustrate, the mishap rate for the US Navy's Pioneer UAS was 334 per 100,000 flight hours compared with an average rate of 1.9 per 100,000 for the US naval aviation over 5 years (Naval Safety Center, 2008). Williams (2004) analyzed US Army, Navy, and Air Force UAS mishaps. The percentage of human factors mishaps varied across UASs from 21% to 68%. Those that involved causal human factors tended to involve issues with alerts/alarms, display design, procedural errors, or skill-based errors. Tvaryanas et al. (2006) analyzed a 10-year cross-section of 221 US Army, Navy, and Air Force UAS mishaps. Overall 60% of mishaps were human related, ranging from 32% to 69% depending on the platform. Further, specific human factors problems varied considerably across systems. Air Force factors tended to involve the operator station and channelized attention. Army factors included overconfidence, crew coordination, communication, and organizational factors related to procedural guidance, publications, and training programs. Navy issues involved organizational and supervision issues, operator station design, and crew factors of channelized attention, oversaturation, distraction, inattention, and complacency.

These reviews reveal at least three important aspects of UAS operations that will impact CRM training. First, human factors are commonly cited in mishap reports indicating that there is ample opportunity to improve safety. Second, problems appear to vary considerably across platforms and organizations. This suggests that Helmreich's and colleagues' threat and error management approach to CRM training content would have merit (see Helmreich, Wilhelm, Klinect, & Merritt, 2001 for more details). Third, the traditional Army, Navy, or Air Force CRM content areas are well represented in the human factors that are emerging as the primary problem areas. However, it is crucial that the training has been tailored to the needs of UAS operators.

As has been found in other CRM applications, simply replacing "aviator" with "UAS operator" and giving standard CRM training is not likely to be successful. If CRM is to be adapted for use in other domains, the training materials must be customized. For the training to be effective it is imperative that the skills that are required have been identified through a training needs analysis, the psychological concepts are translated into the language of the participants receiving the training, and that relevant practical examples and case studies are used to illustrate the concepts. The training is likely to be ineffective unless examples poignant to the particular domain are used. One of the main criticisms of participants of the early civilian aviation CRM courses was that there was too much psychological theory and not enough relevance to aviation. "I am not suggesting the mindless import of existing programs; rather, aviation experience should be used as a template for developing data driven actions reflecting the unique situation of each organization" (Helmreich, 2000, p. 784).

19.5 CONCLUSION

CRM training has become much more widely used in the world's militaries since Prince and Salas' (1993) review. However, as with military hardware, a training program must not remain stagnant or it is in danger of becoming obsolete and ineffective. It is suggested that the world's militaries should revisit their CRM training programs, and reassess where the training continues to be effective, and where it needs to be changed. This will take time and money. However, when one considers both the price of a modern military aircraft (more than US$50 million for an F-18 Hornet E/F; U.S. Navy, 2006) and the cost of training someone to fly it (US$1.5 million for basic jet flight training; About: U.S. Military, 2007), an effective CRM training program is a cost-effective method for improving both safety and mission performance.

REFERENCES

About: U.S. Military. (2007). Air Force aircrew training costs. Retrieved 23 December, 2008 from http://usmilitary.about.com/library/milinfo/blafaircrewcost.htm?terms = student + load + consolidation.

Air Force Safety Center (2018). *Q-1 flight mishap history*. Retrieved 6 February, 2018 from http://www.safety.af.mil/Portals/71/documents/Aviation/Aircraft%20Statistics/Q-1.pdf.

Alkov, R. A. (1991). U.S. Navy aircrew coordination training- a progress report. In R. Jensen (Ed.), *Proceedings of the 6th international symposium on aviation psychology* (pp. 368–371). Columbus: Ohio State University.

Baker, D., Bauman, M., & Zalesny, M. D. (1991). Development of aircrew coordination exercises to facilitate training transfer. In R. Jensen (Ed.), *Proceedings of the 6th international symposium on aviation psychology* (pp. 314–319). Columbus: Ohio State University.

Bower, M. (1966). *The will to manage*. New York: McGraw-Hill.

Brannick, M. T., Prince, A., Prince, C., & Salas, E. (1995). The measurement of team process. *Human Factors, 37*, 641–645.

Chidester, T. R., Helmreich, R., Gregorich, S. E., & Geis, C. E. (1991). Pilot personality and crew coordination: Implications for training and selection. *International Journal of Aviation Psychology, 1*(1), 25–44.

Chief of Naval Operations. (2001). *Crew resource management program, OPNAVINST 1542.7C.* Washington, DC: Author.

Commandant U.S. Coastguard. (1998). *Team coordination training, Commandant Instruction 1541.1.* Washington, DC: Author.

Commandant U.S. Coastguard. (2005). *Auxiliary aviation training manual, Commandant Instruction M16798.5B.* Washington, DC: Author.

Deal, T. E., & Kennedy, A. A. (2000). *Corporate cultures*. New York: Basic Books.

Dekker, S. W. (2005). *Ten questions about human error: A new view of human factors and system safety*. New York: Lawrence Erlbaum Associates.

Department of the Air Force. (2017). *Air Force guidance memorandum to AFI 11-290, Cockpit/crew resource management program*. Retrieved 6 February, 2018 from http://static.e-publishing.af.mil/production/1/af_a3/publication/afi11-290/afi11-290.pdf.

Federal Aviation Administration. (2004). *Advisory Circular No 120-51E: Crew resource management training*. Washington, DC: Author.

Fisher, S.D. (2007). Exploring crew resource Management training and assessing C-130 aircrew attitudes in Air Mobility Command. Unpublished manuscript, Embry-Riddle Aeronautical University, Long Beach Resident Center.

Flin, R., O'Connor, P., & Crichton, M. (2008). *Safety at the sharp end: Training non-technical skills*. Aldershot, England: Ashgate Publishing Ltd.

Flin, R., O'Connor, P., & Mearns, K. (2002). Crew resource management: Improving safety in high reliability industries. *Team Performance Management, 8*(3/4), 68−78.

Gaur, D. (2005). Human Factors Analysis and Classification System applied to civil aviation accidents in India. *Aviation, Space, & Environmental Medicine, 76*, 501−505.

Gibb, R. W., & Olson, W. (2008). Classification of Air Force aviation accidents: Mishap trends and prevention. *International Journal of Aviation Psychology, 18*(4), 305−325.

Grubb, G., Morey, J. C., & Simon, R. (1999). Applications of the theory of reasoned action model of attitude assessment. In R. Jensen (Ed.), *Proceedings of the 10th International Symposium of Aviation Psychology* (pp. 298−301). Columbus: Ohio State University.

Grubb, G., Morey, J. C., & Simon, R. (2001). Sustaining and advancing performance improvements achieved by crew resource management training. In R. Jensen (Ed.), *Proceedings of the 11th international symposium of aviation psychology* (pp. 1−4). Columbus: Ohio State University.

Hanson, W. E. (1996). Beyond bridge resource management: The risk management culture of the U.S. Coast Guard. In A. Chislett (Ed.), *Marine safety and ship maneuverability* (pp. 191−199). Rotterdam: Balkema.

Helmreich, R., Wilhelm, J., Klinect, J. R., & Merritt, A. C. (2001). Culture, error and crew resource management. In E. Salas, C. A. Bowers, & E. Edens (Eds.), *Improving teamwork in organizations: Applications of resource management training* (pp. 305−334). Mahwah, NJ: Lawrence Erlbaum Associates.

Helmreich, R. L. (2000). On error management: Lessons from aviation. *British Medical Journal, 320*, 781−785.

Helmreich, R. L., Merritt, A. C., & Wilhelm, J. A. (1999). The evolution of crew resource management training in commercial aviation. *International Journal of Aviation Psychology, 9*, 19−32.

Hooper, B. J., & O'Hare, D. P. A. (2013). Exploring human error in military aviation flight safety events using post-incident classification systems. *Aviation, Space, & Environmental Medicine, 84*, 803−813.

Kaiser, D., Montijo, G., Spiker, A., Butler, C., Eberhart, J., Vanderford, M., & Walls, W. (2010). Real time cockpit resource management (CRM) training, Contract No. FA8650-08-C-6848, SBIR Phase II Final Report, Air Force Research Laboratory/RHAS.

Karp, R. M., Condit, D., & Nullmeyer, R. (1999). *Cockpit/crew resource management for single-seat fighter pilots. Proceedings of the interservice/industry training, simulation and education conference [CD-ROM]*. Arlington VA: National Training Systems Association.

Kirkpatrick, D. L. (1976). Evaluation of training. In R. L. Craig, & L. R. Bittel (Eds.), *Training and development handbook* (pp. 18.1−18.27). New York: McGraw Hill.

Li, W.-C., & Harris, D. (2006). Pilot error and its relationship with higher organizational levels: HFACS analysis of 523 accidents. *Aviation, Space, and Environmental Medicine, 77*, 1056−1061.

McCarley, J. S., & Wickens, C.D. (2005). *Human factors implications of UAVs in the National Airspace*. Technical Report AHFD-05-05/FAA-05- 01. Atlantic City, NJ: Federal Aviation Administration.

Morey, J. C., Grubb, G., & Simon, R. (1997). Towards a new measurement approach for cockpit resource management. In R. Jensen (Ed.), *Proceedings of the 8th international symposium of aviation psychology* (pp. 676−981). Columbus: Ohio State University.

Naval Safety Center. (2008). Aviation Tables. Retrieved 2 April, 2009 from http://www.safety-center.navy.mil/statistics/aviation/tables.html.

Naval Safety Center. (2014). Department of Defense human factors analysis and classification system: A mishap investigation and data analysis tool. Retrieved 6 December, 2017 from http://www.public.navy.mil/NAVSAFECEN/Documents/aviation/aeromedical/DOD_HF_Anlys_Clas_Sys.pdf.

Nullmeyer, R., Spiker, V.A., Wilson, G., & Deen, G. (2003). Key crew resource management behaviors underlying C-130 aircrew performance. In *Proceedings of the Interservice/ Industry Training Systems and Education Conference*, Orlando, FL.

Nullmeyer, R., Stella, D., Harden, S., & Montijo, G. (2005). *Human factors in Air Force flight mishaps: Implications for change. Proceedings of the interservice/industry training, simulation and education conference [CD-ROM]*. Arlington, VA: National Training Systems Association.

Nullmeyer, R.T., Herz, R., Montijo, G.A., & Leonik, R. (2007). Birds of prey: Training solutions to human factors issues. In *Proceedings of the Interservice/Industry Training Systems and Education Conference*, Orlando, FL.

O'Connor, P., Campbell, J., Newon, J., Melton, J., Salas, E., & Wilson, K. (2008). Crew resource management training effectiveness: A meta-analysis and some critical needs. *International Journal of Aviation Psychology, 18*(4), 353−368.

O'Connor, P., Flin, R., & Fletcher, G. (2002). Methods used to evaluate the effectiveness of CRM training: A literature review. *Journal of Human Factors and Aerospace Safety, 2*, 217−234.

O'Connor, P., Hahn, R., & Nullmeyer, R. (2010). The military perspective. In B. Kanki, R. Helmreich, & J. Anca (Eds.), *Crew resource management*. San Diego, CA: Elsevier.

O'Connor, P., Hahn, R., & Salas, E. (2009). The U.S. Navy's crew resource management program: The past, present, and recommendations for the future. In P. O'Connor, & J. Cohn (Eds.), Human performance enhancements in high-risk environments: Insights developments, and future directions from military research. Shreveport, LA: Paragon Press.

O'Connor, P. & Muller, M. (June 2006). *A novel human factors training curriculum for U.S Navy diving*. Paper presented at the Undersea and Hyperbaric Medical Society Meeting, Orlando, Florida.

Orlady, H.W., & Foushee, H.C. (1987). *Cockpit resource management training*. Technical Report Number NASA CP-2455 Moffett Field, CA: NASA Ames Research Center.

Oser, R. L., Salas, E., Merket, D. C., & Bowers, C. A. (2001). Applying resource management training in naval aviation: A methodology and lessons learned. In E. Salas, C. A. Bowers, & E. Edens (Eds.), *Improving teamwork in organizations: Applications of resource management training* (pp. 283−301). Mahwah, NJ: Lawrence Erlbaum Associates.

Oser, R. L., Salas, E., Merket, D. C., Walwanis, M. M., & Bergondy, M. L. (2000). Can applied research help naval aviation? Lessons learned implementing crew resource management training in the Navy. *Transportation Human Factors, 2*(4), 331−345.

Povenmire, H. K., Rockway, M. R., Bunecke, J. L., & Patton, M. R. (1989). Cockpit resource management skills enhance combat mission performance in a B-52 simulator. In R. Jensen (Ed.), *Proceedings of the 9th international symposium on aviation psychology* (pp. 489−494). Columbus: Ohio State University.

Prince, C., & Salas, E. (1993). Training and research for teamwork in the military aircrew. In E. Wiener, B. Kanki, & R. Helmreich (Eds.), *Cockpit resource management* (pp. 337−366). San Diego: Academic Press.

Salas, E., Burke, C. S., Bowers, C. A., & Wilson, K. A. (2001). Team training in the skies: Does crew resource management (CRM) training work? *Human Factors, 41*, 161−172.

Salas, E., Fowlkes, J. E., Stout, R. J., Milanovich, D. M., & Prince, C. (1999). Does CRM training improve teamwork skills in the cockpit? Two evaluation studies. *Human Factors, 41*(2), 326−343.

Salas, E., Wilson, K. A., Burke, C. S., & Wightman, D. C. (2006). Does CRM training work? An update, extension and some critical needs. *Human Factors, 14*, 392–412.

Shappell, S., Detwiler, C., Holcomb, K., Hackworth, C., Boquet, A., & Wiegmann, D. A. (2007). Human error and commercial aviation accidents: An analysis using the human factors analysis and classification system. *Human Factors, 49*, 227–242.

Shappell, S., & Wiegmann, D. (2001). *Unraveling the mystery of general aviation controlled flight into terrain accidents using HFACS. Proceedings of the eleventh symposium for aviation psychology*. Ohio State University.

Spiker, V. A., Tourville, S. J., Bragger, J., Dowdy, D., & Nullmeyer, R. T. (1999). *Measuring C-5 crew coordination proficiency in an operational wing*. Proceedings of the 20th interservice/industry training systems and education conference *[CD-ROM]*. Arlignton VA: National Training Systems Association.

Stout, R. J., Salas, E., & Fowlkes, J. E. (1997). Enhancing teamwork in complex environments through team training. *Group Dynamics: Theory, research, and practice, 1*, 169–182.

Stout, R. J., Salas, E., & Kraiger, K. (1996). The role of trainee knowledge structures in aviation psychology. *The International Journal of Aviation Psychology, 7*, 235–250.

Thompson, J. S., Tourville, S. J., Spiker, V. A., & Nullmeyer, R. T. (1999). *Crew resource management training and mission performance during MH-53J combat mission training*. Proceedings of the interservice/industry training, simulation and education conference *[CD-ROM]*. Arlignton VA: National Training Systems Association.

Tvaryanas, A. P., Thompson, W. T., & Constable, S. H. (2006). Human factors in remotely piloted aircraft operations: HFACS analysis of 221 mishaps over 10 years. *Aviation, Space, and Environmental Medicine, 77*, 724–732.

US Air Force Safety Human Factors Team (2009). *USAF Aviation safety: FY 2008 in review*. Aero Space Medical Association Annual conference.

U.S. Navy. (2006). F/A 18- Hornet strike fighter. Retrieved 23 December, 2008 from http://www.navy.mil/navydata/fact_display.asp?cid = 1100&tid = 1200&ct = 1.

Wiegmann, D. A., & Shappell, S. A. (1999). Human error and crew resource management failures in naval aviation mishap: A review of U.S. Naval Safety Center data, 1990-96. *Aviation, Space, Environmental Medicine, 70*(12), 1147–1151.

Wiegmann, D. A., & Shappell, S. A. (2003). *A human error approach to aviation accident analysis*. Aldershot, UK: Ashgate.

Williams, K. W. (2004). *A summary of unmanned aircraft accident/incident data: Human factors implications*. Oklahoma City, OH: Federal Aviation Administration.

FURTHER READING

Baker, D., Prince, C., Shrestha, L., Oser, R., & Salas, E. (1993). Aviation computer games for crew resource management training. *International Journal of Aviation Psychology, 3*(2), 143–156.

Dwyer, D. J., Fowlkes, J. E., Oser, R. L., Salas, E., & Lane, N. E. (1997). Team performance measurement in distributed environments: The TARGETs methodology. In M. T. Brannick, E. Salas, & C. Prince (Eds.), *Team performance assessment and measurement. theory, methods and applications*. Mahwah, NJ: Lawrence Erlbaum Associates.

Elliott-Mabey, N. (1999). *The assessment of RAF attitudes to CRM issues: A three year comparison* (PTC/496192/7/CSSB): RAF Command Scientific Branch.

Geis, C. E. (1987). Changing attitudes through training: A formal evaluation of training effectiveness. In R. Jensen (Ed.), *Proceedings of the 3rd international symposium on aviation psychology* (pp. 392–398). Columbus: Ohio State University.

Grau, J. Y., & Valot, C. (1997). Evolvement of crew attitudes in military airlift operations after CRM course. In R. Jensen (Ed.), *Proceedings of the 9th international symposium on aviation psychology* (pp. 556–561). Columbus: Ohio State University.

Katz, L. (2003). Army CRM training: Demonstration of a prototype computer-based program. In R. Jensen (Ed.), *Proceedings of the 12th international symposium of aviation psychology* (pp. 648–650). Columbus: Ohio State University.

Leedom, D. K., & Simon, R. (1995). Improving team coordination: A case for behavior -based training. *Military Psychology, 7*(2), 109–122.

Nullmeyer, R. T., & Spiker, V. A. (2003). The importance of crew resource management in MC-130P mission performance: Implications for training evaluation. *Military Psychology, 15*(1), 77–96.

Secretary of the Air Force (2012). *Cockpit/Crew Resource Management Training Program*, Air Force Instruction 11-290. Washington, DC: Author. Retrieved 6 December 2017 from http://static.e-publishing.af.mil/production/1/af_a3/publication/afi11-290/afi11-290.pdf.

Chapter 20

Cultural Issues and Crew Resource Management Training

José Anca

Faculty of Science, Engineering and Technology, Swinburne University of Technology, Hawthorn, VIC, Australia

INTRODUCTION

Crew resource management (CRM) is the most prolific training intervention of Human Factors in aviation. From its origins in the late 1970s as a countermeasure to "human error," its evolutionary influence in shaping crew behavior and culture has permeated aspects of personnel licensing, safety assurance, and the development of nontechnical skills.

CRM had its roots in the United States. Its success was spelled out by the astute and systematic use of behavioral change intervention and subsequent demonstration of CRM behaviors in the flight simulator. However, a major criticism of CRM lies in its inability to be "culturally calibrated" (Cookson, 2017). While there was worldwide acceptance of CRM training evidenced by the promotion of local civil aviation authority regulations, the training was still largely based on western organizational contexts and Anglo cultures.

There is vicarious evidence suggesting that even foundation CRM topics in aviation such as communication, decision-making, or even attitudes towards automation, can be considered as culture-free. However, nuances exist arising from cultural differentiation, which require examination. Zhu and Ma (2015b) studied the characteristics of Chinese culture and compared the cultural differences between East and West, communication characteristics of Chinese pilots in the flight deck as following four cultural aspects: *harmony*, *relationship*, *face*, and *power*. Cultural differentiation is further observed in Liao's (2015) examination of differences between Chinese and Western pilots:

> A major finding was that the cultural differences strongly influence the pilots' trust and satisfaction with the implementation of a Just Culture, a Reporting Culture, and a Learning Culture in their company. The Western pilots were

Crew Resource Management. DOI: https://doi.org/10.1016/B978-0-12-812995-1.00020-8

more satisfied with those aspects of the Safety Culture model than were the Chinese pilots. Leadership that builds trust, includes a high power-distance, that allows them to maintain harmony with their colleagues in a Reporting Culture which is desired by Chinese pilots. Because it might have generated negative responses from their colleagues, Chinese pilots were more hesitant than were Western pilots to share information and knowledge.

Liao (2015).

In a more controversial study about the influence of cultural differentiation and flight safety, Enomoto and Geisler (2017) asserted a positive correlation between increased power-distance cultures and the propensity towards aircraft accidents. It used regression analysis to estimate the effects of number of flights, GDP, severe weather conditions, and culture on aircraft crashes in 68 countries. The study found per capita GDP and country scores on the cultural dimension of individualism are inversely related to aircraft accidents while power-distance scores and number of flights are directly related to aircraft accidents. Similar conclusions were made by Harris and Li (2008) indicating that high power-distance has been implicated in many aircraft accidents involving Southeast Asian carriers where poor CRM has been identified as a root cause. Harris found that the design of modern flight decks and their standard operating procedures have an inherent Western (low power-distance) bias within them which exacerbates these CRM issues in the Southeast Asian cohort in the study. In all, the analogous findings of Harris, Li, Enomoto, and Geisler underscore the value of continued training for captains and first officers in direct (or straightforward) flight deck communication which can help overcome cultural barriers and reduce accidents.

Similar (and confirmatory) conclusions also surfaced in a cross-cultural study of Omani, Taiwanese, and US pilots, implicating the national culture as a factor in aircraft accidents. Al-Wardi (2017) used the Human Factors Analysis and Classification System (HFACS) framework from the three national cultures to examine mishaps, unsafe events, and human error occurrences. Variations were found between Oman, Taiwan, and the United States at the levels of organizational influence and unsafe supervision. Seven HFACS categories showed significant differences between the three countries. The study concluded that national culture plays a role in aircraft accidents related to human factors that cannot be disregarded.

Sherman, Helmreich, and Merritt (1997) surveyed more than 5,800 pilots across 12 nations which demonstrated a significant difference for preference and enthusiasm for automation on the basis of national culture. Empirical evidence therefore suggests a relationship between cultural nuancing and CRM, which CRM content developers and, overall, airlines could explore to enrich their programs.

As early as 2000, Professor Robert L. Helmreich had made significant explorations on the impact of culture on CRM. His research highlighted the discrete influence of professional, organizational, and national cultures on CRM performance markers such as leadership/followership, communication/ teamwork, and manner in which crews manage threats and errors in the operational arena. There were findings in Helmreich's research where a number of CRM cultural issues were also manifested in other domains such as space exploration and health care.

In respect of national culture differences, survey data from 26 nations on five continents showed highly significant differences regarding appropriate relationships between leaders and followers, in group versus individual orientation, and in values regarding adherence to rules and procedures. These findings replicate earlier research on dimensions of national culture. Data collected also isolated significant operational issues in multinational flight crews. While there are no better or worse cultures, these cultural differences have operational implications for the way crews function in an international space environment. The positive professional cultures of pilots and physicians exhibit a high enjoyment of the job and professional pride. However, a negative component was also identified characterized by a sense of personal invulnerability regarding the effects of stress and fatigue on performance. This misperception of personal invulnerability has operational implications, such as failures in teamwork and increased probability of error. A second component of the research examines team error in operational environments. From observational data collected during normal flight operations, models of threat and error and their management were developed (Helmreich, 2000). The data collected by Professor Helmreich and his team at the University of Texas at Austin, Aerospace Crew Research Center formed the foundations of normal operations monitoring or invariably called LOSA (Line Operations Safety Audits).

Drawing from another prolific domain that has embraced CRM, Tsao and Browne (2015) while applying CRM concepts from nonhealth care domains such as aviation, military, and energy industries where there is a low tolerance for error, noted that adjustments were required to understand CRM concepts, in part from a professional culture level. Similar findings were found with nurses (Sculli et al., 2013), where significant cultural and clinical outcomes were experienced in the implementation of a nursing-focused CRM for the US Veterans Health Administrations National Center for Patient Safety. Associated research by Carney, West, Neily, Mills, and Bagian (2011) used a survey instrument (Safety Attitudes Questionnaire, SAQ) which was administered to pre- and postattendance of a CRM training course called Medical Team Training (MTT) by physicians and nurses from operating rooms in 101 different hospitals. Responses to the six Teamwork climate items on the SAQ were analyzed. In the pre-MTT result, physicians had more favorable perceptions on teamwork climate items than nurses. Physicians demonstrated improvement on all six Teamwork climate items. Nurses demonstrated improvement in perceptions on all teamwork climate items except "Nurse input is well received." Physicians still had a more favorable perception than nurses on all six teamwork climate items at the post-MTT. Despite an improvement in perceptions by physicians and nurses, baseline nurse–physician professional culture differences persisted at completion of the MTT training.

20.1 CULTURAL ISSUES IN CREW RESOURCE MANAGEMENT

A number of CRM training programs include various topics, including culturally adapted CRM training videos, structured learning experiences (SLEs), and group discussion questions that add to its cultural flavor. For instance, personal experience of the author about CRM training design in four non-US airlines attest to the positive impact of cultural adaptations that were built into the course content. By adapting the local culture or otherwise tacit training aids such as flight data recorder readouts and cockpit voice recordings, the CRM course is enhanced and made significantly relevant to its participants.

In another example, local cultural adaptations into line oriented flight training (LOFT) scenario design proved more relevant for simulator learning. Work done by de Carvalho, Saldanha, Vidal, and Carvalho (2016) used an exploratory situated approach for the design, development, standardization, and implementation of LOFT. The situated approach combines a set of methods and techniques that were supported by social construction and cultural adaptation enabling the involvement and participation of different actors of the operational, tactical, and strategic level of the airline. The findings indicate that LOFT situated design, framed by social construction, improves the relevance of LOFT training and can be applied to any airline with a specific culture and organization.

Cultural issues are customs and values that characterize a group, organization, society, or country. These cultural issues govern and predict how individuals and groups will respond when presented with a problem; these include how people perceive risk and deal with threats. Apart from the design of problem scenarios for line operational simulations (LOS), an airline's CRM training course offers the "best seat in the cinema," as it were, to view cultural issues. The author had conversations with various non-US airline CRM practitioners and developers. The conversations identified a few significant cultural issues that shaped the success of their respective airline's CRM course. Likewise, in these conversations, their thoughts about the future of CRM was also obtained.

20.1.1 The Use of Line Pilots as CRM Facilitators

Facilitated learning sessions which use group dynamics and group process techniques are typically delivered by a trained facilitator. The emergence of the CRM pilot facilitator who delivers a course by discussing atypical aviation concepts such as stress management and teamwork dramatically improved the relevance of CRM. The early 1970s CRM Programs were either run by training consultants or retired flight crew. The downside of these courses was that a degree of local content and credibility is lost and relevance suffers because those delivering the course are distant from the airline's local operational experience.

> Using pilots as facilitators was a welcome move, and assigning line pilots to facilitate was even more revolutionary. It added a substantial impact on the efficacy of the program.
>
> H.Y. Khoo, personal communication, 8 April 2009.

An undesired outcome was also sustained by using this cultural issue of having local line pilot facilitators. In airlines that operate in high power-distance cultures where management and line pilot relationships are fraught with mistrust, the selection of line pilots and their subsequent delivery of the program was perceived as a sinister management plot and therefore not to be trusted—using line pilots as CRM facilitators was deemed as a figurative Management "Trojan horse."

Although a worthy intention to use line pilot facilitators, it may fuel suspicion that warrants deeper scrutiny, which at times may become a formidable blocker to the program's success. Fortunately, the operational context of the program and its focus on managing human error almost always liberates the line pilot facilitator. Experience has shown that CRM programs have the capability of raising individual pilot expectations, because suggestions and feedback, including perceptions about the airline's leadership, working conditions, or management systems, such as rostering practices, are often discussed as threats to flight safety. Unfortunately, the line pilot facilitator is caught in between, as it were, in the skirmish:

> It is not the number of times that the same feedback by line pilots is received during the CRM course that is worrying. The letdown is hearing the same responses from management—that they are still studying the issue around the feedback.
>
> E.B. Dulay, personal communication, 8 April 2009.

20.1.2 Strengthening the Role of the First Officer

The Dutch scientist, Professor Geert Hofstede's work on understanding the elements of national culture has often been used in aviation research for the purpose of comparing flight deck culture and gradients of authority. High power-distance cultures like China, Latin America, and some Asian countries stress that respect for rank, elders, and leaders is paramount. It is not surprising that responses about the acknowledgment of the first officer's role in flight safety was a cultural success in the implementation of CRM.

> In line operations, the biggest beneficiary of all is the copilot. He is empowered to be more assertive in the name of CRM. I do feel that CRM has helped to swing the trans-authority gradient in the favor of the first officer. In the pre-CRM days, I felt the TAG (Trans Authority Gradient) was rather steep.
>
> A. Kampli, personal communication, 8 April 2009.

Empowering the first officer while a welcome by-product, was not the intent. Cultures with high power-distance will invariably produce copilots who have a greater tendency of being tacit with an authoritative captain. The logical approach therefore is to include during CRM training interventions to allow first officers to speak up, when in fact the more efficacious approach would be to teach captains to create an atmosphere in the flight deck that allows for open communication including establishing a process to escalate responses to aid the captain's decisions.

It appears that similar experiences regarding the management of authority gradient and communications are observed in health care. Sur, Schindler, Singh, Angelos, and Langerman (2016) conducted interviews of young surgical residents about approaches to raise concerns to their supervisors' clinical decisions using a semistructured guide. The young surgical residents expressed a tension between conceding ultimate decision-making authority to supervisors and prioritizing obligations to the patient. Systemic (e.g., departmental culture, resident autonomy), supervisor approachability, trainee knowledge, and clinical aspects (e.g., risk of harm, quality of evidence) influenced the willingness to voice concerns. Most described verbalizing concerns in question form, whereas some reported expressing concerns directly. Several factors affect surgical residents' management of concerns about supervisors' plans. It was suggested that a tailored curriculum addressing strategies to raise concerns appears warranted to optimize patient safety. Similarly some airlines have adopted a characteristic approach to raise concerns to the captain which is invariably called the "support process"—a series of escalating questions to raise the captain's attention.

Perhaps a most controversial CRM issue involved the evolution of teamwork in the flight deck and the concept of the inevitability of human error. Conversations with Captain Alejandro Camelo highlight this CRM issue:

> CRM taught us to realize the need of teamwork, being aware of our own limitations and those of the other members of the crew. These have improved decision-making and harmony in the working environment. The crew performed more professionally in their different roles.
>
> A. Camelo, personal communication, 13 March 2009.

It is of interest to note that other safety-critical domains are beginning to contend with issues surrounding teamwork and errors in their own workplaces. Barach and Ieee (2016) raise the concerns against preventable patient harm and the lack of high reliability teams in health care. As with Hefner et al. (2017), they found that teamwork and communication dimensions of patient safety culture may be more highly influenced by CRM training than supervisor and management dimensions. Zhu and Ma (2015a) likewise underscore the value of good cockpit—cabin communications and teamwork as a deterrent to human error. The World Health Organization (WHO) learnt from aviation to assemble similar themes to establish medical team training (the CRM variant in health care). To reinforce the learnings taken from CRM in aviation, structuring good communication process using a phasic approach was utilized. MTT training includes the three phases of the WHO protocol to organize communication and briefings: preoperative verification, preincision briefing, and debriefing at or near the end of the surgical case. This training program led to measured improvements in job satisfaction and compliance with checklist tasks, and identified opportunities to improve training sessions (Carpenter, Bagian, Snider, & Jeray, 2017).

20.1.3 CRM Cultural Adaptations

In many instances, a new concept may not necessarily be "new" because linguistically it may have been previously labeled by a less efficacious or less memorable term. For instance, decision-making, communication, teamwork, cooperation, and briefings were preeminent concepts which were performed by rote and habit as a function of flying operations. However, when these concepts were amalgamated to form clusters of what is now called Nontechnical Skills or NOTECHs, the meaning of those words were enhanced and improved. This is best captured in the conversations with Captain Alejandro Covello from Argentina:

> Another is cultural change, it introduced a new vocabulary which was integrated into the manuals. CRM set up a new and fundamental concept legitimated by operational personnel linking various areas. It is the learning of affection through experience that leads to attitudinal change.
>
> A. Covello, personal communication, 13 March 2009.

Because seemingly disparate words were associated and clustered to form an entirely systematic concept such as NOTECHs, processes such as attitude and performance measurement were introduced. A similar conversation went along these lines with Captain Alejandro Camelo:

> The major goal is to achieve quality training based on a continuous improvement concept in which instruction is assessed and checked at every stage, thanks to an analysis that generates real knowledge of the instruction level in the company.
>
> A. Camelo, personal communication, 13 March 2009.

20.1.4 Integration of CRM Into Checking and Training

The conversations about the integration of CRM in the training and checking functions warranted concern. The argument is that CRM concepts have not been integrated adequately into the training and checking functions, due to the lack of endorsements into the check pilot and flight instructors training. It may be that this is more an experience in non-US airlines. As one of the conversations suggested:

> A lot of instructors have a poor idea of CRM principles. Most of them associate CRM mainly to teamwork and communication aspects only.
>
> A. Kampli, personal communication. 8 April 2009.

Conversations with another pilot indicated their airline's difficulty in having instructor pilots attend CRM training, with tensions and connotations about "old school" instructors not being receptive to CRM training being rife. The problem persists in a situation where the CRM program is seen as a line pilot gathering rather than accommodating and introducing check and instructor pilots to CRM and its error management goals.

> A problem we experienced was when we started organising workshops, we started off with a lack of definition regarding the scope of Human Factors and CRM. Therefore, CRM and flight operations checking and training became wide apart.
>
> A. Covello, personal communication, 13 March 2009.

CRM has many linkages with other airline training or competence systems, which if not aligned may prove at the very least, confusing. For instance, CRM research has continuously acknowledged that lack of assertiveness by first officers cannot be fixed by giving more assertiveness training. Rather, the solution is to ensure an atmosphere in the flight deck where open communication is encouraged. Largely, this tone is set by the captain.

One airline provided a dilemma where legacy programs may need to be reviewed in the context of encouraging assertion by first officers. The airline maintains a confidential competence reporting system that is embedded in their command training. This reporting system involves instructors to "check" and submit confidential reports about first officers in assessing their overall command ability and preparedness. Generally, these "checks" are not announced. It is by all accounts a jeopardy system which can have a drastic impact on one's promotion as a captain. As such, when first officers fly with instructors, they tend to be on their guard, closely watching what they do and say since there is a possibility that they could be on "check." Because this system has a stronger impact on one's career with deleterious effects if undesired behaviors (such as being more straightforward) are demonstrated, silence wins in favor of assertiveness.

CRM that remains in the classroom has a greater propensity to decay rather than one that is continuously reinforced in the simulator. One of the conversations reported that initially the inclusion of NOTECHs were useful for simulation training. It provided the context by which scenarios were designed and debriefed. However, anchoring merely on the markers soon lost ground because the markers were repeated and learning soon became dissociated from the scenario itself. Instructor input or curriculum design may have been also a culprit but in any case, the introduction of threat and error management (TEM) as a framework in scenario design and debriefing soon fixed the problem. The integration of CRM countermeasures to address the problems presented in the simulator scenario soon became more relevant.

Again, citing associated experiences in health care, experiments in trauma management suggest that leadership, role competence, conflict, communication, the environment, and the status of the patient all influence the culture of the trauma team (Cole & Crichton, 2006; Hughes et al., 2014). Interpretation of these categories suggests that trauma team education should include human factor considerations such as leadership skills, team management, interprofessional teamwork, conflict resolution, and communication strategies. The experiment further suggests that support systems for role development of junior team leaders should be formalized and inclusion of CRM training to trauma supervisors should be established.

20.1.5   Cultural Mistakes About Extending CRM Training

There is a perceived but unanimous opinion of the positive benefits of extending CRM training, It is generally an uninformed view that CRM is all about working together, being a team, and communicating appropriately— thus missing out on its core objective, which is to understand and use CRM countermeasures to avoid, trap, and mitigate human error. Conversations from a captain where the airline organized a complex seminar using pilots, cabin crew, station management, and engineers as facilitators demonstrated this uninformed view. The dominant theme of the seminar was to make its interdepartmental participants to work together and "fuse" individual efforts to achieve operational goals. While the efforts to implement the training are admirable, strictly speaking it is not CRM training because it lacks the characteristics required of CRM: its error management focus, its need for application in simulation, and its continued reinforcement in check and training functions. The course is by all means an exercise in team-building. The risk is that the true goals of CRM training is diluted as teamwork training. As another airline put it succinctly:

> CRM training can be expanded to all operational areas of staff. If CRM is not expanded to other areas, training is not complete. That is why here in our region, many of us promote the "complete" or corporate training, but we have

made mistakes in our attempts to expand it. We believed that complete training meant expanding training to all company areas, either operations or not; that CRM was the magic pill. Moreover, it was introduced in these workshops, but without clear conception and so it turned from operationally relevant training to cathartics and evangelization of the environment used for different areas to exchange concerns about the other department.

A. Covello, personal communication, 13 March 2009.

Indeed, CRM's success in appropriately defining human error and selecting appropriate countermeasures to meet error constraints proved to be a potentially attractive idea to integrate training with other operating departments. Kemper et al. (2016) supports this view and further found that CRM is most efficacious as nonstand-alone training integrated in other types of operational training.

20.1.6 Cultural Experiences About the Introduction of Threat & Error Management

The initial view about TEM from outside the United States was that it was an approach to replace CRM. Some viewed it as the newest generation of CRM. This view soon subsided and the appropriate context of TEM as a framework was established in a number of CRM courses and indeed defined well in civil aviation regulations. As a result, Line Operations Safety Audits (LOSA) gained popularity and at the same time were understood well as a data collection and analysis tool for monitoring normal operations.

As TEM became more understood worldwide, it refreshed CRM and reshaped its original intent and error management context. Many pragmatic responses to the introduction of TEM were observed:

TEM makes CRM concepts easily understood especially when introduced early on because TEM is specific. It enables the "language challenge" which we sometimes face here in China to be better managed.

R. Mendoza, personal communication, 8 April 2009.

We also have a chance for the rebirth of operative training including TEM as a synthesis instruction, and LOFT as evidence of CRM theory.

A. Camelo, personal communication, 13 March 2009.

We can say that until TEM appeared we only focused on one aspect of the problem, just on human behaviour. With TEM, we can see the scenario where human performance takes place. It must be highlighted that TEM does not replace CRM training but gives us a more ample and complete approach.

A. Covello, personal communication, 13 March 2009.

The use of the TEM framework has had observable benefits likewise in diabetic care management where there were less service omissions by health care workers in administering care to diabetic patients (Taylor, Hepworth, Buerhaus, Dittus, & Speroff, 2007). But also, crucial to frameworks such as TEM, the challenge is to determine linkages between TEM and the application of CRM countermeasures and its influence on safety culture assessment tools (Karanikas, Soltani, de Boer, & Roelen, 2016) and broader goals of safety culture improvement (Ricci & Brumsted, 2012).

20.2   CONCLUSION

It has been more than 40 years since the first experiments that brought forth CRM in the United States. CRM traveled outside of the United States carrying on fundamental concepts about human error, operational teamwork, decision-making, stress management, and communications to name a few. In its journeys, the fundamental concepts remain true but have been enhanced because of cultural adaptations and integrations.

A number of these cultural issues have been discussed in this chapter such as:

- The Use of Line Pilots as CRM Facilitators
- Strengthening the Role of the First Officer
- CRM Cultural Adaptations and the Introduction a New Vocabulary
- Integration of CRM into Checking and Training
- Cultural Mistakes about Extending CRM Training
- Cultural Experiences about the Introduction of TEM.

Associated experiences in other nonaviation domains were presented with a view to establishing similar processes (and journeys) that these other domains are pursuing. Conversations were used from aviation CRM practitioners to understand problems and opportunities that spelled out CRM successes and pitfalls in their own organizations. The upshot is that cultural adaptation, as seen through the different cultural issues presented, has been proven to improve CRM training design and implementation.

20.2.1   The Future of CRM Outside the United States

A significant revelation about responses on the future of CRM outside the United States revealed a preponderance of opinion towards local civil aviation authorities and its importance to the continued maintenance of CRM. Many of the conversations, while extolling the importance of the regulator, also called for greater reinforcement of CRM education and qualification within the regulator's organization, itself.

It is of concern to note that CRM integration into our CAAP is not taken as a primary concern, probably the main reason is that none of those in the hierarchy even have a basic understanding of what CRM is all about and the leadership is politically appointed.

R. Mendoza, personal communication, 8 April 2009.

The lack of institutional resources to invest in CRM education within the regulator will be a perennial barrier towards airlines wanting to advance their programs. Devotion of fiscal resources will suffer even more in the face of economic downturns where supplying basic social needs are more urgent. An avenue to explore in this regard is to gradually increase self-regulation by airlines (with the assistance of the local aviation safety interest groups) to improve their own CRM programs.

Without constant influx of data such as LOSA and CRM training feedback, the program loses its usability as a potent tool for managing harm to lives and assets. CRM therefore becomes static rather than a refreshing experience to learn more about avoiding mistakes. CRM as an operative tool might be denatured and can turn into a bureaucratic obligation to attend a course as part of the annual training.

A. Camelo, personal communication, 13 March 2009.

The important role of the regulator in maintaining CRM cannot be de-emphasized, specifically with its responsibility for assuring its local airline's CRM consistency with both industry practice and ICAO recommendations. The task is daunting. General aviation experiences were not included in this chapter and yet, they too have relative responsibilities to implement and maintain CRM. It is fitting to quote a universal experience of CRM developers not necessarily exclusive to the non-Western world, where hope shapes the face of CRM:

It is always an uphill climb when you take a proactive approach as it is difficult during presentation to management about initiatives to be done when one has no results to justify the ends. Nevertheless, in spite of all these difficulties, the rewards are invigorating as we get the rewards of educating the needful in this field.

R. Mendoza, personal communication, 8 April 2009.

REFERENCES

Al-Wardi, Y. (2017). Arabian, Asian, western: A cross-cultural comparison of aircraft accidents from human factor perspectives. *International Journal of Occupational Safety and Ergonomics*, 23(3), 366–373. Available from https://doi.org/10.1080/10803548.2016.1190233.

Barach, P., & IEEE. (2016). *Designing high-reliability healthcare teams.*

Carney, B. T., West, P., Neily, J. B., Mills, P. D., & Bagian, J. P. (2011). Improving perceptions of teamwork climate with the veterans health administration medical team training program.

American Journal of Medical Quality, *26*(6), 480−484. Available from https://doi.org/10.1177/1062860611401653.

Carpenter, J. E., Bagian, J. P., Snider, R. G., & Jeray, K. J. (2017). Medical team training improves team performance. *Journal of Bone and Joint Surgery-American Volume*, *99*(18), 1604−1610. Available from https://doi.org/10.2106/jbjs.16.01290.

de Carvalho, R. J. M., Saldanha, M. C. W., Vidal, M. C. R., & Carvalho, P. V. R. (2016). Situated design of line-oriented flight training (LOFT): A case study in a Brazilian airline. *Cognition Technology & Work*, *18*(2), 403−422. Available from https://doi.org/10.1007/s10111-016-0367-1.

Cole, E., & Crichton, N. (2006). The culture of a trauma team in relation to human factors. *Journal of Clinical Nursing*, *15*(10), 1257−1266. Available from https://doi.org/10.1111/j.1365-2702.2006.01566.x.

Cookson, S. (2017). Culture in the cockpit: Implications for CRM training. In S. Schatz & M. Hoffman (Eds.), *Advances in cross-cultural decision making* (Vol. 480, pp. 119−131).

Enomoto, C. E., & Geisler, K. R. (2017). Culture and plane crashes: A cross-country test of the gladwell hypothesis. *Economics & Sociology*, *10*(3), 281−293. Available from https://doi.org/10.14254/2071-789x.2017/10-3/20.

Harris, D., & Li, W. C. (2008). Cockpit design and cross-cultural issues underlying failures in crew resource management. *Aviation, Space, and Environmental Medicine*, *79*(5), 537−538. Available from https://doi.org/10.3357/asem.2271.2008.

Hefner, J. L., Hilligoss, B., Knupp, A., Bournique, J., Sullivan, J., Adkins, E., & Moffatt-Bruce, S. D. (2017). Cultural transformation after implementation of crew resource management: Is it really possible. *American Journal of Medical Quality*, *32*(4), 384−390. Available from https://doi.org/10.1177/1062860616655424.

Helmreich, R. L. (2000). Culture and error in space: Implications from analog environments. *Aviation, Space, and Environmental Medicine*, *71*(9), A133−A139.

Hughes, K. M., Benenson, R. S., Krichten, A. E., Clancy, K. D., Ryan, J. P., & Hammond, C. (2014). A crew resource management program tailored to trauma resuscitation improves team behavior and communication. *Journal of the American College of Surgeons*, *219*(3), 545−551. Available from https://doi.org/10.1016/j.jamcollsurg.2014.03.049.

Karanikas, N., Soltani, P., de Boer, R.J., & Roelen, A.L.C. (2016). Safety Culture Development: The Gap Between Industry Guidelines and Literature, and the Differences Amongst Industry Sectors. In P. Arezes (Ed.), *Advances in safety management and human factors* (Vol. 491, pp. 53−63).

Kemper, P. F., de Bruijne, M., van Dyck, C., So, R. L., Tangkau, P., & Wagner, C. (2016). Crew resource management training in the intensive care unit. A multisite controlled before-after study. *BMJ Quality & Safety*, *25*(8), 577−587. Available from https://doi.org/10.1136/bmjqs-2015-003994.

Liao, M. Y. (2015). Safety culture in commercial aviation: Differences in perspective between Chinese and Western pilots. *Safety Science*, *79*, 193−205. Available from https://doi.org/10.1016/j.ssci.2015.05.011.

Ricci, M. A., & Brumsted, J. R. (2012). Crew resource management: Using aviation techniques to improve operating room safety. *Aviation, Space, and Environmental Medicine*, *83*(4), 441−444. Available from https://doi.org/10.3357/asem.3149.2012.

Sculli, G. L., Fore, A. M., West, P., Neily, J., Mills, P. D., & Paull, D. E. (2013). Nursing crew resource management a follow-up report from the veterans health administration. *Journal of Nursing Administration*, *43*(3), 122−126. Available from https://doi.org/10.1097/NNA.0b013e318283dafa.

Sherman, P. J., Helmreich, R. L., & Merritt, A. C. (1997). National culture and flight deck automation: Results of a multination survey. *International Journal of Aviation Psychology*, *7*(4), 311–329. Available from https://doi.org/10.1207/s15327108ijap0704_4.

Sur, M. D., Schindler, N., Singh, P., Angelos, P., & Langerman, A. (2016). Young surgeons on speaking up: When and how surgical trainees voice concerns about supervisors' clinical decisions. *American Journal of Surgery*, *211*(2), 437–444. Available from https://doi.org/10.1016/j.amjsurg.2015.10.006.

Taylor, C. R., Hepworth, J. T., Buerhaus, P. I., Dittus, R., & Speroff, T. (2007). Effect of crew resource management on diabetes care and patient outcomes in an inner-city primary care clinic. *Quality & Safety in Health Care*, *16*(4), 244–247. Available from https://doi.org/10.1136/qshc.2006.019042.

Tsao, K., & Browne, M. (2015). Culture of safety: A foundation for patient care. *Seminars in Pediatric Surgery*, *24*(6), 283–287. Available from https://doi.org/10.1053/j.sempedsurg.2015.08.005.

Zhu, S.X., & Ma, W.L. (2015a). Cockpit/cabin crew communication: Problems and countermeasures. In S. Yingying, C. Guiran, & L. Zhen (Eds.), *Proceedings of the international conference on education, management, commerce and society* (Vol. 17, pp. 508–512).

Zhu, S.X., & Ma, W.L. (2015b). Culture's influence on cockpit communication. In S. Yingying, C. Guiran, & L. Zhen (Eds.), *Proceedings of the international conference on management, computer and education informatization* (Vol. 25, pp. 414–417).

Chapter 21

Airline Pilots, Training, and CRM in Today's Environment

Linda M. Orlady

Orlady Associates, Maple Valley, WA, United States

INTRODUCTION

For basically all airline pilots, there is nothing mysterious about the term crew resource management (CRM). It is a common topic for anyone in aviation. Flight students intent on becoming commercial pilots are exposed to CRM theory and techniques early in their career. At one time, CRM as it applied to single-pilot operation, was referred to as aeronautical decision-making (ADM). Now many flight training academies incorporate CRM into their initial training with topics such as checklist usage, problem-solving, team-building, workload management, and collision avoidance (Turney, 2002). Many airlines evaluate prospective pilots for their CRM skills as well as for their technical flying abilities.

The purpose of the chapter in this third edition is to examine some areas that have changed and to remind the reader of some that have not. It is not intended to be a comprehensive review of airline training programs or training regulations but rather to highlight some of the major change areas and guidance available, and to discuss some new areas such as the role of the manufacturer with CRM. There are also some challenges that have stubbornly remained despite the issues having been raised, sometimes decades earlier. Suffice to say that while we have learned a great deal, there is still a lot to learn.

21.1 TODAY'S ENVIRONMENT AND MARKET FOR PILOTS

To be hired as an airline pilot is different in the market today. There is a great deal of media coverage about pilot shortages. The US pilot retirement age changed to 65 in 2009. However, the FAA increased the qualification for airline transport pilots to 1500 hours of total time. This rule stemmed

Crew Resource Management. DOI: https://doi.org/10.1016/B978-0-12-812995-1.00021-X

from legislative efforts following the Colgan Air 3407 crash in Buffalo, NY in February 2009 which will be discussed in more detail later in this chapter.

One regional US carrier, Great Lakes Airlines, ceased operations in March 2018. As their CEO and founder, Doug Voss stated, "At the end of the day, it's about the pilot-supply issue and how government is managing the consequences of it" (Paul, 2018). Airlines, particularly at the regional level, are offering signing bonuses or "retention payments." For example, Endeavor Air paid pilots hired between 2015 and 2018 an "opportunity" to earn $20,000 for each of their first 4 years of employment. While these retention payments are now incorporated into their current pay rates, a $10,000 training completion bonus is still paid (Endeavor Air, 2018). The topic of pilot "poaching" where a carrier allegedly targets the pilots of another airline for hire, unfortunately, has become a common charge. Further, the pilot shortage trickles down to flight instructors also who are, not surprisingly, quite desirable as potential employees for an airline. The continual turnover and hiring process has an impact which should not be discounted.

It was assumed that by the time pilots began flying in airline cockpits, that they would have a wealth of knowledge and experience from which to draw. Moreover, it was assumed that a pilot would have a fair period of time flying as a copilot or first officer before he/she accepted the command position of captain. The mere thought of a pilot having an extended period, 10—15 years, of flying as a copilot before upgrading to a command position as a captain is something completely foreign to many new airline pilots. It is incompatible with their goals; some pilots are incredulous to learn that such conditions existed.

The cost of training remains a significant factor, and many pilots are dealing with flight training debt of over $125,000. There are some efforts to assist with this cost burden. JetBlue Airlines started a Gateway Program in 2017 that created a defined pathway to becoming a JetBlue first officer. The program is affiliated with a number of accredited universities, and a preferred lender is identified to assist with the financial aspects (JetBlue, 2018). While more traditional ab initio programs have existed for decades in Europe, this topic is fairly new in the United States. American Airlines Cadet Academy announced recently that it will be training prospective pilots for 18 months at the carrier's partner flight schools, "removing financial roadblocks to encourage more to become professional aviators." Once the training is completed, the flight students can interview for a position with three of American Airlines' regional carriers (Silk, 2018).

21.2 SOME EFFECTS OF THE COLGAN 3407 ACCIDENT AND INVESTIGATION

The Colgan 3407 accident in Buffalo, NY in February 2009 was a landmark event for many reasons. Foremost, it was a horrible tragedy with loss of life for 50 individuals. Frequently, accidents and their resulting investigations provide the opportunity to implement new technologies, and/or to pass binding regulatory requirements (Cox, 2017). The "Families of Continental Flight 3407" (Colgan was a code-share with Continental Airlines) formed, worked, and lobbied hard to bring change and legislation, not without some controversy. In this case, a Congressional mandate resulted in the Airline Safety and Federal Administration Extension Act of 2010 (Congressional Record, 2010; FAA, 2013b). The new regulations:

- Required airline pilots to hold an airline transport pilot (ATP) certificate with minimum of 1500 hours total time.
- Required pilots to have a minimum of 1000 flight hours as a copilot in air carrier operations prior to serving as a captain for a US airline.
- Required the FAA to ensure that pilots are trained on stall recovery, upset recovery, and that airlines provide remedial training.
- Established comprehensive preemployment screening of prospective pilots including an assessment of a pilot's skills, aptitudes, airmanship, and suitability for functioning in the airline's operational environment.
- Directed the FAA to update and implement a new pilot flight and duty time rule and fatigue risk management plans to more adequately track scientific research in the field of fatigue. Required air carriers to create fatigue risk management systems approved by the FAA. Note: the creation of CFR Part 117 in 2013 formalized these requirements (Flight and Duty Limitations and Rest Requirements, 2013).
- Required airlines to establish pilot mentoring programs, create Pilot Professional Development Committees, modify training to accommodate new-hire pilots with different levels and types of flight experience, and provide leadership and command training to pilots in command.

As the Subcommittee Chairman, Jerry F. Costello (Illinois), summarized at the hearing:

Our bill is a comprehensive effort to consolidate what we know industry-wide about aviation safety to improve safety performance going forward. The more we looked at these issues, the more it became apparent that information about pilot training and safety programs is not readily available. There is a lot of information regarding industry best practices that is not being shared. This bill not only increased trained standards, but it seeks to identify what airlines are doing right in regard to safety and make this information a resource for others.

Costello (2009).

21.3   REGULATIONS, ADVISORY CIRCULARS, ICAO GUIDANCE

The industry has been busy. In addition to some of the rulemaking highlighted above, the FAA mandated Safety Management Systems (SMS) for Part 121 operators (scheduled air carriers) in 2015 with implementation in 2018 (FAA, 2016a). Voluntary reporting systems are required, as is an effective interface between the certificate holder and the regulator (FAA, 2002). Safety promotion, one of the SMS pillars, is required to provide a framework for a sound safety culture. CRM is mentioned in a number of different documents. Some documents further clarify the term, such as making the distinction between threat and error management (TEM) and CRM in the FAA Advisory Circular on Line Operations Safety Audits (FAA, 2006).

As the aviation safety industry has continued to evolve and as new technologies have been embraced, there are now numerous advisory circulars, regulations, and guidance material on implementation and evaluation. Further, the FAA introduced a new "Compliance Philosophy" to describe their methods of dealing with "unintentional deviations or noncompliance that arise from factors such as flawed systems and procedures, simple mistakes, lack of understanding, or diminished skills" (FAA, 2016b). There is an abundance of information and different companies and vendors available to help with design and implementation. Imagine that you are the airline with compliance, quality assurance, and training responsibilities. Here is a partial list of your resources (or challenges). You might also think of the challenges for the regulator providing oversight.

- FAA AC 120-51E; Crew Resource Management Training (FAA, 2004a)
- FAA AC 120-90; Line Operations Safety Audits (FAA, 2006)
- FAA AC 120-66B; Aviation Safety Action Program (voluntary reporting programs) (FAA, 2002)
- FAA AC 120-92B; SMS for Aviation Service Providers (FAA, 2015)
- FAA AC 120-82 Flight Operational Quality Assurance (FOQA) (FAA, 2004b)
- FAA AC 120-71B—Standard Operating Procedures (SOPs) and Pilot Monitoring (PM) Duties for Flight Deck Crewmembers (FAA, 2017)
- FAA AC 120-103A Fatigue Risk Management Systems for Aviation Safety (FAA, 2013a)
- Transport Canada Advisory Circular 700-042, Crew Resource Management Training Standards (Transport Canada, 2018)
- Guidance on the requirements that pertain to Flight crew for the training and testing of Human Factors under EASA Part-ORO and EASA Part-FCL (CAA, 2016)
- International Civil Aviation Organization Human Factors Training Manual (Doc 9683) (ICAO, 1998)
- European Aviation Safety Agency Decisions on Crew Resource Management Training, 2 presentations from EASA CRM Workshop, 2017 (EASA, 2017)
- Civil Aviation Safety Authority CAAP SMS-3(1); Non-Technical Skills Training and Assessment for Regular Public Transport Operations (CASA, 2011)

- Commercial Aviation Safety Team, Flight Deck Automation Working Group. Operational Use of Flight Path Management Systems—Final Report of the Performance-based operations Aviation Rulemaking Committee/ (CAST, 2013)
- Flight Safety Foundation—A Practical Guide for Improving Flight Path Monitoring (FSF, 2014)
- Skybrary—found at www.skybrary.aero—a superb resource for aviation safety articles (Skybrary, 2018)

21.4 HANDLING BIG DATA AND VOLUNTARY REPORTING SYSTEMS

Airlines receive a great deal of safety and performance data. Many of the latest airplane models generate a plethora of information. For example, the Boeing 787 produces over 500GB of data during every flight. Translating that data into meaningful, actionable information is a challenge. There are numerous vendors with products to "help" interpret. One of the challenges remains understanding that a high incident count in a category does not necessarily translate to the category being the highest risk. For example, the incidence of slow rotation on takeoff could be misinterpreted without also collecting and understanding other variables such as the presence of windshear on the runway.

Some operators have expressed concerns with the templates they are given by some vendors which may fit the aircraft of one manufacturer type better than another. As one safety manager told me, "You don't know what you don't know." It is important to confirm that the models and templates used are valid and reliable for the operation and equipment used. It is vital to have the input of the users, especially as the program is being set up, as well as for periodic reviews.

It is hard to underestimate the value of voluntary reporting programs. The industry—regulators, operators—recognize this fact. It is one of the reasons that a US meeting, InfoShare, has grown to regularly have 500−700 attendees. Today, many airlines have voluntary reporting programs for different employee groups including flight attendants, dispatch, maintenance, and ramp employees. Air traffic controllers have their own air traffic safety action program to voluntarily submit reports.

Not all will recall that one of the first voluntary reporting programs was started by United Airlines in 1974 and called their Flight Safety Awareness Program. One of the submitted reports described an ambiguous approach into Washington Dulles airport where the crew narrowly escaped descending into terrain after being "cleared for the approach" and having an interpretation of the charted approach procedure that was different from that of air traffic control. The submitted report of this incident was shared internally among United's pilots, consistent with the terms of this new and fairly radical safety program. Unfortunately, 6 weeks later, TWA Flight 514 was flying the same approach and also believed they were flying the correct descent path after being cleared for the approach. Unfortunately, they descended below the minimum safe altitude and crashed into a Virginia mountain top, killing all 85 passengers and 7 crewmembers. In their 1975 report of this accident, the NTSB stated that they were "encouraged that such safety awareness programs [as United's] have been initiated...In retrospect, the Board finds it most unfortunate that an incident of this nature was not, at the time of its occurrence, subject to uninhibited reporting...which might have resulted in broad and timely dissemination of the safety message issued by the carrier to its own flight crews" (Harty, 1990; NTSB, 1975; Orlady, 2012). This report eventually led to the creation of NASA's Aviation Safety Reporting System (ASRS).

However, for some operators and for some areas of the world, establishment and maintenance of a voluntary safety program is quite challenging, and may seem to conflict with values of their national culture and/or legal system. One airline, for example, mandated and required pilot participation in their "voluntary" program. They later expressed concerns that the submitted reports of their pilots were de-identified. One of the easiest ways to irreparably harm a voluntary reporting system is to punish the reporter.

For an airline just starting their voluntary programs, there is a fair amount of workload, costs, and protocols to be followed (FAA, 2002). Processing the reports, setting up a gatekeeper, training the event review committee—all of these tasks take time, resources, and a commitment from top management. But, the unique value of this information is that it provides perspectives that are not captured anywhere else—even in the 500GB of date received from a B787.

The information frequently provides insight into interactions—with other crewmembers, with the airplane software, with air traffic control. The reports can highlight CRM strengths and weaknesses—specifically aspects of leadership, followership, monitoring, automation confusion, and fatigue. These reports also can identify new risks in the system. Feeding back the information received from these voluntary reports into training scenarios and company safety publications reinforces the value of the program to those reporting. It sends a clear message to the reporter that it was worth his/her time to submit the report. Frequently, when combined with FOQA information, the voluntary reports enable a much fuller understanding of an event or situation. It should be noted that because manufacturers do not typically receive voluntary reports, it can be difficult for them to understand crew behaviors simply from reviewing FOQA data. Missing this perspective can lead to misinterpretation of information, incidents, and events.

21.5   UNEXPECTED CULTURAL FACTORS

Cultural issues are not all rooted in one's national culture. As the CRM manager for an airline, I presented the following list to a group of bright, enthusiastic check pilots during an annual instructor training session a number of years ago. I had received the list from a line pilot who unceremoniously dropped it on my desk with only the teaser, "I thought you might have interest in this." The list was neatly handwritten on a full page of stationery from a layover hotel. I asked the pilot if I could have a bit more information. His curt response: "I have had a month of hell flying with this captain. This is HIS list that he gave to me this morning on our last trip."

Here is the list:

Items to Improve Cockpit Relations

1. Stop trying to play captain.
2. Don't cry and complain if I use some corrective actions where I deem it is needed. That is what I'm paid to do—conduct a safe operation.
3. Record the departure ATIS on the weight manifest and keep it on the center pedestal over the radar unit where we both can have access to it at any time.
4. Ask me if I am ready to listen for a call to clearance delivery before calling for clearance.
5. Do not operate the radar unit.
6. Do not operate the instrument light switches.
7. Do not request routing changes without asking me.
8. Do not exit the cockpit before the captain, in other words. . .a common courtesy. (Orlady, Orlady, & Barnes, 2002)

The list is quite interesting—but the main point of sharing it here is because of the response that I received from the check pilot group to whom I was presenting. I displayed the list on a large screen and read through them. Asking for their thoughts, one check pilot earnestly asked, "this is a good list; are you going to hand out copies for us?" From the other side of the room, another check pilot was incredulous, wondering if the first pilot could possibly be posing a serious question. He was sure that it was a joke. It was not. Further, the first pilot could not believe that the second pilot did not think it was a great list that should be used on all of their checking and operating experience (OE) flights. Frankly, it was a delightful learning moment.

The point? At that time at this particular airline, there were some definite subcultures in the pilot group which represented different attitudes, procedures, and practices from some mergers, different equipment types, and different routes. What was exceedingly constructive was to use the list as a springboard for some valuable discussion on SOPs, unwritten practices, and norms of behavior.

Today, there are many examples of airlines whose employees represent many national cultures. As an example, Emirates Airlines has stated that they have more than 80 nationalities represented in their pilot group, and over a hundred different nationalities in their flight attendant group. A well-designed CRM and HF program will address these challenges. By acknowledging some of the differences, they are also able to strengthen and reinforce a number of cultural values and the corporate philosophy for their airline. Chapter 20, Cultural Issues and CRM, provides further discussion in this area.

21.6   TRAINING—THE PRIMARY INTERFACE

Many have stated that the most important safety feature on any airplane is a well-trained, highly motivated, and professional pilot (Prater, 2009; Sullenberger, 2009). The training process furnishes the primary interface between manufacturers, the airline operators, the environment in which they must be operated, and the pilots that fly them. The environment in which these airplanes must be operated has become more complex. The airplanes have become both more sophisticated and more expensive. Electronic flight bags and electronic checklists are the standard in many airplanes. The pilot training interfaces between the manufacturers, the airline companies, the pilots, and the environment have become even more important.

Airline pilot training is expensive and represents a significant cost center to the airline. However, it is difficult to underestimate its importance. Training provides a wonderful window of opportunity for an airline. Degani and Wiener described the "Four P's" referring to an airline's corporate philosophy, policies, procedures, and practices (Degani & Wiener, 1994). Instructors and pilots should see a connection in their training (ground, simulator, and operational experience training in the airplane) from the airline's stated philosophy, through the policies stated in manuals, through the procedures, and lastly and perhaps most importantly, through practices in line operations.

The Four P's are the ingredients that constitute the organizational culture or as Professor Richard Hackman referred to it—the organizational shell (Hackman, 1986). An organizational culture with attributes that are consistent, clear, generative, accountable and "just" should result in a robust safety culture at the airline. Put more simply, training should represent "how we fly our airplanes" at a particular carrier. To take advantage of the voluminous safety data collected, it is mandatory that a training department be nimble to highlight and reinforce identified issues, risks, and mitigation strategies.

One challenge with having training embody a corporation's "Four Ps" is that frequently the training is not conducted in-house or by the carrier itself. Sometimes, another company's simulators are used—which may or may not have the same cockpit setup regarding the location of instruments and switches that the pilots will see on the line in their company's aircraft, or even the same checklists. Sometimes, contract instructors are used who may not have a great deal of familiarity with a company's specific procedures. None of this is to suggest that there are not a number of high-quality training organizations, but rather to suggest that this training must be coordinated and differences noted.

21.7 SELECTION OF TRAINING DEVICES

The high fidelity of simulator training devices used today is quite extraordinary. They allow us to have very realistic scenarios. But not all training requires a full-motion simulator. And the simulators should not be modified to the point where they do not respond as the actual aircraft would respond. This point was raised during the NTSB hearing for American Airlines Flight 587 as it was revealed that some simulator parameters had been modified to further amplify some aircraft handling characteristics. The intentions by American clearly were honorable. However, a negative transfer of training will occur if the devices do not represent what will be experienced in the cockpit during line operations (NTSB, 2004).

One of the lessons learned with the advent of glass cockpits is that part-task trainers can be effective for training automation and for practicing CRM behavior such as prioritizing tasks and checklist protocols. Procedural trainers which frequently are simply nonworking cockpit mock-ups can be helpful. Some of these devices are better than others. For example, a single-path device might give the mistaken impression to the pilot that there is only one way to accomplish a task. Some of the first FMC training devices were limited in this regard. It was frustrating as it was clearly obvious to the pilot that there were multiple paths to accomplish the task.

Computer-based training (CBT) is used by many carriers to cover topics such as security issues, carriage of hazardous cargo materials, winter operations, etc. Some carriers also have developed sophisticated CBT for their aircraft ground school which can be accomplished remotely. At some large carriers, pilots cover the entire aircraft ground school using the CBT. Effective training will combine CBT with an instructor interface, whether it is with classroom review sessions or with the use of a part-task trainer or simulator to review and reinforce the CBT and desired CRM behaviors.

The quality of CBT can vary quite a bit. It can be frustrating for the pilot to discover errors in the presentation, to take the time to use the software program to give feedback and point out the errors or discrepancy, only to discover the same errors the following year. Some carriers ensure that the training is tailored to their particular operation, to their checklists, to their procedures—that it supports the company's "Four Ps," as mentioned earlier. It is one of the more important points of training—and one, unfortunately, that is often missed by training designers. The training must represent how the aircraft are flown on the line and the corporate culture of the airline. It is important to note the value of reinforcing the training with a qualified instructor. Otherwise, the training risks being quickly dismissed by pilots who will conclude that it is irrelevant since the training is not consistent with or reflective of actual line operations.

21.8   TRAINING AUTOMATION

Over the years, we have learned a great deal about training automation. It is valuable to recall some of the early questions that were raised as we struggled to understand the appropriate role of automation. In its "National Plan to Enhance Aviation Safety through Human Factors" the Air Transport Association Human Factors Task Force summarized the following in 1989:

> *During the 1970s and early 1980s, the concept of automating as much as possible was considered appropriate. The expected benefits were a reduction in pilot workload and increased safety...Although many of these benefits have been realized, serious questions have arisen and incidents/accidents have occurred which question the underlying assumption that the maximum available automation is always appropriate, or that we understand how to design automated systems so that they are fully compatible with the capabilities and limitations of the humans in the system.*

ATA (1989)

The ATA National Plan also stated, "The fundamental concern is the lack of a scientifically based philosophy of automation which describes the circumstances under which tasks are appropriately allocated to the machine and/or to the pilot" (Graeber & Billings, 1989).

Initially, many airlines developed their own philosophy of automation based on NASA recommendations and industry work. Some airlines developed an introduction to automation course for those making their initial transition to an advanced technology aircraft. Interesting to note the relevance of these courses today, particularly given the fact that so many flight students are exposed to advanced technology cockpits early in their training. Perhaps a course may be needed to familiarize pilots with a standard technology cockpit today as the concept of having to manually set airspeed bugs, for example, would be foreign to some. Manufacturers also included the use of automation in their flight deck design philosophies, which are discussed later in this chapter.

21.9   AUTOMATION SURPRISES

Automation surprises happen to most pilots and have been studied by many researchers. A senior Aer Lingus captain shared a story with this author about approaching New York's John F. Kennedy Airport, arriving from Europe. The crew was forced to abort their approach and execute a go-around due to landing traffic that had failed to clear the runway. As they began their climb to go around, the power levels were not pushed forward sufficiently to be seated in what, for this aircraft, was the takeoff/go-around detent position. As they climbed, the pilots raised the landing gear. However, this action conflicted with the designed logic of the automation.

Since the power levers had not "clicked" into the detent, the aircraft's warning systems believed that the aircraft was still attempting to land and was obviously not in landing configuration as the landing gear now was not "down and locked." Therefore, during this critical flight period and while receiving special go-around instructions from JFK Tower, the aural alerting system began repeatedly announcing very loudly, "TOO LOW, GEAR, TOO LOW, GEAR." The statement of the captain describing the incident was classic, "While I was quite confident that we were not in imminent danger of crashing the aircraft, I really did not know what was going on" (N. Johnston, personal communication, September 9, 2009). There are very few pilots who have not been surprised by automation at some point.

The Asiana 214 accident in San Francisco in July 2013 clearly highlighted some misunderstanding and misinterpretation of the Flight Management systems (NTSB, 2014b). The topic has ramifications for CRM and effective crew behaviors. For example, what callouts should be made? Should all flight mode annunciations (FMA) be verbalized? What actions should the PM take if an appropriate response is not made? Is the main area of concern that the pilots were surprised or startled, or perhaps more importantly, their ability to regroup and recover—individually and as a crew? This is a CRM area as it is vital that both crewmembers understand the recovery actions and, literally, must keep the airplane flying.

Loss of Control (LOC) remains a current topic in the industry. Manufacturers were tasked with developing procedures—primarily pitch attitudes and thrust (power) settings that would keep "the blue side up," that would keep the airplane flying and under control for a brief period of time as the crew figured out what the issues were. Important to note, that for the crew, understanding the cause of the surprise or upset, is not the first priority. Whether mechanically based, an air traffic control conflict, weather phenomena, or an incapacitation from a crewmember—the priority is to fly the airplane and regroup. CRM means making the best use of the resources with the time available. Period.

Some manufacturers follow a "quiet, dark cockpit" philosophy meaning that there are no callouts required if things are going well. One of the challenges with this philosophy is that it does not guarantee that both crewmembers are "on the same page" or have the same mental picture. As an exception to this philosophy and after receiving inputs from many operators, Boeing created a "reversers normal" callout after landing. In the past, if something was operating correctly or "normally," there would have been no callout. However, an investigation of several incidents and input from numerous operators prompted the change. Not surprisingly, it initially was not received well by some operators who strongly believed in the quiet, dark cockpit. It is important for the manufacturer or group with responsibility for checklists to take inputs and change as appropriate, working with regulators for approval.

Frequently, the logic of surprising or unintended automation events, whether caused by the operators or from system design, is not fully understood until after the event. Even the best-designed systems can provide surprises that had not been conceived by the manufacturer nor witnessed in flight testing. Capt. Richard de Crespigny and his crew faced many of these challenges on QANTAS Flight QF32 when the number 2 engine on his Airbus A-380 exploded 4 minutes after departing Singapore on November 4, 2010. To the crew's credit, all persons aboard—440 passengers and 29 crew—survived. Some quotes from Capt. de Crespigny's book, *QF 32* (2012), are particularly salient. "ECAM" refers to Airbus' electronic centralized aircraft monitoring system that can display system information and faults, and specify appropriate steps to take with some malfunctions.

> *I wasn't happy. We'd all become overwhelmed with the sheer number and layered complexity of ECAM alerts, and the 'logical' way ECAM was trying to check and fix the aircraft. (pg. 201).*

> *Months later, when I presented the QF32 story, I would play the soundtrack of the cockpit aural warnings to illustrate to the audience what happens when the ECAM starts issuing piercing alerts and won't shut up. I haven't seen an audience yet that can handle the noise for more than 30 seconds before people screw up their faces and demand that someone switch the sound off. We endured it for much longer-it was like being in a military stress experiment. (pg. 217).*

Sometime after the accident, Capt. de Crespigny asked a senior Airbus test pilot what he and his crew could have done differently. The response, as quoted in his book:

> *Richard, I have no suggestions; we never tested the A380 with the failures that you experience. You were on your own — outside the 10 − 9 safety envelope that certification provides. We designed the A380 to be strong and resilient; you proved it. Everyone at Airbus is proud that our aircraft performed so well. (pg. 325).*

Capt. de Crespigny agreed - and continues to fly the A380.

Training and procedures must prepare crews to remember their priorities, to use checklists as appropriate, but not to abandon basic airmanship or their own cognitive ability to handle situations. With the advent and use of electronic checklists, it can be particularly important, from a CRM perspective, to ensure that both pilots have the same mental and cognitive picture.

21.10 AUTOMATION DOES NOT REDUCE TRAINING REQUIREMENTS

One of the great myths associated with increased automation in air transport operation is that automation reduces training. This is simply not true.

Automation has created training requirements that add to the previous requirements.

Increased automation is a welcome tool and is used by pilots to fly more safely and efficiently. However, the skills and knowledge associated with taking full advantage of increased automation must be added to the training curriculum. All of the former skills and knowledge of professional pilots are still required.

It is simply not possible to monitor a system effectively without knowing how the system is planning to accomplish its task (Billings, 1996). Unfortunately, present training does not always ensure that pilots have this information. Recent accidents and incidents suggest that we do not have an adequate grasp of monitoring as it relates to human performance and limitations. The Flight Safety Foundation recently published "A Practical Guide for Improving Flight Path Monitoring," a collaborative effort by industry members who formed the Active Pilot Monitoring Working Group. Interestingly, the report reinforces the "4P's" concept mentioned earlier and cites the need to have a corporate monitoring philosophy which is supported by senior leadership, written in the operator manuals, and communicated as an organizational standard (FSF, 2014).

21.11   REDUCING LEVELS OF AUTOMATION—WHAT'S CHANGED?

There were some challenges as pilots transitioned to the advanced technology, glass-cockpit airplanes. Sometimes the automation produced surprises; sometimes it accomplished a task, such as leveling off at an assigned altitude, differently than the pilot would have leveled off (e.g., perhaps initiating the level off later than the pilot would have). A good example was some of the early programming on the MD-80 airplane. Aural alerts were designed to be given in a female voice that was colloquially referred to as "Bitching Betty." Suffice to say that "Betty" seemed to fly certain maneuvers (such as level offs) and managed the energy during an approach, in a different manner than many pilots believe they flew. And, "Betty" could be quite vocal, and just plain distracting on some approaches. Attempting to address these concerns, airlines were urged to develop and train their own automation philosophy. They also spent a fair amount of time talking about "reducing levels of automation" as appropriate for pilot control and understanding of a situation. That policy worked well with numerous airplanes. For example, if you reduce the levels of automation on an MD-80, you have basically made it a rope-start, conventional technology DC-9 cockpit.

However, the latest generation of fly-by-wire airplanes have a different architecture, the specifics of which are beyond the scope of this chapter. The airplane systems are integrated as opposed to being independent (sometimes described as "Federated"). Reducing levels of automation on a Boeing 777 or an Airbus 380 can have some dramatic and unintended effects (at least, for the pilot) of reducing or removing some of the flight envelope protection. Put bluntly, there is no such airplane as a "rope-start B777" or "standard technology A380." Some training programs have not discussed this area perhaps as completely as they could. Manufacturers could also potentially provide additional guidance.

The main point is that historically we have trained pilots when surprised or unsure of something with the automatics to reduce the level of automation. Unfortunately, some pilots have not been trained this way. Some mistakenly seem to think that the pilots are there to support the automation! The author is familiar with several cases of low airspeed warning events where the pilots believed that the automation would correct the situation, and, therefore, just waited. It was pointed out in the investigation of the Asiana San Francisco accident that there was confusion and misunderstanding in the flight mode annunciations and operation of the autothrottles. As an example, for many pilots, the "Hold" mode of the autothrottle translated, by their vernacular to "You (the pilot) hold." There was not a belief that the autothrottles would "save the day." As noted by NTSB Board Acting Chair, Christopher Hart, "In this accident, the flight crew over-relied on automated systems without fully understanding how they interacted. Automation has made aviation safer. But even in highly automated aircraft, the human must be the boss." (NTSB, 2014a)

21.12 IMPLICATIONS OF DESIGN PHILOSOPHIES

Airbus, Boeing, Embraer, and Bombardier design and build superb aircraft. Many smart engineers and intelligent design processes work to give pilots airplanes that are both safe and a real pleasure to fly. For example, a 747 or 777 with a strong crosswind handles superbly. Physics in motion! While the superb handling qualities may be due to excellent pilot training and skill, most pilots will laud the superior engineering efforts of the manufacturer. And, certainly the regulatory agencies that certify these aircraft should also receive some credit.

However, pilots have sometimes expressed frustration at procedures and checklists developed by manufacturers. From one particular carrier, and reflecting their culture at the time, some captains created and carried their own checklists. Many operators modified the manufacturer's checklists and procedures to fit their operation. Today, perhaps reflecting the cost and liability of maintaining their own manuals and checklists, more and more operators are using the manufacturer's checklists, procedures, and manuals. Some inputs from operators have prompted manufacturers to change their checklists. One example was changing the timing of setting takeoff flaps—to be accomplished at the gate before taxi as opposed to setting the flaps while taxiing.

Airbus and Boeing have different design philosophies which lend some insight to their cockpit design and flight envelope protection. Dr. Kathy Abbott captured a good summary of these in her chapter, "Human Factors Engineering and Flight Deck Design," in *The Avionics Handbook* (Abbott, 2017).

Boeing has described its high-level flight deck philosophy as follows:

- The pilot is the final authority for the operation of the airplane.
- Both crew members are ultimately responsible for the safe conduct of the flight.
- Flight crew tasks, in order of priority, are safety, passenger comfort, and efficiency.
- Design for crew operations based on pilot's past training and operational experience.
- Design systems to be error tolerant.
- The hierarchy of design alternatives is simplicity, redundancy, and automation.
- Apply automation as a tool to aid, not replace, the pilot.
- Address fundamental human strengths, limitations, and individual differences — for both normal and nonnormal operations.
- Use new technologies and functional capabilities only when:
- They result in clear and distinct operational or efficiency advantages, and
- There is no adverse effect to the human-machine interface.

Airbus has described its automation philosophy as:

- Automation must not reduce overall aircraft reliability, it should enhance aircraft and systems safety, efficiency, and economy.
- Automation must not lead the aircraft out of the safe flight envelope and it should maintain the aircraft within the normal flight envelope.
- Automation should allow the operator to use the safe flight envelope to its full extent, should this be necessary due to extraordinary circumstances.
- Within the normal flight envelope, the automation must not work against operator inputs, except when absolutely necessary for safety.

The value of reviewing this list is to examine the perceived role of the flight crew from the manufacturer's perspective. Particularly in today's flight decks, there are electronic checklists, and electronic flight bags. Crew communication frequently is accomplished through these devices. Does the operation of a competent, well-trained crew reflect these design principles in normal, abnormal, and emergency operations? Would the flight crews agree? What does the incident and accident data show?

21.13 THE MANUFACTURER'S CHALLENGE OF UNDERSTANDING THE OPERATIONAL ENVIRONMENT

It is worthwhile to explore the guidance and expectation of the manufacturers with the operation of their airplanes. Particularly since CRM does not quantify in a typical engineering sense, understanding some of these nontechnical and behavioral aspects (e.g., CRM!) can be challenging for the manufacturer. The following examples perhaps lend some insight.

While working as the Chief Technical pilot for a major manufacturer, one of my responsibilities was to participate in a biweekly technical review board that reviewed different incidents, operator reports, and accident recommendations. One session started with the engineer stating, "a dumb pilot did this, so we have to change our procedure." He continued with the next event: "A dumb pilot did this so now we have to change our checklist." At this particular meeting, there were many "dumb pilot" events to be reviewed. As one of the few pilots in this group and the only airline pilot, I will admit to being taken aback. At the time, I was brand new to this group. My question to them was pretty simple: did they think these pilots were born dumb, or perhaps have the checklists and procedures that they have been writing helped to make the pilots dumb? My question was not received well, or perhaps seemed as though I was speaking Greek. It did provoke some constructive discussions.

Another example: I was told by an engineer that my group did not need to worry about revising the tail strike checklist for a particular airplane. Here is a quick synopsis of our conversation:

Me: "Why?" (don't we need to revise the checklist any longer?)
Engineer: "We are not physically producing a tail skid on that airplane any longer."
Me: "Why?"
Engineer: "It is not needed because pilots will be unable to get a tail strike."
Me: "Why?"
Engineer: "We are changing the software so that the same control movement (pull) will not allow them to strike the tail on landing."
Me: "Are we going to tell the pilots about this software change?"
Engineer: "Why?"

Please do not miss the point that all of the manufacturers design and build some superb airplanes that are a genuine pleasure to operate. However, it is important to examine the understanding from the pilot standpoint and operational perspective as well as from the design engineers. You might think about the numerous devices in today's automobiles—proximity sensors, back-up cameras, automatic lights, automatic shifting into park when removing the key—and the unwelcome surprise that can occur when renting a vehicle without those features—perhaps a dead battery from leaving the lights on when exiting a vehicle. CRM involves making use of all of the resources, being able to communicate effectively, having good situational awareness, and a shared mental model. Some system design changes and "improvements" to "assist" the flight crews unintentionally can disrupt this mental model. It also affects CRM behaviors if the crew is unsure of a particular action or result.

One more example: with the advent of EICAS (engine instrument and crew alerting system) and ECAM (electronic centralized aircraft monitor), many functions are monitored and recommended, and give directed actions to pilots. Imagine that you are at the gate, parking brake on, starting a normal engine sequence. If there is a problem with the start, for example, due to a hot start, pilots know what steps to take. They are going to interrupt the start and stop fuel to that engine (confirming, of course that they have the correct fuel lever). However, present procedures from the manufacturers in most current airplanes direct the pilot to take no action, sometimes described by instructors as "sit on your hands!" until the appropriate EICAS or ECAM message appears. The pilot is to respond to the EICAS or ECAM. These systems, as well as the electronic checklists, have many benefits. There is no doubt that they can help trap potential errors of the crew. However, they also can result in a lack of cognitive awareness and engagement by the crew as they wait to be "told" what to do.

We still have some learning to do about automated systems, crew interaction, startle responses, and CRM behaviors. I recall reading an accident report which described the captain shouting, as the airplane was going out of control, to "get the autopilot on, get the autopilot on." At a different time in our industry, the anticipated call might have been from the captain, "I've got the airplane." We still have learning to accomplish about unintended consequences with the liveware interface and automated systems, particularly in a crew concept environment. CRM behaviors are affected by this design. It is important to have candid, vigorous, and robust discussions and to include qualified and current line pilots. The main point is that the designers and users should understand both the context of the design as well as the operational environment.

21.14 COCKPIT WORKLOAD

Cockpit workload is an important and elusive concept (Wiener & Curry, 1980; Wiener, 1985). What is often forgotten is the importance of training as it applies to evaluating the workload that is imposed on operating pilots. Put simply, a task that is very difficult for a poorly trained person can be a simple task for one adequately trained (Orlady, 1991).

Pilots need to understand workload and how it affects their performance. They need to recognize task saturation and overload—both in themselves and in the fellow crewmember. One of the key tenets for most CRM programs is workload management. We learned a great deal about workload and crew coordination with the introduction of advanced technology aircraft. It was (and is) very easy to become preoccupied, for example, with programming the flight management computer (FMC) or trying to comply with the instructions of the electronic checklist. It is important to have standard operating procedures that clarify programming responsibilities. It is easy for an incompetent or confused PM to greatly complicate a situation, and, consequently, to significantly increase the workload for the PF. It also is very easy for the PM's workload to dramatically increase if the PF decides to manually fly, particularly without an appropriate briefing to the PM. CRM has an important role here in terms of communicating workload overloads and with setting task prioritization.

21.15 MAINTENANCE OF MANUAL FLYING SKILLS—DO ALL HAVE THE SAME FOUNDATION?

It is agreed by about all that manual piloting skills degrade if they are not used. It can be somewhat distressing even to experienced pilots transitioning, for example, from a more advanced Boeing 777 aircraft to an earlier automation level aircraft like the Boeing 757, and observing that their basic instrument scanning skills have degraded. It is easy to become dependent on a primary flight display that basically displays all flight information during normal flight on one single display. In this case, the degradation is caused by a rusty instrument scan and is normally quickly recovered, particularly with good instruction. The point is that there is a transition and that manual skills degrade when not used or when used differently.

There has also been concern expressed about the manual skill foundation for today's pilots. Dr. Charles Billings asked several prescient questions in his excellent book *Aviation Automation: The Search for a Human-Centered Approach*, which, although published in 1996, seems eerily appropriate today:

- Will pilots who have never had to acquire the finely tuned manual skills that older pilots take for granted be able to demonstrate such skills at an acceptable level if they must transition to another aircraft that lacks these advanced features?
- Similarly, will they have learned the cognitive skills necessary for unassisted navigation if the flight management software fails?
- Finally, and perhaps most important given the high reliability of today's aircraft, will they acquire the judgmental skills and experience that alone can enable them to make wise decisions in the face of uncertainty or serious mechanical or environment problems? (Billings, 1996)

Pilots are encouraged to use automation, and most pilots like using automation—to varying degrees. The use of automation is supposed to reduce workload and allow pilots, especially in the busy terminal airspace, to monitor more effectively and to scan for other aircraft. Many airlines have procedures recommending use of automated systems and even requiring their use during certain conditions, such as for a very low visibility approach and landing. For example, some airlines do not allow their pilots to disconnect the autothrottles. Some airlines also train and discuss reducing levels of automation without losing some of the protective provisions that have been designed into the software.

Pilots flying long-haul international routes face a special dilemma. They may be flying schedules that do not have many takeoffs and landings due to the long segment length. On the longer flight segments, the aircraft is scheduled with additional flight crew who serve as relief pilots and who are trained and rated in the aircraft. However, frequently there simply are not enough flight segments for all pilots to stay current with the FAA minimum of three takeoffs and landings within 90 days. The long-haul pilots at one airline used to joke that CRM on their fleet was excellent—because of the challenges with staying current and that the crew inputs were both needed and appreciated. Some airlines bring their long-haul flight crews back for a recurrent simulator session every 90 days. Some airlines have gone a step further and are keeping track of actual aircraft landing currency as opposed to landing currency met with a landing in a simulator session. A few airlines are even scheduling additional no-jeopardy simulator sessions for the pilots simply to manually fly. These sessions are also helpful from a CRM standpoint as the monitoring workload of the PM changes when the PF has turned off some of the automatics and is manually flying the airplane.

21.16 PILOTS WANT AND NEED MORE SYSTEM KNOWLEDGE

At many airlines, pilots want and need more systems knowledge. They want to understand both how systems operate, and more importantly, the logic behind the design of the system. They do not want to be simply checklist readers and executors of procedures, seemingly dependent on a checklist or procedure to "save" them in an irregular or emergency operation. Thoughtfully designed checklists and procedures have huge contributions to make. But dependence without contextual understanding can lead to misinterpretation and unintended consequences.

Pilots also complain about the reduction in "approved" training materials that are provided. Economics surely is a factor, but often the response from instructors or management is that, "if we put the material in the manual, then you are responsible in a check ride for that material." As stated in the previous version of this chapter, that perspective is neither acceptable nor satisfactory. Emergency and irregular operations that occur in actual line operations, unfortunately, are not limited to "what's in the manual." The amount and depth of systems material remains an issue, and one that warrants a balanced discussion with pilots, trainers, and oversight regulators.

As a quick historical note, a NASA-sponsored researcher came to my airline for some cockpit observations on actual line flights. After four or five jumpseat observations, she stopped at my office to share her high level of concern that the pilots did not seem to understand all of the different modes of vertical navigation available on this particular airplane. Her observation was correct. Sometimes the introduction of new technologies was not thought out completely. As I recall, there were five choices for vertical navigation at the time. The VNAV mode was not formally taught, but a pilot might be exposed to it during their line operating experience—if their check pilot had received training. This airline varied from directing its pilots to only use two modes, then three modes, then all five modes, and then back to three modes. It seems humorous now, but the observations, understandably, were quite alarming to the researcher.

Pilots are the product of the information and training that they receive. They frequently do not receive enough information on the automated systems to understand the design and contextual use. This lack of knowledge affects their crew coordination and teamwork. Some airlines are addressing this need, providing a differences section to address pilots transitioning from one manufacturer's airplane to another. This area is perhaps one that the manufacturers could also address and provide material for training.

21.17 INTENTIONAL NONCOMPLIANCE WITH PROCEDURES

Unfortunately, even if training is improved, minimum standards raised, and more training materials provided, there remains the question, "Why do experienced and well-trained aircrews sometimes act against their experience and training and have accidents?"

This question is not new. It has probably been around since Standard Operating Procedures (SOPs) were first developed and their use required. The Flight Safety Foundation Icarus Committee examined this question formally in 1992 at their first meeting. Their discussion of enabling factors, latent factors, and, basically, what lies behind mistaken actions, resulted in the publication of 18 findings and 10 recommendations (Pinet & Enders, 1994). Orlady and Orlady discussed procedural noncompliance or the "willful deviator" in their book *Human Factors for Multi-Crew Flight Operations*. They list some common reasons as to why pilots choose not to comply with established standard operating procedures:

- The pilot may think the established procedure is simply wrong.
- The pilot may think the established procedures are okay for the "average" pilot, but that he/she is different (and yes, frequently superior!).
- The pilot may think his/her procedure is either just as good or better than the one established.
- The pilot may think the procedure is not important or not necessary—or just not worth the bother—just this once, frequently, or always.
- Lastly, in some instances, the pilot does not really object to the established procedure but consciously or subconsciously just wants to defy "them"—that is, meaning management or authority in general (Orlady & Orlady, 1999).

It should be a priority for an airline both to minimize and to learn from non-compliance with established procedures and to incorporate what they learn into their training. It should also be a priority to communicate observations, findings, and corrective actions developed with the pilots that may help them understand their own actions or those of another crewmember. It remains one of this author's pet peeves to read a company report describing an incident with a summary statement that "the crew failed to comply with SOPs." And, frankly, that distaste increased working with a manufacturer who seemed to regard "did not comply with manufacturer's procedure" as the stop point of an investigation. Why? Was there an error of commission or omission based on an intentional action based on the list above? As Sidney Dekker and others have noted, there almost always is "more to the story" that a "failed to comply with SOPs" will not capture (Dekker, 2006). It is vital not to miss these types of learning opportunities.

One airline that is attempting to gather information and learn from procedural differences is FedEx. They are collecting data through a quality assurance collection process of line observations. Of particular note, the observers are recording what is preventing the crews from performing their job. They are noting exceptions and gaps in their procedures and exceptionally good techniques. The observations are nonevaluative; the information collected de-identified. The program is still evolving; it will be interesting to see what they do with the data collected.

SOPs, if they are sound, appropriate to the situation, and developed with the input of those using them, are vital in today's operations. The level of SOP noncompliance can also be a measure of organizational health. That employees would adopt an attitude supporting "why bother having procedures if they are not to be followed" should surely trigger a reexamination of a number of basic tenets and influence of the "Four Ps."

21.18 CURRENT CRM AND HUMAN FACTORS AIRLINE PROGRAMS

I had a recent opportunity to hear 10–12 airlines describe their efforts in CRM and in HF at an industry meeting. There were some common tenets in their excellent and thoughtful presentations. I was reminded of an old list, quite well-known to those who have been in the CRM field for some time. This list, titled, "How to Kill a CRM Program," was compiled by Bill Taggart, a NASA/University of Texas researcher on aviation psychology, at a meeting in Australia (Taggart, 1993). It is interesting to see the relevance of his list today.

How to kill a CRM program

1. Not integrating CRM into LOFT, PT and other operational training.
2. Failing to recognize the unique needs of your own airline's culture.
3. Allowing the CRM zealots to run the show.
4. Bypassing research and data gathering steps.
5. Ignoring the checking and standards pilots.
6. Having lots of diagrams, boxes, and acronyms.
7. Make the program a one-shot affair.
8. Using pop psychology and psychobabble.
9. Turing CRM into a therapy session.
10. Redefining the C to mean charismatic.

What was common in the airline presentations at this meeting in April 2018:

1. They had a program that they thought was tailored for their specific airline, their culture, their employees.
2. They were quite excited about the program.
3. They had support from top management.
4. They had line pilots involved in the design, execution, and review of their programs, and, not infrequently, as instructors.
5. The models and acronyms used in their programs were simple—not simplistic!
6. The programs made sense to the pilots and other employee groups in their airline.
7. They were using the data collected—whether from "first look" or LOSA or "quality assurance" jump seating.
8. The important of voluntary incident reports was stressed and reinforced. Feedback and lessons learned were apparent to the line employees.
9. They were doing better at looking at issues of noncompliance in terms of trying to understand why and whether or not there was something they could do better.
10. They knew that the programs were a process that should continue to evolve.

Some carriers are able to offer joint CRM training sessions with flight attendants and pilots. I have participated in and observed numerous joint training scenarios. The scenarios were excellent, based on real events; the session facilitated by some excellent instructors and received favorably by the participants. Scheduling can be challenging because there are so many more flight attendants than pilots at an airline, and the flight attendants may have training at a location where pilots are not trained. If possible, it is a practice highly recommended—and one which frequently provides very useful feedback to the trainers.

One stubborn issue remains the timing of the CRM training whether for new hires, recurrent, captain upgrade, or for instructors. The timing of the training seems to vary quite a bit, or more positively framed, to be customized at each carrier. New hire CRM training occurs at different points in indoctrination. Some airlines have courses in their initial indoctrination; some will bring the pilots back for training after they have some line experience.

Most, but not all, airlines have a specific captain CRM course or captain command course. There are two points of interest with these captain courses. Some airlines have designed an extensive 4-day course where the new captains are briefed on many of the corporate aspects of the airline and have a chance to interact with some top executives as well as learning more about their command responsibilities and leadership skills. Not surprisingly, the experience is viewed quite positively by the new captains. The course represents a significant corporate investment and commitment. But, there are many pilots who upgraded before these courses were created and have not been exposed to this type of training experience. Is there a way for these "veteran" captains to reap the benefits of the course material? Secondly, so many captains are upgrading at some carriers that it can be difficult to schedule these courses. One airline told me that it can take 3 years to get scheduled. That time delay seems a bit excessive in terms of delivering information that is supposed to help the new captain be the best he/she can be. Recurrent CRM training for instructors is another area that seems to be challenging in terms of scheduling and resources. The instructor group—simulator instructors and line check pilots—are a critical group. The inputs and feedback that they bring is as important as any material that might be delivered to them.

One last area that is being thoughtfully developed are numerous mentoring programs. As mentioned earlier in this chapter, this was one of the recommendations flowing from the Colgan accident. As then FAA Administrator, Randy Babbitt, stated, "The people with the experience need to make sure they're mentoring the ones who don't have it. This needs to become part of our professional DNA [generic code]" (Babbitt, 2009). The mentoring programs have been supported and developed with the assistance of the labor associations in many cases. Reports seem to indicate a "win—win" result for both the pilots being mentored and for those mentoring. The programs are a worthy investment by the airline.

21.19 FINAL THOUGHTS

This chapter has attempted to briefly raise a number of critical and sensitive training issues as they relate to CRM. While CRM provides some great tools, it does not solve everything nor diminish the requirement for technical competency. I recall a story often told by my late grandfather, Colonel Horace Orlady, who soloed in 1916 and flew in the U.S. Signal Corp, the predecessor to the U.S. Army. Their unit had a record of ordering an exceptionally high number of replacements parts (wings, landing gear, etc.), which, frankly, were tied to their dismal accident rate. An army efficiency expert was dispatched to address the issue. Observing so many aircraft in disrepair on his initial tour of the airfield, he queried the sergeant as to the cause. The sergeant succinctly responded, "bad landings, sir." The efficiency expert quickly addressed the situation with a large sign posted in the flight operations area the next day that stated, "There will be no more bad landings at this airfield" (Orlady & Orlady, 1999).

Unfortunately, we do not have a sign to post, nor would anyone think that it would be an effective means to address what are complicated and dynamic issues. Training must be tailored to reflect the specific background and experience of the pilots being trained. It must also accurately reflect the airline's operation, culture and safety reporting systems. The airlines, regulators, and manufacturers are collecting more operational and safety information than probably at any other time in the industry. We know a great deal more now about CRM, training, crew performance, system safety, monitoring, and the performance of highly reliable organizations as some of the earlier chapters have described. The industry's current safety record is excellent. But we must continue efforts to understand how the different components of our aviation system work together, of the interface between the operators, machine, and environment, and of the organizational influence on an operation. And we must continue efforts to protect and share voluntarily reported data so that others might learn and to avoid unintended consequences. CRM is a superb tool and provides a framework for learning and understanding many behaviors. However, it is but one component of the aviation system. We still have lots to learn.

REFERENCES

Abbott, K. (2017). Human factors engineering and flight deck design. In C. Spitzer, U. Ferrell, & T. Ferrell (Eds.), *Digital avionics handbook* (3rd ed.). Boca Raton, Florida: CRC Press, pp. 15–1, 15–16.

ATA. (1989). *Air transport association. national plan to enhance aviation safety through human factors improvements*. New York: Air Transportation of America.

Babbitt, J. (2009). *"We can't regulate professionalism", invited speech at the ALPA's 55th Air Safety Forum*. Washington, D.C: Air Line Pilots Association.

Billings, C. (1996). *Aviation automation: The search for a human-centered approach*. New Jersey: Erlbaum Associates, Inc.

CAA. (2016). Guidance on the requirements that pertain to Flightcrew for the training and testing of Human Factors under EASA Part-ORO and EASA Part-FCL. Standards Document 29, Version 7. United Kingdom. Civil Aviation Authority (CAA).

CASA. (2011). Non-Technical Skills Training and Assessment for Regular Public Transport Operations. Civil Aviation Advisory Publication, CAAP SMS-3(1), Canberra, Australia, Civil Aviation Safety Authority (CASA), Australian Government.

CAST, Flight Deck Automation Working Group (2013). Operational Use of Flight Path Management Systems; Final Report of the Performance-based operations Aviation Rulemaking Committee/Commercial Aviation Safety Team Flight Deck Automation Working Group. Washington, D.C. Federal Aviation Administration.

Congressional Record. (2010). Public Law 111-216-Aug.1, 2010. Airline Safety and Federal Aviation Administration Extension Act of 2010. Retrieved from <https://www.congress.gov/111/plaws/publ216/PLAW-111publ216.pdf>.

Costello, J. (2009). *Hearing Before the Subcommittee on Aviation of the Committee on Transportation and Infrastructure, House of Representatives, September 23, 2009, 111-62.* Washington, DC: U.S. Government Printing Office.

Cox, R. (2017). *Making a Difference in Aviation Safety: Colgan Flight 3407 Nine Years Later, ISASI 2017 Annual Seminar. International Society of Air Safety Investigators (ISASI).* Sterling, VA: International Society of Air Safety Investigators.

de Crespigny, R. (2012). QF 32, Sydney, Australia, Macmillan.

Degani, A., & Wiener, E. (1994). *On the Design of Flight-Deck Procedures (NASA Contractor Report 177642).* California. NASA: Ames Research Center.

Dekker, S. (2006). *The field guide to understanding human error.* Surrey, United Kingdom: Ashgate Publishing Limited.

EASA. (2017). Crew Resource Management in Practice. Cologne, France. EASA. Retrieved from <https://www.easa.europa.eu/document-library/general-publications/crm-training-implementation>.

Endeavor Air. (2018). Offering Unprecedented Pilot Pay. Retrieved from Endeavor Air website: <http://www.endeavorair.com/content/endeavorair/en_us/careers/pilots/Pilot_Compensation.html>.

FAA. (2002). *Aviation Safety Action Program (ASAP), (Advisory Circular 120-66B).* Washington, DC: Federal Aviation Administration.

FAA. (2004a). *Crew Resource Management Training, (Advisory Circular 120-51E).* Washington, DC: Federal Aviation Administration.

FAA. (2004b). *Flight Operational Quality Assurance, (Advisory Circular 120-82).* Washington, DC: Federal Aviation Administration.

FAA. (2006). *Line Operations Safety Audits (Advisory Circular 120-90).* Washington, DC: Federal Aviation Administration.

FAA. (2013a). *Fatigue Risk Management Systems for Aviation Safety, (Advisory Circular 120-103A).* Washington, DC: Federal Aviation Administration.

FAA. (2013b). *Press Release — FAA Boosts Aviation Safety with New Pilot Qualification Standards.* Washington, DC: Federal Aviation Administration.

FAA. (2015). *Safety Management Systems for Aviation Service Providers, (Advisory Circular 120-92B).* Washington, DC: Federal Aviation Administration.

FAA. (2016a). *Safety Management System, SMS for 121 Operators.* Washington, DC: Federal Aviation Administration. Retrieved from: https://www.faa.gov/about/initiatives/sms/specifics_by_aviation_industry_type/121/.

FAA. (2016b). *Compliance Philosophy.* Washington D.C: Federal Aviation Administration. Retrieved from https://www.faa.gov/about/initiatives/cp/.

FAA. (2017). *Standard Operating Procedures and Pilot Monitoring Duties for Flight Deck Crewmembers, (Advisory Circular 120-71B).* Washington D.C: Federal Aviation Administration.

Flight and Duty Limitations and Rest Requirements, 14 CFR Part 117. (2013). Retrieved from <https://www.gpo.gov/fdsys/pkg/CFR-2013-title14-vol3/pdf/CFR-2013-title14-vol3-part117.pdf>.

FSF, Active Pilot Monitoring Working Group. (2014). A Practical Guide for Improving Flight Path Monitoring, Final Report of the Active Pilot Monitoring Group. Alexandria, Virginia, Flight Safety Foundation.

Graeber, C., & Billings, C. (1989). *Human-Centered Automation: Development of a Philosophy.* Mountainview, California: NASA Ames Research Center.

Hackman, J. R. (1986). Group Level Issues in the Design and Training of Cockpit Crews. Cockpit Resource Management Training, Proceedings of the NASA/MAC Workshop (NASA Conference Publication 2455). Ames Research Center, California.

Harty, R. (1990). *Callback, NASA's Aviation Safety Reporting System.* Washington, DC: Smithsonian Institution Press.

ICAO. (1998). Human Factors Training Manual, Doc 9683, Montreal, CA. ICAO.

JetBlue Airlines. (2018). The Universal Gateway Program. Retrieved from JetBlue website: <http://pilots.jetblue.com/university/>.

NTSB. (1975). Aircraft Accident Report, Trans World Airlines, Inc, Boeing 727-231, N54328, Berryville, Virginia. Report Number: NTSB-AAR-75-16. Washington, D.C. National Transportation Safety Board.

NTSB. (2004). Aircraft Accident Report, American Airlines Flight 587, Airbus Industrie A300-605R, N14053, Belle Harbor, New York Report Number: NTSB-AAR-04-04. Washington, D.C. National Transportation Safety Board.

NTSB. (2014b). Descent below Visual Glidepath and Impact with Seawall, Asiana Airlines Flight 214, Boeing 777-200ER, HL7742, San Francisco, California, July 6, 2013. NTSB/AAR/14/01, PB2014-105984. Washington, D.C. National Transportation Safety Board.

NTSB News Release. (2014a). NTSB Find Mismanagement of Approach and Inadequate Monitoring of Airspeed Led to Crash of Asiana Flight 214, Multiple contributing factors also identified. Washington, D.C. National Transportation Safety Board. Retrieved from <https://www.ntsb.gov/news/press-releases/Pages/PR20140624.aspx>.

Orlady, H. (1991). Advanced cockpit technology in the real world. In Proceedings of the Royal Aeronautical Society Conference "Human Factors on Advanced Flight Decks." England.

Orlady, H., & Orlady, L. (1999). *Human Factors in Multi-Crew Flight Operations.* Aldershot, England: Ashgate Publications.

Orlady, H., Orlady, L., & Barnes, R. (2002). Human Factors, What do I really need to know? WATS Aircrew Training Conference, Dallas, TX.

Orlady, L. (2012). *Human Factors and Aviation Safety − Do we have new questions.* Seattle, WA: Royal Aeronautical Society Presentation.

Paul, J. (2018). Great Lakes Airlines suspends flights at DIA, across its route network. *The Denver Post,* March 27, 2018.

Pinet, J., & Enders, J. (1994). *Human factors in aviation: A consolidated approach. Flight Safety Digest December 1994.* Virginia: Flight Safety Foundation.

Prater, J. (2009). Statement submitted before the Subcommittee on Aviation, the Committee on Transportation and Infrastructure, the US House of Representatives, June 17, 2009, Washington, DC.

Silk, R. (2018). American Airlines launching pilot training program. Travel Weekly. April 24, 2018, Secaucus, NJ. Northstar Travel Group. Retrieved from <http://www.travelweekly.com/Travel-News/Airline-News/American-Airlines-launching-pilot-training-program>.

Skybrary. (2018). Retrieved from <https://www.skybrary.aero/index.php/Crew_Resource_Management>.

Sullenberger, C.B. III. (2009). Testimony submitted before the Subcommittee on Aviation, the Committee on Transportation and Infrastructure, the US House of Representatives, February 24, 2009, Washington, DC.

Taggart, W. R. (1993). How to kill off a good CRM program. *The CRM Advocate*, *93.1*, 11–12.

Transport Canada. (2018) Advisory Circular 700-042, Crew Resource Management Training Standards. Montreal, Canada. Civil Aviation Standards, Transport Canada.

Turney, M. A. (2002). Guidelines for Incorporating CRM in the First Stages of Flight Training. *Journal of Aviation/Aerospace Education & Research*, *11*(3). Retrieved from https://commons.erau.edu/jaaer/vol11/iss3/6.

Wiener, E. (1985). Human Factor of Cockpit Automation: A Field Study of Flight Crew Transition (NASA Contractor Report177333). (1985) Ames Research Center: California.

Wiener, E., & Curry, R. (1980). Flight-deck automation: Promises and problems. *Journal Ergonomics*, *23*(10).

Chapter 22

The Future of CRM

Thomas R. Chidester[1], Barbara G. Kanki[2] and José Anca[3]

[1]*Civil Aerospace Medical Institute, Federal Aviation Administration, Oklahoma City, OK, United States,* [2]*Retired, NASA Ames Research Center, Moffett Field, CA, United States,* [3]*Faculty of Science, Engineering and Technology, Swinburne University of Technology, Hawthorn, VIC, Australia*

The chapters making up this volume review history and current conceptualizations of CRM, offer guidance for best practices, and identify areas of incomplete knowledge where additional research is required. As editors, we have an opportunity to hypothesize how our field will evolve from that body of experience. At the outset, let us stipulate the work collected here is extensive. The three of us entered this field shortly after its pioneers (John Lauber, Robert Helmreich, Earl Wiener, Clay Foushee, and others) articulated the crew-level challenges on the flight deck. The work accomplished by those who contributed to this volume, and those whose work is cited in each chapter, is extensive, deliberative, solution-oriented, and enables the development of theory. Having seen this evolution in our adult lifetimes is remarkable. And the collective work, aligned with other industry and regulatory changes, has allowed us to approach a "near-zero" accident rate. How do we accomplish more? What challenges will face us? In this chapter, we offer three complementary areas of thought, comment, or speculation.

First, we believe current guidance is sound and consistent with research findings. Practitioners should continue to respond to regulations and the associated advisory circulars and national and international guidance documents. These include Advisory Circulars on CRM (FAA, 2004) and LOS (FAA, 2015) in the United States. Harmonized regulations have also been established in ICAO (2013), the UK CAA (2017), and EASA (2017). This raises a question for those countries that do not have the resources, culture, or determination for CRM. How might our field better communicate, adapt, or enable application of what has been learned (Helmreich & Merritt, 2001)? Enomoto and Geisler (2017) explored the relationship of a country's socioeconomic factors, culture, and the propensity to aircraft accidents. It found that countries with low gross domestic product (GDP) per capita, low individualism index, and the possession of a culture with high power-distance tended to have a greater incidence of aircraft accidents. It is in these countries where the very purpose of CRM countermeasures—that of active and involved coordination between two pilots may actually spell an accident or safe outcome. The "Gladwell hypothesis" (2008) aptly captures the conditionality of aircraft accidents against teamwork and cooperation in the flight deck:

"And for a long time, it's been clear that if you have two people operating the airplane cooperatively, you will have a safer operation than if you have a single pilot flying the plane and another person who is simply there to take over if the pilot is incapacitated." We acknowledge the complexity of influencing countries about the benefits of CRM countermeasures, especially appropriate communication and teamwork, where the corporate practices, regulatory frameworks, and national culture prove resistant to revolutionary safety change. Yet, in another domain where CRM was spawned by aviation (but not regulated through compliance) in the health care industry, reaping the benefits of good teamwork and communication continue to be empirically recorded and extolled (Haerkens et al., 2015; Hefner et al., 2017; Ricci & Brumsted, 2012; Sax et al., 2009). This could prove that advocacy towards good practice of CRM may be sufficient even without the need for regulations in such countries where culture, determination, and resources may be wanting.

Second, we believe Safety Management Systems will drive evolution of CRM. Much of the guidance in early versions of CRM were borrowed from applied theory about small group psychology (Foushee, 1984). Current generations based on a Threat and Error Management framework evolved from hard-won operational experience (Helmreich, Klinect, & Wilhelm, 1999). Likewise, the data streams implemented through Safety Assurance processes under SMS (FOQA, ASAP, LOSA, AQP, etc.) inform us of challenges encountered by crews and how they resolved them with ease or difficulty. Our theory-driven approaches to policy, procedure, and training must grow by incorporating empirical experience. But beyond a theoretical discussion about SMS, there is growing evidence of the linearity of SMS process and Safety outcomes. In a study of eight European airlines, it was found that the more SMS process and activity is employed, the better the outcome of safety performance—and clearly, CRM countermeasures training is at the core of SMS education (Kaspers et al., 2017). Practitioners in the airlines and regulatory agencies responding to SMS feedback and CRM training design will be the front line of this continuing evolution.

Third, our field will continue to be challenged by technological innovation. Two FAA working groups (1996, 2013) documented how the introduction and advancement of aircraft avionics have added new dimensions to the proficiency of pilots, some of which were not anticipated in design and were understood only in observation of error. The phenomena they describe might be construed as challenging, perhaps undermining, the expert knowledge base of pilots that is fundamental to much of their decision-making (Chapter 5: Flight Crew Decision-Making). Through experience, these technologies and their implications are incorporated into policy, procedure, and training—perhaps not yet to the extent needed. But, our industry has only just begun to innovate in a technological sense. The Federal Aviation Administration and US airlines are introducing NextGen applications. European nations are implementing products of the *Single European Sky ATM Research (SESAR)* initiative. Harmonization efforts are in progress between the two. Both will incrementally and disruptively impact pilot knowledge and training requirements. They can be construed as reengineering the processes by which pilots, controllers, and airline operations controllers/dispatchers navigate, communicate, and accomplish surveillance of air traffic. Innovations include transitioning from aircraft navigation by reference to ground-based facilities to satellites supplemented by aircraft inertial and local augmentation systems; from tactical communications by voice to strategic communications and negotiations of trajectories by datalink; and from observing aircraft position primarily by radar and transponders to receiving broadcasts of precise position and trajectory directly from each aircraft. Because precursor systems have been put in place, such as Flight Management Systems in aircraft and new Air Traffic Management systems (ERAM in the United States, for example), these innovations are phased-in as a series of increasing capabilities. That approach makes their integration less of a leap of human performance in each workgroup, but change always presents the opportunity for errors we may not predict. SMS functions have guided what has been introduced so far, but automation surprises (Sarter, Woods, & Billings, 1997) in piloting and air traffic control are likely. As CRM programs, including simulation, were called upon to correct or improve performance at the airlines following the introduction of FMS-generation aircraft (Chidester, 1999), a similar function can be anticipated following NextGen innovations. Lest this be taken as Luddite-level cautiousness, let us also acknowledge that pursuing a next generation of technology also removes realized risks of older systems. It presents opportunities to reconsider the roles of pilots and controllers and the automated systems we provide to support them. We may take advantage of the unique and creative capabilities of these living, breathing people and guard against the limitations of their physiology and cognitive capacity. CRM must evolve to accommodate the crew-level changes in policy, procedure, and training that will naturally follow; and better, that we should anticipate them.

REFERENCES

CAA. (2017). Practical Crew Resource Management (CRM) Standards: The Handy Guide. *CAP 1607*. London: Civil Aviation Authority.

Chidester, T. R. (1999). Introducing FMS aircraft into airline operations. In S. Dekker, & E. Hollnagel (Eds.), *Coping with computers in the cockpit*. Aldershot, U.K: Ashgate.

EASA. (2017). *Crew Resource Management in Practice. Version 1, December 2017*. Accessed 9.2.18.

Enomoto, C. E., & Geisler, K. R. (2017). Culture and plane crashes: A cross-country test of the gladwell hypothesis. *Economics & Sociology*, *10*(3), 281–293. Available from https://doi.org/10.14254/2071-789x.2017/10-3/20.

Federal Aviation Administration (FAA). (2004). *Crew resource management training* (Advisory Circular 120-51E). Washington, DC. Retrieved from <http://www.faa.gov/documentLibrary/media/Advisory_Circular/AC120-51e.pdf>.

Federal Aviation Administration (FAA). (2015). *Flightcrew member line operational simulations: Line-oriented flight training, special purpose operational training, line operational evaluation* (Advisory Circular 120-35D). Washington, DC. Retrieved from <http://www.faa.gov/documentLibrary/media/Advisory_Circular/AC_120-35D.pdf>.

Foushee, H. C. (1984). Dyads and triads at 35,000 feet -- Factors affecting group process and aircrew performance. *American Psychologist*, *39*(8), 886–893.

Haerkens, M., Kox, M., Lemson, J., Houterman, S., Hoeven, J. G. D., & Pickkers, P. (2015). Crew Resource Management in the Intensive Care Unit: a prospective 3-year cohort study. *Acta Anaesthesiologica Scandinavica*, *59*(10), 1319–1329. Available from https://doi.org/10.1111/aas.12573.

Hefner, J. L., Hilligoss, B., Knupp, A., Bournique, J., Sullivan, J., Adkins, E., & Moffatt-Bruce, S. D. (2017). Cultural transformation after implementation of crew resource management: Is it really possible. *American Journal of Medical Quality*, *32*(4), 384–390. Available from https://doi.org/10.1177/1062860616655424.

Helmreich, R. L., Klinect, J. R., & Wilhelm, J. A. (1999). *Models of threat, error, and CRM in flight operations. Proceedings of the tenth international symposium on aviation psychology*. Columbus, OH: The Ohio State University.

Helmreich, R. L., & Merritt, A. C. (2001). *Culture at work in aviation and medicine* (2nd ed.). London: Routledge.

ICAO. (2013). *Manual of evidence-based training. DOC 9995*. Montreal, Canada: International Civil Aviation Organization.

Kaspers, S., Karanikas, N., Piric, S., van Aalst, R., de Boer, R. J., & Roelen, A. (2017). *Measuring safety in aviation: Empirical results about the relation between safety outcomes and safety management system processes, operational activities and demographic data*. Wilmington: Iaria Xps Press.

Ricci, M. A., & Brumsted, J. R. (2012). Crew resource management: Using aviation techniques to improve operating room safety. *Aviation, Space, and Environmental Medicine*, *83*(4), 441–444. Available from https://doi.org/10.3357/asem.3149.2012.

Sarter, N. B., Woods, D. D., & Billings, C. E. (1997). Automation surprises. In G. Salvendy (Ed.), *Handbook of human factors/ergonomics* (2nd ed.). New York: Wiley.

Sax, H. C., Browne, P., Mayewski, R. J., Panzer, R. J., Hittner, K. C., Burke, R. L., & Coletta, S. (2009). Can aviation-based team training elicit sustainable behavioral change?. *Archives of Surgery*, *144*(12), 1133–1137. Available from https://doi.org/10.1001/archsurg.2009.207.

FURTHER READING

CAA. (2014). Flight-crew human factors handbook. *CAP737 (December 2016 version)*. London: Civil Aviation Authority.

EASA (2015) *ED Decision 2015/027/R Implementation of evidence-based training (EBT) within the European regulatory framework*. Accessed 16.2.18 <https://www.easa.europa.eu/document-library/agency-decisions/ed-decision-2015027r>.

Gladwell, M. (2008). *Outliers: The story of success* (pp. 184–185). New York, Boston, London: Little, Brown & Co.

Index

Note: Page numbers followed by "*f*" and "*t*" refer to figures and tables, respectively.